Latino Education
An Agenda for Community Action Research

A Volume of the National Latino/a Education Research and Policy Project

Edited by

Pedro Pedraza

Melissa Rivera

Center for Puerto Rican Studies, Hunter College,
City University of New York

 LAWRENCE ERLBAUM ASSOCIATES, PUBLISHERS
2005 Mahwah, New Jersey   London

Senior Acquisitions Editor:	Naomi Silverman
Assistant Editor:	Erica Kica
Cover Design:	Kathryn Houghtaling Lacey
Textbook Production Manager:	Paul Smolenski
Full-Service Compositor:	TechBooks
Text and Cover Printer:	Hamilton Printing Company

This book was typeset in 10.5/13 pt. Palatino Roman, Bold, and Italic.
The heads were typeset in Palatino, Palatino Bold, and Palatino Bold Italic.

Lawrence Erlbaum Associates, Inc., Publishers
10 Industrial Avenue
Mahwah, New Jersey 07430
www.erlbaum.com

Library of Congress Cataloging-in-Publication Data

Latino education : an agenda for community action research / edited by Pedro
    Pedraza, Melissa Rivera.
        p.   cm.
    "A Volume of the National Latino/a Education Research and Policy Project."
    Includes bibliographical references and index.
    ISBN 0-8058-4986-6 (casebound)—ISBN 0-8058-4987-4 (pbk.)
    1. Hispanic Americans—Education.   2. Action research in
education—United States.   3. Educational equalization—United States.
4. Educational change—United States.   I. Pedraza, Pedro, 1946–
II. Rivera, Melissa, 1971– III. National Latino/a Education Research and Policy
Project.   IV. Title.

    LC2669.L36   2005
    371.829′68073—dc22   2005012014

Books published by Lawrence Erlbaum Associates are printed on
acid-free paper, and their bindings are chosen for strength and
durability.

Printed in the United States of America
10 9 8 7 6 5 4 3 2 1

This volume is dedicated to Dr. Enrique (Henry) Torres Trueba for the countless hours you gave to those who needed your help, for the compassionate manner and humane mentorship you offered, for the humor and joy you brought to gatherings, and for the *cariño* and *respeto* you shared with all who crossed your path.

Contents

Foreword

The invitation to write the foreword for this volume was originally offered to Dr. Enrique (Henry) Torres Trueba. Unfortunately, his fight with cancer precluded his writing it, and we are honored to have been asked to write it for him. Dr. Trueba passed away peacefully at his Houston home on Saturday, July 22, 2004.

The lifetime scholarship of Dr. Trueba has inspired and motivated hundreds of Latino/a students, teachers, university faculty, and community people. His lifelong commitment to social justice and dedication to issues of equity is legendary in academia. Dr. Trueba's legacy will serve forever as a benchmark of excellence in scholarship and advocacy for the next generation of Latino/a research scholars.

This book is evidence of the powerful, important, and burgeoning changes in the academy for Latino/a researchers compared to when Dr. Trueba began his career as an educational ethnographer in the early 1960s. Although too many Latino/a communities continue to be marginalized and lack access to educational success and economic independence, a growing number of nationally recognized Latino/a scholars now have positions of impact and influence at research and teaching universities throughout the country. These academics are disseminating their work in major mainstream publishing venues in order to provide historically neglected and underrepresented perspectives in traditional areas of study.

It is not easy for authentic transformation to take place inside the academy. The work in this volume bears witness that the bureaucratic and often racist practices and rigid infrastructures of higher educational institutions (i.e., hiring, tenure, publication, grants, funding, etc.)

although daunting, have failed to keep out or silence the strong voices of societal change and fairness. That is one of the common threads in all of the pieces. Dr. Truebas's well-known book, *Raising Silent Voices*, is an apt description for this volume.

We were blessed to have a final audience with Dr. Trueba several weeks prior to his death. In his bed, lying immobile, and in excruciating pain, Dr. Trueba shared a lifetime of wisdom. He pointed to his heart, and as only a sage can, emphatically whispered, "In the end, this is all you have. I have my love, affection, and my integrity."

Dr. T.'s masterful vision and scholarly insights have illuminated the pathway for those of us who have the privilege to serve our communities in our respective academic arenas. This book is offered in the spirit of a man who died the way he lived—with love, affection, and integrity. *Gracias, profesor.*

—José Cintrón and Lila Jacobs
California State University, Sacramento

Preface

Welcome to the National Latino/a Education Research and Policy Project's (NLERAP) collective journey to create a vision and research action plan for improving the education and well-being of Latino/a children, families, and communities. This volume provides the sociohistorical landscape and conceptual foundation for this research framework and agenda, situating NLERAP's efforts within a political and cultural context and illustrating how the agenda can offer important ideas about Latino/a education.

The essays contained in this volume are written primarily by Latino/a scholars who have worked on the complex and dynamic educational issues of U.S. Latino/a communities for decades. Their perspectives go beyond conventional paradigms, discourses, arguments, and sociopolitical standpoints. In addition to exposing the historical and current dehumanizing and destructive ideologies and injustices of education policies and practices, these authors provide a visionary orientation that promises a future beneficial to all, one in which democratic ideals are realized and a nation becomes truly prepared for participation in an interdependent global society.

We invite you to use this volume in your classrooms, community organizations, and professional gatherings as a resource and catalyst for debate and discussion. Ultimately, we hope that you are inspired to action—to use your individual and collective voice, talents, insights, and efforts to improve public education.

OVERVIEW OF THE VOLUME

We have been honored with a Foreword by two longtime students and friends of Dr. Enrique (Henry) Torres Trueba, written on his behalf (Cintrón and Jacobs). His legendary wisdom and pioneering spirit have inspired the authors of this book (and many others) and the entire NLERAP pilgrimage. Thank you, Dr. Trueba. We humbly commit ourselves collectively to continue to struggle for justice and create new spaces for unlimited imagination.

NLERAP's story is one of transformative and critically conscious healing and collective rebirth. Like skilled and creative artisans, the scholars weave a tapestry of insight and innovation, helping to illuminate possibilities for true freedom of the human spirit to learn and evolve.

Imagine for a moment a literary theater production, opening with *Act I: The Dawn*, in which the vision of a collective is illumined. Pedraza and Rivera begin the tale by sharing, in this introductory section, *Creating the Collective Vision*, the origins of NLERAP, highlighting the genesis and development of this community action effort. Mercado and Santamaría then situate the NLERAP initiative within a broader context of educational agendas, focusing on the power of a collective voice.

In *Act II: The Storm*, the pain, destruction, and ravages of imperialism and practices of domination are revisited with a critical lens. This second section, *Sociohistorical Revisioning*, presents a sociopolitical analysis of the history of U.S. Latino/a students' public schooling experiences (MacDonald & Monkman) and reviews the educational research literature on Latinos/as over the past century (Flores; Montero-Sieburth).

Act III: The Aftermath exposes the institutional and instructional wounds created from these dehumanizing structures imposed on Latino/a communities, offering insights into possibilities for change. This section, *Exposing the Colonizing Effects of Reform*, focuses on the present educational reality of Latinos/as, including the current demographic situation of U.S. Latino/a students (Cordero-Guzmán) as well as potently troublesome policies and practices significantly affecting our communities, such as the standardization movement and teacher education (González; Rueda; Márquez-López; Grinberg et al.).

Act IV: New Soil invites us to experience moments of hope through stories of resistance, resilience, and renewal, in which efforts to decolonize minds and humanize the educational process are described.

Collapsing the Paradox, Imagining New Possibilities challenges the previous section's detrimental ideologies by presenting visionary theories, methodologies, and programs for reshaping Latino/a education (Tejeda et al.; Moll & Ruiz; Vásquez; De Jesús).

Act V: The Sowing offers new theories of education for Latino/a communities, in which all dimensions of children, young people, and their communities are considered. The section, *Actualizing the Future*, explores new paradigm development for conceptualizing NLERAP's collective efforts toward more equitable, democratic, transformative, and humane education for Latino/a communities (Hidalgo; Padilla; Rocco).

Act VI: The Harvest invites us to consider a new, uncharted landscape for Latino/a education. This final section, *Realizing the Power of Community Action*, imagines a world with limitless possibilities by first offering various changes needed in order to realize NLERAP's agenda in action and then sharing thoughts about true collaborative research for liberating education (Pedraza). In the Afterword, Nieto discusses how NLERAP is an agenda, that offers "a new research paradigm, one that is respectful and collaborative, purposeful and humble, hopeful and visionary."

In our Appendix, we include NLERAP's agenda document and methods statement so you can more directly engage with the vision of hundreds of scholars, educators, and community advocates. The agenda includes NLERAP's guiding principles, approach to research, initial areas of research, and action plan. The NLERAP initiative is centered on revisioning past educational reform efforts and creating holistic and innovative relationships, theories, and approaches for improving Latino/a education.

With this visionary intellectual foundation and engaged spirit of transformation, we hope the chapters in this volume will inspire you to seed fertile gardens in your schools and neighborhoods and harvest the fruits of educational equity and social justice for Latino/a communities.

—Pedro Pedraza and Melissa Rivera
Center for Puerto Rican Studies, Hunter
College, City University of New York
National Latino/a Education Research
and Policy Project (NLERAP)

ACKNOWLEDGMENTS

We would like to thank our colleagues, friends, and family members who have supported and nurtured NLERAP's efforts and especially the creation and production of this volume. Thank you to the following people and organizations: all of the contributing authors; NLERAP board members; NLERAP regional meeting participants and methods statement co-authors; our editor Naomi Silverman, her assistant Erica Kica, and everyone at Lawrence Erlbaum Associates; Matthew Byrd and TechBooks; the Ford Foundation; the Rockefeller Foundation; the Annie E. Casey Foundation; the Hazen Foundation; the Spencer Foundation; Dr. Felix Matos Rodríguez, Vicky Nuñez, and the *Centro de Estudios Puertorriqueños* at Hunter College; Dr. Barbara Flores, Dr. Albert Karnig and California State University, San Bernardino; and Dr. Enrique Murillo, Dr. Susana Flores, and the *Journal of Latinos and Education*.

PART I

Introduction—Creating the Collective Vision

1

Origins of the National Latino/a Education Research and Policy Project (NLERAP)[1]

Pedro Pedraza
Melissa Rivera
Center for Puerto Rican Studies, Hunter College,
City University of New York
National Latino/a Education Research and Policy Project
(NLERAP)

The National Latino/a Education Research and Policy Project (NLERAP) is the story of a collective journey of informed and actively engaged members of the Latino/a education community.[2] It is a story of resistance and renewal, about more than 200 people who have become sufficiently incensed by U.S. backlash education policies and practices to act. It is a tale of struggle, transformation, transcendence, and

---

[1]The authors would like to thank NLERPP project associate Vicky Núñez for her contributions to this chapter.

[2]NLERAP began in February 2000 as the National Latino/a Education Research Agenda Project with the goal of developing a research agenda for U.S. Latino/a public education with community members, school practitioners and university researchers. Once our collective agenda document was published in 2003 (please see Appendix A), NLERAP's advisory board renamed NLERAP, the National Latino/a Education Research and Policy Project to encompass NLERAP's broader efforts, including its community action research projects and policy work.

proposed liberation; a response to incendiary and suffocating educational politics; and a statement about a vision for truly holistic learning for Latinos/as and others. How can we transcend the violence of our educational policies and classroom practices and instead cloak our communities with peaceful and passionate exploration of self and others within a more humane and just world? It is in this spirit that NLERAP was birthed.

RATIONALE

The National Latino/a Education Research and Policy Project (NLERAP) is an initiative that has developed over the past 5 years to create a vision for transforming U.S. Latino/a education. NLERAP's goal is to articulate a Latino/a perspective on research-based school reform and to use research as a guide to improve the public school systems that serve Latino/a students and communities.

Why craft a research agenda for Latino/a education? The first motivation for NLERAP's work, including this collective volume, is to respond to the fact that the Latino/a community has historically been underserved by U.S. public school systems. This miseducation of Latino/a communities, reflective of larger sociohistorical and economic inequalities, has resisted various reform efforts over the decades. As a result, by most measures of academic success, large numbers of U.S. Latino/a students are failing miserably, or rather, as NLERAP believes, U.S. public schools are miserably failing Latino/a students. As we begin a new century, more attention to these educational issues is required because of the tremendous population increase and projected growth of Latino/a communities in the United States. This reality reinforces a sense of urgency within our community and informs the desperate need to create schools and educational spaces that are responsive to an increasingly multicultural, multilingual, and transnational population.

Beyond responding to the oppressive educational situation of Latinos/as, NLERAP participants and these volume authors also gathered to envision and collectively create more just, equitable, and humane educational experiences for U.S. Latino/a communities. For decades, research that sought to improve education for Latino/a students was conducted by non-Latino/a scholars on issues ranging from immigration to bilingual education to standardized testing and has been based on unquestioned assumptions about the educational needs of Latino/a communities. That research has shaped both public opinion and social policy regarding the educational issues affecting Latino/a students and has left our community with the challenges imposed by the legacy of oppressive theories (such as deficit models, among others). Given our formative experiences as Latino/a researchers, educators, and activists, governmental and philanthropic infrastructures have not been designed in ways that allow Latino/a communities (nor other nondominant communities) to assess or define our own educational issues. Such approaches have served to marginalize the perspectives of Latino/a community members. We believe that the maintenance of poor educational outcomes for Latino/a students attending U.S. public schools is partly related to the existing, culturally myopic research practices and policy-making structures in the United States. Because the Latino/a community now possesses the human and intellectual capital in the form of academic researchers, educators, and community advocates, we believe it is imperative that we work within a framework that we create and own. To this end, NLERAP began a national dialogue with the aim of constructing a framework and plan for the design, implementation, and assessment of pedagogical innovation, liberating practice, and more democratic educational policy, by and for Latinos/as.

THEORETICAL FRAMEWORK

The theoretical framework for the National Latino/a Education Research and Policy Project is grounded in three overlapping areas of scholarship and activism that are reflected within the collection of chapters in this volume: (a) critical studies, illuminating and analyzing the status of people of color (and other oppressed peoples) in the United States; (b) Latino/a educational research, capturing the sociohistorical, cultural, and political schooling experiences of U.S. Latino/a communities; and (c) participatory action research, exemplifying an action-oriented methodology for truly transformative education.

Critical Studies

This literature (which includes critical race theory, critical pedagogy, feminist theories, resistance theories, and others) provides a framework for understanding Latinos/as' status in the United States, including our historical and current social, political, and economic marginalization and the resultant inequitable access to and engagement with quality education. Authors in this volume use this critical standpoint to unearth the colonial and oppressive situation of Latinos/as and create a new vision for transformative possibilities (for examples, please see Chapters 11 and 14, Tejeda and Gutierrez, and De Jesús, respectively).

Latino/a Educational Research

Over the past three decades, Latino/a scholars have engaged in innovative research efforts to explore the sociocultural, political, linguistic, educational, and community aspects of life in U.S. Latino/a families, schools, and neighborhoods. Some of these pioneering, indigenous activist academics share their theories and research in this volume, including Trueba's longtime efforts applying anthropological perspectives to education research; Nieto's research on multicultural, Puerto Rican, and teacher education; Moll, Ruiz, Mercado, and others' work on community knowledge and educational sovereignty; Gutierrez and others' theories on the impact of public policy reforms on Latino/a students; Vásquez and others' research on community action after-school programs; among others. This collective body of work on Latino/a education has shaped and influenced the vision for NLERAP's agenda and action plan.

Participatory Action Research

NLERAP is committed to a research approach that seeks to uncover the emancipatory potential of education. Thus research methodology, that is, how the research is designed, conducted, and analyzed, is central to our work. Some key characteristics of NLERAP's methodology have been identified, including our commitment to collaborative and participatory, interdisciplinary, longitudinal processes that encourage reflection, transform research and teaching, generate new understandings and theories that support the improvement of Latino/a education, influence educational public policy, and are responsive to, maintain, and protect the integrity of human rights.

NLERAP is thus grounded in principles of developmental, participatory action research, especially its philosophical and ideological commitment, which holds that every person has the capacity to know, analyze, and reflect on reality in order to become true agents in their own lives (Fals-Borda & Rahman, 1991; Hinsdale et al., 1995; Maguire, 1987; Park, 1989). For instance, Hinsdale et al. (1995) describe the approach as seeking

to eliminate monopolistic control over knowledge creation. Participatory research respects people's own capability and potential to produce knowledge
and to analyze it and expects the community to participate in the entire
research process. It becomes a means of taking action for development and
is an educational process of mobilization for development. (p. 340)

The actual process of developing the NLERAP agenda adhered to these
principles of collaboration and democratic participation, incorporating
several hundred participants in discussion and consensus building.

THE ORIGINS OF NLERPP

The NLERAP Process

The NLERAP initiative began with an initial planning meeting in February 2000. At this seminal gathering, educators, policy advocates, foundation representatives, and community activists decided that in order
for this effort to be most meaningful and productive for our communities as well as educational contexts in general, we would have to
embrace a new approach. Participants affirmed that the agenda development process would be supremely important to the outcome of
the document. That is, what the agenda said (its vision and priorities)
would be determined by how it was created and who participated in
its creation. Thus began the two-year process of gathering hundreds of
people involved in and impacted by the education of Latino/a communities to discuss, imagine, and innovate.

In March 2000, an advisory board was developed for NLERAP with a
commitment to equitable representation via gender, ethnicity, culture,
region, and diversity of roles within the educational process. Our board
members include university researchers, policy advocates, school faculty and personnel, education administrators, community organization
representatives, local activists, and artists from various Latino/a cultural groups (including Chicanos/as and Mexican Americans, Puerto
Ricans, South and Central Americans, Cubans and Dominicans, and
others) from nine U.S. regions, including Puerto Rico (see appendix B
for list of board members).

Between April 2000 and January 2002, NLERAP gathered educators and advocates from nine regions into focus groups (including
the Northwest, Southern California, the Midwest, the Southwest, the
Northeast, the New York metropolitan area, the Washington, DC area,

the Southeast, and Puerto Rico). These focus groups created spaces to initiate dialogues among participants about what is most needed in research about Latino/a educational communities. Although there were some regional variations, overall, a consensus arose about K–12 educational research for Latinos/as and is outlined in NLERAP's agenda document (please see appendix A). Our hope is that the research framework and agenda will advise and guide researchers, policy makers, educators, and institutions on important educational issues impacting Latino/a communities. Mostly, we hope it will inspire readers like you to actively engage in efforts to improve the education and lives of Latinos/as and others.

NLERAP's Vision and Action Plan

What emerged from the participatory and democratic 2-year process was a clear need for a collaborative and action-oriented approach to Latino/a educational research. This approach includes four guiding principles: (1) honor sociocultural perspectives; (2) recognize the sociocultural, political, economic, and historical context of Latino/a education; (3) *co-educar comunidades*; and (4) promote social justice and democratic ideals. These principles developed from lively discussions about how NLERAP's plan of research would differ from others, in essence, what this collective effort could contribute to both Latino/a communities and national educational practices and policies. The approach is also grounded in a participatory methodology, illuminating our commitment to developmental, community-engaged, action-oriented research that aspires to address issues of educational equity and social justice. This orientation toward community participation and collective movement is the soul of NLERAP's vision for action (please see appendix A).

NLERAP board members and regional meeting participants worked to first develop a framework for all research (as evidenced by the guiding principles and methodology). Eventually, some areas of research were prioritized in order to begin projects with schools, communities, and universities. Some questions that guided the development of our areas of research include: What are the current, important issues to which we must respond as a community? What local issues do we have information about that can and should be shared with broader audiences? What questions do we have that few others are asking and that would benefit our communities? The four areas of research that were identified include: (a) assessment and accountability; (b) teacher and administrator education and professional development; (c) arts in education; and (d) sociocultural, political, economic, and historical context of Latino/a education.

Some areas of research (for instance, assessment and accountability) emerged in response to widespread, destructive practices and policies severely impacting Latino/a students and communities. Others (such as arts in education) emerged organically from the indigenous wisdom within Latino/a communities' history and culture of practice in human development. That is, there was a simultaneous top-down (response to imposed structures and processes) and grassroots (affirmation of our communities' knowledge and assets) perspective on the selection of these areas of research. This list was conceived as a starting point for our collective work, and, by no means, as a comprehensive list of issues NLERAP community researchers will address.

All of NLERAP's research efforts will seek to initiate change on three different levels: (a) educational institutions that serve Latino/a students, meaning create more effective schools and educational policies; (b) instructional practices that can improve classroom environments; and (c) interpersonal relations between schools and Latino/a communities that can allow schools to better appreciate and use Latino/a community resources and assets.

NLERAP also developed an action plan for implementing the collective vision of the agenda, including the development of action research projects with local communities in Latino/a schools. The design and implementation of research projects that carry out the agenda will constitute a cohesive national Latino/a educational research program, responsive to local conditions and needs via a unifying focus on practice and policy. This effort will build, whenever possible, on existing collaborations with local and national education reform efforts in order to facilitate a national infrastructure to support the agenda. The aim of NLERAP's research efforts is to contribute to classroom and school practices, local community issues, state educational policies, and the field of educational research.

Ultimately, the NLERAP initiative is a collective act of faith in the human spirit to be free and whole. Our hope is that in our collaborative struggles and efforts, democratic, inspiring, and inviting educational spaces are created for Latino/a children, young people, families, and communities to learn, evolve, and soar. The volume is NLERAP's conceptual story, exposing and exploring the life-crushing history of U.S. Latinos/as, unmasking the debilitating and rigidly confining current landscape, and encouraging our collective imaginations to envision a boundless future for Latino/a minds and souls. Thank you for journeying with us.

REFERENCES

Fals-Borda, O. & Rahman, M. A. (1991). *Action and knowledge: Breaking the monopoly with participatory action research*. New York: The Apex Press.

Hinsdale, M. A., Lewis, H. M., and Waller, S. M. (1995). *It comes from the people: Community development and local theology*. Philadelphia: Temple University Press.

Maguire, P. (1987). *Doing participatory research: A feminist approach*. Amherst, MA: The Center for International Education, School of Education.

Park, P. (1989). *What is participatory research? A theoretical and methodological perspective*. Northampton, MA: Center for Community Education and Action, Inc.

A New Vision for Latino/a Education: A Comparative Perspective on Research Agendas

Carmen I. Mercado
Hunter College, City University of New York

Lorri Johnson Santamaría
California State University, San Marcos

INTRODUCTION

> To improve education in enduring ways, we will need to strengthen educational research, and to do that, we must change the circumstances that have historically constrained the development of educational study. (Lagemann, 2000, p. xv)

Despite its limitations (see Kaestle, 1993 for an incisive analysis), "research can and must play a central role in strengthening our educational system" (Rita Colwell, director of the National Science Foundation, 1999). For the past three years, overwhelming national attention has been given to No Child Left Behind (NCLB, 2002) legislation mandating the use of "scientific based research," specifically randomized experiments, as the tool of choice for improving education for all of America's schoolchildren and youth. Many reputable scholars have voiced concern that federal sponsorship of one specific approach to educational research fails to recognize the unique and complex nature of educational science (See Berliner and others in the theme issue on Scientific Research in Education of *Educational Researcher*, 31(8), November 2002).

Historically, independent scholars from diverse communities have voiced similar reactions long before the civil rights movement of the 1960s. Although little known, George I. Sanchez (1906–1972) has been described as the father of the movement for quality education for Mexican Americans, and was among the first to conduct research that questioned the use of standardized tests for Spanish-speaking Mexican-American children in the 1930s and 1940s. Presently, these enduring concerns are energizing local forces and giving rise to new types of social movements coalescing around needs that include but go beyond education. One such movement is the National Latino/a Education Research Agenda Project (NLERAP), an independent national collaborative of practitioners, community leaders, foundation officers, and academicians with broad experience and expertise, who have joined voluntarily to exercise intellectual leadership in formulating an organized, comprehensive, and coordinated response to the economic hardships and educational challenges U.S. Latino/a communities continue to face. It is an initiative that arises in times of a "conceptual-based economy," in which "people's livelihoods are depending less on what they are producing with their hands and more on what they are producing with their brains" (Colwell, 1999). To this day, the promise of "ending poverty" and attaining "social justice" made in the aftermath of civil rights struggles remain an elusive goal.

African American, American Indian/Alaska Native, and Latino/a children continue to receive an inferior preparation; and those who manage to earn high school degrees, and many do not, are at best prepared for low-paying menial jobs in the labor market. Research continues to demonstrate combined effects of standards-based high-stakes testing that reduce the intellectual challenge of the curriculum, augment the achievement gap between Whites and non-Whites, and exacerbate dropout rates among Latino/a and other "minority" youth. Appearing to be sensible solutions to real educational problems that respond to public concerns for government and school accountability, these measures do not auger well for life chances of students from communities already experiencing high levels of poverty, attendant social problems, and unemployment, in the new global and information economies. Meanwhile, programs proven successful according to local criteria are overlooked in policies and practices of the federal government's reactionary school reform efforts (What Works for Latino/a Youth, September 2000; Delpit, 2003).

In keeping with the view which describes education as local responsibility, the National Latino/a Educational Research Agenda Project (NLERAP) seeks to reframe prevailing debate and thinking on school reform by defining an agenda that harnesses the power of scientific research and local expertise to determine the best ways to educate children for betterment of Latino/a communities and our society. Specifically, the NLERAP seeks to

a. synthesize and make accessible the best available knowledge to address the educational needs of Latino/a students;

b. organize and coordinate collaborative, cross-disciplinary research on critical topics applying theoretical frameworks and methodological procedures generating valid and robust knowledge of practical and theoretical significance;

c. and provide guidance and advice on what constitutes quality educational research for Latino/a students.

How different is this agenda from others that surfaced on the educational landscape in recent years? In this chapter, we draw comparisons between NLERAP and other relevant, influential, or potentially influential educational research agendas of the past two decades, situating them historically in order to highlight what is distinctive about NLERAP. First, we draw comparisons between the NLERAP agenda and the National Research Council's *Improving Schooling for Language-Minority Children: A Research Agenda* (August & Hakuta, 1997), the most influential national agenda giving direction to federally sponsored research on the education of Latino/a students. We then compare NLERAP to two independent agendas that are the result of local advocacy and concerns about the needs of African American and American Indian/Alaska Native communities, namely 1991's American Educational Research Association's *Commission on Research in Black Education* (CORIBE), and a set of agendas emanating from U.S. indigenous communities, including the *National Dialogue Project on American Indian*

Education (1987–1988), the *American Indian and Alaska Native Education Research Agenda* (2001), and the *National Congress of American Indians Critical Initiatives* (2003). Specifically, comparative analyses will examine

    a.   agenda setting processes;

    b.   identified research priorities;

    c.   and theoretical frameworks and methodological approaches of each agenda presented.

In addition to establishing ways in which NLERAP is different from featured agendas, each analysis is framed in response to the National Research Council's Latino/a research agenda, which has as its foundation federal U.S. support. From the framework provided by this agenda, areas of consensual agreement among other agendas will be identified, underscoring strong commonalities resulting from independent efforts and potential for joint future educational research endeavors. This work begins, with the premise that the federal government has been largely responsible for generating major research agendas affecting the education of Latino/a students, shaping the debate and thinking on research benefiting Latino/a students by providing financial support for the study of issues and topics with implications for federal policy and practices.

THE FEDERAL GOVERNMENT AND RESEARCH ON LATINO/A STUDENTS

Historical Overview

From the 1960s to the 1970s, the federal government assumed an unprecedented role in initiating and supporting educational research in minority communities as a form of social policy (Kaestle, 2001; Lagemann, 2000). Efforts to improve schooling for students from Latino/a communities (and other marginalized populations) has a long history, most evident in the independent school movement that grew in response to school segregation (or the prohibition of schooling), and has proven successful with African American and Latino/a populations. As San Miguel (1987) eloquently states, Latinos "have been active participants in shaping their own destinies" (p. 468). However, the social and political movements of the 1960s and 1970s, which demanded educational equity through litigation and legislation in civil rights and bilingual education, brought national attention to the issue. Unusual by today's standards, the response of Lyndon Johnson's administration (1963–1969) to a complex problem was swift: to focus both on "economic opportunity" and on "educational opportunity" through social welfare programs known as the Great Society and War on Poverty (Kaestle, 2001).

For the first time in the nation's history, the Elementary and Secondary Education Act (ESEA, 1965), considered the centerpiece of the War on Poverty, offered grants and services to schools serving low-income areas, bilingual communities, and American Indians. In 1968, ESEA (Goals 2000 during the Clinton administration and the NCLB 2002 Act under Bush II) was amended to include Title VII, better known as the Bilingual Education Act. The 1978 reauthorization of ESEA added a research agenda for English language learners (ELL), which was congressionally mandated and produced the beginnings of knowledge on and about the education of Latino/a children. The infrastructure for research resulting from this change has played a significant role in shaping this fundamental information base. It was an infrastructure superimposed on an existing structure, which included the National Institute for Education (NIE) and the Center for Educational Statistics (CES) as central components. Created in 1972 during the Nixon administration and under the advice of Daniel Patrick Moynihan, the president's chief advisor for domestic affairs, NIE's mission was to conduct research for purposes of improving education (Cohen & Barnes, 1999).

August and Kaestle (1997) describe how the federal research infrastructure changed to address the research needs of Latino/a communities. According to these authors, Section 742 of the 1978 reauthorization directed the (then) Office of Education to develop a national research program for bilingual education, coordinating the research activities with the NIE, the Office of Bilingual Education (later, OBEMLA when the Department of Education was created), the National Center for Educational Statistics (NCES), and other appropriate agencies. The Education Division Coordinating Committee, which became known as the "Part C Committee," was created in the spring of 1978. The committee organized requests for research identified in the legislation into three general categories: (a) studies to assess national needs for bilingual education; (b) studies designed to improve quality and effectiveness of services for students; and (c) studies designed to improve Title VII program management and operations. Therefore, studies resulting from

Part C were conducted in the context of justification and accountability. As an interagency committee, the Part C Committee represented competing interests, as control over the Part C research funds shifted over time, for example, from NIE-funded basic research studies to evaluation studies funded under the Office of Planning, Budget, and Evaluation (OPBE).

NIE (reorganized as part of OERI in 1985, and as of November 5, 2002, the Academy of Education Sciences) began to prosper through the sponsorship of research on schools, teaching, and learning (Cohen & Barnes, 1999). Basic research by esteemed cultural anthropologists such as Courtney Cazden at Harvard, Fred Erickson at the University of Pennsylvania, and Shirley Heath at Stanford and sociolinguists such as John Gumperz and Dell Hymes, broadened our understandings of language, culture, and learning in diverse school contexts. Through the quality of work they produced, NIE researchers also socialized a new generation of Latino/a and other ethnic scholars to the power and significance of ethnographic and microethnographic approaches to understand fundamentally social processes such as teaching and learning in minority communities. The concept of "culturally responsive teaching" is one construct that emerged as a by-product of litigation—the *Lau v. Nichols* case that sought to address access to quality education for culturally and linguistically diverse learners. The Lau Remedies mandated instructional accommodations for culturally and linguistically diverse learners, thereby reflecting the view that suggests how we teach should be adapted to how children learn. To this day, "culturally responsive pedagogy" continues to be developed even as the imposition of a standardized, core curriculum impedes or subverts its application. It is instructive, although not surprising, that "culturally responsive education" has been a construct of great saliency to Latino/a and African American researchers and not to those considered part of mainstream educational research, in general, and research on teaching, illustrating the importance of theoretical frameworks orienting educational research in nonmainstream communities (Ladson-Billings, 2001).

However, the research program that began to flourish as part of President Johnson's social programs came to a screeching halt. As the educational historian Ellen Lageman (2000) reports, Johnson was a strong believer in education and education became the tool of choice for addressing what were fundamentally economic problems: issues of unemployment and minimum wage. Johnson appointed John W. Gardner, president of the Carnegie Foundation, as chair of the task force charged with planning the administration's initial education policies, and subsequently appointing Gardner as his secretary of health, education, and welfare. In contrast, Kaestle (1993) reports the Reagan administration's policies and priorities were shaped by policy recommendations crafted by the Heritage Foundation under the title "Mandate for Leadership." The mission of this conservative think-tank is "to formulate and promote conservative public policies based on the principles of free enterprise, limited government, individual freedom, traditional American values, and a strong national defense" (http://www.heritage.org).

A Nation at Risk (1983), arguably the most influential of the educational manifestos of the last two decades, was one result of the influence of Reagan's educational advisors. *A Nation at Risk* brought back the idea of standards, which had surfaced as a concern in the aftermath of World War II, and high-stakes testing based on "common sense" rather than research. Two decades later recommendations from this report affect educational policies in states throughout the nation, and these policies, in turn, are now affecting the lives of all children and teachers in the nation's public schools, for better or worse.

By 1984, the Part C Committee was disbanded by Secretary Terrence Bell. The following year (1985), the National Institutes for Education was shut down and the level of funding for educational research sharply decreased. This was an unfortunate turn of events because, as Ellen Lagemann, president of the National Academy of Education, comments, during the 1970s and 1980s researchers moved toward more powerful understandings of and approaches to research (2000). In particular, the use of interpretive studies of educational processes brought culture into more central view. Efforts also were made to link scholarship more closely to practice designed to address educational inequalities. One federally funded study with major impact on classroom teachers is the study of community knowledge and classroom practice, popularly known as "funds of knowledge." This study is noteworthy because its innovative research design combined both basic and applied research, two usually independent components in the research cycle referred to as research and development. In doing so, it responds to the concerns of classroom teachers who are congnizant that waiting for the instructional applications of basic research may not allow them to appropriately address the needs of a diverse and constantly changing student population.

Although the federal government has been the biggest sponsor of educational research, and no doubt influential studies impacting teaching-learning processes in Latino/a and other ethnic communities have resulted from this sponsorship, all too often, research is vulnerable to political influences. Research is affected by funding and policy priorities, which, in turn, affect the type and quality of research produced and the usability and impact of this scholarship. One outcome of these political entanglements is federally sponsored research of the highest practical and theoretical significance according to local criteria, is often the very work dismissed by policy makers. This brief overview (see Box 2.1) also makes clear the need for a new and independent infrastructure for supporting research on the education of children from minority communities and NLERAP represents one step in this direction.

Box 2.1:

A Chronology of Post–World War II Initiatives Affecting Latino Communities

1956 The Council on Basic Education established to strengthen the academic curriculum of the nation

1957 Russians launch sputnik

1958 National Defense Education Act

1964 Civil Rights Act called for the orderly desegregation of schools; Economic Opportunity Act provides job training and employment for the poor

1965 Title I of the Elementary and Secondary Education Act (ESEA), the centerpiece of the War on Poverty, focuses on the educational needs of students from disadvantaged backgrounds (meaning poverty)

1966 Coleman's controversial Equality of Educational Opportunity Survey finds students' academic performance most affected by their families' social and economic status, their race, and their incoming school achievement

1967 Housing and Urban Development (HUD) created to promote urban renewal, public housing

1968 Bilingual Education Act of 1968 (P.L. 90-247) or Title VII of ESEA acknowledges the needs of language minority children

1972 NIE created within the U.S. Department of Health, Education and Welfare, with the purpose of improving education by investigating how schools worked and other issues raised by Coleman's study

1972 *Lau v. Nichols* case; schools must make accessible meaningful education for U.S.-born language minority children though appropriate instructional accommodations

1978 Legislative mandate for the first major substantive research agenda for bilingual education

1979 Department of Education created to improve primary and secondary education; Significant Bilingual Instructional Features Study funded for 3 years by NIE to identify instructional practices with language minority students and to investigate linguistic, cognitive, and social processes involved

1980 The Office of Educational Research and Development (OERI) created in U.S Department of Education, the primary source of research funding in the study of education for language minority children

1983 *A Nation at Risk* is published

1984 The Part C Research Committee disbanded

1984 Title VII reauthorized with expanded support for English immersion; an 8-year multimillion dollar study to compare the effectiveness of structure immersion, early exit bilingual, and late exit bilingual program models is funded.

1984 NIE reorganized out of existence as part of the reorganization of the Office of Educational research and Improvement (OERI) and the federal role in research shrinks to next to nothing

1987 Social Science Research Council forms committee for research on urban underclass

1992 Stanford Working Group advocates for the right of language minority children to an equal opportunity to learn; Title I and VII now make funds available for LMS

1994 Title VII moves away from remedial, compensatory model of bilingual education to enrichment and innovation; ESEA renamed *Improving American School's Act, establishing 8 broad goals for education nationwide*
Educational Research and Improvement Act

1995 Linda Darling-Hammond appoints Task Force on the Role and Future of Minorities

1996 AERA institute on alternative theoretical and epistemological approaches to research in minority communities

NATIONAL LATINO/A EDUCATION RESEARCH AND POLICY PROJECT (NLERAP) AND NATIONAL RESEARCH COUNCIL (NRC) AGENDAS: A COMPARISON

The Agenda-Setting Process

Best described as grassroots, bottom-up, democratic, and participatory, from the beginning NLERAP seeks aggressively to be open and inclusive, cross-disciplinary, and dialogic. Under the direction of Pedro Pedraza of the Center for Puerto Rican Studies of the City University of New York, and guided by a national advisory board that includes academic scholars, practitioners, and community activists, NLERAP goes to great lengths to draw on local knowledge and expertise, acknowledging the importance of perspective and point of view in educational inquiry (Green, 1994) but also the inseparability of theory from practice. Thus, NLERAP relies on local networks of informants to assure representation of the expertise and viewpoints of the entire spectrum of the education community—parents, students, teachers, community leaders, administrators, educationists, academics, government agencies, and foundations. In light of diversity of contexts, NLERAP also seeks representation of demographic trends, settlement patterns, and geography (urban-rural), holding nine distinct regional meetings in the United States and Puerto Rico over a two-year period. Through processes of dialogue and reflection across different roles and perspectives, issues and concerns are presented and discussed, local and national agreements on critical topics are derived, even when consensus is not always possible.

Gatherings in which disciplinary scholars, such as sociologists, anthropologists, economists, political scientists, and historians, engage with local practitioners, leadership, and representatives from philanthropic foundations in conversations about research do not always result in mutual understanding but always produce deep conversations about issues and concerns, and competing practical and theoretical lenses are negotiated. Even though all NLERAP participants share a similar commitment to understanding and addressing the educational experiences of Latino/a students, there are broad differences in backgrounds and experiences among them.

Possibly because of this, participants in NLERAP have come to recognize dialogue and reflection across difference as essential to identification of critical topics of importance to local communities and nationally. NLERAP participants also come to appreciate these processes that are at the core of collaborative research and needed to understand and represent complex educational phenomena holistically, taking into account economic, sociopolitical, cultural, and historic factors.

As will become clear, other locally initiated agendas reviewed in this chapter follow, to a modified degree, a similar path. The approach, however, represents a sharp contrast to the way agendas are typically set, as is the case with the National Research Council's (NRC) 1997 Agenda for Language Minority Children (refer to Table 2.1). The council "was organized by the National Academy of Sciences in 1916 to associate the broad community of science and technology with the Academy's purpose of furthering knowledge and advising the federal government." The National Academy of Sciences is "a private, nonprofit, self-perpetuating society of distinguished scholars engaged in scientific and engineering research" (August & Hakuta, 1997). Although the report provides few details as to the agenda-setting process, we know participants were primarily academicians representing the discipline of psychology, and the number of publications and research awards determine scholarship and, therefore, "expertise." Once convened, the panel of "experts" meets in mostly private meetings to craft an agenda, basically from the top down, and with the freedoms the federal government accords to any of its advisory groups. Who is invited to sit at the table determines the character of the conversations, the viewpoints that are legitimized in the research, and consequently the knowledge base that we use to understand and address educational concerns.

Research Priorities

Not surprisingly, much of the knowledge base on Latino/a students has an unbalanced emphasis on the development of English language proficiency among newly arrived immigrant students, even though Latinos are a diverse population including recent and long-term Americans from Mexico, Puerto Rico, Cuba, Central and South America, and the Dominican Republic. This is the inevitable result of federally sponsored research and congressionally mandated studies of bilingual education giving priority to the acquisition of English language proficiency. Even so, the NRC agenda acknowledges the need for a comprehensive

TABLE 2.1

Comparisons Between NLERAP and the NRC Agenda

Name	Source	Procedures	Purpose	Research Priorities
Improving Schooling for Language Minority Children: A Research Agenda (1994–1997)	The Committee on Developing a Research Agenda on the Education of Limited English proficient and Bilingual Learners was formed to conduct this NRC study.	A 12-member commission that met to set the agenda includes five Ph.D.s in psychology, three in education, and one sociolinguist. Nine are experts in language development, cognitive development, bilingual education, immigrant education, and student demographics.	-Review knowledge base on linguistic, cognitive, and social processes in educating ELLs and Bilingual Learners; -Examine knowledge on effective programs to identify issues worthy of research -Evaluate research methodologies; -Recommend research priorities, the infrastructure, & the use of scientific evidence to inform policy and practice.	-Content area learning, English literacy (in L2), intergroup relations, and social learning context; Focus on young children, older students with little/no formal schooling; and former LEP's; English language acquisition among non-Latinos; -Effective programming, assessments, and teacher education for ELLs with disabilities; -Research questions of strong constituencies; -Build the nation's capacity for high-quality research
National Education Latino/a Research Agenda	An initiative of El Centro de Estudios Puertorriqueños at Hunter College	A National Advisory Board of Representatives nine Regional Meetings held over 2-year period in geographically distinct areas of United States and Puerto Rico o identify context specific needs through dialogic processes engaging a broad range of stake holders, including community activists, teachers, parents, cross-disciplinary scholars.	To give voice to Latino/a perspectives on school reform and the knowledge base needed to sustain positive social change	Areas of Research: *Standards and Assessment Practices *Teacher and Administrator Education and Professional Development *Sociopolitical and Historical Context of Latino/a Education * Arts in Education

framework that explores literacy acquisition and development for the range of Latino/a learners—from those who are new to English to those who have lived in multilingual, multidialectal communities all their lives—across the developmental continuum and in different contexts of use. Among the highest priority areas for future research in the NRC agenda are (a) content area learning, (b) second language literacy (c) intergroup relations, and (d) the social context of learning. Other areas of importance where there are existing research bases include assessment and teacher preparation.

Although there are overlaps between the NRC agenda and the NLERAP agenda, the highest priority concerns identified by NLERAP participants are (a) assessment, (b) high-stakes testing, (c) teacher preparation, and (d) the arts in education. It is worth reemphasizing these broad categories with corresponding concerns were identified through dialogic processes engaging between 200–300 participants representing a broad range of expertise, including lived experiences, across different regions of the country. No attempt was made to forge consensus, although the consensus that emerged naturally is impressive. African American and American Indian research agendas came out of similar collaborative processes unique to their populations and sociohistorical time of inception.

Theoretical Framework and Methodological Approaches

Most NLERAP participants agree knowledge is a social and historical product, facts are theory-laden, and the task of science is to invent theories to explain the real world (House, 1991). Consequently, although cross-disciplinary collaborations are complex, they are essential to generate robust knowledge of practical and theoretical significance for the schooling of students from marginalized communities. If it is true "no such tradition exists" as García and Otheguy (in Moll, 1992) claim, then NLERAP is constructing a framework to guide this type of research, adding to tasks having yet to be completed but not diminishing enthusiasm for morally imperative work. The project is establishing a new theoretical and epistemological tradition in the study of Latino/a students by Latinos in the context of Latino/a communities inclusive of economic sociopolitical, cultural, and historical factors that can be used interdisciplinarily, depending on research questions and modes of inquiry. Members of the Research and Methods Working Committee of NLERAP have spelled out five principles of Participatory Action Research (PAR) that represent the methodological approach advocated by the group. Accordingly, PAR is an approach to carrying out research that can involve any one of a number of specific methods. PAR is not a method per se. Thus, principles of PAR have been applied to both qualitative and quantitative research that involve many different methods. Five suggested principles include:

1) Involve the group(s) most directly affected by the research in framing the research questions;

2) Develop skills of critical inquiry in the group of research participants who are working on the research project;

3) Share a draft of the written research results with the affected community before the research is published;

4) Negotiate reciprocity with the community most directly affected by the research;

5) Make sure that the work connects locally with the affected community and up from there, to either a district, statewide, or national level.

Sonia Nieto describes this kind of work as Latinos "cracking the code" (p. x) of their cultural-historical experience, knowledge, research, and appropriate implications shifting Latinos from the position of "being studied" from the outside, to the role of being firsthand researchers of their lives and experiences as experts from the inside (2001). An excellent example of a research approach in which Latinos collaborate in the study of their communities is the "funds of knowledge" approach as previously discussed (see, for example, Mercado [2000] in New York, Rueda [2004] in Los Angeles, Olmedo [1997] in Chicago). Through participation in this collaborative approach to research and development pre- and in-service teachers generate theoretical knowledge based on direct examination of culture as lived experience, which is then applied to transform classroom learning building on and extending the cultural resources for learning in students' homes and communities. African American, American Indian, and Alaska Native researchers who work within their ethnic communities also find value in applying the cultural-historical approach when thinking about theoretical alternatives for research (Tippeconnic, 2000; Yazzie, 2000).

THE AMERICAN EDUCATIONAL RESEARCH ASSOCIATION'S (AERA) COMMISSION ON RESEARCH IN BLACK EDUCATION (CORIBE)

Similar to the underlying premise for the betterment of Latino/a communities of NLERAP, the Commission on Research in Black Education (CORIBE) was designed to further the economic and educational survival and development of people of African descent. CORIBE, however, operates under the assumption the Black cultural knowledge base is neither divisive nor a "minority" issue. Like NLERAP, the Commission was designed to bring together a diverse group of visionary leaders (commissioners) and participants including researchers, graduate students, practitioners, policymakers, and community educators to voluntarily produce research and disseminate findings reflective of global educational issues affecting Black people. Unlike the NRC, CORIBE's purpose is not to advise the federal government as much as it is to advise the African American and perceived minority communities in the United States. CORIBE values research conducted by researchers of African American descent benefiting African American individuals and communities and seeks to identify additional resources, convening regularly to modify, adapt, and fine-tune the process.

The Agenda-Setting Process

Unique from NLERAP's bottom-up grassroots inception and NRC's nationally sanctioned Agenda for Language-Minority Children, CORIBE was initiated in 1999 by the American Educational Research Association (AERA), the premier international professional organization responsible for advancing educational research and its practical applications. The commission was an outgrowth of the Research Focused on Black Education Special Interest Group (SIG) aspiration to establish a new AERA division on Black education. In a 2001 report, *Facing the New Millennium: A Transformative Research in Action Agenda and Black Education,* CORIBE frames their agenda-setting process, research priorities, theoretical frameworks, and methodological approaches of the organization's agenda (King, 2001).

CORIBE is comprised of an Elders Council providing commissioners with wisdom and history to guide the process of improving Black education issues and 13 commissioners appointed by AERA presidents.

Commission goals include: (1) enhancing the work of the AERA Research Focused on Black Education (SIG); (2) advocating for AERA responsiveness to Black education issues; (3) increasing funding opportunities for research to increase legitimacy of issues concerning Black education; (4) identifying, generating, and supporting interests in research in Black education across the organization; and (5) the close examination of international and different U.S. contexts of Black education.

Founding commissioners worked diligently at developing an aggressive agenda using a small grant provided by AERA. Central to the commission's agenda included the preparation of research papers for publication, the development of a working colloquium, the procurement of additional funds for the work, and the creation of an Internet presence.

Research Priorities

The newly formed commission developed a research agenda out of the central question: How can education research effectively improve the lives of Black people and advance human understanding? Unlike the NRC research agenda (1997) but as in the case of NLERAP, this question was to be answered holistically, across multiple levels and in various sociohistorical contexts. Based on this question, themes for research papers were identified in the initial planning group's proposal. The papers, including comments and responses from invited scholars representing Latino/a, White, and African American perspectives, were presented and discussed during the 2000 AERA annual meeting. At this meeting, elders and commissioners recommended developing a more transformative agenda prioritizing applied research inclusive of the entire Black community (churches, parents, advocacy organizations, artists, writers, actors, etc.) utilizing advanced technology in a variety of ways addressing Black education globally, including the importance of recognizing spirituality in Black education research. This evolving community-based grassroots approach was more similar to the current work of the NLERAP agenda.

At the AERA 2001 meeting CORIBE presented a multimedia symposium featuring 10 research-based "best practices" across academic disciplines serving learners in primary through post-secondary education in diverse cultural contexts. Cultural groups represented included Haitian, Native Hawaiian, South Carolina–Gullah, and urban and rural communities nationwide. Interethnic relations among people of African descent emerged as a research area worthy of further review as noted by NLERAP researchers in acknowledging important differences between groups of Latinos living in the United States from specific countries (e.g., Mexico, Puerto Rico, Cuba, the Dominican Republic, El Salvador) as well as generational and regional differences. CORIBE's Web site has several links to American Indian Web sites, corroborating the intraethnic dialogue suggested in the Latino/a research agenda and an interactive CD-ROM was developed and disseminated as a result of this work.

CORIBE accomplishments to date include the preparation of four research papers and six brief commentary research reports, a model research priority panel community discussion, various meetings, AERA symposium, a working colloquium, and an interactive Web site that includes, among other things, an online institute for graduate student research training, and an online database. Other multimedia resources include videotapes and audiotaped meetings. At this time, NLERAP is seeking funding to develop a comprehensive Web site to accommodate research activities, community outreach, inter- and intragroup interactions, as well as interactive member participation. By making good use of technology the NLERAP and CORIBE usher people of color directly into the "digital divide" challenging assumptions around the notion of access, while harnessing the power of technology to democratize the research process.

Theoretical Frameworks and Methodological Approaches

In 1997 Edmund Gordon reported on task force findings on the role and future of minorities in AERA. Gordon argues for AERA support for approaches to knowledge construction grounded in alternative realities. According to Gordon, issues concerning people of color are not important solely for minority scholars but for the entire association's (AERA) membership.

Gordon's report provides the framework for methodological and theoretical premises of CORIBE and in agreement with the NLERAP's position on the necessity for diverse scholars to construct more appropriate frameworks for conceptualizing research on youth of color being taught in U.S. mainstream educational systems. Linda Tillman (2002) further substantiates this work by suggesting scholars of color "implement new strategies, begin new discourses, and create paradigms and models of educational research not only inclusive of culturally sensitive research approaches for African Americans but also have potential to change lives and communities in emancipatory ways" (p. 9).

CORIBE describes a culturally nurturing process-building methodology wherein graduate students and participating scholars are involved in opportunities for collaborative reflection, empirical inquiry imaginative in nature, and other collaborative action. The NLERAP research agenda describes this approach as being interdisciplinary as well as generated for Latinos by Latinos (Nieto, 2003). Of similar importance is the inclusion of African American studies, black intellectual traditions, and African or African American spirituality in research on or about Black people, generated by Black scholars. In this way, there are various contexts in which to think about Black education research and practice in which African culture and knowledge and wisdom of elders is respected and celebrated. Along this vein, for African American researchers, a form of cultural praxis with "Africanist principles" is embraced, epitomized by a metaphor likened to jazz, including the notion of embracing the paradox, coolness, and polycentrism (King, 2001; Ladson-Billings, 2003). These tenets of CORIBE's research agenda are in contrast to mainstream research in the way it democratizes the research process with values including reciprocity, mutuality, and truth-telling prevalent in African American culture (King & Mitchell, 1990/1995), akin to Nieto's idea of Latinos being able to crack the code regarding ELLs in U.S. schools.

CORIBE's research agenda thrives on a culture-systemic theoretical framework. NLERAP describes alternative epistemological, theoretical, and methodological frameworks inclusive of economic, sociopolitical, cultural, and historical factors employed interdisciplinarily depending on the scholar research questions or modes of inquiry. CORIBE describes this type of alternative appropriate for whichever group engages in the research and dissemination process. Transformative research in action is set apart from mainstream research in this manner. Research conducted for the people by the people will look very different than traditional research based on hegemony of the past. The focus on universal human interests, survival, and development make this research relevant for all of humanity (Gordon, 1997).

THE NATIONAL DIALOGUE PROJECT ON AMERICAN INDIAN EDUCATORS AND THE AMERICAN INDIAN AND NATIVE ALASKAN EDUCATION RESEARCH AGENDA

American Indians and Alaska Natives have had to operate as collaborative, dialogue-based, consensus-building tribes and forced intertribal entities as long as they have been violated, oppressed, and marginalized by various European and U.S. governments. Latinos and African Americans in the United States have had their share of similar treatment, but not entirely on their homeland and not to the point of near extinction and invisibility. The Indian Nations at Risk Report (1991) describes 20 years of progress from the 1970s to the 1980s yet describes sustained lack of progress in the area of American Indian education. As in the case for Latino/a groups in the United States, early research with an American Indian or Alaska Native focus has come largely as a result of federal initiatives to improve conditions for AI/AN people to increase opportunities for mainstream success. Like NLERAP and CORIBE, the National Dialogue Project on American Indian Education (NDPAIE), the American Indian and Alaska Native Education Research Agenda (AIANERA), and the National Congress of American Indians (NCAI) 2003 *Critical Initiatives* each describe ways in which American Indian groups find common ground, identify core issues, and develop research priorities with and without the help of the federal government.

The Agenda-Setting Process

The National Dialogue Project ran from 1987 to 1988 and was initiated by collaboration between the American Indian Sciences and Education and the College Board's Equality Project. It involved 7 regional dialogue sessions representing 87 tribes, and 150 American Indian students, parents, tribal leaders, and educators. Much like the NLERAP and CORIBE in its evolution, the NDPAIE was determined to develop an agenda addressing the economic, social, and emotional problems of youth needing to function in what leaders in the project called "two worlds."

The development of the AIANERA, by contrast, is more similar to the National Research Council's agenda for language-minority children (1977), as it was assigned to the U.S. Department of Education's Office of Educational Research and Improvement (OERI) and Office of Indian Education (OIE) in 1991 by Executive Order (13096). Working groups came from various U.S. departmental offices (e.g., Department of Education, Bureau of Indian Affairs), representatives of the Administration for Native Americans, the NCAI, and included ideas and comments from Native and non-Native educators and researchers.

In 2003, the NCAI published *Critical Issues*, which support the agenda described in the AIANERA, including public education and communication issues, the call for a research institute, a digital divide initiative, and an Indian Education focus on NCLB (2002) legislation. NCAI is an important entity because it is the oldest, largest, and most representative American Indian and Alaskan Native organization in the United States with over 250 member tribes and thousands of United States members.

Research Priorities

Sovereignty and self-determination are at the forefront of all research efforts affecting American Indian/Alaska Native (AI/AN) peoples (Lomawaima & McCarty, 2002) and all efforts to stop the legacy of conventional colonizing research paradigms described by Smith (1999) are being pursued. Like research on students who are Latino/a and African American, educational research on students who are American Indian and Alaska Native (AI/AN) needs to focus on individual student success rather than success as measured by criteria established by the majority culture (i.e., expected standardized high-stakes test results). Researchers also should respect tribal sovereignty as well as be sensitive to tribal differences inherent to indigenous people in the United States (AIAERA, 2001). Similarly, inter- as well as intragroup, linguistic, and geographical differences come to mind when considering research on students who are Latino/a and African American as well.

In direct response to these concerns, the NDPAIE identified nine concerns to inform research priorities (1987–1988). These concerns began with community-based research and included teacher reeducation and the inclusion of American Indian perspectives in courses, standardized tests as one indicator, legislative support for school reform, holistic curriculum, emphasis on high standards, and a merger of culture and education. Like the Latino/a and African American research agendas described, those involved in the dialogue seek to challenge mainstream assumptions about their AI/AN children by conducting community-based research from the inside versus "empirically based" research from the outside.

More recently, the federally supported AIANERA describes a research agenda which comes out of the U.S. Department of Education under the direction of a Federal Interagency Task Force given the responsibility for developing a research agenda for AI/AN learners in response to the Executive Order 13096. The Executive Order which concerns American Indian and Alaska Native learners states the agenda will (a) establish baseline data on academic achievement and retention of students to monitor improvement, (b) evaluate promising practices, and (c) evaluate the role of language and culture in the development of educational strategies. Agenda language in this initiative is "progress" and "benchmark" laden in areas, and absent from the agenda is the notion of community-based work. The agenda does seem to reflect the idea of looking more closely at ties between language and culture, suggesting a closer look at the whole student.

The National Congress of American Indians (NCAI) as collaborator with the AIANERA, "serves to secure and preserve rights for AI/AN people;...to enlighten the public toward a better understanding of Indian people; to preserve tribal rights;...and to promote the common welfare of American Indians and Alaska Natives" (NCAI, 2003). As part of its charge, the NCAI looks to address gaps in information, education, and technology through dialogue-based partnerships and relationships. The NLERAP describes like dialogue sessions in the development of their research priorities. Through a proposed research institute to gather and assess data on conditions and trends for AI/AN, the group hopes to develop ideas and options for community-based approaches to federal American Indian policy and tribal governance. The group is in the process of developing a tribally driven "think-tank" for proactive strategy development. In addition, similar to CORIBE's technology focus, NCAI has developed a Web site using an Indian-owned and operated Web development firm and endeavors to improve telecommunications and information technology by going after private and federal funds to support their technology efforts. The NCLB (2002) Act is also on NCAI's agenda as members are committed to assisting American Indian tribes to implement the Act within Indian schools by way of a partnership with the National Indian Education Association.

According to the AIANERA, there are seminal issues needing resolution before carrying out and organizing the AI/AN research agenda.

These include definitional issues that should be resolved by AI/AN tribes; finding researchers with demonstrated knowledge of Native cultures; identifying quality research (design standards as well as researcher understanding of cultural context), and the ability to generalize findings. The prevalence of research on AI/AN conducted by non-Native researchers is mentioned as is the notion suggesting these cultures are less sophisticated than U.S. mainstream culture and the need to dismantle this underlying assumption. The AIANERA describes six priority research categories for the research agenda: educational outcomes; Native language and culture; teachers, schools, and resources; children with special needs; early educational needs; and standards and assessments to explore the AI/AN research agenda.

Theoretical Frameworks and Methodological Approaches

Comparable to calls made by Latino/a and African American community-based researchers about their participation in and production of ethnic research, AI/AN scholars describe a need for recognition and publication by more American Indian scholars and researchers (Swisher, 1996), while at the same time acknowledging respectable collaboration with non-Native researchers (Lomawaima & McCarty, 2002). When AI/AN researchers engage in this work, it is necessary they examine their own histories and understandings of education, culture, and self-determination (Yazzie, 2000) in order to reconsider how cultural conflict resulting in knowledge negotiation and adaptation (Lipka, 1998) can lead to what Joel Spring calls deculturalization (2001). AI/AN scholars describe a kind of critical pedagogy and way of thinking about themselves in relation to their own education and research endeavors from a perspective that directly embraces critical race theory (Ladson-Billings & Tate, 1995). In fact, Latino/a and African American scholars need to go through similar processes in order to reverse historical methods of education as colonization perpetuated through the culture of testing and standards-based mainstream knowledge present in U.S. schools today.

The absence of indigenous knowledge systems in "empirical" research is noted by AI/AN scholars and speaks volumes of the value of a group such as CORIBE's Elders Council. In order for AI/AN groups to take ownership of knowledge and research to benefit their communities, they need to apply truths empirical to AI/AN for specific communities in specific time, space, and geographic location arising out of particular realities of "indigineity." The "funds of knowledge" approach is embraced by Latino/a, African American, and AI/AN inquiry communities alike as a common yet specific, inclusive yet particular, theoretical framework with which to view the "repositories of knowledge residing in their communities frequently overlooked in Western science and school curriculum" (Lomawaima & McCarty, 2002, p. 3).

AI/AN research should be based on cultural strengths and integrity if sustainability is to be achieved (Deyhle & Swisher, 1997). Both NLERAP and CORIBE participants echo these concerns related to building on solid cultural foundations appropriate for their students as a means to authenticate research results. Tribal influence in every aspect of research development, design, and methodology is crucial to the applicability of results and sound conclusions (Tippenconnic, 2002). Latinos and African Americans have come to similar conclusions based on theoretical frameworks developed by NLERAP and CORIBE. All groups reject the notion of one truth or one way of conducting research based on the perpetuation of objects unity by mainstream research trends. Lomawaima (2000) describes a shift in power or mental models in Indian country where tribes are currently exercising more control, autonomy, and responsibility in research resulting in an anticipated move to Indian scholars giving back to their tribal communities (Swisher & Tippenconnic, 1999). Latino/a and African American communities have exercised this kind of autonomy in the past, but mostly in isolation, and mostly at the whim of federal funding and governmental legislative trends. Punitive legislation like the NCLB Act (2002) can act as a catalyst for diverse researchers to reexamine priorities, "reframe" research areas, and create powerful shifts in knowledge and practice in the interest of all children of color.

COMMON GROUND

Although each Latino/a, African American, and American Indian/ Alaska Native agenda reviewed in this chapter represents independent initiatives, convergence among them is striking (refer to Table 2.2). Despite differences, convergence is strong in terms of the following.

TABLE 2.2
Community-Initiated Research Agendas

Name	Source	Procedures	Purpose	Research Priorities
National Dialogue Project on American Indian Education (1987–1988)	The American Indian Sciences & Education Society & The College Board's Equality Project	Seven regional dialogues representing 87 tribes and 150 American Indian students, parents, tribal leaders, and educators	Develop an agenda to address the economic, social, and emotional problems of youth who need to function in two worlds; call to reorient basic competencies	Major concerns: e.g., community-based research; Teacher reeducation and the inclusion of Indian perspectives in courses; standardized tests as only one indicator; legislative support for school reform; holistic curriculum; emphasis on high standards and merger of culture and education.
National Education Latino/a Research Agenda	An initiative of El Centro de Estudios Puertorriqueños at Hunter College	A National Advisory Board of Representatives nine Regional Meetings held over 2-year period in geographically distinct areas of US and PR identify context specific needs through dialogic processes engaging hundreds of stake holders, including community activists, teachers, parents, cross-disciplinary scholars,	To give voice to Latino/a perspectives on school reform and the knowledge base needed to sustain positive social change	Areas of Research: *Standards and Assessment Practices *Teacher and Administrator Education and Professional Development *Sociopolitical and Historical Context of Latino/a Education * Arts in Education

Name	Source	Procedures	Purpose	Research Priorities
A Transformative Research and Action Agenda in Black Education (1999–2001)	The AERA Commission on Research in Black Education (CORIBE) was established in 1999 to stimulate research (including funding for research), its dissemination and policy-making to improve education for and about people of African ancestry.	Elders council (6), commissioners (13), scholars (25); planning team (8). Work plan to address education holistically; commission four state-of-the-art papers; -Working colloquium analyzes gaps in knowledge and conceptual and analytical research tools and Web site as research and dissemination tool	Crisis in black education; how research can improve the lives of Black people and advance human understanding; -Reorient research thru culturally responsive analytical tools and conceptual frameworks and international perspectives -Identify culturally nurturing best practices -Computer-based digital technologies for community development	-Well-funded large and small-scale applied research on culture as an asset in student-teacher learning and development; -Community impact -The relationship between alienation and achievement -Relationship between cognition and political-economic goals; between coping and cognition -Dynamics between funds of knowledge and activity structures across contexts and knowledge domains -Models of in-service teacher development that promote conceptual shifts

Self-Help and Self-Determination

There is a long history of struggle predating the civil rights movement to act in the best interest of our children and our communities. We agree with Smith (1999) that research is a significant site of struggle and agency. Research is at the service of improving the quality of life and education in local communities. It is a way of taking back or claiming ownership to the right to determine what is in the best interest of our communities.

Creating a Broad-Based Participatory Process

We are community-oriented people and collective work comes naturally. Broad-based participation in the knowledge construction process democratizes the research process, and enables us to examine and interrogate how we make sense of social phenomena, to determine what counts as quality research and to advance human understanding in ways likely to make a difference in our communities. However, there are many impediments to building and sustaining communities across professional, social, and ideological boundaries, even among people who have a shared vision. The struggle to find ways to address or mitigate the effects of these challenges is ongoing, but we "embrace the conflict" and tensions that arise because of benefits derived from coming together.

The Centrality of Culture and Language

Culture is our lived experience, tradition, and values that nurture and sustain us. Culture speaks in honoring the knowledge and wisdom of our elders; in the expression of self through words, music, artistic expression, and movement; in the importance of spirituality in our lives; and in the values of mutuality and reciprocity. Culture is central to how we conduct research and it is central to how our children learn. Therefore, culture is an asset both in research and education.

The Influence of Context

Regarding local contexts, independent schools, alternative public schools, and community-based organizations are examples of three different educational contexts that have met success in educating

Latino/a, African-American, and American Indian students. Studies need to be conducted describing the influence and impact of these learning contexts on healthy human development.

However, we are mindful that all activities are embedded socio-political, cultural, historical, or sociohistorical contexts, webs of power relations constraining or facilitating possibilities for action. Each research agenda reviewed described ways in which contexts affect research and implications.

Holistic Education

Latino/a, African American, American Indian, or Alaska Native children, and all youth of color "come to school with a wide variety of needs, and therefore should be treated as whole people rather than detached receptacles for academic knowledge" (Sanacore, 2001). People who come from indigenous cultures see their children in their entire team as ready and able, not broken or deficient, or at risk in any way.

New Epistemological Frameworks

As expressed to each research agenda, educational research in Latino/a/minority communities requires the development of alternative theoretical frameworks powerful enough to examine and analyze complex social and educational phenomena from cross-disciplinary perspectives. For example, oppression has been framed as we-they but seldom as we-we. Furthermore, the design of contrastive case studies are needed to examine the differential experiences of varied language and racial minorities so as to better understand the diverse character of our American educational heritage, including inter- and intraethnic differences and similarities among Latino/a, African American, American Indian, or Alaska Native people in the United States, resulting from geographic, linguistic, and cultural factors.

Economic Empowerment and Community Development

Poverty is the root cause of many of the social and educational problems impeding healthy human development in formal learning contexts.

Our concern is not with increasing scores on standardized tests; it is about economic empowerment for historically marginalized communities. Although people of color are often made to compete for limited resources provided by such educational acts as the ESEA of 1965, Goals 2000, and the NCLB (2002), research agendas previewed in this chapter suggest a collective rise above this polarizing and overall destructive mental model that does not serve us well.

CONCLUSIONS AND RECOMMENDATIONS

The answer to why we need another research agenda does not simply come from an examination of the content of different agendas. It comes from understanding the bigger picture. As Popketwitz and other critical theorists suggest, research on the education of Latinos is embedded in a web of power relations which needs to be understood (1992). We need to use empirical evidence to unmask how power relations shape discourse and research on the education of Latinos, African Americans, American Indians/Alaska Natives in ways that speak to the interests of the American public.

Furthermore, as Peter Senge suggests, we need to use systemic thinking to address complex problems and issues (1990). We also need to understand that in a complex system there is no one source of power. Collectively, we are the system and we need to act with this awareness. In this manner, we can harness the strength that comes from collective action to transform who we are, to transform education, and the conditions of our communities.

This is precisely what the National Latino/a Education Research Agenda Project is all about—it is about forming alliances with a broad base of stakeholders and sponsoring multidisciplinary, longitudinal action research projects addressing in a more strategic and holistic manner the gravest concerns of our communities. Collaborative action is what CORIBE describes and models in its transformative research practice and call for action of Black people on a global scale, transcending language and culture, and in calling for a more inclusive research agenda. Additionally, research agendas for underrepresented groups need to include collaborative endeavors with individuals who come from other groups including the value of work from allegiances with White allies. To the extent this chapter demonstrates commonalities, we are in a better position to form alliances to continue to and further build the strong base of support merited by this endeavor.

Historically, coalitions of African Americans, American Indians, Chicanos, and other disenfranchised groups successfully struggled in the civil rights movement to attain valued social, economic, and educational goals. Present conditions in our communities call for the same unity of purpose and action. Our common ground compels us to connect to each other, to learn from each other, and to engage in collaborative research projects allowing us to study educational issues and concerns with greater depth and rigor in a cost-efficient manner. Much is already known about "best practices," even though this information has been marginalized. Opportunities for ethnic groups to develop competence, skill, and proficiency in inter-/intraethnic dialogue need to be valued, created, sought after, and maximized.

IMPLICATIONS

This chapter provides a comparative perspective on research in Latino/a communities, past, present, and future from divergent viewpoints and voices. It is evident there is a great deal of common ground in what is being said, but there are differences in the epistemologies framing each agenda, theoretical perspectives, and methodological procedures guiding the framing of the agendas depending on unique characteristics of each agenda reviewed. One thing is for certain: Scholars of color and those interested in social justice and equity need to challenge several mainstream assumptions about our youth and schools in order to impact action, social justice, and equity sooner rather than later. Educationally based assumptions needing challenge include: (1) the United States as a meritocratic system; (2) the notion racism has been "solved"; (3) educational tracking as neutral; and (4) the purpose of schooling as assimilation (Cochran-Smith, 2003).

Research quality is also an issue wherein agendas reviewed express concern for improving the quality of research. As mentioned earlier, one of the factors affecting research quality is the lack of funding. Another is research crossing class, ethnic, and racial boundaries requires a multidisciplinary perspective, demanding skills and expertise exceeding preparation provided in graduate and postgraduate studies. Moreover, educational research within minority and working-class communities in the United States has, for the most part, become the domain of an ethnically diverse group of researchers, many who have entered educational research through what are considered nontraditional avenues. For example, many are former teachers and school administrators who bring valuable insights based on firsthand knowledge of schools, classrooms, and communities, but who have had relatively fewer opportunities to participate as members of research communities.

This contribution suggests the need for collaborative studies engaging senior scholars who may have less knowledge of local contexts working side by side with junior colleagues who bring other types of expertise. It also demonstrates possibilities and sets an example for inter- and interethnic collaboration. Successful collaborative work not withstanding, fund-raising to support these efforts is critical. Basic and applied research needs to be funded, preferably by foundations, professional organizations, and universities who are willing to commit to longitudinal research for purposes of generating new knowledge in high-priority local communities.

Underrepresented groups in the United States need to recognize when times are crucial for discourse and single-mindedness on behalf of children of color in school systems. However, because research is complex, costly, and time-consuming, efforts to address the needs of diverse learners also may have to be made on moral and ethical grounds, not simply on the basis of data-driven information and processes. It is up to scholars and researchers of color to collectively identify possibilities for Latino/a, African American, American Indian, and Alaska Native students, and other educationally marginalized children in our country. When scholars and researchers of color and like-minded allies come together around these issues, it will be like waking a sleeping giant in U.S. school system reform.

REFERENCES

August, D. G., & Hakuta, K. (Eds.). (1997). *Improving schooling for language-minority children. A research agenda*. Washington, DC: National Research Council.

August, D. G., & Kaestle, C. (1997). Improving the infrastructure for research on English language learners and bilingual education. In D. August & K. Hakuta (Eds.), *Improving schooling for language minority children. A research agenda* (pp. 363–411). Washington, DC: National Research Council.

Berliner, D. C. (2002, November). Educational research: The hardest science of all. *Educational Researcher, 31*(8), 18–20.

Cochran-Smith, M. (2003, April). Equity and accountability issues in teacher education. In J. A. Banks & C. A. McGee Banks (Chairs), *Diversity, accountability, and equity: Findings and insights from the second edition of the Handbook of Research on Multicultural Education*. Presidential invited session at the annual meeting of the American Educational Research Association, Chicago, IL.

Cohen, D. K., & Barnes, C. A. (1999). Research and the purposes of education. In E. C. Lagemann & L. S. Shulman (Eds.), *Issues in education research* (pp. 17–41). San Francisco: Jossey-Bass.

Colwell, R. (1999). Remarks made to the National Educational Research Policy and Priorities Board, Department of Education, Washington, DC. Retrieved March 18, 1999, from http//www.nsf.gov/od/lpa/forum/colwell/rc990318doe.htm

De la Luz Reyes, M., & Halcón, J. J. (Eds.). (2001). *The best for our children: Critical perspectives on literacy for of Latino students.* New York: Teachers College Press.

Delpit, L. (2003, April). Touched by their fire, blinded by their brilliance: Reinventing education for African American children. Dewitt Wallace-Readers Digest Distinguished Lecture at the annual meeting of the American Educational Research Association, Chicago, IL. April 22, 2003.

Deyhle, D., & Swisher, K. (1997). Research in American Indian and Alaska Native educations: From assimilation to self-determination. In M. W. Apple (Ed.), *Review of research and education* (pp. 113–194). Washington, DC: American Educational Research Association.

Feuer, M. J., Towne, L., & Shavelson, R. J. (2002). Scientific culture and education research. *Educational Researcher, 31*(8), 4–14.

Foster, M. (2000). *Teaching Black students: Best practices.* (CORIBE-Briefs). Paper retrieved May 24, 2003, from http://www.coribe.org/PDF/MFosterA.pdf

Freeman, K. (2001). *Black populations globally: The costs of the underutilization of Blacks in higher education.* (CORIBE-Briefs). Paper retrieved May 24, 2003, from http://www.coribe.org/PDF/free_BLACKPOP.pdf

Gordon, E. W. (1997, April). Task force on the role and future of minorities. *Educational Researcher, 44*–53.

Greene, M. (1994). Epistemology and education research: The influence of recent approaches to knowledge. In L. Darling-Hammond (Ed.), *Review of research in education* (pp. 423–464). Washington, DC: AERA.

Gutiérrez, K., Baquedano-Lopez, P., & Alvarez, H. H. (2001). Literacy as hybridity: Moving beyond bilingualism in urban classrooms. In M. de la Luz Reyes & J. J. Halcón (Eds.), *The best for our children: Critical perspectives on literacy for of Latino students* (pp. 122–141). New York: Teachers College Press.

House, E. R. (1991, August–September). Realism in Research. *Educational Researcher, 20*(6), 2–9.

Indian Nations at Risk Task Force. (1991). Indian nations at risk task force: An educational strategy for action: *Final report of the Indian nations that risk task force.* Washington, DC: U.S. Department of Education. (ERIC Document Reproduction Service No. ED343753)

Kaestle, C. F. (2001, Feb.). Federal aid to education since WWII: Purposes and politics. In J. Jennings (Ed.), *The future of the federal role in elementary and secondary education* (pp. 13–36). Washington, DC: Center for Educational Policy.

Kaestle, C. F. (1993, January–February). The awful reputation of educational research. *Educational Researcher, 22*(1), 26–31.

King, J. E. (2001). *Facing the new millennium: A transformative research and action agenda and black education.* The report of the AERA Commission on Research and Black Education submitted to the American Educational Research Association, June 2001.

King, J. E., & Mitchell, C. A. (1999/1995). *Black mothers to sons: Juxtaposing African American literature with social practice.* New York: Peter Lang.

Ladson-Billings, G. (2001). *Crossing over to Canaan: The journey of new teachers in diverse classrooms.* San Francisco: Jossey Bass.

Ladson-Billings, G. (2003, April). Critical race theory and multicultural education: Implications for equity and accountability. In J. A. Banks & C. A. McGee Banks (Chairs), *Diversity, accountability, and equity: Findings and insights from the second edition of the handbook of Research on multicultural education.* Presidential invited session at the annual meeting of the American Educational Research Association, Chicago, IL.

Ladson-Billings, G., & Tate, W. F., IV. (1995). Toward a critical race theory in education. *Teachers College Record, 97*(1), 47–68.

Lagemann, E. C. (2000). *An elusive science: The troubling history of education research.* Chicago: University of Chicago Press.

Lee, C. D. (2001). *This state of knowledge about the education of African Americans.* (CORIBE-Briefs). Paper retrieved May 24, 2003, from http://www.coribe.org/PDF/BlackEd.pdf

Lipka, J. (1998). *Transforming the culture of schools: Yup'ik Eskimo examples.* Mahwah, NJ: Lawrence Erlbaum Associates.

Lomawaima, K. T. (2000). Tribal sovereigns: Reframing research in American Indian communities. *Harvard Education Review, 70*(1), 1–21.

Lomawaima, K. T., & McCarty, T. L. (2002). Reliability, validity, and authenticity in American Indian and Alaska native research. *Special edition ERIC digest.* Washington, DC: U.S. Department of Education. (ERIC Document Reproduction Service No. EDORC0204)

Mercado, C. I. (2000). The learner: "Race," "ethnicity," and linguistic difference. In V. Richardson (Ed.), *Handbook of research on teaching.* (668–694) Washington, DC: AERA.

Moll, L. C. (1992, March). Bilingual classroom studies and community analysis: Some recent trends. *Educational Researcher, 21*(2), 20–24.

Moll, L. C., Amanti, C., Neff, D., & González, N. (1992). Funds of knowledge for teaching: Using a qualitative approach to connect homes and classrooms. *Theory Into Practice, 31*(2), 132–141.

Moll, L. C., & Ruiz, R. (2002). The schooling of Latino children. In M.M. Suarez-Orozco & M.M. Paez (Eds.), *Latinos remaking America* (pp. 362–374). Cambridge, MA: Harvard University Press.

Moll, L. C., & Ruiz, R. (2003, April). Contemporary issues and schooling of Latino students. In P. Pedraza & M. Rivera (Chairs) Part 2: National Latino/a education research agenda project. *Imagining new possibilities for Latino/ communities.* Session at the annual meeting of the American Educational Research Association, Chicago, IL.

A Nation at Risk. (1983). *A nation at risk: The imperative for educational reform.* From the National Commission on Excellence in Education. Washington, DC: U.S. Department of Education. Report retrieved May 24, 2003, from http://www.ed.gov/pubs/NatAtRisk/

National Congress of American Indians. (2003). *2003 Critical initiatives.* Report retrieved May 24, 2003, from www.indian.senate.gov/2003hrgs/022603hrg/hall.PDF

National Educational Research Policy and Priorities Board, U.S. Department of Education. (2000). *Investing in learning: A policy statement with recommendations on research in education.* Washington, DC: Author.

Nieto, S. (Discussant). (2003, April). Part 2: *National Latino/a education research agenda project.* Imagining new possibilities for Latino/communities. Session at the annual meeting of the American Educational Research Association, Chicago, IL.

Nieto, S. (2001). Foreword. In M. de la Luz Reyes & J. J. Halcón (Eds.), *The best for our children: Critical perspectives on literacy for of Latino students* (pp. ix–xi). New York: Teachers College Press.

No Child Left Behind. (2002). *No child left behind: A desktop reference.* Prepared by the Office of the Undersecretary. Washington, DC: U.S. Department of Education.

NSF's Interagency Educational Research Initiative

Olmedo, I. M. (1997). Varces of our past: Using oral history to explore funds of knowledge within a Puerto Rican family. *Anthropology and Education Quarterly, 28*(4), 550–573.

Pedraza, P., & Rodriguez, M. (2003, April). *Dialogues in Black and Brown: conversations with the commission on research in Black education and the National Hispanic research agenda.* In

R. Ruiz (Chair), Session at the annual meeting of the American Educational Research Association, Chicago, IL.

Popketwitz, T. S. (1992). A political/sociological of teacher education reforms: Evaluation of the relation of power and knowledge PDF available from http://www.ncela.gwu.edu/resabout/research/tempall.html

Report of President's Advisory Commission on Educational Excellence for Hispanic Americans. (2003, April). Report retrieved June 4, 2003, from http://www.ed.gov/PressReleases/04-2003/04092003a.html

Rueda, R., Monzo, & Higareda, I. (2004). Appropriating the sociocultural resources of Latino/a paraeducators for effective instruction with Latino students. *Urban Educational, 39*(1), 51–90.

Sanacore, J. (2001, March 5). Needed: Caring schools. *Education Week.* Retrieved April 26, 2005 from www.edweek.org/articles/2001/03/07/25sanacore.h20.html

San Miguel, G. (1987). The status of historical research on Chicano education. *Review of Educational Research, 57*(4), 467–480.

Santamaría, L. J. (2003, April). Multicultural education, English language learners, and academic achievement in elementary school: moving theory into practice. In G. A. Duncan (Chair), *Committee on scholars of color in education: New member paper session.* At the annual meeting of the American Educational Research Association, Chicago, IL.

Senge, P. M. (1990). *The fifth discipline: The art and practice of the learning organization.* New York: Currency Doubleday.

Smith, L. T. (1999). *Decolonizing methodologies: Research and indigenous peoples.* New York: Zed Books.

Spring, J. (2001). *Deculturalization and the struggle for equality* (3rd ed.). New York: McGraw-Hill.

Swisher, K. G. (1996). Why Indian people should be the ones to write about Indian education. *American Indian Quarterly, 20*(1), 83–90.

Swisher, K. G., & Tippeconnic, J. W., III (Eds.). (1999). *Next steps: Research and practice to advance Indian education.* Charleston, WV: ERIC.

Tillman, L. C. (2002). Culturally sensitive research approaches: An African-American perspective. *Educational Researcher, 31*(9), 3–12.

Tippeconnic, J. W. III, (2000). Reflecting on the past: Some important aspect of Indian education to consider as we look toward the future. *Journal of American Indian Education, 39*(2), 1–12.

Watkins, W. H. (2000). *Colonial education in Africa: Retrospects and prospects.* (CORIBE-Briefs). Report retrieved June 4, 2003, from http://www.coribe.org/PDF/watkins_Colonial.pdf

Wertsch, J. (1991). *Voices of the mind.* Cambridge, MA: Harvard University Press.

Yazzie, T. (2000, May). *Holding a mirror to "eyes wide shut": The role of Native languages and cultures in the education of American Indian students.* Presented at the National Indian Education Research Agenda Conference, Albuquerque, NM.

PART II

Sociohistorical Revisioning

3

Setting the Context: Historical Perspectives on Latino/a Education

Victoria-María MacDonald
Florida State University

Karen Monkman
De Paul University

INTRODUCTION

The contemporary issues engaging scholars and practitioners of Latino/a education are rooted in a long and complicated sociohistorical context. This chapter provides an overview of the most salient themes in the history of Latinos and education from the 16th century Spanish presence in North America to the present. Several themes and tensions are recurrent throughout the history of Latino/a education. First, the relationships between Latinos and others in society, namely, the positioning of Latinos in society; the various ways in which social categories and social relations have been structured (particularly by the United States, Mexico, and Spain); and the ways in which agency of Latinos has conditioned, challenged, and altered those categories and social relations. Social structures constrain and also enable, as we can see in the legal system that defines who is in which ethnic or racial category and how people deemed members of those categories are accorded or denied rights and benefits in society. Agency is also clearly at work, as we will see from the segregation of children who "looked Spanish" into substandard classrooms, to the changes during the 1960s and 1970s because of the Chicano movement. Power and its negotiation are central in these dynamics; power relations condition the ways that ethnic and racial peoples have been able to participate in society, to challenge its inequities, and to change it from the inside out.

Second, schooling and its role in social and cultural change are clearly evident in this historical overview. Schools can be tools of social reproduction, replicating the inequitable social structures in society (Willis, 1977). Similarly, they often promote assimilation with narrow assumptions of Anglo-conformity embedded in the processes of schooling (Spring, 1994). Conversely, however, schools also can be locuses of change wherein inequitable social and cultural structures and practices are challenged, resisted, refused, coopted, and altered (Levinson & Holland, 1996). We need only look at the many examples in the other chapters in this book at the ways in which teachers, parents, and children have engaged in struggles to improve their schooling experiences. When such experiences become frequent and commonplace, schools become changed entities and more equitable forces in society.

For instance, we can look at educational reforms such as bilingual education for Puerto Ricans in New York City during the 1960s and 1970s, and how successfully implemented bilingual educational programs produce bilingual, bicultural citizens who fully engage in multiple aspects of society. Similarly, Trujillo (1996) recounts the ability of Chicanos in "Aztlán City" to alter the power relations and gain control of the school board and the city council in 1970 in their struggle for equal educational opportunity. The work of COPLA (*Comité de Padres Latinos*) has improved the experience of children in a Mexican immigrant community through united efforts of parents, teachers, and school administrators (Delgado-Gaitan, 2001). Initiatives such as these expect educational experiences to be "additive" and not "subtractive." Additive schooling is about seeing language and ethnic identity as assets that "figure precisely in what it means to be educated in U.S. society" (Valenzuela, 1999, p. 270). It is about the maintenance of community and culture and at the same time expanding one's ability to engage fully in additional cultures and communities. Former students become economic actors in society, without abandoning their cultural roots. In contrast, subtractive schooling, the most common historical practice imposed on Latinos in American public schools, promotes an assimilative process wherein minority children abandon their first languages and cultures as they acquire the dominant language and culture. This practice thereby cuts off Latinos' ability to communicate and participate across cultural and language boundaries. Furthermore, it prevents the possibilities of building on the strengths of one's first culture and language.

Third, we see a rich texture in the changing notions of just what it means to be Latino/a in the United States (Trueba, 1999; Suárez-Orozco & Páez, 2002). Throughout this chapter, we show how broad notions such as "Latino" or "Hispanic" have been interpreted by the powers that be in the United States (and, formerly, Spain and Mexico). Although we know that the terms Latino/a and Hispanic are not synonymous, nor equally embraced by everyone (we hear Hispanic more in Florida but Latino/a more in California, for example), we will not directly discuss the political issues involved in labeling (Oboler, 1995) in this chapter. Choices of using these broader terms versus more specific terms such as Mexican American, Cuban American, Guatemalan, Hispano, Tejano, Chicano, and Nuyorican are problematic because of differentiated subgroup experiences in this country.

In this historical chapter, we reveal the changing ways in which ethnicity, race, and culture have come to be categorized and conceptualized. Ethnic, cultural, and racial categories are social constructions and so change over time and in different places. Because they are socially constructed, their meaning can be altered. As this chapter reveals, in both individual and collective forms, such as the creation of the League of United Latin American Citizens in 1929 (LULAC), and through the energies of individuals such as Antonia Pantoja in New York City, that participation has been influential in moving us toward a society that is more integrated and more diverse.

In summary, constructing a "usable past" for Latino/a education empowers students, teachers, and scholars with a foundation of how policies have shaped today's educational opportunities (Hansot & Tyack, 1982). Latino/a schooling, a relative newcomer to the field of educational history, is situated in this chapter within the context of U.S. expansionism, imperialism, Cold War ideology, and the politics of immigration during the 19th and 20th centuries (MacDonald, 2001).

The history of Latino/a education in this chapter is divided into several chronological eras. From the colonial era in the Southwest and the Southeast (1521–1821) to the conquest of Mexico in 1848 by the United States and to the arrival of Puerto Ricans to New York and Cubans in Florida in the 20th century—these numerous eras reflect the diverse demographic and regional history of schooling for Latinos. These demarcations in historical eras are often fluid, of course, but at least provide a framework for understanding the long and diverse expanse of Latino/a education (MacDonald, 2004). Policies that shaped this Latino/a educational experience are intertwined with the social, economic, legal, and political status of Latinos. Throughout U.S. history, Latinos have demonstrated how collective action, legal channels, and philanthropy can be utilized to change the course of history. As other scholars will demonstrate in this volume, educational opportunity and achievement for Latinos is within reach. The question remains to what extent we can create schools and a society that benefits from, includes, and is shaped by the strengths of cultural diversity while diminishing the inequities inherent in a stratified society.

COLONIAL SCHOOLING IN THE SOUTHWEST AND SOUTHEAST, 1521–1821

Formal and informal education in northern New Spain (roughly today's southwestern states) occurred within the context of Spanish exploration, conquest, and settlement. Conquistadores carried out these activities under the name of both the crown and the church. As David Weber (1992) explained, the explorers believed they could "serve God, Country, and themselves at the same time." The search for gold and other riches was no less a part of Spain's intent as it rose to international power in the 15th and 16th centuries. Although the quest for material wealth was disappointing to the Spaniards who pushed into the American Southwest, they created a permanent imprint on Native American culture. The Spanish imposed their language in verbal and written forms, along with the beginnings of formalized European education. The collision of cultures, languages, and religions over three centuries produced a new people who are the ancestors of today's southwestern Latinos.

Conquest in the Caribbean islands and Latin America began in the late 1400s and early 1500s. Exploration in modern-day United States dates back to Juan Ponce de León's arrival in Florida in 1513. Financed at first by the Spanish government, and later with private funds, explorers settled the New World. On reaching a settlement of Native Americans, the Spanish would issue a *requerimiento* or notification. The requerimiento ordered natives to accept Spanish rule and Christianity or risk their lands, lives, and liberty (Weber, 1992). The Spanish government provided financial and military support for the religious conversion of Native Americans, a chief vehicle for the imposition of Spanish language and culture. By 1526 at least two priests were required to accompany any exploration parties to New Spain. Catholic orders, chiefly from the Franciscan, Dominican, and Jesuit orders, created a network of missions that extended northward up California's Pacific Coast and westward through modern-day Texas and inward to New Mexico and Arizona. A short-lived series of missions also were created in the Southeast starting with the founding of St. Augustine, Florida, in 1565. The missionaries began the intertwined task of fulfilling their duty to the church to Christianize the natives and their duty to the Spanish empire—to teach them the Spanish language and loyalty to the Crown.

During the long period of Spanish reign, local conditions and Native American rebellion shaped colonial policies. The Council of Indies, located in Spain, was the governing body for all colonial activities. The council issued reforms such as the 1573 Royal Orders for New Discoveries, prohibiting explorers from conquering and physically harming Native Americans. However, the distance from authorities in Spain, opportunities for exploitation, and religious zeal limited the effectiveness of these reforms (Weber, 1992).

The Spanish conquest had a devastating impact on Native American populations. Infectious European diseases (particularly smallpox), abuse of the *encomendero* (a system in which Natives involuntarily worked Spaniard's lands), enslavement, and forced relocation into missions, permanently altered the demographics of the Americas. Close contact between Europeans and Native Americans in the mission compounds often resulted in alarmingly high rates of mortality (Sweet, 1995).

Furthermore, colonial policies dictated the land, civil, and political rights of individuals in New Spain based on their skin color, race, ethnicity, and national origin (Menchaca, 2001). European-born *peninsulares* occupied the highest legal and social status in New Spain. The second tier consisted of *criollos*, individuals born in New Spain of pure Spanish parentage. Legally, Native Americans occupied the third tier. In return for accepting colonial rule, land rights were accorded and the church became their legal protector (Menchaca, 2001, p. 81). Socially, Native Americans were below both African slaves and free Blacks (Haas, 1995, p. 29).

Adding to the complexities, however, of long centuries of settlement, many soldiers and settlers entered into unions (legitimately or illegitimately) with Indian women. The children of these unions were called *mestizos*. Mestizos occupied a nebulous legal and political status in the eyes of the Spanish crown. Depending on factors such as the status of the father and whether the parents were married in the church, some mestizos eventually "passed" into society as criollos (Mörner, 1967). In the status-conscious New Spain, these legal, social, and political distinctions impacted educational opportunities.

During the 1600s and 1700s, Spanish explorers pushed northward from central Mexico into lands that form the contemporary United States. Both settlers and missionaries carried out formal and informal educational activities after the rudiments of living were established. Three discernible forms of education—settlers' schools, missions, and informal education—emerged simultaneously, each reflecting the hierarchical nature of Spanish colonial society. Settlers' schools, charged with the preservation of Spanish language, culture, and religion in the New World, represented the first type. Run by either secular teachers or under the auspices of the missions, this formal education for cultural transfer was initially reserved only for the children of Spanish settlers, civil leaders, and military officers. Over the course of time, these schools also included children born in the New World, many of whom were mestizos.

The second and most prevalent type of formal education occurred in the missions. Missions were generally enclosed compounds run by priests and lay brothers to Christianize and "civilize" the Native Americans, as will be described in detail later in this chapter. The educational function of the missions was reserved exclusively for Native Americans as colonial policy dictated the separation of Whites from Indians in the missions (Burns, 1908, p. 507). Unlike the social purpose of cultural transmission in settlers' schools, mission education was purposefully designed to *replace* Native American languages, religions, dress, and other cultural attributes with the Spanish language, Roman Catholic faith, and European mores and customs. Although some priests learned native languages, the mission's role in the deculturalization of Native Americans was extensive (Menchaca, 1999).

Informal education occurred throughout New Spain, and represents the third form of learning evident in the colonial era. Similar to any frontier situation, settlers brought books, pamphlets, and other means of noninstitutional learning to share with their families and fellow settlers. The copious letters between officials in Spain and New Spain preserved in the royal archives reveal a high level of literacy among the officers and elite explorers. Although the Spanish Inquisition attempted to censor books considered heretical, works such as Miguel de Cervantes's 1605 *Don Quixote* were favorites listed in the ship's registers headed for the New World (Leonard, 1949).

Schooling in colonial New Spain was generally aimed at reproducing Spanish society. With increasing unions across racial and cultural boundaries, new social categories, for example, mestizos, were created that complicated earlier divisions in society.

THE MEXICAN ERA OF INDEPENDENCE, 1821–1848

Latin Americans grew increasingly dissatisfied with Spain's rigid and hierarchical colonial policies, particularly its political and economic favoritism toward Spanish-born individuals. As a result, Latin American countries rebelled, demanding more equitable rights for Latin American–born and indigenous peoples. Mexico declared independence from Spain in 1821, opening an era of political and financial instability, particularly for the far northern areas of Mexico. Political changes in the liberal Mexican government profoundly affected education during this era. The independence movement democratized Spain's rigid caste system. The new constitution's 1822 "Plan de Iguala" stipulated that *all* classes of Mexicans were citizens and the three former legal Spanish classifications—Spanish, mestizo, and Indian—were abolished. Because the primary function of the missions had been to use education as a way of Christianizing and Hispanicizing Native Americans, this political shift and the Mexican government's mandated secularization of the missions greatly weakened the Catholic Church's role. The Mexican government withdrew subsidies for missions and ordered the return of church-controlled lands to the public domain. These financial and political changes during the 1820s and 1830s had a devastating impact on some churches, limiting their ability to provide education at the same levels as under Spanish rule (Martinez & Alire, 1998).

At the same time that financial support for church schools was being withdrawn, another Mexican constitution in 1824 required education for all children but left funding and other administrative matters to the state and territorial governments (Berger, 1947). Recent historians have not thoroughly examined school records from this era but the general sense is that although the paper decrees and laws for educational support existed, the actual number of schooling opportunities decreased or stayed the same (Berger, 1947; Menchaca, 1999).

In 1834, for example, the Mexican government sent 20 teachers to open schools in California, still part of Mexico. The teachers dispersed throughout the territory and some taught in the mission schools (Menchaca, 1999). Additional schools during this era included The Young Ladies Seminary in San José (run by the Sisters of Charity), a mission school in San Rafael, and San Francisco's Church of Saint Francis School. A total of more than 1,000 pupils were attending schools in California prior to the Mexican War (California Dept. of Public Instruction, 1865). New Mexico's educational facilities also were meager during the Mexican Era, except for the efforts of private teachers such as Father Antonio José Martinez, who wrote and published textbooks for schoolchildren (Menchaca, 1999).

In sum, this early period of Mexican independence revealed the persistence of Catholic schools as favored educational institutions, and the beginning, at least on paper, of public support for schools. The long intertwined history of Catholicism and schooling would create difficulties under more secularized forms of education introduced when the Southwest territories became part of the United States. Furthermore, the limited funds for public schooling during Mexican independence gave Anglo settlers coming from the eastern United States the false impression that education was little valued. These beliefs led to the marginalization and dismissal of alternative forms of education in favor of the Anglo-Saxon Protestant, middle-class public school reform movement of the mid-19th century (MacDonald, 2004).

AMERICANIZATION AND RESISTANCE: CONTESTED TERRAIN DURING THE ERA OF CONQUEST AND IMPERIALISM, 1848–1912

The United States–Mexican War, 1846–1848

Beginning in the mid-19th century, the United States began an era of expansionism, supported ideologically by the notion of Manifest Destiny. The concept of Manifest Destiny provided a justification for the United States to spread from coast to coast and initiate the Mexican War. The Mexican War's resolution with the Treaty of Guadalupe Hidalgo in 1848 resulted in the acquisition of vast territories. Mexico ceded 500,000 square miles—including the contemporary states of California, New Mexico, Arizona, Utah, Nevada, and parts of Colorado and Wyoming—for $15 million. The United States also agreed to assume debts and honor the property rights of current inhabitants. After the Treaty of Guadalupe Hidalgo, Menchaca (2001) points out that Latino/a and Native American populations became racialized again, this time under U.S. definitions of ethnicity and race. Educational opportunities for Southwestern Latino/a children under U.S. territory and statehood varied depending on location and the economic and legal status of their parents. The draw of gold in California after 1849 and the opening of land for slave-owners in Texas led to faster Anglo occupation and settlement in those two states resulting in more Americanization measures. In contrast, Latinos in the areas of northern New Mexico and Colorado, often called *Hispanos*, wielded more economic and political power, and subsequently could more readily maintain bilingual/bicultural public schools for a longer period (Donato, 1999; Getz, 1997).

Within the broad range of educational experiences for Latinos in the Southwest from the Treaty of Guadalupe Hidalgo until statehood of the last territory (i.e., Colorado in 1912) themes from the colonial era resurface but with different ramifications. Specifically, contests over language and religion and between local communities and state agencies dominated this era. These controversial issues typified educational reform efforts in the Midwest and Northeast but took a different shape and form in the Southwest (Cremin, 1980; Kaestle, 1983). The widespread and accepted view of public schools as vehicles of Americanization among Anglo-Saxon Protestant reformers ultimately triumphed in the Southwest but not without decades of compromise and fluidity.

Texas and California rapidly adopted statehood in 1845 and 1850 respectively. Settlers from the previously independent Republic of Texas (1836–1845) and easterners drawn by the California Gold Rush of 1849 crowded into the western states, causing tensions between older Latino/a populations and the new Anglos. After the Treaty of Guadalupe Hidalgo in 1848, the pattern of racialization previously begun under Spanish rule was resurrected. Suffrage was only granted to Mexicans considered of the White race. Mestizos, Native Americans, African Americans, and Afro-mestizos were denied political rights in the new state constitutions. Furthermore, these groups were barred by statute from practicing law, becoming naturalized citizens, and, in many cases, marrying Anglos. Despite assurances in the treaty that the land rights of Spanish settlers would be preserved, scores of Mexican landholders in California (called *Californios*) and Texas (*Tejanos*) lost their land and means of subsistence (Griswold del Castillo, 1990). These discriminatory measures, according to Menchaca (1999), resulted in increasingly reduced political clout for Latinos in Texas and California to fight for equal educational opportunities. Furthermore, conditions for Mexican Americans were particularly harsh in Texas. As a Southern slave state, ideas of racial inferiority extended not only to African Americans but to Mexican Americans as well (Horsman, 1981).

During the first years of statehood in California (1850–1866), Catholic schools continued to educate Mexican Americans, and were often provided with public funds for their efforts. Section 10 of California's 1851 school law permitted religious schools to receive "compensation from the Public School fund in proportion to the number of its pupils, in the same manner as provided for district schools by this act" (California Dept. of Public Instruction, 1865, p. 244). By 1853 these measures were under attack. For instance, Bishop Joseph S. Alemany asked the California Superintendent of Public Instruction in that year to continue supporting the Catholic schools, "I beg leave to ask you to aid us with your great influence, that the reported schools may not be altogether cut off from the public fund." According to Bishop Alemany, 12 schools with a total of 579 pupils were being instructed in English, French, and Spanish languages in Catholic schools throughout California (State of California, 1853, Appendix C). The 1855 revised school law permanently removed the option of public funds for private religious schools. One last effort was made in 1860 when Hon. Zack Montgomery of Yuba County introduced a bill to the Assembly permitting Catholic schools to receive a portion of the funds. It was argued vigorously in the California Assembly but defeated (California Dept. of Public Instruction, 1865).

According to San Miguel (1999), the popularity and spread of Catholic schools in the Southwest even after public schools were created was the result of three main reasons. First, Catholic schooling was seen as a form of preserving Latino/a identity because of the closely intertwined nature of religion in Latino/a culture. Second, the Catholic Church was willing to permit the speaking of Spanish in school and allow Mexican Americans to preserve other cultural traditions. For example, when the Sisters of Loretto were recruited to work in New Mexico in the 1850s, "the Sisters applied themselves to the study of the Spanish language." Within one year, their school, Our Lady of Light, had 20 boarders and 22 day pupils (Abreu, 1932, p. 47). Finally, the recruitment of teaching orders provided an inexpensive method of staffing schools, and some of them were native Spanish speakers from Spain or Mexico.

In the 1850s, 1860s, and even early 1870s Spanish was still used in many of the public schools in Texas and California. San Miguel and

Valencia (1998) call the inclusion of Spanish a form of "additive Americanization," meaning that it did not strip Latinos of their culture. Texas superintendent of Public Instruction J. C. De Gress, for example, noted that a former ruling disallowing Spanish and German in the schools was repealed in 1872. He argued that the "large proportion of citizens of German and Spanish birth and descent in our State" rendered the introduction of rule 7 necessary. Rule 7 permitted German, French, and Spanish to be taught in the public schools "provided the time so occupied shall not exceed two hours each day" (State of Texas, 1872, p. 10). In California, school reports from the 1850s continued to report public schools with Spanish classes. In 1866 California began its policies of "subtractive" education with passage of a school law mandating in Section 55 that "All schools shall be taught in the English language" (California Dept. of Public Instruction, 1866, p. 17). In Texas and California the existence of laws promoting English did not completely eradicate the use of Spanish, however. As late as 1886 complaints were filed with the superintendent of schools in Texas that public schools were conducted in Spanish and German (State of Texas, 1886).

Spanish-medium schools and the use of public funds for Catholic schools persisted even longer in the sparsely settled territories of New Mexico (1848–1912), Arizona (1848–1912), and Colorado (1848–1876). In 1874, for instance, among the New Mexico Territory's 128 public schools, 40 were conducted in English and Spanish and 88 solely in Spanish (Territory of New Mexico, 1874). The *School Laws of New Mexico (Leyes de Escuelas de Nuevo Mexico)* were printed with alternate pages in Spanish and English. In 1889 the laws permitted school directors to "adopt textbooks in either English or Spanish, or both." As Donato (1999) has found in northern Colorado, and Getz (1997) in New Mexico, the political participation of Latinos as elected school officials resulted in better educational conditions and less subtractive policies than other southwestern states.

The long territorial decades of New Mexico and Arizona combined with the slow development of public schools, an increasing number of Anglo settlers from the east, and divisions within the Catholic Church, opened the door for an additional influence on Southwestern Latino/a education—Protestant missionary schools. The Presbyterian Church, under the leadership of missionary superintendent Sheldon Jackson, viewed late-19th-century New Mexico as a field ripe with possibilities. Jackson wished to seize the area in the late 19th century for Protestantism as the Spanish had, centuries earlier, replaced the Aztec religion in Mexico with Catholicism (Bender, 1996). Yohn (1995) and Bender (1996) reveal the high price Latino/a children paid if they attended the Protestant missionary schools, however. Children were stigmatized in their communities, and local Catholic priests threatened parents with excommunication. At the same time, Yohn points out the long-term benefits to children attending Presbyterian schools, particularly young men. Hispanos, especially those who converted to Catholicism, became the "recipients of whatever largesse the mission enterprise had to reward" and were introduced to networks of Anglo individuals who promoted their education and could help them secure employment (Yohn, 1995, pp. 171–172). These advantages are reinforced by the status of both the Catholic and public schools in New Mexico during the 1870s and 1880s. According to Banker (1993), Yohn (1995), and others, most public school classes were conducted in Spanish and Catholic school classes in both languages. As a result, the missionary schools offered upwardly mobile Hispanos entry to the language, values, and milieu of the English-speaking Protestant, Anglo world.

We see in this era reflection of how schooling is used for nation-building purposes. When the Southwest was part of Mexico, the Spanish language and Catholicism were prominent. As northern European influence increased so, too, did the requirements of English and the introduction of so-called secular but really pan-Protestant public schools or Protestant missionary schools. Americanization was thus promoted through both additive and subtractive acculturation processes, depending in part on the underlying agenda of local social institutions and political processes.

Education and Imperialism at the Turn of the Century in the United States

The belief in Manifest Destiny that had gripped many U.S. politicians and citizens and provided support for the Mexican War in the 1840s also characterized U.S. policies and sentiments during and after the Spanish-American War of 1898. The Treaty of Paris concluding the war resulted in U.S. acquisition of Puerto Rico, Guam, and the Philippines. Cuba was first governed directly and then under the 1901 Platt Amendment Cuba remained an American protectorate until 1934. U.S. imperialistic views toward newly acquired Puerto Rico set the stage for an abrupt and rigid enforcement of Americanization in its schools. According to Nieto (2000), these early subtractive policies are an important legacy that contributes toward understanding contemporary Puerto Rican underachievement. Imperialistic, anti-Spanish, and anti-Catholic attitudes permeated the writings of Anglo military officers and administrative officials. On seizing Puerto Rico, General Nelson A. Miles declared, for example, that its people would now have "the advantages and blessings of enlightened civilization" (MacDonald, 2001, p. 371). These attitudes profoundly influenced the rapid implementation of assimilationist policies in the schools.

Specifically, territorial governor General Guy V. Henry established a Code of School Laws in 1899 that urged districts to organize public schools. A circular dated January 19, 1899, required that teachers "shall be expected to learn English," and in new appointments English-speaking teachers "shall be preferred." Furthermore, all candidates for teacher diplomas must pass examinations in English (Negron de Montilla, 1975, pp. 9–10). Community criticism of the new laws arose immediately and even U.S. policy makers acknowledged that Henry's mandate was more adapted to the "school system of Massachusetts" (Negron de Montilla, 1975, pp. 9–10).

In both Cuba and Puerto Rico, the U.S. government tapped the experience of officials who had worked in Native American boarding schools or on behalf of African Americans as part of the Freedmen's Bureau in the South during Reconstruction. Some of these measures were based on U.S. experience in education of other "conquered peoples," including the championing of industrial education as an appropriate curriculum. For instance, one form of Americanization involved sending youth to mainland colleges to become inculcated with American values (MacDonald & García, 2003). The Puerto Rican colonial government sponsored approximately 45 "poor young men of robust constitution and good conduct" per year between 1901 and at least 1907 to attend colleges in the United States. The colonial legislation (Section 73) narrowly specified the institutions available, "The colleges or institutions designated to which the said students shall attend are Hampton Institute, Hampton, VA. and Tuskegee Institute, Tuskegee, Ala., and such other similar educational institutions as the commissioner of education may from time to time specify" (U.S. Commissioner of Education, 1907, p. 331). Tuskegee and Hampton, African American industrial education colleges, also were the recipients of advanced students from Native American reservations (Lindsey, 1995).

A loophole in the colonial legislation enabled the commissioner to permit some Puerto Rican scholarship students to attend institutions with broader academic missions than Tuskegee and Hampton. In 1903–1904, the commissioner of education in Puerto Rico reported 18 students in their third academic year at institutions as varied as Haverford, Rutgers, Cornell, Wesleyan, MIT, University of Michigan, University of Maryland Medical School, and Lehigh University (U.S. Commissioner of Education, 1907, p. 332). By 1905, almost 500 Puerto Ricans were attending American institutions as a means of building pride in the United States and educating officials to staff the colonial government (Rodriguez-Fraticelli, 1986). Despite the exception of some students who attended more academic higher educational institutions, part of the colonial legacy was thus an attempt to narrow educational opportunities for Puerto Rican youth into government-approved institutions for industrial training. The utilization and development of a stratified system led to differences in skills and knowledge between the Latino/a population and the Anglo dominant group.

THE SOUTHWESTERN LATINO/A EDUCATIONAL EXPERIENCE UNDER SEGREGATION: INTRAGROUP VARIATION AND INTERPRETATION, 1900–1965

Whereas students in newly colonized Puerto Rico were being Americanized on their own island or sent to the United States for advanced training, children of Mexican descent in the Southwest experienced increasing segregation after 1900. According to Gonzalez (1990), several factors contributed to this increase. These include Anglo fear of the rapid influx of Mexican Americans into Southwestern communities (particularly after the 1910 Mexican Revolution), residential segregation, racism, and a political economy willing to provide only a rudimentary level of schooling for the agricultural workforce.

Unlike the rigid, de jure segregation of African Americans from Whites in Southern public classrooms, statutes for Southwestern school districts rarely included segregation clauses. Rather, Anglo school administrators utilized vague and often unwritten justifications to place Mexican children into separate classrooms or entirely separate schools from their Anglo peers. Administrators justified segregation based on the perception that the children possessed deficient English language skills, scored low on intelligence tests, and possessed deficient personal hygiene (Gonzalez, 1990). Although many school districts argued that

Mexican children were only segregated in the early grades, the reality was that they were rarely transferred to the upper grades in Anglo schools (MacDonald, 2004).

Reliance on migrant agricultural workers in the southwestern economy also resulted in nonenforcement of compulsory school attendance laws for Mexican-origin children. One study of selected southwestern counties in the 1930s revealed that attendance among White children ranged from 71 to 96%, whereas school attendance for Mexican children only ranged from 39 to 89% (Donato, 1997, p. 30). Furthermore, among Mexican Americans who were in school, 85% attended segregated schools in the 1930s and expenditures and supplies overwhelmingly favored the White schools (Gonzalez, 1990; Donato, 1997). Among other features designed to maintain an inequitable system, Mexican American children were given used textbooks from the White schools, and Mexican American athletic teams could not compete in Anglo leagues.

San Miguel (1987) documented how the Mexican American community in Texas reacted with agency, not passive acceptance, to the increasingly inequitable educational opportunities of the 20th century. Through the creation of grassroots organizations such as LULAC (League of United Latin American Citizens) in 1929, and a shifting coalition of community, state, and regional organizations (the post–World War II GI Forum, for example), Mexican Americans responded proactively to protect the future of their children in a rapidly changing U.S. economy and society. San Miguel (1987) showed that with the exception of the campaign of Little Schools of 400 (a pre–school program designed to prepare children for public schools), political circumstances resulted in a far "narrower approach" to the pursuit of educational opportunity than most organizations had anticipated.

In her ethnographic history, Martha Menchaca chronicles Mexican American life in segregation-era Santa Paula, California. An anthropologist by training, Menchaca brings our attention to the humiliating practices enforced by schools that required Mexican students to "bathe in showers constructed especially for them" before entering the public school classroom (1995, p. 68). Increasing segregation and discrimination toward Mexican Americans dating from the late 19th century created, according to Menchaca, a present-day community of "social apartness." In the Santa Paula community, schooling reproduced inequality, served the agricultural needs of citrus growers and was thus one more dimension of the persistently divided Anglo/Mexican worlds of California.

Historians of the Mexican American experience, similar to historians of African American history, have emphasized agency and the positive aspects of segregated schools. San Miguel (2001), for example, described how Mexicans in Houston during the segregation era did not necessarily view the creation of a "Mexican" school in their community as a form of oppression. Instead, he argues that the building of Lorenzo de Zavala School in 1920, named after a Mexican patriot, was "heartily supported" by the Mexican population and witnessed dramatic enrollment increases. San Miguel also documents the presence of successful Mexican American youth in Houston's secondary schools and colleges, thus raising questions "about the popular and historical interpretation of the Mexican experience in education" in which "all Mexican origin children were non-achievers" (p. 26). Similarly, Cinthia Salinas's emerging work on private schools created by Mexican Americans exhibits the level of leadership and self-initiative undertaken in Texas when public schools were unsatisfactory (Salinas, 2002).

Rubén Donato (1999) and Lynn Marie Getz (1997) also explore the relationship between the Hispano population and public schools in New Mexico and Colorado under segregation. As mentioned earlier, *Hispanos* are Hispanic Americans descended from 17th-century settlers of northern New Mexico and southern Colorado. During the late 19th century, when Mexican immigration increased and with it, prejudices toward Latinos, Hispanos emphasized their distinct heritage as something to be celebrated and to avoid discrimination. In their studies, both authors found considerable political power among this group. As a result, Hispano public schools could determine who taught and administered, could dictate the nature of social and academic environments and determine which students should prepare for college.

The potential to train role models for Latino/a youth also was operable in New Mexico. For instance, the state legislature founded in 1909 the Spanish-American Normal School at El Rito. The legislature charged the institution to educate "Spanish-speaking natives of New Mexico for the vocation of teachers in the public schools of the counties and districts where the Spanish language is prevalent" (New Mexico Dept. of Ed. 1918, p. 30). The school enrolled over 100 students by 1918. In the 1930s, the bilingual state teacher training college was still open and eventually absorbed into the New Mexico higher education system (Getz, 1997). As is often the case, on further examination of seemingly negative dynamics, one finds a more nuanced experience that includes both benefits and obstacles.

The inequitable conditions for Latino/a children in the pre–Civil Rights era nonetheless contributed to the formation of grassroots organizations and a series of lawsuits in the 20th century such as *Alvarez v. Lemon Grove, CA* (1932). Many of these lawsuits preceded African American attempts for integration and are not yet fully incorporated into mainstream educational history (MacDonald & Beck, 2000).

As early as the 1920s, Latinos formed associations to pressure Anglo communities for more equitable opportunities. LULAC, for example, whose members were mostly middle-class Texas citizens, favored bilingual education and attacked discrimination and segregation in the public schools (San Miguel, 1987). The first case LULAC brought to the courts was *Independent School District v. Salvatierra* (1930/31), which challenged segregation of Mexican children. Although the case was lost because it was determined that Spanish children could be segregated because of their "special language needs," it opened the door for more successful lawsuits. In Lemon Grove, California, Mexican American parents refused to send their children to a separate school that was located in a renovated barn and decided to boycott the school. The resulting suit against the school board, *Roberto Alvarez v. Lemon Grove* (1931), successfully secured the right for Mexican Americans to have their children attend the White school. *Lemon Grove* also established a precedent for both the NAACP's racial integration efforts and subsequent Latino/a suits.

A decade before *Brown v. Board of Education*, Mexican Americans were locally successful in eliminating segregation. In *Mendez et al. v. Westminster School District of Orange County, California* (1946), the court ruled that Mexican Americans did not belong in the category of "Negro, Mongolian, and Indian children" who were legally segregated from Whites. The judge also ruled "evidence clearly shows that Spanish-speaking children are retarded in learning English by lack of exposure to its use by segregation." The Texas case of *Delgado v. Bastrop Independent School District* (1948) also ruled in favor of Mexican Americans, stating that segregating children was illegal except for in the first grade. Unfortunately, the judge ruled that Black children must continue to attend separate schools in that district. Despite these early local successes at desegregation, by 1966, Donato (1997) argues, 66% of children with Spanish surnames were still attending schools predominantly Mexican American.

MAINLAND PUERTO RICAN AND CUBAN
EDUCATION IN THE POST–WORLD WAR II ERA:
A STUDY IN CONTRASTS

Whereas school conditions for Southwestern Mexicans remained fairly static during the 1930s, 1940s, and 1950s, Puerto Ricans and Cubans, the second and third largest Latino/a subpopulations, began arriving on the U.S. mainland. Because the growing presence of Puerto Ricans and Cubans was in areas outside of the Southwest, there was increased national attention to the linguistic and scholastic needs of Latinos.

Small numbers of Puerto Ricans and Cubans had lived in the United States in the 19th and early 20th centuries. The period of greatest migration, however, began after World War II. Politics and economics distinctly shaped the unique and continuing Cuban and Puerto Rican migrations. The circumstances surrounding each of these populations' arrival to the United States profoundly impacted their contrasting educational experiences and opportunities on the mainland.

In 1940, almost 70,000 Puerto Ricans lived on the mainland. By 1950, that number had increased to 300,000, and in 1960 was 887,661. New York City and surrounding areas absorbed most of this immigration (Sánchez Korrol, 1994, p. 21). Most historians agree that the following factors spurred migration to the mainland: the Jones Act of 1917, which granted U.S. citizenship to Puerto Ricans; the Johnson Acts of 1921 and 1924, which curtailed European immigration; labor shortages in the United States during World Wars I and II; and relatively inexpensive transportation costs to the United States (Sánchez Korrol, 1994).

Both Weinberg (1977) and Sánchez Korrol (1994) emphasize the years before World War II as ones in which Puerto Ricans established strong networks, created communities, and formed mutual aid associations. Concerns regarding the public schools were explored through avenues such as the Puerto Rican association *Madres Y Padres Pro Niños Hispanos* (Mothers and Fathers in Support of Hispanic Children) during the 1930s and early 1940s. This organization, for example, questioned the school officials' use of intelligence testing, which channeled Puerto Rican children into classrooms for "backward" children rather than recognizing the inherent language bias in such testing. The 1940s and 1950s witnessed a sharp jump of Puerto Rican children in the New York City schools. In 1949, there were only 29,000 Puerto Rican children in the schools and only 4 years later they numbered about 54,000. By 1968, almost 300,000 Puertorriqueños attended New York City schools. In response to these rapid increases the city commissioned an intensive, multiyear investigation, *The Puerto Rican Study, 1953–1957*. In this study, researchers recommended extensive bilingual preparation of teachers and support staff. According to Weinberg (1977), school authorities ignored the important recommendations. As a result, teachers and administrators were overwhelmed in the late 1950s and 1960s by new arrivals—it was estimated that less than one quarter could speak English (Weinberg, 1977).

Sánchez Korrol (1996) emphasizes the positive influence of Puerto Rican women hired as Substitute Auxiliary Teachers (SAT) in New York City of the 1940s and 1950s. Although there were few in number compared to the demand, these teachers were engaged in a "struggle" to "provide alternative modes of instruction for the increasing numbers of Spanish-speaking youngsters arriving to this city" (p. 83). Furthermore, Sánchez Korrol persuasively demonstrates how the SATs lent "recognition" and "legitimacy" to the introduction of alternative methods of teaching English-language proficiency. Her analysis of the SATs and other struggles of the post–World War II era document both the problems of the times and the involvement of Puerto Ricans in the search for solutions.

The creation of organizations for the betterment of education dating from the 1930s; the establishment of the Puerto Rican–founded ASPIRA (the Spanish word "aspire") in 1961; and the militancy of the late 1960s, form the basis for Sánchez Korrol, Nieto, and others to conclude that "contrary to popular opinion, the education of children has long been a primary objective in continental Puerto Rican communities" (Sánchez Korrol, 1996, p. 283).

During the decades of the 1950s and 1960s when Puerto Ricans in New York City and Chicago were beginning to fight for educational opportunity, Cubans arriving in the United States posed a contrasting challenge to educational policy makers (Padilla, 1985). Until the 1960s, the official policy of the New York City public schools mandated "English-only instructional programs steeped in convention and inflexibility" for the Spanish-speaking American citizens (Sánchez Korrol, 1996, p. 86). The arrival of Cuban refugees in the late 1950s and early 1960s generated a different policy response than that toward Puerto Ricans. Situated within the context of Cold War politics, school policies toward the Cuban refugees departed from strict Americanization measures characteristic of earlier eras, and permitted more flexibility and openness toward bilingual education.

The history of Cuban migration to the United States in the post–
World War II era is typically divided into three waves. The first wave
of one quarter of a million Cubans arrived between 1959 and 1962. These
Cubans, sometimes called the "Golden Exiles," disproportionately represented the urban, educated professional and business classes. For instance, although only 4% of all Cubans in 1959 had received high school
diplomas, 36% of this wave of exiles held high school degrees (Olsen &
Olsen, 1996). The second wave of Cubans began during the "freedom
flights" of 1965 and extended until 1973 when Fidel Castro ended them.
The social and economic composition of this second wave has been described as working-class and less educated than the initial "golden
exiles." The third wave of 1980, pejoratively named the "marielitos"
(Mariel, Cuba, was the port of departure), received its negative reputation because Castro announced that he had sent the worst elements of
Cuba in the boatlift. The controversial arrival of the first group to have
lived under Castro's communist regime brought an additional 125,000
Cubans to the United States during 1980 (García, 1996, p. 6).

The strikingly different U.S. policies for Puerto Ricans versus Cubans
was noted as early as the 1960s. Activists at the 1968 New York City
conference sponsored by ASPIRA and the Puerto Rican Legal Defense and Education Fund "knew that the political and institutional
establishment had backed bilingual programs for Cuban refugees in
Miami—a move prompted by Cold War politics—and now they wanted
similar educational alternatives to be available to Puerto Rican children" (Sánchez Korrol, 1994, p. 231). Indeed, Puerto Ricans experienced
stricter classroom English-only policies and discrimination against hiring Puerto Rican teachers (even with baccalaureate degrees) because
of their accents. At the same time, these measures were not applied to
the new Cubans and waivers were provided for those seeking teaching
certificates.

Through the creation in 1961 of the Cuban Emergency Refugee Center under the administration of the Department of Health, Education,
and Welfare (HEW), federal funds were channeled to agencies throughout southern Florida. One of these HEW programs included hiring and
training Cuban professionals to work as bilingual teacher aides in the
Dade County public schools. Another sizeable HEW grant allowed
the University of Miami to open the Cuban Teacher Training Program
in 1962 (García, 1996, pp. 26–28). Careful observers also noted that
whereas Puerto Ricans had been discouraged from receiving bilingual
schooling, pilot programs at Coral Way Elementary School and other

southern Florida sites were opened without controversy and with adequate staffing and funding for Cuban students. This aid also extended to higher education. HEW's Office of Education created a college loan program for Cuban students in 1961. By 1966, Maria Cristina García notes that more than 5,500 Cuban Americans had taken advantage of this program.

Not only Puerto Ricans in New York City and Chicago but also African Americans in southern Florida viewed the extension of educational and other economic opportunities to Cubans with dismay. The generous aid packages and direct federal grants to Dade County public schools exceeded the regular funds provided for needy U.S. citizens (García, 1996). Although *Brown v. Board of Education* had ruled segregation illegal in 1954, Miami, like most urban areas, still practiced racial segregation in the 1960s. One African American minister in Miami, observing that racially mixed and Afro-Cuban refugees were attending White schools, wrote, "The American Negro could solve the school integration problem by teaching his children to speak only Spanish" (García, 1996, 29).

The contrasting mainland experiences of Puerto Ricans and Cubans after World War II have potentially impacted educational outcomes. Federal documents such as *Our Nation on the Fault Line* (U.S. Government, 1996) and the National Council of La Raza's (1998) study of Latino/a education note the disparate achievements between groups such as Puerto Ricans and Cubans. Ogbu (1978) explains why some groups achieve more success in our schools, according to one's membership in cultural groups that are either "involuntary" or "voluntary" minorities. The former include African Americans, Native Americans, Mexican Americans, and Puerto Ricans; the latter include most Asian immigrant groups, and Cubans (among others). Voluntary minorities came to the United States voluntarily and have maintained a dual frame of reference (to the United States as well as to their country of origin), and are better able to react to discrimination and develop or maintain a sense of independence from U.S. cultural and social dynamics. Most of these groups see education as a route to economic well-being. Involuntary minorities are American by virtue of conquest or involuntary migration such as slavery. Their cultural identity is developed in opposition to mainstream U.S. cultural norms, including a stance toward the relevance, or irrelevance of schooling. In many ways Ogbu's model helps us to understand why Cuban Americans do well in school whereas Mexican Americans and Puerto Ricans do less well, although he doesn't explain why Mexican Americans are considered involuntary immigrants when the majority in the United States now, numerically, are here because of voluntary immigration and not conquest (descent from peoples in the Southwest when it was the northwest region of Mexico). Researchers will continue to investigate further how these historical legacies shape contemporary educational opportunity and sociocultural dynamics that interact with school experiences.

THE FIGHT FOR EDUCATIONAL OPPORTUNITY IN THE SOUTHWEST

The inequitable schooling conditions for Latinos during most of the 20th century were not passively accepted but fought through a series of legal actions, collective agency, and finally through pressure on the federal government. One thorny issue surrounding desegregation movements in the Southwest was that segregation was often de facto by tradition but not by any legal statute such as those that regulated the separation of Black and White children in southern states. Thus, as explored earlier, some of the lawsuits prior to the 1950s had focused specifically on categorical identity issues. Were Mexican Americans Indians? Were they Black? Were they White? These issues have dogged legal interpretations since the 1840s and continue into the 21st century as seen in controversies over the 2000 Census classifications.

The persistence of segregation and hurtful language policies combined with the broad Civil Rights era of the 1950s and 1960s led to more successful and widespread fights for educational equity. MALDEF, the Mexican American Legal Defense and Educational Fund, was founded in 1967 and played a crucial role in numerous lawsuits. In the same year, La Raza Unida also was formed and provided more resources and personnel to the causes of Mexican Americans through the Chicano movement. Boycotts, student blowouts, and numerous grassroots activities fought for bilingual education, the hiring of Latino/a teachers, inclusion of Latino/a history in the curriculum, and the end of racist practices in schools. The passage of the 1968 federal Bilingual Education Act was one of the successes of this era, affirming the right for non-English speaking children to receive appropriate instruction, curricular materials, and federal funds for this purpose. The Supreme Court's ruling in the 1974 case *Lau v. Nichols* upheld the notion that failure of a school district to teach a child in a language he or she could understand was a violation of his or her civil rights.

In 1970, *Cisneros v. Corpus Christi* marked a turning point for desegregation. In this case the court ruled that Mexican Americans were an ethnically identifiable minority group and could not be utilized to racially integrate schools. As San Miguel argued in *Brown, Not White* (2001), using Mexican students to satisfy federal orders to integrate Black schools was a final insult to Chicanos being used as "pawns, puppets, and scapegoats" for the convenience of desegregation compliance by the Houston Independent School District.

Before the Civil Rights era, Mexican children were punished for speaking Spanish at public schools, few Latino/a teachers were hired as role models, and neither Puerto Rican nor Mexican-origin children could see themselves in their textbooks or the school curricula. Furthermore, intelligence tests and outright racism permitted the tracking of students into nonacademic classes, limiting options for higher education. The efforts of individuals and collective action put an end to the most blatant discriminatory practices of the segregation era. With increased numbers of Latinos arriving in the United States in the 21st century, the permanence of these reforms will be challenged.

NEW LATINOS IN THE SCHOOLS: THE POST-1965 IMMIGRATION WAVE

In recent decades immigration has been more varied, with increased migration from Central and South America and the Caribbean. Since 1965, when U.S. immigration laws were liberalized, Latinos and Asians have comprised the fastest growing immigrant groups to the United States. The 2000 U.S. Census revealed that Latinos and Blacks are virtually equal in number, with Latinos expecting to outnumber blacks in the first decade of the 21st century. The Black-White paradigm that has dominated the historical research of American schools has been permanently altered (MacDonald & Beck, 2000). In addition, Latinos have been immigrating to parts of the United States unaccustomed to non-English speakers such as the South. Working in poultry processing plants or picking Vidalia onions in Georgia and North Carolina, the new Latino/a immigrants disrupt the traditional Black-White Southern dichotomies (Wortham, Murillo, & Hamann, 2002).

The recent arrival of Latino/a immigrants has not occurred without tensions. During the 1980s and 1990s, states such as California passed measures targeted at immigrants. English-Only movements,

Proposition 227, and the elimination of Affirmative Action in the California and Texas University systems are examples of the backlash against rapid demographic changes. How will the next generations fare? Historically, we have seen patterns of inclusion and exclusion, of purposeful segregation among Latinos to preserve their culture and language, and of strategies which sought integration into White society. This historical perspective on Latino/a education points to the need for constant vigilance on the part of advocacy groups, the federal government, researchers, and citizens. Latinos individually and collectively have changed over time what it means to be American. We can expect the richness and diversity of Latino/a cultures to alter the social fabric for all of us.

REFERENCES

Abreu, M. (1932). Denominational and private schools in New Mexico. *Biennial report of the New Mexico schools, 1930–1932*. 45–51. Santa Fe: State Superintendent of Public Instruction NM.

Banker, M. (1993). *Presbyterian missions and cultural interaction in the far southwest, 1850–1950*. Urbana: University of Illinois Press.

Bender, T. (1996). *Winning the west for Christ: Sheldon Jackson and Presbyterianism on the Rocky Mountain frontier, 1869–1880*. Albuquerque: University of New Mexico Press.

Berger, M. (1947). Education in Texas during the Spanish and Mexican periods. *Southwestern Historical Quarterly, 51*, 41–53.

Burns, J. (1908). *The Catholic school system in the United States: Its principles, origin, and establishment*. New York: Benziger Brothers.

California Department of Public Instruction. (1853). Second annual report of public instruction of the state of California. Sacramento: George Kerr, State Printer.

California Department of Public Instruction. (1865). Historical sketch of the public school system of California. In *First biennial report of the superintendent of public instruction of the state of California for the school years 1864 and 1865*. Sacramento: author.

California Department of Public Instruction. (1866). Revised school law, approved March 24, 1866. Sacramento: O. M. Clayes, State Printer.

Cremin, L. (1980). *American education: The national experience 1783–1876*. New York: Harper & Row.

Delgado-Gaitan, C. (2001). *The power of community: Mobilizing for family and schooling*. Lanham, MD: Rowman and Littlefield.

Donato, R. (1997). *The other struggle for equal schools: Mexican Americans during the Civil Rights era*. Albany: State University Press of New York.

Donato, R. (1999). Hispano education and the implications of autonomy: Four school systems in southern Colorado, 1920–1963. *Harvard Educational Review, 69*, 117–149.

Fisher, M, Pérez, S., González, B., Njus, J., & Kamasaki, C. (1998). *Latino education: Status and prospects: State of Hispanic America*. Research Report for the National Council of La Raza. Wash. DC: NCLR.

Gallegos, B. (1992). *Literacy, education and society in New Mexico 1693–1821*. Albuquerque: University of New Mexico Press.

García, M. C. (1996). *Havana USA: Cuban exiles and Cuban Americans in South Florida, 1959–1994.* Berkeley: University of California Press.

Getz, L. M. (1997). *Schools of their own: The education of Hispanos in New Mexico, 1850–1940.* Albuquerque: University of New Mexico Press.

Gonzalez, G. (1990). *Chicano education in the era of segregation.* Philadelphia: The Balch Institute Press, and London and Toronto: Associated University Presses.

Griswold del Castillo, R. (1990). *The Treaty of Guadalupe Hidalgo: A legacy of conflict.* Norman: University of Oklahoma.

Haas, L. (1995). *Conquests and historical identities in California, 1769–1936.* Berkeley and Los Angeles: University of California Press.

Hansot, E., & Tyack, D. (1982). A usable past: Using history in educational policy. In Ann Lieberman & Milbrey W. McLaughlin (Eds.), *Policy making in education: Eighty-first yearbook of the National Society for the Study of Education* (pp. 1–22). Chicago: The National Society for the Study of Education/University of Chicago Press.

Horsman, R. (1981). *Race and manifest destiny: The origins of American racial Anglo-Saxonism.* Cambridge, MA: Harvard University Press.

James, G. (1927). *In and out of the old missions.* Boston: Little, Brown & Company.

Kaestle, C. (1983). *Pillars of the republic: Common schools and American society, 1780–1860.* New York: Hill & Wang.

Leonard, I. (1949). *Books of the brave: Being an account of books and of men in the Spanish conquest and settlement of the 16th-century new world.* Cambridge, MA: Harvard University Press.

Levinson, B. A., & Holland, D. (1996). The cultural production of the educated person: An introduction. In Bradley A. Levinson, Douglas E. Foley, and Dorothy C. Holland (Eds.),*The cultural production of the educated person: Critical ethnographies of schooling and local practice.* Albany: SUNY Press.

Lindsey, D. (1995). *Indians at Hampton Institute, 1877–1923.* Urbana: University of Illinois Press.

MacDonald, V.-M. (2001). Hispanic, Latino, Chicano, or "Other"?: Deconstructing the relationship between historians and Hispanic-American educational history. *History of Education Quarterly, 41,* 365–413.

MacDonald, V.-M. (2004). *Latino education in the United States: A narrated history, 1513–2000.* New York: Palgrave/MacMillan.

MacDonald, V.-M., & Beck, S. (October, 2000). *Educational history in black and brown: Paths of divergence and convergence, 1900–1990.* Paper presented at the meeting of the History of Education Society, San Antonio, TX.

MacDonald, V.-M., & García, T. (2003). Historical perspectives on Latino access to higher education, 1848–1990. In Lee Jones & Jeanett Castellanos (Eds.), *The majority in the minority: Expanding the representation of Latina/o faculty, administrators, and students in higher education.* Sterling, VA: Stylus Publishing.

Martinez, J. J., & Alire, J. C. L. (1998). The influence of the Roman Catholic church in New Mexico under Mexican administration, 1821–1848. In Thomas J. Steele, Paul Rhetts & Barbe Awalt. Eds. *Seeds of struggle/harvest of faith: The papers of the Archdiocese of Santa Fe Catholic Cuarto Centennial Conference: The history of the Catholic Church in New Mexico* (pp. 329–344). Albuquerque: LPD Press.

Menchaca, M. (1995). *The Mexican outsiders: A community history of marginalization and discrimination in California.* Austin: University of Texas Press.

Menchaca, M. (1999). The Treaty of Guadalupe Hidalgo and the racialization of the Mexican population. In Jose F. Moreno (Ed.), *The elusive quest for equality: 150 years of Chicano/Chicana education* (pp. 3–29). Cambridge, MA: Harvard Educational Review.

Menchaca, M. (2001). *Recovering history, constructing race: The Indian, black, and white roots of Mexican Americans*. Austin: University of Texas Press.

Mörner, M. (1967). *Race mixture in the history of Latin America*. Boston: Little, Brown & Company.

Navarro, J.-M. (1995). *Creating tropical Yankees: The "spiritual conquest" of Puerto Rico, 1898–1908*. Unpublished doctoral dissertation, University of Chicago.

Negron de Montilla, A. (1975). *The public school system and the Americanization process in Puerto Rico, 1900–1930*. Río Piedras, Puerto Rico: Universidad de Puerto Rico, Editorial Universitaria.

New Mexico Department of Education. (1918). *Twenty-seventh and twenty-eighth annual reports of the state superintendent of public instruction to the governor of New Mexico for the Years 1917–1918*. Albuquerque: Central Printing Co.

New Mexico, Territory of. (1874). *Education in New Mexico: Report of Hon. W. G. Ritch to the commissioner of education, for the year 1874*. Santa Fe: Manderfield & Tucker Printers.

New Mexico, Territory of. (1889). *Compilation of the school laws of New Mexico*. East Las Vegas, NM: J. A. Carruth.

Nieto, S. (Ed.). (2000). *Puerto Rican students in U.S. schools*. Mahwah, NJ: Lawrence Erlbaum Associates.

Oboler, S. (1995). *Ethnic labels, Latino lives: Identity and the politics of (re)presentation in the United States*. Minneapolis: University of Minnesota Press.

Ogbu, J. (1978). Understanding cultural diversity and learning. *Educational Researcher 21*, 8, 5–14, and 24.

Olson, J., & Olson, J. (1995). *Cuban Americans: From trauma to triumph*. New York: Twayne Publishers.

Orfield, G. (1999). Politics matters: Educational policy and Chicano students. In Jose F. Moreno (Ed.), *The elusive quest for equality: 150 years of Chicano/Chicana education* (pp. 111–122). Cambridge, MA: Harvard Educational Review.

Padilla, F. (1985). *Latino ethnic consciousness: The case of Mexican Americans and Puerto Ricans in Chicago*. Notre Dame, IN: University of Notre Dame Press.

Rodríguez-Fraticelli, C. (1986). *Education and imperialism: The Puerto Rican experience in higher education, 1898–1986*. New York: Centro de Estudios Puertorriqueños, Hunter College of the City University of New York.

Salinas, C. (April, 2002). *Things are different here: The schooling experiences of Tejanos in Jim Hogg County, 1930–1970*. Paper presented at the meeting of the American Educational Research Association, New Orleans, LA.

San Miguel, Jr., G. (1987). *Let all of them take heed: Mexican Americans and the campaign for educational equality in Texas, 1910–1981*. Austin: University of Texas Press.

San Miguel, Jr., G. (1999). The schooling of Mexicanos in the Southwest, 1848–1891. In Jose F. Moreno (Ed.), *The elusive quest for equality: 150 years of Chicano/Chicana education* (pp. 31–52). Cambridge, MA: Harvard Educational Review.

San Miguel, Jr., G. (2001). *Brown not white: School integration and the Chicano movement in Houston*. College Station: Texas A&M Press.

San Miguel, Jr., G. & Valencia, R. (1998). From the Treaty of Guadalupe Hidalgo to Hopwood: The educational plight and struggle of Mexican Americans in the Southwest. *Harvard Educational Review, 68*, 353–412.

Sánchez Korrol, V. (1994). *From colonia to community: The history of Puerto Ricans in New York City, 1917–1948*. Berkeley: University of California Press.

Sánchez Korrol, V. (1996). Toward bilingual education: Puerto Rican women teachers in New York City schools, 1947–1967. In Altagracia Ortiz (Ed.), *Puerto Rican women and work: Bridges in transnational labor* (pp. 82–104). Philadelphia: Temple University Press.

Shea, J. (1886). *History of the Catholic Church in the United States, with portraits, views, maps and facsimiles*. (vol. IV). New York: D.H. McBride & Co.

Spring, J. (1994). *Deculturalization and the struggle for equality: A brief history of the education of dominated cultures in the United States*. New York: McGraw-Hill.

Suárez-Orozco, M., & Páez, M. (Eds.) (2002). *Latinos remaking America*. Berkeley: University of California Press.

Sweet, D. (1995). The Ibero-American frontier mission in Native American history. In Erick Langer & Robert H. Jackson (Eds.), *The new Latin American mission history* (pp. 1–48). Latin American Studies Series. Lincoln: University of Nebraska Press.

Texas, State of. (1872). *First annual report of the superintendent of public instruction of the state of Texas for the year 1871*. Austin, TX: J. G. Tracy, State Printer. (Wisconsin State Historical Society)

Texas, State of. (1873). *Second annual report of the superintendent of public instruction of the state of Texas, 1872*. J. C. DeGress, superintendent of public instruction. Austin, TX: James P. Newcomb and Company. (Wisconsin State Historical Society)

Texas, State of. (1886). *Fifth biennial report of the superintendent of public instruction for the scholastic years ending August 31, 1885, and August 31, 1886*. Benjamin M. Baker, superintendent Public Instruction. Austin, TX: State Printing Office.

Trueba, E. (1999). *Latinos unidos: From cultural diversity to the politics of solidarity*. Lanham, MD: Rowman and Littlefield.

Trujillo, A. (1996). In search of Aztlán: Movimiento ideology and the creation of a Chicano worldview through schooling. In Bradley A. Levinson, Douglas E. Foley, & Dorothy C. Holland (Eds.), *The cultural production of the educated person: Critical ethnographies of schooling and local practice*. Albany: SUNY Press.

United States Bureau of the Census. (2000). *Census 2000*. Retrieved February 14, 2005, from http://www.census.gov

United States Commissioner of Education. (1907). Report of the commissioner of education for the year ending June 30, 1905. Volume 1. Washington: Government Printing Office.

United States Government. (1996). *Our nation on the fault line: Hispanic American education*. President's Advisory Commission on Educational Excellence for Hispanic Americans. Washington, DC: Author.

Valenzuela, A. (1999). *Subtractive schooling: U.S.-Mexican youth and the politics of caring*. Albany: SUNY Press.

Weber, D. (1992). *The Spanish frontier in North America*. New Haven, CT: Yale University Press.

Weber, D. (1999). *What caused the Pueblo revolt of 1680?* Boston: Bedford/St. Martin's Press.

Weinberg, M. (1977). *A chance to learn: A history of race and education in the United States*. Cambridge: Cambridge University Press.

Willis, P. (1977). *Learning to labour: How working class kids get working class jobs*. Farnborough, England: Saxon House.

Wortham, S., Murillo, E., & Hamann, E. (Eds.). (2002). *Education in the new Latino/a diaspora: Policy and the politics of identity*. Westport, CT: Ablex.

Yohn, S. (1995). *A contest of faiths: Missionary women and pluralism in the American Southwest*. Ithaca, NY: Cornell University Press.

4

The Intellectual Presence of the Deficit View of Spanish-Speaking Children in the Educational Literature During the 20th Century

Barbara M. Flores
California State University, San Bernardino

INTRODUCTION

By tracing the educational research literature from a historical perspective (Flores, 1982), we will see how Spanish-speaking children have been depicted from a cultural and linguistic deficit view and how these "deficiencies" purportedly have been the culprits of "these" children's educational failure during the 20th century. Early in the 20th century, Latino/a children came to be considered a "problem" to educators, particularly in the Southwest. Historically, Latino/a students' underachievement in school has been explained from an intrinsic cause-and-effect point of view. Usually, it has been attributed to their cultural or linguistic background or both.

In the Southwest, this underachievement and low educational attainment among Latino/a students commonly had been referred to as a "Mexican problem." In the 1920s, the "Mexicans" were intentionally segregated from their Anglo counterparts because their Spanish language was assumed to retard their achievement in English-language instruction. In the next decade, the 1930s, the "Mexican problem" began to appear increasingly in the educational literature (Manuel, 1930; Reynolds, 1933). This trend continued into the 1940s and 1950s as evidenced when Tireman (1948) and Burma (1954) reported that the educational problems of the Mexican American students included their language inabilities, high dropout rates, low achievement, and intelligence scores. However, despite these negative accounts, George I. Sanchez, in *Forgotten People* (1940) and Carey McWilliams, in *North From Mexico* (1949), began to question the so-called Mexican problem.

In the 1960s, Mexican American students' nonachievement was attributed to what were characterized as linguistic (Englemann and Bereiter, 1966) and cultural (Reissman, 1962) deficiencies. In the 1970s, the Latino/a students' underachievement also was commonly attributed to their limited English language, cultural differences, and low socioeconomic level. To date, these "deficiencies" have evolved into present-day "limited English language" problems to be "remedied," "fixed," and "compensated." A plethora of federal programs (Compensatory Education, Migrant Education, Title I, and Bilingual Education [Title VII] since the 1960s were established to improve the English language development of "limited English speakers." All of these programs were/are based on the assumption that it is some "deficiency" in the Latino/a students that causes their low achievement. Garcia (1977) summarized the deficit educational view in the following statement: "The research and documents of the first six decades of [the 20th] century, in effect, rendered the Mexican American and his bilingualism—which have a history of more than two hundred years of linguistic and cultural development—speechless and cultureless" (p. 3).

In order to substantiate and document the validity of this statement, a systematic review of the educational literature was undertaken for the purposes of this study. The earliest documentation can be traced to 1922 (Young, 1922). Most of the early educational research was devoted to intelligence testing (Garretson, 1928; Garth, 1925; Sheldon, 1924). Vaca (1970) critiques and gives a detailed account of these psychological studies. High rates of mental retardation among Mexican Americans soon became an identifiable label and "problem." Since the early 1920s, the genesis of the deficit view can be traced. What follows is a characterization of the intellectual presence of the deficit view of

Spanish-speaking children in the educational literature during the 20th century by decade.

THE 1920s: THE "PROBLEM" IS "MENTAL RETARDATION"

With the rise of psychologists' interests in intelligence testing and instrument development in the 1920s, it is not surprising that the results by Mexican Americans became an anomaly to be studied and rationalized. As a group, Mexican children did not do well on these tests (Garth, 1923), nor did they do well on achievement tests.

Correlations between low intelligence scores and low scholastic achievement scores soon became the explanation for the "Mexican" child's lack of success in school. Reynolds (1933) reported various studies that were related to the question of mental retardation (e.g., Garretson, 1928; Mitchell, 1927; Taylor, 1927). These comparative studies between Anglo children and their Mexican American counterparts investigated either the relationship of language difficulty to intelligence and retardation or achievement in reading.

These tests used in these research studies were treated as reliable and valid even though the population they were administered to had not been included in the reliability and validation process of the test development. However, despite these questionable research practices, the myth of "mental retardation" because of "language difficulty" among Spanish-speaking children was born. The researchers reasoned that their "language difficulty" stemmed from knowing Spanish and then having to learn English in school. This, therefore, produced an educational "problem." The "bilingual problem" of Mexican American children was intrinsically rooted within the children and their families, not the school, nor societal prejudices. Consequently, lack of achievement was blamed on the child. The causes were "language difficulty" (Manuel & Wright, 1929), which resulted in low intelligence. According to Manuel (1930, p. 150), language instruction was ". . . one of the major aspects of the 'Mexican' problem."

THE 1930s: THE "PROBLEM" IS "BILINGUALISM"

During the decade of the 1930s, the shift from "mental retardation" as a cause for the lack of achievement among Spanish-speaking children changed to a direct "language" cause. However, Nieto (2000) reports

that the New York City Chamber of Commerce in 1935 reported that
Puerto Rican children were considered "slow learners" based on intelligence testing, which of course, were given in English, a language
the children did not know. Reynolds (1933), Kelly (1936), and Burbeck
(1939) specifically note that the educational problem facing the schools
was "bilingualism." For example, Burbeck (1939, pp. 49–50) stated that:
"The problem of bilingualism has not always received sufficient consideration in the public school. . . . The Spanish speaking nationalities
and the Japanese seem to be our greatest bilingual problem. The problem of bilingualism might be considered as that of acquiring a second
language." This author presented the views that the acquisition of a
second language was problematic and that learning to read and speak
English was an undertaking with "appalling difficulties." Although
she asserted that learning a second language was difficult, no scholarly
investigations in the support of the contention were offered.

Not only was learning to speak English as a second language viewed
as a "problem" for Spanish-speaking children, so was learning to read
(Kelly, 1936, p. 209): "Bilingualism and its effects upon the reading
aspects of language is a problem of vital significance to education in
the southwest. Large groups of the population are bilingual." Again,
unfounded and broad generalizations were made without the appropriate evidence. Correlational studies do not purport cause-and-effect
generalizations. They only suggest a relationship.

Kelly's statement rendering the negative effects of bilingualism on
reading was based on a study of 629 Spanish-speaking and English-
speaking students who took the Iowa Silent Reading Test in three
northern Arizona cities. The results revealed "that the deficiencies of
the Spanish speaking were not confined to any one phase of reading
ability" (p. 211). Notably, the validity, reliability, and appropriateness
for the population of this standardized reading test were not reported.
Using syllogistic reasoning, test performance was equated with reading competence and deficiencies were assumed to have been "proven."
This is a gross misinterpretation of standardized test results along with
making statements about unexamined assumptions of language use
and language competence.

Tireman, Dixon, and Cornelius (1935) and DeVargas (1937) focused
on teaching methodologies for the acquisition of English vocabulary
prior to learning to read. It was reasoned that "in non-English speaking communities the vocabulary becomes of first importance. Reading cannot be introduced at once but must wait until the proper oral

background formed" (Tireman et al., 1935, p. 118). Proper oral background is equated with having the appropriate English vocabulary. Again, an unexamined assumption is made, that is, that command of oral language is prerequisite in order to read in one's second language. No distinction was made between receptive control (listening and reading) and productive control (speaking and writing). Nor was there any consideration for the child's strength in his/her own language. The focus was on "lack of vocabulary" in the second language, English.

This negative perspective that bilingualism was detrimental to the acquisition of a second language as well as reading is clearly erroneous. Everywhere else in the world, bilingualism is prized as an asset. In fact, in many countries, students learn four or five languages during their schooling. Bilingualism means that one can use two languages to communicate. Thus, knowing two languages is an asset not a deficit. However, if one believes the contrary, then it will become the reality. The 1930s surely inculcated educators, the general public, and most of all the Latino/a population in the United States into believing that bilingualism was problematic. It is unfortunate that bilingualism and multilingualism was/is viewed as a "problem" instead an asset.

THE 1940s: THE "PROBLEM" IS TO "CHANGE" MEXICANS THROUGH EDUCATION

Faced with more Spanish-speaking children attending schools in the 1940s, the school responded by declaring that "the problem of education of the Mexican children in our schools [was] a serious one..." (Andras, 1943, p. 328). Bilingualism continued to be a "...challenging problem to the educator in general and to the speech pathologist in particular" (Lynn, 1945, p. 175). It is interesting to note that during the 1940s bilingualism was still seen here as a problem when throughout the world it is considered a prized asset, particularly in business. The view of bilingualism as a problem in this country is rooted in socioeconomic, political-linguistic, and historical events.

At the turn of the 20th century, waves of poor immigrants with different languages and cultures came to America. They provided the cheap labor of America's expanding industrialization. Working-class status, poverty, and lack of formal education contributed to their low social status. But, with the thrust to attain the democratic ideal of education for all (now known as "equal educational opportunity"), assimilation of immigrants through massive public education became "the challenging problem" for schools. "Mexicans" were both original settlers and immigrants to the Southwest. They have a history of being "conquered" and economically "exploited" (Acuña, 1972). Distorted perceptions of the Mexican soon became widely accepted stereotypes and prejudices (Romano, 1968). In contrast, the Puerto Rican "migration" was considered problematic in New York City and "their" children were rendered "invisible" (Nieto, 2000).

In the 1940s, these prejudices surfaced in the educational literature as evidenced by the following quote by no less a Latino/a (Rojas, 1946, p. 204):

> Bilingual children, in general, are the children of cultural and racial minorities . . . from the educational point of view, however, language is the most conspicuous, and probably the most fundamental problem. . . . It is the only problem over which the schools have direct and complete control. The schools cannot change the socioeconomic status of the bilingual nor alter his appearance, but they can help him overcome his language disability.

It is apparent that the logic of reasoning is that schools should change what they can about the minority bilingual child. And, language was/is what they could/can change. The child's language was clearly seen as "problematic." It is a sad commentary that this statement was made by a Latino/a scholar. Now, even Hispanic Americans and scholars began to think and write about this "language disability" of their own children! This "conspicuous and fundamental problem" was compounded by another issue—that language could be directly controlled by the schools. Within this decade there were several articles (Dann, 1940; Finnochiaro, 1949; Flicker, 1947; Tireman, 1941; and Wedberg, 1942) and books (Tireman, 1948; and others) that gave specifics about how a teacher could change "bilingual" children through education.

The suggested practices ranged from training the ear to overcoming "foreign accents" to acquiring isolated vocabulary to mastering oral English before reading. Likewise, imitation, drills on isolated units of speech and language and repetition of patterned sentences were advocated. Given the knowledge base at the time related to how language is learned, it is not surprising that these practices were sanctioned. Although there were conflicting views about learning theory, behaviorism prevailed and influenced many of these practices of language teaching.

Certainly, the educational solutions to the "bilingual" problem were based on the knowledge base available, but they also were greatly influenced by historical attitudes, prejudices, racism, classism, and bigotry. Segregation existed as sociopolitical policy. It was also sanctioned as an acceptable pedagogical practice. Thus, the "language" problem became a basic justification to continue the practice of segregation, turning what had become an unconstitutional activity into one that could appear to have a rational basis. The rationale given for segregating centered on the fact that first grade Spanish-speaking students needed special attention in learning English; therefore, in order to give them special attention and not hold back their English-speaking counterparts, they needed to be segregated. They would get separate but equal education. Even though this practice was becoming recognized as illegal, school systems continued to use it. Attempts to discontinue segregation practices were reported in the literature, but still little progress was indicated. In one particular Los Angeles school it was reported that "segregation" of Mexican Americans was discontinued this year. However, because "many of the first grade Mexican children do not speak English or do not speak it well, thirty-three of them have been segregated until they learn the language which requires about a year" (Jeidy, 1947, p. 203).

Strickland and Sanchez (1948) questioned the practice of segregation and called it prejudicial and discriminatory. They surveyed 10 school systems in Texas in order to determine: (1) the extent to which segregation was being practiced; (2) the rationale for the practice; and (3) the degree to which the practices really upheld the reasons. They found that: (1) 8 out of the 10 schools "employed" segregation practices; (2) "segregation" was carried out on a purely arbitrary basis, determined solely by local custom, tradition, and prejudice (p. 23); (3) the "practices [did not] correspond to the reasons given for segregation" and that "no pedagogically defensible techniques or procedures were employed for the determination of those youngsters needing segregation because of language handicaps or other special needs" (p. 23); and (4) "segregation instead of being designed for furthering the education of Spanish surnamed children, was discriminatory and prejudicial to their educational development" (p. 23).

Segregation practices coupled with the view that Spanish-speaking children had a "language bilingual" problem resulted in perpetuation of the nonachievement view of Spanish-speaking children. In addition, an unconstitutional practice, segregation, was sanctioned as a pedagogical solution to the "language" problem of "these" children to the educational system.

THE 1950s: THE "PROBLEM" IS A "DUAL HANDICAP" AND "LANGUAGE BARRIER"

Not only was segregation still an issue in the 1950s (Edwards, 1952) but bilingualism became a "dual handicap" (Chavez & Erikson, 1957; Rowan, Kendall, & Strough, 1950) and a "language barrier" (Teel, 1954). To confront these "language handicap" and "language barrier" explanations for the causes, practical solutions and remedies began to appear.

For example, Tireman (1955) elaborated the view of education as compensation for deficiency. He stated that "the reading problems of most bilingual children arise, generally from the home situation" (p. 33). His solution was to remedy the "meager experiences" of the home environment with school "compensating with a rich and satisfying program." This, in turn, would solve the children's vocabulary problems in English reading.

Chavez and Erikson (1957) also attributed "poor health and discouraging economic and environmental situation" as explanations for the "low level of attainment" among Spanish-speaking children. Their solution to this problem was the need for expert teachers. They reasoned that "children who are handicapped by inadequate knowledge of English require the best that can be had in instruction" (p. 201). Abraham (1957, p. 475), in addition, called for teachers who understood "why they, [the students] won't talk, or are often late, or dress shabbily." In addition to needing "enriched school environments," "expert teachers," and "understanding" to resolve the "bilingual language handicap problem," Rowan, Kendall, and Stroud (1950, p. 426) suggested that ". . . persistent patience is required."

These authors were setting the stage for the "cultural" and "linguistic" deficit advocates of the 1960s. Abraham stereotyped; Rowan, Kendall, and Stroud mislabeled; Chavez and Erikson created a deficit term, "handicapped"; and Tireman continued to perpetuate the notion of an internal basis for "reading problems of non English speaking children." The works of these authors is not research based. Their conclusions are speculations about why a particular group of children in American society appear to do poorly on tests. Unfortunately, these generalizations have become accepted truths and common misconceptions. The historical evolution of racist manifestations in our educational system and among educational writers and researchers is understandable yet alarming. Even in the 1950s, Wallace (1956) stated that there wasn't enough conclusive research to finding concrete solutions for the educational problems of bilingual children. Even he was still viewing bilingualism as a problem.

To summarize, this decade is an extension of the view of the "Mexican" as a "problem" in the schools in the United States. Culture and home environment had now been added to language in the list of "causes" for "retardation," lack of school attainment, and reading problems. The saga of the "deficit" view continued to grow with each decade adding its own negative labels.

THE 1960s: THE "PROBLEM" IS "CULTURAL" AND "LINGUISTIC" DEPRIVATION

> "Hey, I'm Depraved because I'm Deprived."
> *West Side Story*

During the decade of the 1960s, the concepts of "cultural" (Reissman, 1962) and "linguistic" (Englemann & Bereriter, 1966) "deprivation" greatly influenced educators, researchers, Congress, and the general public. The blame for continued underachievement and low educational attainment still rested on the Latino/a child's so-called inabilities. Latino/a children's home life and language were now firmly established as the primary causes of school failure. The genesis of the previous decade's deficit view had gained wider acceptance. The child's "language problem," "bilingual disability," "mental retardation," "dual handicap," and "language barrier problems" were relabeled "deprivation." Carter and Segura (1979, pp. 27–28) describe this decade:

> More general interest and massive financial investment in solutions to educational and social problems of the Mexican American characterized the 1960's. The Chicano movement played a key role in supporting the demands for equal educational opportunity and self-determination. Rationales of cultural deprivation gained ascendancy, as did compensatory programs based on the concept.

Federal programs such as Head Start, Compensatory Education, Migrant Education, Title I, and Title VII (Bilingual Education) were funded in order to "remedy" the "deprivation" of minority children including Mexican Americans. What resulted was nationwide institutionalization of the "deficit view." By getting to the child "early," Head Start programs would intervene positively where the family couldn't. The program would provide the child with the "rich experiences" that his/her family "lacked." For older children, where it was too late, "compensatory" and "remedial" programs would try to lessen the achievement gap by supplanting current educational practices with intensified versions of the same practices. The Elementary and Secondary Education Act of 1965 primarily focused on helping "disadvantaged" children. Title I was aimed at providing additional help in the basic skills, whereas Title VII was specifically for the "limited English" speaker.

Likewise, Migrant Education was created in order to expand the schools' responsibilities. High absenteeism and transient behavior characterized the migrant Mexican child. The itinerant lifestyle was/is not compatible with conventional school expectations. The itinerant patterns that characterized our nation's migrant workers, the essential gatherers of fresh fruit and vegetables, had supposedly shortchanged their children's life experiences. The school neither understood nor accepted these workers' lifestyle. Usually travel is associated with broadening one's knowledge of the world; however, a migrant farmworker's traveling experiences and knowledge were not recognized or valued. "They've only seen the world from the back of a migrant worker's truck," said one report. Most school programs adopted a clinical view, that is, they viewed the child as without any strengths, inflicted with a sickness to be cured, with only symptoms of weakness and with deficiencies that need to be compensated for.

Educators during this decade, in general, continued to view the Latino/a child as "handicapped," "limited," "disadvantaged," and "problematic." For example, Ching (1965, p. 22) echoes Tireman's earlier unfounded generalization: "Teachers who work with bilingual children are often confronted with pupils who have handicaps in relation to the language backgrounds necessary for successful reading. . . .Before the child with a language handicap can begin to read successfully, he must command a meaningful English vocabulary."

This decade is rampant with unfounded generalizations about language learning and language development. For example, the child's Spanish competence was not even considered; instead it was regarded as a "handicap." Hoben (1966, p. 28) not only restated that Mexican American children ". . . come to school with a language handicap . . ." but also added that "often the child who is experiencing difficulty in school has not mastered even one language." The latter statement is a commonsense assertion and paradoxically, it is not at all supported by any scientific evidence. All children, by the time they come to school, are able to communicate their needs. Mastery of a language is often judged by an elitist's yardstick, for only he/she who judges holds the evaluative power. And, then, those who would be judged also must be complicit, that is, believe it, for it to be accepted as a truth.

Perales (1965, p. 99) also said that "students of Latino/a descent possess a limited Spanish vocabulary and they will borrow from their equally limited English vocabulary to complete their expressions." He also was interested in "correcting" their Spanish errors. Calderon (1963) concentrated on recommending the eight "most common" mistakes made by Spanish-speaking children and advocated that these mistakes could be corrected, for example, the "sh" and "ch" confusion. These "mistakes" were viewed as deficiencies and not as dialectical features. These misconceptions about dialectical differences parallel views in the same period on Black English and other low-status English dialects.

Arnold (1968, p. 634) focused on the widespread condition of the "disadvantaged" Mexican American children by stating that "mass failure and deficient reading appear symptomatic of a more fundamental problem. Many of these children have little knowledge of English, the language of instruction in the schools." The focus was still on knowing the English language; however, not all educators held such deficiency attitudes. No one denies the fact that immigrants to this country need to learn English, but must they be humiliated and dehumanized because of their language and culture? A child comes to school willingly and ready to learn. She/he comes with a wealth of knowledge based on his/her cultural and linguistic assets. So, to continually "blame the victim" is a one-sided argument.

Fortunately, new views began to emerge based on new research building on insights from linguistics and psycholinguistics. Kaufman (1968), Modiano (1968), and Krear (1969) advocated initially teaching literacy to Spanish-speaking children in their mother tongue. Teaching Spanish-speaking children to read in their language became a controversial educational practice in bilingual education. However, as long as it was seen as transitional and English as a Second Language also was a curricular component, the practice was not seriously challenged. Any solution to the Latino/a child's "language problem" was welcomed.

Rosen and Ortego (1969) reported that poorly trained and unsophisticated teachers with cultural biases and profoundly ignorant notions concerning how language is learned were tragically too common in the schools. Goodman (1969) also advocated that there was definitely an urgent need to modernize teacher knowledge, behaviors, and attitudes pertaining to the language differences of their pupils. Knowledge and acceptance of the child's language were being called for at the end of this decade, but still the "deprivation" view lingered. Its remnants remained in the decade of the 1970s as well.

The 1960s were greatly influenced by the Civil Rights movement, the War on Poverty, the student movement, and "el movimiento Chicano." These historical events were a catalyst for mobilizing masses of people wanting and demanding their civil rights, educational opportunity, and social legitimacy. The nation's very constitutional foundation was being tested and challenged. Minorities wanted more than tolerance and an end to discrimination. They demanded the right to their own language and culture while learning and adopting the language of their new/old country as well as the right to be accepted as themselves. They rejected the melting pot notion that dominated school programs for immigrants. In other words, they wanted to keep their sociocultural and language identity and also adopt this nation's language and culture. They did not want to reject/replace their parents' and grandparents' language and culture at the expense of losing their cultural and linguistic identity. Instead, they advocated adding English and the American culture to their repertoire.

THE 1970s: THE "PROBLEM" IS EQUAL EDUCATIONAL OPPORTUNITY FOR THE CULTURALLY AND LINGUISTICALLY "DIFFERENT" CHILD

Carter's (1970) book, *Mexican Americans in Schools: A History of Educational Neglect*, begins the decade and Carter and Segura's (1979) book, *Mexican Americans: A Decade of Change*, ends it. In the interim much activity ensued in the forms of: (1) national studies about the status of the Mexican American student in education, for example, the United States Commission on Civil Rights (1971, 1973, 1974); (2) significant legislation, both federal and state (Title I, Title VII, Head Start, Migrant Education); (3) landmark litigations (see Teitlebaum and Hiller, 1977); and (4) continued support of federal programs and research.

Equal Educational Opportunity and desegregation practices characterized this decade's enormous goals for educational equality. However, achievement and school attainment among Latino/a students still was disproportionately low. Test scores on standardized achievement tests continued to be the single criterion for evaluation despite their narrow scope and growing criticism toward their use. The "back to basics" movement influenced educators and created a crisis view among our nation's parents, teachers, legislators, and the general public. Legal precedents were set, for example, *Lau v. Nichols* (1974), *Aspira v. School Board of New York* (1974), *Serrano v. Priest* (1971), and so on. The deficiency view still prevailed but was now disguised as the "culturally" and "linguistically" different "problem." The teaching of English was still an issue. However, the deficiency view was seriously questioned and challenged by many scholars (Arciniega, 1973; Brischetto & Arciniega, 1972; Carter and Segura, 1979; Ginsburg, 1972; Vaca, 1970; and Weinberg, 1977).

During the 1970s, the expansion and growth of bilingual education for our nation's "language" minorities marked a turning point away from the United States' political "ethnolingualcentric" stance. The turning point, though, was still basically founded on the compensatory framework of 1960s federal legislation. It must be noted that bilingual education was supported but was expected to prove itself in a short span of time.

The "limited English" terminology in the federal guidelines represents again the "language problem" concept that saw its birth in the 1930s. Several key works on language and education became the basic resources, for example, Anderson and Boyer's (1970) *Bilingual Schooling in the United States*; Williams' (1970) *Language and Poverty*; Spolsky's (1972) *The Language Education of Minority Children*; Engle's (1973) *The Use of Vernacular Languages in Education: Revisited*; Saville and Troike's (1971) *Handbook of Bilingual Education*; Paulston's (1974) *Implications of Language Learning Theory for Language Planning*; and Turner's (1973) *Bilingualism in the Southwest*; and many, many more.

The boom in professional staff development, curriculum development, teacher preparation programs in institutions of higher education, and the implementation of Title VII programs in elementary and secondary schools preceded needed research and planning. But despite the many obstacles, the "bilingual movement" made significant strides in beginning to provide equal educational opportunity for decades of "educational neglect." Clearly, this decade made significant growth and change regarding the quality and equal educational opportunities of Latino/a students. At the beginning of the decade, concrete plans and implementation to disseminate information and conduct national research had begun, for example, the new bilingual research center at the Southwest Regional Lab, SWRL; the establishment of the National Clearinghouse for Bilingual Education; the establishment of the new Office of Bilingual Education and Minority Affairs in the new Department of Education at the federal level; and the establishment of the National Association of Bilingual Educators, NABE. Also, many statewide and local chapters formed to support the Bilingual Education movement. Congress also established the National Institute for Education that was designated to orchestrate national research.

Despite growing movements to build positive attitudes among some educators about bilingualism and Spanish/English speakers, many educators were still clouded by misconceptions about language use, language learning, language development, and language acquisition. And, despite the growing knowledge explosion in linguistics (Chomsky, 1965), sociopsycholinguistics (Goodman, 1970; Goodman & Goodman, 1978; Goodman, Goodman, & Flores, 1979), sociolinguistics (Halliday, 1978; Krashen, 1978), sociocultural traditions (Moll & Diaz, 1987; Scribner & Cole, 1981; Vygotsky, 1978), critical pedagogy (Freire, 1970; Freire and Macedo, 1978; Giroux, 1983; McClaren, 1993), child language and thought development (Ferreiro & Teberosky, 1979, 1982; Macedo & Bartolome, 1991), and educational linguistics, educators resisted the new knowledge. They were still greatly influenced by decades of "deficitness" thinking. They still embodied many *habitudes* (habitual unexamined attitudes) (Flores, 1982) about Spanish-speaking children's language and culture. Without a doubt, "English language" achievement on a standardized test still seemed to be the focus and often the single yardstick used for determining educational achievement and success.

THE 1980s: THE "PROBLEMS" WERE "SEMILINGUALISM" AND "LIMITED ENGLISH PROFICIENT" (LEP) STUDENTS

The advent of the concept of semilingualism was potentially dangerous. It was a new label for cognitive deficiency, that is, if a child did not learn some basic concepts in his first language, then he/she would be cognitively deficient in L2 as measured by a standardized achievement test (Skutnaubb-Kangus, 1976). The basic assumption, again, was focusing on the negative, placing an emphasis on weakness and assuming a resultant deficiency. By the way, the standardized test was given in the child's second language. The logic of reasoning was clearly faulty and syllogistic as evidenced in the 1920s with the intelligence tests given to the children in another language that wasn't their mother tongue. The confusion with how language and thought expand and develop was evident; that is, it was assumed that learning concepts solely depends on language. However, this does not mean that language does not play an important part, but it is not language alone that determines concept development. Language provides a naming of the concept. Likewise, the assumption that a standardized test score can determine cognitive development is also very narrow and limiting.

The nature of the growth and development of language and thought still needed/needs to be further explored. The Piagetians, Vygotskians, the Gardeners (multiple intelligence), and the sociopsycholinguists of the world began systematically to document and generate new knowledge that impacted the development of pedagogy. And, fortunately, the advocates of this concept of semilingualism lost their momentum in creating yet another new label for old practices, that is, relabeling and mislabeling minority children's "lack of achievement" in schools. Unfortunately, "Limited English Proficient" speaker became one of the icons used to label Spanish-speaking children. They would call them "LEPs," "FEPs," and "NEPs." These terms still exist. It seems so dehumanizing to call a child by these labels. But, when "these" children are "dehumanized," then they are no longer seen as vibrant children eager to learn; they become objects and problems to be dealt with (Freire, 1970). After all, "they come from homes where they have language and cultural problems."

According to Nieto (2000), this decade marks a significant paradigmatic shift from the educational liberal reform movements of the 1960s and 1970s to a conservative retrenchment. She states that "during the previous 2 decades educational concerns had focused on educational equality by challenging the deficit theories popularized in the 1960s [and decades before] and through strategies such as busing, integration, ethnic studies, and bilingual, cross-cultural multicultural education" (p. 22). Unfortunately, this marks the beginning of the demise of many educational innovations and effective schooling practices that had been in place. However, in spite of these setbacks, different pockets of local success have been sustained (e.g., Mercado, 1992, 2001; Torres-Guzman, 1989), but these lessons of success need to become widespread. In the *Best for Our Children* (2001), edited by Maria de la Luz Reyes and John Halcon, many Latino/a scholar activists present theoretical frameworks, research studies, and pedagogical solutions for the successful academic schooling of Latino/a children and students.

THE 1990s: THE "PROBLEM" IS THAT THESE CHILDREN ARE "AT RISK"

This decade lies more in our recent memories. When *A Nation At Risk* (1983) appeared on the scene, it set the stage for continuing the deficit tradition. Now, Spanish-speaking students were classified as "at risk." Their parents are the culprits because they don't care, can't read or write, neglect their children, and don't speak English. This "blaming the victim" syndrome continued throughout this decade despite many efforts by Latino/a scholars and other scholars who rejected the deficit view (Flores et al., 1991; Valencia, 1997). For example, Richard Valencia's edited volume (1991), *Chicano School Failure and Success: Research and Policy Agendas for the 1990s* documents the sociopolitical and sociohistorical educational policies and practices that were/are based on segregation, racism, and unequal treatment of Chicano students in schooling practices such as standardized testing, psychological testing, institutionalized tracking, and ability grouping. The results of these institutionalized schooling practices have resulted in devastating high dropout rates among not only Chicano students but the majority of Latino/a students nationwide. And, the second edition of *Chicano School Failure and Success* (2002) begins the 21st century by documenting current realities of Chicano schooling experiences, language perspectives on Chicano student achievement, cultural and familial perspective on Chicano student achievement, educational testing and special education issues germane to Chicano students, and, finally, the big picture of Chicano school failure and success with solid roadmaps toward Chicano students' school success.

According to Martha Menchaca (1997), these educational practices toward racial minorities are rooted historically in the socioeconomic subordination of people of color by White business owners who "rationalized their actions . . . by claiming the moral right to govern racial minorities in that the latter were either animals or were culturally inferior" (pp. xii–xiii). According to Menchaca (1997), this historically deficit way of thinking and policy making can be traced between the 1600s and 1800s. Likewise, she documents that public schooling was denied to children of color for more than a century because of dominant White economic interests and controls. And when children of color finally were granted public schooling, "... such schooling for students of color typically was segregated and inferior—thus demonstrating the pernicious impact of deficit thinking on schooling practices" (p. xiii). So, today we still are facing these inequitable schooling policies and practices. As we enter the 21st century, we face ultraconservative movements (English Only, Back to Basics, standardization of curricula, high-stakes standardized testing, etc.), public policies (banning of bilingual education in states such as California, Massachusetts, New York; high school exit exams; No Child Left Behind) and big corporate interests (McGraw-Hill, Houghten Mifflin, Open Court) in the effort to continue these deficit views and schooling practices of Latinos and children of color in general. Educating the masses would indeed unbalance the economic power brokers. Access to knowledge is a threat to the status quo. However, in spite of these attempts to maintain the status quo, the Latino/a population's earning and spending power now exceeds $800 billion just in the United State alone. They are a growing economic base whose time has arrived. In a democratic nation such as the United States, there is no reason now to continue this deficit thinking, schooling practices, or inequitable educational treatment. A democratic society is maintained by its educated citizenry.

The following table (4.1) provides an overview and summary of the history of "The Intellectual Presence of the Deficit View of Spanish-Speaking Children in the Educational Literature During the 20th Century." The focus of the "problem" and the most common myths, fallacies, and habitudes are included for each decade (Flores, 1982).

The genesis of the deficit point of view as an explanation for Latinos' "lack of success in school and educational achievement" is deeply rooted in the historical, cultural, and educational mystique. Romano (1967, p. 8) explains that "... no matter from which group they come, those in power describe their own station in life as resulting directly from goal-oriented behavior, a competitive urge ... in short, they place the reasons or causes of their 'success' somewhere within themselves." Others who do not fit or who are not successful are labeled as inferior; "... the reasons or causes of 'inferior' status [are placed] somewhere within the minds, within the personalities, or within the culture of those who are economically, politically, or educationally out of power" (p. 7).

By naming the problem and by having interrogated the genesis of the deficit view of Latinos in this nation, we have to continue to transform the linguistic and cultural deficit myths (Flores, Diaz, & Cousin, 1991; Nieto, 2000; Valencia, 2002) that negatively impact not only our Latino/a children but all children of color. We have to create public policies,

TABLE 4.1

The Intellectual Presence of the Deficit View
of Spanish-Speaking Children in the Educational
Literature During the 20th Century

Decade	Focus	Myths, Fallacies, and Habitudes
The 1920s	The "Problem" Is "Mental Retardation"	a. Spanish-speaking children are mentally retarded because of language difficulty as determined by an I.Q. test.
The 1930s	The "Problem" Is "Bilingualism"	a. Spanish-speaking children do not achieve in school because they are bilingual. b. Learning English is difficult. c. "Bilingualism and its effects upon the reading aspects of language is a problem."
The 1940s	The "Problem" Is to "Change" Mexicans Through Education	a. The Mexican could be changed through schooling. b. The bilingual child's language is a problem; therefore, it is the only problem that the schools have direct and complete control over. c. Because Mexican children have a language problem, they must be segregated.
The 1950s	The "Problems" Are a "Dual Handicap" and "Language Barrier"	a. The school must compensate for the Mexican children's deficiencies by providing "a rich and satisfying program." b. Bilingual children's reading problems arise generally from their home situations.
The 1960s	The "Problem" Is "Cultural" and "Linguistic" Deprivation	a. Home and language are the primary causes of school failure. b. The school must remedy the deprivation of Spanish-speaking students. c. Before the child with a language handicap can begin reading successfully, he must command a meaningful English vocabulary.
The 1970s	The "Problem" Is Equal Educational Opportunity for the Culturally and Linguistically "Different" Child	a. The "Limited English Proficient" child must be helped. b. English language achievement on a standardized test is the only yardstick used for educational success. c. Bilingual children must not mix their languages. If they do, it is an indication that they "know" neither well. They are said to be "alingual," "nonlingual," or "semilingual."
The 1980s	The "Problems" Are "Semilingualism" and "Limited English Proficient" (LEP) students	a. If children don't learn concepts in their native language, they will be cognitively deficient when learning those concepts in a second language. b. Semilingualism is determined by a score on a standardized achievement test given in English. c. The "LEP" child needs special education in order to learn English. d. Bilingual children need to be taught in their primary language, then transitioned into English.

Table 4.1 (continued)

Decade	Focus	Myths, Fallacies, and Habitudes
The 1990s	The "Problem" Is That These Children Are "At Risk"	a. In order to prevent failure in schooling, we must intervene early. b. "These" children come from very dysfunctional families and need additional help. c. "These" children's parents don't care, can't read and write, and neglect their children.
The 2000s	The "Problem" Is Lack of English	a. "These" children continue to fail in school because they have been in bilingual education. b. The inability to learn English prevents "these" students from succeeding.

legislation, and schooling practices that are beneficial not only to our children but to society in general. We have to educate our communities to actively participate in their own governance, in their own political and economic realities, in creating their own destinies.

We must resist and continue to right the wrongs; we must prevail and plant the seeds for the generations to come; we must unite in our efforts to construct and maintain a just society; we must act or we will perish by our own lack of courage, by our own collusion, or by our own will to remain as part of the status quo. The National Latino/a Educational Research Agenda is a formidable step in the educational future of Latino/a children and students in the United States.

REFERENCES

Abraham, W. (1957). Bilingual child and his teacher. *Elementary English, 34,* 474–478.

Acuña, R. (1972). *Occupied America: The Chicano's struggle toward liberation.* San Francisco: Cornfield Press.

Anderson, T., & Boyer, M. (1970). *Bilingual schooling in the United States.* Austin, TX: Southwest Education Development Laboratory.

Andras, E. P. (1943). Workshop studies: Education of Mexican Americans. *California Journal of Secondary Education, 18,* 328–330.

Arciniega, T. (1973). The myth of the compensatory education model in the education of Chicanos. In R. D. de la Garza, Z. A. Kruszewski, & T. Arciniega (Eds.), *Chicanos and Native Americans.* Englewood Cliffs, NJ: Prentice Hall.

Arnold, R. D. (1968). English as a second language. *The Reading Teacher, 21,* 634–639.

Aspira of New York Inc., v. Board of Education of the City of New York, 72 Civ. 4002 (S.D.N.Y. April 30, 1974).

Brischetto, R., & Arciniega, T. (1972). *Examining the examiners: A look at educators' perspectives on the Chicano student.* Unpublished paper presented at the Rocky Mountain Social Science Association, Salt Lake City, Utah.

Burbeck, E. (1939). Problems presented to teachers of bilingual pupils. *California Journal of Elementary Education, 8,* 49–54.

Burma, J. H. (1954). *Spanish speaking groups in the United States.* Durham, NC: Duke University Press.

Carter, T. P. (1970). *Mexican Americans in schools: A history of educational neglect.* New York: College Entrance Examination Board.

Carter, T. P., & Segura, R. D. (1979). *Mexican Americans in school: A decade of change.* New York: College Entrance Examination Board.

Chavez, S. J., & Erikson, T. L. (1957). Teaching American children from Spanish speaking homes. *Elementary School Journal, 57,* 198–203.

Ching, D. C. (1965). Methods for the bilingual child. *Elementary English Elementary School Journal, 42,* 22–27.

Ching, D. C. (1976). *Reading and the bilingual child.* Newark, DE: International Reading Association.

Chomsky, N. (1965). *Aspects of theory of syntax.* Cambridge, MA: MIT Press.

Dann, J. A. (1944). Introducing English to a bilingual majority group. *Elementary English Review, 17,* 18–22.

DeVargas, D. (1937). Teaching Mexicans an English vocabulary. *Elementary English Review, 14,* 31.

Edwards, N. (1952). Segregation of Spanish-speaking children in public schools. *Elementary School Journal, 52,* 31–81.

Englemann, S., & Bereiter, C. (1966). *Teaching disadvantaged children in the preschool.* Englewood Cliffs, NJ: Prentice Hall.

Engle, P. (1973). *The use of vernacular languages in education revisited.* Arlington, VA: Center for Applied Linguistics.

Ferreiro, E., & Teberosky, A. (1979). *Los sistemas de escritura en el desarrollo del nino.* Mexico: Siglo XXI.

Ferreiro, E., & Teberosky, A. (1982). *Literacy before schooling.* Portsmouth, NH: Heinemann Publishers.

Finnochiaro, M. (1949). Suggested procedures in the teaching of English to Spanish speakers. *High Points, 31,* 60–66.

Flicker, J. (1947). Classes for Spanish speaking children. *High Points, 29,* 58–62.

Flores, B. (1982). *Language interference or influence: Toward a theory of Hispanic bilingualism.* Unpublished dissertation, University of Arizona, Tucson.

Flores, B., Cousin, P., & Diaz, E. (1991). Transforming deficit myths about learning, language, and culture. *Language Arts, 68,* 369–379.

Flores, B., Diaz, E., & Cousin, P. (1991). Transforming deficit views in language, learning and culture. *Language Arts.*

Freire, P. (1970). *The pedagogy of the oppressed.* New York: Herder & Herder.

Garcia, R. L. (1977). *Language and reading development of bilinguals in the United States.* ERIC (ERIC Document Reproduction Service No. ED145449).

Garretson, O. K. (1928). A study of causes of retardation among Mexican children in a small public school system in Arizona. *Journal of Educational Psychology, 19,* 31–40.

Garretson, O. K. (1928). Study of the causes of retardation among Mexican children. *Journal of Educational Psycbology, 19,* 31–40.

Garth, T. R. (1923). A comparison of the intelligence of Mexican and mixed and full blooded Indian children. *Psychological Review, 30,* 388–401.

Ginsberg, H. (1972). *The myth of the deprived child.* Englewood Cliffs, NJ: Prentice Hall.

Giroux, H. (1983). *Theory and resistance in education.* South Hadley, MA: Bergin & Garvey Publications.

Goodman, K. (1970). Psycholinguistic universals in the reading process. *Journal of Typographic Research.* Spring, 103–110.

Goodman, K. (1986). *What's whole in whole language?* Portsmouth, NH: Heinemann Publishers.

Goodman, K. (1996). *On reading.* Portsmouth, NH: Heinemann Publishers.

Goodman, K., & Goodman, Y. (1978). Reading of American children whose language is a stable rural dialect of English or a language other than English. Final Report. Project NIE-C-00-3-0087. Washington, DC: Department of Health, Education, & Welfare/National Institute of Education.

Goodman, K., Goodman, Y., & Flores, B. (1979). *Reading in a bilingual classroom: Literacy and biliteracy.* Rosslyn, VA: Clearinghouse for Bilingual Education.

Goodman, K. S. (1969). Dialect barriers to reading comprehension. In J. C. Baratz & R.W. Shuy (Eds.), *Teaching Black children to read.* Washington, DC: Center for Applied Linguistics.

Goodman, Y. (Ed.). (1991). *How children construct literacy.* Newark, DE: International Reading Association.

Halliday, M. A. K. (1978). *Learning as a social semiotic: The social interpretation of language and meaning.* Baltimore, MD: University Park Press.

Herbert, C. (1972). *The bilingual child's right to read.* ERIC (ERIC Document Reproduction Service No. ED062841)

Hoben, N. (1966). Help the language handicapped! *Texas Outlook, 50,* 28–29.

Jeidy, P. (1947). First grade Mexican American children in Ventura County. *California Journal of Elementary Education, 15,* 200–208.

Kaufman, M. (1968). Will instruction in reading Spanish affect ability to reading in English? *Journal of Reading, 11,* 521–527.

Kelly, V. H. (1936). The reading abilities of Spanish and English speaking pupils. *Journal of Educational Research, 15,* 200–211.

Krashen, S. (1981). *Principles and practice in second language acquistion.* London: Prentice-Hall International.

Krear, S. E. (1969). Role of the mother tongue at home and at school in the development of bilingualism. *English Language Teacher, 24,* 2–4.

Lau, et al. v. Nichols et al., 483 F. 2d 791 (9th Cir. 1974).

Lynn, K. (1945). Bilingualism in the Southwest. *Quarterly Journal of Speech, 31,* 175–180.

Macedo, D., & Bartolome, L. (1991). *Dancing with bigotry.* New York, NY: St. Martins Press.

Manuel, H. T. (1930). *The education of Mexican and Spanish speaking children in Texas.* Austin: The Fund for Research in the Social Sciences, The University of Texas.

Manuel, H. T., & Wright, C. E. (1929). Language difficulty of Mexican American children. *Pedagogical Seminary and Journal of Genetic Psychology, 36,* 458–468.

McLaren, P. (1993). *Schooling as a ritual performance.* London: Routledge.

McWilliams, C. (1949). *North from Mexico: The Spanish speaking people of the United States.* New York: J.B. Lippincott Company.

Menchaca, M. (1997). Early racist discourses: Roots of deficit thinking. In R. Valencia (Ed.), *The evolution of deficit thinking.* New York: Falmer Press.

Mercado, C. (1992). Researching research. In A. Ambert & M. Alvarez (Eds.), *Puerto Rican children on the mainland: A research view.* New York: Garland.

Mercado, C. (2001). The learner: Race, ethnicity, and linguistic difference. In V. Richardson (Ed.), *Handbook of research on Teaching.* (4th ed.). Washington, DC: American Educational Research Association.

Mitchell, A. J. (1927). The effect of bilingualism in the measurement of intelligence. *Elementary School Journal, 38,* 29–37.

Modiano, N. (1968). National and mother language in beginning reading: A comparative study. *Research in the Teaching of English, 2,* 32–43.

Moll, L. (1990). *Vygotsky and education.* London: Cambridge University Press.

Moll, L., & Diaz, E. (1987). Change as the goal of educational research. *Anthropology and Educational Quarterly, 18*(4), 300–311.

Moll, L., & Diaz, S. (1987). Change as the goal of educational research. *Anthropology and Educational Quarterly, 18*(4), 300–311.

The National Commission on Excellence in Education. (1983). *A nation at risk: The imperative for educational reform.* Washington, DC: United States Department of Education.

Nieto, S. (Ed.). (2000). Puerto Rican students in U.S. schools: A brief history. In *Puerto Rican students in U.S. Schools.* Mahwah, NJ: Lawrence Erlbaum Associates.

Paulston, C. (1974). *Implications of language learning theory for language planning.* Arlington, VA: Center for Applied Linguistics.

Perales, A. M. (1965). Audiolingual approach and the Spanish speaking student. *Hispanic, 48,* 99–102.

Reissman, F. (1962). *The culturally deprived child.* New York: Harper & Row.

Reynolds, A. (1933). *The education of Spanish speaking children in five southwestern states.* Washington, DC: United States Government Printing Office.

Rivera, M., & Pedraza, P. (2000). The spirit of transformation: An education reform movement in a New York City Latino/a community. In S. Nieto (Ed.), *Puerto Rican Students in U.S. Schools.* Mahwah, NJ: Lawrence Erlbaum Associates.

Rojas, P. M. (1946). Reading materials for bilingual children. *Elementary School Journal, 47,* 204–211.

Romano, O. I. (1967). Minorities, history and the cultural mystique. *El Grito, 1*(1), 5–11.

Romano, O. I. (1968). The anthropology and sociology of the Mexican Americans: The distortion of Mexican history. *El Grito, 2*(2), 13–26.

Romano, O. I. (1969). The historical and intellectual presence of Mexican Americans. *El Grito, 2*(2), 32–46.

Rosen, C. L., & Ortego, P. D. (1969). Problems and strategies in teaching the language arts to Spanish speaking Mexican Americans. ERIC (ERIC Document Reproduction Service No. ED025368).

Rowan, B., Kendall, E., & Stroud, M. (1950). The teaching of bilingual children. *Education, 70,* 423–426.

Sanchez, G. I. (1940). *Forgotten people: A study of New Mexicans.* Albuquerque: The University of New Mexico.

Saville, M. R., & Troike, R. C. (1971). *A handbook of bilingual education.* Washington, DC: Teachers of English to Speakers of Other Languages.

Scribner, S., & Cole, M. (1981). *The psychology of literacy.* Cambridge, MA: Harvard University Press.

Serrano et al. v. Ivy Baker Priest, 96 California Reporter. 487 P. 2d 1241 (1971).

Sheldon, W. H. (1924). The intelligence of Mexican children. *School and Society, 19,* 139–142.

Skutnabb-Kangus, T., & Toukomaa, P. (1976). *Teaching migrant childrens' mother tongue and learning the language of the host country in the context of the socio-cultural situation of the migrant family.* Helsinki: The Finnish National Commission for UNESCO.

Spolsky, B. (1972). *The language education of minority children.* Rowely, MA: Newbury House.

Staats, A. W., & Staats, C. K. (1971). *Child learning, intelligence, and personality: Principles of a behavioural interaction approach.* New York: Harper & Row.

Strickland, V. E., & Sanchez, G. I. (1948). Spanish name spells discrimination. *Nations Schools, 41*, 22–24.

Taylor, M. C. (1927). Retardation of Mexican children in the Albuquerque schools. Unpublished master's thesis. Stanford, CA: Stanford University.

Teel, D. (1954). Preventing prejudice against Spanish speaking children. *Educational Leadership, 12*, 94–98.

Teitlebaum, H., & Hiller, R. J. (1977). Bilingual education: The legal mandate. *Harvard Educational Review, 47*(2), 138–170.

Tireman, L. S. (1941). Bilingual children. *Review of Educational Research, 11*, 340–352.

Tireman, L. S. (1942). School problems created by the foreign speaking child. *Texas Outlook, 26*, 19–20.

Tireman, L. S. (1943). Teaching Spanish in the high school. *Hispania, 26*, 35–40.

Tireman, L. S. (1944). Bilingual children. *Review of Educational Research, 14*, 273–278.

Tireman, L. S. (1945). A study of fourth grade reading vocabulary of native Spanish speaking children. *Elementary School Journal* (December), 223–227.

Tireman, L. S. (1948). *Teaching Spanish speaking children.* Albuquerque: University of New Mexico Press.

Tireman, L. S. (1955). Bilingual child and his reading vocabulary. *Elementary English, 32*, 33–35.

Tireman, L. S., Dixon, N., & Cornelius, V. (1935). Vocabulary acquisition of Spanish speaking children. *The Elementary English Review, 12*, 118–119, 144.

Thonis, E. W. (1970). *Teaching reading to non-english speakers.* New York: MacMillan.

Thonis, E. W. (1976). *Literacy for America's Spanish speaking children.* Newark, DE: International Reading Association.

Torres-Guzman, M., & Martinez Thorne, Y. (2000). Puerto Rican/Latino student voices: Stand and deliver. In S. Nieto (Ed.), *Puerto Rican students in U.S. schools.* Mahwah, NJ: Lawrence Erlbaum Associates.

Turner, R. (1973). *Bilingualism in the southwest.* Tucson, AZ: University of Arizona Press.

United States Commission on Civil Rights. (1971). *Report 1: Ethnic isolation of Mexican Americans in the public schools of the Southwest.* Washington, DC: United States Government Printing Office.

United States Commission on Civil Rights. (1972). *Report 3: The excluded student: Educational practices affecting Mexican Americans in the Southwest.* Washington, DC: United States Government Printing Office.

United States Commission on Civil Rights. (1974). *Report 6: Toward quality education for Mexican Americans.* Washington, DC: United States Printing Office.

Vaca, N. C. (1970). The Mexican American in the social sciences: 1912–1970. *El Grito, 3*(3).

Valencia, R. (Ed.). (1991). *Chicano school failure and success: Research policy agendas for the 1990s.* London: Falmer Press.

Valencia, R. (Ed.) (1997). *The evolution of deficit thinking: Educational thought and practice.* London: Falmer Press.

Valencia, R. (Ed). (2002). *Chicano school failure and success: Past, present, and future.* London: Routledge/Falmer, a Taylor & Francis Group.

Vygotsky, L. (1978). *Mind in society: The development of higher psychological process.* (M. Cole, V. John-Steiner, S. Scribner, & E. Souberman, Trans. & Eds.). Cambridge, MA: Harvard University Press.

Wallace, A. (1956). Bilingualism and retardation. *Elementary English, 33*, 303–304.

Wedberg, A. (1942). Teaching of speech to Mexican children. *California Journal of Elementary Education, 10*, 216–222.

Weinberg, M. (1977). *A chance to learn.* New York: Cambridge University Press.

Williams, F. (1970). *Language and poverty.* Chicago, IL: Markham Publishing Company.

Young, K. (1922). Mental differences in certain immigrant groups. *The University of Oregon Publications, 1*(11).

Ziros, G. I. (1976). Language interference and teaching the Chicano to read. *Journal of Reading, 19*(4), 248–288.

5

Explanatory Models of Latino/a Education During the Reform Movement of the 1980s[1]

Martha Montero-Sieburth

University of Massachusetts-Boston

INTRODUCTION

This chapter focuses on the explanatory models used for Latinos from the pre- and posteducational reform initiatives that arose from the publication in 1983 of *A Nation at Risk: the Imperative for Educational Reform*, a study of the quality of American education during President Ronald Reagan's administration. Without a doubt, *A Nation at Risk* became the most seminal critique and call[2] to action in American education, credited with setting into motion the major reforms of the past 20 years (Bell and Crosby, 1993). Its bellicose language, reflected by statements such

---

[1]This chapter is dedicated to the memory of Alicia Cuevas de Montero, my mother, who was 98 years old when she passed away while I was completing this manuscript. Her life has been and will remain a source of inspiration, fortitude, and rectitude—of open kindness, laughter, and soulful commitment to me, my scholarly research, and community work. Her life was dedicated to issues of social justice that in turn helped me to understand the educational needs of Latinos. May her spirit continue to be my spiritual and daily guide.

[2]The reform referred to here is about the educational initiatives that were common during the 1900s to 1980s, and to the changes that have taken place and are in vigor since the 1980s and apply to the first decade of the 21st century.

as "if an unfriendly foreign power had attempted to impose on America the mediocre educational performance that exists today, we might well have viewed it as an act of war" (The National Commission on Excellence in Education, 1983), became emblemic of the waves of reform frenzy that followed.

Crafted by a commission of educators, school board presidents, policy makers, and researchers, the report in its findings condemned the cumulative mediocrity that had passed as actual learning during the 1980s (Ravitch, 1999). The impoverishment of American education and loss of its competitive edge among other industrialized countries, and, most important, its world-class-status power were blamed on the decline of learning standards, lowered teacher expectations, the "dumbing down" of content and vocabulary, and the lack of parental commitment to education (Bell, 1993).

Yet, in its condemnation about the devaluation of American education, *A Nation at Risk* failed to address any of the ideological, social, cultural, and economic conditions that affect teachers and the performance of students. Instead, it focused on the administrative functions of schooling; the need to enforce a series of recommendations directed at developing teachers around competency-based skills; an emphasis on testing; evaluations based on outputs; standardized curriculum; and accountability from schools, teachers, and parents—all factors that are a focus today.

Underrepresented students, with poor educational achievement, limited reading and writing, and high dropout rates became the target of the report. Under the disadvantaged or at-risk rubrics, Latinos[3] were identified along with African Americans and other groups, as having deficient education. Instead of the remediation or compensatory education suggested during the 1960s and 1970s, the commission instead made several recommendations that would directly address equitable treatment of diverse populations and high quality schooling. Among these were proposed changes in content, creation of standards and development of high teacher expectations, use of time, professional development of teaching and leadership, and fiscal support that would assure underrepresented students that once such educational

---

[3]Although the term "Latinos" is used as a generic label, it also includes the term "Hispanics," as it is widely used in the research literature. Specific groups and nationalities such as Mexicans, Cubans, island- and U.S.-born Puerto Ricans, Salvadorans, Hondurans, Guatemalans, Costa Ricans, Nicaraguans, and nationalities from South America are identified throughout this chapter in recognizing the variability within Latino/a groups.

excellence was attained, African Americans, Latinos, and other disadvantaged students, needed to only take advantage of such learning opportunities in order to achieve (Crosby, 1993).

High school graduation requirements were to be strengthened by students completing 4 years of English, 3 years of mathematics, 3 years of science, 3 years of social studies, and one semester of computer science and for those pursuing college, 2 years of foreign language study. Schools from K to 12 to colleges and universities were to adopt more rigorous and measurable standards with higher expectations. Admissions requirements were to be raised for college entry. More time was to be devoted to the basics and to homework completion. Teaching would become more professional in terms of salaries, differentiated staffing patterns, hiring, and leadership at the school level (Crosby, 1993). This was the proposition behind the first wave of reform. However, under the recommendations made by *A Nation at Risk* and subsequent reports, the issue of how such reform was to impact the education of Latinos under successive waves was altogether ignored, and failure within the home, caused by the lack of parental nurturance and motivation became the preferred explanations among stakeholders for describing the educational needs of Latinos. Teachers were among the first to be blamed for the educational state of affairs. Administrators, managers, and finally students and parents followed. Finally, accountability in all aspects of schooling became the modus operandi.

Twenty years later, it seems not only necessary, but also imperative to write about the pre- and posteducational reform movement of the 1980s for its impact on Latino/a education.[4] The reasons are obvious: The Latino/a population has now become a majority in several states, thereby creating greater demands for education.[5] Latinos across the nation are gaining leadership positions which give them stakes in decision

---

[4]In 1993, a 10-year analysis of *A Nation at Risk* appeared in *Phi Delta Kappan*, presenting different opinions and positions as to the outcomes of the recommendations that were made in 1983. Both the progress in schools, with regard to teacher professional development, higher credentialing, and standards, as well as systemwide reform efforts were presented along with the limitations of such educational reform, mostly represented by the use of eschewed statistics. Complementing this study, the Center for Education Reform presented their views over a 15-year period, which reported that the generations of students and in particular Latinos were still at risk.

[5]Carlos Molina and Marilyn Aguirre-Molina (1994) report on the growth of the Latino/a population in an article entitled "Latino populations: Who are they?," in *Latino Health in the U.S.* They state: "The United States now ranks sixth in terms of the number of Latinos residing within its borders; only Mexico, Spain, Colombia, Argentina, and Peru have larger Latino/a populations" (p. 3). Similarly, the Tomas Rivera Center also has a representative map that identifies 23 states out of the 50 with majority Latino/a populations today.

making and power to influence education.[6] Latino/a immigrants have become a major concern affecting the future enrollment and completion of schooling for children attending kindergarten to twelfth grade.[7] Economic remissions by Latino/a immigrants to their countries of origin are in the billions and that affects not only the country of origin's infrastructure and education, but the level of productivity of the immigrants in the United States.[8] Latinos are participating at higher levels than ever before in the workforce, yet, without education, they will continue to work at the lower echelons of society, providing much of the needed public and social services but not moving up into better paying positions.[9] Dual citizenship for many Latinos has now created a comfort level that allows for them to be "here" and "there," and this mobility affects the circular migration of groups, their reintegration into different contexts, and adaptation to schooling for their children.

Yet, beyond these reasons, there is the critical issue of whether the reform initiatives of the 1980s have trickled down and indeed helped Latinos to attain a better education, on the one hand, and, on the other, whether the perspectives by which Latinos have been perceived, understood, and situated in American society also have changed in a positive way as a consequence of the reforms (Darder, Rodríguez-Ingle, & Cox, 1993; Darder, Torres, & Gutierrez, 1997). I consider these concerns the focus of this chapter.

---

[6]See Carol Hardy-Fanta's research at the Center for Women in Politics and Public Policy at the University of Massachusetts-Boston on the rise of Latinos politicians over the past 35 years: *Directory of Latino/a Candidates in Massachusetts*, 1968–1994; *Speaking from Experience: A Handbook of Successful Strategies by and for Latino/a Candidates in Massachusetts*, 1996; Latino/a *Politics in Massachusetts: Struggles, Strategies and Prospects*, written with Jeffrey Gerson (New York: Routledge, 2002); and *Latina Politics, Latino/a Politics*, 1993.

[7]Marcelo Suárez-Orozco at Harvard University, Georges Vernez at the Rand Corporation, Nancy Foner at SUNY, Ruben Rumbaut at University of California, Irvine, Mary C. Waters at Harvard University, and George Sanchez at the University of Southern California are among the researchers studying the growing immigration literature.

[8]The remittances to Latin America, according to different sources, including the Tomas Rivera Center, are anywhere from $6 billion to $15 billion a year, which has a tremendous impact on the country's economic infrastructure. Mexico is the leading country, sending close to $900,000 million (Prepared statement by Dr. Manuel Orozco, public director, Central American Inter-American Dialogue, U.S. Committee on Banking, Housing, and Urban Affairs. Oversight Hearing on "Accounting and Investment Protections Issues Raised by Enron and Other Public Companies." Washington, DC. February 28, 2002. Also by Orozco, "Remittances and Markets: New Player and Practice." Working Paper, June 2000, Los Angeles, The Tomas Rivera Policy Institute).

[9]There is a growing research literature on the economics of working-class Latinos in terms of their participation in such services as restaurants, cleaning, housekeeping, childcare, and hospitals as well as nursing-home kitchens. See the Gaston Institute of the University of Massachusetts for publications that address this issue.

How have such reforms helped to further the educational achievement of Latinos? In what ways have these reforms provided for equitable access and advancement while opening social, economic, and political opportunities for their future?

To uncover the trajectory of the impact of reforms on Latino/a education, these reforms need to be understood in a larger context. This requires delving into the historical past to understand the present, and understanding the types of educational explanations that have been proffered for Latinos. Thus, I examine the impact of the reforms on the education of Latinos of the past 20 years but include an overview of the periods from the 1920s to the 1960s, and from the 1960s to 1980s as a historical backdrop, referred to previously in published research written by Michael Batt and me (Montero-Sieburth & Batt, 2001).

By tracing how Latinos have fared during earlier periods in the educational process, how they have been included or excluded, and how the social sciences have been able to describe their education, the access, quantity, and quality of educational opportunities that have impacted Latinos can critically be examined. Only then can we ascertain whether an analysis of the policies and practices of the reforms have met or not met the needs of Latino/a students.

This chapter therefore attempts to identify the meaning of reform for Latino/a education with the underlying research paradigms and ensuing descriptions of such education as a primary goal. In addition, the descriptions formulated as explanations or models over the past 60 years and those that have followed the reforms initiated after 1983 are presented along with an analysis of the reforms to date. The impact of these reforms on the education of Latinos is then addressed in terms of its saliency and significance. Finally, the implications of the types of expectations and responses that the education of Latinos might have in the early decades of the 21st century to other reforms are also analyzed and described. The chapter is organized around the following questions:[10]

- What have the focus of research and the responses of educators and policy makers been in assessing the educational attainment and achievement of K–12 Latino/a students?

- How have Latinos been discussed in the educational reform movement research literature? And how have their educational experiences been described?

---

[10]The views herein presented are those of the researcher based on extensive reviews of the research on the education of Latinos. They do not necessarily represent the position of the National Latino/a Educational Research and Policy Project.

- What are the current and operant explanations about Latino/a education? What have been the prevalent theories and paradigms that have emerged from this research to explain the education of Latinos?

- What are the implications for policy and practice from the reform and explanations for Latinos and their education? What implications can we derive from the reform movement's educational policies and practices that best prepares Latinos in their educational advancement in the next decades of this century?

In answering these questions, the nature of educational reform in the United States and its constructs as well as a generic overview of reform since the 1920s, that identifies some of the patterns that have reappeared today is presented. The ways that Latinos have fared through different waves of reform are highlighted through a brief synthesis of the historical record and the explanatory models that have been used to characterize the learning potential of Latino/a groups. From these explanations and reform agendas, an assessment is made about the impact of these reforms on Latino/a education, and from these, implications about the future of Latino/a education during the first decades of the 21st century are drawn.

THE NATURE OF EDUCATIONAL REFORM IN THE UNITED STATES

Educational reform in the United States has not been easily understood by many of its proponents, opponents, or stakeholders. David Tyack and Larry Cuban (1995, p. 7) explain that:

> Not all reforms are born equal; some enjoy strong political sponsors while others are political orphans. But even reforms with strong supporters do not always become embedded in the schools. Outside forces shape the course of school reform, but schools are also in some respects autonomous, buffered institutions. Educators have variously welcomed, improved, deflected, coopted, modified, and sabotaged outside efforts at reform.

In fact, the underlying motives for creating reforms are not readily understood, because they require investigation, are pronounced from positions of power, and are often created out of the reach of schools and classrooms. Policy makers as well as researchers, educators, and the public at large, obsessed with finding out "what works" often succumb and accept some of the following assumptions as the reasons change and reform take place: There is the assumption that the educational system is "not working," and needs fixing through revitalization, reinvention, or drastic overhaul of the organization, curricular structure, administration, teachers, and the ways students are assessed.

It is also assumed that reform will bring order into a disorganized system and make it functional, that is, change should be visible and produce organized systems. Moreover, reform initiatives are assumed to be understood by all of the stakeholders involved, and hence believed to be implemented in a logical and rational manner. This means that there is a sequence that is evident in which gains can be measured. The reforms of schools and education are assumed to have positive consequences that inevitably benefit all students, irrespective of their socioeconomic, linguistic, and cultural backgrounds (McNeil, 2000). These assumptions characterize what Tyack and Cuban (1995) describe as the "progress and regress" of educational reform. On the one hand, the idea that better schools guarantee a better society has fostered a sense of continuous progress in schooling. On the other hand, severe criticisms of current schooling all point to a need for federal interventions and major changes as an effective way to right the wrongs of education. But as they point out, either of these positions are highly politically embedded, so much so that they acknowledge that "In an age when 'accountability' is measured more and more by scores on standardized tests, 'progress' in enrolling previously excluded youth in high schools and colleges seems to lead to 'regress' in academic achievement" (Tyack & Cuban, 1995, p. 29). They further argue that schools remain as one of the more effective and stable public institutions in need of teaching students to think critically and to participate in a civic society.

Whereas the goals inherent in these assumptions are laudable in their desired outcomes, the fact of the matter is that educational reform has rarely been linear in its development or implementation. It tends to occur in bits and spurts and at different times and is not altogether readily accepted by those involved. In point of fact, actual reform may not be evident except to those in the throes of change within a school or unit. Reform initiatives may silently begin without even being noticed by the central office of a given school district or classroom. The intent of such reforms may be to create egalitarian forms of communication involving everyone in accomplishing the stipulated changes, as is the case of school-based management, or bottom-up decision making. Yet, given the hierarchical nature of schooling, greater acceptance of reform may occur when the decisions and policies to be implemented emanate from dictums from the top that are carried forth at the bottom and directly from central administration.

Administrators and teachers may not even consciously buy into the rationale and expected practices of a given reform unless evident tangible results or trade-offs such as high student achievement scores, or excellent school rankings based on examination outcomes are present. Teachers have been known to be some of the worst resisters to change, requiring several years of retraining and retooling before being willing to accept or adapt the introduced reforms. Tyack and Cuban (1995) point out those policy initiatives into institutional trends require: (1) the *time lag* between advocacy and its actual implementation; (2) the *uneven penetration* of reforms in different educational arenas; and (3) the *different impact* of reforms on social groups.

Who benefits from the reform? In what ways? What are the tradeoffs? And what are the short-term and long-term consequences? These are questions often left unanswered by the reform process—all of which have serious implications for the education of Latinos. The next section presents an overview of how the reforms prior to 1983 have evolved followed by a subsection on how Latinos have been included or excluded by such reforms.

Pre-1983 Overview of School Reform Efforts

School reform in the United States is not a recent phenomenon. In fact, American educational history has been characterized by a variety of reforms from the early 20th century derived from egalitarian influences of the 19th century (Steinberg, 1997; Rothstein, 2002). Schools were to provide a common education that cut across ethnic, religious, and class differences and reflected America's democratic ideals.

The early 1900s became the heyday of curriculum reform, the professionalization of administrators and teachers, the formation of the common school, and the massive integration of numerous immigrants from eastern and southern Europe during 1840 to 1880.[11] Post-1880, the

---

[11]Ewa Morawska (1995, p. 187) says in "The Sociology and Historiography of Immigration," in *Immigration Reconsidered*, that between 1820 and 1940 well over 40 million immigrants arrived in the United States and, from 1940 to 1990, close to 15 million. Moreover, during

English, Irish, and Germans who arrived, according to Oscar Handlin (1982), were differentiated from the earlier groups by being more inclined to schools. Schools were viewed as the sites of class equalization and places where the new generations would be molded by education. Standardization of curriculum and learning along with bureacratization of schooling and organizational systems and assimilation of immigrants became the basis on which schools functioned. According to Madaus and Tan (1993, p. 58), "curriculum became differentiated according to student 'ability' level, often with disastrous consequences for minorities and non-English speakers."

The overall purpose of schooling was to Americanize newcomers in the American ways. This was such a reality for the massive waves of immigrants arriving from Ireland, southern Europe, and the pogroms of Russia between 1840 and 1924. Whereas many Jews arrived as families, the majority, according to Morawska (1990), were young men who came as migrant laborers with the idea that they would make sufficient monies to return and better their conditions at home. Yet the overall numbers of immigrants expected to stay, and welcomed the opportunity to be schooled, a practice that was not often available in their countries of origin. Mary Antin's (1912) depiction of her experiences in Chelsea, Massachusetts, and her yearning to learn English in *The Promised Land* became the banner for many immigrants (Antin, 1912).[12] Yet there were also adverse effects of schooling on immigrants, where schools were such stultifying places that students preferred working in the sweatshops than attending classes (Rossi & Montgomery, 1994).

Horace Mann promoted the promise of universal education through the creation of the common school with the belief that such schools could provide the equal footing needed by the newcomers (Karier, 1986). Issues of social justice and democratic motives spurned much of the reform movement, yet as part of the Americanization process, intolerance of divergent ideas, languages, and customs prevailed (Montgomery & Rossi, 1994).

1900–1910, 85–90% of the entering Italian, Slavic, Hungarian, and Mexican peasants and 65% of the Jews were manual workers, and 1–2% professional. Seventy-five percent of Chinese and Japanese immigrants during the same period were classified as laborers and 2% were in professional occupations.

[12]Pamela Nadell, in her introduction to Mary Antin's book, *From Plotzk to Boston*, published in 1985, points that for Antin, Americanization was akin to Zionism and hence she supported Louis Brandeis's notion that "to be a good American, one must be a good Jew, and to be a good Jew, one must be a good Zionist" (1985, p. xvi).

Normative culture using mechanistic learning and rote memorization allowed schools to train extensive numbers of immigrants throughout the 1920s until the 1930s, when progressive educators began to use experiential learning as the basis of their programs. David Tyack (1974) points out that children who were to work in the factories in low-wage positions learned the basic skills, discipline, and work habits that would prepare them for such jobs. Exposure to high-order thinking was simply not a priority.

According to Oscar Handlin (1982), the decade of the 1920s eased pressures on schools from the flow of newcomers, but at the same time fomented the values of Americanism. As public schools expanded, they drew much of their teachers and administrators from the immigrant groups, but schools provided one fragment of the wider system of acculturation. Immigrant families sought out other institutions besides schooling to mold their children and to ethnically socialize them.[13] On the one hand, reformers had hoped that schools could transform the society yet maintain homogeneity in arriving ethnic groups. On the other hand, there was push and pull for immigrants who wished to retain their cultural ways while also integrating into American society (Tyack, 1974).

Yet even with the emphasis on integration through Americanization, an undertow of anti-immigrant sentiment also was growing. In 1882, the Chinese Exclusion Law prohibited the entry of Chinese laborers for 10 years, and, according to Sucheng Chan (1990, p. 62), it "was the first congressional attempt to bar would-be immigrants on the basis of race or color."

This was followed by an act in 1888, which denied entry to any Chinese laborer who had returned to China, and later the Scott Act that curtailed the reentry of laborers altogether, making Chinese exclusion permanent by 1904, and later repealed in 1943 (Chan, 1990). The Immigration Act of 1924 created a permanent quota system that reduced the numbers entering the United States and limited each foreign-born group living in the United States in 1890 from 3% to 2%. Whereas the period of the 1920s and 1930s focused on issues of efficiency and expenditures as their school reform, by the 1960s and 1970s, this had shifted

---

[13]In Chelsea, Massachusetts, for example, there were over 150 ethnic fraternities at the turn of the century that provided immigrants with opportunities to listen to operas, musical repertoires, perform dances, and maintain their cultures and languages. See Edward Kopf's dissertation on *The Intimate City: The Social Order of Chelsea, 1906–1915,* 1974 (University of Michigan Microfilm).

to equity (Callahan, as reported by Reyes & Valencia, 1995). The 1930s was the post–Great Depression era and also a time when those leaving America outnumbered those entering.

The early 1940s were marked by reform policies leading to consolidation of the great masses under the New Deal policies of Roosevelt. Kantor and Lowe (1995) point out that the New Deal paid more attention to African Americans than any other administration in unprecedented ways, by having greater awareness and including them in federal agencies, but did not specifically meet their needs nor understood the relationship of poverty to race nor the need to focus on education in more than marginal ways.

The aftermath of World War II provided opportunities for many adults, particularly Latinos. Those who partook of the educational system were mostly the offspring of adult immigrants who reaped the payoffs of their parents in the second generation, when the GI bill after World War II made it possible for many to advance their education by attending college. Sputnik's flight into space in 1957 and the scientific advances of the Russians spurned Americans into creating federal legislation. The learning of science, math, and foreign languages was reintroduced with fervor, and became a means to compete with the Russians in the midst of the Cold War. Even though testing had been used as a local education policy since the 1840s according to George F. Madaus and Ann G. A. Tan (1993), the passage of the National Defense Education Act (NDEA) in 1958 marks its importance as a national policy.

Prior to the 1960s, and unbeknown to many, the education of Latinos consisted primarily of district segregated schools with limited human and material resources, where discrimination was rampant, teachers held low expectations of Latino/a students, schools were saturated with exclusionary policies and practices, and the curriculum was irrelevant to their lives (Arias, 1986; Carter & Segura, 1979; Donato, 1999; Romero, Hondagneu-Sotelo, & Ortiz, 1997; San Miguel, 1987).[14]

---

[14]For a detailed bibliography by state on the publications of Mexican Americans, see the holdings on Latinos and education of research centers such as Center for Mexican American Studies, UT, Austin; Center for U.S.-Mexican Studies, UC, San Diego; Chicano and Chinas Studies Program at UNM; Chicano Studies Research Center at UCLA; Center for Chicano Boricua Studies, WSU; Julian Samora Research Institute at MSU; Latino/a Alumni Network, LAN; Mexican American Studies and Research Center, UA; Stanford Center for Chicano Research; Southwest Hispanic Research Institute (SHRI), the Tomas Rivera Center, Claremont; CUNY Dominican Center; The Center for Puerto Rican Studies, Cuban Research Institute, FIU; Mauricio Gaston Institute for Latino/a Community and Public Policy Studies, UMass-Boston; and the Inter-University Programs for Latino/a Research.

Revisionist researchers such as Rubén Donato (1999), Genaro Gonzalez (1991), David Montejano (1992), and Guadalupe San Miguel (1987), who have been documenting the educational history of Latinos with a particular focus on segregated districts and schools in different parts of the United States, have identified factual and contextually bound data that explains the access that Latinos actually had in education and the responses they made to inequitable and discriminatory practices. Donato (1999) has traced the educational practices of Mexican Americans in the Southwest demonstrating that instead of being passive, as the omission of historical facts has shown, they actively protested and defended the education of their children. In another study, Donato (1999) shows that depending on whoever controlled the schools, decisions about who administered and taught in schools became the determinants of Latino/a students' futures.

In fact, Guadalupe San Miguel (1987) argues that the picture of passive reactions from Latinos in their communities was more the exception, whereas activism has been more the norm. Because segregation of Mexican children in the Southwest was based on local customs and controlled by school board policies, it was unlike the segregation of African Americans, which was sanctioned by state laws. The education of Mexican Americans was discouraged because their employers could control them. This, in fact, led to strengthening the cultural identification and cohesiveness of Mexican Americans, surmises San Miguel. He further argues that much of the segregation in schools was because of residential segregation in Los Angeles during the 1920s and 1930s.

Much of the research of this period provides the image of Latinos and education in relation to the success and failure of diverse ethnic groups in contrast to the dominant European White and middle-class mainstream students (Erickson, 1994). The nature of failure in schooling of underrepresented groups becomes an intense focus of study taken on by social scientists with fervor since the 1960s. Ethnic groups and their educational achievement are studied between culturally dominant and subordinate groups as well as between subordinate groups and even within similar groups.

The educational achievement of Asians, Blacks, Latinos, and Native Americans is studied in comparison and contrast to the successes of European White Anglo students.[15] Asian students are compared to Latinos

---

[15]In addressing Latinos, I am not collapsing all the subgroups but focus primarily on Mexican Americans and Puerto Ricans, who are most extensively discussed in the research

and Blacks, and the "model minority" myth of Asians among under-represented groups emerges, giving rise to a series of explanations where Asians are considered to be more educable than any other group (Bodnar, 1987). The within-group differences in educational achievement become linked to acculturation, assimilation, and integration processes for Mexican Americans, Cubans, Puerto Ricans, Caribbeans, and now Central and South Americans. Often contrasted are Cubans with the other Latino/a subgroups, an issue that tends to show sharp disparities in the first generations of Cubans, and fewer disparities with the second and following generations (Fernandez & Shu, 1988).

Nevertheless, the literature on Latinos and education abounds with fragmented descriptions, where they are characterized as one monolithic group, superficially analyzed in terms of their educational conditions, and stigmatized regarding their human agency in education. Mexican Americans and Puerto Ricans are described most often as being deficient or disadvantaged, in terms of their demonstrated abilities in schools and their home cultures in comparison to the experiences of their Anglo counterparts (Arias, 1986). Yet, the reality identified by Molina and Aguirre-Molina (1994, p. 16) is that

> Latinos have less than 5 years of schooling than African Americans and Whites (12% vs. 5% and 2%, respectively).... The two groups with the lowest levels of schooling in the United States are foreign-born Mexicans, who average approximately 11 years of schooling, and Puerto Ricans, who average approximately 8 years.

Such a "problem" can only be eradicated by exposing Latino/a students to the education and social capital (literacy, numeracy, and knowledge about accessing the social and educational systems) of White middle-class mainstream students. By acquiring the required competencies and abilities to perform at an appropriate level, Latino/a students are presumed to be able to compete in the social and economic spheres of American society. Unfortunately, a causal link is made between this theoretical assumption and the culture of students and homes, which implies that their capacity for achieving academically is determined by their home lives. In this manner, a student's culture

---

literature in education. Cubans of the first wave do not fit the descriptors for Mexicans and Puerto Ricans, but later generations of Cubans, even those in general education programs, as has been shown by research conducted by Fernandez and Shu (1988), exhibit some of the same dropout patterns of their Latino/a counterparts.

becomes linked to a pathological and endemic explanation for their academic failure (Gallenstein, 1998). This results in a no-win situation, where the loser is the Latino/a student.

Other researchers also have attempted to focus on the explanations leveled at Latinos as they are compared to southern European immigrants at the turn of the century. The comparisons are about how well the European immigrants integrated and became assimilated, how well they learned English and gained an education in comparison to the outcomes of Latinos today. The belief has been that if immigrant Italians, Jews, French, and Irish learned English through "sink or swim" schooling and were readily assimilated, became permanent residents, then Latinos, using the same strategies, should be able to follow in their footsteps and reap the economic, social, and educational benefits found in America.

Such comparisons have been questioned over time, and are currently unraveling under the pressure of social science research findings that provide more fine-tuned descriptions based on new methodologies and revisionist analyses of such realities (Montero-Sieburth & Lacelle Peterson, 1991; Perlmann, 2002). Quite to the contrary, researchers such as Nancy Foner, Rubén Rumbaut, Steven Gold (2000), Joel Perlmann (2002), Hans Vermeulen (2001), Vermeulen and Perlmann (2000), Alejandro Portes and Ruben Rumbaut (1996), Ewa Morawska (1995), Yans-McLaughlin (1990), as well as others, are demonstrating that such immigrants actually faced odds that have been romanticized, but that they in fact experienced differentiated access and mobility and returned to their countries of origin in higher numbers than had been assumed.[16] In *Polish and Italian Schooling Then, Mexican Schooling Now? U.S. Ethnic School Attainment across the Generations of the 20th Century*, Perlmann (2002, p. 4) states that:

> The educational attainment of Mexican immigrant parents were somewhat lower than those of Italian or Polish parents, and this factor would have

---

[16]Morawska (1995, p. 195) indicates in "The Sociology and Historiography of Immigration," in *Immigration Reconsidered*, that "...no less than 35 percent of Poles, Serbs, Croatians, and Slovenes, 40 percent of Greeks, and over 50 percent of the southern Italians, Magyars, and Slovaks from northeastern part of Austria-Hungary returned to Europe...even the Jews...returned, during the period between 1880 and 1900, at the considerable rate of over 20 percent. Among the early Asian immigrants on the West Coast and Hawaii, departures were...two thirds—caused by expulsion acts between 1882 and 1903....Mexican immigrants, estimated at about 20 percent during the first two decades of this century, increased to over 80 percent in the interwar period...as a result of deportations during the depression."

affected the children; but this difference is surely the least important reason for the huge difference between the educational handicaps of second-
generation Mexican[17] Americans and second-generation Italians or Polish
Americans.... Mexicans were concentrated in the rural southwest, where
expansion of secondary schooling was slow, while Italians and Poles were
concentrated in the urban north, where secondary schooling was booming.
Second, discrimination against Mexicans in southwestern schools was much
more institutionalized than discrimination against Italians and Poles in the
cities in the north.

He also points out how misleading it is to speak of the Hispanic or
Mexican educational levels in the United States today, because immigrant educational levels are considered along with native educational
attainment as one and the same and they have striking differences depending on the education that immigrants completed before their arrival. The Department of Education's annual survey includes race and
ethnic educational attainment data, which erroneously is reported in
the same manner (Perlmann, 2002).

The period between the 1960s and 1970s has been referred to by
Donato and Lazerson (2000) as the "golden age" because historical interpretations overrode older interpretations, social movements gave rise
to new scholarship, and an anti-institutional and anti-establishment
rebellion prevailed. This became the period of Civil Rights reform,
when the United States' history of racial exclusion and unequal education as well as educational opportunities were openly challenged
by African Americans. The leadership of the African American communities helped push the Great Society policies of Lyndon B. Johnson
into the foreground. Moreover, the findings of the Coleman Report
(1966) pointed out that family influences were greater than physical
resources and other influences for the academic achievement of underrepresented students. According to Madaus and Tan (1993), through

---

[17]Perlmann (2002) distinguishes between the first generation and second generation by
identifying as first generation those born in Mexico who immigrated to the United States
at an age greater than 10. The 1.5 generation includes those who immigrated to the United
States at age 10 or younger and who have profited from schooling in the United States, and the
second generation are U.S.-born individuals who have parents born in Mexico. This second
generation refers to U.S.-born individuals with one parent who was born in Mexico and the
other parent who was not born in Mexico, maybe of U.S.-born Mexican origin, U.S.-born of
other origins, or foreign-born from another country. The 2.5 generation refers to those who
had one immigrant parent from Poland, Italy, or Mexico and one parent born in the United
States of whatever origin, or native born of mixed parentage. Third generation would then
consist of those whose parents were both born in the United States.

the 1960s quality of schools was focused on inputs, that is, teachers, and school finances as measures of quality. By the late 1960s, after Coleman Report's (1966) findings came out that schools mattered little on a student's achievement irrespective of his/her background and social context, the focus shifted toward outcomes. Harvey Kantor and Robert Lowe (1995, p. 4) point out:

> Whereas prior to 1960 the federal government played a relatively minor role in education, between 1960 and 1970 federal aid to elementary and secondary schools increased from about a half a billion dollars to $3.5 billion a year, and the number of federal education programs expanded more than sixfold, from 20 to 130, many designed to improve education for low-income, minority, and "educationally disadvantaged" students.

Catapulted by the Supreme Court's decision in *Brown v. Board of Education* regarding racial segregation in school as unequal, African Americans and other underrepresented students became the focus of remedial and compensatory education. The prevailing belief was that by providing additional classes, reading materials, tutoring, and educational programs that would allow students to eventually move into general tracks, these students would succeed. Such solutions were to provide not only access but also equal footing for these students in order to put them on par with White European Americans. Head Start became one of the major reforms of this period, and its focus on early childhood learning as an entry point to further the education of underrepresented students, including Latinos, became the basis for other programs that followed. The impact of such compensatory programs, were to be measured by extensive use of standardized tests.

African Americans, who expected major changes in education, grew tired with desegregation because it was not only slow in changing schools but also took several decades to be implemented. Not relying on the federal government's push for desegregation, African Americans turned to their communities for control and created the social and political platforms that would gain them standing.

The Chicano movement followed on the footsteps of African Americans and gained momentum from the Civil Rights Movement. Chicanos held similar positions and challenged the unequal treatment and lack of rights in land ownership, education, health, work experienced by Hispanics. Among the issues that Chicanos or Mexican Americans raised were their disproportionate representation in the casualty rates of the

Vietnam and Korean wars; their lack of education; the erosion of their ethnic backgrounds, languages, and cultures; poverty; and police brutality (Rochín & Valdés, 2000). Although many more Latinos were going to school in the 1960s than ever before, few were graduating from high school and continuing with higher education. Those who were able to attend community colleges ended up completing terminal degrees (Gándara, 1995). These concerns later became the impetus for the creation of Hispanic Association of Colleges and Universities (HACU) to serve the needs of Latinos beyond high school and community colleges by creating pipelines into higher education and the creation of many of the Chicano studies programs across the country's universities.

In 1968 the Bilingual Education Act was passed as a discretionary federal program under the Elementary and Secondary Education Act. As such bilingual educational programs were directed at helping linguistically and culturally different students to achieve in schools using native language instruction as a vehicle to acquire English language proficiency. These programs were buttressed by the court ruling of the *Lau v. Nichols* initiatives, allowing Chinese-speaking students and other similar students with language needs to special instructional approaches that would transition them into English-speaking mainstream programs using different classes in their native languages and in English (Crawford, 1989). Experimentation of different models for transition and even maintenance dual language programs took place throughout the country, and second language research was widely conducted during the next 30 years (Arias & Casanova, 1993). Massachusetts became the first state in 1968 to enact transitional bilingual education legislation. Other states followed, including Florida, California, Texas, Louisiana, Arizona, New Mexico, Colorado, and employed pull-out, early and late exit, and dual-language programs.

However, from its inception, bilingual education emerged in the minds of policy makers and educators as a political issue,[18] with debates occurring between those who supported bilingual education, its language usage and its methodologies, to those who opposed bilingual

---

[18]I believe that because bilingual education was part of the Title III legislation directed at providing poor families with monies, it irreparably became associated as being the "educational programs" for the poor, setting bilingual education up in a no-win position. Bilingual education in the United States has become an education of questionable power, and the very use of first and second language learning using mother tongue has been undermined. Interestingly, the use of more than one language in other parts of the world is viewed as necessary, viable, and legitimate.

education for not stressing the learning of English as its most significant goal. The camps became clearly spelled out during the early 1980s between the "English Only" proponents who considered English to be the official and national language of the United States, using English immersion as the appropriate methodology and criticizing those in support of bilingual education for being anti-American to the "English plus" advocates who view the learning of English as an intended goal of bilingual education yet view the need to use mother tongue as a means to learn a second language. By the 1990s, bilingual education programs reached a climax when Ronald Unz, a California entrepreneur, put English immersion programs on the ballots of the state of California, through Proposition 227; in Arizona; and in Massachusetts through Ballot 2—all of which were passed.[19]

Today, bilingual education remains one of the most volatile issues in American education signaling in many respects, the power of Latinos in using Spanish and considering the United States a bilingual nation, to opponents who see Latinos using bilingual education as a platform for gaining political power and for eroding the English language and American values (Crawford, 1989).

During the 1960s, studies of Latino/a families began to emerge under the influence of national character studies in the field of anthropology. Under the influence of Margaret Mead and Ruth Benedict studies of cultural groups emerged with strong generalizations about behavior and development. Whereas the focus of national character studies was initially of "exotic" cultures such as Samoans and the Japanese people, the research quickly gravitated to studies of Caribbean and Meso-American groups. Studies such as that portrayed by Oscar Lewis (1966) about the *Children of Sanchez* for Mexicans and *La Vida: A Puerto Rican Family in the Culture of Poverty—San Juan and New York* (1965) for Puerto Ricans provided characterizations of Latinos through the lens of the culture of poverty theory. Such characterizations described Latinos and their families as being pathologically deviant, problematic, and uneducable based on their conditioning by a culture of poverty—stereotypes that persist into the present.

---

[19]The indictments made by Ronald Unz against bilingual education as a barrier to English language learning has captured the interest of not only White voters, but many Latinos. As new arrivals, Latinos are more likely to view the speaking of English as a means to secure jobs and attain mobility. Hence, bilingual education using mother tongue will more likely be viewed as a deterrent. It is therefore no surprise that some Latinos, particularly those with the ability to vote, would favor the passage of English immersion.

The power of these descriptions and explanations of how African Americans, Latinos, and other underrepresented groups fared in education flourished and gained explanatory significance, in the sense that they were used indiscriminately as "empirical" statements and "evidence" to describe educational experiences. For the most part, these models viewed Latinos as part of the deficit and disadvantaged explanations made prevalent during the 1960s, and the research on "at-risk students" during the 1970s and 1980s. The condemnation of Latino/a cultures to the conditioning effects of the culture of poverty theory linked Latinos to cultural deficit and culturally deprived models of education. Educational remediation and compensatory programs were to compensate for their academic limitations. By providing reading materials, literacy programs, and the learning of mathematics and science, greater emphasis was placed on the achievement of the "disadvantaged." Yet, the questions that remain are: *When was remediation sufficiently achieved? Or at what point had there been sufficient compensation of education to gain equal entry into the mainstream education?*

The effects of these reforms have no doubt contributed to linking Latinos to education in negative ways and with explanations difficult to overcome, now ingrained in the social sciences and education. The very need to explain an ethnic group's potential already disadvantages such a group, especially when it is done from those in a position of power and privilege over those without these attributes. It is evident that even with the years of research available on Latinos and education and the plethora of publications that exists, an entrenchment in understanding the educational needs of Latinos persists.

After the 1960s, and into the 1970s, the educational needs of the poor and disenfranchised including the needs of Latinos, was less of a priority, although the issues remained the same. National declines on the SAT scores gave rise to major emphasis on minimum competency testing. As Arias (1986), Darder, Torres, and Gutiérrez (1997), Orfield (1997), and others have shown, Mexican Americans and Puerto Rican students were segregated in impoverished inner-city schools, where budgetary constraints and lack of interest diffused the need to reform. Tracking became commonplace as a system for creating ability groups (Oakes, 1994). More significantly, Puerto Ricans suffered the worst effects of poverty, which have persisted to the present.

Charles Silberman's explosive book entitled, *Crisis in the Classroom: The Remaking of American Education* during the 1970s, criticized American education by signaling its obsession with credentialing and degree status over active learning. Silberman echoed the need for learners in schools to become critical thinkers, aware of social injustices and the need for humanity. His critique questioned how far the educational pendulum should swing between the learning of basic skills and reflective thinking.

Many of the educational reforms that were implemented prior to the 1980s, emanated from state policies that influenced classroom practices and teacher development. These reforms swung between "back to basics" learning, and the use of critical thinking and child-centered learning. Latinos negatively experienced many of the effects of these educational swings, partly because they were grouped with other underrepresented groups making their presence invisible, and partly because attention to their educational history was limitedly understood. The existence of such exclusionary practices, in general, define the prereform period because they describe the educational situation of Latinos and set the stage for their education until 1983.[20]

Post-1983 Overview of Reform Efforts

By 1983, a call to action in reforming schools became the basis on which *A Nation at Risk* was published (National Commission on Excellence in Education, 1983). American students were comparatively achieving at lower levels than their counterparts of industrialized nations. The fear of losing ground as the most powerful nation in the world compelled policy makers and educators to require reform that would overcome the mediocrity of schools and would help America compete in a growing global economic market. Strident throughout this and other reports that followed such as the American Association for the Advancement of Science (1998), and the National Research Council (1989), was the message that compared to Japan and other industrialized countries, schools were not producing effective learners with world-class standards. Reform was viewed as a panacea for economic issues and private sector interventions in education. In fact, Michael Apple suggests that instead of holding the private sector and business industry accountable

---

[20]I distinguish between educational reform and restructuring, which often are used synonymously. I define restructuring as the specific strategies, which are employed by school administrators in effecting educational reform and which can be systemic—changing issues schoolwide—or specific—changing the current curriculum. When applied to the reform movement, these strategies tend to be identified as policies and processes.

for the economy, the schools have become the sites where employment concerns and competitiveness are to be found. Shaping students, especially those who are poor and underrepresented, for the workforce became a vocalized goal (Apple, as cited by Montgomery & Rossi, 1994).

Starting with 1983 and continuing into the 1990s, with the passage of major bills, policies, and initiatives, major restructuring of schools has taken place. This post-reform period unfolds through a series of waves of reform with each wave focusing on specific issues and specific groups—the organization and management of schools, administrators' leadership, professional development of teachers, student achievement, parental involvement, schoolwide systemic changes, curricular policies, and instructional programs.

Whereas each wave is defined differently, there have at least been nine waves of reform, all moving toward greater control and decision making at the school level. Under the Reagan and Bush administrations, the locus of control in education shifted from the state level to the federal and national levels through the myriad of national initiatives undertaken. National standards in education in different subject areas were created, leading to local interpretations of these into frameworks and curricular designs. Yet, even though the Clinton administration expanded excellence in education and supported federal funding shifts to state and block grants, the political power of the national government to the states began to disperse. Some programs survived whereas others disappeared. In some states, English immersion programs replaced bilingual education. Nevertheless, both administrations made education center stage, a feat that had been unprecedented with the exception of the 1960s.

During the first wave of reforms, the focus was on the organizational structures of schools. Reforms at different levels, from top-down to bottom-up, partial and systemic, and in small learning communities have been experimented with (The Jossey-Bass Reader on School Reform, 2001). Concerns with issues of excellence, quality, and management by objectives, professional development, and later curricular and systemic changes, addressing national and local standards as well as assessment, evaluation, and accountability characterize the second set of waves directed at teachers and administrators. Without doubt, the influence of the private sector requiring highly competent workers also worked its way into the school curriculum, school-to-work programs, as well as entrepreneurial skill building in high school course content were incorporated into the curriculum of many public schools. National

Goals 2000 became the capstone defining criteria for changes in schools, curriculum, and professional development. The idea that all children were to be ready to come to school and be able to read by 2000 became the goals that schools attempted to achieve.

This impetus was followed by a series of other policies, all pointing to knowledge, skill development (reading readiness, literacy development, computer abilities, and math and science grounding) representing the technological, scientific, and business and competitiveness of a capitalist society. Attitude formation, based on family values, was represented in programs of character education. The latter waves have targeted the role of parents, families, and communities, focusing on students and their rights to excellence and parents and families in partnering with schools. Finally, technological and cybercommunication as a basis for parents and schools to maintain contact have become everyday common buzzwords.

The concerns raised by such waves have shaped much of the current debate about schooling. Educational research conducted during the previous 30 years became the basis for many of the changes implemented by much of these reforms (Lockwood & Secada, 1999). This research focused on the organization of schools, the decision-making processes of administrators, classroom management, and teaching and learning under "best practices." These findings also became the basis for the reports that followed *A Nation at Risk*.[21] From such reforms, a series of programs demonstrating achievement in performance outcomes have emerged, all promising that all students can learn using different approaches. Among some of the most notable of these approaches are the James Comer Family and Community program, the Accelerated Schools program devised by Henry Levin, the Coalition of Essential Schools of Theodore Sizer, Deborah Meier's program in New York and now in Boston, Robert Slavin's Success for All reading program, America's Schools based on standards assessment and action plans introduced by Marc Tucker with standards-based curricular developments by Judy Carr and Douglas Harris (2001).[22]

---

[21] Among the contributors to reports that followed were the National Research Council (1989) and the American Association for the Advancement of Science (1998).

[22] It should be noted that there are far more approaches that have been developed than have been included herein. The list is extensive but, for the purpose of this chapter, only those approaches that have gained notoriety in the field of education have been included. The omission of other programs does not preclude their being significant.

To be sure, the planning and design of educational reforms emanated from different policies at the federal level, such as the standards movement, high-stakes testing, and performance assessment, but they were implemented at the state and local levels through curriculum frameworks, testing, program development, and accountability factors and their significance to learning and teaching is actually being tested in the classroom. Rather than organizing the policies and changes in a chronological manner, or identifying these through each of the different waves of reform, I prefer to subsume these changes under the educational orientation they fostered. Of these orientations, the following have been the most salient.

• *Issues of Quality and Excellence* were identified by educators as some of the major concerns in the early part of the first waves of reform. Excellence in learning was sought in educational programs that did not lower academic standards or the high expectations of teachers. This meant that criteria for developing such excellence needed to be stipulated so that such criteria could be understood and interpreted by all schools. Excellence came to be measured by high achievement outcomes, high reading scores, mathematical prowess, and delivery of programs with results. Quality was to be demonstrated in the value-added aspects of learning that accrued beyond those gained through basic education.

• *Professional Development of Teachers* took on from the start enormous emphasis, as teachers were one of the groups most assailed for their lack of competency in teaching students, their low expectations, and, most important, their knowledge base and credentials to teach. Under such pressures, professional development through extended coursework, pre- and in-service programs grew phenomenally. State requirements making mandatory testing of teachers have become commonplace.

• *Management Issues and Organization of Schools* were considered fundamental in making reform work. The initial wave of reform was mostly targeted at organizational and managerial concerns within schools. Management by objectives taken from the business world was adopted and emulated by schools. Competency based education also was fostered, particularly in meeting the needs of underserved students. Training in MBO became widespread with each school district participating to a greater or lesser degree depending on the resources available.

• *Standards and Curriculum* discussions prevailed, with some districts adapting their curriculum to national standards, whereas others rephrased the standards into frameworks and basic curricular guidelines. World-class standards in which students could compete in their given areas of knowledge, in any context based on the education of industrialized countries, have become benchmarks for many schools. Most important, education in America shifted toward meeting the competitive edges of world market economies, technology, and scientific endeavors.

The education of English language learners in some states followed the basic standards and in other cases, became reinterpreted for such students. Confusion prevailed at first between the role of standards and that of curriculum, but as administrators and teachers began to interpret the standards, they became familiar with developing benchmarks for the standards, rubrics for assessing learning, and, most recently, the understanding for design curriculum developed by Grant Wiggins and Jay McTighe (1998) and Project Zero (Blythe & Associates, 1998) at the Harvard Graduate School of Education as well as differentiated curriculum by Carol Ann Tomlinson (2001).

• *Assessment and High Stakes Testing* assumed major proportions in the educational reform movement under the assertion that all students could attain "world-class standards" in mathematics, science, English, history, and geography. Assessment was no longer about including different evaluation formats such as formative and summative but, more important, about figuring out how students are learning and how they are able to demonstrate such learning through performance outcomes and minimum competency testing. High-stakes testing, particularly with batteries of tests provided at different grade levels, have become commonplace means for promoting students and for quantifying their knowledge base before graduating from high school.

The Massachusetts Comprehensive Assessment System (MCAS) which tests students at different grade levels in order for students to be able to graduate, is one of the most hotly debated issues.[23] Likewise the Texas Assessment of Academic Skills (TAAS), which tests students

---

[23] Early studies conducted by Miriam Uriarte from the University of Massachusetts-Boston for the Gaston Institute in Latino/a and Community Development, demonstrated that 70% of the Latino/a students in Massachusetts were apt to fail the required graduation tests using MCAS. In the 1998 round of tests in math, English, and science, Latino/a children failed at rates nearly double that of Massachusetts's White population (Gaston Institute for Latino/a Community Development and Public Policy).

at third, fifth, and eighth grades, would determine after three opportunities, if students could pass on to the next grade. Proponents state that such high-stakes testing determines future graduates are well prepared, whereas opponents complain about the use of single tests as the only determinants of student learning. These opponents point out not only that the potential cultural and linguistic biases of standardized tests when used for "high-stakes" testing for promotion can have disproportionately negative effects on English language learners, but retention and grade repetition increase the likelihood of students dropping out in subsequent grades (Rodríguez, 1999).[24]

• *Parental Involvement* in schools and directly in the education of their children also has been one of the most emphasized issues relating to reform. Every reform agenda stipulates the need to involve parents as partners in educating students. The expectation is that parents who are actively involved, are participatory, vocal, and democratic in their commitments to schools, and will support schools in positive ways. Thus having parents in local school councils is greatly emphasized, because such practices also help parents to become leaders and to assume responsibility in education.

• *Accountability Measures* of schools have become large scale in their dimensions. Schools are being held responsible for the learning of students, and are being asked to set up measures of accountability by which they can be evaluated, improved, or shut down. A reemphasis on the United States' competitiveness with other countries and the poor performance in testing scores in math and science allowed the president and governors of the nation to set up America 2000 with six goals that included world-class standards and a national testing program used to monitor progress toward meeting the goals and attaining the standards (Madaus & Tan, 1993). Such a stake in outcomes-directed testing has continued to the present.

Today, the federal policy enacted during the first term of President George W. Bush, *No Child Left Behind Act of 2001, Title I*, is the latest to foster accountability in this series of reforms. Under this policy, based on a standard of accountability, and the goal that all students perform

---

[24] According to Rodriguez, statistics from the National Academy of Sciences shows that 20% to 30% of students in the United States have already been retained by the third grade and in urban centers the percentage is closer to 40% to 50%. When related to Latino/a dropout rates of 30% in urban public schools, the picture presented is grim.

at a proficient and advanced level in mathematics and English by 2014, each state now has to measure improvement of schools through comprehensive testing systems. Parents have the choice to pull students out of schools if they do not reach their improvement goal, place their children in another public or charter school, or, if the school underperforms for two cycles, schools must provide supplemental services, including tutoring.

In addition, Title III, directed at *Language Instruction for Limited English Proficient and Immigrant Students*, spells out the creation of programs for family literacy, professional development, data collection and dissemination, research, assistance to Native Americans, systemic reform, improvement of accountability systems, English language proficiency, "...and to the extent possible, the native language skills of such children." Under such policy, immigrant children are to be tested after being in the United States for no more than 3 years. Schools are required to meet the annual measurable achievement objectives during a 2-year period, if the school fails, then an improvement plan that addresses specific obstacles will be put into practice (Congress of the U.S., Title III: Language Instruction for Limited English Proficient and Immigrant Students, 2001).

The notion of the disadvantaged student has once again reappeared in the title of the research center of James Coleman in Chicago, the Center for Research in Education of Students Placed at Risk (CRESPAR) with the collaboration from Johns Hopkins University and Howard University (Slavin & Calderon, 2000) and even in *No Child Left Behind: Improving the Academic Achievement of the Disadvantaged*.

THE IMPACT OF EDUCATIONAL REFORMS ON LATINOS

Left unstudied in these reform efforts have been the responses of Latino/a students and parents to the reforms, the impact that the reforms have had in advancing their educational achievement, and the influence that the reforms have had on Latino/a communities.

A few studies reflecting on the relationship between reform and Latinos have responded to these issues (Valdivieso & Nicolau, 1992; Reyes & Valencia, 1995). Reyes and Valencia (1995) argue that the schools of the 1980s and 1990s ignored the demographic changes taking place in the student populations and in so doing that led to marginalization and alienation of Latino/a students. They identify several assumptions that hurt Latinos: (1) schools are marketplaces, whereby tuition tax credits or voucher policies can be used by parents in selecting schools which may not be the case for Latino/a parents who do not know what to expect; (2) schools need limited change, which applies to the idea that the structure of schools do not need to change and, hence, Latinos are left in a quandary about what constitutes actual change; (3) students and schools are homogeneous and, hence, uniformity and conformity should operate well—left out of this assumption is the fact that students and schools are not the same, the notion of one size fits all simply does not work for Latinos; (4) schools are economically uniform, which means that they have the adequate resources available to students. On the contrary, the schools that most Latinos attend are without resources. The consequences of such assumptions, they allege, set up Latinos for school failure, retention, stratification, and provide Latinos with no equitable opportunities to learn. They also allege that the commission that prepared the report of *A Nation at Risk* ignored language minority students throughout the 40 commissioned reports. They conclude that because the school reforms initiated in the 1980s did not consider equity, they have provided those who already have an education with additional support, and weakened those who most need such an education.

Steinberg (1997, p. 184) concurs by singling out that school reform has failed students and their families in the United States because "... the school reform movement [failed] to reverse the decline in achievement ... due to its emphasis on reforming schools and classrooms, and its general disregard of the contributing forces that, while outside the boundaries of the school, are probably more influential."

Researchers and policy makers have made their concerns about the education of kindergarten to twelfth grade known during the past century through reports of local communities, state reports, and extensive publications in social and educational research (Chapa, 1996; General Accounting Office, 1994, Ginorio & Huston, 2001; Los Angeles County Commission on Human Rights, 1989; Mizell & Vernez, 2001; Oakes, 1994; Perez & Martinez, 1993; Rodriguez, 1999).[25] Initial studies in

---

[25]See the Chicano literature for extensive documentation on Californian and Southwestern communities that include descriptions of educational experiences. In addition, the repositories of the University of California, Los Angeles, and the Centers for Chicano and Latino/a Studies at different centers across the nation have extensive data on such an issue.

educational research during the 1970s to the present focused on bilingual education and language issues, mostly at the elementary levels, since these were the areas under attack by opponents to bilingual education. In attempting to satisfy the public's demand for "what works," an inordinate number of large-scale studies on the evaluation and significant issues of bilingual education were conducted.[26] Wayne Thomas and Virginia Collier's (1999) longitudinal study of effective bilingual programs has become seminal in the field and so have the studies conducted by Kenji Hakuta (1986). James Cummins's (1986) research in Canada also has widely contributed to the understanding of bilingual students and to providing a framework for their empowerment in schools. However, even with 30 years of continuous research, bilingual education continues to be questioned and devalued, although promotion of bilingual abilities are among the skills most required in the economic competitive markets of the world.

The ongoing studies about Latinos and education have focused on different aspects that include from issues of classroom learning, administration, community schools and development, newcomers, to adolescents and immigrants in different generations (Garcia, 2001; General Accounting Office, 1994; Ginorio & Huston, 2001; Montgomery & Rossi, 1994; Perez & Martinez, 1993). Few have addressed secondary schools, after-school programs, and the lives of Latino/a students, yet the research being conducted is now yielding several studies on adolescents that are making their invisibility visible (Montero-Sieburth & Villarruel, 2000; Villarruel et al., 2002).

There is also a wealth of historical documentation that sheds light on some of the educational concerns of many Latino/a communities. Yet although this literature is extensive and significant, the lack of follow through at the federal or national levels beyond the blue ribbon commissions and committees set up by different presidents to conduct such reports is all but glaring. Several commissions were asked to report on the status of Latino/a education during the 1990s. Among these are *No More Excuses*, published in 1998, after being commissioned in 1995 identifying the dropout issues for Hispanics and a call to action (Secada

---

[26]Jim Cummins has demonstrated that it is impossible to state "what works" in bilingual education because evaluation of bilingual education programs cannot be set up with control or experimental groups, because there is such variability from group to group and class to class. Instead, he suggests that it is the transference of languages attained by native language instruction that is significant and the opportunities that speakers have to use native language equally along with second languages that positively influences language learning.

et al., 1998). In 1996, the President's Advisory Commission on the Educational Excellence for Hispanic Americans presented the shortcomings of the educational system serving Latinos and the resulting achievement gap in *Our Nation on the Faultline: Hispanic American Education*. A second follow-up report was made to raise the educational performance of Hispanic students to the same level of achievement of other students by the year 2010 in *Creating the Will, Hispanics Achieving Educational Excellence*.[27] All of these reports identify the same issues already identified before and the recommendations tend to repeat the same concerns, yet they all use language that cries for attention such as "a call to action, creating the will, energizing the nation." Certainly, the invisibility of Latinos is not because of lack of research on their educational needs, or the unwillingness of the Latino/a community to make their issues evident, instead it is more the response of the educational system that has failed and begs the question: *What will it take for Latinos to become visible and responded to in their educational needs by the educational establishments?*

In summary, there has been a great deal of reform and such reform has been and currently is, instrumental in defining American education. The themes of equity, excellence, and relevance dominate the discussion of reform today as they have in the past and each wave of reform from the 1900s on is connected to underlying educational philosophies that gravitate among teacher-centered, content-centered, or child-centered curriculum, the political mood of the times, budgetary concerns, the role of newcomers and immigrants, and American education in global contexts, as seen in the Third International Mathematics and Science Study (TIMSS).

Nevertheless, because reform initiatives are highly contingent on the prevailing politics of the times, like a pendulum they are susceptible to the administrations in power and in their choices. Education has swung from "back to basics learning" to the more holistic approaches inherent in constructivist thinking and learning. That being said, the issue of how Latinos have fared in education from a historical overview is depressing and dismal, overcome only by strident efforts conducted by single Latino/a communities to gain power over the education of their children. Examples of these initiatives are El Puente School Program in New York City, the South End's Inquilinos Boricuas en Acción in Boston, just to name a few. Multiple efforts at creating charter schools,

---

[27]These are only a few of the many reports that have been issued repeating the same issues for more than 85 years.

alternative schools, after-school programs, and community schools responsive to Latinos have flourished throughout the United States.[28] Schools such as El Puente, or programs such as ALAS and AVID are educational programs that provide alternatives to educate Latino/a students without depriving students of their connections to their linguistic and cultural roots.[29] Yet reforms are not insular but take place in contexts and in that respect, to understand their impact, the explanations that have arisen from the research literature for Latinos becomes critical.

TYPES OF EXPLANATORY MODELS USED FOR LATINOS AND EDUCATION

In the coedited publication with Michael Batt, we sought to identify the most salient explanatory models that emanated from the social science research and theoretical frameworks of the past 40 years, from the 1960s to the 2000s. In such a review, the educational achievement of Latinos is discussed through several perspectives and theoretical models, some of which are in use today. We included among these: (1) the cultural deprivation or cultural deficit model; (2) the cultural difference model; (3) the voluntary immigrant and involuntary minorities explanation; (4) the bilingual education model; (5) the economic explanatory models; (6) the cultural capital model; (7) the theory of resistance model; (7) the coethnic peer communities model; (8) the dual frame of reference explanations; (9) the academic failure explanations of "at-riskness"; and (10) the success factors explanation that highlights cultural patterns and resilience as being significant in determining educational achievement.

Rather than repeat from the previous publication, or portray these as the only available explanations, I prefer to organize these explanations

---

[28]See Francisco A. Villarruel, Michigan State University; Martha Montero-Sieburth, University of Massachusetts-Boston; Corliss Wilson Outlay, University of Minnesota; Christopher Dunbar, Michigan State University entitled "Dorothy, there is no yellow brick road:" The paradox of community youth development approches for Latino/a and African American Urban Youth. In J. L. Mahoney, R. W. Larson, & J. Eccles (Eds.), *After School Activities: Contexts of Development*. Sage Publications, 2005, pp. 111–130.

[29]There are many programs that have successfully helped Latinos make transitions between remedial to regular programs across the country. Each varies in its approach, but all have as a goal, helping Latinos aspire to the same benefits as other students. Among some of these programs are the following: Project Theme between University of California and a California School District, AVID, Achievement for Latinos through Academic Success, (ALAS), San Diego Urban School District: Project "Write," Project Prism: The International High School, New York; Project AVANCE, Early Outreach, and MESA.

and include others around the focus of research that has taken place for Latinos through specific frameworks in kindergarten through twelfth grades. I cluster several of the past explanations in this chapter around more overlapping themes that have been used to typify the central issues or to solve the problems in Latino/a education. Among the prevailing frameworks are the following: Cultural Explanations, Language Functions and First and Second Language Frameworks, Macro-Societal Frameworks, Economic Frameworks, Social Theory Frameworks, Culture of Failure Frameworks, Cultural Analysis Frameworks, and Transnational and Comparative Studies Frameworks.

Cultural Explanations Framework

Among the *cultural explanations* that have been used for Latinos, not only is the cultural deficit model present but so is the cultural disadvantaged and even cultural difference model in that they all use culture as the core concept from which comparisons between and within groups are made. The concept of culture used is derived in these cases from middle-class standards of appropriateness or, as Hugh Mehan stated, in making competent students.[30] These cultural models, widely used during the 1960s and 1970s, were a departure from earlier genetic explanations of inferiority used to explain the reason why some children from underrepresented groups failed to succeed in schools. Failure in this regard was identified as not being able to read, write, or compute at the level of White mainstream students and the analysis of students' success or failure was based on using White middle-class standards as normative culture. The way to offset such deficits was by identifying the ways in which African American families and Latinos could use reading materials, emphasize certain behaviors leading to effective learning, and preparedness and readiness to go to school.

Obviously such a model did not take into consideration that in making the comparisons between ethnic groups, the underrepresented students would rarely catch up with their mainstream counterparts because they had already been marked as being disadvantaged and often did not have access to the cultural capital needed to succeed. Moreover, the solutions were for the most part middle-class solutions hardly attending to the more critical social and economic factors affecting

---

[30]See Hugh Mehan (1980). The Competent Student. *Anthropology and Education Quarterly,* *11*, pp. 131–152.

learning. Second, when the notion of culture was extended into the cultural difference model, differences in speaking, communication, and cultural conventions appropriate to a given group, but inappropriate in school settings were emphasized. Of particular importance was the microethnographic research that focused on classroom interactions and linguistic match or mismatches between teachers and students depicted by Susan Phillips (1993) through participant structures, by Erickson and Mohatt (1982) between teachers and Native American students, and by John Gumperz in *Crosstalk*, a film that depicted cross messages of communicative competence even in the use of English.

Language Functions and First and Second Language Frameworks

The second framework can be clustered around *language functions and first and second language acquisition* explanations. The seminal book on *Functions of Language in the Classroom*, edited by Courtney Cazden, John P. Vera, and Dell Hymes (1972), characterized the study of language in social contexts and included nonverbal communication, language varieties and verbal repertoires, communicative strategies delving into styles of learning and teaching to language and cognition as well as communicative competence. Through the use of language functions, studies of differential language use became prevalent and were applied to Latinos whose lack of academic achievement was attributable to the use of different codes and language patterns evident between Latinos and their mainstream dominant Euro-White culture teachers (see the research of Cazden, Carrasco, Maldonado-Guzman, & Erickson, 1980). Among the notable longitudinal studies of this vein conducted during the 1980s by the Centro de Estudios Puertorriqueños and headed by John Attinasi, Pedro Pedraza, Shana Poplack, and Alicia Pousada, is *Intergenerational Perspectives on Bilingual*.[31]

Although the research on bilingualism has been extensive for over 40 years, misconceptions about first and second language acquisition, the time needed to learn a second language, and the contexts in which language learning occurs are evident. Underlying these misconceptions is a subtle if not obvious disregard for the importance of native

---

[31]The Center for Puerto Rican Studies at Hunter College has one of the most extensive list of publications dealing with community-based sociolinguistic and cultural research and interventions of Latinos in their education.

language use in the education of Latinos, particularly at the elementary and secondary levels. Even when research presents that languages are learned in social and academic contexts that positively support such learning; that there are several approaches that can be used at different stages of language learning to help students become bilingual, biliterate, and bicultural; and that language status and policies influence the degree to which a first and second language is attained, there is a subtractive, rather than additive conceptualization of bilingual education. The end result is one of monolingualism and monoculturalism prevailing over bilingualism. The underlying message is that issues of language have become so politicized that the explanatory models have become targeted to specifically address the academic achievement of mostly bilingual students, and not all students who could benefit from being bilingual.

Given that rationale, explanations about language learning tend to be ignored. The focus in many of the educational explanations derived from sociolinguistic research turns to identifying those institutional or structural factors that contribute to Latino/a students' limited academic attainment and achievement and not the cognitive flexibility that is present in bilingualism.

Cultural-Ecological Frameworks of a Macro-Dimension

Had John Ogbu's research, criticizing the limitations of sociolinguistic and microethnographic studies of interactions in the classrooms because they did not focus on the macro-dimensions and socioeconomic conditions of underrepresented students, not appeared, we would probably not have understood the structural conditions that affect Latinos and education in a broader sense. Ogbu's (1987) early research in Stockton, California, presents a structural and economic explanation that defines the ceiling of opportunities made available to underrepresented students. He expands his theory with other comparative studies of what he calls voluntary or immigrant, and involuntary or nonimmigrant minorities, the former referring to immigrants who of their own will arrive in the United States for economic and educational gains and do so because they serve their groups and communities back home. The latter refers to those immigrants whose own group has been subjugated by conquest, colonization, or domination and hence develop a limited sense of their opportunities, particularly to succeed in schools.

This pattern appears to be borne out in Ogbu's (1992) later research after he studied groups in different contexts such as the Hairy Ainu in Japan, who are rejected in Japan, but accepted in other parts of the world. His research has given rise to what he has identifies as a cultural-ecological model of success and failure in schooling based on students' sense of survival, and of "making it." For such a process to be able to foster success, supportive conditions for achieving success as defined through a coherent curriculum, well prepared teachers, and responsive schools need to be present. Margaret Gibson also explored the notion of accommodation with Punjabi students and jointly published with Ogbu (Gibson & Ogbu, 1991).

Ogbu's research, although criticized for its tendency to generalize about ethnic groups without accounting for the variability within groups, and even for some of the historical grounding of groups so that they do not conveniently fall under his category of conquered groups, points to a third framework that has dominated social science since the 1970s and 1980s and is commonly used today.

Economic Frameworks

Despite the economic interplay that is suggested by Ogbu, between the institutional and individual's economic opportunities, there also appears to be a set of competing explanations in the research of Latino/a education that focuses on the socio as well as economic meanings that can be understood through social theory. Such an *economic framework* is based on the research by Pierre Bourdieu and Jean Passeron of the concept of cultural capital, James Coleman's social capital, Samuel Bowles and Herbert Gintis's (1976) correspondence theory, and Paul Willis's (1972) resistance theory. Later, the concept of underclass as used by William Julius Wilson (1978) became applied not only to African Americans but also to Latinos. By focusing on the quantification factors of knowledge as a capital to be invested through access to learning and predispositions learned at home, the set of economically driven explanations demonstrate how sorting of students into different slots functions as part of the economic and social structure. Moreover, the value of social or cultural capital brings into question the type of class or underclass differences, which are schematically developed over time and reinforced and reproduced through schooling.

The criticism leveled at such economically deterministic explanations made it evident that students were not passive actors, as attested by Willis's study of the lads, in *Learning to Labour*, but that resistance to schooling is evident in the way that students respond. This has led to the formulation of what has been called postresistance studies within the field of critical theory and refinements of students' actions and behaviors as representative of active and not passive agents in their learning.

Social Theory Frameworks

Such refinement can best be clustered around several *social theory explanations*: (1) the structural limitations theory—referring to social ceiling limitations, the lack of opportunity beyond one's education; (2) the studies on the burden of acting White, often referred to as "dumbing down," in which underrepresented students hide their academic potential among their peers so as to be included within the peer culture; (3) the research on oppositional behaviors, and counter cultural responses described by Fordham and Ogbu (1986), and Matute-Bianchi (1991); and (4) accommodation theories explained through the research of Margaret Gibson for the Punjabi (1988).

These theories have been applied to Latinos as well as African Americans, yet the focus for Latinos has been on the oppositional behaviors as displayed in gang membership (Vigil, 1999), gender differences in education, dropping out, and the "at-risk" syndrome. Some research has attempted to identify what have been the responses of schools to students, and how Latinos have understood education through their own experiences. (Montero-Sieburth, 1993, 1996; Montero-Sieburth & Villarruel, 2000).

Psychological Frameworks

The next set of explanatory models falls under a *psychological framework* in that these explanations have outgrown the previous culture of poverty theory and national character generalizations and become refined with the "new immigrants." The explanations advanced under this framework address what Suárez-Orozco, based on De Vos's theories, identifies as *dual frames of reference*. In his early research on Central Americans, Suárez-Orozco (1987) found that students from El Salvador, in particular, tend to exist with the idea of being here but also being back home. Part of their motivation for learning is fostered by the responsibility engendered by the group, and by the constant reference to how things are here in comparison to back home. As can be seen, such explanations, unlike previous ones, begin to be more sophisticated in advancing notions of the complexities faced by Latino/a students. Rather than only emphasizing language and cultural issues, which was the prevalent research during the late 1980s and continued to the present at the elementary rather than secondary levels, this research begins to show the adaptability of immigrant Latino/a students in light of Latino/a students born in the United States and the push and pull dimensions of immigration. The initial research by the Suarezes and others has made bold distinctions between diverse groups of Latinos, Central Americans initially and later, U.S.-born and immigrant Latinos with regard to their achievement (Suárez-Orozco & Suárez-Orozco, 1995). Their later research begins to shed light on the "plasticity" of Latinos and their diverse adaptive patterns (Suárez-Orozco & Paez, 2002). The Suárezes (2001) advocated for the realization of hybrid identities and bicultural competencies. Concurring with this premise, I prefer to refer to the acceptance of Latinos as the legitimization of their "hybrid power."

Ethnographic and more extensive and longitudinal studies of Latino/a students, have presented more complex explanations such as the *peer coethnic existence model*, which highlights the importance of peer membership for Latinos. The research of Rumbaut and Portes (2001) as well as others demonstrates that peers with whom Latinos associate often determine their chances at having opportunity to learn. This peer coexistence model presents the notion of segmented assimilation by which, depending on the leadership evident, color, and location of individuals in Eurocentric contexts, their adaptation becomes differentiated by generations. For those not sharing in their parents' cultural ways and outlooks, assimilation occurs in oppositional ways, whereas for those who maintain ethnic connections, educational support may be garnered (Portes & Zhou, 1993).

The Culture of Failure Frameworks

Irrespective of the explanations proffered for Latinos in general, such explanations support assumptions of failure or as Ray McDermott has said, a *culture of failure* (Varenne & McDermott, 1998). Using this explanation, Latinos tend to be viewed as being uneducable, often relegated to what Jorge Chapa (1996) has identified as a two-tiered educational system, one for those who can access the benefits attributed to mainstream students within their own generation through being educated, and another defined by poverty, lack of education, and low socioeconomic status (SES), which keeps such a generation of students locked into self-fulfilling prophecies of failure. The sheer concentration of Latinos in the lowest math and science courses across schools in the United States attests to the use of tracking as a sorting device (Oakes, 1994). Moreover, the overrepresentation of Latino/a students in special education classes begs the questions of how is this possible? and why?

Consequently the issue of mainstreaming Latino/a students from bilingual education classes, without any social or instructional support, almost guarantees higher dropout rates and retention rates for Latinos. Dropouts are worst among Latino/a students of all SES backgrounds than any other ethnic or racial group.[32] Yet the analysis of dropouts conducted in several studies by Michelle Fine (1995) and others calls attention to the lack of social responsibilities and structural inequities that continue to persist in schools. Only now has there been greater scrutiny of this myth in the past 15 years with large-scale federally funded research projects such as those conducted by CREDE and the Center for the Research of Students Placed at Risk (CRESPAR) of Johns Hopkins and Howard University and numerous qualitative ethnographic studies by anthropologists, educators, sociologists, and psychologists such as Michelle Fine, Henry Trueba, Luis Moll, Francisco Villarruel, Ricardo Stanton-Salazar, and others. It is no wonder that being "at risk" has been associated from national survey studies to language-speaking abilities, SES, and ethnicity in the case of Latinos, even though several ethnographic case studies demonstrate the contrary (Montero-Sieburth, 1993; Nieto, 1993). Failure has become so endemically associated with Latinos that being "at risk" for one single factor already places a student at risk (Bempechat, 1999).

Absent from the framework supporting the culture of failure is research about (1) the way that Latino/a parents have been treated by schools in the education of their children; (2) the way that assessments and evaluations are carried on; (3) the curricular structure; (4) the way that Latino/a community knowledge is understood; and (5) the types of intergenerational learning that can be generated with and for Latino/a students.

At the school level, unless Latino/a parents know how the system operates, administrators and teachers hold them at arm's length, often

---

[32]See *No More Excuses: Hispanic Dropout Project* and the writings of Olatokunbo S. Fashola and Robert Slavin on Effective Dropout Prevention and College Attendance Programs for Latino/a Students (http://www.ncbe.gwu.edu/miscpubs/used/hdp/hdp-4.html).

being excluded for not exhibiting democratic behaviors. Latino/a parents are expected to participate and vote in school committees as other parents within the system. Yet they may not have been socialized into democratic decision-making processes if they emigrated from highly paternalistic and hierarchically stratified countries (Montero-Sieburth, 2001). Assessment and testing also are secret issues that are rarely understood by Latino/a parents, because their knowledge of the way that schools are organized or the curriculum functions is not accessible to them.

Cultural and Community Analysis

Community funds of knowledge (Moll, Amnti, Neff, & Gonzalez, 1992) is another arena that is separate from schools, particularly because the outreach of schools is limited to the children and their parents, but not to the contexts in which they live. The role that cultural analysis has in determining achievement outcomes for Latino/a students has been studied among several researchers such as Angela Valenzuela (1999) and Henry Trueba (1987). Finally, the ways that learning can occur through different generations is also absent from the research on the normative culture of schools. Focusing on the mobility factors of one to another generation is useful in describing their academic attainment and in forecasting their school completion (Portes & Rumbaut, 1996; Perlmann, 2002).

Transnational and Comparative Studies

Transnational and comparative studies are the latest wave of explanations that can be used with Latino/a students. The transnational nature of many of the Latino/a students' experiences has brought a focus to the learning that occurs in their countries of origin and that follows them once in the United States. Interestingly, it is the field of comparative studies that has produced much of this articulation, particularly in comparative and contrastive studies from one country to another. The need to understand the social identities being acquired as people migrate and settle in new parts of the world, also carries with it the interpretation of what that diaspora means in the lives and education of migrants, emigrants, and immigrants. Thus, capturing the levels of accommodation, integration, or what Portes calls modes of incorporation, allows us to better ascertain the types of educational models that make sense for Latinos.

In sum, all of these frameworks, which cluster different explanatory models, either condemn Latinos, identify complexities of their adaptation, identify rejection, and only a few relate to specific areas of success. For the most part, the impact of these accepted truths over the past 60 years has been enormously damaging, with characterizations of whole populations as being "at risk" or deficient, with families blamed for not providing adequate learning environments, with teachers incapable of working with "these students," and with students being in need of major adjustments in order to academically achieve.

Although today the labels may have changed, the meanings behind these research paradigms from which many of the explanations have arisen and been sustained, still tend to describe the education of Latinos as being based on models of failure and "at risk." *How can the academy as well as the research field break away from such models towards more promising policies and practices?*

IMPLICATIONS OF THE ANALYSIS OF EXPLANATORY MODELS AND REFORM INITIATIVES ON LATINO/A EDUCATION FOR POLICIES AND PRACTICES

In the past 20 years, ethnographic studies conducted by Latino/a researchers such as Henry Enrique Trueba (1987), Patricia Gándara (1995), and Ricardo Stanton-Sálazar (1997), to name just a few, have begun to shed light on the educational successes of Latinos using cultural analysis, resilience theory, and critical empowerment theories. Although cultural analysis explanations have persisted, alternative explanations of Latinos have only recently emerged deriving much of their impetus from the literature of resilience, critical empowerment, and political analysis. Given the trajectories of the explanations used for Latinos in the past, it is notable that in recent years, more benign and positive outlooks have emerged regarding Latinos and education. Such a transformation raises the following questions in my mind:

Are Latino/a researchers today analyzing educational issues not seen or understood before by Latino/a and non-Latino researchers? Are there new methodologies being used that show different perspectives than those presented during the 1960s and 1970s?

Or have new paradigms begun to emerge from the research of Latinos that explain education differently than that described by non-Latinos?

Although these are complex and difficult questions, the answers most likely lay somewhere between the contexts and perspectives of Latino/a and non-Latino researchers, as well as the paradigms and research in which these studies have taken place. Like other Latino/a colleagues, I believe that Latinos (1) have been made invisible in much of the social science research (Montero-Sieburth & Villarruel, 2000); (2) have been undermined in terms of the contributions they make to the field of research; and (3) have had a silencing effect leveled on them by other researchers and educators that only recently identifies that Latino/a researchers have come of age.[33] The invisibility of Latinos and lack of realistic descriptions of their education and hence of relevant reforms are most likely because of several factors.

The Operant Contexts of Research

From the 1930s to the 1970s, Latino/a researchers who attempted to describe their communities often were dismissed as not being capable of presenting an objective nor scientific perspective, were too embedded in their communities to be able to present objective interpretations, and because they had not gained entry into the White mainstream-dominated research field. In other words, Latino/a researchers had not yet come of age. Thus, the descriptions of non-Latinos conducted by anthropologists, sociologists, and educators, who were considered to be outsiders and hence more objective, gained favor in the academic realm.[34] In fact, single group imposition has led to the assumption that all educational experiences of Latinos, including Mexican Americans, the largest of the subgroups, have been the same, undifferentiated by context.

The lack of disaggregated data also obscures needed data on each subgroup. The experiences of all Latinos become subsumed under one group or heading in national studies or are presented as a general

---

[33]The silencing effect can be noticed in that social science publications still appear in which Latino/a researchers are subsumed under the analysis of more known mainstream researchers and are often spoken for rather than being allowed to speak for themselves.

[34]See the controversy between William Madsen and Octavio Romano regarding their perspectives in researching Mexican Americans in Texas. Madsen represented Mexican American culture as the root cause of Mexican Americans' inability to succeed in America. Romano considered serious ethnographic distortions evident and felt there was a need to contextualize Chicano culture (Menchaca, 2000).

statistic in a quantitative format, not depicting the subtle differences that exist among each subgroup. For some Cubans, their background experiences and entry into the educational system are clearly different than that of Puerto Ricans learning in the Bronx or Mexican Americans in the valley of Texas. Being immigrant or U.S.-born Latino/a as well as age of entry to schooling, education of parents, and particularly of the mother, and use of mother and second languages—all have significant bearings on education, yet such distinctions between groups and within groups are often obliterated by the research literature.

The Perspectives Held by Researchers

Many of the social science studies stem from research conducted from the perspectives of non-Latino researchers, many of whom studied Latino/a communities from afar, without much of the cultural knowledge and insights of diverse Latino/a researchers. Although backed by their professional titles, several of these researchers have ended up describing Latinos through the perspective of "outsiders," creating stereotypes that persist and in effect, are not only colorblind but more insidiously promote negative images that fail to erode even when research conducted by "insiders" of those same cultures presents an alternative view. What often began as a cultural generalization about a given ethnic group became "scientific" explanations. Their persistence in the literature and use over time provided these descriptions with a status of explanatory power and strength, uncontested by academia.[35]

Without a doubt, the legacy of postcolonialism and post-slavery perspectives as well as paternalistic and condescending statements abounds throughout much of the early research on Latinos. How such a perspective changes or is tempered by social science research is a topic that is heated and often discussed at the American Anthropological Association, or the American Educational Research Organization. Yet, in this century, that perspective will likely tend to dissipate, and become replaced by multiple and collective perspectives, if not because it is intended, certainly because it will be influenced by the power of Latino/a numbers and their positions in social science research.

---

[35] As I have mentioned elsewhere, there is a prevailing epistemological imperialism evident in that only one way of knowing is imposed on all others. This notion is credited to Professor Mariella Bacigalupo at Princeton University.

The World Views or Paradigms Underlying
the Research Undertaken

Traditional research paradigms, representing quantitative, Western, and European-centered perspectives of some non-Latino researchers and how they view education and Latinos, have recently given way to less traditional perspectives shared by Latinos researchers (Rosaldo, 1993). Whereas non-Latino researchers have comparatively character-ized the education of Latinos with middle-class Anglo perspectives, and with an eye toward identifying failure, Latino/a researchers during the past century have been investigating these factors within their own communities. Unlike the "new" explanations that are unquestioned or become unstudied truths, often becoming epistemological statements from those in power to explain those without power or "education," the explanations that Latinos share are connected to the communities they study; are holistic in nature; socially, economically, and culturally prob-lematize issues; focus on the psychosocial aspects of an ethnic group; and are embedded within a political and critical theory framework.

By and large, Latinos have been characterized by the literature as being "dependent on the education of Whites, incapable of succeeding, and often being immobilized by poverty, speaking Spanish, and even their own cultures in advancing their education."[36] Not having a voice to speak about education, it is noteworthy that today social scientists approximate the meaning of *educación* as lifelong learning, as a new discovery of Latino/a cultures, yet such a meaning has always been present within Latino/a cultures.[37]

The Situationality of Latinos Between Blacks
and Whites

The situationality of Latinos, which relates to how Latinos are perceived and see themselves particularly often being placed between Blacks and White Europeans, as part of the Census identification, and also in terms of economic and political dimensions, tends to blur their participation in schooling. More important, such standing defies the peripheral status

---

[36]These are my own words, collected from much of the research literature over the span of 30 years.

[37]The term *educación* among Latinos presumes that learning is lifelong and not only takes place in the formal school settings but in informal settings as well, and the community mem-bers are all participants in such education.

attributed to Latinos by signaling the centrality of education for the growing numbers of the Latino/a population. Without doubt, Latinos care about the education of their children, but often do not have the knowledge or tools to access its opportunities, except for those who acquire the social and cultural capital in education.

The Lack of Grounding of Latino/a U.S. Research in Its More Global, Comparative, and Transnational Meanings

Transnational education of Latinos is just one of these outcomes, studied widely at institutions of higher learning, and becoming part of the global social science analyses. Studies of the diasporas of Latinos have also begun to shed myths about their homogeneity and adaptation in different contexts (Torres & Velásquez, 1998). Subtle and accurate articulation of mobility factors, labor issues, and immigrant status are beginning to demonstrate a different face for Latinos than that represented in the "deficit explanations." More complex issues between each generation are being studied, from 1 to 1.5 to 2 generation using Census data in different ways. Comparative analysis has also begun to focus on more detailed analysis of Latinos rather than glib comparisons (see Suárez-Orozco & Paez, 2002; Vermuelen, 2001; Waldinger, 2001). Latinos, once defined by quotas, Spanish-surname, nationality, citizenship, or country of origin, can today be characterized as being not only immigrant, U.S.-born, first-, second-, and third-generation but also transnational and panethnic in relation to their seamless mobility between borders and their global diasporas.

Hence, in discussing the educational models that Latinos have experienced throughout history, it is important to understand their experiences *from their perspectives and from various sources,* and to view them not as a generic group, but as diverse subgroups with different educational trajectories.

RESPONSES NEEDED FOR REFORMS THAT WILL EFFECTIVELY IMPACT LATINOS

Whereas much of the reform presented herein has been directed at "helping minorities overcome their educational limitations," "compensating for their home life by providing remedial education," "reducing their disadvantaged status," bringing quality and excellence into their learning, or "making sure that all children can learn," the rhetoric behind these statements stands in sharp contradiction to the high numbers of dropouts, ineffectual education often cited by the media and research, overrepresentation of students in lower level math and science classes, documentation of poor or limited education, and the undeserved and inequitable treatment experienced by many Latinos described by revisionist historians.[38] Yet as has been analyzed in this chapter and throughout the explanations that have arisen and the underlying paradigms that support them, there are evident implications for educational policies and practices that need to be considered for Latino/a education to become a reality.

Recipients of Reform Need to Be at the Center of Reform

Changes in education without the recipients of reform being center stage will remain ineffectual. Latinos cannot continue to be perceived as invisible given their numbers, growing power, and economic promise. They cannot be viewed as minorities, or as victims in the process of education but, rather, as being at the center of the reform movements. Latinos have been and today remain at the periphery of the educational reform discourse. They are maintained at arm's length in the reform agenda, even though they are central in the discussion of high dropout and repetition rates, are underrepresented in math and science and talented programs, and overrepresented in special education and bilingual education. Throughout the reforms that have occurred in U.S. educational history, Latinos have not been central in the articulation, nor the formulation of changes and reforms that would benefit them. Given the enormity of the new immigrants, how they are to be educated is an eminently important question that affects not only Latinos but also more significantly, Americans in their well-being.

The Economic and Social Conditions of Latinos Must Realistically Be Understood

Reforms without understanding the economic conditions of Latinos from one generation to another will be truncated in developing realistic

---

[38]There is ample research on the overrepresentation of Latinos in bilingual education and special education and evidence of their underrepresentation in gifted and talented programs.

policies and even practices. The lack of understanding between reform and social and economic issues cannot continue to go unchecked or misunderstood for Latinos.

The research of Card, Di Nardo, and Estes (1998, p. 37) compared the 1940 and 1970 and the 1994–1996 Census data in *Current Population Surveys*, and found that there are important intergenerational links between the economic status of immigrant fathers and the economic status and marriage patterns of their native-born sons and daughters. Children of better-educated immigrants have higher education, earn higher wages, and are more likely to marry outside of their father's ethnic group. They report that "the rate of intergenerational 'assimilation' in educational attainment has remained stable over the last 50 years, and that the rate of intergenerational 'assimilation' in earnings has also remained constant, apart from an effect of widening overall wage inequality." Thus, the advantages for children of immigrants (second generation), they state, is associated with greater socioeconomic success in the United States, but with greater economic disparities for the "natives" or third generation.

More studies of this nature are needed that begin to identify the intersections at which Latinos experience upward mobility and higher educational access. Some of the recent studies by the Henry Kaiser Foundations on a 2002 National Survey of Latinos presents an optimistic picture of what is possible (Brodie, Steffenson, Valdez, & Levin, 2002).[39] Moreover, recent research conducted by Lindsay Lowell and Roberto Suro (2002) indicates that the educational profile of Latino/a immigrants is improving and that the educational gap with natives is actually closing in high school education. Latino/a immigrants will be increasing their secondary education in their countries of origin and that will distinguish them towards a higher educational profile. At the same time, older less educated immigrants will be aging.

According to Richard Rothstein (2002) how schools affect society and how society affects schools is out of balance. This arises from the assumption "... that schools are independent actors whose ability to generate student outcomes and through them, to affect other social and economic institutions is limited only by schools' own effort and skill ... we have assumed that improved academic performance of elementary and secondary students can and should be the cure for all

---

[39]See Mary Brodie, Annie Steffenson, Jaime Valdez, & Rebecca Levin. (2002). *National survey of Latinos*. Menlo Park, CA: Henry J. Kaiser Family Foundation and Pew Hispanic Center.

economic and social ills, irrespective of the influence of families or of the broader economic policies . . . " (p. 1). Kantor and Lowe (1995) alert us to consider that:

> current reforms in education will remain truncated unless it too addresses the long-standing political and economic accords that set the contours of educational policy and underclass. Our analysis of the development of educational policy today as well as in the past includes a consideration of the social and economic arrangements beyond schooling itself that structure the processes of policy formation in education, it will remain impossible to clarify the limits and possibilities educational policy makers now confront . . . (p. 10)

The Growing Research on Latinos Needs to Be Strongly Supported and Experimentation of Programs Needs to Continue

Reform without inclusion of growing research of Latinos will continue to support deficit explanations of Latinos and education and diminish their contributions to the understanding of Latino/a communities. Support for researching the issues that are most salient and well understood by the Latino/a community needs to be ever present, rather than promised. Latinos know what they need and understand the complexity of their own communities, and the dimensionality of the push and pull, as well as assimilationist and pluralistic trends they have experienced. The type of research that is now needed extends beyond the borderlands and the barrios to the more generative research of created social and cultural identities, as being experienced in El Barrio of New York City between Puerto Ricans and incoming Mexicans and other groups. We need to know how Latinos will not discriminate among themselves and gain a sense of their own civic empowerment and can move beyond having to fight for the "crumbs" or being in the "crab barrel, where each crab in climbing, pulls the other one down."

There is also a reported need to continue to experiment with programs that indicate that the interventions they make on educational attainment of program participants have impact. The evaluation study of Lee Mizell and Georges Vernez (2001, p. 29) on *Increasing the Education Attainment of Hispanics: Program Effectiveness* shows that early childhood, high school dropout prevention, and college-going programs have a positive effect on the educational attainment of participants. They cite that:

> early childhood programs increase in-grade retention from 3 to 75 percent among high risk children and . . . also increase the high school graduation rate from 26 to 37 percent. . . . School and community based high school dropout prevention programs decreased the dropout rate from 23 to 92 percent among students with a 12 to 29 percent pre program probability of dropping out of high school. . . . Finally, college-going programs were found to increase college going in a range from 7 to more than 70 percent.

Certainly these outcomes make a case for supporting these programs and for expanding them as well. In addition, a recent analysis by Lucy Hood (2003), *Immigrant Students, Urban High Schools: The Challenge Continues*, for the Carnegie Corporation highlights the importance of small-school settings, English as a Second Language instruction, one-to-one contact between adults and students, and interested and committed teachers as key components in impacting immigrant students.

In terms of policy implications of these points, it should be noted that with the research knowledge also comes the training of younger generations to access such knowledge. Cadres of researchers, policy makers, and community members need to be developed and platforms of civically empowered individuals need to emerge, in similar fashion to that of African American educators and researchers. These possibilities can only be achieved when Latinos are listened to and their research continues to be legitimately accepted and practiced.

The Heterogeneity of Latinos and Decision-Making as Part of Reforms Needs to Be Understood

Reform without comprehending the changes in Latino/a populations in terms of vast heterogeneity, mobility, adaptation patterns, language patterns, religions, and so on will continue to maintain stereotypes and condemn Latinos to an underclass. The fixation on homogeneity as a reality needs to yield to acknowledging the heterogeneity of Latinos as a template for then understanding different routes to decision making and to the development of democratic citizenry. Thus, reforms have to model the different approaches that can be used to achieve common and collective goals. To assume that Latinos already know how to participate in a democracy given the mobility of immigrants and the residential segregation of Latinos in the United States, is to dismiss the opportunity they have in generating a multicultural democracy, one in which the educated citizen is highly valued.

Reform Policies and Practices Need to Acknowledge Latinos as a Visible Force

Throughout the reforms that have occurred in U.S. educational history, Latinos have not been central in the articulation nor the formulation of changes and reforms that would benefit them, except for the reforms and recommendations that they have generated through commissions, their own organizations, and grassroots efforts or community-based initiatives steeped in the social, economic, and cultural realities of Latinos. Because Latinos make up part of the intended minorities who will benefit from reform, they are implicitly addressed in many of the reform policies but become explicit insofar as they are presented in terms of dropout rates, repetition, and retention indexes. Such exclusionary but at the same time inclusionary policies and practices, are total contradictions. Reform that does not view Latinos as a visible, powerful force to be listened to in developing educational policy will place the outcomes of Latino/a research on education on the back burner. In point of fact, except for grassroots Latino/a community interventions, in which the parents and community members have had a voice in the education of their children, Latino/a education has been for most of the past century ineffectual, poor in quantity and quality, compensatory in nature, unsubstantial, deficient, experienced negatively by Latino/a students and their families, and undeserved.

The Adaptation of Diverse Latinos' Needs to Be Understood in Its Complexity

Reform without understanding the complexity of adaptation of Latinos, will continue to create barriers rather than enhance their learning. This means that different patterns of their adaptation, by generation, by education, by the influences of the community, culture, and language need to be taken into account rather than subsumed under one type of explanation. The very diversity of Latinos calls for more careful analysis of their communities and the way they gain access to education and have mobility from one generation to the other. Furthermore, the continuity or discontinuity of home to school and school to home transitions need to be understood in terms of their impact on learning. A mixed message about home life and the parents' role in education does little to support the student's own negotiation of these spaces. Thus, what is required is a clearer understanding of who are today's Latinos in the United States, what each generation carries into U.S. society, and in what ways, and what kind of education responds to their current and future needs.

Unless praxis is practiced whereby there is reflection to action on the research of kindergarten through twelfth grade for Latinos, derived from community input, and unless that research is used by the very communities of Latinos to make education their own process, then empowerment and actions to commit, unlearn, and deconstruct what has been a discriminatory system of education against Latinos, will not take place. We cannot afford to wait for future explanations of success to appear. It is time that Latinos speak for their children's education and their future, knowing that they can draw on the social, cultural, linguistic, economic, and resilient strength that permeates all Latino/a cultures.

REFERENCES

Antin, M. (1985). *From Plotzk to Boston*. New York: Markus Wiener Publishing.

Arias, B. (1986). The context of education for Hispanic students: An overview. *American Journal of Education, 3*, 25–56.

Arias, B., & Casanova, U. (1993). *Bilingual education: politics, practice and research*. Ninety Second Yearbook of the National Society for the Study of Education, Chicago: University of Chicago Press.

Attinasi, J., Pedraza, P., Poplack, S., & Pousada, A. (1988). Intergenerational perspectives on bilingualism: From community to class. New York: Centro de Estudios Puertorriqueños, Hunter College.

Bell, T. (1993). Reflections one decade after a nation at risk. *Phi Delta Kappan, 74*(8), 592–597.

Bell, T., & Crosby, E. (1993). A nation at risk: 10 years later. *Phi Delta Kappan, 74*.

Bempechat, J. (1999). Learning from poor and minority students who succeed in school: Children's views on success and failure have a big impact on their learning. *Harvard Education Letter, 15*(3), 1–3.

Blythe, A., and Associates. (1998). *The teaching for understanding guide*. San Francisco, CA: Jossey Bass.

Bodnar, J. (1987). *The transplanted: A history of immigrants in urban America*. Indianapolis: Indiana University Press.

Bourdieu, P., & Passeron, C. (1990). *Reproduction in education, society and culture*. Thousand Oaks, CA: Sage Publication.

Bowles, S., & Gintis, H. (1976). *Schooling in a capitalist America: Educational reform and contradictions of economic life*. New York: Basic Books.

Bowles, S., & Gintis, H. (1976). *Schooling in a capitalist America*. New York: Basic Books.

Brodie, M., Steffenson, A., Valdez, J., & Levin, R. (2002). *National survey of Latinos: 2002* Menlo Park: CA: Henry J. Kaiser Family Foundation, Washington, DC: Pew Hispanic Center.

Card, Di Nardo, & Estes (1998). *Current population surveys.* Washington, DC: U.S. Census Bureau.

Carter, T., & Segura, R. (1979). *Mexican Americans in school: Decade of change.* New York: College Entrance Examinations Record.

Cazden, C., Carrasco, R., Maldonado-Guzman, A., & Erickson, F. (1980). The contribution of ethnographic research to bicultural bilingual education. In J. E. Alatis (Ed.), *Georgetown University roundtable on languages and linguistics* (pp. 64–80). Washington, DC: Georgetown University Press.

Cazden, C., Vera, J., & Steiner, S. (1972). *Functions of language.* Rowley, MA: Newbury Press.

Chan, S. (1990). European and Asian immigration into the United States in comparative perspective, 1820s to 1920s. In V. Yans-McLaughlin (Ed.), *Immigration reconsidered* (pp. 37–78). New York: Oxford University Press.

Chapa, J. (1996). *Mexican American education: First, second and third generation adaptations.* Cambridge, MA: Current Issues in Educational Research Workshop, Harvard University Graduate School of Education.

Coleman, J. (1988). Social capital in the creation of human capital. *American Journal of Sociology, 94*, 95–120.

Coleman, J., Campbell, S. E., Hobson, C. J., McPartland, J., Mood, A. M., Weinfield, F. D., & York, R. L. (1966). *Equality of educational opportunity.* Washington, D.C. Office of Education, U.S. Department of Health, Education and Welfare, U.S. Government Printing Office.

Congress of the U.S. (2001). Title III: Language instruction for limited English proficient and immigrant students.

Crawford, J. (1989). *Bilingual education: History, politics, theory and practice.* Trenton, NJ: Crane.

Crosby, E. A. (1993). The "at risk" decade. *Phi Delta Kappan, 74*(8), 598–604.

Cummins, J. (1986). Empowering minority students: A framework for intervention. In J. Kretovics (Ed.), *Transforming urban education* (pp. 327–346). Boston: Allyn and Bacon.

Darder, A., Rodríguez- Ingle. Y., & Cox, B. G. (Eds.). (1993). *The policies and the promise: The public schooling of Latino children.* Claremont, CA: The Tomas Rivera Center.

Darder, A., Torres, R. D., & Gutierrez, H. (Eds.). (1997). *Latinos and education: A critical reader.* New York: Routledge.

De Vos, G., & Suárez-Orozco, M. (1990). *Status inequality: The self in culture.* Newbury Park, CA: Sage.

Donato, R. (1999). Hispano education and the implications of autonomy: Four school systems in Southern Colorado, 1920–1963. *Harvard Educational Review, 69*(2), 117–148.

Donato, R., & Lazerson, M. (2000). New directions in American educational history: Problems and prospects. *Educational Researcher, 29*(8), 4–15.

Erickson, F. (1994). Transformation and school success: The politics and culture of educational achievement. In J. Kretovics & E. J. Nussel (Eds.), *Transforming urban education* (pp. 375–395). Boston: Allyn and Bacon.

Erickson, F., & Mohatt, G. (1982). Cultural organization of participation structures in two classrooms of Indian students. In G. Spindler (Ed.), *Doing the ethnography of schooling* (pp. 133–174). New York: Holt, Rinehart and Winston.

Fernandez, R., & Shu, G. (1988). School dropouts: New approaches to an enduring problem. *Education and Urban Society, 20*(4), 363–386.

Fine, M. (1995). The politics of who's at risk. In B. Blue Swadener & Lubeck, S. (Eds.), *Children and families "at promise": Deconstructing the discourse of risk* (pp. 76–96). New York: SUNY.

Foner, N., Rumbaut R., & Gold, S. J. (2000). *Immigration research for a new century: Multi-disciplinary perspectives.* New York: Russell Sage Foundation.

Fordham, S., & Ogbu, J. (1986). Black students school success: Coping with the burden of acting white. *Urban Review, 18*(3), 176–206.

Gallenstein, N. (1998). Educational challenges of hispanics: Cultural literature review. *Information Analyses,* ERIC DIGESTS, 1–31.

Gándara, P. (1995). *Over the ivory walls: The educational mobility of low income Chicanos.* Albany: SUNY.

Garcia, E. (2001). *Hispanic education in the United States: Raices y alas.* New York: Rowan and Littlefield.

General Accounting Office. (1994). *Hispanics' schooling: Risk factors for dropping out and barriers to resuming education.* Washington, DC: U.S. Government Printing Office.

Gibson, M. (1988). *Accommodation without assimilation: Sikh immigrants in an American high school.* New York: Cornell University Press.

Gibson, M., & Ogbu, J. U. (1991). *Minority status and schooling: A comparative study of immigrant and involuntary minorities.* New York: Garland Publishing Com.

Ginorio, A., & Huston, M. (2001). *Si, se puede, Yes we can: Latinas in school.* Washington, DC: American Association of University Women.

Gonzalez, G. (1991). Hispanics in the past two decades, Latinos in the next two: Hindsight and foresight. In M. Sotomayor (Ed.), *Empowering Hispanic families: A critical issue for the 1990s* (pp. 1–20). Milwaukee, WI: Family Service America.

Hakuta, K. (1986). *Mirror of language.* New York: Basic Books.

Handlin, O. (1982). Education and the European immigrant 1820–1920, In B. Weiss (Ed.), *American education and the European immigrant, 1840–1940* (pp. 3–16). Chicago: University of Illinois Press.

Hood, L. (2003). *Immigrant students, urban high schools: The challenge continues.* New York: Carnegie Corporation of New York.

The Jossey-Bass Reader on School Reform (2001). San Francisco, CA: Jossey-Bass.

Kantor, H., & Lowe, R. (1995). Class, race, and the emergence of federal education policy: From the New Deal to the Great Society. *Educational Researcher, 14*(3), 4–11.

Karier, C. (1986). The common school era. *The individual, society, and education. A history of American educational ideas* (2nd ed., pp. 43–67). Chicago: University of Illinois Press.

Lewis, O. (1965). *La vida: A Puerto Rican family in the culture of poverty—San Juan and New York.* New York: Random House.

Lewis, O. (1966). The culture of poverty. *Scientific American, 218,* 19–25.

Lockwood, A. T., & Secada, W. (1999). *Transforming education for Hispanic youth: Exemplary practices, programs, and schools.* Washington, DC: National Clearinghouse for Bilingual Education.

Los Angeles County Commission on Human Rights. (1989). *The effects of school reform on black and Latino students in Los Angeles County.* Los Angeles, 1–25.

Lowell, L., & Suro, R. (2002). *The improving educational profile of Latino immigrants.* A Project of the Pew Charitable Trust and USC Annenberg School for Communication, Washington, DC: Pew Hispanic Center.

Madaus, G. F., & Tan, A. G. (1993). The growth of assessment. In *Challenges and achievements of American education.* G. Cawelti (Ed.). Washington, DC: Association of Supervision and Curriculum Development, pp. 33–79.

Matute-Bianchi, M. (1991). Situational ethnicity and patterns of school performance among immigrants and non-immigrant Mexican-descent students. In M. Gibson & J. U. Ogbu (Eds.), *Minority status and schooling: A comparative study of immigrant and involuntary minorities* (pp. 205–247). New York: Garland.

McNeil, L. (2000). Creating new inequalities: Contradictions of reform. *Phi Delta Kappan,* 728–734.

Mizell, L., & Vernez, G. (2001). *Increasing the education attainment of Hispanics: Program effectiveness.* Santa Monica, CA: Rand Education.

Molina, C., & Aguirre-Molina, M. (1994). "Latino populations: Who are they?" *Latino Health in the U.S.: A Growing Challenge.* American Public Health Association, pp. 3–27.

Moll, L., Amnti, C. C., Neff, D., & Gonzales, N. (1992). Funds of knowledge: Using a qualitative approach to connect homes and classrooms. *Theory Into Practice, 31*(2), 132–141.

Montejano, D. (1992). *Anglos and Mexicans in the 21st century.* Julian Samora Institute, (Eds.). Michigan State University.

Montero-Sieburth, M. (1993). The effects of schooling process and practices on potential at risk Latino high school students. In R. Rivera & S. Nieto (Eds.), *The education of Latino students in Massachusetts: Issues, research and policy implications* (pp. 217–242). Amherst: Mauricio Gaston Institute and University of Massachusetts.

Montero-Sieburth, M., & Batt, M. (2001). An overview of the educational models used to explain the academic achievement of Latino students: Implications for research and policies into the new millennium. In R. Slavin & M. Calderon (Eds.), *Effective programs for Latino students* (pp. 331–368). Mahwah, NJ: Lawrence Erlbaum Associates.

Montero-Sieburth, M., & Lacelle Peterson, M. (1991). Immigrants and schooling: An ethnohistorical account of political and family perspectives in an urban community. *Anthropology and Education Quarterly, 22*(4), 300–325.

Montero-Sieburth, M., & Villarruel, F. A. (Eds.). (2000). *Making invisible Latino adolescents visible: A critical approach to Latino diversity.* New York: Falmer Press.

Morawska, E. (1995). The sociology and historiography of immigration. In V. Yans-McLaughlin (Ed.), *Immigration reconsidered* (pp. 187–238). New York: Oxford University Press.

The National Commission on Excellence in Education. (1983). *A nation at risk: The imperative for educational reform. A report to the nation and the secretary of education.* Washington, DC: National Commission on Excellence in Education.

National Research Council. (1989). *Everybody counts. A report to the nation on the future of mathematics education.* Washington, DC: National Academy Press.

Nieto, S. (1993). Creating possibilities: Educating Latino students in Massachusetts. In R. Rivera & S. Nieto (Eds.), *The education of Latino students in Massachusetts: Issues, research, and policy Implications* (pp. 243–261). Mauricio Gaston Institute for Latino Community Development and Public Policy, University of Massachusetts. Boston: University of Massachusetts Press.

Oakes, J. (1994). Tracking, inequality, and the rhetoric of reform: Why schools don't change. In J. Kretovics & E. Nussel (Eds.), *Transforming urban education* (pp. 146–164). Needham Heights, MA.

Ogbu, J. U. (1987). Variability in minority school performance. *Anthropology and Education Quarterly, 18,* 312–334.

Ogbu, J. U. (1992). Understanding cultural diversity and learning. *Educational Researcher, 22,* 5–14.

Ogbu, J. U., & Matute-Bianchi, M. E. (1986). Understanding sociocultural factors: Knowledge identity and school adjustment. In *Beyond language* (pp. 73–142). Los Angeles: California State University Evaluation, Dissemination and

Assessment Center. Sacramento: Bilingual Education Office, California State Dept. of Education.

Orfield, G. (1997). Deepening segregation in American public schools: A special report from the Harvard Project on School Desegregation. In *Equity and excellence in education* (pp. 5–24). Philadelphia, PA: Taylor & Francis.

Padilla, A. M. (1995). *Hispanic psychology: Critical issues in theory and research.* Thousand Oaks, CA: Sage Publications.

Perez, S., & Martinez, D. (1993). *State of Hispanic America 1993: Toward a Latino anti-poverty agenda.* Washington, D.C.: National Council of La Raza.

Perlmann, J. (2002). *Polish and Italian schooling then, Mexican schooling now? U.S. ethnic school attainments across the generations of the 20th century.* Washington, DC: Russell Sage Foundation, Working Paper, No. 350.

Phillips, S. (1993). *The invisible culture.* Prospect Heights, IL: Waveland Press.

Portes, A., & Rumbaut, R. (Eds.). (1996). *Immigrant America: A portrait.* Berkeley: University of California Press.

Portes, A., & Zhou, M. (1993). The new second generation: Segmented assimilation and its variants. *Annals, 530,* 75–96.

Ravitch, D. (1999). Student performance: The national agenda in education. *Brookings Review* (Winter), 12–16.

Reyes, P., Scribner, J. D., & Scribner, A. P. (Eds.). (1999). *Lessons from high performing Hispanic schools.* New York: Teachers College.

Reyes, P., & Valencia, R. R. (1995). Educational policy and the growing Latino student population: Problems and prospects. In A. Padilla (Ed.), *Hispanic psychology: Critical issues in theory and research* (pp. 303–325). Thousand Oaks, CA: Sage Publications.

Rochín, R. I., & Valdés, D. N. (2000). *Voices of a new Chicana/o history.* East Lansing: Michigan State University Press.

Rodríguez, R. J. (1999). In *search of high academic achievement: The policy drive to end social promotion.* Washington, DC: National Council of La Raza, 1–5. (http://nclr.policy.net/proactive).

Romero, M., Hondagneu-Sotelo, P., & Ortiz, V. (Eds.). (1997). *Challenging fronteras: Structuring Latina and Latino lives in the U.S.* New York: Routledge.

Rosaldo, R. (1993). *Culture and truth: The remaking of social analysis.* Boston: Beacon Press.

Rossi, R., & Montgomery, A. (1994). *Education reforms and students at risk: A review of the current state of the art.* Washington, DC: U.S. Department of Education. Accessed April 6, 2005 at www.ed.gov/pubs/EdReformStudies/EdReform/title.html

Rothstein, R. (2002, January 24–25). *Out of balance: Our understanding of how schools affect society and how society affects schools.* Conference Proceedings. 30th Anniversary Conference: Traditions of Scholarship in Education. Spencer Foundation. Chicago, Il.

Rumbaut, R., & Portes, A. (Eds.). (2001). *Ethnicities: Children of immigrants in America.* New York: Russell Sage Foundation.

San Miguel, G. (1987). The status of historical research on Chicano education. *Review of Educational Research, 57*(4), 467–480.

Science and Technology for the Nation: Issues and Priorities for the 106th Congress. (1998, December 16). Views from the Science and Technology Community on the House Science Committee's Report. Unlocking our Future: Towards a New National Science Policy, Symposium of the Science AAAAS Committee on Engineering and Public Policy. Washington, DC: American Association for the Advancement of Science.

Secada, W., Chavez-Chavez, R., Garcia, E., Munoz, C., Oakes, J., Santiago-Santiago, I., & Slavin, R. (1998). *No more excuses: The final report of the Hispanic dropout project.* Washington, DC: U.S. Dept. of Ed.

Slavin, R., & Calderon, M. (Eds.). (2000). *Effective programs for Latino students*. Mahwah, NJ: Lawrence Erlbaum Associates.

Stanton-Sálazar, R. (1997). A social capital framework for understanding the socialization of racial minority children and youths. *Harvard Educational Review, 67*(1), 1–40.

Steinberg, L. (1997). *Beyond the classroom: Why school reform has failed and what parents need to do*. New York: Touchstone.

Suárez-Orozco, M. (1987). Becoming somebody: Central American immigrants in U. S. Inner City Schools. *Anthropology and Education Quarterly, 18*, 287–299.

Suárez-Orozco, M. (1998). *Crossings: Mexican immigration in interdisciplinary perspectives*. Cambridge, MA: David Rockefeller Center for Latin American Studies and Harvard University.

Suárez-Orozco, M., & Paez, M. M. (Eds.). (2002). *Latinos remaking America*. Berkeley: University of California Press, and Cambridge, MA: David Rockefeller Center for Latin American Studies.

Suárez-Orozco, C., & Suárez-Orozco, M. (Eds.). (1995). *Transformations: Migration, family life, and achievement motivation among Latino adolescents*. Stanford, CA: Stanford University Press.

Suárez-Orozco, C., & Suárez-Orozco, M. (2001). *Children of immigration*. Cambridge, MA: Harvard University Press.

Suro, R. (1999). *Strangers among us: Latino lives in a changing America*. New York: Vintage Press.

Thomas, W., & Collier, V. (1999, April). *Evaluation that informs school reform: Study, design and findings from the Thomas and Collier (1998) National School-Based Collaborative Research on School Effectiveness for Language Minority Students*. Paper presented at the American Educational Research Association Meeting, Montreal.

Thomlinson, C. A. (2004). *The differentiated classroom: Responding to the needs of all learners*. New York: Prentice Hall.

Torres, A., & Velásquez, J. E. (1998). *The Puerto Rican movement: Voices from the diaspora*. Philadelphia, PA: Temple University Press.

Trueba, H. E. (1987). *Critical ethnographic praxis for the study of immigrants*. Unpublished manuscript, at Harvard Graduate School of Education.

Trueba, H. E. (Ed.). (1987). *Success or failure? Learning and the language minority student*. Cambridge, MA: Newbury House.

Tyack, D. (1994). *The one best system: A history of American urban education*. Cambridge, MA. Harvard University Press.

Tyack, D. (2000). Reflections on histories of U.S. education. *Educational Researcher, 29*(8), 19–20.

Tyack, D., & Cuban, L. (1995). *Tinkering toward utopia: A century of public school reform*. Cambridge, MA: Harvard University Press.

Valdivieso, R., & Nicolau, S. (1992). *Look me in the eye: A Hispanic cultural perspective on school reform*. Washington, DC: U.S. Department of Education, Office of Educational Research and Improvement.

Valenzuela, A. (1999). *Subtractive bilingualism: U.S. Mexican youth and the politics of caring*. New York: SUNY.

Varenne, H., & McDermott, R. (1998). *Successful failure: The school America builds*. Boulder, CO: Westview Press.

Vemeulen, H. (2001). *Culture and inequality. Immigrant cultures and social mobility in long-term perspective*. Amsterdam, Netherlands: Institute for Migration and Ethnic Studies.

Vermeulen, H., & Perlmann, J. (Eds.). (2000). *Immigrants, schooling and social mobility: Does culture make a difference?* New York: St. Martin's Press.

Vernez, G., & Abrahmse, A. (1996). *How immigrants fare in U.S. education.* Institute on Education and Training. Center for Research on Immigration Policy. Santa Monica, CA: Rand Corporation.

Vigil, J. D. (1997). Personas Mexicanas: Chicano high schoolers in a changing Los Angeles: Ft. Worth, TX: Harcourt Press.

Vigil, J. D. (1999). Streets and schools: How educators can help Chicano marginalized gang youth. *Harvard Educational Review, 69*(3), 270–288.

Villarruel, F., Montero-Sieburth, M., Wilson Outlay, C., Dunbar, C. (2005). "Dorothy, there is no yellow brick road": The paradox of community youth development approaches for Latino and African American urban youth. In J. L. Mahoney, R. W. Larson, & J. Eccles (Eds.), *After-school activities: Contexts of development* (pp. 111–130). Thousand Oaks, CA: Sage.

Villarruel, Francisco, & Walker, Nancy E. with Pamela Minifee, Omara Rivera-Vazquez, Susan Peterson, Kristen Perry (2002). *¿Dónde esta la Justicia? A call to action on behalf of Latino and Latina youth in the U.S. justice system.* Commissioned by Building Blocks for Youth Initiative. East Lansing: Institute for Children, Youth and Families, Michigan State University.

Waldinger, R. (2001). *Strangers at the gates: New immigrants in urban America.* Berkeley: University of California Press.

Wiggins, G., & McTighe, J. (1998). *Understanding by design.* Alexandria, VA: Association for Supervision and Curriculum.

Willis, P. (1972). *Learning to labour: How working class kids get working class jobs.* Westmead, UK: Saxon House.

Wilson, W. J. (1978). *The declining significance of race: Blacks in a changing America.* Chicago: University of Chicago Press.

Yans-McLaughlin, V. (1990). *Immigration reconsidered: History, sociology and politics.* New York: Oxford University Press.

PART III

Exposing the Colonizing Effects of Reform

6

Latinos and Education: A Statistical Portrait

Héctor R. Cordero-Guzmán
City University of New York

THE LATINO/A POPULATION IN THE UNITED STATES

Over the last decade, the growth and increasing visibility of Latinos have become evident to a larger segment of the U.S. population. The Latino/a population has doubled between 1980 and 2000 in expected places such as Los Angeles, New York (60% growth, in fact), Chicago, Miami, Houston, and many other large cities, but it also has grown significantly in many other areas such as Raleigh, Atlanta, Orlando, Las Vegas, Portland, Washington, DC, and in many small towns and cities all over the United States.

The Latino/a population includes significant diversity by national origin (from countries in Latin America and the Caribbean) and migration status (from recent arrivals to families that have lived in the United States for generations). It also includes significant variation by socioeconomic status and place of residence. A recent report by the U.S. Department of Education (2003) includes one of the most comprehensive analyses ever produced of data on Latino/a education. Unfortunately, the report does not disaggregate the information by national origin, but it still allows us to get a concrete picture of the main indicators of Latino/a education.

The Latino/a population is large, growing, and relatively young. In 2000, the Census counted approximately 35.2 million Latinos in the United States, or 12% of the population, and a total of 98.2 million Latinos (24.3% of the U.S. population) are expected by the year 2050. There were 22,338,311 Latinos (or close to 63%) of Mexican origin followed by 3,539,988 (or 10%) from Puerto Rico; 1,312,127 (or 4%) from Cuba; around 999,561 (or 3%) from the Dominican Republic; 2,435,731 from Central America (or 7%) including 1 million from El Salvador; about 1,847,811 (or 5%) from South America, including 653 thousand from Colombia; and 2,764,952 (8%) classified as "Other Hispanics" (or persons that specified that they were Latino/a but did not provide any other indication of a particular national origin).

The median age for Latinos is 26.6 years compared to 35.9 years for the total population (38.6 for Whites and 30.6 for Blacks) and almost one out of every three Latinos in the country is less than 15 years of age. In fact, there were 11.4 million Latino/a children under 18 years of age and approximately 15% of children in the United States are of Latino/a origin. By the year 2020 projections indicate that there will be close to 18.1 million Latino/a children, or 23% of the population less than 18 years of age, out of a total youth population of 77.1 million.

Latino/a children and youth are among the fastest growing segments of the U.S. population. The Latino/a population grew by 43% between 1990 and 2000 and is expected to grow by an even larger 58% between 2000 and 2020. Unfortunately, however, the Latino/a population is also quite poor as measured by annual income and poverty rates. Close to 7.2 million Latinos, or 21%, live below the poverty level compared to 11% for the total U.S. population. Latino/a children are particularly likely to live under poverty. Out of a total of 11.6 million poor children in the United States, close to 3.3 million (or 28%) are Latino/a , and 28% of all Latino/a children live below poverty (compared to 31% of Black children and 9% of White children).

Lack of health insurance among many families (it is estimated that close to 31% of Latino/a families and 25% of Latino/a children do not have health insurance) and lack of access to preventive clinics and programs have a significant impact on the health and the education of Latino/a families and children. In many parts of the country, Latino/a children also suffer disproportionately from higher rates of infant death and low birth weight. The prevalence of asthma and other diseases is quite high and, although they are moving in the right direction, teen pregnancy and mortality rates (particularly homicides and suicides) are still high. At the national level, the birth rate for Latinas 15 to 19 years of age in 1997 was 94 births per 1,000 compared to 33 per 1,000 for Whites, 82 per 1,000 for Blacks, and 22 per 1,000 for young Asian women. Approximately one quarter of births to teens 15 to 19 in the United States were to Latinas.

Higher poverty rates mean that Latino/a children are disproportionately exposed to what the U.S. Department of Education considers "risk factors" including: (a) mother with less than high school, (b) living in a family that received welfare or food stamps, (c) living in a single parent household, and (d) parents whose primary language is not English. Data from the U.S. Department of Education indicates that only 28% of Latino/a children in kindergarten had no "risk factors," similar to the 28% rate for Black children but alarming when compared to the 71% of White children with no risk factors. Conversely, the percentage of Latino/a and African American children with one or more risk factors was 71% and close to 33% (or one in three) Latino/a children had two or more risk factors.

TRENDS IN SCHOOL ENROLLMENT

In 1999, 26% of Latino/a 3-year-olds, 64% of 4-year-olds, and 89% of 5-year-olds were enrolled in a center-based program or kindergarten compared to 60%, 81%, and 99% of Black children and 47%, 69%, and 93% of White children, respectively. Although family care is more prevalent among Latinos, it is important that efforts are made to include and tailor early childhood development programs and initiatives to Latino/a children.

Latino/a enrollment in public schools has skyrocketed over the last two decades. In 1990 close to 32.4% of public school students were minority and 11.7% were Latino/a . By the year 2000, close to 38.7% of public school students in K–12 were minority and 16.6% were Latino/a. Whereas the growth and expansion of the Latino/a population throughout the United States accelerated in the 1990s, Latino/a students are a significant proportion of students in particular regions (west, south, and northeast, respectively), particular states, and cities. Latinos account for more than 16% (their national average) of students in New Mexico (50%), California (43%), Texas (41%), Arizona (34%), Nevada (26%), Colorado (22%), and Florida and New York (both with 19%).

Latinos also constitute significant proportion (41%) of students in the 10 largest urban school districts such as Los Angeles Unified (71%), Dade County (Miami) in Florida (56%), Houston Independent School District (55%), New York City (38%), and the city of Chicago (35%). Latino/a students also are significantly segregated. Estimates indicate that 38% of Latino/a students (and 37% of Blacks), for example, go to a school that is more than 90% minority, whereas 43% of White students go to a school that is less than 10% minority.

EDUCATIONAL PROGRESS AND HIGH SCHOOL COMPLETION

Although many educators have serious and legitimate reservations about the increasing use and reliance on standardized tests for educational measurement, the Department of Education measures and compares assessments at the national level with the National Assessment of Educational Progress (NAEP). Latino/a scores on the NAEP at ages 9, 13, and 17 in reading, math, and science have improved in the range of 10 to 20 points over the last 25 years. The gap between Latino/a and White students, however, is still significant and persistent. The score difference in reading for 17-year-olds, for example, was 24 points, in mathematics it was 22 points, and in science it was 30 points. For 13-year-olds, the score difference in reading was 23 points, in mathematics it was 24 points, and in science it was 39 points. Resources matter as, for example, close to 28% of Latino/a and Black children in grades 1 through 12 reported having a computer in their household in 1998, compared to 70% of White children.

Another way to measure educational outputs is by examining the dropout (or push-out) rate defined as the percentage of 16- to 24-year-olds who are not in school and did not graduate from high school. In 1972 close to 21.3% of Latinos (compared to 12.3% of Blacks) were considered drop-outs and this number declined to 13.2% by 1990 (compared to 9% for Blacks). In the decade of the 1990s, Latino/a drop-out rates have remained at around 13%. The percent of Latino/a 16- to 24-year-olds who are not in school and did not graduate from high school differ significantly by birthplace and recency of migration. For Latino/a 16- to 24-year-olds born outside of the United States, the percentage is 44.2%; for those born in the United States with at least one parent born abroad, the rate lowers to 14.6%, whereas for Latinos born in the United States of U.S.-born parents the rate is 15.9%.

The high school completion rate for Latinos 18 to 24 years old that are not enrolled in high school has shown some improvements between 1972 (56.2%) and 1992 (62.1%) compared to Whites and Blacks in 1972 (86.0% and 72.1%, respectively) and 1992 (90.7% and 85.2%). But, by the year 2000, the graduation rate was still very low at 64.1% compared to 83.7% for Blacks and 91.8% for Whites. This means that over one third, or 35.9% of Latinos 18 to 24 years old, have not completed high school.

LATINOS AND HIGHER EDUCATION

Close to 7% of Scholastic Aptitude Test (SAT) takers in 1991 and 9% in 2001 were Latino/a. Whereas average SAT scores have remained the same at 451 in verbal and 458 in math for Mexicans and 460 in verbal and 465 in math for other Latinos, the scores of Puerto Ricans seem to have improved to 457 in verbal (or 21 points) and 451 in math (or 12 points). The gap between Whites and Latinos, however, remains significant, as the average scores for Whites also improved over the decade to 529 in verbal and 531 in math in 2001.

In 1999 there were close to 14.8 million persons enrolled in all 2-year and 4-year colleges and universities in the United States and 1.3 million were Latinos. Although enrollment in colleges and universities increased by 7% between 1990 and 1999, Latino/a enrollment rates increased by 68% from 782,449 in 1990 to 1.3 million in 1999. Enrollment in Hispanic Serving Institutions (HSI) increased by 14% to 1,398,687 students of which 587,720 were Latinos.

Close to 81% of all college students in 1980 were classified as White. By the year 2000, 68% of college students in 2000 were White: 64% of students in 2-year colleges and 71% of students in 4-year colleges. Although only 4% of college students in 1980 were Latino/a (6% of 2-year colleges and 3% of 4-year colleges) the number had increased to 10% by the year 2000 and Latinos were 14% of students in 2-year colleges and 7% of students in 4-year colleges.

If we examine college enrollment as a percentage of 18- to 24-year-olds, the data indicate that 39% of Whites were in college, 31% of Blacks, and 22% of Latinos (31% for U.S. citizen Latinos). The proportion of 18- to 24-year-old Latinos enrolled in college increased steadily throughout the 1990s. If we analyze enrollment as a percentage of 18- to 24-year-olds who have completed high school, we find that 44% of Whites were in college compared to 39% of Blacks and 36% of Latinos (and 43% for U.S. citizen Latinos) in that age group and with a high school degree.

Of the 1,237,875 bachelor's degrees conferred by U.S. universities in 2000, 74,963 (or 6.1%) went to Latinos, a 105% increase over the 36,612 Latino/a degrees in 1991. Latinos received 9.1% of the associate's degrees, 4.2% of the master's degrees, and 4.8% of first professional degrees. Of the 44,780 doctorate degrees awarded in the United States that year, Latino/a students received 1,291 (or 2.9%). Faculties at U.S. colleges and universities are still overwhelmingly White (85.6%) and 2.9% of faculty members in 1999 were Latinos. But, Latino/a college faculty were unevenly represented in the educational hierarchy with 4.8% of instructors reporting Latino/a origin and only 2.5% of associate professors and 1.8% of full professors.

The percentage of 25- to 29-year-olds that completed college among Latinos has remained at the 9 to 10% range since statistics were first complied in 1975, whereas the percentage for Whites and Blacks increased, respectively, from 24% and 11% in 1975 to 34% and 18% in 2000. The proportion of persons more than 25 years old in the United States with a bachelor's degree or more is 25.7%. The rate for Whites is 28.1%, 16.6% for Blacks, and 10.6% for Latinos, and the trend persists for master's, first professional, and doctorate degrees, where Whites are three times and Blacks almost two times more likely to have completed those degrees than Latinos.

LATINO/A CHILDREN AND AMERICA'S FUTURE

The increasing presence and visibility of Latino/a children throughout the United States provides the nation with an opportunity and a challenge. Latino/a enrollments in school are increasing, as are high school graduation, enrollment in college, and college graduation rates. But we also know that the graduation and educational attainment gaps between Latinos and other groups are significant, large, and persistent. As the articles in this volume suggest, improving the educational status of Latinos involves the students, their parents and families, changes in classroom practices and teacher involvement, improvements in school administration, increases in the levels and use of resources, changes in pedagogical practices, and a more sustained involvement of the school in the community and the community in the school.

Latino/a children and youth are there in numbers, but they are missing from planning, design, research, reporting, and policy on education and youth programs. We know a lot about what works for all children and what needs to be done to improve Latino/a education in particular.

We know that WIC works, that prenatal care works, that childhood immunization works, that preschool education and Head Start work, that compensatory education works, that early intervention for students with disabilities works, that home visits and daycare work, that parent training works, that graduation incentives work, that juvenile crime prevention works, that youth employment and training works, and that substance abuse programs work. But we still need to know much more about how to replicate best practices, how to build and maintain organizational networks that support education, and how better to reach and service the growing Latino/a community. As educators, it is essential that we continue to point out that a concerted effort and sustained involvement in Latino/a education is in the national interest and a necessary investment in the future of America.

REFERENCES

Llagas, C., & Snyder, T. D. (2003). *Status and trends in the education of Hispanics* (NCES2003-008). Washington, DC: U.S. Department of Education, National Center for Education Statistics.

7

Standards-Based Reform and the Latino/a Community: Opportunities for Advocacy

Raúl González[1]
National Council of La Raza

INTRODUCTION

Standards-based reform is now a central feature of the education policy landscape. However, few of the recommendations for implementing standards-based reform have looked specifically at the conditions that would make it an effective strategy for Latinos. This is the case even though the standards-based movement was founded on the recognition that economically disadvantaged and minority children lag behind their more affluent and White peers in most measures of educational well-being, particularly in achievement test scores, and that previous attempts at closing the achievement gap have failed.

Standards-based reform includes three major theoretical components. First, high standards will motivate students to improve their

---

[1] Raul González is legislative director with the National Council of La Raza (NCLR). Sonia M. Pérez, NCLR's Vice President for Research and Strategic Initiatives, provided substantive edits and oversaw preparation of this paper.

performance if they are challenged by rigorous academic courses. Second, assessments will be used to measure improvement and make important decisions about students. Third, this reform will lead to school system accountability by providing parents, policy makers, and advocates information about their local schools.

In this chapter, I examine how standards-based reform affects Latino/a students. First, I provide a brief background on the standards movement, including why the low educational status of Latino/a and other disadvantaged students provided impetus for reform. I also discuss recent policy developments and the impact they may have on the standards movement. I then describe some challenges to proper implementation of standards-based reform, as well as elements critical for successful implementation. Finally, I suggest a new lens through which educators and advocates may view strategies for improving the schooling of Latinos.

BACKGROUND

The Advent of Title I

The Elementary and Secondary Education Act (ESEA) is the federal law related to education in grades pre-kindergarten through 12. Because nearly every school district in the United States receives funding through ESEA programs, this legislation often sets the tone for state and local education reforms. Title I is the most significant section of the ESEA because it is the single largest source of federal funding for public schools.[2] The program has undergone several revisions since its creation in 1965 and has evolved into what is now recognized as standards-based reform.

The Title I program was created because poor children in this nation were not receiving educational opportunities equal to that of other children. Earlier versions of this program relied almost exclusively on providing additional resources to schools serving these students. Without real performance standards, however, these schools simply provided already low-performing students with remedial instruction. As a result, an environment of low expectations and poor results now

---

[2]Federal funding constitutes about 7% of all public school funding. The balance is provided through state and local budgets, and other sources.

pervades many schools attended by Latino/a, African American, and other economically disadvantaged students.[3]

The 1994 Reforms

In 1994, Congress passed the Goals 2000: Educate America Act (Goals 2000, P.L. 103–277) and the Improving America's Schools Act (IASA, P.L. 103–382) to encourage high standards at the state level. Passage of these laws was possible in part because of the belief that under the "old Title I," schools focused too much on providing basic services to disadvantaged students and that this strategy failed to close the achievement gap between these students and their more affluent peers (Citizens' Commission on Civil Rights, 1998). The "new Title I," contained in the IASA, was designed to encourage states to raise academic standards for all students, including English Language Learners (ELLs) and children with disabilities. Specifically, the IASA required states to show that they developed or adopted challenging standards and high-quality assessments. Furthermore, schools and school districts were to be held accountable for demonstrating that students in schools receiving Title I funds made progress as measured by the new assessments. For example, school districts and schools that did not make "adequate yearly progress" were subject to "corrective action" under that law.[4] The Goals 2000 program provided grants to states to assist them in developing their academic standards and student performance benchmarks.

Recent Policy Developments

In January 2002, President George W. Bush enacted the No Child Left Behind Act (NCLB), which provides further momentum to the standards movement. This legislation reauthorizes the ESEA and

---

[3]In its 1998 report, *Title I in Midstream: The Fight to Improve Schools for Poor Kids*, the Citizens' Commission on Civil Rights argues that Latino/a and other minority children often perform at low levels in part because of low standards and expectations set by schools they attend.

[4]As contained in the IASA, Adequate Yearly Progress (AYP) meant "continuous and substantial" school and district improvement as measured by student scores on performance assessments. Corrective action included withholding of funds and reconstitution of school and school district personnel. In the No Child Left Behind Act (NCLB), these definitions are largely unchanged. However, the corrective action provisions in the NCLB focus on improving specific areas of weakness related to a school's failure to improve outcomes for students.

encourages states and school districts not only to "stay the course" with standards-based reforms but also to intensify them through ambitious new requirements designed to close the achievement gap that exists between low-income, minority, and ELL students and their more affluent, White, and English-proficient peers. Achievement will be measured primarily by reading and mathematics assessments in grades 3 through 8. States and school districts are required to increase test score results for all students in these grades, but particularly for students at the low end of the test-score gap. The NCLB also requires states to increase the number of qualified teachers and to provide parents with information about the qualifications of teachers. Furthermore, the NCLB places a focus on improving the academic achievement and English proficiency of ELL students.

Although the NCLB increases the emphasis on testing, it does not represent a philosophical shift away from the IASA reforms. However, it does send a clear signal to the public schools that they will be held accountable for helping all students make academic progress. In addition, it devolves a great deal of decision making about implementation of this Act to the states. For example, whereas the NCLB provides an accountability framework based principally on testing, it allows state and local education agencies to use other measures to show that schools are helping students make academic progress.[5] However, the NCLB does not require states and school districts to use all of these other measures.

This element of the NCLB should be one of great interest for those who advocate on behalf of Latino/a students. The flexibility granted to state departments of education by the NCLB will largely determine how the legislation will be implemented. As the debate on the NCLB unfolded in Congress, proponents of increased flexibility argued that states should have the freedom to use federal funds for purposes they identify as important for their states (Rotherham, 1999; Shokraii Rees, 1999). Skeptics of this approach countered that scarce federal funds should be targeted to enhancing educational opportunities for economically disadvantaged students and those students at the low end of the test-score gap (Citizens' Commission, 1998). The compromise in the NCLB provides states with a set of requirements for academic

---

[5]Under the NCLB, AYP must be based on each state's academic standards and shall be measured primarily by the state assessments, and may include other measures, such as other assessments, grade retention, attendance rates, and participation in gifted and advanced courses. High schools must use graduation rates in describing how they meet AYP requirements.

outcomes, such as those noted earlier. The NCLB also provides states with a framework for providing disadvantaged students with a high-quality education, including a definition of what constitutes good testing practices.[6] As such, the NCLB contains what Congress and the Bush Administration have identified as the elements of good schooling.

However, the NCLB also gives states the flexibility to leverage the NCLB to improve the educational experiences of Latinos or simply to meet the basic requirements of the law. Thus, the advocacy challenge now moves from the federal level to the state and local levels. This means that advocates will have the opportunity to influence how the NCLB takes shape in local schools. The next section discusses challenges that advocates may face as they attempt to influence implementation of the NCLB.

IMPLEMENTATION OF STANDARDS-BASED REFORM IN LATINO/A COMMUNITIES: CHALLENGES EXIST

NCLB believes that standards-based reform can improve schooling for Latinos but only if policy makers and school administrators address serious challenges and ensure that the conditions necessary for success are in place. If the theory is applied properly, it holds promise, particularly if it provides greater access to learning opportunities, engenders richer learning environments, and encourages appropriate testing practices. However, simply raising the academic bar will not improve Latino/a student achievement. The assumption that higher standards will automatically lead to better academic outcomes ignores the realities faced by students, teachers, and others involved in the business of public education. In fact, many variables affect whether Latino/a and other students can meet higher academic standards—or whether teachers can adequately provide instruction and administrators can provide the basic elements that need to be in place to meet them.

As outlined here, inadequate learning opportunities and inappropriate use of assessments may pose barriers to proper implementation of standards-based reform as the authors of the NCLB envision it.

---

[6]The state tests required by the NCLB must be: aligned with state academic standards, valid and reliable for the purposes for which they are being used, consistent with nationally-recognized professional and technical standards, useful for diagnostic purposes (although not restricted to this use), and must allow for test data to be disaggregated by race, ethnicity, English proficiency, gender, migrant status, disability, and socioeconomic status.

Inadequate Learning Opportunities

Too often, Latino/a and other economically disadvantaged students do not receive sufficient opportunities to meet high expectations of performance and knowledge. Some of these barriers include:

Inequitable Funding of High-Poverty Schools

Students must be provided the quality of instruction, resources, and facilities necessary to meet the new standards. Unfortunately, these conditions exist in few school systems, and are especially rare in those with large low-income and minority populations. In fact, school districts with the largest concentration of economically disadvantaged students spend about $1,000 less per student, on average, than districts with few poor students (Education Trust Data Bulletin, 2001).

Little Access to Challenging Curricula

Latino/a and African American students are less likely than Whites to be placed in education tracks with rigorous curricula that adequately prepare them to meet performance and content standards and go on to college (Haycock, Jerald, & Huang, 2001). For example, about one in five Latino/a and African American eighth-grade students takes algebra, compared with more than one in four of their White peers (The Education Trust, 1998). Among 17-year-olds, only 8% of Hispanics and 4% of Blacks have taken precalculus or calculus, compared with 15% of Whites (National Center for Education Statistics, 2000). In Massachusetts, a state with a standards-based reform system in place, Latino/a students are seldom enrolled in math classes that place them on course to pass the math portion of that state's high school exit exam. For example, in 1999, only 37% of Latino/a students in the Boston school district were enrolled in "grade-level" math classes,[7] compared with 62% of White students (Upshur & Vega, 2001).

Poorly Trained or Unqualified Teachers

If students are to meet more challenging academic benchmarks, they must have access to high-quality instruction. Yet, minority students

---

[7]The term "grade-level" courses is used to describe those courses that would prepare students to take more advanced work later in their school careers. For example, students should take pre-algebra by eighth grade in order to be prepared for algebra in ninth grade and more advanced courses in higher grades.

are more likely than White students to be in schools with unqualified, often ineffective teachers. For example, about two thirds of Latino/a, African American, and Native American eighth-grade math students have teachers who do not have an undergraduate degree in mathematics, compared with half of all White students (Haycock, 1998).

Ineffective Parent Involvement Strategies

There is agreement that parent participation is important to ensure the success of reform efforts (Johnson, 1996). Given that Latino/a students are concentrated in low-performing schools that will be required to raise standards, Latino/a parents and communities should especially be included in the development of standards-based reforms. Unfortunately, there is not a good track record in this regard. In fact, although 96% of Americans with school-aged children believe that parents should be familiar with the academic standards in their children's schools, only 38% of Latino/a parents believe that schools are adequately providing this information (Council For Basic Education, 1998). Latinos and African Americans particularly believe that parents should be in a position to understand standards and hold schools accountable. For example, 83% of Latinos and 90% of African Americans strongly believe that parents should be able to compare local academic standards to national recommendations, compared with 74% of Americans overall (Council For Basic Education, 1998).

Inappropriate Use of Assessments

Tests are the principal method by which educators assess student knowledge and progress, and the standards-based reform movement clearly prescribes a significant role for tests. Proponents of large-scale testing argue that more rigorous exams will lead to more challenging curricula and will force schools to improve services to minority and economically disadvantaged students (Haycock, Jerald, & Huang, 2001). In addition, they believe that test results can provide data to parents, teachers, and policy makers showing whether or not schools are helping students improve academically (No Child Left Behind Blueprint). As noted earlier, the NCLB would require states and school districts to rely on tests to a greater extent than under the previous ESEA to measure whether or not students are meeting new standards.

Although there should be a role for assessments in school reform, skeptics of test-driven reforms believe that tests must be used appropriately and not be viewed as the sole measure of student achievement.[8] Advocates and educators are also concerned that the growing emphasis on high-stakes[9] tests is negatively affecting curriculum development and instructional freedom by shifting the focus of the education of students to simply helping them pass these exams (McNeil & Valenzuela, 2001).

In addition to general concerns with test design, such as validity and reliability, specific issues with assessments related to the education of Latinos include test inaccuracy, test misuse, and weakened instructional services. As state education departments and school districts plan to implement testing systems, advocates should urge them to consider these issues that can reduce the effectiveness of assessments in improving educational outcomes for Latinos.

Test Inaccuracy

Some standardized tests may not effectively assess student aptitude and achievement, especially those of ELLs. The National Research Council (NRC) indicates in a report on high-stakes testing that some test scores may be more directly linked to the quality of teacher instruction than to student ability (Heubert & Hauser, 1998). In the same report, the NRC found that ELLs are even more likely to receive inaccurate scores, concluding that "when students are not proficient in the language of assessment (in this case, English), their scores on a test will not accurately reflect their knowledge of the subject being assessed (except for a test that measures only English proficiency)." (Heubert & Hauser, 1998).

Inappropriate Educational Treatments

Test results can sometimes be used to make decisions about children which do more harm than good. For example, high-stakes testing often results in negative educational outcomes, such as increased grade retention and dropout rates (Clarke et al., 2000). These "educational treatments" are being made based on test results, even though the research

---

[8]See August 11, 2000, Letter from the Leadership Conference on Civil Rights to Norma V. Cantu, assistant secretary, Office for Civil Rights, U.S. Department of Education, providing comments on *The Use of Tests When Making High-Stakes Decisions for Students: A Resource Guide for Educators and policy makers.*

[9]High-stakes tests, including gatekeeping tests, result in significant consequences for students or for schools (e.g., tracking, grade promotion, and graduation are consequences for students, whereas financial rewards or loss of accreditation are consequences for schools).

shows that decisions such as tracking, grade promotion or retention, and graduation should not be made solely on the results of standardized tests (Heubert & Hauser, 1998). Educators must consider that low test scores for Latino/a, ELL, and other students may not be an accurate measure of a student's ability to master the curriculum, but may be directly tied to ineffective instruction or lack of proficiency in English. Moreover, Latinos are more likely than Whites to attend schools with inexperienced, ineffective teachers and less likely to have access to rigorous, properly aligned curricula. These factors may help to explain low Latino/a test scores, which may be misused to retain students in grade, deny them high school diplomas, or assign them to lower tracks or less rigorous education programs.

Watered-Down Curricula

"Overtesting" may actually water down curricula and place restrictions on pedagogy. Using a test to drive instruction involves teachers providing students with instruction related to information and concepts contained in tests, without using test questions. However, evidence is emerging that some schools are "teaching to the test,"[10] rather than providing students with the full range of the curriculum promised by standards-based reform proponents. In fact, this may be happening in schools with the lowest test scores, which means that students attending these schools are being denied access to the full curriculum. Many administrators, policy makers, and teachers are under enormous pressure to make sure that their students score well on exams. To achieve this, they are spending more class time on test preparation, at the expense of quality teaching and learning. As a result, although they may pass their exams, these students may not have the academic skills necessary to succeed in college (Kato, 1998).

IMPLEMENTATION OF STANDARDS-BASED REFORM IN LATINO/A COMMUNITIES: EIGHT ELEMENTS OF SUCCESS

There is support in the Latino/a community for setting high expectations within the context of a *comprehensive* approach to standards. Specifically, standards should be applied to everyone involved in the

---

[10] "Teaching to the test" refers here to focusing classroom instruction on the format, content, and style of a test, in order to achieve favorable results. This does not always result in mastery of skills, content, or analytical thinking.

education of children—not just imposed on students. School district administrators, principals, teachers, parents, and families, as well as students are responsible for all students' performances and outcomes. In order for standards-based reform to have a positive impact on Latino/a educational outcomes, educators and advocates should hold state- and local-level policy makers and administrators accountable for putting the following elements in place.

Equitable Resource Distribution

Prior to instituting a standards-based reform regime, policy makers must ensure that all children, especially disadvantaged students, are provided the resources necessary to receive a high-quality education and a meaningful opportunity to learn. This is especially true in states with large numbers of Latino/a students. Unfortunately, some states have failed to provide schools serving large numbers of poor and minority students with the funding needed to help students meet tougher state standards.[11] State funding formulas should not be developed in a vacuum. Instead, policy makers should consider that some students have been deprived of equitable opportunities for their entire school careers, which may explain why they are at the low end of the achievement gap. Thus, state funding formulas should be designed to provide extra assistance to schools serving these students.

Alignment of Curricula and Instruction
With Standards and Assessments

There must be consonance among the various elements of school reform. The curriculum must be aligned with the standards to ensure that students are prepared to meet higher performance benchmarks. Similarly, the assessments used to measure student performance must be aligned with the curriculum to ensure that they accurately measure student learning. Appropriate instructional materials must be available to all students who will be subjected to more challenging performance standards. For example, states with new science standards

---

[11] For example, see http://www.edlawcenter.org and http://www.cfequity.org for information on school finance equity litigation in New Jersey and New York, respectively. In both states, the implementation of standards-based reform led to favorable court decisions requiring a shift in state funding practices to provide increased funding to low-income school districts. The New York State case was overturned on June 25, 2002.

should ensure that all schools have properly equipped laboratories. Teachers also must be allowed the time and provided the resources to learn the new curriculum and adjust their pedagogy if necessary. Policy makers and administrators must provide adequate funding—and set aside time—for alignment of the standards-based reform components, as well as for professional development activities.

A High-Quality Teacher Corps

School administrators must provide the most needy students with the best instruction. Specifically, administrators must assign the most effective teachers to schools where low-income and minority students attend, particularly where there are large numbers of ELLs. Policy makers must provide incentives for those who teach in these schools, including equalizing urban and suburban teacher salaries, college loan forgiveness, and ongoing professional development and support. In addition, institutions that prepare teachers, especially teachers who will work in Latino/a-serving schools, should ensure that preservice preparation and in-service training evolve from the content standards dictated by reform. In this way, teachers will have the skills to teach the new curriculum to Latino/a students and make good use of test results.

Appropriate Test Use

Policy makers and administrators must understand that a test used to lead the curriculum or to hold schools accountable should not be used to make high-stakes decisions about students, and that a test of student mastery may not be appropriate for system accountability. Moreover, they should understand that test results might not always provide precise and conclusive evidence of student mastery (Heubert & Hauser, 1998). Thus, policy makers and administrators should ensure that tests are used only for the specific purpose for which they were designed.

Utilization of Multiple Measures of Student Performance for Making High-Stakes Decisions

Policy makers and administrators should devise state and district accountability systems that do not rely on a single test. Important decisions, such as grade retention and promotion, tracking, and graduation, should not be made solely on the basis of test results, but should take into account multiple sources of information about students, such as classroom grades, teacher and parental input, child development, and school attendance. Moreover, administrators must ensure that such decisions provide educational benefits for students. For instance, because grade retention has been shown to lead to dropping out of school, and Latinos are often retained in grade and drop out at a high rate, school leaders must be certain that high-stakes tests are used to reverse these trends rather than contribute to them (Heubert & Hauser, 1998).

Fair Treatment of Special Populations

School districts may have an incentive to exclude ELLs and children with disabilities from exams in an effort to inflate district- and school-level student test scores artificially. Therefore, policy makers and administrators should require that all students are included in assessments, including students in alternative and charter schools, and that reasonable accommodations are provided where necessary for students with special needs.

Supportive School Organization and Culture

Latino/a and other minority children often attend schools in which the environment itself is a barrier to learning. For example, in 1999, Latino/a and African American public high school students were more likely than White students to report that there were gangs in their schools and that they feared being attacked in school (National Center for Education Statistics, 2001). To give these students optimum chances to learn, policy makers and administrators should ensure that schools have enough physical space to accommodate all their students safely, including reducing school and class size, and the school culture should foster learning and demonstrate concern for students' well-being, including promoting respect for diversity and protecting students from discrimination (Schwartz, 1995).

Active Parent and Community Participation

Although most school reform advocates agree that parents and communities should be more involved in helping students improve test scores, school districts and schools have not done enough to ensure this. In tandem with a standards-based system, policy makers and administrators should provide information in a language that is easily understood by parents and community members explaining, at least

- Whether or not assessments are aligned with standards, curriculum, and pedagogy
- How test results will be used to improve instruction and learning
- Individual student scores
- School- and districtwide scores disaggregated by race, ethnicity, socioeconomic status, language status, gender, and migrant status
- How parents and community members can help improve student performance (Johnson, 1996).

Once this information is made available, educators and advocates must work with parents to fill other knowledge gaps about the school system and the NCLB. The NCLB creates a new Local Family Information Centers (LFICs) program that can help community-based organizations (CBOs) fill this role. The LFICs program would provide grants to CBOs that inform parents about important education issues, including state standards, assessments, and accountability mechanisms. The LFICs can, therefore, prepare parents to hold schools accountable for closing the achievement gap.

CONCLUSION: A NEW ADVOCACY STRATEGY

The sheer number of Latino/a students attending U.S. public schools demands attention to reforms that will improve their academic outcomes. The proportion of the student population that is Latino/a increased by 150% in the last 25 years (U.S. Census Bureau, 2000). In 1975, approximately three million Latinos were attending public schools, accounting for 6.7% of the kindergarten-through-grade-12 student population. By 1999, more than 7.5 million Latinos were enrolled in grades kindergarten through 12 in the public schools, accounting for 16.2% of all such students. Thus, a system cannot be deemed "successful" if it fails a large number of Latinos. In addition, because Latinos will represent a large proportion of the future workforce, our nation's ability to maintain our economy, homeland security, Social Security, and other government operations will be largely dependent on the quality of education available to Latinos.

Given that the NCLB will probably affect state and local policy options for the next decade, eliminating large-scale student assessments will not be an option for advocates.[12] However, the NCLB provides some leverage to ensure that schools do not ignore Latinos, requiring that student test scores are disaggregated by different student categories, including race, ethnicity, and English proficiency. Thus, schools will have to pay attention to these students because they will be part of their accountability "bottom line." The legislation also mandates state report cards that must provide information about schools, including student achievement data disaggregated by race, ethnicity, and English proficiency; the percentage of students not tested; high school graduation rates; and professional qualifications of teachers in the state. Although by no means an end-all solution, this type of information provides a vehicle for advocates to ask important questions about how standards-based reform is working in Latino/a-serving schools.

This does not mean that we should stop trying to mitigate the negative effects of testing. We must continue to investigate ways to minimize the negative impacts of high-stakes testing, including advocating for appropriate testing practices, such as encouraging the use of multiple measures and appropriate accommodations for ELL and special-needs students. Now that it appears that testing is here to stay, the question for Latino/a advocates is: Where do we go from here? In this section, we examine some of the advocacy opportunities presented by the NCLB and ways in which Latino/a researchers and advocates can influence implementation.

Advocacy Opportunities

Pursuing "Authentic Accountability"

With passage of the NCLB, proponents of test-driven accountability can claim some measure of victory. But how can advocates use tests to encourage accountability and improve achievement? The NCLB requires the school system to close the achievement gap through

---

[12]Before passage of the NCLB, advocates fought to end testing because of its harmful impacts on Latino/a and African American children. In Congress, Senator Paul Wellstone (D-MN) and Representative Bobby Scott (D-VA) introduced legislation in 2001 to ensure that federally mandated tests are used appropriately and do not harm students. Although this has helped focus the debate on how tests should be used, including describing how they can be misused in a way that increases grade retention and dropout rates, it is clear that testing will continue to be a reality in our schools.

disaggregated reporting of test results. If this is done right, it can be part of a comprehensive plan to close the gap. If it is not, then the places where it is going wrong can be identified. Researchers have demonstrated that some accountability systems can mask increased dropout rates (McNeil & Valenzuela, 2001). Advocates should use the reporting requirements required by the NCLB to praise the system if it works, and provide constructive criticism if it fails.

Closing School Finance Gaps

Court cases in New Jersey and New York have resulted in court-ordered remedies to close the "opportunity gaps" between rich and poor schools (Rebell, 1999). Standards-based reform in these states clarified for the courts what specific benchmarks students needed to reach in *every* school in the state. The courts were then able to specify the resources poor schools needed to help their students meet new academic standards. The reporting requirements in the NCLB, including those related to teacher quality, can help local advocates to identify where the "opportunity gaps" exist and to apply pressure to state and local school boards to close such gaps. In addition, advocates have leverage under the NCLB to pressure state- and district-level policy makers to target more funding to students, including ELLs, who may have the most difficulty meeting the academic benchmarks in the NCLB.

Enhancing Community Involvement

Underlying standards-based reform are the theories that students will meet higher benchmarks if they are challenged, and if they do not their parents will march into the schools and demand change. We understand that it is going to be a challenge to help some students to pass new standardized tests if they have never had a qualified teacher or a math textbook they could call their own. Clearly, some students are going to need extra tutoring, and parents will need to be prepared to use information about their children's schools to hold the system accountable. CBOs can help.

CBOs are the lifeblood of the Latino/a community. They provide culturally competent services, including academic enrichment, to Latinos in their own communities. Moreover, the community-based education sector acts as a safety net for Latino/a students. As the high Latino/a dropout rate makes clear, many Latinos are not receiving the services they need in the traditional public schools. These schools have failed to reach these students. Latino/a CBOs are currently providing education programming to thousands of Hispanic children who would otherwise leave the public school system altogether. Rather than competing with public schools, CBO-run programs can serve as models of innovation by offering small class sizes, curricula and instruction tailored to individual student needs, and effective parental involvement strategies.

Yet, many policy makers, school administrators, and public school advocates are unaware of the services provided by CBOs. Others are openly hostile to the idea of such groups providing education services. For Latino/a students and their parents, these CBOs can play an important role in achieving real education reform.

In addition, to think that the average parent can march into a school and connect the dots between state standards, state assessments, and Title I is fantasy. Parents need to get information from an accessible source that can help parents understand the complicated school system, particularly as it relates to the new requirements in the NCLB. CBOs can play a significant role in providing parents with the training they need to advocate on behalf of their children and to hold schools accountable for helping all children learn. They can help parents learn what questions to ask, such as why certain schools have good test scores but do not test certain children or why their school has such a high dropout rate.

Roles for Researchers and Advocates

Filling Important Research Gaps

As noted earlier, the NCLB places particular emphasis on raising the academic achievement of ELL students. The law does provide some guidance to educators, including a clear policy statement that schools will be held accountable for helping ELLs learn English and meet the same academic benchmarks as their English-proficient peers. However, the NCLB specifically—and the standards-based reform strategy in general—is missing certain key elements. For example, it is well known that there are problems concerning assessing ELLs and including them in accountability programs, but clear strategies for remedying these concerns are rarely even articulated, much less implemented. Thus, many ELLs are either inappropriately assessed or not tested at all. Latino/a researchers should seek answers to the critical questions of "What is the most effective method for assessing ELLs" and "When is it appropriate to use their test scores for system-wide accountability."

Answering these questions would give policy makers and the public schools the tools required to close the achievement gap.

Perhaps a more pernicious concern is "gaming" by schools, particularly in the design of accountability systems based on assessments. Such gaming includes deliberately increasing grade retention rates to provide some students with an extra year of test preparation, engaging in practices that "push out" students who may lower aggregate test scores, and mass exemptions of ELL students from assessment or accountability systems. For ELL students, gaming of the system creates the worst of both worlds—it masks low achievement by certain students and therefore undermines effective accountability, and often simultaneously inhibits effective instruction would help students meet more challenging standards. Researchers should "unmask" such gaming so that Latino/a parents and others can more effectively hold schools accountable.

Monitoring and Shaping NCLB Implementation

Educators, advocates, and policy makers should understand how they can shape implementation of the NCLB. Specifically, they should participate in the development of state education department plans to

- Serve ELL and other students at the low end of the test-score gap
- Recruit and place qualified teachers in schools serving these students
- Put in place assessment and accountability systems that are used to improve teaching and learning, not to punish students and teachers

In addition, the debate on the NCLB began during a period in which states began to experience budget shortfalls, after nearly a decade during which state coffers were relatively robust. The NCLB testing and accountability provisions require a significant investment not just in test development and administration, but also in teacher training, particularly as it relates to ELLs. Thus, it is unlikely that the public schools will meet the requirements of the NCLB unless Congress provides sufficient funding to implement the reforms contained in the legislation (National Council of La Raza, 2002).

Further, the NCLB includes provisions to enhance community involvement in school reform. For example, the NCLB requires states and school districts to create report cards showing whether or not students are making progress toward meeting state achievement standards. Educators and advocates should monitor these report cards and provide this information to parents and families of Latino/a students. In addition, the NCLB allows CBOs to provide after-school services under the 21st Century Community Learning Centers (21st Century) program.[13] Advocates should make sure that state departments of education give CBOs a fair portion of 21st Century funding.

Congress and the Bush Administration have raised the bar on standards-based reform. There is no question that the NCLB's testing and accountability requirements will affect public education for the next decade, and that this will pose challenges for educators and advocates concerned about equity for Latino/a students and families. However, the chief responsibility for implementing the NCLB lies with state education departments and local school districts. Although the NCLB is intended to close the achievement gap that exists between economically disadvantaged and minority children and their more affluent and nonminority peers, the legislation provides state and local education agencies with a degree of latitude regarding how they will attempt to close the gap. Thus, the advocacy challenge has moved to a large degree from the U.S. Congress to state capitols and local school boards. That is where Latino/a researchers and advocates must focus a greater degree of their attention. And that is why the National Council of La Raza (NCLR) intends to work with the National Latino/a Education Research and Policy Project to perform research in schools and Latino/a communities to answer the critical questions that will help Latino/a advocates and parents become well-informed participants in the effort to improve the schooling of Latino/a children.

REFERENCES

The Citizens' Commission on Civil Rights (1998). *Title I in midstream: The fight to improve schools for poor kids*. Washington, DC.

Clarke, M. Haney, W., & Madaus, G. (2000, January). *High stakes testing and high school competition*. Chestnut Hill, MA: The National Board on Educational Testing and Public Policy, Boston College.

Council for Basic Education (1998). *Findings from the council for basic education's national poll of public attitudes toward rigorous academic standards*, Washington, DC.

---

[13]The 21st Century program provides funds to states for after-school services. States then grant funds to school districts and CBOs that provide these services.

The Education Trust (1998). *Education watch: The education trust 1998 state and national data book.* Washington, DC.

Education Trust Data Bulletin (2001, May 6). *The other gap: Poor students receive fewer dollars.* Washington, DC: The Education Trust.

Haycock, K. (1998). *Thinking K-16: Good teaching matters a lot.* Washington, DC: The Education Trust.

Haycock, K., Jerald, C., & Huang, S. (2001, Spring). *Thinking K-16, closing the gap: Done in a decade.* Washington, DC: The Education Trust.

Heubert, J. P., & Hauser, R. M. (1998). *High stakes: Testing for tracking, promotion, and graduation.* National Research Council. Washington, DC: National Academy Press.

Johnson, J. (1996). Assessment as a tool for improving student achievement, Support for Texas Academic Renewal (STAR) Center at the Charles A. Dana Center Web site. http://www.starcenter.org/articles/assessment.html.

Kato, B. (1998, September). Testing focus distorts teaching. *Catalyst.*

McGinn, D. et al. (1999, September 6). The big score. *Newsweek.*

McNeil, L., & Valenzuela, A. (2001). The harmful impact of the TAAS system of testing in Texas: Beneath the accountability rhetoric. In Gary Orfield & Mindy L. Kornhaber (Eds.), *Raising standards or raising barriers? Inequality and high-stakes testing in public education.* Washington, DC: Century Foundation Press.

National Center for Education Statistics (2000, August). *NAEP 1999 trends in academic progress: Three decades of student performance.* Washington, DC: U.S. Department of Education.

National Center for Education Statistics (2001). *Indicators of school crime and safety: 2001.* Washington, DC: U.S. Department of Education.

National Council of La Raza (2002, March). *Analysis of president' FY 2003 budget plan.* Washington, DC.

No Child Left Behind Blueprint. U.S. Department of Education Web site: http://www.ed.gov/offices/OESE/esea/nclb/part3.html.

Rebell, M. (1999, Fall). *Blueprint for better schools.* New York: Campaign for Fiscal Equity.

Rotherham, A. (1999, April). *Toward performance-based federal education funding: Reauthorization of the elementary and secondary education act.* Washington, DC: Progressive Policy Institute.

Schwartz, W. (1995). *Opportunity to learn standards: Their impact on urban students.* Washington, DC: U.S. Department of Education, ERIC/CUE Digest No. 110, ERIC Clearinghouse on Urban Education.

Shokraii Rees, N. (1999, June). *Accountability + freedom = straight A's.* Washington, DC: Heritage Foundation.

Upshur, C., & Vega, R. (2001, Summer). *New study finds few Latinos prepared for MCAS, The Gaston Institute Report.* Boston: The Gaston Institute.

U.S. Census Bureau (2000, October). *Enrollment status of the population 3 years old and over, by age, gender, race, Hispanic origin, nativity, and selected educational characteristics.* Washington, DC.

8

Student Learning and Assessment: Setting an Agenda

Robert Rueda
University of Southern California

INTRODUCTION

Hardly a day goes by when a public figure does not call out for greater accountability for public schools. Office-holders and office-seekers, from both inside and outside of education, are likely to mention the improvement of public education as part of their agenda. Most recently, this concern with education and improving public schools, the education reform agenda, has almost become synonymous with large-scale and high-stakes assessment especially as embodied in the No Child Left Behind Act of 2001 (H.R.1). Significantly, one of the four "pillars" of this national education reform blueprint is accountability and testing (the others include flexibility and local control, funding for what works, and expanded parental options). This legislation, in which accountability plays a major role, represents a comprehensive overhaul of existing federal law (Elementary and Secondary Education Act enacted in 1965 and the Improving America's Schools Act of 1995) and is the principal federal law affecting K–12 education today. Among the accountability features of the new legislation are stringent requirements for states including:

1. States must develop "adequate yearly progress" (AYP) statewide measurable objectives for improved achievement for all students and for specific groups: economically disadvantaged students, students from major racial and ethnic groups, students with disabilities, and students with limited English proficiency

2. The objectives must be set with the goal of having all students at the "proficient" level or above within 12 years (i.e., by the end of the 2013–2014 school year)

3. AYP must be based primarily on state assessments but also must include an additional academic indicator

4. The AYP objectives must be assessed at the school level. At the end of 2 years, schools that have failed to meet their AY objective for 2 consecutive years will be identified for improvement

5. School AYP results must be reported separately for each group of students identified above so that it can be determined whether each group of students met the AYP objective

6. At least 95% of each group must participate in state assessments

A related stipulation of this legislation is that states establish performance standards for their tests. As Linn, Baker, and Betebenner (2002) note, some states set high standards not knowing that these would be used to determine AYP objectives. Moreover, virtually no state is close to meeting the goals being set, and in many cases it is not realistic to expect that states will be able to meet the standards. Although this is problematic for all states, it is especially troublesome for states with large numbers of Latino/a students where finding appropriate assessments is challenging and where the mechanisms for impacting student progress are not well conceived or implemented.

Arguments against accountability are tantamount to speaking out against motherhood or the flag. Yet, although this focus on improving schools and learning is commendable, it does have critical ramifications for Latino/a students. One, for example, is the use of English-only standardized assessments where significant consequences are attached either to students themselves, their teachers, their schools, or their districts. Although recent syntheses on teaching and learning have

suggested the importance of culture and language in the learning process, for the most part this has not translated into the current debates
or implementation of assessment (American Psychological Association
Board of Educational Affairs, 1995; Bransford, Brown, & Cocking, 1999;
Donovan, Bransford, & Pellegrino, 1999; Lambert & McCombs, 1998).
Another problematic issue in the current move toward accountability is holding students accountable to standards without also taking
into account opportunity to learn (Clare Matsumura, Garnier, Pascal,
& Valdes, 2002) or providing mechanisms to address low performance
other than economic or other sanctions.

Although the use of high-stakes large-scale assessment for school accountability is not new, the current emphasis on their widespread use is.
This increasing emphasis is arguably the most visible manifestation of
assessment concerns that have both potential and actual ramifications
for Latino/a students. However, there are other areas that, although
less visible in current public discussions, have particular importance
for Latino/a students, especially those who are English learners. One
area has a longer history, yet still continues to be an area of concern:
assessment for special education placement. Another area is the use
of testing and assessment processes related to entrance into postsecondary educational institutions. This chapter will examine the issues
surrounding each of these areas, and try to provide suggestions related
to formulating a research agenda that addresses them. First a bit of background on each of these areas will be provided, outlining the issues,
and then a discussion of how these translate into areas of concern for a
research agenda will be provided. The purpose here is not to provide a
definitive review of each area, but to provide a brief review of key issues
in each domain and how they hold particular importance for Latinos.

LARGE-SCALE HIGH-STAKES
ACCOUNTABILITY MEASURES

One important component of the effort to reform schools is the use of
rigorous learning standards for all students (Lachat, 1994). The basic
idea is that standards should be public, clear, and hold high expectations for students, serving as a key tool to improve schools and student
outcomes (National Council on Education Standards and Testing, 1992;
National Education Goals Panel, 1993). A majority of states are tying
state-mandated testing programs to new or revised state curriculum
standards. Moreover, 48 states have statewide assessment programs,

and almost all report making revisions in their state tests to align them more closely with specific state standards (Education Week, 2000).

The new federal education legislation just passed also includes new requirements for states and school districts in terms of demonstrating student achievement. Annual testing based on state standards in reading and mathematics will be required for all students in grades 3 through 8. Increasingly, these test results are tied to significant consequences. As of 1996, for example, at least 23 states reported connecting explicit consequences to state test results, such as funding cuts, warnings, mandatory assistance from outside experts, loss of accreditation, or state takeover (Bond, Roeber, & Braskamp, 1996). Similarly, the new federal education legislation permits parents to transfer students in failing schools to successful public or charter schools.

In the best of circumstances, these standards should serve as tools of equity and excellence, assuring that every stakeholder concerned with the educational process is working toward the same worthwhile goals while serving as a guide for what should be taught, how progress should be monitored, and what should be assessed. Under these ideal conditions, the tracking and placement of certain groups of students such as poor or non-English speaking students would decrease or disappear. However, there are many problems, both real and potential, that serve to diminish the promise of these otherwise commendable goals. Urban schools, that have disproportionate numbers of students from low SES and diverse cultural and linguistic backgrounds, have disproportionately felt the negative impacts of testing policies (Darling-Hammond, 1994).

As one example, Buly and Valencia (2002) conducted a study in Washington State that looked at students who failed the state reading assessment. She found that whereas English Language Learners represented 11% of the population taking the test, they represented 43% of those students who failed the test. Likewise, although low SES students represented 47% of those taking the test, they represented 67% of those who failed. More important, she did an analysis of the patterns of performance of those who failed, and was able to distinguish clusters of students based on error profiles. For example, "automatic word callers" were able to identify words fluently, but did not understand what they read, whereas "slow comprehenders" could identify words and understood them but were not fluent. As Valencia noted, each of the various subgroups identified would require different instructional interventions to perform better. Valencia concluded that scores on state assessments mask important group and individual differences, and may be especially problematic with poor and non-English proficient students. Normally, only summative scores are attended to for accountability purposes, while the types of detailed analyses more useful for instructional purposes are ignored.

Some of the criticisms and problems are not directly focused on Latino/a students per se but affect them nevertheless. For example some have argued that many state-mandated tests emphasize obscure knowledge of isolated facts or vocabulary, which then has the effect of forcing teachers to narrow the curriculum and deemphasize higher-order critical thinking skills (McNeil, 2000; Yeh, 2001). Yet as Darling-Hammond has noted, this is particularly apt to take place in urban schools populated by Latino/a and other students of diverse backgrounds (Darling-Hammond, 1995).

Others have noted that tests should not be used to gauge innate ability or make inferences about potential academic success under conditions of unequal opportunity to learn. Many poor Latino/a students and other students of color are exposed to less challenging curricula, have less access to resources, less high-quality instruction, and have a higher likelihood of being in unsafe or unsupportive school environments (Darling-Hammond, 1994; Nettles & Nettles, 1995).

Other areas of concern related to standards and high-stakes tests include the following:

- Standards may not include or address the needs of all students such as English learners
- In the development of tests and assessment indicators, provisions may not be made for English learners or students from diverse cultural backgrounds, so that the tests become de facto language test or test of cultural familiarity
- There may be no alignment between state or district standards and assessment methods, so that assessments do not provide a true picture of what was learned. In high-stakes situations, the consequences for low performance may be significant. In this context, high-stakes situations are those educational contexts where student performance is related to long-term, real-life consequences such as placement in special education, graduation from high school, college entrance, and so on.
- Assessments may be too narrowly focused and restrict curriculum, especially for groups that traditionally score low
- Test results are increasingly tied to rewards and punishments, resulting in a situation where some students or groups (traditional

"low achievers") are less valued—one potential outcome is that the neediest schools are staffed by the least qualified teachers

- Assessments may be used only for accountability purposes, but not used to improve instruction or in the reallocation of resources
- Political considerations become the driving force in the development and implementation of standards and assessment. (Smith, Heinecke, & Noble, 1999).

It has been convincingly argued that most current assessments are not designed to capture the full range of what English language learners know and much of what they are able to do (LaCelle-Peterson & Rivera, 1994). There have been various attempts to deal with this shortcoming. One approach, the default position, has been to simply exclude students who do not speak English from tests. For those interested in accountability issues and monitoring students' performance over time, however, this is not satisfactory, as it excludes these students from the same expectations and challenges of high standards of other students. As an example, one study in 1994 found that of the 48 states responding, 44 permitted exemptions for English language learners. The reasons varied from recent arrival status (usually from 1 to 3 years), teacher recommendation, and even participation in an ESL program, although this situation has begun to change (Olson & Goldstein, 1997).

Another approach has been to use test accommodations, or modifications in test administration procedures. Butler and Stevens described a taxonomy of test accommodations that fall into two categories: modifications of the test (use of native language, text change in vocabulary, change in linguistic complexity, use of visual supports, glossaries, dictionaries) and modifications of the procedure (extra time, breaks, administration over several sessions, directions given in native language, and so on) (Butler & Stevens, 1997b). They further point out that the use of accommodations is complex and argue the need to match assessment accommodations to the specific characteristics of individual students or subpopulations. Although this body of work is not large, it does suggest caution against blanket statements about the general effectiveness or lack of effectiveness of a particular form of accommodation for any individual or subgroup (Abedi, Lord, & Hofstetter, 1998).

Still another approach is the use of the native language in assessment, either through the development of parallel assessments or translating existing English assessments. Some critics have pointed out that the issue of equivalency of item difficulty is problematic, and this approach may interact differentially with the language in which the child has been instructed (Figueroa, 1990). One complication is that English-language learner status is not a single entity (LaCelle-Peterson & Rivera, 1994; Valdes & Figueroa, 1994).

Butler and Stevens proposed a comprehensive framework for unpacking some of the variability surrounding English learners, including variables related to the home, community, school, educational background, language factors, and personal characteristics (Butler & Stevens, 1997a). In addition, they stressed the need to consider three critical background variables that impact performance and should be considered in thinking about accommodations: academic English language proficiency (see Bailey, in press, for an excellent discussion of this issue), prior education, and length of time in the United States. At present, there is a lack of information related to high stakes assessment with Latino/a students and this is clearly an important priority given the importance that such assessment has come to play in the national education agenda. Current standardized assessments are heavily loaded with academic English language proficiency but ignore the other dimensions noted by Butler and Stevens.

SPECIAL EDUCATION ASSESSMENT

One consequence of low academic achievement and low test scores, especially at the early grades, is referral for special education placement or remedial programs. There are a whole set of assessment issues that accompany this area, the most prominent being the role of ability testing and the problem of overrepresentation in certain categories for certain subgroups of the general population, in particular African American and Latino/a students (for a comprehensive review of the assessment issues involved, especially involving the use of IQ tests, see Valencia & Suzuki, 2001). This disproportional representation issue will be briefly discussed later.

The issue of disproportionate representation of minority students in special education has haunted the education field for almost 35 years. An early study by Mercer (1973) documented disproportionate representation in classes for students with mild retardation (educable mentally retarded [EMR]) and raised other issues regarding biased assessment and placement practices. These practices included, for example, inappropriate testing in English of students not proficient in the language, use of on-the-spot translations, and inappropriate norms that did not include representative samples.

A short time later the National Academy of Sciences convened a panel on this issue of overrepresentation of minority students in special education. The ensuing report reaffirmed earlier placement patterns and criticisms of existing assessment and placement practices (Heller, Holtzman, & Messick, 1982). As part of the panel's work, a review of the available Office for Civil Rights (OCR) data found that minority students were overrepresented in classes for the mentally retarded (EMR and trainable mentally retarded [TMR]) as well as in classes for the emotionally disturbed (Finn, 1982). These analyses documented effects for district size and size of minority enrollment, and disproportionate representation rates were found to be related to the presence or absence of bilingual programs. A major recommendation of the panel was to deemphasize individual differences in achievement and to focus more on assessing the validity of instructional settings. Importantly, the panel also recommended greater attention to assessing problems before a child accumulates a long history of failure and before formal testing for special education diagnosis.

There have been many changes since these early reports, but in many ways things have not changed much at all. There have been significant legal battles fought over these issues; there have been significant changes to education law; there have been significant changes in demographics in many school districts and states; there have been significant educational initiatives such as the school reform movement and the current emphasis on reading (Rueda, Artiles, Salazar, & Higareda, 2002).

Unfortunately, there are indications that disproportionate representation, especially in the "judgmental" categories of special education, remains a problem.[1] Because of the continuing nature of this problem, more recently a second panel from the National Academy of Science was convened on this same issue (Donovan & Cross, 2002). This just-released report found that at the national level, whereas 5% of Asian students are identified for special education, the rate for Hispanics is

---

[1]Generally the disability categories involved include mild mental retardation, emotional/behavioral disorders, and specific learning disabilities. Usually, the defining characteristic of students with these labels includes low academic performance and/or atypical social behavior. These categories are called "judgmental" because students appear normal in most arenas outside of classroom and test situations in contrast to more severe disabilities where students manifest identifiable characteristics such as with Down syndrome, autism, deafness, and so on.

11%, for Whites, 12%, for American Indians 13%, and for Blacks over 14%. More specifically, Black students are overrepresented in the category of mental retardation and emotional disturbance, and underrepresented in gifted and talented programs, and

- the greatest disproportion is in MR, where Black children are more than twice as likely as all other students to be assigned. About 2.6% of all Black children are identified as MR.
- about 1.5% of Black students are labeled ED—about twice the rate for all other students.
- although about 6% of all students are labeled gifted and talented, only 3% of Black students are so labeled.

The report also found that while Hispanic students were not overrepresented in the categories of mental retardation or emotional disturbance, they were underrepresented in gifted and talented programs. More specifically, only about 3.5% of Hispanic students are placed in gifted programs, about half the rate for White students.

American Indian/Alaskan Native students were overrepresented in the learning disabilities category—(White, Hispanic, and Black student placement rates hover between 6 and 6.5%, whereas American Indians are at almost 7.5%) and underrepresented in gifted and talented programs, with just under 5% placed. In contrast, Asian students are about half as likely as other students to be labeled as students with mental retardation, and about a third as likely to be labeled as students with emotional disturbance or learning disabilities. Yet almost 10% of Asian students are placed in gifted and talented programs; this is three times the rate for Blacks and Hispanics, and a 30% higher rate than for White students.

Like its predecessor, this report recommended that assessment focus on features of the context rather than simply the individual, including prior educational history, quality of instructional environments, access to resources, teacher quality, and so on. In addition, the report suggested much greater emphasis on early intervention, trying to identify problems way before a formal referral is necessary, and providing ample additional instructional help, especially in early reading. Significantly, the report went on to recommend that special education eligibility should be determined on the basis of resistance to high-quality interventions rather than to performance on arbitrary tests. Specifically, it recommended that an IQ-achievement discrepancy should be eliminated as a requirement for determining that a child has a learning disability, thus eliminating one of the major uses of IQ tests in the eligibility determination process, and proposed noncategorical classifications that focus on matching a student's specific needs to an intervention strategy, thus removing the need for traditional labels.

Although on the surface these developments may seem positive, there are still significant imbalances in special education placements, as the national data indicate. Although the specific patterns and categories may have changed over time, the major issue is that the consistency and systematic nature of disproportionate representation is reason for concern and these are not random patterns.

Somewhat more troubling is that there are some data that suggest that when more local analyses are done, the problem of disproportionate representation may be more significant than the nationally aggregated data would suggest (Oswald, Coutinho, Best, & Singh, 1999). For example, the size of a school district and of the special education programs as well as the size of the representation of the ethnic group in the district can also shape the problem (Artiles & Trent, 2000; Reschly, 1997). The need for disaggregated data is evidence that one potential result of English-only mandates may be related to increased rates of special education placement for English learner and immigrant students (Artiles, Rueda, Salazar, & Higareda, 2000).

Although the call to focus on intervention (especially reading) rather than just type of special education placement or label is commendable, little of the intervention research in the area of reading has "unpacked" variables such as language proficiency—little is known about reading acquisition for ELL students (Garcia, 2000). The call to focus on reading instruction as an answer may ignore the critical distinction between reading and literacy, focusing on reading without equal concern for the wider issue of literacy (Rueda & McIntyre, 2002). As is noted in this chapter, while the focus on instruction and intervention is a good one, other developments threaten to become problematic issues, including the standardization of instruction and materials, and universality of approaches—all three of these issues translate quite easily into problems which have major implications for the domain of assessment. Although some have pointed to alternative assessment procedures such as performance-based assessment as a potential solution to some of these long-standing issues, some have wisely cautioned that alternative procedures are not inherently equitable, and caution must be taken regarding how and why they are used (Darling-Hammond, 1996).

TESTING AS A GATEKEEPER
FOR HIGHER EDUCATION

The effects of problematic assessment procedures do not stop in the early elementary years. In fact, the issues related to tests and assessment may have a significant impact on student careers much further down the academic pipeline. For example, although Latino/a students have made some gains in postsecondary education over the past half century, helped in part by tools such as affirmative action, there are still wide discrepancies among various groups in terms of access to higher education (Garcia, 2001). Just over one million Hispanic students were enrolled in institutions of higher education in 1998, twice as many as a decade earlier (National Center for Educational Statistics, 1998). Still, Latino/a students are half as likely to graduate from college as White students (National Center for Educational Statistics, 1995). Whereas a variety of factors have been examined with respect to this problem, assessment (especially entrance exams such as the SAT taken during students' high school years) has been a key factor. These high-stakes tests are normally taken during the later years of students' K–12 school careers. Entrance exams have become increasingly important with the withering support for affirmative action programs and policies (Bowen & Bok, 1998). Specifically, they play an increasingly large gatekeeping role, particularly in key states such as California and Texas.

Although a complete treatment of the complex issues surrounding affirmative action and the role of standardized entrance exams in relation to access to higher education is beyond the scope of this chapter, a recent study is informative (see Garcia, 2001, for a more comprehensive review of the issues). The study in question was conducted in California, a state that is heavily Latino/a and also the location of the first major rollback of affirmative action in postsecondary education. This was spurred by the passage of Proposition 209 in the state, which eliminated the consideration of race, ethnicity, and gender in public employment, public contracting, and education. The University of California system approved policies consistent with this mandate that went into effect in the spring quarter of 1997–1998.

Koretz, Russell, Shin, Horn, and Shasby recently conducted a study that focused on this major university system to explore how eliminating affirmative action in college admissions affects the diversity of admitted students (Koretz, Russell, Shin, Horn, & Shasby, 2002). The study sought to compare the effects of changing admissions from a period before the affirmative action ban to the race-neutral admissions policy later put into force. Although the study was complex and addressed a number of related issues, one finding was that admissions processes that were race-neutral and relied solely on SAT and GPA had major effects at the most selective campuses in the University of California system, although the effects were smaller at the less selective campuses. Importantly, none of the alternative admissions models that were analyzed in the study could replicate the composition of the student population that existed in the system prior to the elimination of affirmative action.

As access to higher education becomes increasingly test-dependent, it is critical that considerations of fairness and equity be taken into account and that close monitoring of both access to and graduation from quality institutions of higher education be monitored. Whereas concerns about fairness and equity are commonly cited when considering high-stakes tests for students in the early grades, it is equally important at the other end of the educational continuum. Especially critical is the secondary school period of a student's career, because course-taking, counseling, test preparation, and other factors are related to later outcomes.

CONCLUSION

Although the current focus on education is a positive development, it has often led to a desire for quick fixes that are unrealistic and without promise for meaningful change. With respect to low achievement, for example, some common responses have included

- a market-driven approach with an emphasis on privatization;
- standardization of (and often mandated) curricula, instructional materials, teaching approaches;
- retention;
- remedial programs, either supplementing or replacing ongoing programs;
- accountability, often operationalized by single measure high-stakes standardized tests.

Accountability is one of the key elements of the recently passed federal blueprint for school reform. Yet, the time frame producing results is increasingly short and the consequences are increasingly punitive. This is of great concern for students who are English learners.

The No Child Left Behind Act is remarkable in its single-minded call that limited English proficient students receive English-only instruction and in the failure to promote bilingual education or primary language development as equally viable instructional approaches to support the development of English language and content skills with limited English proficient students. If students are to be held accountable to challenging standards, they must be given appropriate opportunity to master the standards.

Recently, researchers have begun to call for balance in the context of instruction, particularly in the areas of reading and literacy. Policies that mandate a single approach to instruction have caused concern in this respect. For example, Pearson and Raphael have called for balance in the following areas (Pearson & Raphael, 1999):

- Authenticity—the balance between doing school-like activities versus those with some connection to everyday life
- Classroom Discourse—the balance between adult versus child control over topics and turn taking
- Teachers' Roles—the balance between the amount of teacher control over student activity on a continuum from explicit instruction to co-participating
- Curricular Control—the balance between local control and external control over what is taught

The discussion in this chapter of some of the assessment issues of importance to Latinos suggests that a similar call for balance can be applied to assessment. What are some of the dimensions of assessment that might need to be considered? A preliminary list of such considerations is presented here.

Achievement and Ability Versus Opportunity to Learn

There is some controversy about the distinction between achievement and ability tests. In general, ability tests give information about what one has learned measured at this point in time, whereas ability tests try to assess the underlying psychological aptitudes that are considered to be more stable and predictive of performance in the future.

An example of the latter would be IQ tests. However, most large-scale standardized tests used for accountability purposes are usually ability tests. Although these may be useful for comparative purposes, that is, to differentiate one student from another along one or more dimensions, they typically do not provide information about opportunity to learn. Opportunity to learn can be defined as a range of variables likely to influence student performance, including access to resources, access to high-quality instructional content and processes, extra-school opportunities, and direct preparation for the test being administered (Herman, Wakai, Wakai, & Heath, 1997). It is increasingly clear that without information on opportunity to learn, it is difficult to interpret the performance of students of diverse backgrounds and make comparisons. An important area to consider in the future will be taking opportunity to learn issues into account in the design and interpretation of assessment instruments and also addressing opportunity to learn as a worthwhile issue in its own right.

Reading Versus Literacy

Consistent with a recent major report on reading from the National Research Council (Snow, Burns, & Griffin, 1998), this chapter points to the need to differentiate reading and literacy. The former focuses on the individual psychological processes involved in decoding and comprehending text, or "... the use of the products and principles of the writing system to get at the meaning of a written text" (Snow et al., 1998, p. 42). Literacy, however, includes reading, but also focuses more broadly not only on the act of reading but on the beliefs, attitudes, and social practices that literate individuals and social groups engage in a variety of settings and situations, including those involving technology (Pearson & Raphael, 1999). Although the underlying individual cognitive processes underlying decoding text may be more universal in nature, the social practices underlying various types of literacy are more culturally bound. It is the combination of both that defines the adult who uses the tools of reading and writing in sophisticated ways. With respect to assessment, it is important to assess both dimensions to assure that not only basic skills are mastered, but that the actual uses of literacy in school and beyond are appropriately developed. The complex social and cognitive processes underlying the uses of literacy in everyday life are just as critical as basic skills and facts, and future assessments should focus on both dimensions.

Participation Versus Accuracy

There is currently much debate over how to treat students of diverse abilities and languages on large-scale high-stakes assessments. As noted earlier in this chapter, early approaches followed the strategy of simply excluding particular groups of students such as non-English speakers. However, because this strategy also reduces the degree to which such students can be monitored in terms of educational outcomes, more focus has shifted to accommodations in testing. Researchers at the Center for Research on Educational Standards and Student Testing (CRESST) at the University of California at Los Angeles have done especially useful work in this regard. However, as some (Shepard, 2001) have noted, there is a great deal of inconsistency in terms of how different states deal with these accommodations More-over, as Shepard (2001) notes, there is some question regarding this work in terms of the balance between participation and accuracy. That is, whereas it is important that particular subgroups of students not be excluded (and, thus, schools not be held responsible for their outcomes), there is also a need that assessments provide accurate information. For students who do not speak the language, for example, the assessment becomes a de facto language assessment in spite of what the test purports to measure. This is an issue that will have to be closely monitored as accountability measures become attached to higher and higher consequences.

Accountability Versus Instruction

Whereas the thrust of new federal legislation and various state initiatives focus on accountability issues, there is a trade-off in terms of a focus on assessment as a tool to inform teaching. Large-scale accountability measures are not designed to directly inform day-to-day instruction, and they are not used by teachers in this way (except where they drive teach-to-the-test practices). However, good instruction is informed by constant assessment and monitoring which is used to modify instruction. Teachers need to be supported with professional development activities that inform them of new developments in classroom-based techniques such as performance assessments and other means to improve their teaching. In the rush to focus on large-scale accountability measures, budgets need to be examined to assure that teachers are supported with assessment more closely linked to instructional activities.

Single Versus Multiple Indicators

Whereas public discourse regarding accountability primarily focuses on accountability *measures*, assessment specialists are increasingly talking about accountability *systems*. The idea is that because of various sources of error, no single measure is a good index of performance. Rather, an integrated system of related measures is more likely to provide a more accurate and complete account of performance. This is especially critical for Latino/a populations, where measures are much more likely to occur because of the interplay of language, culture, and socioeconomic factors with specific test characteristics. Especially critical will be the means to hold the accountability systems *themselves* accountable. Baker, Linn, Herman, and Koretz (2002) have developed a comprehensive set of Standards for Educational Accountability Systems that address five domains, including system components, testing standards, stakes, public reporting formats, and evaluation. Among the selected items of concern to this chapter are the following:

- Accountability expectations should be made public and understandable to all participants in the system
- Accountability systems should employ different types of data from multiple sources
- Accountability systems should include the performance of all students, including subgroups that historically have been difficult to assess
- Decisions about individual students should not be made on the basis of a single test
- If tests are to help improve system performance, there should be information provided to document that test results are modifiable by quality instruction and student effort
- If test data are used as a basis of rewards or sanctions, evidence of technical quality of the measures and error rates associated with misclassification of individuals or institutions should be published
- Evidence of test validity for students with different language backgrounds should be made publicly available

What are some previously ignored dimensions that require attention in the future? Past assessment has tended to focus assessments entirely on the individual student at a single point in time. There is a fundamental rule in assessment that is often overlooked—when students are being compared and inferences made about ability or potential, *comparisons are only valid when they have had equal opportunity to learn the material and acquire the skills covered in the test.* What other aspects are relevant to assessment if we broaden our focus beyond the individual? The following dimensions remain largely unexamined in current assessment work.

Opportunity to Learn

What is the nature of present and past instructional environments and social mediation have students had access to? What is the quality, type, amount, and range of school-like and non-school-like literacy activities and artifacts students have had access to?

Sociocultural Context

What is the social organization of learning settings and features of important social contexts in students lives, including materials, activities, and people?

Sociopolitical Considerations

What are the local dynamics in terms of past and current power (economic, political) relationships among various groups in specific communities and schools? How are these embedded in important social institutions such as schools and classrooms? How are these perceived and experienced by individual students and their families? How do these ultimately impact classroom relationships, attitudes toward schooling, and ultimately school achievement?

Whereas tests and assessment systems often have been narrowly construed and have served as roadblocks and negative factors in the educational and life outcomes of many Latino/a students, it does not have to be that way. When assessment systems are well conceptualized and comprehensively designed, and administered and used in appropriate ways, they can be tools used as powerful tools for accountability as well as instructional purposes. However, there are also many reasons for concern, as noted in the chapter, so that past abuses are not repeated. The factors and issues outlined in this chapter can form the foundation for an agenda for future research and development.

REFERENCES

Abedi, J., Lord, C., & Hofstetter, C. (1998). *Impact of selected background variables on students' NAEP math performance* (Center for Research on Evaluation, Standards, and Student Testing). Los Angeles: University of California, Los Angeles.

American Psychological Association Board of Educational Affairs. (1995, December). *Learner-centered psychological principles: A framework for school redesign and reform.* Washington, DC: American Psychological Association.

Artiles, A., Rueda, R., Salazar, J., & Higareda, I. (2000, November). *Factors associated with English learner representation in special education.* Presented at the Minority Issues in Special Education Conference. Boston, MA: Law School, Harvard University.

Artiles, A., & Trent, S. (2000). Representation of culturally/linguistically diverse students. In C. Reynolds & E. Fletcher-Jantzen (Eds.), *Encyclopedia of special education, Vol. 1 (2nd ed.)* (pp. 513–517). New York: John Wiley & Sons.

Bailey, A. L. (in press). From *Lambie* to *Lambaste*: The conceptualization, operationalization and use of academic language in the assessment of ELL students. In K. Rolstad (Ed.), *Rethinking school language.* Mahwah, NJ: Lawrence Erlbaum Associates.

Baker, E. L., Linn, R. L., Herman, J. L., & Koretz, D. (2002, Winter). Standards for educational accountability systems. *The CRESST Line*, 1–4.

Bond, L., Roeber, E., & Braskamp, D. (1996). *Trends in state student assessment programs fall 1996.* Washington, DC: Council of Chief State School Officers.

Bowen, W., & Bok, D. (1998). *The shape of the river: Long term consequences of considering race in college and university admissions.* Princeton, NJ: Princeton University Press.

Bransford, J., Brown, A., & Cocking, R. (1999). *How people learn: Brain, mind, experience, and school.* Washington, DC: National Academy Press.

Buly, M. R., & Valencia, S. (2002). Below the bar: Profiles of students who fail state reading assessments. *Educational Evaluation & Policy Analysis, 24*(3), 219–239.

Butler, F., & Stevens, R. (1997a). *Considerations in addressing large-scale assessment issues for language minority populations* (National Center for Research on Evaluation, Standards, and Students Testing (CRESST), Center for the Study of Evaluation (CSE), Graduate School of Education and Information Studies,). Los Angeles: University of California, Los Angeles.

Butler, F., & Stevens, S. (1997b). *Accommodation strategies for English language learners on large-scale assessments: Student characteristics and other considerations* (Center for the Study of Evaluation (CRESST), National Center for Research on Evaluation, Standards, and Student Testing, Graduate School of Education). Los Angeles: University of California, Los Angeles.

Clare Matsumura, L., Garnier, H. E., Pascal, J., & Valdes, R. (2002, November). *Measuring instructional quality in accountability systems: Classroom assignments and school achievement.* CSE Technical Report 582. Los Angeles: Center for the Study of Evaluation and National Center for the Study of Evaluation, Standards, and Student Testing.

Darling-Hammond, L. (1994). Performance-based assessment and educational equity. *Harvard Educational Review, 64*, 5–30.

Darling-Hammond, L. (1995). Inequality and access to knowledge. In J. Banks & C. Banks (Eds.), *Handbook of research on multicultural education* (pp. 465–483). New York: Macmillan.

Darling-Hammond, L. (1996). Performance-based assessment and educational equity. In E. Hollins (Ed.), *Transforming curriculum for a culturally diverse society* (pp. 245–272). Mahwah, NJ: Lawrence Erlbaum Associates.

Donovan, M., Bransford, J., & Pellegrino, J. (1999). *How people learn: Bridging research and practice.* Washington, DC: National Academy Press.

Donovan, M., & Cross, C. (2002). *Minority students in special and gifted education.* Washington, DC: National Academy Press.

Education Week. (2000). *Quality counts 2000: Who should teach?* Bethesda, MD: Editorial Products in Education, Inc.

Figueroa, R. (1990). Assessment of linguistic minority group children. In C. Reynolds & R. Kamphaus (Ed.), *Handbook of psychological and educational assessment of children: Intelligence and achievement.* New York: Guilford Press.

Finn, J. (1982). Patterns in special education placement as revealed by the OCR surveys. In K. Heller, W. Holtzman, & S. Mesick (Eds.), *Placing children in special education: A strategy for equity* (pp. 322–381). Washington, DC: National Academy Press.

Garcia, E. (2001). *Hispanic education in the United States: Raices y Alas.* Lanham, MD: Rowman & Littlefield.

Garcia, G. (2000). Bilingual children's reading, Vol 3. In M. Kamil, P. Mosenthal, P. Pearson, & R. Barr (Eds.), *Handbook of reading research* (pp. 813–834). Mahwah, NJ: Lawrence Erlbaum Associates.

Heller, K., Holtzman, W., & Messick, S. (1982). *Placing children in special education: A strategy for equity.* Washington, DC: National Academy Press.

Herman, J. T., Wakai, D. C. D., Wakai, S. T., & Heath, T. (1997). *Assessing equity in alternative assessment: An illustration of opportunity-to-learn issues.* Technical Report No. 440. Los Angeles: UCLA, Center for the Study of Evaluation.

Koretz, D., Russell, M., Shin, C., Horn, C., & Shasby, K. (2002). Testing and diversity in postsecondary education: The case of California. *Education Policy Analysis Archives, 10*(1), 1–34.

LaCelle-Peterson, M., & Rivera, C. (1994). Is it real for all kids? A framework for equitable assessment policies for English language learners. *Harvard Educational Review, 64,* 55–75.

Lachat, M. (1994). *High standards for all students: Opportunities and challenges.* South Hampton, NH: Center for Resource Management.

Lambert, N., & McCombs, B. (1998). *How students learn: Reforming schools through learner-centered education.* Washington, DC: American Psychological Association.

Linn, R. L. (2000). Assessments and accountability. *Educational Researcher, 29*(2), 4–16.

Linn, R. L., Baker, E. L., & Betebenner, D. W. (2002). *Accountability systems: Implications of requirements of the No Child Left Behind Act of 2001.* CSE Technical Report No. 567. Los Angeles, CA: Center for the Study of Evaluation and National Center on Evaluation, Standards, and Student Testing.

McNeil, L. (2000). *Contradictions of school reform: Educational costs of standardized testing.* New York: Routledge.

Mercer, J. (1973). *Labeling the mentally retarded: Clinical and social system perspectives on mental retardation.* Berkeley, CA: University of California Press.

National Center for Educational Statistics. (1995). *The educational progress of Hispanic students: The condition of education, 1995.* Washington, DC: U.S. Department of Education.

National Center for Educational Statistics. (1998). *Annual report, 1998.* Washington, DC: U.S. Department of Education.

National Council on Education Standards and Testing. (1992). *Raising standards for American education.* Chestnut Hill, MA: Author.

National Education Goals Panel. (1993). *Setting standards, becoming the best* (Chapter 1, Vol. 1). Washington, DC: Author.

Nettles, M. T., & Nettles, A. L. (1995). *Equity and excellence in educational testing and assessment.* Boston: Kluwer Academic Publishers.

No Child Left Behind Act of 2001, Pub. L. No. 107–110, 115 Stat. 1425 (2002).

Olson, J., & Goldstein, A. (1997). *The inclusion of students with disabilities and limited English proficient students in large-scale assessments: A summary of recent progress.* Washington, DC: National Center for Education Statistics, U.S. Department of Education.

Oswald, D., Coutinho, M., Best, A., & Singh, N. (1999). Ethnic representation in special education: The influence of school-related economic and demographic variables. *Journal of Special Education, 32,* 194–206.

Pearson, P., & Raphael, T. (1999). Toward a more complex view of balance in the literacy curriculum. In W. D. Hammond & T. E. Raphael (Ed.), *Early literacy instruction for the new millenium* (pp. 1–21). Grand Rapids: Michigan Reading Asociation.

Reschly, D. (1997). *Disproportionate minority representation in general and special education: Patterns, issues, and alternatives.* Des Moines: Iowa Department of Education.

Rueda, R., Artiles, A., Salazar, J., & Higareda, I. (2002). An analysis of special education as a response to the diminished academic achievement of Chicano/Latino students: An update. In R. Valencia (Ed.), *Chicano school failure and success: Research and policy agendas for the 1990's* (pp. 310–332). London: Falmer Press.

Rueda, R., & McIntyre, E. (2002). Toward universal literacy. In S. Stringfield & D. Land (Eds.), *Educating at risk students: One Hundred-first Yearbook of the National Society for the Study of Education* (pp. 189–209). Chicago, III: The University of Chicago Press.

Shepard, L. A. (2001). The role of classroom assessment in teaching and learning. In V. Richardson (Ed.), *The handbook of research on teaching,* 4th Ed. Washington, DC: American Educational Research Association.

Smith, M., Heinecke, W., & Noble, A. (1999, Winter). Assessment policy and political spectacle. *Teachers College Record, 101*(2), 157–191.

Snow, C. E., Burns, M. S., & Griffin, P. (1998). *Preventing reading difficulties in young children.* Washington, DC: National Academy Press.

Valdes, G., & Figueroa, R. (1994). *Bilingualism and testing: A special case of bias.* Norwood, NJ: Ablex Publishing Corporation.

Valencia, R., & Suzuki, L. (2001). Race/ethnicity, intelligence, and special education. In R. Valencia & L. Suzuki (Eds.), *Intelligence testing and minority students: Foundations, performance factors, and assessment issues* (pp. 187–207). Thousand Oaks, CA: Sage Publications.

Yeh, S. (2001). Tests worth teaching to: Constructing state-mandated tests that emphasize critical thinking. *Educational Researcher, 30*(9), 12–17.

9

California's Standards Movement: How English Learners Have Been Left Out of the Equation for Success

Teresa I. Márquez-López
University of California, Riverside

INTRODUCTION

This chapter examines how the California Educational Reform Movement of the late 1990s, and recent policy changes, have had a detrimental effect on English learners who comprise more than one fourth of the state's school-age population. The BTSA-ELL Project was developed for use throughout the state. After 3 years of successful implementation, the BTSA-ELL Project was not adopted by the state for English learners and their teachers. This article cites the need to reconsider how California's Educational Reform Movement addresses the needs of English learners.

The Beginning Teacher Support and Assessment Program (BTSA) is California's, 2-year teacher induction program that is designed to be part of the teacher credentialing process. The BTSA-ELL Project was initiated in 1999, to prepare new teachers to meet the educational needs of English learners through professional development. At a time when politics overshadows students' educational needs the positive outcomes of a successful program were shelved rather than built into California's Educational Reform agenda to produce positive outcomes for teachers of English learners and their students.

CALIFORNIA'S STANDARDS MOVEMENT

California has joined the national trend to implement educational reforms using a standards-based model with high levels of accountability for teachers and students. A wave of initiatives in our state has placed increased pressure on educators to improve student academic performance as measured by standardized tests. Annual student test scores evaluate educators' performance. However, California officials ignored the instructional needs of its 2.2 million language minority students (California Department of Education, 1999a). The result has produced an environment that limits the professional discretion of educators. California leads the nation with the largest number of English learners. Educators in the state need to be prepared to provide instruction that assists English learners to meet the goals of the standards movement. Currently, the annual assessments administered to students demonstrate that English learners are failing to meet the state's new standards. How California succeeds or fails to resolve this issue will be examined closely by states like New York, Florida, Texas, and Illinois with high percentages of English learners, in addition, to states with increasing numbers of language minority students entering their schools.

NEW STANDARDS FOR TEACHERS
AND STUDENTS

In the late 1990s the California Department of Education (CDE) began to implement a series of educational initiatives for teachers and students that constitute the foundation of the state's educational reforms. In 1997, the California Standards for the Teaching Profession (CSTP) were adopted to define what California classroom teachers should know and skills they must possess. In 2002, new Teacher Education and Teacher Induction Standards were adopted with the objective of improving teacher quality. Next, a review of the state's curricula and the publication of the state-adopted Subject Matter Content Standards defined the content students should be taught and mastered by kindergarten through twelfth grade. The Standards included the adoption of the Reading-Language Arts Framework in 1997, the Science Framework in 1998, the Mathematics and English Language Development Frameworks in 1999, the History-Social Studies Framework in 2000, and the Visual and Performing Arts Framework in 2001. Class size reduction was another initiative that was implemented in the primary grades and specified secondary classes. It reduced the number of students assigned per teacher from thirty or more to twenty. However, class-size reduction lead to an increased demand for more teachers to fill the increased number of classes. Districts worked aggressively to hire qualified teachers and implement each of these reform initiatives to improve student academic performance.

THE CHALLENGE OF RETAINING
QUALIFIED TEACHERS

Nationally approximately 20% of teachers do not remain in teaching for more than five years (McCreight, 2000). The resulting teacher shortage cuts across all teaching fields and geographic areas (Sweeney & Whitworth, 2000). A fundamental cause of inadequate student achievement is the failure of schools to staff classrooms with qualified teachers (Ingersoll, 2001). The research literature, states "no other intervention can make the difference that a knowledgeable, skilled teacher can make in student achievement" (Darling-Hammond, 1999, p. 5). The quality of teachers, specifically their ability, experience, and education is the most important in-school factor for improving student achievement (Chatham Education Foundation, 2000; Ferguson, 1991).

The high turnover of teachers is an important issue that has received more attention in recent years. Teacher turnover rates highlight potential staffing problems that can be disruptive to the quality of the school community and its performance. The turnover rates also draw attention to the failure to ensure that elementary and secondary schools are staffed with qualified teachers (Ingersoll, 2001).

Some of the most common reasons teachers give for leaving the teaching profession are poor working conditions including limited support for new teachers (Center for the Future of Teaching and Learning, 2001). Moreover, in California where one out of every four students is an English learner, teachers' lack the preparation to effectively teach English learners may be one more reason they consider leaving teaching. An analysis of the 1998 BTSA Statewide Evaluation Survey Report indicates teachers did not feel prepared or competent to instruct

English learners. New teachers also reported they received limited support in meeting the diverse needs of language minority students (Mitchell, Scott, Hendrick, & Boyns, 1998). Another reason teachers leave the profession is the practice of placing new teachers in some of the most challenging classroom assignments. This often includes teaching English learners. Teachers placed in these assignments that are not adequately prepared, find themselves in a difficult situation and are left to cope or fail. By contrast, when appropriate support is provided these teachers can successfully instruct English learners.

Teacher attrition is exacerbated by the teacher shortage that has continued to grow since the late 1990s (Lugg, Bulkley, Firestone, & Gardner, 2002).

> After decades of having a reliable stream of teachers and principals, many school districts are facing shortages (Educational Research, 1998; Hussar, 1999). The National Center for Education Statistics project that the U.S. will need anywhere from 1.7 million to 2.7 million public school teachers by the 2009 school year . . . The current and projected shortages are largely due to retirements, a growing student population, career change, and large teacher and administrator turnover in some areas (ERS, 1998; Hussar, 1999). Rising student enrollments in general and a growing need for teachers in specialty areas such as special education, bilingual education and science education may further exacerbate these shortages (p. 34).

The practice of placing new teachers in the most challenging classroom assignments is a factor in teacher attrition. For example, new teachers are often assigned to multigrade classrooms, English learners, special education students, students with behavior problems, or a combination of the aforementioned. New teachers often have limited training in English learner instructional methodology and are developing their pedagogical practice, hence, are not yet equipped to manage multiple challenges. School officials need to recognize that assigning new teachers to difficult assignments places them at high risk of leaving the profession and places students at high risk for academic failure.

After gaining a few years of teaching experience teachers often transfer to a more affluent school or district to work in a less challenging environment. This pattern of attrition most often negatively impacts students of color and English learners often attending urban or rural schools in poor communities. California's teacher population, like that of most other states, is primarily White (84%) and middle class (Toppo, 2003). These teachers need professional development to effectively teach the diverse student population attending California's public schools. A transfer to a suburban school allows teachers to move away from working in schools with high numbers of English learners, economically disadvantaged children, and students from cultural and economic backgrounds substantially different from their own. The dynamics of teacher attrition highlight the staffing problems that undermine school performance for schools with English learners.

HOW CALIFORNIA'S STANDARDS MOVEMENT HAS NEGATIVELY EFFECTED ENGLISH LEARNERS

Reform efforts have largely left English learners out the equation for success. Teacher quality has been a matter of great concern since the publication of the National Commission on Teaching and America's Future (1996). California's certification that authorizes teachers to instruct English learners is the Crosscultural, Language and Academic Development Certificate (CLAD). The CLAD Certificate prepares teachers to implement effective methods and strategies while teaching English learners. At the height of California's Educational Reform implementation the CLAD requirements were reduced. Prior to 2002, the CLAD was comprised of four modules: (1) Language Structure and Development; (2) Second Language Methodology; (3) Culture; and (4) two Second Language courses in the target language (Spanish, Vietnamese or another language). With the implementation of the 2042 Standards for Teacher Education and Teacher Induction programs in 2002, the two target language classes required were eliminated. By doing away with the two 30-hour classes in Spanish, teachers no longer experience the challenges involved in acquiring a second language. Consequently, without language learning experiences teachers are not able reference the pedagogical practices demonstrated in the courses, nor are teachers able to apply them to their instructional practice.

The Spanish language courses helped teachers to establish communication between non-English speaking parents and themselves. Although for many teachers the level of Spanish proficiency they acquired was basic, they found that parents appreciated their effort to communicate, and were more involved in their children's education! Eliminating this requirement substantially reduced the preparation and qualifications of teachers assigned to English learners. Likewise, teachers' ability to communicate with non-English-speaking parents also was reduced. "All students deserve a highly qualified teacher" is the mantra of the current educational reform movement. Reducing professional development requirements for teachers of English learners in an era of high standards and accountability is a contradiction that detracts from teachers' ability to provide rigorous meaningful instruction to English learners, hinders student achievement, and reduces teacher quality.

POLICY AND POLITICAL CONSTRAINTS

Although it is well documented that teacher quality is a key component of student academic success, English learners are hindered by multiple constraints. Rumberger and Gándara (2000) reported that 25% of teachers of English learners are not fully certified. That study shows that English learners are twice as likely to have an uncredentialed teacher. In California where one out of every four students is an English learner, and at the elementary level where one out of every three children is an English learner, teachers need more preparation. It is extremely difficult to improve academic performance and create positive outcomes in low performing schools without adequate support. The tremendous challenge of constantly recruiting and training teachers to meet the needs of students places schools and districts in a position of managing the constant flow of new teachers that pass through their schools. The lack of qualified teachers and the instability of the school faculty place students in further jeopardy. Students instructed by teachers who do not have a strong command of the subject matter content and English learner methodology over 2 to 3 years can prove to be academically fatal for students (Haycock, 1998). A teacher population that is in constant flux relegates students to an inferior education.

In California, the state policies under Proposition 227 limit the exercise of a teacher's professional discretion on the part of school officials (Unz & Tuchman, 1998). Teachers and administrators have been adhering to policy that prescribes that English learners be placed in an "English language classroom ... in which the language of instruction used by the teaching personnel is overwhelmingly the English language" and that teachers use structured English immersion methods. Consequently, educators are pressured to, "focus on what is measured, teach to the test, and rely on scripted lessons 'that work,' and there is less room for professional discretion in the classroom" (Sykes & Millman, in Goldring & Greenfield, 2002, p. 11; Uriarte, 2002).

Districts statewide, for the most part, have not encouraged parents to exercise their right to waive English-only instruction for their children and select an alternative program including enrichment models such as dual language/two-way bilingual immersion programs and alternative bilingual education models of instruction. These options were widely requested by parents prior to the passage of Proposition 227. Post–Proposition 227, confusion was widespread among new and veteran teachers and was exacerbated by the hostile climate that lingered after the highly charged political campaign. Veteran bilingual teachers were afraid to speak a language other than English to their students because they were concerned about being the target of litigation for not adhering to the new policy. Overall, policy and accountability mechanisms have had a chilling effect at the local level, reducing local discretion, autonomy, and creativity in addition to narrowing curriculum and constraining teaching pedagogy (Toenjes, Dworkin, Gary, Jon, & Antwanett, in Goldring & Greenfield, 2002, p. 10; Uriarte, 2002).

THE UNREALIZED PROMISE
OF PROPOSITION 227

Proposition 227 was widely promoted by promising to improve English language development for English learners, but it has failed to do so. The Rumburger and Gándara study (2000) shows that in 1998, approximately 29% of English learners were receiving primary language support. After the passage of Proposition 227 in June 1998, native language instruction in California's classroom declined to 12%. In the 2000–2001 academic year it was reported to be less than 10%. Three years later with 90% of English learners receiving instruction conducted by Proposition 227 guidelines English learner reclassification rates to fluent English proficient have not increased significantly. Maxwell-Jolly and Gándara (2002) present California data reporting English learner redesignation rates from limited English proficient (LEP) to fluent English proficient (FEP) at 7% prior to the passage of Proposition 227 followed by an increase 2 years later to 7.6%. This slight gain nonetheless cannot be directly attributed to the implementation of Proposition 227 guidelines since multiple initiatives such as the Public Schools Accountability Act, new Subject Matter Content Standards, class size reduction, and teacher induction programs were all introduced at the same time. Because English-only instruction has not substantially increased the academic performance of English learners the state must move beyond this limited and ineffective solution to models that have demonstrated success for English learners. For English learner outcomes to meet California's requirements, students must be prepared to meet the state-adopted

Subject Matter Content Standards, pass California's English Language Development Test, the California High School Exit Examination, and score well on the state mandated California Achievement Test (6th Edition).

CALIFORNIA'S PLAN TO PREPARE TEACHERS OF ENGLISH LEARNERS AND SPECIAL EDUCATION STUDENTS

In order to improve the teacher retention and attrition rates, the California State Department of Education expanded the 2-year induction program for new teachers called the Beginning Teacher Support and Assessment (BTSA) Program. BTSA's induction program has three overarching goals: (1) to assist school districts in retaining newly recruited beginning teachers; (2) to improve students' academic achievement by providing well-prepared and supported beginning teachers; and (3) to offer a professional role for veteran teachers in mentoring novice teachers during their first 2 years in the teaching profession. In 1999, the BTSA Program dedicated funding to develop specialized professional development for teachers of English learners and Special Education students. Both BTSA Programs were designed to meet the needs of the growing English learner and Special Education population and to retain these teachers once prepared to meet the unique needs of their students.

Our program consortium members included the University of California, Riverside; California State University, San Bernardino; Riverside County Office of Education; and the San Bernardino County Superintendent of Schools Office. The Design Team was funded by the *English Language Learner (ELL) Augmentation Grant* from the California Department of Education (CDE) and the California Commission on Teacher Credentialing (CCTC). The members were Dr. Rocio Flores Moss, Dr. Teresa Marquez-Lopez, and Dr. Esteban Diaz. Our design team developed an English Learner Professional Development Model with training for mentor teachers based on a strong theoretical and pedagogical framework designed to assist beginning teachers to implement an effective instructional program for English learners. *The California Formative Assessment and Support System for Teachers* (CFASST) provides the structure for BTSA training statewide. The design team developed an English Learner Instructional Guide and materials to add to the CFASST events that included reflective practice and assessment components for daily lessons. Ultimately the design team strove to remedy the lack of training teachers described in the *1998 State Evaluation Study*.

The primary goal of our professional development program was to assure that mentors and beginning teachers of English learners received the critical elements of professional development in order to improve instruction. These elements included English Language Development (ELD) Standards, state-adopted Subject Matter Content Standards, Specially Designed Academic Instruction Delivered in English (SDAIE) methodology, and the opportunity to review local district policy in light of Proposition 227's defining the role of primary language instruction to access the core curriculum. In addition, mentors and beginning teachers were given the opportunity to explore the descriptions and experiences of students of varying characteristics and backgrounds most often associated with English learners. Some of these characteristics included diverse cultural, linguistic, socio-economic and educational factors that affect school adjustment, academic achievement and the process of second language acquisition. The BTSA-ELL Program highlighted the methodology and pedagogical practices to be used specifically by teachers for English learner instruction. Figure 9.1 presents a prototype of the guide and sample of teacher's reflective and assessment practices.

In January 2000, the first cohort of 35 BTSA-ELL mentors attended ELL Professional Development offered by the design team. Mentors were trained to assist the 32 beginning teachers that had been assigned to them during their 1st year of teaching. The BTSA-ELL Program sought teachers who held Bilingual Certification so that new teachers could be mentored by a teacher with extensive training and experience working with English learners. The next group of teachers targeted to participate as mentors were CLAD Certified teachers with broad experience teaching English learners. In a few cases, mentor teachers participated in the project because of their interest even though they did not have bilingual or CLAD certification. This first cohort of mentors and beginning teachers was selected from a large, local school district with a high percentage of English learners. The cohort was comprised of elementary and middle school teachers. The design team presented the methods developed to assist new teachers and guided discussions about the various strategies mentors could use to support their beginning teacher. Mentors met with their novice teacher on a regular basis throughout the week, or on a weekly basis. In September 2000, a second cohort of 31 mentors and 37 beginning teachers began participating in the BTSA-ELL Program. The second cohort was comprised of kindergarten through high school teachers from districts throughout Riverside and San Bernardino counties.

ELL INSTRUCTION PLAN AND REFLECTION

Grade/Class _____ Subject Matter _____

Date _____

DIRECTIONS: Use this form to design an instructional experience that meets the instructional needs of your ELL students. Use the left side to plan the experience and the right side to reflect on the instructional impact of the experience. Select two ELL students that are working at different ELD levels. Collect evidence of learning for each student to include as evidence for this inquiry.

ELL INSTRUCTION EXPERIENCE PLAN To be completed prior to the implementation of the experience	REFLECTION To be completed following the implementation of the experience
CONTENT STANDARDS GOAL(S)	CONTENT STANDARDS GOAL(S)
What Standard(s) did you select for ELL student(s)? What do your students need to know and do? What assessment have you selected? What is acceptable evidence? What specific strategies will you use to support ELL students and their level of proficiency in teaching this lesson? What resources are available to you? Class:	In what ways were the Standard(s) appropriate for your ELL students? Were your students highly engaged in the lesson? Which strategies assisted students in achieving the learning goals? Were available resources helpful? Were the Standard(s) met or will you need to re-teach? Class:
Student 1:	Student 1:
Student 2:	Student 2:
How do the learning goals build on student's prior academic knowledge and interests? Class:	In what ways did student prior academic knowledge, experiences, and interests aid their learning? Class:
Student 1:	Student 1:
Student 2:	Student 2:

FIG. 9.1.   Sample ELL Guide.

Professional Development for Mentor Teachers

BTSA-ELL mentors attended five days of the CFASST professional development. This portion of the professional development is the model delivered to all mentors participating in BTSA statewide. In addition, the BTSA-ELL mentors participated in ELL Professional Development. The ELL Professional Development program began by reviewing the dramatic demographic shift in California's student population, focusing on these trends in Riverside and San Bernardino counties, where the English learner student population had grown by approximately 30%, twice the rate of the statewide English learner population (California Department of Education, 1999). The ELL Professional Development Program focused on the new *California Standards for the Teaching Profession, California's English Language Development (ELD) Standards* and demonstrated the alignment between the ELD Standards and the *State-Adopted Language Arts Framework*. The ELD Standards were presented as a critical link to the *Language Arts Framework*. Teachers were trained to first use the ELD Standard to build the listening, speaking, reading, and writing skills that English learners need as a foundation to successfully begin learning the Language Arts Framework Standards. Specially Designed Academic Instruction in English (SDAIE) methodology was demonstrated as an integral part of lesson plan design. Mentor teachers reviewed their respective school districts' policies in relation to the role of primary language instruction to assist English learners to access the core curriculum. Reviewing districts' language policies was critical in light of the passage of Proposition 227. Districts had written new policies that were not uniformly implemented nor clearly articulated. The review of Proposition 227 allowed teachers to understand how the new policy was being interpreted in their district and allowed them to use the students' primary language according to their district's guidelines.

English Language Learner Standards Based on the California Standards for the Teaching Professional

In 1997, the California Standards for the Teaching Profession (CSTP) were introduced to teachers to define and articulate the professional role of the state's teaching force. Dr. Rocio Flores Moss developed a parallel version of the CSTP for the BTSA-ELL teachers. The English learner CSTP is entitled, English Language Learner Standards (see Figure 9.2). It assists teachers to view the CSTP through the instructional lens of

STANDARD ONE	STANDARD TWO
ENGAGING AND SUPPORTING ALL STUDENTS IN LEARNING	CREATING AND MAINTAINING EFFECTIVE ENVIRONMENTS FOR STUDENT LEARNING
1-1 Connecting student's prior knowledge, native language, level of English proficiency, life experiences, and interests with learning goals. 1-2 Using a variety of instructional strategies and resources to respond to student's diverse needs, assure that students comprehend core content, and use English for authentic communication in academic and social contexts for varied purposes and audiences. 1-3 Facilitating learning experiences with appropriate language modifications, by understanding when and how to focus on oral and written language that promote autonomy, interaction and choice. 1-4 Engaging students in problem solving, critical thinking, and other activities appropriate to their levels of English proficiency that make subject matter meaningful. 1-5 Promoting self-directed, reflective learning for all students, incorporating higher order thinking strategies appropriate for English Language Development levels that involve all students in assessing their learning.	2-1 Creating a language and print-rich physical environment that engages all students in relevant activities that support learning academic content and language skills. 2-2 Establishing a climate that minimizes anxiety, promotes fairness and self-esteem to motivate student participation and respect for diversity. 2-3 Promoting social development and group responsibility that involves students in collaborative work to learn important content, concepts, and skills. 2-4 Establishing and maintaining standards for student behavior that are centered around meaningful learning. 2-5 Planning and implementing classroom procedures, routines, and an integrated approach to language learning in a variety of grouping configurations to support student learning. 2-6 Using instructional time effectively to incorporate learning modalities and the student's native language promoting mastery of content and language.

STANDARD THREE	STANDARD FOUR
UNDERSTANDING & ORGANIZING SUBJECT MATTER FOR STUDENT LEARNING	PLANNING INSTRUCTION & DESIGNING LEARNING EXPERIENCES FOR ALL STUDENTS
3-1 Demonstrating knowledge of subject matter content, student development, and instructional strategies that address students' linguistic proficiency levels and diverse academic needs. 3-2 Organizing curriculum to support student understanding through instructional strategies that are appropriate to the subject matter, English language proficiency levels, and relevant to the learner. 3-3 Interrelating ideas and information within and across subject matter areas by reinforcing language learning while teaching content. 3-4 Developing students' understanding through instructional strategies that contextualize lessons and are appropriate to subject matter. 3-5 Using materials, resources, technologies, and hands-on activities with students in a variety of ways to gather and record data, making subject matter accessible to all students.	4-1 Drawing on their student's background and valuing experiences, native language, level of English proficiency, and developmental learning needs to promote understanding in a meaningful and supportive context. 4-2 Establishing and articulating goals for students learning by scaffolding information and using a communication-based approach that integrates English language learning with academic content. 4-3 Developing and sequencing instructional activities and materials for both content and language acquisition with ample opportunities to practice, demonstrate, apply, reflect, assess understanding, and when needed provide intervention and re-teaching. 4-4 Designing short-term and long-term plans to foster students learning by providing multiple and varied opportunities to practice new language learning and to understand and internalize new content and skills. 4-5 Modifying instructional plans to adjust for student needs, varying instructional activities with appropriate transitions and pacing that promote active participation in valuable learning.

STANDARD FIVE	STANDARD SIX
ASSESSING STUDENT LEARNING	DEVELOPING AS A PROFESSIONAL EDUCATOR
5-1 Establishing and communicating learning goals for all students using standards and English Language Development (ELD) benchmark performance indicators. 5-2 Collecting and using multiple sources of information to assess students' learning, using formal and authentic assessments, and making frequent checks for understanding. 5-3 Involving and guiding all students in assessing their own learning by modeling purposeful feedback and asking students to observe their depth of understanding toward mastering skills and content. 5-4 Using the results of assessments to guide instruction, provide intervention and re-teaching to address incomplete learning and understanding, and record English learners progress on ELD proficiency levels as an evaluative measure for redesignation. 5-5 Communicating with students, families, and other audiences about student progress and eliciting assistance from family members and bilingual professionals to support student achievement.	6-1 Reflecting on teaching practices and planning professional development to improve language skills, diversity/cross-cultural knowledge and appropriate use of content and strategies for educating all students. 6-2 Establishing professional goals and pursing opportunities to refine approaches that make the curriculum accessible to every student. 6-3 Working with communities to improve professional practice, incorporate student's cultural and linguistic background, and dynamics of students' cultural and linguistic background, and dynamics of students' communities. 6-4 Working with families to improve professional practices, build language skills outside of instruction time, nurture parents as partners in the education of their children, and develop an understanding of families' racial, cultural, and socioeconomic backgrounds. 6-5 Working with colleagues to improve professional practices, creating a support network that supports beginning and experienced teachers to address all students' diverse learning needs and build success across content, programs, and grade levels. 6-6 Balancing professional responsibilities, maintaining motivation, demonstrating professional conduct and integrity in the classroom and school l community, and extending knowledge about legal responsibilities for students' learning, behavior and safety.

FIG. 9.2.   English Language Learner Standards. *Source:* Based on the California Standards for the Teaching Professional.

the English learner. This tool allowed teachers to review each standard and strategically plan instruction to connect with their students' life experiences and interests.

An example of how the English Language Learner Standards is used by teachers can be seen for Standard 2-2, *Establishing a climate that minimizes anxiety, promotes fairness and self-esteem to motivate student participation and respect for diversity.* Teachers are reminded to consider the challenges involved with learning a second language and encouraged to create a positive climate for promoting learning opportunities that enhance student learning. One first year teacher reported, "instead of using the regular social studies or science books I add more visuals along with peer tutors, and hands-on activities to help my students." Another beginning teacher stated, "English learners in my class are at different levels. I have non-English and limited English proficient students. Because of the variety of levels I must conduct small group instruction using total physical response methods along with realia and other materials." Each standard addresses how new teachers can help students to negotiate learning to create positive outcomes. Standard 1-4 focuses on *Engaging students in problem solving, critical thinking and other activities appropriate to their levels of English proficiency that makes subject matter meaningful.* Teachers described how they communicate and monitor this learning goal for their students using a variety of strategies. A beginning teacher focusing on Standard 1-4 described her instructional strategies, "First, the activities are appropriate to their levels of English proficiency. I presented an abstract concept and an activity involving vocabulary building and logic building skills. The use of supplementary materials created a visual dimension to the lesson and made the subject matter meaningful." The design team encourages teachers to set goals for students using group assignments, research skill, asking "what if" questions, acting out meaning to help students develop the skill outlined in Standard 1-4. Figure 9.2 shows the English Language Learner Standards used by project participants.

ELL GUIDE AND SUPPORTING MATERIAL

The ELL Guide offers a structure for beginning teachers to examine their classroom and school context. In partnership with their mentor teacher, new teachers consider school, district, and community resources to meet the needs of their students. Beginning teachers organize their grade level curriculum and their classroom setting while being supported in accessing school and district resources. The ELL Guide served as a tool to support mentors and beginning teachers through this process of organizing instruction to meet the California Standards for the Teaching Profession. A beginning teacher described her experience by stating, "The program is great. I learned to reflect on my practice and became more involved in my school. My mentor is really open to help, offer ideas and provide me with materials. This year I have put in practice many suggestions that came from my mentor and colleagues."

The ELL Guide combined with the English Language Learner Standards helped teachers monitor various assessment strategies when planning, instructing, and evaluating student progress. The sample of an ELL Guide in Figure 9.1 demonstrates a number of questions posed to the beginning teacher while planning their lessons including: What Standard(s) did you select for ELL student(s)? What do your students need to know and do? What assessment have you selected? What is acceptable evidence? What specific strategies will you use to support ELL students and their level of proficiency in teaching this lesson? What resources are available to you? After the lesson has been taught the teacher is asked to reflect on the instructional lesson responding to a number of question to assess the effectiveness of their instructional practice. When a beginning teacher in the project was asked about planning instruction, selecting standards, and building expectations her comment was, "A student who is very limited in English is still developing the language and needs to be supported in his first language to learn the content with the rest of the students. The teacher can translate as vocabulary is being developed or acquired. However, academic goals should be set equally for all students. Language will develop and academic achievement will be automatically translated into English. Language is not, and should not, be a limitation for students' academic growth." The following are samples of the questions presented to beginning teachers to help them reflect on the lesson after it was presented to students. In what ways were the Standard(s) appropriate for your ELL students? Were your students highly engaged in the lesson? Which strategies assisted students in achieving the learning goals? Were available resources helpful? Was the Standard(s) met or will you need to re-teach? Beginning teachers began to reflect on their practice through the use of this tool with the help of their mentor teacher. Teachers began to understand that using the ELL Guide as a tool for reflection helped them assess their own practice. One mentor stated, "the ELL Guide is well laid out, easy to follow, and a ready reference for new teachers." Another mentor stated, "I found that my own teaching methods improved and my knowledge of the availability of teacher materials and outside resources available increased." It should be noted that each of the six Standards are address throughout the ELL Professional Development with the support of the ELL Guide allowing beginning teacher the time to learn how to implement the English Language Learner Standards in their daily instruction.

ELL Follow-Up Sessions

Mentors attended five follow-up sessions annually. The follow-up sessions offered mentors professional development to assist them in supporting their beginning teacher. The design team modeled how mentors could help beginning teachers to use specific strategies in the ELL Guide. The ELL Guide focused on organizing the classroom, planning instruction, and assessing student progress. During the follow-up sessions mentors shared their knowledge about English learner pedagogy and discussed the issues they confront as a mentor helping a beginning teacher. The mentors were given the tools and strategies to assist new teachers to face their challenges, resolve difficult issues, and enhance instruction for students.

As new education initiatives were introduced to the state, the BTSA-ELL Professional Development added new components to keep teachers well informed. For example, in 2001, California introduced the *California English Language Development Test (CELDT)* for all English learners. The CELDT evaluates English learners' listening, speaking, reading, and writing skills in English. A CELDT component was added to the professional development. Mentor teachers were prepared to interpret assessment results and assist beginning teachers to inform their classroom instruction using this new data. The data allowed teachers to place students in appropriate instructional programs and monitor their progress in each of the four areas. The CELDT training component preceded the May 2001 implementation of CELDT testing in school districts throughout the state.

To examine the effectiveness the BTSA-ELL program I designed a study to answer the following research questions:

1. What are the effects of BTSA-ELL augmentation (professional development and ELL Guide) on participating beginning teachers and their English learner students?
2. What are the effects of the BTSA-ELL augmentation on mentors working with participating beginning teachers?

In June 2001, after both cohorts had participated through a full cycle of attending ELL Professional Development, statewide training, and the use of support materials, a survey was developed for beginning teachers and mentors. The BTSA-ELL Survey asked questions about their experiences participating in the ELL Professional Development, their use of ELL Guides, Follow-up Sessions, supplementary materials, and other forms of support they received from the design team members. The survey was administered to both groups to examine the full effects of each of the professional development components. A total of 69 surveys were sent to beginning teachers and 66 mentors. The qualitative data comprised approximately 50% of the survey questions. The qualitative data was analyzed to identify broad issues as well as smaller emerging issues related to the research questions.

MENTORS' VIEWS ON THE BTSA-ELL SUPPORT

Mentor teachers reported five areas of effective support that the BTSA-ELL Program offered them as mentors supporting a 1st year teacher. Mentors also noted how the program influenced their own classroom practice.

1. The ELL Guide offered a framework to reference effective instructional methodology and practices for English learners.
2. The Design Team offered follow-up sessions and 3 full days of professional development during the school year to prepare mentors by demonstrating effective instructional practices to be used for English learners.
3. The Design Team offered copies of the Professional Development materials to participating mentors to enable them to initiate other mentors in their district. The Design Team's professional development served as a Trainer-of-Trainers model for some school districts allowing them to effectively prepare many other mentors.
4. By participating in the BTSA-ELL Program mentors met on a regular basis with mentors from their district and neighboring school districts to engage in authentic problem solving about language policy, implementation of new state initiatives, and local school site issues.
5. The BTSA-ELL Program created a collaborative community of veteran educators that were able to update their pedagogical knowledge for English learners and refocus their own practice

framed by their new knowledge. They became informed of available resources and materials in their own district and were now part of a broader community of support including two local universities and county Offices of Education.

BTSA-ELL Mentors' Views on the ELL Guide

The mentors that participated in the ELL Professional Development were committed to support their beginning teachers. This was demonstrated through their insightful observations while supporting teachers and the statements written on the survey about their experiences helping them. The following quotes from the mentor survey illustrate the comments echoed by several mentors. "The ELL Guide thoroughly focused on the academic needs of English learners and reminded beginning teachers to hold all students to high Standards." "The ELL Guide focus on English learners' special needs and planning for instruction helped beginning teachers to increase the frequency of assessment for students." Mentors observed that after an assessment was completed, beginning teachers often adjusted their lesson plans and instruction according to students' performance. The organization of the ELL Guide was found to be "very specific and encouraged new teachers to be reflective and use a variety of instructional strategies." The mentors valued becoming a member of a community of learners. "The opportunity to network and share ideas with other mentors was a valuable experience that enhanced my own teaching." Other statements made by mentors included, "The ELL Guide needs to be a regular part of the statewide BTSA Program," and "This program holds teachers accountable." Another mentor described the BTSA-ELL Program as "an excellent program, the best English learner program I've ever participated in because of its concentration on teaching strategies, identification of needs, and assessment tools for beginning teachers." An important observation made by a mentor describes her observation of new teachers in the ELL program, "a benefit of this program is that beginning teachers hold themselves to a higher standard. They frequently asked themselves, 'How can I get better?' Beginning teachers identified their own strengths and weaknesses. From their reflection they attempted to improve their instruction." The comments written by mentors were of the same nature as those made during professional development sessions and individually to the design team.

BTSA-ELL MENTOR RECOMMENDATIONS

BTSA-ELL mentors were asked to comment on their concerns and/or suggestions regarding the ELL Professional Development and ELL Guide. Given that many of the mentors were experienced veteran teachers they provided valuable insight into the range of issues across school districts. Their recommendations were given important consideration and professional development sessions often added components to address issues raised through this process. Mentors stated that they wanted more training in the area of English Language Development Standards, CELDT Assessment, student reclassification post-Proposition 227, and lessons on multiculturalism.

Mentors who had earned a Crosscultural Language and Academic Development (CLAD) or Bilingual Crosscultural Language and Academic Development (BCLAD) Certification expressed a need to update their knowledge with new research and theory to improve their instruction. Many of these teachers had earned their CLAD and BCLAD certification 10, 15, and 20 years earlier, and felt that they could not rely on what they had learned in college. First and foremost, they wanted to continue to do their best for English learners. The need to revitalize their instruction with new strategies was viewed as being an important priority and a critical part of the BTSA-ELL mentor professional development. This demonstrated to the design team the level of commitment the mentors placed on their own professional development and how they relied on the ELL Program to enhance their growth. They saw the ELL Program as an opportunity not only to help beginning teachers but also to improve their personal knowledge base for English learner instruction.

BEGINNING-TEACHERS' VIEWS ON THE
BTSA-ELL SUPPORT

Beginning teachers reported five areas of effective support that the ELL Professional Development offered them as first-year teachers. They were provided with

1. a mentor highly knowledgeable in English learner methodology and equipped with an organizational and planning framework for supporting a new teacher.

2. a mentor who met on a regular basis with the new teacher to assist them to effectively organize their classroom environment, plan instructional lessons, and evaluate the presentation of their instruction and student academic progress.

3. the ELL Guide that presented a framework and reference when the beginning teacher organized the classroom and planned lessons independently. The ELL Guide helped them focus on strategies for English learners.

4. the ELL Guide to help beginning teachers prepare for classroom observations by their mentor and school administrators. The ELL Guide outlined questions to discuss during the observation conference. Teachers were prepared and able to reflect on their own teaching practice.

5. a mentor that helped them become knowledgeable and competent teachers of English learners and helped them become an integral part of their new school community.

Beginning teachers shared that the ELL Guide helped them to identify English learners and plan according to their special needs. The ELL Guide prompted more ideas and ways of using materials to effectively teach and assess students. The ELL Guide was found to be beneficial because it provided an outline for planning. Mentors helped the beginning teachers to go back and reflect on instruction, drawing out valuable insight and information for teaching students from various backgrounds. The ELL Guide and supporting materials were viewed as a "great" structure to guide the lessons presented during mentor observations. Beginning teacher and mentor discussions that followed each observation were an important means of communication and for planning instruction. The ELL Guide was credited for helping to frame and support the beginning teacher and mentor relationship. The mentors were described by beginning teachers as willing "to help, offer ideas, and provide additional materials."

BTSA-ELL Beginning-Teacher Recommendations

The BTSA-ELL Survey asked beginning teachers to comment on their concerns or suggestions regarding the ELL Professional Development and ELL Guide. The recommendations were carefully considered and suggestions were often integrated into the professional development sessions. Some of the recommendations included the need for more opportunities to observe the classrooms of experienced teachers of English learners and for opportunities to share ideas with these other teachers.

One of the most valuable recommendations came from beginning teachers assigned to mentors without CLAD or Bilingual Certification. Their recommended was that it be mandatory for ELL mentors to have CLAD or Bilingual Certification. These beginning teachers felt that the mentoring relationship was hindered because mentors without a CLAD or BCLAD certificate had limited knowledge of English learners methodology and this restricted the mentor's ability to adequately assist the new teacher. Teachers described the need for support in planning, developing teaching strategies, assessment issues, assistance in the use of the ELL Guide but because their mentors had few experiences to draw from they did not receive the full extent of the support they needed. Beginning teachers said "the mentor's lack of prior English learner experience hampered their ability to offer suggestions, or to teach the beginning teachers methods and strategies that would help their English learners." They felt that sufficient prior English learner experience should be a prerequisite for mentors to be assigned to new teachers with English learners in their classroom.

After 2 years of implementing the BTSA-ELL Program for teachers and mentors significant progress was being achieved for both groups. Moreover, mentors felt that the support the program offered made a significant difference to the beginning teachers they mentored, their students, and themselves. A strong foundation had been put in place to continue to address the needs of teachers instructing English learners.

BTSA-ELL IMPLEMENTATION CREATES POSITIVE GAINS

In 1999, prior to the development of the BTSA-ELL Program, the *Statewide RIMS-BTSA Evaluation* (Mitchell, Scott, & Boyns, 1999) showed the RIMS-BTSA Program provided beginning teachers with limited guidance in helping them with instructional planning and teaching strategies for ELL students. Figure 9.3 shows the responses of new teachers and their mentors. New teachers were asked to rate the extent to which BTSA helped them to meet the needs of English learners. The mean response to this question on a 5-point scale, with 1 indicating low agreement, was 2.26 (N = 521). In 2000, 1 year after implementation of the BTSA-ELL the mean score increase to 2.69 indicating a statistically

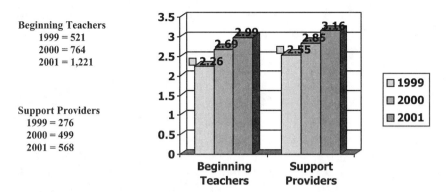

Beginning Teachers
1999 = 521
2000 = 764
2001 = 1,221

Support Providers
1999 = 276
2000 = 499
2001 = 568

FIG. 9.3. RIMS-BTSA efficacy in preparing teachers to instruct English learners.

significant difference (N = 764). The positive trend continued upward in the 2nd year (2000) of the BTSA-ELL for beginning teachers with a mean of 2.99 (N = 1,221) reported. These gains were achieved even with a dramatic increase of new teachers from 521 to 1,221. The mean scores of mentors working with the new teachers showed a similar pattern. In 1999, their mean was 2.55 (N = 276) and then increased to 2.85 (N = 499) in 2000. This was surpassed in 2001 with a mean of 3.16 (N = 568). The number of mentors more than doubled from 276 to 568 two years later. The Statewide RIMS-BTSA Program Survey Evaluation conducted longitudinally by Mitchell et al. (1999, 2000, 2001) demonstrates measured improvement in the way the BTSA-ELL Program support helped to meet the needs of ELL students over time. Although there were statistically significant gains over this 3-year period the highest mean score for beginning teachers was 2.99. This mean score is in the mid-range on a 1 to 5 scale, indicating that beginning teachers are aware that they must do more to be successful teacher of English learners but are not confident in knowing how to accomplish this task.

DILEMMAS AND ANOMALIES

In 2001, during the second year of the implementation of the BTSA-ELL Program California's Department of Education authorized the revision of BTSA Professional Development materials. The BTSA-ELL Program and the BTSA Special Education Program were developed as a prototype for statewide adoption to be included in the revision of BTSA Professional Development materials. The Evaluation Research Study for the BTSA-ELL Program was conducted to measure its effectiveness and showed positive results for both beginning teachers and mentors. The BTSA Special Education Program did not conduct a study to evaluate its effectiveness. Despite the lack of a formal evaluation, it is the case that the BTSA Special Education Program was adopted and is currently being used by new Special Education teachers throughout California. However, because of the overwhelming needs of the 2.2 million English learners in the state and the limited success they are experiencing achieving the academic standards, the state the BTSA-ELL Program was not adopted. The use of the ELL Professional Development materials is restricted from dissemination for use by districts throughout the state. The result was that less than 10% of the materials developed were added to the 2002 revised CFASST professional development materials for beginning teachers. With the failure to implement the BTSA-ELL Program the state has yet to provide a comprehensive solution for teachers of English learners and denies students the added support the BTSA-ELL Program provided to help them to succeed in school. A clear response from state officials why the BTSA-ELL Program was not adopted for use statewide while the BTSA Special Education Program was implemented was never clearly articulated. A few vague comments were delivered secondhand about the political tension post Proposition 227 in Sacramento and the lack of political will to clearly address the need of English learners beyond the restriction of languages other than English. New teachers of English learners and their mentors were clearly disappointed along with school districts outside the region that were unable to use the materials.

The same study surveyed BTSA beginning teacher of English learners that were not introduced to the ELL components. This sample of beginning teachers stated that they did not recall there being any English learner content in the CFASST events nor were they sure what materials were available to them. One beginning teacher wrote, "When English learners are placed in my class I do not modify instruction, but we all learn together." This comment demonstrates how beginning teachers without the benefit of the ELL Professional Development are not able to articulate differentiated instructional strategies that support English learners' instruction. Recognizing their own weakness in this area, some of their recommendations were that, "As part of the CFASST events, first year teachers should complete a number of observations and interviews with an experienced teacher of English learners." An additional suggestion from a beginning teacher was that it would have been helpful to have a "real ELL program" at their school site. A general concern expressed by teachers was that there was not sufficient support for English learners in their district and at their school sites. Beginning teachers were still at a loss in trying to improve instruction for English learners.

Finally, teachers felt that English learners' success in school was dependent on the beliefs that teachers held about their students and their capacity to learn. They shared that students were most successful when teachers were well trained, but teachers felt that they were learning on the job rather than entering their assignment prepared to teach English learners!

OUTCOMES AND IMPLICATIONS

The 1999 National Center for Educational Statistics report, *The Condition of Education,* confirmed that, "Approximately 70% of all teachers recently surveyed said they felt moderately or not at all prepared to address the needs of students from diverse backgrounds including students with limited English proficiency." Locally, the *Statewide RIMS-BTSA Evaluation* (Mitchell et al., 1999) revealed teachers felt critically limited in their ability to meeting the needs of English learners. The BTSA-ELL research findings demonstrated that the ELL professional development and support materials provided essential support to both veteran and beginning teachers of English learners. BTSA serves a region whose English learner population is increasing at 30% annually. The training has been received with great enthusiasm and served to answer many post–Proposition 227 questions in regard to providing effective instructional services for English learners. Feedback from the beginning teachers and their mentors was consistently positive concerning the ELL Guide, ELL Professional Development, ELL Follow-up Sessions, and supplementary materials.

The BTSA-ELL Survey findings indicated that ELL beginning teachers agree that the ELL Guide is specific enough to guide beginning teachers in developing a repertoire of skills and knowledge necessary to begin using a number of strategies in planning instruction for English learners. Beginning teachers were assisted in identifying ELL students, to considering their special needs, and in using effective instructional strategies and materials in a variety of ways. The ELL Guide was found to be an effective tool to direct the observation and follow-up conferencing, and to support the beginning teacher and mentor discussions about student learners, and to foster the mentoring relationship. The BTSA-ELL Program provided veteran CLAD and BCLAD trained mentors with updated training. The BTSA-ELL Program addressed new policy issues and procedures that varied across school districts post–Proposition 227. The ELL Professional Development addressed new initiatives such as the California Standards for the Teaching Profession, State-Adopted Subject Matter Content Standards, English Language Development Standards, the California English Language Development Test. The professional development prepared mentors to take a leadership role in their schools to address these new initiatives. Veteran BCLAD and CLAD trained teachers felt more knowledgeable and better prepared to address these policy issues and state initiatives.

If English learners are going to be academically competitive they must be prepared to pass the California English Language Development Test, meet the state-adopted Subject Matter Content Standards, pass the California High School Exit Exam, and earn a high school diploma. Success in these areas will open the door to competitively enter higher education, which means meeting California State University and University of California eligibility requirements. Teachers and administrators must receive more rigorous professional development that provides them with the knowledge and skills to effectively teach English learners. Currently, students are being held accountable through these policies and will soon be penalized for not achieving the standards outlined by the California Educational Reform Movement. How accountable are the state, teachers, and school district administrators who are entrusted with the role of helping English learners meet these standards? Much more needs to be done on behalf of English learners to allow them an equal opportunity for success.

ACKNOWLEDGMENT

The UCR-RIMS-BTSA-ELL Program was supported through a grant funded by the California Department of Education and the California Commission on Teacher Credentialing. Additional funding for the UCR-RIMS-BTSA Research Project was granted by the University of California Linguistic Minority Research Institute (UC LMRI) under the UC LMRI Grants Program. Opinions reflect those of the author(s) and do not necessarily reflect those of the grant agencies.

REFERENCES

Bushman, J., Goodman, G., Brown-Welty, S., & Dorn, S. (2001). Educational leadership: Making standards work, Vol. 59, No. 1, September 2001.

California Department of Education. (1998). *Proposition 227: Educating English learners for the twenty-first century*. Sacramento: CA. Retrieved January 16, 2001, from http:// www.cde.ca.gov/el/

California Department of Education. (1999a). *California R30 report*. Sacramento: CA. Retrieved July 25, 1999, from http://www.cde.ca.gov/demographics/

California Department of Education. (1999b). *English language development standards, July 1999*. Sacramento: CA. Retrieved December 1, 2000, from http://www.cde.ca. gov/standards/

California Department of Education. (1999c). *Language arts framework, 1997*. Sacramento: CA. Retrieved December 1, 2001, from http://www.cde.ca.gov/standards/

California Department of Education. (2002). *California High School Exit Exam (CAHSEE) for Mathematics and English Language Arts (ELA) by Program Combined 33 Riverside County and 36 San Bernardino County*. Retrieved July 20, 2002, from http:// data1.cde.ca.gov/dataquest/ExitProf2.asp?cSelect=33,RIVERSIDE&cYear=2001-02 &TestType=E&cAdmin=C&tDate=000000&Pageno=1

Center for the Future of Teaching and Learning. (2001). *Teaching and California's future: The status of the teaching profession*. The California State University Institute for Educational Reform; Policy Analysis for California Education; The University of California, Office of the President; WestEd.

Chatham Education Foundation. (2000). *Teacher retention survey 2000*. Chatham, NC: Chatham Education Foundation.

Darling-Hammond, L. (1999). *Professional development for teachers: Setting the stage for learning from teaching*. The Center for the Future of Teaching and Learning. Santa Cruz, CA.

Ferguson, R. (1991). Paying for public education: New evidence on how and why money matters. *Harvard Journal on Legislation, 28, Summer*, 465–498.

Goldring, E., & Greenfield, W. (2002). Understanding the evolving concept of leadership in education: Roles, expectations, and dilemmas. In J. Murphy (Ed.), *The educational leadership challenge: Redefining leadership for the 21st century*. National Society for the Study of Education, Part 1 (pp. 1–19). Chicago: University of Chicago Press.

Haycock, K. (1998). Good teaching matters: How well-qualified teachers can close the gap. *Thinking K–12, 3*(2), 1–14. http://wwwedtrust.org/main/main/reports.asp

Ingersoll, R. M. (2001). *Teacher turnover, teacher shortages, and the organization of schools*. University of Washington: Center for the Study of Teaching and Policy.

Johnson, S. M. (2000). Teaching's next generation. *Education Week on the Web*. Retrieved September 2001, from www.edweek.org/ew/ewstory.cfm?slug+39johnson.h19 &keywords=Susan?Moore %Johnson.

LA Times. (2003, July 10). http://www.latimes.com/news/education/la-me-exit10jul10, 1, 4804851.story?coll= la-news

Lugg, C. A., Bulkley, K., Firestone, W. A., & Gardner, C. W. (2002). The contextual terrain facing leaders. In J. Murphy (Ed.), *The educational leadership challenge: Redefining leadership for the 21st century*. National Society for the Study of Education, Part I (pp. 20–41). Chicago: University of Chicago Press.

Maxwell-Jolly, J., & Gándara, P. (2002). A quest for quality: Providing qualified teachers for California's English learners. In Z. F. Beyknot (Ed.), *The power of culture: Teaching across language differences* (pp. 43–70). Cambridge, MA: Harvard Education Publishing Group.

McCreight, C. (2000). *Teacher attrition, shortage, and strategies for teacher retention*. Texas A&M University: Department of Professional Programs. (ERIC Document Reproduction Service No. ED444986)

Mitchell, D., & Boyns, D. (2001). *The California beginning teacher support and assessment program: State evaluation study.* Riverside, CA California Education Research Cooperative and the University of California, Riverside.

Mitchell, D., Scott, L., & Boyns, D. (1999). *The California beginning teacher support and assessment program: State evaluation study.* Riverside: California Education Research Cooperative and the University of California, Riverside.

Mitchell, D., Scott, L., & Boyns, D. (2000). *The California beginning teacher support and assessment program: State evaluation study.* Riverside: California Education Research Cooperative and the University of California, Riverside.

Mitchell, D. E., Scott, L. D., Hendrick, I. G., & Boyns, D. (1998). *The California beginning teacher support and assessment program: State evaluation study.* Riverside: California Education Research Cooperative and University of California, Riverside.

National Center for Educational Statistics (NCES). (1999). *The condition of education report.* Washington, DC: U.S. Department of Education.

National Commission on Teaching & America's Future. (1996). *What matters most: Teaching for America's future.* New York: Teachers College, Columbia University.

Rumberger, R., & Gándara, P. (2000). The schooling of English learners. In E. Burr, G. C. Hayward, B. Fuller, & M. W. Kirst (Eds.), *Crucial issues in California education: Are the reform pieces fitting together?* (pp. 23–44). Berkeley: University of California, Policy Analysis for California Education.

Sweeney, J., & Whitworth, J. (2000). *Addressing teacher supply and demand by increasing the success of first-year teachers.* Chicago: Paper published at the Annual Meeting of the American Association of Colleges for Teacher Education.

Toenjes, L. A., Dworkin, A., Gary, L., & Antwanett, N. (2002). *The lone star gamble: High stakes testing, accountability and student achievement in Texas and Houston.* Unpublished manuscript, The Sociology of Education Research Group (SERG), Department of Sociology, University of Houston.

Toppo, G. (2003, July 2). The face of the American teacher, White and female, while her students are ethnically diverse. *USA Today.* Retrieved December 27, 2004, from http:// www.usatoday.com/educate/college/education/articles/20038706.htm.

Unz, R. K., & Tuchman, G. M. (1998). *The Unz initiative.* California Department of Education Web site. Sacramento:CA. [Online]. http://www.cde.ca.gov/el/

Uriarte, M. (2002). *The high stakes of high stakes testing.* in Beykont, Z. F. (Ed.) *The power of culture: Teaching across language difference* (pp. 3–24). Cambridge, MA: Harvard Education Publishing Group.

10

Con Pasión y Con Coraje: The Schooling of Latino/a Students and Their Teachers' Education

Jaime G. A. Grinberg
Katia Paz Goldfarb
Montclair State University

Elizabeth Saavedra
University of New Mexico, Albuquerque

INTRODUCTION

Our three children (Grinberg and Goldfarb) attend public schools and are bilingual in Spanish and English. One of the coauthors of this chapter, Saavedra, is a Chicana from New Mexico who is bilingual and bicultural and the other two coauthors are immigrant, tricultural, and multilingual. Throughout the years, they have encountered numerous situations and misunderstandings on the part of teachers, administrators, and fellow students grounded on assumptions and misconceptions not only about who they are as tricultural people, but also about their linguistic expressions, their diverse ways of knowing, their passionate modes of communicating and expressing their ideas, their ways of relating and connecting with others, and even about their own frustration with not being validated for who they are. Therefore, we are personally invested in the education of teachers because teachers can open or close possibilities, can reinforce and exacerbate conflicts, or can bridge and integrate differences such as those that derive from assumptions and misconceptions. Teachers can shape learning experiences, make them meaningful, exciting, respectful, relevant, and inclusive, or can teach that who the students are and what they bring with them as cultural beings is of no value. Furthermore troubling, they also can teach that in order to succeed in school students must abandon who they are, their heritages, their language, their behaviors, values, cultural norms, and ways of knowing. If we have these concerns about our children and if we are not happy about some of the teachers, administrators, and board of education members, who are an important part of our children's lives and education, then why should we accept these "educators" teaching other children? This chapter explores the education of educators, which not only happens in the university but also happens in the community including all of our children (our own and those members of other families and caregivers). Thus, in a Freirean sense, if the education of teachers happens in specific places such as local communities, then our children not only learn from teachers, they educate teachers, too.

The arguments of this chapter are rather simple: (1) teacher education and professional development fail to address properly the preparation of teachers who work with Latina/o students; (2) one of the reasons for that failure is the lack of authentic and critical experiences that immerse teachers and future teachers in the communities, to work and learn WITH the communities, not to work ON them. The history of changes in teacher education has provided a number of enduring structural issues that disable these curricular efforts to move teacher education in/to the community (Grinberg & Goldfarb, 1998), yet we argue that, (3) in spite of these disabling structural issues, teacher education can prepare teachers who can learn from their students. In short, *school students can and do educate their teachers*. In this case, we explore 2 dimensions of teaching that can be learned from the students regardless of institutional arrangements, practices of oppression, or structural limitations: *pasión* (passion) and *coraje* (courage, rage, anger, or indignation, cheerful disrespect, daring, and "chutzpah"), which are positive forms of resistance, transgression, and transformation because they struggle to alter unjust conditions and to provide possibilities of improvement

(Bourdieu & Hacquant, 1992, Bourdieu & Passeron, 1977; Cresswell, 1996; Foucault, 1988, 2000). *Pasión y Coraje* tend to be dismissed because they are expressions and behaviors based on emotions and feelings, thus, in tension with reason, which is often privileged as the intellectual, balanced, objective, and valued way of learning. As Freire asserted (1998), this is a false dichotomy. Fischman (2000) suggested that:

> Emotions and beliefs are not easily incorporated in educational research, not only because people tend to mask the expression of feelings, but also because emotion and expressions of desire resist the (very often) reductionist preconceived frameworks of researchers. Moreover, in order to imagine a different educational future, researchers need to incorporate the multifaceted dimensions of emotions, bodies, and feelings because ignoring them is impossible when dealing with the real problems of schooling. Furthermore, isolating feelings from thinking and understanding will not be of much help in imagining how to transform the inequalities occurring at schools and in society. (p. 8)

Fischman's argument resonates well with those of us who grew up in cultural contexts that celebrate emotions, creativity, and reasoning as part of the same integral experience. In contrast, their dichotomization exacerbates tensions and conflicts when these different cultures meet or clash, thus forcing a negotiation in which many are not even aware that this has to be negotiated. This happens often in the encounter with schooling: Although there may be gender stratification in privileging one form of knowing over the other—such as rationalistic knowledge over emotional knowledge, or divorced reasoning over integrating feelings, emotion, and body with the mind—it also creates conflicts with students who come from homes where these constructed dichotomies may be present, at least in the same ways. For instance, Nieto (2000) provides numerous examples of what she calls "cultural discontinuities" referring to the incongruence between home or local cultures and that of the school. Nieto uses among other examples from her data, the difference on the concept of being smart or intelligent. Although in the dominant American culture intelligence is an innate quality, for most Latinos/as intelligence is a learning process, often a result of investing time and energy, which demands networks of support such as those provided by family, friends, and communities. The school often represents a break with the values, behaviors, beliefs, and ways of knowing of Latina/o students, thus creating a cultural rupture between

the dominant institution and the dominated, but not necessarily passive and domesticated clients (Grinberg & Goldfarb, 1998; Grinberg &
Saavedra, 2000). Or as McCaleb (1994) has suggested, "Children live
their lives in two worlds: that of the home and community and that of
the school. When these two worlds fail to know, respect, and celebrate
each other, children are placed in a difficult position" (p. vii). Valdez
(1996) argued that these discontinuities or ruptures are often present
in the case of Mexican immigrants, whom she studied, because they
have a clear sense of schooling, expectations, and success in their native communities, but their ways of knowing are not always relevant
to the European-American prevalent middle-class structure of schooling, also discovering that their views and experiences are undervalued,
and often times in conflict with the institutional culture and with the
teachers and staff perceptions of success.

However, building on local knowledge and expertise has been identified as an important strategy to redefine what constitutes the culture of
the school (Goldfarb, 1998; Nieto, 2002; Zeichner et al., 1998). Goldfarb
(1998) argues that practices such as "Grupo de Padres," which has been
institutionalized in a school with a predominantly Latin population,
helps parents (mostly mothers) to gain ownership over the school life
of their children, including policies and services, becoming an "urban
sanctuary" (a safe, trusting, and respectful environment, where their
voice counts). Furthermore, their regular physical presence, including
owning a physical space, has created among the teachers a dynamic of
learning from and with the community. Nieto (2000, 2003a, 2003b) has
clearly advocated for such teacher learning. In her research using case
studies she encountered that Latina/o students reported meaningful
and relevant learning also from teachers who were not from their same
cultural background because "These teachers had either learned the
students' language or were knowledgeable about or comfortable with
their culture..." (2000, p. 298). Furthermore, Zeichner et al. (1998) in
their comprehensive study of the preparation of teachers for cultural
diversity, argued that teachers not only need to have the experiences
and tools to alter unjust social, political, and cultural relations manifested in school life, curriculum, and pedagogy, but they also argued
for the need to prepare teachers who will be systematically grounded
and exposed to "multiple types and sources of knowledge" (p. 169). The
authors suggested that for a teacher education program to be successful
in preparing teachers for cultural diversity, that program should hire

"community members and/or school staff as adjunct teacher education program faculty..." (p. 169).

Villegas and Lucas (2002) supported this approach, and they added that for teachers it is crucial to "...translate those insights into pedagogical practices" (p. 95). For that purpose, they suggested a number of strategies that include (pp. 95–102): helping students to access prior knowledge and beliefs, building on students' interests, using examples and analogies from students' lives, building on students' linguistic resources, using appropriate instructional methods, and tapping community resources. Villegas and Lucas (2002) also suggested that such education of teachers cannot happen solely during their preservice programs, thus advocating for a lifelong learning approach, which in turn, Grinberg (2002) argued, will urge us to make experience a systematic and scrutinized subject matter of study. In addition, Nieto (2000, 2003a) has argued that there is much to learn not only about the students but also from the students. This approach validates what Latina/o students bring to the learning experience by potentially altering asymmetrical power arrangements that historically have worked against them, thus, for a change, Latino/a students become sources of knowledge, beliefs, and feelings. Teaching and learning like this is coherent with Freire's dialogical pedagogy (1970a, 1998), in which the directions in the relationship of the educator and the educated (learner) are both ways; thus, the educator becomes the learner who is being educated by her/his students.

It is in this venue that in this chapter we utilize the concepts of *Pasión y Coraje*, to illustrate the integration of intellectual and emotional ways of knowing that Latino/a students use in educating their teachers. *Pasión y Coraje* are critical ways of knowing that should be added to the lifelong learning process that Villegas and Lucas (2002) advocate in culturally responsive teacher education programs. We also add that this process needs to be aided by a critical reading of power arrangements done through an inquiry-oriented practice or by fostering a practitioner research approach to the understanding of one's contexts (Anderson, Herr, & Nihlen, 1994; Cochran-Smith & Little, 1993). This is coherent with Villegas and Lucas's argument for teacher education as a lifelong learning process because such research renews with new questions and contexts through time and place. Within this perspective, reclaiming feelings, emotions, imagination has to be part of learning to teach in general, and particularly when learning from students, which adds a spiritual dimension to learning to teach (Wexler, 2000). Such learning is also political because it interrupts discourses and practices that discipline and docilize body and mind, as we will see in the critical incidents presented in another section of this chapter.

These interruptions happen within institutional arrangements. Certainly, these teacher education programs may incorporate the right ingredients when educating teachers of Latina/o students in the United States. However, all programs need to be analyzed within their particular institutional contexts. The history of teacher education demonstrates that these institutional and contextual arrangements respond more often to issues outside the conceptual, curricular, and pedagogical debates. First, teacher education programs are not isolated from university contexts, from local and national politics, and from market pressures. Second, the preparation of teachers is not isolated from the context of schooling (Liston & Zeichner, 1990), which tends to be one that stands in conflict and tension with the contemporary constructivist and critical cultures in some preservice teacher preparation programs. Third, the education of teachers in too many programs has a "hidden curriculum" (Ginsburg & Clift, 1990) that, purposely or not, maintains the discourse of neutrality and thus favors the status quo in spite of numerous reforms. Finally, returning to the first point regarding the intrinsic relationship of teacher education to the context of the university, it is important to remark that the education of teachers not only also happens in colleges of arts and sciences, but most of it actually happens in these colleges.

In order to support the argument that although teacher education has failed to prepare teachers for Latina/o students, this can and should be done, in the following section we will expand on the multiple contexts of teacher education from a historical perspective. Then we will address culturally responsive teacher education and social justice. Finally, we discuss teacher education in the communities and Latino/a students and their teachers' education.

CONTEXTS OF TEACHER EDUCATION

This section focuses on some topics in the history of teacher education that will help unpack some disabling issues. Because the education of teachers of Latino/a students is not different from teacher education in general but rather is embedded in teacher education, it is necessary to understand how the field constituted its practices and discourses. The aspects covered here analyze the institutional and social contexts that shaped the curriculum and experiences in teacher education but do not analyze the education that teachers receive when they are already in schools, whether by the school system or by the community and students. These will be partly covered later in this chapter. Thus, the intention here is not to include the whole spectrum of the history of teacher education in the United States but rather to explain enduring aspects that have worked against the education of teachers and have contributed to the cyclical collapse of teacher education reforms (Labaree, 1994, 1997).

Apple (1991) suggested that the failure of reform in teacher education is the failure to unveil the nature of schooling within certain historically developed social arrangements:

> All too many proposals for the education of teachers are formed in a vacuum. They ignore the political and economic context in which education as a whole takes place. . . . In this process, these proposals often fail to challenge the prevailing distribution of economic, political, and cultural power. (p. vii)

Several studies on the history of teacher education identified a set of enduring issues. Some of the issues are the disabling influence of markets in the curriculum and reform of teacher education, the influence of academic politics on the lack of ownership over the curriculum of teacher education, and the gender and class background of prospective teachers. In combination, these factors contributed to a variety of negative characteristics of teacher education: the low status of teacher education students and programs, the narrow view of teacher preparation as instruction, the shaping of the programs into short and easy to enter, quick, and undemanding, and that seem to have lost their sense of mission (Goodlad et al., 1990; Herbst, 1989; Urban, 1990; Warren, 1985).

Market considerations have driven both policies and content of study in teacher education programs (Warren, 1985). The size of the teaching force, its demand and supply, had an impact on the curriculum of teacher education, licensure, and hiring procedures of teachers independent of professional judgment and independent of research knowledge (Sedlak & Schlossman, 1986; Sedlak, 1989). Markets influence who gets into teaching and the quality of the teacher. This is in part what had been called the *disabling legacy* of markets because of their negative effects on the content and quality of teacher preparation (Labaree 1994, 1995). For example, throughout the 19th century and for most of the 20th, there was a shortage of teachers. At the same time, certification became a required norm for employment (Sedlak, 1989). Teacher education programs (particularly normal schools) not only granted teaching credentials that were sponsored by the state but also attempted to satisfy the demand for teachers in a growing society with mandatory schooling (Labaree, 1994). The large numbers of prospective teachers attending teacher education programs needed efficient production. This meant low-cost and high-speed (short-term) programs. This program organization was at the risk that "product" quality could be sacrificed to satisfy employer demand:

> If teacher training took on aspects of mass production, and if the product was not expected to last very long anyway, then the cost of producing each unit had to be kept down in order to sustain the operation. Under these circumstances, an intensive and prolonged process of professional education was difficult to justify to legislators and taxpayers. (Labaree, 1994, p. 18)

Short time in the program, easy courses, and superficial content with focus on few technical aspects were necessary to attract many students and to provide them with a low-cost license in order to respond to state and local district pressures. Historically, normal schools and the institutions that evolved out of them sought to provide a socially efficient way to satisfy the market demand for teachers (Goodlad, 1990).

Another form of market pressure that influenced the quality of teacher education programs has come from consumers. Constituencies attracted to teacher education programs didn't necessarily look forward to a teaching position (Herbst, 1989; Labaree, 1994). Rather, many clients of these programs wanted a credential that would provide access to the larger job market and that would have a broad exchange value. This means that the credential gained as result of a course of studies has certain value because of aspects such as the job market and what kind of jobs can be secured, and not necessarily as a result of what was learned (use value of a credential). Therefore, the result of this process is a dichotomy between the use value and the exchange value of the credential.

The tension emerges when, given the dichotomy between use and exchange values of a credential, the job market doesn't value expertise if it is not attached to a credential and that a credential assumes that such expertise exists—but in the case of teaching such assumption is often false. According to Collins (1979), the job market doesn't respond to expertise but to the power arrangements of the professions that monopolize the provision of credentials. Knowledge and expertise are assumed on the base of a credential. For many consumers of credentials, the interest of investing in a credential is not necessarily expertise and knowledge but, rather, the possibility of securing better jobs and better status than they normally could access without such credential. A better job, a better income, and a better status are elements of upward social mobility. Improving social status and social class are result of several variables, among them a better job (Lipset & Bendix, 1959). To have access to a better job in a credential society depends more on the status and market needs of the credential than on the meaning of the knowledge and expertise. Furthermore, a credential in one profession doesn't limit the access to better jobs only within the profession. For instance, during the latter part of the 19th century, a teaching credential opened opportunities to a wide range of white-collar jobs (Herbst, 1989).

Access to normal schools, which were located mostly in farming areas, also was cheaper and easier to gain than access to the university, often located in larger cities. Although the credentials from normal schools and from universities didn't have the same exchange value in the market, a normal school credential enhanced the possibilities of white-collar jobs for the sons and daughters of farmers and blue-collar workers, thus creating a demand for normal school credentials without intention of using the credential to teach. In turn, the consumers' demand for credentials and social mobility forced normal schools to expand their curriculum in order to satisfy the need for more generic skills besides the traditional concentration on teaching. Opening new courses and later offering new programs in these normal schools produced a shift on the focus of the institution away from teacher preparation into the newly created and expanded programs. Because of both program expansions and consumer pressures, many of these normal schools of the 19th century and of the early 20th century evolved into universities:

> Ambitious school leaders, determined to provide more than training for elementary and/or rural teachers, quickly introduced programs that would lead to a bachelor's degree. By the 1920s (much earlier for some), many

state normal schools had become teachers' colleges, offering a bachelor's degree.... The teacher training mission has also been affected by the several constituencies that normal schools have served.... For example, the tremendous increase in college enrollments following the Second World War further eroded the teacher preparation mission, as former normal schools responded to the demands of predominantly male students for programs in liberal arts and other professions. (Altenbaugh & Underwood, 1990, p. 178–179)

Teacher education, then, lost its importance as the main purpose of these institutions, becoming a prey of academic politics, including competition for enrollments, budgets, and prestige. Teacher education curriculum responded to the internal university pressures that required several courses in the arts and sciences. Some programs in arts and sciences needed students to justify their existence as programs, or at least to maintain faculty lines and budgets. These internal struggles between teacher education and departments in arts and sciences resulted in fewer courses taken in teacher education. This pattern continues to be present in contemporary universities, with the addition of state-mandated limitations for the total number of credit hours required for students' graduation at the undergraduate level and the number of credit hours allowed to be provided in teacher education programs. Given a limited number of credit hours that teacher education students take in order to meet graduation requirements, the more credit hours that are required to take in arts and sciences programs to satisfy general education expectations means less credit hours taken by these same students in teacher education departments. This sacrifice of credit hours in teacher preparation has meant quality decline of programs because of less engagement with the subject matter of the profession. Also, it has meant higher costs for the teacher education program since the production of credit hours was reduced. Thus, students and programs of teacher education were and continue to be shared with programs and faculty with no stake in teacher preparation.

The sharing of responsibility in the preparation of teachers between teacher education programs and other academic units raises another theme that the literature highlights: ownership of programs and responsibility for the quality of such programs. Warren (1985), referring to Professor H. Rugg's ideas, argues that, "No college curriculum could be effective unless it was controlled by the faculty responsible for it" (p. 11).

The shift of institutional focus away from teacher education also produced fragmentation of programmatic coherence because of shared responsibility in the preparation of teachers with faculty and programs with little commitment to this task. For instance, normal schools that grew into institutions offering bachelor's degrees, increased the need for faculty in academic subjects. These new faculty were trained in their own disciplines and their interest was to advance knowledge in their fields. Most of these faculty members were trained in research universities and the mission and institutional expectations of normal schools were foreign to their experiences. Moreover, for some the primary interest was research rather than teaching. As Urban (1990) asserted: "These academic faculty, many of whom were trained in universities, brought university values from their own disciplines into the teachers college setting, values that did not honor the purpose of preparing teachers as the ultimate goal of their work" (p. 65).

Also, most of these university faculties didn't have the same class and gender background of the teachers and future teachers (Lanier & Little, 1986; Ginsburg, 1987). Historically both normal schools and university education departments mostly enrolled female students, many of them from lower-middle-class backgrounds (Altenbaugh & Underwood, 1990; Ginsburg, 1987; Rury, 1989). According to Ginsburg (1987), teacher education programs enrolled a population of students, mostly women from lower-middle-class or working-class backgrounds, which was different from the rest of the student population in universities. This difference created an asymmetric balance of status among students and programs, where teacher education students and programs are at the bottom of the hierarchy.

In short, a low-status program with a watered-down curriculum has to negotiate mostly within itself what content and what experiences will be privileged and at the cost of what other content and experiences. This situation is particularly problematic because not only do the teachers of our children not have a strong preparation in general but also such preparation often neglects a culturally responsive education (Villegas & Lucas, 2002); a critical pedagogy; a preparation for cultural diversity (Zeichner et al., 1998); it is overregulated by the state and by the standardization of the profession; and, as Zeichner noted (2003), the alternative of social justice has not been well addressed in contemporary teacher education dominant reform efforts. Furthermore, Ginsburg and Clift (1990) argued that, "When society and its relation to schooling

are discussed in teacher education, the hidden message is that existing institutions and social relations are natural, neutral, legitimate, or
just given" (p. 457). Such hegemonizing tendency is present because
in teacher education programs students are exposed to "experiences
through which future teachers learn about hierarchies and authority
relations in education...and by different types of educational institutions 'serving' different racial and ethnic groups" (Ginsburg & Clift,
1990, p. 457). For teachers of Latina/o students in particular, developing
a sense of inquiry and critical reflection may enable them to counter
the hegemonizing tendencies of the curriculum and the normalizing
disciplinary practices of schooling (Anderson & Grinberg, 1998). Looking at teacher education as a disciplinary practice helps understand
that whereas discourses and practices may sound progressive, simultaneously they have to compete with their own regimentation, control
techniques, surveillance approaches, and ideological shortcomings. A
disciplinary practice is, in a Foucauldean sense:

> A set of discourses, norms, and routines that shape the ways in which a
> field of study constitutes itself; ... connects with historical, political, cultural,
> and economic contexts but are enacted within specific, local, and contin-
> gent institutional arrangements, and ... entails the establishment of conven-
> tions, agreements, and rules that regulate and legitimize current ways of
> distinguishing among "best practices", desired outcomes, academic rigor,
> and valid knowledge claims. (Anderson & Grinberg, 1998, p. 330)

Therefore, contemporary teacher education is an arena of debate and
struggle, not only for the enduring institutional and market factors outlined earlier but also in terms of what constitutes good teacher education, even within the confines of a few credit hours. During the last
two decades, in particular since the Carnegie report *A Nation at Risk*
(1983) and the report *Tomorrow's Teachers* (Holmes Group, 1986), the
content and pedagogy of teacher education has been interrogated and
proposals for change have been implemented in numerous areas but
seldom in the direction of critical inquiry based practices that will challenge to alter unjust social, political, economic, and cultural relations,
as these two reports represented a narrow decontextualized proposal
to maintain or improve the status of teacher education and teaching as a
profession within a larger agenda of conservative social and economic
programs but not that of culturally, ethnically, or linguistically diverse
and historically marginalized and colonized students.

CULTURALLY RESPONSIVE TEACHER
EDUCATION AND SOCIAL JUSTICE

In a paper that analyzes the discourses of contemporary influential opposing proposals for reforming the preparation of teachers, Cochran-Smith and Fries (2001) argue that such approaches can be framed within two main ideological agendas. The first is: "The agenda to professionalize teaching and teacher education, which is linked to the K–12 curriculum standards movement" (p. 3). The second agenda is the "movement to deregulate teacher education by dismantling teacher education institution" (p. 3). However, a multicultural and social justice critique has raised a number of concerns. Such critiques argue that, on the one hand, there is an overtechnocratization and scientifization of preparation programs, thus neglecting the political, cultural, and historical rights and aspirations of groups, communities, and students who have often been the recipients of a symbolic colonizing curriculum, which also includes silencing and dehumanizing pedagogies. On the other hand, the deregulation advocates respond to a neoliberal ideology that serves at least to maintain the status quo by creating a teaching force with no understanding of pedagogy, curriculum, and students' diversity. Furthermore, these uneducated teachers privilege their knowledge (Popkewitz, 2000), their ways of knowing, and their cultural capital over that of their students who often are constructed as the deprived "other," something that already has been in place in school curricula and pedagogies (Gallegos, 2000; Goldfarb, 1998; Grinberg & Goldfarb, 1998; Grinberg & Saavedra, 2000; Nieto, 2000; Steinberg & Kincheloe, 2001; Valdez, 1996). Advocates of culturally responsive teacher preparation (Villegas & Lucas, 2001, 2002) have argued that given the demographic tendencies in America, unless we prepare teachers who can understand the complexities of diversity and culture, and who can create inclusive environments, we run the risk of betraying the democratic purpose of schooling, thus resorting one more time to the symbolic colonization of the "other" (Carlson, 1997). Explaining the consequences of constructing "otherness" as a form of "symbolic colonization," Grinberg and Saavedra (2000) argued that:

> [T]he dominant language of schooling has referred to minorities, the working and poor classes, and immigrants using labels that indicate inferiority, savagery, deprivation, and difference. This is a common way of constructing the "other," that is, as different from what is established as normal, desired, and dominant, something that challenges homogeneity. Thus, by pathologizing

students, their families, and ethnic and social groups, the project of schooling becomes one of domestication, "civilizing," Westernizing, Americanizing, and normalizing students according to the values, culture, language, and traditions of the dominant classes: in other words, a colonizing project. For us, symbolic colonization is an encompassing and helpful term to describe these practices. The discourse of "English only" is an example of symbolic colonization, since language has been central to imperialistic cultural imposition throughout history. (p. 422)

Furthermore, "educational colonization" has to be named and unpacked as a symbolic practice. Swartz (1997) explained that:

Symbolic practices deflect attention from the interested character of practices and thereby contribute to their enactment as disinterested pursuits. This misperception legitimizes these practices and thereby contributes to the reproduction of the social order in which they are embedded. Activities and resources gain in symbolic power, or legitimacy, to the extent that they become separated from underlying material interests and hence go misrecognized as representing disinterested forms of activities and resources. (p. 90)

By focusing on serving students' "needs" vis-à-vis school success within the mainstream dominant perspectives and standards, such constructions of inferiority and deprivation as well as remedial and "at-risk" pedagogical practices become legitimate normalizing approaches. Evermore, cultural and political critique is contained and silenced, often reduced and constructed as deviant, pathological, or disloyal (Saavedra, 1998). For instance, Grinberg and Saavedra (2000) provided the example of the Southwestern portion of the United States, which

has had a constant history of colonization that began with the Spanish conquistadors and continues through the present in what we term "symbolic colonization," which occurs through our contemporary institutions. Symbolic colonization draws from postcolonial theory and refers to how certain practices maintain an unequal and hierarchical distribution of power and access to knowledge through educational and social relations. Given the legitimate and/or informal rules in place, minorities are continually held at the bottom of the stratified social and economic system without institutional possibilities for advancement or change. (p. 421)

Bourdieu (1994) and Bourdieu and Passeron (1977) referred to educational systems as the primary institutional setting for the production, transmission, and accumulation of the various forms of cultural capital, thus contributing to the maintenance of a nonegalitarian social system by allowing inherited cultural differences to shape academic achievement and occupational attainment. Moreover, education has become the institution most responsible for the transmission of social inequality, cultural resources, and educational credentials. Educational practices that perpetuate privilege of some groups over others exacerbate inequities that persist from generation to generation, without conscious recognition or public resistance because, as Ross (1991) explained as the "Bourdieu effect," a cycle of social reproduction occurs: "They are excluded because they don't know why they are excluded; and they don't know why they are excluded because they are excluded. Or in other words, the system reproduces its existence because it goes unrecognized" (pp. xi–xii).

Such reproduction in teacher education is discussed by students in these programs (Grinberg & Saavedra, 2000), who "acknowledged that university programs have created courses, requirements, and expectations with little relevance for them or the linguistic and ethnic minority students they are serving" (p. 433). Furthermore, one of the students in teacher education argued that:

> I was not prepared for the reality in the schools. We needed to learn about coalition building, community building, and activism to challenge the administration so that we could provide for minority kids. The needy students get the least amount of services and programs. In my teacher preparation program, I didn't learn how to help these kids. We never discussed what our real purpose in working with monolingual or minority kids is all about in any of the classes at the university, particularly the core courses. The core classes that are required didn't address the larger societal issues that I was going to encounter when I started teaching. I never learned how to change the system, or how to get the system to work toward justice for all students. (Grinberg & Saavedra, 2000, pp. 433–434)

Moreover, in teacher education programs, "culture is approached as a superficial treatment toward understanding the client to be served" (Grinberg & Saavedra, 2000, p. 434). This is one of the aspects that culturally responsive teacher education, as outlined earlier, is proposing to change. But can this be enough to counter the historical structural enduring issues in teacher preparation described above?

In concurrence with culturally responsive teacher education and with moving teacher education further into schools and communities, Zeichner (2003) argued for a rethinking of the dominant discourses and practices of teacher education and calls for the alternative discourse of "social justice." Although at times social justice could be an elusive term, Goldfarb and Grinberg (2002) defined it in the context of popular education in Latin America vis-à-vis extreme differences in terms of power, economic distributions, access to knowledge, and generation of knowledge: "We define social justice as the exercise of altering these arrangements by actively engaging in reclaiming, appropriating, sustaining and advancing inherent human rights of equity, equality, and fairness in social, economic, educational, and personal dimensions, among other forms of relationships" (p. 162).

Zeichner (2003) expands on social justice in the context of education in the United States as grounded in a critique of the "cultural gap between teachers and their pupils, advocates of the social justice agenda which is an outgrowth of the social reconstructionist tradition of reform in American teacher education see both schooling and teacher education as crucial elements in the making of a more just society" (p. 507). Furthermore, he challenges the Interstate New Teacher Assessment and Support Consortium (INTASC) standards by proposing three domains: knowledge, performance, and dispositions, which currently are being discussed and addressed by Urban Network to Improve Teacher Education (UNITE) in light of the movement advocating for social justice in teacher education. In a Freirean tradition and congruent with the body of literature cited above, the knowledge domain insists that the teacher understands life in the students' communities and how students use knowledge, interact, and communicate; teachers "know something about the funds of knowledge that exist in these communities" (p. 508). The performance domain refers to the ability of incorporating students' cultural and community contexts to enhance and promote further learning. The disposition domain explains, "The teacher sees resources for learning in all students rather than viewing differences as problems to overcome" (p. 508) and teachers have the belief that they are responsible for making a difference. Yet, Zeichner warns that the social justice agenda needs to address structural issues with concrete proposals beyond pedagogy because, "it is clear that any solution to the problems of inequality and injustice in public education will need to address the larger contexts in which teaching and teacher education exist" (p. 509). He also recommends that, given the lack of diversity and experience in diverse communities among teacher educators, to employ community members as teacher educators. In addition, he calls to prepare all teachers to teach all children.

These proposals for social justice as the ways to frame teacher education have to incorporate two other dimensions. One is that of exploring and problematizing the self, and the other is the education that students provide to teachers.

For example, one aspect of problematizing the self relates to de-essentializing categories such as Latina/o. By essentializing categories, the result is a limited analysis of power relations within these groups. For instance, the educational experience of an educated affluent Latina woman is probably different from the educational experience of the Latina woman who cleans the bathroom of the educated affluent woman. Furthermore, postcolonial critiques (Carlson, 1997; Cordova, 1997; Dhillon, 1999; Fanon, 1952; Gallegos, 1998; Memmi, 1965, 1984) unpacked the dynamics of internal colonization and the role of the colonized minorities that operate as educational brokers in perpetuating oppression, marginality, and asymmetric access to knowledge in order to bring advantage to themselves at the expense of their own ethnic, gender, or racial entourage (Carlson, 1997; Cordova, 1997; Gallegos, 1998; Grinberg & Saavedra, 2000). As an example, the Southwest has been a problematic area to study because many Hispanics are not Mexican Americans but are Chicanos (Mestizos, the mix of Spanish colonizers and American Indians). In northern New Mexico and southern Colorado, many Hispanics consider themselves Spanish Americans who never recognized Mexican sovereignty and who were well settled for almost 300 years before becoming part of the American territory (North American). Thus, for these groups it is not a history of education of immigrants as it is for many Latinos/as but a history of education, colonization, dispossession, and accommodation, in which there were winners and losers not only in terms of Anglo-Hispanic categories but also within Hispanic populations. Moreover, the problem was also one of a struggle of a colonizing, privileged population of aristocratic descendants of Spanish conquerors, and their losing ground to the new colonizer after the Treaty of Guadalupe Hidalgo (Grinberg & Saavedra, 2000). In this equation, some of the old privileged classes maneuvered to maintain their privilege at the expense of their own becoming agents for the new colonizing power. Therefore, although Hispanics had agency, it is important, in a Freirean tradition, to study in favor of whom this agency operated and under what circumstances. At times, this agency perpetuated colonization in a symbolic way by benefiting a class of educational brokers who acted as colonized minorities (Cordova, 1997; Gallegos, 1992, 1998; Grinberg & Saavedra, 2000). In addition, Hispanics and Mexican American educational histories are in some aspects different from Cuban, Dominican, Puerto Rican, or Uruguayan immigrants' educational histories. Thus, analyzing the structural and cultural aspects of localized communities become imperative for understanding the dynamics of schooling and the pedagogical and curricular strategies for social justice.

The education that students provide to teachers, which should be added to a culturally responsive teacher education that fosters and advances social justice, will be discussed in the next section.

TEACHER EDUCATION IN THE COMMUNITIES: LATINO/A STUDENTS AND THEIR TEACHERS' EDUCATION

So, what will it entail to prepare this teacher? Such preparation should be intellectually stimulating, engaging, passionate, and inquiry-based (Grinberg, 2002). Furthermore, such preparation has to take place not only in the university classrooms or the school classrooms, but should also be immersed in the life of the local communities (Grinberg & Goldfarb, 1998; McCaleb, 1994, 1998; Nieto, 2000; Villegas & Lucas, 2001, 2002; Zeichner, 2003; Zeichner et al., 1998). This immersion means to go beyond the ethnographic and inquiry-oriented approaches, which are important aspects of a solid teacher preparation program or principal education program, toward a reflective and critical experiential approach. Furthermore, learning to teach this way means building on the traditional progressive and critical idea (Grinberg, 2002) of tapping on the assets of the community (Nieto, 2000; Villegas & Lucas, 2002), and using members of local communities as co-instructors, guides, and coaches (Zeichner, 2003; Zeichner et al., 1998). These practices also ought to open the possibility of including students as sources of local knowledge. It is to that point that we turn now: Teacher education programs have to provide future teachers with the intellectual and emotional propensities and sensibilities to be also educated by their own students. Here we refer in particular to two sine qua non characteristics of good teaching that relate not only to the pedagogical realm but also in particular address some of the structural aspects of schooling: *Pasión* and *Coraje*, which are congruent with what students of Latina/o heritage understand and value.

In what follows, we will first describe three "critical incidents," in which we were indirectly involved by virtue of being a teacher of the teachers in these events.[1] Then we will briefly analyze these incidents vis-à-vis schooling, and, finally, we will refer to *Coraje* and *Pasión*.

The first incident unfolded as follows: In one of Grinberg's graduate seminars, students were reading materials related to theoretical concepts of "correspondence," "critique," "transgression," and "resistance." One of the students, who at the time was an English teacher, shared her concern about the values and politics of her school's administration. She taught in a school where a significant number of students were immigrants from Mexico and Central America, including some Cuban students. This particular semester she had sections with well above 30 students each. In a school's department meeting that was attended by administrators, she raised her dissatisfaction. The response was astonishing. She was told to be patient for a few weeks since a significant number of Spanish-speaking students will "drop out" anyway and this "natural" process will drastically reduce the class size. The incident does not end with this. The next day after the seminar, she was called to the principal's office. She was reprimanded for voicing in public her concerns about the school and creating a "negative representation" of the school and its administrators. She was told that the school always has to look good. Grinberg wanted to know how the school principal knew about the discussion in the seminar. It was easy to conclude that it was one of the students in the seminar who was doing her administrative preparation internship in that building. After confronting this student about her breach of confidentiality, something

---

[1]Critical incidents are "highly charged moments and episodes that have enormous consequences for personal change and development" (Sikes, Measor, & Woods, 1985, cited in Angelides, 2001, p. 432) to "mostly straightforward accounts of very commonplace events that occur in routine professional practice" (Tripp, 1993, p. 25). Herr (2002) argues that the "analysis of critical incidents invites a probing into workplace norms that help construct institutional realities and can stimulate reflection on institutional practices, exposing underlying motives and structures" (p. 8). Furthermore, Herr adds, "The naming of an event as a critical incident can come from any individual in an institution and signals that an event has occurred that potentially becomes the stimulus for reflection" (p. 8).

Critical incidents are not independent situations. They can present the hidden aspects of an institutional or programmatic culture. In a critical tradition, citing Smyth (1991), Herr (2002) suggests a series of questions when analyzing these events: Who benefits and who loses by the actions taken? What structural and cultural conditions enable and perpetuate the actions? What are the power arrangements? What factors disable possible alternative actions? It is also necessary to understand that critical incidents are not divorced from participants and are not discovered but they are rather constructed by the importance and value participants provide to the situation or event (Tripp, 1993).

that was discussed in class the first day in relation to issues of trust and safety, Grinberg decided to withdraw the student from the seminar. In turn, Grinberg got calls from the school principal, trying to explain that they have a great dropout prevention program, and from the department chair in Educational Administration asking him to reconsider the "withdrawal" of the student, as it may reflect negatively in the programs and because the university works so closely with the schools that this could provoke a public relations problem. Grinberg did not reinstate the student. The reprimanded teacher did write a couple of excellent papers building on this experience and she is now teaching in another state.

The second incident was a walkout of high school students in our neighborhood high school. The students demanded more advanced ESL classes to gain language skills in order to enroll in honor classes, or college preparatory or advanced placement classes, and demanded to have these classes offered in Spanish. Their argument was that the school did not provide them with a fair opportunity to have the education they needed to continue on to college. Furthermore, they claimed that the only available classes were low track and that their preparation was geared only to low-skills, low-paid jobs. The students' parents fully supported their children's challenge to the school. The school district response was twofold. They decided to offer more sections of ESL classes but not content classes in Spanish, and they decided to "reprimand" the teachers in the ESL department at the school for not being able to contain, control, and stop the students' protest. We first became aware of these situations because some of the parents were our neighbors and some of the teachers were our students in our graduate classes.

The third incident was different. A large group of students from another local high school organized themselves to provide their teachers and the new administrators in the building with tours of their community because they perceived that most of their teachers just "didn't get it" in terms of the ethnic, cultural, linguistic, social, political, economic, and geographical background of the local community. These tours included renting a bus and taking the school faculty to places, teaching them about the history of the community, and teaching them about their backgrounds, culture, institutions, traditions, religious and spiritual ceremonies, and languages. This school building is located in an area with a high number of Chicanas/os, and it is the same building where a group of students organized a walkout in support and solidarity with the teacher's union, which was negotiating a new contract at the time.

We become aware of the community tour organized by the students through our graduate students who commented on this event with pride and admiration for the students. Some teachers are writing their theses on this topic. In this school, the "dropout" rate was close to 50%.

Analysis of Incidents

In understanding these critical incidents, it is relevant to consider language as a commodity, and as a colonizing instrument. For instance, although Spanish language served in the colonization, decultural-ization, and subjugation of American Indians in the Southwest, and English is the de facto language of the North American colonization and expansion, immersed in the discourses of Manifest Destiny and Americanization, mastery of both languages became an important economic commodity with a relevant exchange value by the beginning of the 20th century. Therefore, many schools were expected to provide English language skills that could not be acquired at home. During the 1920s, with the context of the American nationalist discourses during the war in Europe, Spanish-speaking programs in schools were limited or nonexistent. Furthermore, for many Chicanos in the 1960s, Spanish was the language to be reclaimed and restored, but it needed to be acquired because only seldom was it spoken. Many Chicanas/os who became teachers and who had the cultural and political critique of the dominant curriculum, not always had the preparation to teach aca-demic content in Spanish. In consequence, it is not a surprise that there were limited options for students who wanted to learn content in other languages rather than English because there were not enough teachers who could teach advanced classes in Spanish and there were not efforts to prepare teachers and hire teachers who could do it. Besides, another tension was present because programs focused mostly in English lan-guage acquisition, but when cultural issues were part of the proposals, they cultivated a heritage that ignored the "mestizo" experience.

An additional important theme was the limited resources, financial and human, to teach college preparatory classes in Spanish. Even if there were noble intentions, historically teachers have not been pre-pared to teach students who are different from their own background or to teach in a different language. Teacher preparation programs did not address the curricular critiques but, rather, focused on language acquisition in its cognitive domain without much attention to the academic content itself. University programs were conceptually and institutionally organized on the base of the knowledge and the structures that were available and affordable, thus limiting what future and practicing school personnel could learn in order to alter unjust school experiences.

Another issue was that schooling served to dominate, also meaning to perpetuate asymmetrical relations of power and access to knowledge. This could suggest that in spite of possible noble intentions, the school system is not ready to alter the pattern of stratification in terms of having or not having access to knowledge (the null curriculum). Therefore, indicating that structural changes may be needed beyond creating seemingly progressive programs. This is exacerbated in the case of the teacher reprimanded for her concerns with the insensitive response of the administration or with the administration's concerns regarding the teachers' inability, or unwillingness, to stop the students from walking out. This incident further invites one to consider that the hidden curriculum of preparation programs and the not so hidden aspects of lifelong learning in the school settings involves the development of a deceiving sense of loyalty.

Loyalty is played as an important aspect of public relations for the institutions. The teachers' loyalties within this view, whether in K–12 schools or in the university, should be with the institution. The institution becomes an entity with its own life, and it is at the expense of loyalty to the students and the local communities that such institutional loyalty is cultivated. It serves as a form of control, containment, docilization, and surveillance. The institution has to look good and the clients could be pathologized if needed. Within this view, the fault of dropping-out or of not having intellectually stimulating programs is with the students, not the school. The teacher has to submit to such evil processes as if she or he was in a Kafkaean story. It is an interesting twist that within this institutional loyalty, voice is also controlled. In his study of loyalty, Hirschman (1970) explained that given the presence of "exit" (the ability or possibility to leave the organization or institution and join another one), "voice" (public sharing of perspectives, concerns, suggestions, and critiques) becomes an important tool for organizations to maintain loyalty. He argued that the exercise of voice develops a sense of investment in the organization/institution and, therefore, in open societies with exit as a choice, institutions should promote voice. Yet, in the incidents where the teachers were reprimanded, voice is under surveillance, thus limiting the sense of investment in the institution. Given the choice of exit, one of the teachers left. However, students do not have the same choice. They don't have exit except for dropping out or attending a private school, which for many are inaccessible and equally alienating (see the study by Herr, 1997). Students' choices are limited because of economic, political, policy, geographical, or cultural factors, which include being close to home and families. This is where the alternative of a constructive resistance could be manifested, as in the case of the students walking out demanding an education or with the students organizing community tours and teaching about their heritage and resources. It is in this spirit that we suggest looking at two important characteristics that these students contribute to teachers, something that is not often taught in university classes, but that teachers could learn from their students: *Pasión y Coraje*. These are not only intellectual dispositions but also are feelings and emotions, something that Freire (1998) explains with clarity:

> It is impossible to teach without the courage to love, without the courage to try a thousand times before giving up.... We must dare, in the full sense of the word, to speak of love without the fear of being called ridiculous, mawkish, or unscientific, if not antiscientific. We must dare ... we study, we learn, we teach, we know with our entire body. We do all these things with feeling, with emotion, with wishes, with fear, with doubts, with passion, and also with critical reasoning. However, we never study, learn, teach, or know with the last only. We must dare so as never to dichotomize cognition and emotion. (p. 3)

Pasión (passion) is often associated with an intense emotion, feeling, and it happens with devotion and dedication, with love, and with physical energy. It also includes a level of risk-taking because it can produce intense suffering. Often during progressive times teachers were instructed to control their passions and not to be too directive of the students' innate interests, to avoid being intrusive (Grinberg, in press). What we are proposing here is that passion is an important element of good teaching, particularly in communities and with students who value and understand pasión and who, themselves, are open about being passionate.

Coraje can be translated in a number of ways. Often it means courage. The courage to take on unpopular positions, the courage to confront authority, the courage to risk one's own privilege, the courage to accept one's own limitations, the courage to confront injustice, the courage to teach everybody's children, the courage to learn from one's students. *Coraje* is also anger, even rage, at least indignation. The conditions of schooling, the historical structural inequities, the expectation that some students will drop out, the perpetuation of "otherness," to name just a few, should provoke coraje. Nieto (2003b) argues that "anger is the other side of hope, and given the conditions in urban public schools today, hope is constantly tested" (p. 392). *Coraje* is also daring, as Freire framed in the earlier quote, and it is in many ways a form of cheerful disrespect toward institution and people who utilize their privilege to maintain asymmetrical relations with students and their families. *Coraje* is also "chutzpah," a way of both daring and cheerfully disrespecting authority, norms, and power arrangements. In the incidents described earlier, *Coraje* and *Pasión* are part of the teachers' education.

We understand that *Pasión* and *Coraje* happen with both teachers and students, and that as much as teachers can teach their students, the students can also teach their educators and each other. *Pasión* and *Coraje* are not aspects or dimensions of learning for teachers in general or for teachers of Latina/o students in particular. *Pasión* and *Coraje* perhaps cannot be taught only through classwork in the university, but if we reconsider where teacher education should take place and what domains of knowledge should be taught and experienced, contextualized, deconstructed, and enacted, if systematic critical inquiry is done with/in communities, not on the communities and students, analyzing how power operates and what alternatives may emerge from within the community, then perhaps we can "test" our hopes one more time and find a sustaining and transforming force.

SUMMARY

Standards, curriculums, and even pedagogies geared to address issues of culture and power, when framed in the discourse of professionalization, function as a disciplinary practice. We argue that the formal education and professional development of these teachers do not prepare them, do not educate them to what should entail to teach. The critical incidents illustrated how a professional discourse risks the development of docilizing practices of loyalty to the institution but not necessarily to the students, the Latina/o students, and to these communities where the schools are located. Furthermore, those teachers who see their teaching as interrupting and resisting the reproducing practices that perpetuate inequities, and who teach by engaging in advocacy, activism, transgression, and transformation, not only are vulnerable to the surveillance of their supervisors and administrators but also risk their relative privilege and risk the disciplining aspects of the hierarchy within school systems and teacher education programs.

The possibilities of advancing an agenda of social justice, fostering culturally responsive teacher education, moving education in/to and with the communities, and integrating emotions, feelings, and body within the realm of what it entails to teach may provide with important alternatives to how and where teachers are educated, and by whom. *Pasión* and *Coraje* are important because these are ways of teaching in and out of the classroom that potentially can interrupt structural injustices, and that can be learned from the students, thus reducing the incongruencies and discontinuities between home, community, and school.

REFERENCES

Altenbaugh, R. J., & Underwood, K. (1990). The evolution of normal schools. In J. I. Goodland, R. Soder, & K. A. Sirotnik (Eds.), *Places where teachers are taught* (pp. 3–39). San Francisco, CA: Jossey-Bass.

Anderson, G., & Grinberg, J. (1998). Educational administration as a disciplinary practice: Appropriating Foucault's view of power, discourse, and method. *Educational Administration Quarterly, 34*(3), 329–353.

Anderson, G., Herr, K., & Nihlen, A. (1994). *Studying your own school: An educator's guide to qualitative practitioner research.* Thousand Oaks, CA: Corwin Press.

Angelides, P. (2001). The development of an efficient technique for collecting and analyzing qualitative data and the analysis of critical incidents. *International Journal of Qualitative Studies in Education, 14*(3), 429–442.

Apple, M. (1991). Series editor's introduction. In D. P. Liston, & Zeichner, K. M. (Eds.), *Teacher education and the social conditions of schooling* (pp. vii–xii). New York: Routledge.

Bourdieu, P. (1994). *Academic discourse.* Stanford, CA: Stanford University Press.

Bourdieu, P., & Hacquant, L. (1992). *An invitation to reflexive sociology.* Chicago: University of Chicago Press.

Bourdieu, P., & Passeron, J. (1977). *Reproduction in education, society, and culture.* London: Sage Publications.

Carlson, D. (1997). *Making progress: Education and culture in new times.* New York: Teachers College Press.

Cochran-Smith, M., & Fries, M. (2001). Sticks, stones, and ideology: The discourse of reform in teacher education. *Educational Researcher, 30*(8), 3–15.

Cochran-Smith, M., & Lytle, S. (Eds.). (1992). *Inside/outside: Teacher research and knowledge.* New York: Teachers College Press.

Collins, R. (1979). *The credential society: An historical sociology of education and stratification.* Academic Press.

Cordova, T. (1997). Power and knowledge: Colonialism in the academy. *Taboo, the Journal of Culture and Education,* Fall, 209–234.

Creswell, T. (1996). *In place, out of place.* Minneapolis, MN: University of Minnesota Press.

Darder, A. (1997). Creating the conditions for cultural democracy in the classroom. In A. Darder, R. Torres, & H. Gutierrez (Eds.), *Latinos and education: A critical reader.* New York: Routledge.

Dhillon, P. (1999). (Dis)locating thoughts: Where do the birds go after the last sky? In T. Popkewitz & L. Fendler (Eds.), *Critical theories in education* (pp. 191–207). New York: Routledge.

Fanon, F. (1952). *Black skin, white masks*. New York: Grove Press.

Fanon, F. (1968). *The wretched of the earth*. Harmondsworth: Penguin.

Fischman, G. (2000). *Imagining teachers*. New York: Rowman & Littlefield.

Foucault, M. (1988). *Politics, philosophy, culture: Interviews and other writings, 1977–1984 (L. Kritzman, Ed.)*. London: Routledge.

Foucault, M. (2000). *Power: Essential works of Foucault, 1954–1984*, volume III (P. Rabinow, Ed.). New York: New Press.

Freire, P. (1970). *Cultural action for freedom*. Cambridge, MA: Harvard Educational Review and Center for the Study of Development and Social Change.

Freire, P. (1970/1992). *Pedagogy of the oppressed*. New York: Continuum.

Freire, P. (1998). *Teachers as cultural workers: Letters to those who dare to teach*. Boulder, CO: Westview.

Gallegos, B. (1992). *Literacy, education, and society in New Mexico, 1693–1821*. Albuquerque: University of New Mexico Press.

Gallegos, B. (1998). Remember the Alamo: Imperialism, memory, and postcolonial educational studies. *Educational Studies, 29*, 232–247.

Ginsburg, M. (1988). *Contradictions in teacher education and society*. New York: The Falmer Press.

Ginsburg, M., & Clift, R. (1990). The hidden curriculum of preservice teacher education. In W. R. Houston (Ed.), *Handbook of research on teacher education* (pp. 450–465). New York: Macmillan.

Goldfarb, K. (1998). Creating sanctuaries for Latino immigrant families: A case for the schools. *The Journal for a Just and Caring Education, 4*(4), 454–466.

Goldfarb, K., & Grinberg, J. (2002). Leadership for social justice: Authentic participation in the case of a community center in Caracas, Venezuela. *Journal of School Leadership, 12* (March), 157–173.

Goodlad, J. I., Soder, R., & Sirotnik, K. A. (Eds.). (1990). *Places where teachers are taught*. San Francisco, CA: Jossey-Bass.

Grinberg, J. (2002). "I had never been exposed to teaching like that": Progressive teacher education at Bank Street during the 1930's. *Teachers College Record, 104*(7), 1422–1460.

Grinberg, J., & Goldfarb, K. (1998). Moving teacher education in/to the community. *Theory into Practice, 37*(2), 131–139.

Grinberg, J., & Saavedra, E. (2000). The constitution of bilingual/ESL education as a disciplinary practice: Genealogical explorations. *Review of Educational Research, 70*(4), 419–442.

Herbst, J. (1989). *And sadly teach: Teacher education and professionalization in American culture*. Madison: University of Wisconsin Press.

Herr, K. (1997). Learning lessons from school: Homophobia, heterosexism, and the construction of failure. *Journal of Gay and Lesbian Social Services, 7*(4), 51–64.

Herr, K. (2005). Administrators mandating mediation: Tools of institutional violence cloaked in the discourse of reconciliation. *International Journal of Leadership and Education, 8*(1), 21–33.

Hirschman, A. (1970). *Exit, voice, and loyalty*. Cambridge, MA: Harvard University Press.

Holmes Group (1986). *Tomorrow's teachers*. East Lansing, MI: Author.

Kincheloe, J., & Steinberg, S. (1997). *Changing multiculturalism*. Philadelphia: Open University Press.

Labaree, D. F. (1994). An unlovely legacy: The disabling impact of the market on American teacher education. *Phi Delta Kappan, 75*(8), 591–595.

Labaree, D. F. (1997). Public goods, private goods: The American struggle over educational goals. *American Educational Research Journal, 34*(1), 39–81.

Lanier, J., & Little, J. (1986). Research on teacher education. In M. C. Wittrock (Ed.), *Handbook of research on teaching* (3rd ed.), (pp. 527–569). New York: Macmillan.

Lipset, S. M., & Bendix, R. (1959). *Social mobility in industrial society.* Berkeley: University of California Press.

Liston, D., & Zeichner, K. (1990). *Teacher education and the social conditions of schooling.* New York: Routledge.

McCaleb, S. (1994). *Building communities of learners: A collaboration among teachers, students, and community.* New York: St. Martin's Press.

McCaleb, S. (1998). Connecting preservice teacher education to diverse communities: A focus on family literacy. *Theory into Practice, 37*(2), 148–154.

Memmi, A. (1965). *The colonizer and the colonized.* New York: Orion.

Memmi, A. (1984). *Dependence: A sketch for a portrait of the dependent.* Boston, MA: Beacon.

National Commission on Excellence in Education. (1983). *A nation at risk: The imperative for educational reform: A report to the Nation and the Secretary of Education, United States Department of Education. United States.* Washington, DC: The Commission.

Nieto, S. (2000). *Affirming diversity: The sociopolitical context of multicultural education.* New York: Teachers College Press.

Nieto, S. (2002). Language, culture, and teaching [electronic resource]: Critical perspectives for a new century. Mahwah, NJ: Lawrence Erlbaum Associates.

Nieto, S. (2003a). *What keeps teachers going?* New York: Teachers College Press.

Nieto, S. (2003b). Challenging current notions of "highly qualified teachers" through work in a teachers' inquiry group. *Journal of teacher education, 54*(5), 386–398.

Popkewitz, T. (2000). *Educational knowledge: Changing relationships between the state, civil society, and the educational community.* New York: State University of New York Press.

Ross, K. (1991). Translator's introduction. In J. Ranciere. *The ignorant schoolmaster: Five lessons in intellectual emancipation* (pp. vi–xxxiii). Stanford, CA: Stanford University Press.

Rury, J. L. (1989). Who became teachers?: The social characteristics of teachers in American history. In D. Warren (Ed.), *American teachers: Histories of a profession at work* (pp. 9–48). New York: Macmillan.

Saavedra, E. (1998). *Against hegemonic unity: Narratives on becoming a public intellectual and provocateur in the academy.* Freeman Butts Lecture presented at the American Educational Studies Association, Philadelphia, PA.

Sedlak, M. W. (1989). Let us go and buy a school master: Historical perspectives on the hiring of teachers in the United States, 1750–1980. In D. Warren (Ed.), *American teachers: Histories of a profession at work* (pp. 257–290). New York: Macmillan.

Sedlak, M. W., & Schlossman, S. (1986). *Who will teach?* Santa Monica, CA: Rand.

Smyth, J. (1991). Problematising teaching through a "critical" approach to clinical supervision. *Curriculum Inquiry, 21*(3), 321–352.

Steinberg, S., & Kincheloe, J. (2001). Setting the context for critical multi/interculturalism. In S. Steinberg (Ed.), *Multi/intercultural conversations* (pp. 3–30). New York: Peter Lang.

Swartz, D. (1997). *Culture and power: The sociology of Pierre Bourdieu.* Chicago: University of Chicago Press.

Tripp, D. (1993). *Critical incidents in teaching.* London: Routledge.

Urban, W. J. (1990). Historical studies of teacher education. In W. R. Houston (Ed.), *Handbook of research on teacher education* (pp. 59–82). New York: Macmillan.

Valdez, G. (1996). *Con respeto: Bridging the distance between culturally diverse families and schools.* New York: Teachers College Press.

Villegas, A., & Lucas, T. (2001). Preparing culturally responsive teachers: Rethinking the curriculum. *Journal of Teacher Education, 53*(1), 20–32.

Villegas, A., & Lucas, T. (2002). *Educating culturally responsive teachers: A coherent approach.* Albany: SUNY Press.

Warren, D. (1985). Learning from experience: History and teacher education. *Educational Researcher, 14*(10), 5–12.

Warren, D. (Ed.). (1989). *American teachers: Histories of a profession at work.* New York: Macmillan.

Wexler, P. (2000). *Mystical society: An emerging social vision.* Boulder, CO: Westview Press.

Zeichner, K. (2003). The adequacies and inadequacies of three current strategies to recruit, prepare, and retain the best teachers for all students. *Teachers College Record, 105*(3), 490–519.

Zeichner, K., Grant, C., Gay, G., Gillette, M., Valli, L., & Villegas, A. (1998). A research informed vision of good practice in multicultural teacher education: Design principles. *Theory Into Practice, 37*(2), 163–171.

PART IV

Collapsing the Paradox, Imagining New Possibilities

11

Fighting the Backlash: Decolonizing Perspectives and Pedagogies in Neocolonical Times

Carlos Tejeda
California State University, Los Angeles

Kris D. Gutierrez
UCLA

INTRODUCTION

In April 2003, the American Educational Research Association (AERA) held its annual meeting in Chicago, Illinois. The week-long conference, housed in several major hotels, was attended by over 10,000 people. Among the thousands were two of this chapter's authors, scholars from Los Angeles who presented their research and participated in numerous conference events. On an early evening that April, we stood outside the entrance of a hotel enjoying the windy chill and debating about taking a taxi to a conference event in another hotel. We decided to walk, agreeing that neither the distance separating the hotels nor the time it would take to traverse it was really an issue. After a few laughs about the fact that we actually contemplated taking a taxi, we walked

261

from one hotel to the other—a 15-minute stroll that included crossing a bridge over the Chicago River.

As we crossed that bridge, we came across a pillar with a sculpted relief that brought us to a standstill of temporal and spatial simultaneity. At the top of the relief, we saw a winged man of European phenotype, clad in the armor of a Spartan soldier and poised like an archangel leading others to a battle and eventual victory. With a flaming torch in one hand and a shield in the other, his facial expression and posture conveyed the confidence of a divinely inspired and invincible warrior. Directly below the Angel-like warrior, we saw a man whose clothing and phenotype clearly identified him as European explorer. He stood confidently looking in the same direction as the angel-like warrior above him. Directly behind the explorer, we saw a European missionary. Although he also gazed in the same direction as the angel-like warrior, he seemed to be looking and thinking beyond the explorer. Below these two figures, we saw six near-naked men of indigenous phenotype. They surrounded the deified figures of European conquest and colonization. Their faces and postures revealed humble indifference, resignation, exhaustion, humiliation, and even defeat, but not the sense of confidence and grandeur of the figures above them. At the very center of the relief, we saw an indigenous body knelt at the feet of the deified figures. It was that brown body in genuflection at the feet of the symbols of Western Colonialism that most strikingly caught our attention: that native on his knees was not only something we saw, it was something we felt.

We stood before the relief experiencing a heterochronology in which our past, present, and potential future was synchronously lived: we felt the weight of a colonial past when a corporal genocide massacred indigenous bodies and a cultural holocaust annihilated indigenous minds, when the survivors of the slaughters were socialized for subservience; we lived the insidiousness of a neocolonial present when essential features of that colonial domination and exploitation continue to structure the social, political, economic, and cultural relations between differing groups, when indigenous bodies die at the alters of Western civilization's institutional arrangements in smaller proportions and from different causes than in past centuries but continue to be sacrificed nonetheless; we felt the anger, desire, and hope for a time that had not come but could be vividly imagined, a time in which public monuments depicting people and places from the past would reference nothing more than relations between people and social spaces that were fully passed. We stood before the relief occupying a heterotopology, inhabiting at once the space of our immediate corporal displacement, the larger spaces of a region and nation, and the dominant and counter narratives of their representation: we were simultaneously elites from the American academy and Natives on our knees in the places of European discovery; we stood as both indigenous to the land and immigrants to the nation; we held the status of both citizens and "illegals"; we were both occupants of privilege and exiles from equality.

The relief on that bridge—a bridge in the heart of affluent Chicago—is meant to commemorate the exploration and settlement of what has come to be known as the Midwestern United States. But on that early evening, we read an entirely different narrative from the surface of the sculpted relief. It was impossible to walk away with the intended meanings of city planners and artists celebrating a narrative of discovery and settlement. We read ourselves through the celebrated history and hierarchy conscious that the signs and symbols projected from the pillar torturously tattooed brown bodies with textualities that devalue and disgrace them in the racial, cultural, and linguistic arrangements of American society.

On that April evening, we made it from the one hotel to the other, but we realized that we continue crossing from the time and space depicted by the sculpted image to a time and space of social justice for indigenous and dominated peoples in Anglo-American society. As conference participants, we belonged to a group of thousands who crossed repeatedly from one location to another arriving at intended events throughout the week-long conference. But as descendants of the survivors of corporal genocides and cultural holocausts, we also belonged to groups of people in a perpetual crossing, people forced to cross languages, cultures, and borders, trampling on accents, identities, bodies of knowledge, and the very sanctity of life.

On the final day of the conference, we boarded an airplane that would cross the midwestern United States and arrive in Los Angeles. We knew, however, that leaving the times and spaces surrounding that sculpture in Chicago would bring us no closer to arriving at social justice in American society. On the contrary, California awaited us with a context of backlash politics and educational policies directed against people from socially, culturally, and linguistically dominated groups— a context of racist political and educational policies and practices directed largely against descendants of yesterday's corporal genocides and cultural holocausts. What we term as backlash politics in California has led to educational policies and practices that we refer to as backlash pedagogies. These conservative and politically motivated policies accept substantial inequality as a neutral baseline and normative referent for educational practice and reform while simultaneously enshrining and institutionalizing the status quo of White privilege and domination commemorated on that concrete pillar in Chicago. In contemporary California, millions of people from dominated groups find themselves trekking the terrains of a backlash that obstructs the progress and threatens the advances of their attempted crossing from the consequences of the social and cultural slaughters of the past to a social and cultural justice in the future.

In this chapter, we discuss the current context of backlash politics and pedagogies directed against people from dominated groups in the state of California. We then argue for a decolonizing perspective and praxis that can serve as a bridge across the terrains of these largely racist and xenophobic politics and pedagogies. Specifically, we argue for resisting and countering backlash pedagogies and their intents with a decolonizing pedagogy—a pedagogy conceptualized from the standpoint of socially, culturally, and linguistically dominated people struggling for social and ideological decolonization.

BACKLASH POLITICS AND PEDAGOGIES

We contend that the contemporary context in the state of California is characterized by a political and pedagogical backlash against people from nondominant cultural and linguistic groups. Susan Faludi (1991) popularized the notion of *backlash* in her analysis of the war against women in American society. Although she is addressing the specific backlash against feminism and the social and political gains of women in the United States, the passage below helps illustrate the essence of what we refer to as backlash politics and pedagogies in California:

> The counterassault is largely insidious; in a kind of pop-culture version of the Big lie.... The backlash is at once sophisticated and banal, deceptively "progressive" and proudly backward.... The backlash has succeeded in framing virtually the whole issue of women's rights in its own language. Just as Reaganism shifted political discourse far to the right and demonized liberalism, so the backlash convinced the public that women's "liberation" was the true contemporary American scourge—the source of an endless laundry list of personal, social, and economic problems. (Faludi, 1991, p. xviii)

The current wave of conservative and politically motivated educational policies, aimed at radically restructuring educational practice in California, blames the State's educational crisis on teachers' "liberal" pedagogies and on poor, immigrant students who speak a home language other than English. The new policies constitute what we refer to as backlash pedagogy and not only ignore the inequality experienced by socially, culturally, and linguistically dominated groups throughout the history of the United States, they function to preserve it. Institutionalized via recent educational reforms, the pedagogical *backlash* has rolled back the small gains achieved in less blatantly xenophobic times.

Our analysis of current educational policies and their effects draws on several theoretical lenses to help us make sense of how political, social, economic, and educational processes coalesce into a backlash pedagogy. We draw primarily on cultural-historical activity theory because it is a theory of learning and development that focuses on the centrality of culture and its relationship to language and human development (Cole, 1996; Moll, 2000; Vygotsky, 1978; Wertsch, 1985). Its dynamic and processual notion of culture calls for a focus on how human beings interact with their social worlds through mediational means. Cultural-historical activity theory and its instrumental notion of culture lead us to understand diversity and difference as resources for learning (Cole, 1998; Engestrom, 1987, 1999; Gutiérrez, Baquedano-López, & Tejeda, 2000; Moll, 2000; Wertsch, 1991). We use cultural-historical activity theory to highlight how the social constructs of race and ethnicity and its proxies, language and ability (or achievement/underachievement) and the social practices of racism, discrimination, and privileging mediate the schooling outcomes of poor immigrant students who are also English-language learners.

We also draw on Critical Race Theory (Gotanda, 1995; Harris, 1993) to understand how the White privilege and domination of an indigenous-annihilating and African-enslaving past are maintained through current formal and informal mechanisms of racial subjugation and inequality. This theoretical perspective brings to view how whiteness becomes the uncontested baseline and normative referent for contemporary educational reform. It helps explain how White privilege and its attempts to nullify difference persevere despite the social, political, and legal victories of the Civil Rights movement and other subsequent struggles.

Our extensive ethnographic research of effective literacy practices in both classrooms and nonformal learning contexts in southern

California has highlighted the necessary and sufficient conditions that help ensure robust learning for students from linguistically diverse learning populations (Gutiérrez, Baquedano-López, & Alvarez, 2000; Gutiérrez, Baquedano-López, Alvarez, & Chiu, 1999; Gutiérrez, Baquedano-López, & Tejeda, 2000; Gutiérrez, & Stone, 1997). The robust learning communities we have studied across school districts have the following features in common: They mediate learning or assist learning in a variety of ways and utilize multiple mediational tools; they employ heterogeneity and hybridity (including hybrid language practices) as organizing principles of instruction; they utilize all the social, cultural, and linguistic resources of the participants; they regard diversity and difference as resources for learning; and, they define learning rather than teaching as the targeted goal (Gutiérrez, 2000). These learning communities redefine the normalizing baseline of traditional classroom communities and serve as a stark contrast to the cognitive and social consequences of the backlash pedagogy we observe today.

Fundamentally, backlash pedagogy rejects diversity and difference as resources for learning; it is characterized by reductive notions of learning—particularly literacy and language learning—that define diversity and difference as problems to be eliminated or remediated. Thus, backlash pedagogy necessarily prohibits the use of students' complete linguistic, sociocultural, and academic repertoire in the service of learning. In this way, backlash pedagogy is an institutionalized and structured response to diversity and difference, without consideration of the sociohistorical context of racism and classism in this country and its manifestation in educational policies, practices, and outcomes.

Backlash pedagogies do not just happen in a vacuum; they are rooted in backlash politics, products of ideological and institutional structures that legitimize and, thus, maintain privilege, access, and control of the sociopolitical and economic terrain. Backlash politics are counterassaults against real or perceived shifts in power. These can be deliberate and intentional campaigns that forthrightly attack changes in society—for example, the politics of white supremacist groups; or, they can be deceptive and cloaked in a language of "progress" that favors the group perceiving a loss in power. Backlash politics do not require an intentionally racist campaign, but can be a collection of ostensibly racially neutral initiatives that result in consolidating racial inequality.

Education in contemporary California is a case study in backlash politics—politics undergirded by a nostalgia for the golden age of entitlement and privilege that existed before the incremental changes of the Civil Rights movement and the state's rapidly changing demographics. Rooted in discomfort and discontent amongst the dominant population, this backlash coincided with several significant trends in California: (1) a marked change in the state economy that led to a general economic recession in the late 1980s and 1990s; (2) the rapidly shifting demographics in the state over the past several decades; (3) the increasing political influence and social presence of people of color, particularly immigrant Latinos and Asians; (4) a perceived loss of entitlement and, in particular, a perceived decrease in access to elite educational institutions and to the marketplace; and (5) an emerging countersentiment informed by a growing body of knowledge that challenges the prevailing orthodoxy that defines diversity and difference as problems to be eliminated or fixed.

In the past decade, voters in California have overturned affirmative action and have eliminated race as a criterion for admission to the University of California, essentially eliminated bilingual education by restricting the use of the primary language in instructional contexts and mandating English-only instruction for English-language learners, and have proposed the elimination of health and educational services for undocumented immigrants (a measure the courts declared as unconstitutional), and have attempted to eliminate the collection of race and ethnicity data essential to the social, educational, and political well-being. These backlash politics are largely a reactionary response to the dramatic demographic shift in California and its public schools. The extraordinary numbers of English-language learners have created a new educational challenge that has been met with resistance from conservative and xenophobic politicians, citizens, and educators that have successfully garnered support from within the general populace. This resistance has been evidenced by a pattern of assault against the largely immigrant and non-English speaking Latino/a population and has resulted in the passage of three consecutive and related Propositions: 187, 209, and 227. Despite the legal rhetoric, these reforms were directed at Latinos and the problems attributed to their growing presence (Macedo, 2000). We argue that it is critical both to expose these reforms for what they intend and to contextualize the overall reform movement within current sentiments about civil rights that are fundamentally ahistorical.

The voter initiatives designed to limit educational access to immigrant, Latino/a, and African-American school-aged students in the form of Propositions 187, 209, and 227 are rooted in ahistorical understandings of the privilege borne of social, cultural, and economic domination in American society. For example, Proposition 227 mandates the elimination of or reduction in the use of students' primary language blatantly while ignoring that bilingual education was a limited educational response to English-only instruction that was not working for linguistically diverse student populations. Before *Lau v. Nichols*, English immersion *was* the pedagogical norm. Nevertheless, the new right, neoconservatives, and liberals point to the "failure" of bilingual education in support of Proposition 227, despite the evidence that the instantiation of bilingual education programs varied significantly in its practices and goals across learning contexts, that English was overwhelmingly the primary language of instruction, and that literacy practices depended on the availability of resources and well-trained staff (August & Hakuta, 1997). Similarly, despite that historically affirmative action laws argued that passive nondiscrimination was insufficient to ensure access and equality, the underlying premise of Proposition 209 (the anti-affirmative action measure) is that gender and racial discrimination and inequity are no longer societal problems requiring redress. Despite hundreds of years of a brutal racial and cultural domination that permeated virtually every social relation and institutional arrangement in American society (not to mention an abundance of statistical data evidencing the continued privileging of Whites), proponents of Proposition 209 argue that affirmative action policies result in discrimination against White men. And more problematic, a significant sector of the general populace has been persuaded by this argument.

A defining characteristic of the backlash politics and pedagogies in California has been a deceptive and disguising discourse that has allowed proponents to garner support among significant sectors of the state's electorate. Omi and Winant (1994) put forth that the new right objective to dismantle the incremental political gains of racial and linguistic minorities cannot be easily achieved without consequences. Hence, a key device is to reframe the project using code words, phrases, and symbols that refer indirectly to racial themes but do not directly challenge popular democratic or egalitarian ideas, for example, justice and equal opportunity. For example, the various initiatives in California never mentioned race or racism directly, but instead proposed these changes as sound and fair-minded public policy leading ultimately to economic development through the most efficient economic means (rational choice decision making). The rollbacks to civil rights gains were rearticulated as beneficial to the larger populace in that they would redistribute much needed resources more equitably (state funds and places in elite institutions). The discourse of backlash politics pedagogies has helped frame these insidious measures into acceptable and even equity-oriented reforms: for example, Proposition 227 was known as "English for the Children" (Unz & Tuchman, 1997), Proposition 209 was titled the "Civil Rights Initiative," Proposition 54 was known as the Racial Privacy Initiative.

The passing of such reactionary measures was also facilitated by a period of renewed interest in educational reform. Not since the publication of *A Nation at Risk* (National Commission on Excellence in Education, 1983) has education assumed such an increasingly prominent position in national and state policies and politics. This publication and its related forum helped to intensify the critique of our nation's failing schools and the declining achievement of our nation's students. Despite research exposing the inaccurate characterization and causes of the educational crisis (Berliner & Biddle, 1995), the national discourse of reform nevertheless continues to be fueled by gross misunderstandings of the reasons for the declining state of the American educational system. This trend is mirrored in state politics. Everyone is an educational candidate, from the presidential nominee to the local city council candidate. But nowhere is the reform fervor more frenzied than in California. Not since the passage of Proposition 13 in 1978—which capped property tax rates, created rigid budget spending parameters, and reduced dramatically funding resources for education—has education become the centerpiece of local and statewide politics.

The popular initiative process flourishes today as a way of reshaping public policy. The sheer number of educational reforms currently being implemented and proposed is unprecedented. In addition to those initiatives we have previously discussed, since 1994 the educational and political establishment, including the popular media such as *the Los Angeles Times*, have initiated new reforms that address new statewide standards in subject matter areas such as language arts and mathematics, new statewide reading initiatives, and new policies that reduced class size in K–3 classrooms and in ninth grade English classes. Such initiatives demanded a renewed focus on accountability and resulted in a newly mandated statewide assessment program (SAT 9), teacher and administrator accountability measures, and a prohibition on the practice of social promotion. Indeed, there is a boon in educational reform. Yet just as these initiatives became law, the state's electorate (predominantly comprised of White, middle-aged homeowners with a rapidly diminishing percentage of children in public schools) defeated Proposition 26, which would have overturned Proposition 13 and earmarked state revenue for school construction.

At face value, one would be hard pressed to argue against the seeming intent of some of these educational measures. Who could deny, for instance, that smaller classes may lead to better learning or that we should have high standards of learning for all students? But such reforms often mandate the type of immediate action that usually precludes formal or institutional attention to long-term cognitive, social, and political consequences for teachers, students, and their communities. Class size reduction was a mandated quick fix that resulted in a dramatic teacher shortage. Not surprisingly, the poorest, most overcrowded and low-achieving schools required the largest percentage of new teachers. Although these schools fulfilled the legislative mandate, they did so by hiring the least trained and experienced teachers for students with the greatest learning need, especially in the context of 227. In short, English-language learners simultaneously were immersed in English-only or "English-only-like" learning contexts without the support of their primary language and they were placed in classrooms with largely monolingual and inexperienced teachers with little to no experience teaching English-language learners. What's more, the coinciding push to increase reading achievement in the early grades has placed these same students in district mandated reading programs developed for English dominant students. Many of these reforms are unsubstantiated in research about effective instruction, language, and literacy learning for English-language learners, or situated practice. These reforms might be understood simply as leading to bad practice that results in ineffective learning, but given the history of schooling's role in the deculturalization of dominated groups the perpetuation of educational inequality for linguistic and cultural minorities in the United States, these current policies and practices can be seen as having a much more sinister effect.

Historically, backlash practices have used race as the primary screening device for categorizing and marginalizing sectors of the population. In this current political climate, backlash politics and its pedagogy create other surrogates, such as language and ability, for the larger category of race. Refining the categories of difference makes it easier to identify and subsequently "normalize" and "socialize" the so-called deviant population. The contradiction here, of course, is that structured racial privilege is attained by simultaneously categorizing and then negating these categories. In their analysis of Proposition 187, for example, Chang and Aoki explain the double bind that minorities experience in public policy:

> We might question legal doctrines such as equal protection and their role in producing racialized identities while simultaneously mandating color-blindness on the part of public actors. (Chang & Aoki, 1997, p. 313)

Proposition 227, the prohibition of the primary language in instruction, is perhaps the most salient component of backlash pedagogy and also exemplifies this double bind. First, language becomes the primary screening device for recategorizing the student population, but the law also requires that schools ignore this difference by mandating a one-size-fits-all approach to language and literacy learning: English-only.

Consider this typical scenario in a California classroom. One child is White and English language dominant, a second is Latino/a and Spanish language dominant. Both are emergent literates in their primary language. Yet, academic reform in California assumes these two students participate on a level playing field, and ostensibly treats them identically pedagogically. However, this mandated pedagogy simultaneously limits the Spanish-speaking child from using her complete linguistic and sociocultural repertoire to learn and, once again, privileges the English dominant student in the learning environment. In this context, instruction is geared toward the acquisition of oral English speaking skills and English is used primarily in content area instruction. Such practices belie the vast knowledge base about the role of language in the learning process. We know that language is the primary tool we use to express and make sense of our experiences; a tool that can help transform our thinking and understanding (Gutiérrez, Baquedano-López, & Turner, 1997). Indeed, language is the considered *the tool of tools* (Cole & Engeström, 1993); the most powerful sense-making tool humans use. What then are the cognitive consequences for children who are not allowed to draw from their complete linguistic tool kit in learning activities?

We address this question in our ongoing work about effective learning communities for Latino/a children (Gutiérrez, Baquedano-López, & Alvarez, 2000; Gutiérrez, Baquedano-López, Alvarez, & Chiu, 1999; Gutiérrez & Stone, 1997). This body of work helps us see the de facto inequality in both the individual and collective set of reforms we term backlash pedagogy. In the thriving learning communities we study, no single language or register is privileged, and the larger linguistic repertoires of participants become tools for participating and making meaning in learning activity. Moreover, the participants regularly utilize hybrid language practices—that is, the strategic use of multiple codes and registers—that enhance the possibility of dialogue, interpretation, and thus learning. Such practices build local interpretive practices and communities that necessarily draw on local knowledge, cultural practices (e.g., the funds of knowledge about which Moll [2000] writes), personal experience, and different ways of demonstrating competence (Gutiérrez, Baquedano-López, & Tejeda, 2000). Thus, instead of focusing on the children's language designation or fluency in either Spanish or English, the practices of these rich communities facilitate movement across languages and register toward particular literacy learning goals.

These, however, are far from the normative literacy practices of most classrooms, especially in the post-227 era. Even when the use of the primary language is permitted, many classrooms instantiate the reforms in the most reductive literacy practices. In defiance to what we know about how children learn and become literate, reductive literacy practices organize learning in ways that make oral English language fluency the target of instruction, and thus equate oral English fluency with proficiency in academic English. Reductive literacy practices also define literacy learning as an individual accomplishment where skills are taught in isolation of meaning-making literate practices. Of consequence is that Latino/a children are socialized to reductive notions of literacy and its practices. As Luis Moll (2000) explains:

> Concurrent biliteracy (not solely biligualism) is not required or expected of any other children [other than Latino/a] in this country, with the possible exception of Cuban children in Florida (See Garcia & Otheguy, 1985). And when it occurs, it is constrained by the limiting characteristics of working-class schooling, which reduce to basic elementary functions what the children can do with literacy. Furthermore, Latino/a children in the United States are schooled within a neo-colonial educational system that always seeks to fulfill other people's purposes and interest, not theirs. (p. 265)

Backlash pedagogy, then, is much more than a set of methods or practices for teaching and learning. Clothed in the rhetoric of reform, backlash pedagogy becomes the judicial arbitrator of who gets "sound" educational practices and in what form. Thus, backlash pedagogy is a political intrusion that makes it professionally and, in some cases legally, risky for educators to implement what they know about teaching in an effective and culturally responsible way. Of critical significance, as we have just illustrated, is that backlash pedagogy tries to impose a radical color-blindness on pedagogy and thus erases differences that we know make a difference in learning. Racial and class differences have no valence in the educational equation of backlash pedagogy.

Linguistic difference, primarily language use, is at the center of backlash pedagogy and, thus, has particular consequences for linguistic minorities and the policies directed at them. The largely anti-Latino/a reform package, that is, 187, 227, 209, effectively employed a language of reform that both devalued the Spanish (and other) language, its utility, and thus, its community. This sentiment is inherent in backlash pedagogy, which ignores the significant socializing power of language, and the role of language in shaping racialized ideologies.

Nullifying the language of the Latino/a community is an overt attempt to nullify its collective and individual identity. This is a largely uncontested practice in liberal democratic societies in which the language of a particular community is devalued, making "discrimination on linguistic grounds publicly acceptable where the corresponding ethnic or racial discrimination is not. For example, although penalizing a student for being African-American may be illegal, penalizing a student for speaking African-American Vernacular English is not" (Woolard, 1998, p. 19). Such devaluing of one's language can help call into question, or render suspect, the legitimacy of one's claim to citizenship (Blommaert & Verschueren, 1998). This reform is more than which language to use in educational settings; it is about the social reconstruction of identities so that they do not pose a threat to White dominance (Chang & Aoki, 1997). Language choice is not solely a technical choice but is always a political issue linked to mechanisms of social controls (Woolard, 1998). Although the backlash campaign uses language as a sorting device to marginalize and neutralize populations, it also influences individual constructions of self and the Other.

In the post-227 context, then, English-only becomes the normative baseline of educational policies and practices, and defines educational competence, both in how we participate, and how we are evaluated. More significantly, English-only, bolstered by its sister educational reforms gives rise to a backlash pedagogy that hastens and strengthens the normalizing of teachers, students, and their practices.

The challenge for us is to resist this wave of backlash politics and pedagogy, to historicize its origins, intents, and possible effects, and to construct a pedagogical practice that assists students from socially, culturally, and linguistically dominated groups to cross from the times and spaces of corporal genocides and cultural holocausts of the past, through the times and spaces of social, cultural, and linguistic domination in the present, and into a time and space of social justice in the future. It is with this in mind that we argue for the politics and praxis of a decolonizing pedagogy.

CONTESTING AND CONSTRUCTING PEDAGOGIES FROM A DECOLONIZING POLITICS AND PRAXIS

To understand why California's electoral process and educational system can be employed against the human rights of specific populations, it is necessary to focus on happenings in the present while gazing at the horrors of the past. From this vantage, one can see that the migrating and toiling population of unwelcomed "Latinos/Hispanics" targeted by recent propositions in California is largely descendant from indigenous populations that have been killed, conquered, converted, and renamed by European conquerors, colonists, and capitalist statesmen throughout the past 5 centuries. One also can see that the racist nature of contemporary political processes, educational policies, and their sustaining discourses has a genealogy whose origins can be traced back centuries to the political, educational, and ideological frameworks of the "Indian"-annihilating and African-enslaving imperialisms of a Spanish monarchy and an Anglo-American democracy (Aldama, 2001; Horseman, 1997; Seed, 2001; Spring, 2001; Williams, 1995). What's more, one sees that wherever conquest, colonization, and capitalist exploitation found indigenous and African peoples in the hemisphere, a deculturalizing education that schooled them toward subservience shortly followed. From a vantage in the present that intently gazes at the past, we see that what openly transpired long ago insidiously haunts our contemporary times.

In A *Little Matter of Genocide*, Churchill (1997) reminds us of the holocaust and horrors of that past. He asks us to recall that between

1492 and 1892 the population of approximately 125 million indigenous people in the hemisphere was decimated by more than 90%:

> The people had died in their millions of being hacked apart with axes and swords, burned alive and trampled under horses, hunted as game and fed to dogs, shot, beaten, stabbed, scalped for bounty, hanged on meathooks and thrown over the sides of ships at sea, worked to death as slave laborers, intentionally starved and frozen to death during a multitude of forced marches and internments, and, in an unknown number of instances, deliberately infected with epidemic diseases. (p. 1)

His work and that of other scholars further reminds us that for those who managed to survive, life under the conquering sword was not necessarily better than a death at its end. From the very beginning, survivors of what became a centuries-long onslaught of European conquest and colonization were brutally victimized by social practices and institutional arrangements that sought their labor, geographical removal, and/or "civilization"/religious conversion (Brown, 1981; Deloria & Lytle, 1983; Galeano, 1989; Churchill, 1997; Seed, 2001).

Indigenous and African peoples that were not fatally brutalized or banished were systematically socialized for subservience—that is, those that were not eradicated by the colonizers were educated into their proper place within the colonial order they imposed. In the 1540s, the Dominican priest Bartolome de Las Casas and the Aristotelian philosopher Juan Gines de Sepulveda debated the most effective methods to "civilize" and convert the "barbarous" and "childlike" "Indian" within the Spanish Empire (Hanke, 1959, 1974). A hundred years later, in the not-too-distant colonies of an expanding British Empire, pressure from England prompted the missionary John Elliot in the colony of Massachusetts to propose that Indians converted to Christianity should be taken from their villages and placed in reservations called praying towns (Spring, 2001). That same year, the Massachusetts General Court declared that any "Christian or pagan [referring to Indians]... wittingly and willingly... deniing [sic] the true god, or his creation or government of the world... shalbe [sic] put to death" (as cited in Spring, 2001). More than 2 centuries later, having inherited from the British empire the tasks of conquering and converting "Indians," the imperialist democracy of an emerging capitalism in the United States was enacting the Indian Removal Act of 1830 and forcibly removing "Indian" children from their families; the children were placed in boarding schools in an attempt to exterminate "Indian" culture, instill a capitalist ethos, and teach subservience to the U.S. government (Adams, 1995). At about the same time, landowners and government officials in the conquered territories of Texas and California debated the education of Mexicans. Although Anglo farmers wanted to keep Mexican children out of schools and ignorant to insure a steady supply of wage-labor, public officials wanted them in segregated schools so they could be "Americanized" (Spring, 2001).

Gazing down historical paths of conquest, colonization, and capitalist expansion, we see that the corporal genocide that massacred the indigenous body was everywhere and always accompanied by a cultural holocaust that annihilated the indigenous mind. What the former accomplished by the swinging of the sword, the latter completed through the schooling of the subject. With the killing, conquest, and conversion came the imposition of colonial institutional arrangements and the imposition of European worldviews and epistemological traditions of what Foucault referred to as the "cultural archive" of the West (1972). Looking at the present from the vantage of the past, Tuhiwai Smith reminds us that the cultural archive that served to train colonial elites and subdue indigenous peoples "has come to structure our own ways of knowing" (1999, p. 59). From the same vantage, Willinsky points out that the West's cultural archive was vastly expanded as bodies of knowledge and disciplines were born and developed at the service of imperialist expansion and colonial rule, and that given the enormity of imperialism's educational project (its production and imposition of knowledge) one can only expect that it lives on "as an unconscious aspect of our education" (1998, p. 3). He insists that we need to learn "how five centuries of studying, classifying, and ordering humanity within an imperial context gave rise to peculiar and powerful ideas of race, culture, and nation that were, in effect, conceptual instruments that the West used both to divide up and educate the world" (p. 2). Speaking specifically about the contemporary consequences of those conceptual instruments, Deloria explains that regardless of what indigenous peoples say about "their origins, their migrations, their experiences with birds, animals, lands, waters, mountains, and other people," Western science controls the definition of "respectable and reliable human experience" in a manner that allows it to reduce indigenous peoples to "a pre-human level of ignorance" and to reject their knowledges and worldviews as mere "superstition" (1997, p. 7). Deloria, Willinsky, and Tuhiwai Smith remind us that we are descendants of institutions and ideas that have yet to fully pass, and that the consequences of those institutions and ideas imposingly inhabit our contemporary context .

We contend that the contemporary context of what is now referred to as the United States is essentially characterized by an *internal neocolonialism* (Almaguer, 1974; Barrera, 1979) that has its origins in the mutually reinforcing systems of colonial and capitalist domination and exploitation that dispossessed indigenous populations and enslaved Africans throughout the 17th, 18th, and 19th centuries. Hence, we see the present, in which indigenous peoples are reduced to ontological foreigners and nondominant groups are increasingly assaulted by racist politics and policies, as a dynamic extension of a colonial and imperialist past that included the corporal genocide and cultural holocaust of indigenous and African peoples. From this perspective, we contend that the struggle against today's backlash politics and pedagogies against dominated peoples should be tied to a struggle for a politics and praxis of decolonization in the mutually constitutive terrains (e.g., the economic, the cultural, the political, and the educational) of our social experience.

Although our decolonizing perspective acknowledges that the past is not the present, it argues that the former can neither exist nor be understood outside of the latter. It is impossible for social subjects to be ontologically disconnected from time and space; their being in the world cannot be detached from and unaffected by the chronologies and spatialities of their *cultural-historical* (Cole, 1996) existence—an existence in which the present is directly born from and sustained through cultural practices inherited from the past. We do not, of course, argue that we are living the actual colonial domination or capitalist exploitation of the 17th, 18th, or 19th centuries. It is clear that many of the processes and practices of early colonial domination and capitalist exploitation have been altered, abandoned, or legally terminated, but essential features of that domination and exploitation continue to structure the economic, social, political, and cultural relations between differing groups in contemporary "American" society. What's more, the corporal genocide and cultural annihilation of indigenous and nonwhite peoples is far from over. Although the sounds of the dismantling of educational and linguistic rights implied by aforementioned propositions loudly remind us of the ongoing annihilation, the sight and smell of decomposing corpses along the U.S.-Mexico border force us to recall the continuing genocide (see Eschbach, 1999).

In contemporary times, brown bodies die at the altars of Western colonialism's economic, political, and cultural arrangements in smaller proportions and from different causes than in past centuries, but they continue to be sacrificed nonetheless. It is in response to the sacrificial slaughters in the social spaces of the border, the workplace, the class-room, and the mind that we call for a decolonizing politics and praxis that can help us cross from the times and spaces of a colonial past to the times and spaces of a decolonized existence. In response to the back-lash pedagogies we currently encounter, we specifically propose the politics and praxis of a decolonizing pedagogy.

FUNDAMENTAL PREMISES OF A DECOLONIZING PEDAGOGY

The decolonizing pedagogy we propose sets out to assist students to actively reflect, critique, and work against the existing forms of do-mination and exploitation in the United States while simultaneously preparing them for the concrete exigencies of its educational and/or professional spaces. It is a pedagogical approach that is anticolonial, anticapitalist, antiracist, antisexist, and antihomophobic. It under-stands that the dominant curricular design, instructional practice, and forms of assessment in schools function to sustain and reproduce neo-colonial domination, capitalist exploitation, a *difference of domination*[1] and the ideological frameworks that sustain these. Hence, it argues

---

[1]Tejeda (in press) explains the concept of *difference of dominations* as follows: Difference implies the juxtaposition of phenomena. When difference is referenced with regards to people it usually refers to their juxtaposition on the basis of sexual, racial, cultural, and/or linguistic characteristics or features. There is difference between people that is *actual* and difference that is *supposed*—that is, difference that is genetically mandated (such as the physiological difference between males and females), and difference that is socially constructed (such as the difference in value between males and females supposed in certain cultures). Within Western binarist logic, difference usually implies a construction of opposites in which one of the features or characteristics being differentiated is set up as superior or more desirable than the other, in which one of the opposites is used to measure, evaluate, or define the other. Actual or natural difference should be acknowledged and celebrated. Difference that is socially constructed and implies hierarchies in which features or characteristics are compared in order to subordinate or define as lacking should be rejected. Because difference in our social world exists along both these lines, it is fundamentally important to clearly establish which of the two we are referring to when discussing difference in our conceptualizations or commentaries. I employ the term *difference of domination* to refer to difference that (be it ideologically constructed, or naturally given and then ideologically recoded) functions to establish, reproduce, or legitimize the domination of some groups over others.

for a pedagogy that challenges the dominant practices of schooling and makes schools concrete sites for the development of a critical consciousness of social existence and the possibility of its transformation in the interests of working class, indigenous, and nonwhite peoples.

A basic premise of our call for a decolonizing pedagogy is that the dominant economic, cultural, political, judicial, and educational arrangements in contemporary "American" society are those of an *internal neocolonialism* produced by the mutually reinforcing systems of colonial domination and capitalist exploitation that have organized social relations throughout the history of the United States. Our concept of internal neocolonialism is indebted to the work of Barrera (1979) and Almaguer (1974). Barrera employs the concept in the development of a theory of racial inequality that is proposed as an alternative to the theories of deficiency, theories of bias, and theories of structural discrimination that attempted to explicate the issue of Chicana/o inequality in the United States. In outlining this theory, he offers a discussion of colonialism and internal colonialism that is essential to the notion of internal neocolonialism we propose:

> Colonialism is a structured relationship of domination and subordination, where the dominant and subordinate groups are defined along ethnic and/or racial lines, and where the relationship is established and maintained to serve the interests of all or part of the dominant group. (p. 193)

Internal colonialism is distinguished from colonialism in the following terms:

> Internal colonialism is a form of colonialism in which the dominant and subordinate populations are intermingled, so that there is no geographically distinct, "metropolis" separate from the "colony." (p. 194)

Almaguer (1974) links internal colonialism in the United States to advanced monopoly capitalism in a manner that is also essential to our developing concept of internal neocolonialism. In his examination of Chicana/o oppression in North America, Almaguer calls for a simultaneous analysis of capitalist and colonial structures, arguing that both the historical process of colonization (be it classical colonialism, neocolonialism, or internal colonialism) and the rise and spread of capitalism should be viewed as fundamental in the organization of social and economic power in the United States. He explains that the histories of oppressed peoples have been largely formed both by the rise of capitalism and the expansion of colonial domination, and he further theorizes that there is a dialectical relationship in the development of monopoly capitalism and the development of internal colonialism. He describes this relationship as follows:

> The colonial expansionism by which the U.S. absorbed vast territories paved the way for the incorporation of its non-white colonial labor force. This contributed in turn to the accelerated process of capital accumulation. Necessary for the development of modern capitalism...not only did internal colonialism and monopoly capitalism develop concurrently, but both processes are intimately interrelated and feed each other. At the same time that the utilization of non-whites as a controlled, colonized labor force contributed to the development of the U.S. as a major metropolis of the international capitalist system, the attendant class system in the U.S. provided a means of reinforcing a racially and culturally defined social hierarchy. (p. 42)

As this passage explains, capitalism did not simply develop side by side with internal colonial domination; it became inextricably interrelated with it. More significantly, Almaguer contends that capitalism is now the dominant mode of production and that it continues to systematically perpetuate a colonial domination in which the brunt of its oppression and class contradictions "have been largely carried over on racial terms and fall on the backs of colonized people of color" (1974, p. 42).

We define the dominant condition characterizing social existence in the United States as a colonial one because there continues to be a structured relationship of cultural, political, and economic domination and subordination between Europeans, on the one hand, and indigenous and nonwhite peoples, on the other. What's more, this relationship (which was imposed and institutionalized throughout the 17th, 18th, and 19th centuries and has been maintained, in essence, up to the present) continues to serve primarily the interests of a dominant White, English-speaking, and Christian population. We qualify it as an *internal* colonial condition because the colonizing/dominant and colonized/subordinate populations coexist, are often socially integrated, and even share citizenship within the same national borders. What's more, we see this internal colonial condition, its forms of social organization, and its institutional apparatuses as inextricably tied to and perpetuated by capitalism and capitalist social relations—a capitalism that Almaguer discussed as advanced monopoly capitalism and we currently see as global capitalism (McLaren & Farahmandpur, 2000; Stromquist & Monkman, 2000). Our conception of internal colonialism, then, assumes the fundamentality of capitalism and capitalist social relations in the various dimensions of our neocolonial condition and social interaction.

We expand the concept from internal colonialism to internal *neo*colonialism to distinguish between the forms of domination, oppression, and exploitation of the internal colonialism of the 17th, 18th, and 19th centuries, and the forms of domination, oppression, and exploitation that have characterized the internal colonialism of the 20th and 21st centuries. It is fundamentally important to understand how landmark legislation and its effects (e.g., the Emancipation, Proclamation, the Fourteenth Amendment to the U.S. constitution, the Indian Citizenship Act, Brown v. Board of Education, the Civil Rights Act, the Voting Rights Act, the Indian Self-Determination and Education Assistance Act, and the Native American Languages Act) have altered the domination and exploitation of subordinated groups.

Our understanding of the continuity of colonial relations rejects simplistic representations of colonizing and the colonized populations. We are cognizant that the population of settling/invading Europeans was defined by difference and division along ethnic, linguistic, gender, and social class lines, and that not even the dominant population of Anglos was socially homogenous. Similarly, we recognize that there was tremendous diversity among both indigenous populations and African people brought as slaves. We are well aware that in referring to Indigenous people, African slaves, or their descendants, we reference people from a plurality of groups with differing cultures, languages, and forms of social organization. Similarly, our conception of the processes and practices (both past and present) of colonialism acknowledges that not all European groups (nor differing social groups within the dominant Anglo population) have been equally complicit in the colonial relations of domination and exploitation that have defined social relations in the Americas. Not all European groups have benefited equally from the establishment and perpetuation of colonial and neocolonial relations. We also are aware that not all indigenous or nonwhite peoples and their descendants experienced or are experiencing colonialism/neocolonialism in a uniform manner.

Another fundamental premise of our call for a decolonizing pedagogy builds on Marx's and Engels's (1973; 1978; 1884) materialist philosophy and theorization of human practice. We understand that the condition of differing groups in American Society is a product of the everyday practice and activity of social subjects—both subjects who dominate and exploit and subjects who are dominated and exploited. From this perspective, we understand that people live an internal neocolonial domination and capitalist exploitation because they engage in and instantiate these in the very production and reproduction of their material existence and its cultural expression; the past, present, and future condition of the differing groups in the United States is materialized in the practice of their everyday lives, through the labor and mundane displacements of their very bodies. We also understand, however, that people do not simply choose to engage in processes and practices that make and remake their condition; they engage in everyday activity and relate to others in the production and reproduction of their social existence with the weight of a colonial and capitalist past squarely on their backs and sharply in their minds. Contemporary people create the condition of their existence within material and ideological circumstances inherited from a past that haunts them in the present.

Building further on a materialist philosophy and theorization of human practice, decolonizing pedagogy insists that people are not condemned to continue making and remaking the condition of their existence according to the circumstances imposed by the historicality, sociality, and spatiality inherited from their past. Those circumstances can be changed instead of merely reproduced and made anew; the very practice that makes possible people's existence and instantiates their domination, exploitation, and difference holds the potential to radically transform them. Mere practice, however, will not lead to this transformation; it must be practice that is grounded in a critical consciousness of the current circumstances and the very possibilities of their transformation. Hence, the idea that social reality can be transformed through *praxis*—guided action aimed at transforming individuals and their world that is reflected on and leads to further action—is fundamentally important to our conception of a decolonizing pedagogy.

This understanding of the malleability of social reality and the transformative potential of human practice finds clear expression in Freire's (1990) pedagogy for the oppressed:

> Just as objective social reality exists not by chance, but as the product of action, so it is not transformed by chance. If men[/women] produce social reality (which in the "inversion of praxis" turns back upon them and conditions them), then transforming that reality is an historical task, a task for men[/women]. [...] The latter, whose task it is to struggle for their liberation together with those who show true solidarity, must acquire a critical awareness of oppression through the praxis of this struggle. One of the gravest obstacles to the achievement of liberation is that oppressive reality absorbs those within it and thereby acts to submerge men's[/women's] consciousness.

Functionally oppression is domesticating. To no longer be prey to its force
one must emerge from it and turn upon it. This can be done only by means
of the praxis: reflection and action upon the world in order to transform it.
(p. 36)

From this view, an end to the internal neocolonial condition that under-
girds California's racist propositions and backlash pedagogies requires
that we develop the ability to perceive critically the circumstances of
our existence in the world—that we develop a critical consciousness
of our social existence. Our action in the world is largely determined
by the way we see ourselves within it, and a correct perception necessitates an ongoing reflection on our world and our positioning within
it. Neither mere action nor mere reflection and critical consciousness,
however, can effectively contest internal neocolonialism and its political and pedagogical manifestations. This can be achieved only through
"praxis: the action and reflection of men in the world in order to transform it" (Freire, 1990, p. 66).

Hence, Freire argues for an educational practice that engages with
the oppressed in a reflection that leads to action on their concrete reality. He calls for a pedagogy that makes oppression and its causes
the objects of a reflection that will allow the oppressed to develop a
consciousness of "their necessary engagement in the struggle for their
liberation" (1990, p. 33). He emphasizes the essential importance of critical consciousness to transformative action and attributes to education
a fundamental role in developing such consciousness:

In order for the oppressed to be able to wage the struggle for their liberation,
they must perceive the reality of oppression not a closed world from which
there is no exit, but as a limiting situation which they can transform. This
perception is a necessary but not a sufficient condition for liberation; it must
become the motivating force for liberating action. (p. 34)

In problem posing education, men[/women] develop their power to perceive
critically the way they exist in the world with which and in which they find
themselves. They come to see the world not as static reality, but as reality in
process, in transformation. Although the dialectical relations of men with the
world exist independently of how these relations are perceived (or whether
or not they are perceived at all) it is also true that the form of action men
adopt is to a large extent a function of how they perceived themselves in the
world. Hence the teacher-student and the students-teachers reflect simultaneously on themselves and the world without dichotomizing this reflection
from action, and thus establish an authentic form of thought and action.
(p. 71)

Building on Freire, we argue that "critical consciousness is developed through the struggle against internal neocolonialism in the spaces of both the classroom and the larger social context" (p. 20), and we insist that educators bear a responsibility to initiate, assist, and nurture the development of this consciousness.

The decolonizing pedagogy we call for is informed by a theoretical heteroglossia that strategically utilizes theorizations and understandings from various fields and conceptual frameworks to unmask the logics, workings, and effects of internal colonial domination, oppression, and exploitation in our contemporary contexts. At present the most significant of these have been *postcolonial studies* (Said, 1978; Ashcroft, Griffiths & Tifflin, 1995; Mongia, 1996; Moore-Gilbert, 1997; Gandhi, 1998; Singh & Schmidt 2000), *spatial theory* (Foucault, 1980, 1986; Soja, 1989, 1996; Lefebvre, 1991; Spain, 1992; Keith & Pile, 1993; Rose, 1993; Ligget & Perry, 1995; Daniels & Lee, 1996; Hamnett, 1996), *critical pedagogy* (see Giroux, 1981, 1983, 1988; Apple, 1982, 1990; McLaren, 1988, 1995, 1997, 1998; Leistyna, Woodrum, & Sherblom 1996; Wink, 1997), *critical race theory* (Crenshaw, 1995; Delgado, 1995; Delgado & Stefancic, 1997; Solorzano, 1997, 1998; Solorzano & Yosso, 2000), and *cultural-historical activity theory* of learning and human development (Vygotsky, 1978; Wertsch, 1985, 1991; Cole & Engeström, 1993; Cole, 1996; Engeström, Miettinen, & Punamaki, 1999; Gutierrez, 2000; Gutierrez, Baquedano-Lopez, & Tejeda, 2000; Moll, 2000).

THE CURRICULAR CONTENTS OF A DECOLONIZING PEDAGOGICAL PRAXIS AND ITS CULTURAL-HISTORICAL CONCEPTION OF LEARNING AND COGNITION

What is the subject matter of a decolonizing pedagogy? What do teachers and students engaged in decolonizing pedagogical praxis teach and learn from one another? We contend that developing a critical consciousness of our internal neocolonial condition and its possible transformation is fundamental to what teachers and students do in decolonizing pedagogical spaces. This requires explicit attention to the history and contemporary manifestations of internal neocolonialism in a manner that clearly explicates their social origin and rejects the inevitability of their historical consequence. It also introduces students to robust theories and conceptual frameworks that provide them the analytical tools to excavate history and examine the present. It is a pedagogical content that must be guided by a conceptually dynamic worldview and a set of values that are anticapitalist, antiracist, antisexist, and antihomophobic.

We view the contents described above as necessarily contingent and context-specific. Although internal neocolonialism indelibly marks all social existence and largely defines every dimension of life, it assumes diverse forms and is experienced differently in the various social spaces of "American Society." Hence, we contend that the specific history and specific manifestations of neocolonialism that students and teachers engage should be determined by the particular social spaces of their existence—the specific places and social contexts where they experience internal neocolonialism. Likewise, the specific theorizations and conceptual frameworks that students and teachers engage should be determined by the specificity of neocolonial domination and exploitation in the social spaces they inhabit. The content of a decolonizing pedagogical praxis on an Indian reservation, for example, would necessarily be different than the content of a decolonizing pedagogical praxis in the urban spaces of metropolitan Los Angeles. In other words, the content is situated and contingent and thus open to continuous modification and expansion.

Although history and social science courses are seemingly ideal and most immediately relevant for addressing the history and current manifestations of internal neocolonialism, we call for decolonizing pedagogical praxis across the curriculum. All curricular subject matter (e.g., the social sciences, the humanities, and the natural sciences) can be used to examine neocolonial conditions or can be engaged in a manner that addresses the neocolonial production, utilization, and/or effects of its related bodies of knowledge. Whether we engage students in the learning of mathematics, history/social studies, language arts, chemistry, physics, or vocational skills, the content of our pedagogy highlights, examines, and discusses transforming the mutually reinforcing systems of neocolonial and capitalist domination and exploitation in the United States. Our proposed pedagogy also necessarily addresses how working-class indigenous and nonwhite teachers and students are assaulted by multiple and mutually constitutive forms of violence in the various dimensions of their daily lives. In this way, a decolonizing praxis seeks to provide students a rich theoretical, analytical, and pragmatic toolkit for individual and social transformation.

Although we call for a specific curricular focus, we are also committed to ensuring students the opportunity to master the traditional curriculum necessary for academic success within the present system of schooling. We do not call for ignoring or replacing the official curricular content for which students are held accountable. Although we see the need to problematize and expose the official curriculum's complicity with neocolonial domination and exploitation, we know that failing to prepare students in the mastery of this curriculum only sets them up for academic failure and its related social consequences. The decolonizing pedagogical praxis we propose sets out, for example, to prepare high school students to dynamically critique and actively work against neocolonialism while preparing and making themselves eligible for admission to and success at the most prestigious universities in the United States. Such contradictions are inevitable in internal neocolonial contexts.

DECOLONIZING PEDAGOGICAL PRAXIS AND THE CULTURAL-HISTORICAL CONCEPTION OF LEARNING AND COGNITION

A decolonizing pedagogical praxis challenges not only the forms, content, and intent of backlash pedagogies and their historical antecedents but also requires a complete reconceptualization of the social organization of learning in classrooms and educational institutions. Such a reconceptualization calls for a transformation in the social and intellectual relationships among participants in both schools and the particular communities in which the schools reside. From our perspective, the most productive theory of human development—one that aligns with a decolonizing perspective that focuses on the present while gazing at the past— is cultural-historical activity theory (Cole, 1996; Gutierrez, 2000; Moll, 2000; Vygotsky, 1978; Wertsch, 1985, 1991). At its core, cultural-historical or sociocultural theory recognizes the fundamentally relational nature of teaching and learning, the microgenetic, sociohistorical, and cultural planes of human activity, and the centrality of culture in human development. Its dynamic and processual notion of culture requires a focus on everyday practice within larger systems of activity that are, of course, always socially and culturally organized. As Cole and Engestrom argue, "A natural unit of analysis for the study of human behavior is activity systems, historically conditioned systems of relations among individuals and their proximal, culturally organized environments" (1993, p. 8). From our perspective, these practices and their larger activity systems are inescapably organized within particular neocolonial spaces of domination and exploitation. And more importantly, it is through the practices and activity systems of everyday life—those of the workplace, the classroom, the household, and the pubic forum—that neocolonial domination and exploitation are learned from one generation to the next, moved along from times and spaces that have passed to times and spaces that are currently lived, and reproduced anew.

From this perspective, teaching and learning cannot be disconnected from the larger contexts of their development, from the microgenetic or moment-to-moment and its larger sociohistorical context. This simultaneous focus on historicity and the quotidian requires us to understand the practices of schools as inseparable from our contemporary neocolonial contexts. For us, cultural-historical activity theory provides both a theoretical lens and methodological toolkit for examining and understanding how cultural artifacts that are both material and ideational mediate human beings' interaction with their social worlds. As such, tools or artifacts are never neutral and always a particular politic.

Conceptualizing teaching and learning as fundamentally situated and socially mediated forces us to always ground instructional practices in the present and past realities of teachers and students and to organize learning in ways that promote and assist their potential. Inherent in cultural historical theory is a pedagogy of potential in that its primary concern is on what students can accomplish with assistance in robust contexts of learning (Gutierrez, Baquedano-López, & Tejeda, 2000). But here we argue not for contexts that treat all contents, practices, and ways of organizing learning as neutral but, rather, we argue for contexts in which knowing and knowledge lead to a critical consciousness that guides action toward a transformation of our neocolonial condition.

Within a decolonizing perspective, cultural-historical activity theory can be used to examine and expose the ways the social constructs of race and ethnicity and its proxies, language and ability, achievement and underachievement, as well as the social practices of racism, discrimination, and privileging mediate the schooling outcomes of students from culturally and linguistically dominated groups. (Gutierrez, Asato,

Santos, & Gotanda, 2002). In doing so, we create new social relations and systems of activity that move toward a fundamentally
different instantiation of social justice—one that is defined by dominated peoples engaged in the politics and praxis of decolonization.

CONCLUSION

Sculpted reliefs in the Midwest and backlash politics and pedagogies
in California remind us that the effects and institutional arrangements
of yesterday's colonialism persist and are clearly manifest in the social,
cultural, and linguistic domination of millions in American society—
millions who are forced to divest their accents, identities, and knowledges in pursuit of educational opportunity; millions for whom a cultural holocaust continues as they struggle for social justice and equality.
We believe that the challenge before us is to interrogate the narratives
that naturalize and commemorate Euro-supremacy in the Americas; to
resist the current backlash politics and pedagogies by historicizing and
exposing their origins, intents, and effects; and, to construct a politics
and pedagogy that assists students from dominated groups to cross
from the times and spaces of corporal genocides and cultural holocausts in the past, through the times and spaces of social, cultural, and
linguistic domination in the present, and into a time and space of social
justice in the future. And we propose confronting this challenge from a
decolonizing perspective and the politics and praxis of a decolonizing
pedagogy that sets out to assist students to actively reflect, critique, and
work against the existing forms of domination and exploitation in the
United States while simultaneously preparing them for the concrete
exigencies of its educational or professional contexts. Such pedagogies
and praxis are possible and they flourish in the academic programs we
develop for students from migrant farmworker backgrounds and for
immigrant and other poor children in our after-school club. Such decolonizing perspectives and practices rupture the status quo of inequality
and make possible a social justice in the present.

ACKNOWLEDGMENT

The authors would like to acknowledge Manuel Espinoza and Jolyn
Asato, graduate students at UCLA who contributed to developing some
of the ideas presented in this chapter and have collaborated on earlier
publications where those ideas have been presented.

REFERENCES

Acuña, R. (1981). *Occupied America: A history of Chicanos*. 2nd ed. New York: Harper and Row.

Adams, D. (1995). *Education for extinction: American Indians and the boarding school experience, 1875–1928*. Lawrence: University Press of Kansas.

Afzal-Khan, F., & Seshadri Crooks, K. (Eds.). (2000). *The preoccupation of postcolonial studies*. Durham, NC: Duke University Press.

Aldama, A. J. (2001). *Disrupting savagism: Intersecting Chicana/o, Mexican immigrant, and Native American struggles for self-representation*. Durham, NC: Duke University Press.

Allen, J., & Pryke, M. (1996). The production of service space. In S. D. R. Lee (Ed.), *Exploring human geography: A reader*. New York: Halstead Press.

Almaguer, T. (1974). Historical notes on Chicano oppression: The dialectics of racial and class domination in North America. *Aztlan* 5 (1 & 2): 27–54.

Almaguer, T. (1994). *Racial fault lines: The historical origins of white supremacy in California*. Berkeley: University of California Press.

Apple, M. W. (1982). *Education and power*. Boston: Ark Paperbacks.

Apple. M. W. (1990). *Ideology and curriculum*. (2nd ed.). New York: Routledge.

Apple, M. (1996). *Cultural politics and education*. New York: Teachers College Press.

Ashcroft, B., Griffiths, G., & Tifflin, H. (Eds.). (1995). *The post-colonial studies reader*. New York: Routledge.

August, D., & Hakuta, K. (1997). *Improving schooling for language-minority children: A research agenda*. Washington, DC: National Academy Press.

Barnes, T., & Gregory, D. (Eds.). (1997). *Reading human geography: The poetics and politics of inquiry*. New York: Arnold.

Barrera, M. (1979). *Race and class in the Southwest: A theory of racial inequality*. Notre Dame: University of Notre Dame Press.

Behdad, Ali. (2000). Une practique sauvage: Postcolonial belatedness and cultural politics. In F. A.-K. K. Seshadri-Crooks (Ed.), *The pre-occupation of postcolonial studies*. Durham, NC: Duke University Press.

Berliner, D., & Biddle, B. (1995). *The manufactured crisis: Myths, fraud, and the attack on America's public schools*. Reading, MA: Addison-Wesley Publishing Company, Inc.

Blauner, R. (1972). *Racial oppression in America*. New York: Harper and Row.

Blommaert, J., & Verschueren, J. (1998). The role of language in European nationalist ideologies. In B. Schiefflelin, K. Woolard, & P. Kroskrity (Eds.), *Language ideologies: Practice and theory* (pp. 189–210). New York: Oxford University Press.

Brown, D. (1981). *Bury my heart at Wounded Knee: An Indian history of the American West*. New York: Washington Square Press.

Bulhan, H. A. (1985). *Frantz Fanon and the psychology of oppression*. New York: Plenum Publishing.

Camarillo, A. (1979). *Chicanos in a changing society: From Mexican Pueblos to American barrios in Santa Barbara and Southern California, 1848–1930*. Cambridge, MA: Harvard University Press.

Campbell, J., & Oakes, J. (1995). The invention of race: Rereading White over Black. In R. D. J. Stefancic (Ed.), *Critical White Studies: Looking behind the mirror*. Philadelphia: Temple University Press.

Chang, R., & Aoki, K. (1997). Centering the immigrant in the inter/national imagination. *La Raza Law Review, 10*, 309–361.

Chomsky, N., & Herman, E. S. (1979). *The Washington connection and Third World fascism*. Boston: South End Press.

Churchill, W. (1997). *A little matter of genocide: Holocaust denial in the Americas 1492 to the present*. San Francisco: City Lights Books.

Cole, M. (1996). *Cultural psychology: A once and future discipline*. Cambridge, MA: The Belknap Press of Harvard University Press.

Cole, M. (1998). Can cultural psychology help us think about diversity? *Mind, Culture, and Activity, 5*(4), 291–304.

Cole, M., & Engeström, Y. (1993). A cultural-historical approach to distributed cognition. In G. Salomon (Ed.), *Distributed cognitions: Psychological and educational considerations* (pp. 1–46). New York: Cambridge University Press.

Crenshaw, K. (1995). Mapping the margins: Intersectionality, identity politics, and violence against women of color. In N. G. Kimberlé Crenshaw, G. Peller, & K. Thomas (Eds.), *Critical race theory: The key writings that formed the movement*. New York: New Press.

Cruz, C. (2001). Toward an epistemology of a brown body. *QSE: The International Journal of Qualitative Studies in Education, 14*(3), 657–669.

Daniels, S., & Lee, R. (Eds). (1996). *Exploring human geography: A reader*. New York: Halstead Press.

Davis, P. C. (1995). Law as microaggression. In R. Delgado (Ed.), *Critical race theory: The cutting edge*. Philadelphia: Temple University Press.

De Leon, A. (1983). *They called them greasers: Anglo attitudes toward Mexicans in Texas, 1821–1900*. Austin: University of Texas Press.

Delgado, R. (1995). The imperial scholar: Reflections on a review of civil rights literature. In N. G. Kimberlé Crenshaw, G. Peller, & K. Thomas (Eds.), *Critical race theory: The key writings that formed the movement*. New York: New Press.

Delgado, R. & Stefancic, J. (Eds.). (1997). *Critical white studies: Looking behind the mirror*. Philadelphia: Temple University Press.

Deloria, V. (1997). *Red earth white lies: Native Americans and the Myth of scientific fact*. Golden, CO: Fulcrum Publishing.

Deloria, V., & Lytle, C.M. (1983). *American Indians, American justice*. Austin: Texas University Press.

Dirlik, A. (1996). The postcolonial aura: Third world criticism in the age of global capitalism. In Padmini Mongia (Ed.), *Contemporary postcolonial theory: A reader*. New York: Arnold.

Driver, F. (1996). Geography's empire: Histories of geographical knowledge. In S. D. R. Lee (Ed.), *Exploring human geography: A reader*. New York: Halstead Press.

Duran, E., & Duran, B. (1995). *Native American postcolonial psychology*. Albany: State University of New York Press.

Engestrom, Y. (1987). *Learning by expanding*. Helsinki, Finland: Orienta-Konsultit Oy.

Engestrom, Y. (1999). Activity theory and individual and social transformation. In Y. Engestrom, R. Miettinen, & R. Punamaki (Eds.), *Perspectives on activity theory* (pp. 19–38). Cambridge, UK: Cambridge University Press.

Engestrom, Y, Miettinen, R., & Punamäki, R. (Eds.) (1999). *Perspectives on activity theory* New York: Cambridge University Press.

England, V. L. (1997). Getting personal: Reflexivity, positionality, and feminist research. In T. B. D. Gregory (Ed.), *Reading Human Geography: The poetics and politics of inquiry*. New York: Arnold.

Eschbach, K. (1999). Death at the border. *International Migration Review, 33*(2).

Faludi, S. (1991). *Backlash: The undeclared war against American Women*. New York: Crown Publishers.

Fanon, F. (1963). *The wretched of the earth* (C. Farrington, Trans.). New York: Grove Press.

Foucault, M. (1972). *The archeology of knowledge*. New York: Pantheon.

Foucault, M. (1980). *Power/knowledge: Selected interviews and other and other writings 1972–1977*. (Colin Gordon, Ed.). Pantheon Books: New York.

Foucault, M. (1986). Of other spaces. *Diacritics, 16*, 22–27.

Franklin, J. H., & Moss, A. A. (1988). *From slavery to freedom: A history of Negro Americans.* 6th ed. New York: Alfred A. Knopf.

Fredrickson, G. (1997). White images of black slaves (is what we see in others sometimes a reflection of what we find in ourselves?). In R. Delgado & J. Stefanic (Eds.), *Critical white studies: Looking behind the mirror.* Temple University Press: Philadelphia pp. 38–45.

Freire, P. (1990). *Pedagogy of the oppressed.* (M. B. Ramos, Trans.). New York: Continuum.

Freire, P. (1998). *Pedagogy of freedom: Ethics, democracy, and civic courage.* (P. Clarke, Trans.). Lanham, MD: Rowman & Littlefield.

Galeano, E. (1989). *Las venas abiertas de América Latina.* Mexico City: Siglo Veintiuno Editores.

Gandara, P., Maxwell-Jolly, J., Asato, J., Curry, J., Garcia, E., Gutiérrez, K., & Stritkus, T. (2000). The initial impact of proposition 227 on the instruction of English learners. *Linguistic Minority Research Institute Newsletter, 9*(3), 1–2.

Gandhi, L. (1998). *Postcolonial theory: A critical introduction.* New York: Columbia University Press.

Garcia, O., & Otheguy, R. (1985). The masters of survival send their children to school: Bilingual education in the ethnic schools of Miami. *Bilingual Review / Revista Bilingue, 12*(1–2), 3–19.

Giroux, H. A. (1981). *Ideology, culture, and the process of schooling.* Philadelphia: Temple University Press.

Giroux, H. A. (1983). *Theory and resistance in education: A pedagogy for the opposition.* New York: Bergin & Garvey Publishers.

Giroux, H. A. (1988). *Schooling and the struggle for public life: Critical pedagogy in the modern age.* Minneapolis: University of Minnesota Press.

Gotanda, N. (1995). A critique of "Our Constitution Is Color-Blind." In K. Crenshaw, N. Gotanda, G. Peller, & K. Thomas (Eds.), *Critical race theory: The key writings that formed the movement* (pp. 257–275). New York: The New Press.

Gutiérrez, K. (November, 1999). *Backlash pedagogies: When reform creates unsuccessful practice.* Paper presented at the annual conference of the National Council of Teachers of English. Denver, Colorado.

Gutierrez, K. (2000). Teaching and learning in the 21st Century. *English Education, 32*(4), 290–298.

Gutierrez, K. (2001). Using hybridity to build literacy in urban classrooms. In M. Reyes & J. Halcon (Eds.), *The best for our children: Latina/Latino voices on literacy* (pp. 122–141). New York: Teachers College Press.

Gutiérrez, K., Asato, J., Santos, M., & Gotanda, N. (2002). Backlash pedagogy: Language and culture and the politics of reform. *The Review of Education, Pedagogy, and Cultural Studies, 24*, 335–351.

Gutiérrez, K., Baquedano-López, P., & Alvarez, H. (2000). The crisis in Latino education: The norming of America. In C. Tejeda, C. Martinez, & Z. Leonardo (Eds.), *Charting new terrains of Chicana(o)/Latina(o) education* (pp. 213–232). Cresskill, NJ: Hampton Press Inc.

Gutiérrez, K., Baquedano-López, P., & Alvarez, H., & Chiu, M. (1999). A cultural-historical approach to collaboration: Building a culture of collaboration through hybrid language practices. *Theory into Practice, 38*(2), 87–93.

Gutierrez, K., Baquedano-Lopez, P., & Asato, J. (2001). English for the children: The new literacy of the old world order. *Bilingual Review Journal, 24*(1&2), 87–112.

Gutiérrez, K., Baquedano-López, P., & Tejeda, C. (2000). Rethinking diversity: Hybridity and hybrid language practices in the third space. *Mind, Culture, and Activity, 6*(4), 286–303.

Gutiérrez, K., Baquedano-López, P., & Turner, M. G. (1997). Putting language back into language arts: When the radical middle meets the third space. *Language Arts, 74*(5), 368–378.

Gutierrez, K., & Larson, J. (1994). Language borders: Recitation as hegemonic discourse. *International Journal of Educational Reform, 3*(1), 22–36.

Gutiérrez, K., Rymes, B., & Larson, J. (1995). Script, counterscript, and underlife in the classroom: James Brown versus *Brown v. Board of Education. Harvard Educational Review, 65*(3), 445–471.

Gutiérrez, K., & Stone L. (1997). A cultural-historical view of learning and learning disabilities: Participating in a community of learners. *Learning Disabilities: Research and Practice, 12*(2), 123–131.

Hamnett, C. (1996). *Social geography: A reader.* New York: Arnold.

Hanke, L. (1959). *Aristotle & the American Indians: A study in race prejudices in the modern world.* Chicago: Henry Regnery Company.

Hanke, L. (1974). *All mankind is one: A study of the disputation between Bartolomé de Las Casa and Juan Ginés de Sepúlveda in 1550 on the intellectual and religious capacity of the American Indians.* DeKalb: Northern Illinois University Press.

Harris, C. (1993). Whiteness as property. *Harvard Law Review, 106*(8), 1709–1791.

Haymes, S. (1995). *Race culture and the city: A pedagogy for black urban struggle.* New York: State University of New York Press.

Horseman, R. (1997). Race and manifest destiny: The origins of American racial Anglo-Saxonism. In R. D. J. Stefancic (Ed.), *Critical white studies: Looking behind the mirror.* Philadelphia: Temple University Press.

Jacobs, J. (1996). *Edge of empire: Postcolonialism and the city.* New York: Routledge.

Keith, M., & Pile, S. (Eds.). (1993). *Place and the politics of identity.* New York: Routledge.

Lefebvre, H. (1991). *The production of space* (D. Nicholson-Smith, Trans.). Cambridge: Blackwell. (Original work published 1974)

Leistyna, P., Woodrum, A., & Sherblom, S.A. (Eds.). (1996). *Breaking free: The transformative power of critical pedagogy.* Cambridge, MA: Harvard Educational Review, Reprint Series No. 27.

Let's fix our schools: Majority Rule Act (1999). Retrieved March 31, 2000 from http://www.letsfixourschools.com/voterinfo//vi_mra_p.html

Ligget, H., & Perry, D. C. (Eds.). (1995). *Spatial Practices: Critical explorations in social/spatial theory.* Thousand Oaks, CA: Sage.

Lipsitz, G. (1998). *The possessive investment in whiteness: How white people profit from identity politics.* Philadelphia: Temple University Press.

Macedo, D. (2000). The colonialism of the English Only movement. *Educational Researcher, 29*(3), 15–24.

Marx, C. (1978). *El dieciocho brumario de Luis Bonaparte.* Pekin: Ediciones Lenguas Extranjeras.

Marx, K. (1973). *Karl Marx on society and social change.* (N. J. Smelser, Ed.). Chicago: University of Chicago Press.

Marx, K., & Engels, F. (1984). *The German ideology.* (C. J. Arthur, Ed.). New York: International Publishers.

Massey, D. (1984). Geography matters. In J. Allen (Ed.), *Geography matters! A reader.* Cambridge: Cambridge University Press.

McLaren, P. (1988). On ideology and education: Critical pedagogy and the politics of education. *Social Text* (19&20), 153–185.

McLaren, P. (1995). *Critical pedagogy and predatory culture: Oppositional politics in a post-modern era*. New York: Routledge.

McLaren, P. (1997). *Revolutionary multiculturalism: Pedagogies of dissent for the new millennium*. Boulder, CO: Westview Press.

McLaren, P. (1998). *Life in schools: An introduction to critical pedagogy in the foundations of education*. 3rd ed. New York: Longman.

McLaren, P., & Farahmandpur, R. (2000). Critical multiculturalism and globalization: Transgressive pedagogies in gringolandia. In C. Tejeda, C. Martinez, & Z. Leonardo, (Eds.), *Charting new terrains of Chicana(o)/Latina(o) Education*. Cresskill: Hampton Press.

Moll, L. (2000). Inspired by Vygotsky: Ethnographic experiments in education. In C. Lee & P. Smagorinsky (Eds.), *Vygotskian perspectives on literacy research: Constructing meaning through collaborative inquiry* (pp. 256–268). New York: Cambridge University Press.

Moll, L., Amanti, C., Niff, D., & Gonzalez, N. (1992). Funds of knowledge for teachers: Using a qualitative approach to connect homes and classrooms. *Theory into practice, 31*(2), 132–141.

Mongia, P. (Ed.). (1996). *Contemporary postcolonial theory: A reader*. New York: Arnold.

Moore-Gilbert, B. (1997). *Postcolonial theory: Contexts, Practices, Politics*. New York: Verso.

National Commission on Excellence in Education. (1983). *A nation at risk: The imperatives for educational reform*. Washington, DC: U.S. Department of Education.

Omi, M., & Winant, H. (1994). *Racial formation in the United States: From the 1960's to the 1990's*. New York: Routledge.

Popkewitz, T. (2000). Reform. In D. Gabbard (Ed.), *Knowledge and power in the global economy: Politics and the rhetoric of school reform* (pp. 33–42). Mahwah, NJ: Lawrence Erlbaum Associates.

Rose, G. (1993). *Feminism and geography: The limits of geographical knowledge*. Minneapolis: University of Minnesota Press.

Said, E. (1978). *Orientalism: Western conceptions of the Orient*. London: Penguin.

Seed, P. (2001). *American pentimiento*. Minneapolis: University of Minnesota Press.

Singh, A., & Schmidt, P. (2000). *Postcolonial theory and the United States: Race ethnicity and literature*. Jackson: University Press of Mississippi.

Soja, E. (1989). *Postmodern geographies: The reassertion of space in critical social theory*. New York: Verso.

Soja, E. (1996). *Thirdspace: Journeys to Los Angeles and other real and imagined places*. Cambridge, UK: Blackwell Publishers.

Solorzano, D. (1997). Images and words that wound: Critical race theory, racial stereotyping, and teacher education. *Teacher Education Quarterly, 24*, 5–19.

Solorzano, D. (1998). Critical race theory, racial and gender microaggressions, and the experience of Chicana and Chicano scholars. *International Journal of Qualitative Studies in Education, 11*, 121–136.

Solorzano, D., & Yosso, T. (2000). Toward a critical race theory of Chicana and Chicano education. In C. Tejeda, C. Martinez, & Z. Leonardo (Eds.), *Charting new terrains of Chicana(o)/Latina(o) Education*, Cresskill: Hampton Press.

Spain, D. (1992). *Gendered spaces*. Chapel Hill, NC: The University of North Carolina Press.

Spring, J. (1992). *Images of American life: A history of ideological management in schools, movies, radio, and television*. Albany: State University of New York Press.

Spring, J. (2001a). *The American school: 1642–2000*. 5th ed. San Francisco: McGraw-Hill.

Spring, J. (2001b). *Deculturalization and the struggle for equality: A brief history of dominated cultures in the United States*. 3rd ed. San Francisco: McGraw-Hill.

Steinhorn, L., & Diggs-Brown, B. (1999). *By the color of our skin: The illusion of integration and the reality of race*. New York: Penguin Books.

Stromquist, N. P., & Monkman, K. (Eds.). (2000). *Globalization and education: Integration and contestation across cultures*. Landham, MD: Rowman & Littlefield.

Tejeda, C. (2000). Toward a spatialized understanding of the Chicana(o)/Latina(o) educational experience: Theorizations of space and the mapping of educational outcomes in Los Angeles. In C. Tejeda, C. Martinez, & Z. Leonardo (Eds.), *Charting new terrains of Chicana(o)/Latina(o) Education*. Cresskill: Hampton Press.

Tejeda, C. (in press). Decolonizing pedagogy and critical multiculturalism in the classroom: Reading the word and the world of American schooling with teacher candidates. *Multicultural Education*.

Trouillot, M. R. (1995). *Silencing the past: Power and the production of history*. Boston: Beacon Press.

Tuhiwai Smith, L. (1999). *Decolonizing methodologies: Research and indigenous peoples*. New York. Zed Books.

Unz, R., & Tuchman, G. (1997). *English language education for children in public schools*. Retreived March 31, 2000, from http://www.onenation.org/fulltext.html

Vygotsky, L. S. (1978). *Mind in society: The development of higher psychological processes*. M. Cole & U. J. Steiner (Eds.). Cambridge, MA: Harvard University Press.

Wertsch, J. (1985). *Vygotsky and the social formation of mind*. Cambridge, MA: Harvard University Press.

Wertsch, J. (1991). *Voices of the mind: A sociocultural approach to mediated action*. Cambridge, MA: Harvard University Press.

Williams, R. A. (1995). Documents of Barbarism: The contemporary legacy of European racism and colonialism in the narrative traditions of federal Indian Law. In R. Delgado (Ed.), *Critical race theory: The cutting edge*. Philadelphia: Temple University Press.

Willinsky, J. (1998). *Learning to divide the world: Education at empire's end*. Minneapolis: University of Minnesota Press.

Wink, J. (1997). *Critical pedagogy: Notes from the real world*. New York: Longman.

Wood, G. (1983). Beyond educational cynicism. *Educational Theory, 32*(2), 55–71.

Woolard, K. (1998). Introduction: Language ideology as a field of inquiry. In B. Schiefflelin, K. Woolard, & P. Kroskrity (Eds.), *Language ideologies: Practice and theory* (pp. 3–47). New York: Oxford University Press.

Zentella, A. (1997). *Growing up bilingual*. Malden, MA: Blackwell.

Zinn, H. (1995). *A people's history of the United States: 1492—present*. New York: Harper Perrennial.

12

The Educational Sovereignty of Latino/a Students in the United States[1]

Luis C. Moll
Richard Ruiz
University of Arizona

In one of his last papers, our late friend and colleague David Smith (Smith, 2000) reflects on research he conducted in Philadelphia and elsewhere, and mentions how ethnographic research has difficulty in addressing the "real" issues in education: disparities in relations of power. He wrote as follows:

> A challenge facing urban ethnography today is not only to surface the narratives of oppression, resistance and resilience [but to] develop approaches that put these narratives to use in addressing the oppressive equations. It is not enough to uncover local "funds of knowledge"... nor to incorporate these into our pedagogical repertoire, but they must become the basis for a radical new pedagogy, one that is based on and privileges these narratives and local knowledge. (p. 16 in manuscript)

---

[1]This paper is a revised version of a keynote address delivered by L. C. Moll at the Ethnography Forum, Graduate School of Education, University of Pennsylvania, March 1, 2002; it is also a revised version of Moll and Ruiz (2002).

In this chapter we want to present and elaborate a concept that attempts to respond, at least in some respects, to David's challenge. The concept is that of educational sovereignty. This is a term inspired by the work of colleagues doing research in and with indigenous communities, addressing the need to challenge a long history of control and coercion in the education of Indian students (e.g., Lomawaima, 2000; McCarty, 2002; Warner, 1999; see also Henze & Davis, 1999).

WHAT IS EDUCATIONAL SOVEREIGNTY?

We use the term "educational sovereignty" to capture the need to challenge the arbitrary authority of the "white" power structure and reestablish within the Latino/a communities themselves the structures and norms by which to determine the essence of education for Latino/a (and other minority) students (see Moll & Ruiz, 2002). It is, in other words, a term of both resistance and affirmation, signaling the recognition of a negative history to be challenged and the hope of a positive future to be grasped. But we are not proposing "sovereignty" in the sense of creating strict and arbitrary boundaries of separation, the way it is done to mark, chauvinistically, and often on the basis of conquest, the territory of a nation/state. That concept of sovereignty, despite the recent nationalistic rhetoric in the United States about "homeland defense," is becoming obsolete because of "the emergence of a new political order, one which would permit overlapping authority structures" (Wright, 2000, p. 79). This new order is being created in large part by the requirements of a global economy, the transnational character of immigration, and the emergence and strengthening within the past half century of supranational authorities intervening in the affairs of putatively sovereign states.

The obsolescence of the notion of territorial sovereignty, the purpose of which is to separate "us" from "them," is demonstrated clearly in the contradictions inherent in the juxtaposition of calls for border-free economic spaces, on the one hand, and insistence on strict border control to keep immigrants out, on the other. "The emergence of a new economic regime," Sassen (1999) writes, "sharply reduces the role of national governments and national borders in controlling international [economic] transactions." "Yet," she continues, "the framework for immigration policy in these countries remains centered on older conceptions of the nation-state and the national borders" (Sassen, 1999, pp. 4–5; cf. Held, McGrew, Goldblatt, & Perraton, 1999).

As important to the decline of the territorially sovereign nation-state is the growing importance of supranational and regional authorities such as the United Nations, the International Court of Justice, and the various regional and subcontinental conventions that compete for legitimacy with traditional nations. Indeed, such entities exist in large part to intervene in the affairs of states on behalf of individuals or groups, deriving their authority from the application of principles "higher" than those embodied in the laws of the state.

The International Nuremberg tribunal (1946 and following); the UN's International Bill of Human Rights (1948); the European Convention for the Protection of Human Rights (1950); the Helsinki Declarations of Human Rights (1992); and the UN International Criminal Court (1998) are powerful influences against the laws of individual states even though they have little if any enforcement capacity beyond public humiliation. These and similar authorities have been used to contravene long-standing sovereignty agreements between states, as well, as when the British House of Lords used the 1984 Torture Convention to justify the extradition of General Pinochet to answer charges of human rights abuses in Chile (Held, 1995; Wright, 2000).

The challenge to the traditional view of sovereignty as strict boundedness is captured nicely in the literature on interdisciplinarity and international education, and we can use it here to some advantage. In their edited book on boundaries and theoretical integration, Sil and Doherty (2000) include papers that argue against rigid divisions at the same time that core aspects of disciplinary traditions are both acknowledged and valued. Huntley (2000), for example, uses the term "threshold" (as opposed to boundary) to characterize the separation or compartmentalization of disciplinary traditions in the social sciences. "Whereas the concept of 'boundary' connotes forced separation and perhaps antipathy, the concept of 'threshold' inheres [sic] suggestions of both separation and joining—one 'crosses' a threshold" (p. 178). Nor does he bemoan the proliferation of thresholds, seeing it as a natural development of knowledge, what he calls the "geography of human knowledge":

> The emergence of thresholds is providing an ever more detailed map of this geography, viewing which requires only the development of our own capacity to rise above perceiving these thresholds as "boundaries." Our judgments as to topics of attention, epistemological viewpoints, and the like, thus can serve to locate us, rather than limit us, if only we can rise above the choices themselves. (Huntley, 2000, p. 197)

Other writers make similar distinctions. Fardon and Furniss (1994), for example, suggest the use of "frontiers," implying the "interpenetration of phenomena," rather than "boundaries," which suggest "exclusive and distinct phenomena," in discussions of language communities (p. 3). Such use of the concept of "frontier," although embedded, is also evident in work by Bixler-Márquez (1998), who describes how indigenous communities on both sides of the Mexico-U.S. border use electronic media to convey information on health, political reform, education, and language to each other. The control they have over the dissemination of essential information is an exercise in educational sovereignty: it affords them the opportunity to decide how and to what degree they will interact with the communities around them.

Perhaps the best examples of the type of educational sovereignty we are proposing can be found in the literature on indigenous schooling. One such example is provided by Vick-Westgate (2002), who presents a detailed history of the struggle for good schooling for Inuit children against the Quebec government. She describes a situation in northern Canada in which native communities have started to take control of the education of their children. By "control," she means having decision-making authority over curriculum, methods and materials, staffing, calendar, and assessment, among many other things—in other words, the essence of schooling. She describes the need for greater appropriation of schooling by the local community with a quote from a 1992 task force report on Inuit schooling:

> The education system in Nunavik should be restructured and refocused to make it work for us, to ensure that it prepares us to handle the problems and opportunities of living that we actually face—not just the ones the school board has been mechanically structured to deal with. We are not asking someone else to create this system for us. Creating it ourselves is a necessary step to self-government in Nunavik. Self-government and education go hand in hand just as independence goes with wisdom. (Vick-Westgate, 2002, p. 236)

The situation in Nunavik is different from those of most minority communities in North America in that they have retaken control of not only their social institutions but also their territory (Inuits selected "Nunavik" as the name of their territory in 1987, although the resolution of property rights and governmental structure is ongoing). Even here, however, it is important to note that the greatest obstacle to their independence, as in most colonial situations, is not territorial but psychological.

Even having control over a bordered piece of property does not ensure control of their educational and social institutions, as native communities in the United States are well aware. To help in the reorientation process and to objectify a sense of internal control, the community established a formal body, the Satuigiarniq Committee ("Satuigiarniq" is an Inuit word meaning "reclaiming"). The committee expressed the need for such an attitudinal change:

> Community involvement and empowerment will come only from the development of a sense of ownership of the process. Our aim is not to do the consultation for the communities but rather to help them develop the leadership skills necessary to design and conduct their community's consultation and to develop the attitude of self-reliance and a level of competence which will truly lead to their community's reclaiming of the educational system. (Vick-Westgate, 2002, p. 229)

An essential dimension of educational sovereignty is the extent to which communities feel themselves to be in control of their language behaviors. The considerable recent work on language retention and revitalization from the inside (see, for example, Grenoble & Whaley, 1998; Ostler & Rudes, 2000; Fishman, 2001; May, 2001, and many others) is testimony to the salience of such issues. The multitude of examples precludes a comprehensive review of this work here. We will mention only two. Nora England's work among several Maya communities in Guatemala (in Grenoble & Whaley, 1998) reveals the difficult processes of language preservation in a highly minoritized community. She chronicles the work of the Mayan Language Academy (established in 1991) that established a number of principles and assumptions under which it proceeds: Mayan control of language decisions; standardization of Mayan languages; expansion of the domains of Mayan language use; use of Mayan languages in schools as media of instruction, not primarily as instruments of castellanization; and the eventual recognition of the Mayan languages as official within their regions. Although these communities recognize that the demarcation of formal borders around the areas they inhabit (territorial sovereignty) is not feasible nor perhaps even desirable, they do affirm their right and responsibility to take control of the development of their language (linguistic sovereignty) and the uses to which it is put in schools (educational sovereignty).

Similarly, Martinez (2000) describes the situation of native Pueblo communities in North America. She explains that the motivation of these people to teach children the heritage language is because this is valuable for their own reasons, not merely as a means to learning English: "The reason Pueblo adults wish for children to learn their heritage language has nothing to do with the acquisition of English. It is so that the children can participate knowledgeably and appropriately in the maintenance of their traditional culture and religion" (2000, p. 217) She also mentions the need for future leaders of the communities to know the traditional language and values of the people, and the importance of recognizing the "intrinsic value" of Pueblo languages. Finally, she makes the connection between linguistic and educational sovereignty: "... educators must understand that if Pueblo languages are taught in schools, they should be used in ways that are appropriate to the cultures they represent, and not as poor translations of English language curriculum" (p. 217).

It is important to reiterate that we are not using the term "educational sovereignty" to signal the need for an act of separation. We mean by it almost the opposite—the strength and power a social setting like a school can garner by developing strategic social networks to create "cultural spaces" that will enhance its autonomy, mediate ideological and programmatic constraints, and provide additive forms of schooling for its students. In relation to Latino/a children and their teachers, consonant with the international examples mentioned earlier, educational sovereignty also means reclaiming their language rights, in the midst of their oppression, and the aggression perpetrated by the dominant society (more on this later).

In particular, we emphasize the type of agency that considers the schooling of Latino/a children within a larger education ecology, with an eye toward the transnational potential of such schooling, and that respects and responds to the values of education possessed by Latino/a families (see, e.g., Goldenberg & Gallimore, 1995). This larger ecology, then, includes not only schools but also the social relationships and cultural resources found in local households and community settings, and the potential connections created with other schools and communities in the Americas.

What follows is, first, a somewhat cursory review of the status quo for hundreds of thousands of Latino/a students, very diverse in their own right, but mostly from low-income families (see Moll & Ruiz, 2002). It will seem very oppressive for those not familiar with the current conditions of Latino/a education. In fact, no White, middle-class child will ever face the pressures, abuses, and restrictive learning conditions imposed on these children.

Although emphasis of these comments is on the education of Latino/a children, there are many cognate issues with the situation of other marginalized groups, especially African American children. There are very few studies, however, that attempt to address jointly the education issues of these two groups. These studies are badly needed. Let us keep in mind that Latino/a and African American children now constitute the majority population in most urban school districts in the country.

This initial summary, then, will serve to highlight the "encapsulation" of these children's schooling, resulting in various forms of what Valenzuela (1999) has called "subtractive" schooling: forms of schooling that are not only forcibly (and punitively) assimilative, but that deliberately exclude the social, cultural, or linguistic resources of the students. We then present three promising responses, among many others that could be reviewed, to this encapsulation of schooling by dominant policies, practices, and ideologies, which illustrate attempts at educational sovereignty. Each example is taken from projects in which we have participated and in which an ethnographic understanding of issues plays a pivotal role. To conclude, we identify four areas of study essential to elaborating the concept of educational sovereignty.

THE STATUS QUO CONSIDERED

All contemporary issues of education for Latino/a students must be understood, in one way or another, in the context created by demographic changes. Los Angeles is a case in point. For example, Rumbaut (1998; see also Portes & Rumbaut, 2001) has estimated that 62% of the population of Los Angeles, approximately six million people, is of "immigrant stock," most of them Latinos.[2] A current estimate is that the Latino/a population of the city and county of Los Angeles ranges from 40 to 45% of the total population. In the county this represents a total of over four million people, the majority population of Los Angeles, with about 40% between the ages of 0 and 17, or school age; moreover, about 63% of young children (ages 0–5) in the county are Latinos

---

[2]Rumbaut defines "immigrant stock" as the sum of the first and second generations of the U.S. populations.

(Children Now, 1999). All issues in Los Angeles, then, political, economic, or educational, are now framed and mediated by this demographic reality (see Rocco, 1996).[3]

Furthermore, the great majority of this population, whether recent
immigrants, second generation, or later, could be considered as either
working-class or poor, and very likely to remain that way (see, e.g.,
López, Popkin, & Tellez, 1996; Ortíz, 1996; Treiman & Lee, 1996). The
Latino/a population nationally is also overwhelmingly working class
and low income. Consider just two national indicators: In 2002, 28% of
Latino/a children younger than 18 (school-age) live below the poverty
level (compared to 9.5% for Whites); and 21.4% of Latinos were living in
poverty (7.8% for Whites) (Ramirez & de la Cruz, 2002). The sociologist
Vilma Ortíz (1996), in a study done of Latinos in Los Angeles, concluded
that, given existing structural and economic conditions, this population
would remain permanently in the low working class. Whether her pre-
diction is accurate or not, the point is that this low social class status is a
more or less stable, a more or less "fixed" structural condition of Latinos
in urban settings. This socioeconomic standing, as is well known, has
major implications for the schooling of children (Lee & Burkam, 2002).

The schools reflect these broader demographic changes. For example, the Latino/a population of the LAUSD (as of 2002–2003), according
to District data, is well over half a million students (537,136), or 72%
of the total student population (746,852); in contrast, the White student population is 9.4% (70,031).[4] Taking into account the other ethnic
groups, this school district is approximately 90% "minority," if such a
term is still applicable.

Furthermore, 75% of students in the district are eligible for free or
reduced lunch services, the great majority of these students Latinos.
In addition, of the total number of students in the District, about 43%
are designated as English Learners (EL), about 300,000 of these students being Spanish speakers. Nearly all of these (EL) students are in
the free or reduced lunch program, among the poorest students in the
district.

---

[3] As of January 1, 2002, the population of the City of Los Angeles: 3,80,400; the County of Los
Angeles: 9,824,800. Source: Office of the City Administrative Officer, 2003, City of Los Angeles Economic and Demographic Information; see http://www.cityofla.org/CAO/econdemo.
htm

[4] All data about LAUSD were obtained from the following California Department of Education websites: see, http://www.ed-data.k12.ca.us/welcome.asp; http://www.lausd.k12.
ca.us/; http://cahsee.cde.ca.gov/2002/

The teaching corps, however, remains largely White (47.7%), with 27.2% Latino/a and 14% African American. Statewide in California, we should point out, the discrepancies are larger: the Latino/a student population is at 45% (34% White) whereas 74% of teachers are White and only 14% are Latinos. Thus, Latinos are the majority at LAUSD and statewide; students are mostly working class and poor, but the teaching corps is primarily White and middle class, and English monolingual as well.

The academic performance of Latino/a students is generally low. Without belaboring the point, the dropout rate (grades 9–12) for Latinos, and for African Americans, is very high;[5] for example, the 4-year derived rate, an estimate of the percent of students who would drop out in a 4-year period based on data collected for a single year (2002–2003), is 36% for Latinos, and 43% for African Americans. Furthermore, the academic achievement of these students is the lowest in the district. For example, Latinos have the lowest percentage (55%) of students passing the state's English language arts high school exit exam; the percentage of passing scores for the math exam are even lower (27%). These high dropout rates, combined will the low achievement, are a consistent finding in all school districts nationally with comparable socioeconomic profiles.

One would figure that in a school district with such a dominant Latino/a population, issues affecting these children would take precedence, but nothing could be further from the truth, which helps illustrate the neocolonial conditions of their schooling. If anything, Los Angeles Unified has become one of the most restrictive districts anywhere. Consider the following issues.

- Bilingual education is virtually banned (statewide), Spanish is banished as a language of instruction, under penalty of law, and the teachers threatened with lawsuits if they use Spanish in school.

---

[5]Beginning in 2002–2003, the California Department of Education (CDE) adopted the National Center for Educational Statistics (NCES) Dropout definition, which is a follows: [A student who] (1) Was enrolled in grades 7, 8, 9, 10, 11, or 12 at some time during the previous school year and left school prior to completing the school year and has not returned to school as of Information Day; or, (2) Did not begin attending the next grade (7, 8, 9, 10, 11, or 12) in the school to which they were assigned or in which they had preregistered or were expected to attend by Information Day.

A similar law was passed by initiative and is now in place in Arizona and Massachusetts, and is being considered in other states, such as New York and Texas. Consider the coercive ideological context that such a law perpetuates, establishing Spanish as a pariah language in the schools while privileging English exclusively, and showing how only the interests of the Anglo monolingual community can be represented in the schools. Sadly, this ideology is confined neither to California nor to the present context; see MacGregor-Mendoza's (1998) historical analysis of what she calls the "criminalization of Spanish in the United States."

- Highly restrictive and regimented reading curricula are put in place district wide, and without any evidence of their appropriateness, imposed on teachers by law, focusing primarily on the children pronouncing phonemes in isolation as the principal if not sole pedagogy of early reading, severely curtailing or prohibiting alternative (meaning-driven) instructional approaches.

- Mandatory mass (high-stakes) testing is implemented, despite the failure of such systems to narrow the gap between majority and minority students. These tests leave little to no room for more formative forms of assessment that may lead to increased professional development of teachers, precisely what is needed to address the needs of a diverse and largely poor group of students, and result in increased rote instruction of a narrow group of subjects.

- The referral of Latino/a students to special education increases with the onset of English-only practices. The most common reason for referral is early reading difficulties, particularly common when non-English speakers are being taught to read in English by English-monolingual teachers using mandated phonics methods. These lessons become, in essence, prolonged dialect correction lessons.

- The district implements a no-social-promotions policy, as part of the standards movement, with retention rates estimated as high as 50%.

- The district implements a mandatory class reduction program. A consequence, given a shortage of teachers, is that uncertified teachers are routinely assigned to teach in the poorest schools with large populations of English language learners.

Therefore, if you are a young Latino/a student entering the LAUSD, you are likely to (1) engage a low-level academic curriculum, befitting your low social class status, that will limit your opportunities for academic advancement; (2) suffer the indignity and psychological violence of having Spanish, your home language, banned in school by the edict of white strangers; (3) spend hours every week doing language drills on nonsense phonemes, with little time devoted to understanding what you read; (4) face the strong likelihood of being labeled retarded or learning disabled for the rest of your school career; (5) be flunked for not passing tests of questionable validity but that are politically expedient; or (6) risk being taught by teachers with limited or no qualifications.

The point is that these constraints are not just isolated issues that coincide. It is vital to recognize the organized political forces and language ideologies that guide these activities as part of a broader social and educational policy of control and coercion, in the context created by immigration and the changing demographics. Moreover, none of these structural and ideological conditions is likely to change in the near future; in fact, they are likely to become more oppressive, given the changing demographics of the school population.

Our claim is that the situation as described, although with considerable variation, represents the status quo for Latino/a students in the United States, a population that is overwhelmingly working class and poor, growing demographically, and suffering the consequences of their growth and their position in the social order.

THE STATUS QUO MEDIATED:
THREE APPROACHES

What follows are examples taken from three projects, all featuring additive forms of agency that may mediate these constraints by tapping into existing cultural resources in both local and distant communities to situate and redefine teaching and learning within a broader educational ecology (see Moll & Ruiz, 2002).

Funds of Knowledge

This work involves close collaboration with anthropologists and teachers to develop a pedagogical approach that builds on the cultural resources of local communities, mostly working-class, Latino/a neighborhoods. We refer to these cultural resources as "funds of knowledge," those bodies of knowledge that underlie the productive (and other) activities of households. We have been particularly successful in helping teachers, as well as others, approach, understand, and define their school's community in terms of these funds of knowledge. What characterizes the approach is the work of teachers conducting research in their students' households, and then discussing and analyzing their data in conjunction with other teachers and researchers as part of study-group settings. In contrast to other approaches that emphasize home visits, the teachers in our studies visit their students' households to learn from the families, and they enter households with a theoretical perspective that seeks to understand the ways in which people make sense of their everyday lives. The goal is to gain an appreciation and understanding of how people use resources of all kinds, most prominently their funds of knowledge, to engage life. We sustain that through firsthand research experiences with families, teachers come to develop a representation of their school's community as possessing ample resources for learning, which help create many possibilities for positive pedagogical actions (González, Moll, & Amanti, 2005).

In addition to the possibilities of forming new classroom practices, what is also important is that teachers come to know the households not only intellectually but also personally and emotionally. Moreover, just as important as the concrete social relations established through the visits, are the "imagined" relations that can be formed with other families in the school or community. The point is that it becomes easy to imagine that other families in the community also possess ample funds of knowledge. These *imagined communities*, a term we borrow from Anderson (1991), become important cultural artifacts, for they help us mediate in important ways our actions and our thinking about (low-income) children, their families, their lives, and their prospects within schools, even if we have not met them personally.

Therefore, the process of documenting funds of knowledge is not only an empirical but also a theoretical activity. The empirical information that teachers collect from households is the starting point; expanding and sharing insights from these visits with other teachers is part of the theoretical work done at the study-group settings. In other words, through the visits, and through the deliberate elaboration of the concept of funds of knowledge, we appropriate theoretically the families' lived experiences. As such, as with any theoretical enterprise, our conclusions are always tentative, temporary, and subject to revision by further study or scrutiny (for details, see González et al., 2005).

There is one additional point about this work that we want to emphasize for present purposes. Given the importance of social class in the schooling of children and the work of teachers, one could consider treating social class as a primary theoretical or conceptual tool, exactly the way we have treated funds of knowledge. In collaborating with teachers, we prepared diligently to conduct the work by doing the required theoretical and methodological readings to establish the ethnographic nature of the concept. As part of this preparation we highlighted the relation of funds of knowledge to the history of labor of the families and to the household economy, with the understanding that both were related primarily to the working-class segment of the labor market. Ideally, we could also have developed, as part of the same study-group discussions, a more sophisticated understanding of social class as it helps determine household and classroom dynamics, the production of knowledge, and the relationships between these settings.

That is, just as the teachers came to develop a theoretical language about funds of knowledge in the process of conducting research and in making their findings pedagogically viable, they (and we) could also have developed a language to talk about class relations as the major source of inequalities in education.

Additive Schooling

In our most recent work we are extending our previous research by concentrating on two important aspects. One is the development of biliteracy, how young children become literate in two language systems and accomplish this feat routinely, as a mundane task. This is an important point. In the elementary school that is our study site, a Spanish-immersion school (K–5), all children, regardless of social and language background, graduate from the school literate in English and Spanish. Part of our analytic task is to document, through various means, but especially participant observations, the developmental trajectories of the students in each language. Our primary strategy has been to develop longitudinal case studies of twenty such students, what we call an integrated case-study analysis, out of a sample of 80 children.

We take biliteracy development in children, then, as the clearest index of additive schooling. Simply put: If you are a parent and your child is not graduating elementary school literate in two languages, you are being shortchanged by the school system; the system is serving somebody else's needs and interests, but not yours. Although we emphasize this goal for all children, it is all the more to be expected for immigrant and other bilingual children—children who come to school with pre-existing proficiencies and cultural contexts for acquiring additional languages. That is, for those children whose first or heritage language is other than English, rather than lowering our expectations for them, as has been the norm, we should instead fully expect that their schooling experience would result in at least bilingualism and biliteracy. They are, after all, in the best position of all to develop into highly proficient bilinguals: their first language is supported by the home environment and their second by the social environment. It remains for the school to promote such advantageous conditions. But such promotion rests on a reorientation—a sense that these children have been gifted culturally and linguistically (Portes & Hao, 2002), and that they, their languages and culture, their communities, and their traditions are a great value that we squander unless we develop them fully (Ruiz, in press).

There is no magic in helping children learn to read and write fluently in two languages. It takes a committed principal, well-trained instructional staff, sound bilingual pedagogy, and the wherewithal to mediate constraints imposed on schools. For example, the school received complaints from parents that the levels of beginning Spanish reading were too low for Spanish speakers because these levels were tailored to the English-monolingual students. The school, with the participation of all teachers, responded by creating "Exito Bilingue" (EB), a series of cross-age Spanish reading groups ($1^{1}/_{2}$ hours a day; 3 days a week) into which the students were placed according to their reading proficiency in Spanish. The entire school staff participated in these sessions; there are currently about 14 such groups. We feared the program would turn into a static tracking program, but that has not been the case. The students are continually assessed, both formally and informally, and the groups rearranged accordingly. This innovation has allowed for prolonged and concentrated (meaning-based) literacy instruction in Spanish for all students. For the English-dominant speakers EB has provided extra support in their weaker language; for the Spanish-dominant students it has provided accelerated development in Spanish that has created a sort of "zone of proximal development" for their English reading.

A second aspect of study has been to analyze how language ideologies, an inescapable aspect of the schooling of Latino/a students, come to mediate the biliteracy development of students. Two unanticipated developments have shaped our work. One is that the voters of Arizona

approved Proposition 203, the evil twin of a similar antibilingual education proposition in California that targets Latino/a children and
families, and which has placed the school ideologically under siege.
As in California, Latino/a (and American Indian) voters opposed the
proposition by about the same proportion as Anglo voters favored it,
around 65%.

During the whole campaign and election period we were able to document how the school became a site of resistance to such oppression.
The campaign became a defining moment for the school, as teachers,
students and their parents became political activists in defending their
school. Even after passage of the proposition into law, the school, with
the support of the parents, has remained a site of defiance, as it has
continued to offer its curriculum, what they consider not only a pedagogical but also a moral choice for the students, while adjusting to the
new legal conditions.

A second development is that we noticed, more than we had anticipated in designing the study, how the children develop their own
versions of language ideologies, which influence their dispositions for
literacy in one language or another. These ideologies, if we can call
them that, may have little to do with their parents' attitudes or beliefs
about language, but a lot to do with peer relations at the school. The
following example illustrates how language ideologies do their work
(from Moll, 2000). We have found how, especially for Latino/a children,
language ideologies arouse strong feelings about Spanish and English
from the very beginning of their formal education.

As we initiated the study we learned of a 5-year-old girl, Veronica,
who while in kindergarten expressed quite clearly her feelings about
English and Spanish (from Carmichael, 1998). Veronica, who was born
in Tucson and lives in the barrio in which the school is located, is the
oldest of four children. Her mother immigrated (legally), along with
her parents, from Sonora, Mexico in 1986, when she (the mother) was
14; her father also was born in Mexico and immigrated (legally) when
he was 14. Her parents married at the age of 17; her mother was, at the
time of the interview, 27 years old and her father 28.

In an initial interview, this Spanish-monolingual girl told her teacher,
Cathy, that she (Veronica) enjoyed speaking English more than Spanish,
and predicted that she would soon stop speaking Spanish because she
didn't like it much. In fact, this young girl imagined herself speaking
only in English in just 3 or 4 years, when she would be in the interme-
diate grades. She also expressed that one can learn more in English, a

stance based on her observation that most grown-ups speak English (Carmichael, 1998, pp. 7–11). In her view, a person who doesn't learn English will suffer dire consequences: "He has to be out on the street begging for food . . . because when he went to school he didn't hear anything and he stayed dumb" ("*Tiene que andar en la calle pidiendo comidas . . . porque cuando iba a la escuela no oía nada y luego se quedó burro*").

We also found, however, that the sources of Veronica's and other children's ideologies did not depend on a lineal transmission model from adults to child. For example, Veronica's mother expressed very clearly that she wanted her child to retain her Spanish and become bilingual: "I don't want her to focus only on English, nor only on Spanish. I want both (languages) to go with her [in life] ("*No quiero que se enfoque no más en inglés, ni tampoco en el español. Yo quiero que los dos vayan.*"). The mother also expressed that she considered Spanish the language of the family (something that Veronica acknowledged), and emphasized that Spanish was intimately tied to her Mexican cultural identity.

Nevertheless, even in the context of a Spanish-language immersion school, one that makes every effort to privilege Spanish in the school, in a classroom in which the teacher uses only Spanish and conveys through her actions and attitude the importance of knowing the language well, with a mother who wants her to retain her Spanish while developing her English, and who considers Spanish the language of their family and the language of their identity, this little girl was already planning to speak English and only English in the near future.

What was going on with Veronica? We had some hints from the initial interviews. One is that she was a limited English speaker (according to the school's language assessment instrument), and was eager to learn the language, for it is the first language of most of the children at school. As just one of four Spanish speakers in her class of 20 children, she considered English the language of the school for it dominated her peer relations, regardless of Spanish being the obvious language of instruction. She also felt that English is the language of grown-ups, of people on the street, that is, the public language, and people would understand her better if she spoke English, and even that one can learn more in that language. She knows that her mother did not learn English as a child and figures that is why she cannot speak English fluently now. And finally, she wanted to learn English to teach her little sister, who could not speak it very well.

Veronica already embodies and articulates competing language ideologies, as linked to the larger context of Spanish-speakers in the Tucson borderlands area, indeed to the larger context of Latinos in the United States, and to specific forms of life and schooling. We have suggested, as Luykx (1996) has asserted, that "rather than simply being inculcated with a prefabricated ideology, students bring their own meanings, practices, and values to the pedagogic situation, and the outcome is a conflictive mixture of what they bring and what they encounter there" (p. 264). Thus, it is important to consider how ideologies function as mediating devices, and how they help give meaning to the actions of becoming a biliterate in a school setting, with both positive or negative consequences for the children's learning, including their language development.

This key point needs a bit more elaboration. Central to our analysis is how language ideologies can be linked to several semiotic systems and social interactions central to the schooling processes, thus becoming inescapable for the students and teachers. Therefore, in a Vygotskian sort of way, language ideologies may function as "cultural resources" with differential influences on actions by adults and children. In particular, as van Dijk (1996) proposes, a key dimension of ideologies is their cross-situational potential as socially shared resources for thinking, for both groups and individuals, that can be drawn on (or not) and applied in different contexts. The example of Veronica, then a kindergarten student, illustrates how a child may come to restrict herself, determine her future, and delineate her identity by decisions she makes about language. Notice how she comes to consent, to acquiesce, to the dominant social ideologies about language, in this instance English, even before she can speak the language. As such, we are struck by how language ideologies, in several mediated ways, are always involved in the process of the students' personal production, that is, in the production of who they are becoming as persons.

Children, then, form their subjectivities, who they are as persons, and reconstitute them, using the cultural resources and social processes available to them. These subjectivities, which are always fluid, are simultaneously "deeply singular," for no two children have identical social histories, and "deeply social," for they are always embedded in the dynamics of particular systems of social interaction. In this respect, one must consider that children actively create and re-create themselves, within domains and communities not necessarily of their choosing, but with social, semiotic, and ideological aspects specific to their particular status as children, especially if they are minority children.

Norma González (2001), in her research with Mexican American children and families, also has addressed the identities that children construct when they use language(s) in particular ways. She does so in relation to what she calls the "emotion of subalternity," that is, how minority status itself provides an "infrastructure" for child language socialization, and mediates the children's construction of meaning and identity. She writes that "these evocative dimensions of race/class and minority status have been absent in language studies of children" (p. 54), yet they represent a formative force in language socialization. Thus, for Latinos, as for African American children, ambiguity and contradiction, and competing language ideologies, are always a backdrop to their language socialization and development, especially in relation to schooling.

Mediating Structures

The third example (adapted from Moll, 2001) refers to work that attempts to create activities within community contexts as additional settings for the learning and development of children and adults. The example is from the work of Vásquez and colleagues, and the activity setting they refer to as "La Clase Mágica" (see Vásquez, 2003). This setting forms part of a group of related projects called the Fifth Dimension, all community-based, after-school programs (see, e.g., Cole, 1996). In brief, all of these projects share a particular social structure, combining play with educational activities, and containing a special set of rules, activities, artifacts, and relationships among participants, including work and computer-mediated connections with local universities.

The programs are all conducted after school, meeting in the afternoons, usually 3 days a week for 2 hours, at a community site such as a youth club, library, or other community setting. All of the participants are volunteers, including the school children that attend the program. The adults in the setting typically represent an intergenerational mix of undergraduate students, enrolled in psychology or education courses at local universities, who act as on-site tutors and research assistants; graduate students majoring in the social sciences; family members of the children in the program or local community members, and university faculty who supervise the implementation of activities and conduct research at each site.

La Clase Mágica is a bilingual setting (English and Spanish), so that children, or adults, can participate in all activities in either language, or in both. Vásquez (1993) explains it as follows:

> Transforming the Fifth Dimension was not a simple act of translation from English to Spanish but a fundamental change in the approach to the organization of the pedagogical activity. Although informed throughout by traditional Mexican cultural knowledge, the Fifth Dimension's evolution into La Clase Mágica was not based solely on the children's home culture. Rather it tapped the multiple knowledge sources available in the children's everyday life. Whenever possible, content knowledge and skills from such learning domains as the family, church, sports, and dance groups were written into tasks accompanying the games. The goal was to build upon the background knowledge of the children at the same time that a new set of experiences and a second language were introduced. (p. 208)

La Clase Mágica represents, therefore, a fundamentally new cultural setting, one that borrows strategically but differs significantly from the children's home culture and from other institutional cultures such as the school. The children's experiences and background knowledge form part of the foundation of the site, something that is recognizable by all participants and validated daily through the routines and practices that constitute the setting. In this sense, perhaps the most notable characteristic of this site is the internal distribution of languages. An important consequence of the particular cultural arrangement of La Clase Mágica is that, to a remarkable extent, language designations, especially in relation to English fluency, which are so powerful in sorting children in schools, become irrelevant within the site. The specific language characteristics of the child, considered temporary, never become a barrier to full participation within the site, nor do they control or limit involvement because both languages are found everywhere, fostered, and used routinely in the performance of tasks.

Another consequence has to do with the connections created with the local community. La Clase Mágica is an open cultural system where the participation of local residents is encouraged and vital to the success of the site. The local residents, especially the children's families, represent not only an additional resource for teaching, contributing their knowledge and experiences, but help establish on a daily basis the cultural identity of the site, that is, how La Clase Mágica defines itself culturally through the nature and content of its routines. The long-term existence of such a nonschool setting depends crucially on the network of support it can generate, and how it can mediate existing constraints, especially given fluctuations in funding. The involvement of parents becomes an essential strategy to help perpetuate the site within its host setting, be it a local club, library, or church.

FUTURE RESEARCH THEMES

This section contains four issues or themes (there are certainly many more) that might help shape a future educational agenda (adapted from Moll & Ruiz, 2002). All four themes take into account the growing population of Latinos in the United States, which serves as the broader context for education issues, and the need to create strategic alliances in enhancing the educational landscape and sovereignty of these students. These themes also hold considerable theoretical potential, for their investigation can motivate new concepts and propositions.

Interethnic Relations

An important characteristic of the schooling of Latino/a children is their predominance in "minority dominant" schools. As such, the issues that we have summarized in this paper are also relevant to the schooling of other groups, in particular African American children. Put another way, the character and dimension of the schooling of Latinos should be analyzed not independently, as is usually the case, but in relation to the situation of African American children, for they both share similar political environments in urban areas. There are few recent studies in the literature addressing jointly issues of education for both Latinos and African Americans (but see Dávila & Rodríguez, 2000; Hout, 2001; MacDonald & Beck, 2004). There are, however, recent studies pointing to the negative interethnic perceptions and to potential serious conflict among these and other groups (see Johnson, Farrell, & Guinn, 1999), although Latino/a and African American relations may vary considerably depending on urban area, political and economic history and arrangements, and specific social issues, as shown by Mollenkopf (1999) and Rodríguez (1999). Clearly, education is an issue that lends itself to intergroup analysis. Urban schools may have become mostly irrelevant to Whites, as it seems from the demographics. Nevertheless, these institutions remain crucial for both Latinos and African American communities, so that collaboration may be in both groups' mutual interest, and an important if undertheorized subject of study.

Transnational Communities

This issue reflects one of the most interesting developments in Latino/a (and other immigrant) communities across the country. It refers to the social networks that facilitate more or less continuous links between the societies of origin and settlement. To be sure, this is not a new phenomenon, especially with Mexicans living in the borderlands, or among Puerto Ricans and their "circular" migration to and from the island, a dynamic popularly known as "*el vaivén.*" However, as Portes (1996) has pointed out, contemporary transnational communities seem to have developed a new character, as defined by three features: (1) the large number of people involved and the variety or diversity of the Latino/a groups implicated in transnational enterprises; (2) the near instantaneous character of long-distance communications across national borders, as characterized by the constant use of cell phones and electronic mail for instant communication; and (3) that cumulative participation in this transnational process helps make it a "normative" phenomenon, instead of anomalous, among certain immigrant groups.

The social, economic, or political activities that these international social networks facilitate may be creating novel paths of adaptation (into U.S. society) unlike previous immigrations, with potential implications for the formation of identities and for education (see, e.g., Guerra, 1998). Note the possible variations in these transnational arrangements: (a) communities along the border (Texas-to-California), characterized by geographical proximity to Mexico, may be inclined to reduce transnationalism to actual physical contacts—shopping, shipping, working, and so on; (b) cyclical migrants (e.g., Puerto Ricans or Dominicans who travel back and forth to the island) may have political allegiances, sentimental attachments, and some economic interests in maintaining their ties; (c) economic elites with Internet and other technological connections may be able to establish such communities wherever they may be, even far from the traditional centers of Latino/a concentrations; (d) such communities may be more motivated to maintain and develop their first languages, thereby giving increasing perceptions of economic, cultural, and social threat among those who argue that such communities pose irredentist dangers.

One consequence of these transnational dynamics may be the creation of a strong "linguistic marketplace," where language proficiency is seen as real capital in the global economy (see, e.g., Skutnabb-Kangas, 1999). In the United States, perhaps the strongest case for the economic benefits of dual language proficiency has been made by Fradd and her colleagues (e.g., Fradd & Lee, 1998), who have documented the economic benefits of fluent bilingualism, especially in south Florida. These outcomes may help establish the desirability of bilingualism and biliteracy for all populations, but especially for Latinos. In a sense, these transnational activities extend the borders of the countries in question, and within these contexts, Latinos in the United States are hardly a minority, forming instead part of a much larger and international community.

The Uses of Technology

The rapid spread of new technologies in the home and workplace, and as the bases for economic development, has had a differential impact on the wealthy versus the poor. The use of computers in schools reflects the stratification of the system, with the wealthier schools doing the most interesting intellectual work with the technology. Similarly, the use of the Internet, for example, is mostly a middle-class phenomenon, hardly influencing working-class life and work; and even when social class is taken into account, there are differential uses of this resource by different ethnic groups. Few studies are available that analyze successful applications of technological solutions to the schooling of Latino/a children. The issue remains not how to adapt the technology to existing circumstances but, rather, how to use the technology to create fundamentally new circumstances for the children's schooling.

Linguistic Human Rights

The last few years of the 20th century have seen a virtual explosion in scholarly interest in the issue of how to extend rights to language minority communities, especially those in large, multinational states. This is evidenced by the number of books, chapters, and articles in scholarly journals (e.g., May, 2001; Kontra, Phillipson, Skutnabb-Kangas, & Varady, 1999; Skutnabb-Kangas & Phillipson, 1995), new journals on the question (e.g., International Journal on Minority and Group Rights), international conferences and conventions (e.g., The Hague Recommendations Regarding the Educational Rights of National Minorities in 1996), and Web sites (e.g., terralingua.org). The issue has become so central and familiar to scholars in a multiplicity of fields, from language planning to law to sociology and political science, that it is known most popularly by its initials, LHRs (linguistic human rights). Although the interest emerged most dramatically out of concern for saving the world's dying indigenous languages (see, e.g., Krauss, 1998), it has been broadened to portray the language rights of immigrant and other minority communities as essential civil rights, regardless of the status of the languages (cf. Hernández-Chávez, 1995; Grin, 1995). This will surely be a matter of great concern with respect to Latinos in the United States as the Spanish-speaking population grows to be the largest minority group in the country.

CONCLUSION

We have proposed the concept of "educational sovereignty" to capture the agency needed to challenge the legacy of control and impositions that characterizes the education of Latino/a students in this country. Educational sovereignty requires that communities create their own infrastructures for development, including mechanisms for the education of their children that capitalize on rather than devalue their cultural resources. It will then be their initiative to invite others, including those in the academic community, to participate in such a creation (cf., Lomawaima, 2000). These forms of education must address Latino's self-interest or self-determination, while limiting the influence of the anglocentric whims of the majority that historically have shaped their schooling.

At a minimum, educational sovereignty must (1) attend to the larger historical structures and ideologies of schooling, with the goal of making educational constraints, especially those related to social class, visible and unstable; and (2) develop social agency that situates teaching and learning as part of a broader education ecology and that taps into existing social and cultural resources in schools, households, and communities in promoting change.

REFERENCES

Anderson, B. (1991). *Imagined communities: Reflections on the origin and spread of nationalism* (2nd ed.). London: Verso.

Bixler-Márquez, D. (1998). Multilingual, long-distance community education in Mexico's Sierra Tarahumara. *La Educación, Año XLII*, No. 129–131, I–III, pp. 121–139.

Carmichael, C. (1998). *Hablar dos veces: Talking twice: Language ideologies in a dual-language kindergarten*. Unpublished project paper.

Children Now (1999). *California county data book: How are youngest children are faring*. Los Angeles, CA. Available online at http://www.childrennow.org

Cole, M. (1996). *Cultural psychology*. Cambridge, MA: Harvard University Press.

Dávila, R., & Rodríguez, N. (2000). Successes and challenges of relations between African Americans and Latinos. In L. Huntley (Ed.), *Beyond racism: Embracing an interdependent future* (pp. 36–48). Atlanta, GA: The Southern Education Foundation.

Fardon, R., & Furniss, G. (Eds.). (1994). *African languages, development and the state*. London: Routledge.

Fishman, J. A. (Ed.). (2001). *Can threatened languages be saved? Reversing language shift revisited: A 21st century perspective*. Clevedon: Multilingual Matters.

Fradd, S., & Lee, O. (Eds.). (1998). *Creating Florida's multilingual global work force: Policies and practices in assessing and instructing students learning English as a new language*. Tallahassee: Florida Department of Education.

Goldenberg, C. N., & Gallimore, R. (1995). Immigrant Latino parents' values and beliefs about their children's education: Continuities and discontinuities across cultures and generations. In P. Pintrich & M. Maehr (Eds.), *Advances in motivation and achievement* (Vol. 9, pp. 183–227). Greenwich, CT: JAI.

González, N. (2001). *I am my language: Discourses of women and children in the borderlands*. Tucson: University of Arizona Press.

González, N., Moll, L. C., & Amanti, C. (Eds.). (2005). *Theorizing practices: Funds of knowledge in households, communities, and classrooms*. Cresskill, NJ: Hampton.

Grenoble, L. A., & Whaley, L. J. (Eds.). (1998). *Endangered languages: Current issues and future prospects*. Cambridge: Cambridge University Press.

Grin, F. (1995). Combining immigrant and autochthonous language rights: a territorial approach to multilingualism. In T. Skutnabb-Kangas & R. Phillipson (Eds.), *Linguistic human rights: Overcoming linguistic discrimination* (pp. 31–48). Berlin: Mouton de Gruyter.

Guerra, J. (1998). *Close to home: Oral and literate practices in a transnational Mexicano community*. New York: Teachers College Press.

Held, D. (1995). *Democracy and the global order*. Cambridge, UK: Polity.

Held, D., McGrew, A., Goldblatt, D., & Perraton, J. (1999). *Global transformations*. Cambridge: Polity.

Henze, R., & Davis, K. (1999). Authenticity and identity: Lessons from indigenous language education. *Anthropology and Education Quarterly, 30*(1), 3–21.

Hernandez-Chavez, E. (1995). Language policy in the United States: A history of cultural genocide. In T. Skutnabb-Kangas & R. Phillipson (Eds.), *Linguistic human rights: Overcoming linguistic discrimination* (pp. 141–158). Berlin: Mouton de Gruyter.

Hout, M. (2001). Educational progress for African Americans and Latinos in the United States from the 1950s to the 1990s: The interaction of ancestry and class. *Working paper*. Survey Research Center, University of California, Berkeley.

Huntley, W. L. (2000). Thresholds in the evolution of social science. In R. Sil & E. M. Doherty (Eds.), *Beyond boundaries? Disciplines, paradigms, and theoretical integration in international studies* (pp. 177–205). Albany: SUNY Press.

Johnson, Jr., J., Farrell, W. C. Jr., W. and Guinn, C. (1999). Immigration reform and the browning of America: Tensions, conflicts, and community instability in metropolitan Los Angeles. In C. Hirschman, P. Kasinitz, & J. DeWind (Eds.), *The handbook of international migration: The American experience* (pp. 290–310). New York: The Russell Sage Foundation.

Kontra, M., Phillipson, R., Skutnabb-Kangas, T., & Várady, T. (Eds.). (1999). *Language: A right and a resource. Approaching linguistic human rights*. Budapest: Central European University Press.

Krauss, M. (1998). The condition of Native North American languages. *International Journal of the Sociology of Language, 132,* 9–21.

Lee, V., & Burkam, D. (2002). *Inequality at the starting gate: Social background differences in achievement as children begin school.* Washington, DC: Economic Policy Institute.

Lomawaima, K. T. (2000). Tribal sovereigns: Reframing research in American Indian communities. *Harvard Educational Review, 27*(1), 1–21.

Lopez, D., Popkin, E., & Tellez, E. (1996). Central Americans: At the bottom, struggling to get ahead. In R. Waldinger & M. Bozorgmehr (Eds.), *Ethnic Los Angeles* (pp. 279–304). New York: Russell Sage Foundation.

Luykx, A. (1996). From Indios to Profesionales: Stereotypes and student resistance in Bolivian teacher training. In B. Levinson, D. Foley, & D. Holland (Eds.), *The cultural production of the educated person* (pp. 239–272). Albany: State University of New York Press.

MacDonald, V. M., & Beck, S. (2004, April). *Paths of divergence and convergence in black and brown educational history.* Paper presented at the American Educational Research Association Annual Meeting, San Diego, CA.

MacGregor-Mendoza, P. (1998). The criminalization of Spanish in the United States. In D. Kibbee (Ed.), *Language legislation and language rights* (pp. 55–67). Amsterdam: John Benjamins.

Martinez, R. B. (2000). Languages and tribal sovereignty: Whose language is it anyway? *Theory into Practice 39*(4), 211–220.

May, S. (2001). *Language and minority rights: Ethnicity, nationalism, and the politics of language.* Harlow, UK: Longman/Pearson.

McCarty, T. L. (2002). *A place to be Navajo: Rough Rock and the struggle for self-determination in indigenous schooling.* Mahwah, NJ: Lawrence Erlbaum Associates.

Moll, L. C. (2000, April). *Mediating matters: The importance of forms of life.* Paper presented at the symposium, Diversity matters: New perspectives from sociocultural theory, Annual Meeting of the American Educational Research Association.

Moll, L. C. (2001). Through the mediation of others: Vygotskian research on teaching. In V. Richardson (Ed.), *Handbook of research on teaching* (4th ed.) (pp. 111–129). Washington, DC: American Educational Research Association.

Moll, L. C., & González, N. (2004). Engaging life: A funds of knowledge approach to multicultural education. In J. Banks & C. McGee Banks (Eds.), *Handbook of research on multicultural education* (2nd ed.) (pp. 699–715). New York: Jossey-Bass.

Moll, L. C., & Ruiz, R. (2002). The schooling of Latino students. In M. Suárez-Orozco & M. Páez (Eds.), *Latinos: Remaking America* (pp. 362–374). Berkeley: University of California Press.

Mollenkopf, J. (1999). Urban political conflicts and alliances: New York and Los Angeles compared. In C. Hirschman, P. Kasinitz, & J. DeWind (Eds.), *The handbook of international migration: The American experience* (pp. 412–422). New York: The Russell Sage Foundation.

Ortíz, V. (1996). The Mexican-origin population: Permanent working class or emerging middle class? In R. Waldinger & M. Bozorgmehr (Eds.), *Ethnic Los Angeles* (pp. 247–278). New York: Russell Sage.

Ostler, N., & Rudes, B. (Eds.). (2000). *Endangered languages and literacy* (Proceedings of the Fourth Foundation for Endangered Languages Conference). Bath, UK: Foundation for Endangered Languages.

Portes, A., & Hao, L. (2002). The price of uniformity: Language, family, and personality adjustment in the immigrant second generation. *Ethnic and Racial Studies, 25,* 889–912.

Portes, P. (1996). Globalization from below: The rise of transnational communities. In W. P. Smith & R. P. Korczenwicz (Eds.), *Latin America in the world economy* (pp. 151–168). Westport, CT: Greenwood Press.

Portes, P., & Rumbaut, R. (2001). *Legacies: The story of the immigrant second generation.* Berkeley: University of California Press, and New York: Russell Sage Foundation.

Ramirez, R., & de la Cruz, P. G. (2002). *The Hispanic population in the United States: March 2002*, Current Population Reports, P20-545. Washington, DC: U.S. Census Bureau.

Rocco, R. (1996). Latino Los Angeles. In A. Scott & E. Soja (Eds.), *The city: Los Angeles and urban theory at the end of the twentieth century* (pp. 365–389). Berkeley: University of California Press.

Rodriguez, N. (1999). U. S. immigration and changing relations between African American and Latinos. In C. Hirschman, P. Kasinitz, & J. DeWind (Eds.), *The handbook of international migration: The American experience* (pp. 423–432). New York: Russell Sage Foundation.

Ruiz, R. (in press). *Language as resource: Language planning and the wealth of nations.* Clevedon and Philadelphia: Multilingual Matters.

Rumbaut, R. (1998, March). *Transformations: The post-immigrant generation in an age of diversity.* Paper presented at the Annual Meeting of the Eastern Sociological Society, Philadelphia.

Sassen, S. (1999). *Guests and aliens.* New York: New Press.

Sil, R., & Doherty, E. M. (Eds.). (2000). *Beyond boundaries? Disciplines, paradigms, and theoretical integration in international studies.* Albany: State University of New York Press.

Skutnabb-Kangas, T. (1999). Linguistic diversity, human rights and the "free" market. In M. Kontra, R. Phillipson, T. Skutnabb-Kangas, & T. Várady (Eds.), *Language: A right and a resource. Approaches to linguistic human rights* (pp. 187–222). Budapest: Central European University Press.

Skutnabb-Kangas, T., & Phillipson, R. (1995). Linguicide and linguicism. In R. Phillipson, & T. Skutnabb-Kangas (Eds.), *Papers in European language policy* (pp. 83–91). ROLIG papir 53. Roskilde: Roskilde Universitetscenter, Lingvistgruppen.

Smith, D. (2002). The challenge of urban ethnography. In E. Trueba & Y. Zou (Eds.), *Ethnography and schools: Qualitative approaches to the study of education* (pp. 369–387). Lanham, MD: Rowman & Littlefield Publishers.

Treiman, D., & Lee, H. (1996). Income differences among 31 ethnic groups in Los Angeles. In J. Baron, D. Grusky, & D. Treiman (Eds.), *Social differentiation and social inequality: Essays in Honor of John Pock* (pp. 37–82). Boulder, CO: Westview.

Valenzuela, A. (1999). *Subtractive schooling: U.S.-Mexican youth and the politics of caring.* Albany: State University of New York Press.

van Dijk, T. (1996). *Discourse, racism and ideology.* Islas Canarias, Spain: RCEI Ediciones, Universidad de La Laguna.

Vásquez, O. (1993). A look at language as a resource: Lessons from La Clase Mágica. In M. B. Arias & U. Casanova (Eds.), *Bilingual education: Politics, practice, and research* (pp. 199–224). (Ninety-second Yearbook of the National Society for the Study of Education, Part 2.) Chicago: University of Chicago Press.

Vásquez, O. (2003). *La Clase Mágica: Imagining optimal possibilities in a bilingual community of learners.* Mahwah, NJ: Lawrence Erlbaum Associates.

Vick-Westgate, A. (2002). *Nunavik: Inuit-controlled education in Arctic Quebec.* Calgary: University of Calgary Press.

Warner, S. (1999). Kuleana: The right, responsibility, and authority of indigenous peoples to speak and make decisions for themselves in language and cultural revitalization. *Anthropology and Education Quarterly, 30*(1), 68–93.

Wright, S. (2000). *Community and communication: The role of language in nation state building and European integration.* Clevedon: Multilingual Matters.

13

Social Action and the Politics of Collaboration[1]

Olga A. Vásquez
University of California, San Diego

INTRODUCTION

In an age when the global is ever present in the local, when diversity is an increasing constant in the classroom and when communication across institutions is a necessity rather than a choice, collaboration is ever more consequential. To function in isolation as an individual or an institution is foolhardy if not virtually impossible in today's new society. The new social conditions heralded by advances in communication technology, the diversification of society and the demands and excesses of the new economy have not replaced the need for human contact in building long-term, trusting relationships, even when these relationships are conducted across cultures, systems, or geographical locations (Castells, 1996). The social webs through which individuals and institutions typically operate continue to require tending and nurturing. Dyke (2000), for example, asserts that, "technology cannot

[1] Funding for the collaborative educational project described in this chapter was provided by the University of California, San Diego's Center for Education and Teaching Excellence (CREATE) and by the Office of the UC President. Without this support, this experiment in collaboration would not have been possible.

replace the need for strong leadership and human interactions" (p. 19). Online communication supplements rather than replaces human contact in many areas of everyday life according to Castells and others. Even participants who spend most of their times in virtual worlds and communities must reenter RL (real-life) to reengage in social relations (Turkle, 1995).

To be effective in the 21st century, educational collaborative efforts must continue a "hands-on" approach. Real-life social interaction affirms and sustains long-lasting, trusting relationships initiated or maintained across distance learning projects (Cummins & Sayers, 1995), and network communities (Foot, 1999). Thus, the detachment and hierarchy characteristic of old forms of collaboration has given way to an emphasis on personal attention by key individuals. In its place, one finds an "integrative" form of collaboration that rests on the value and practice of the principles of equitable participation and accords a greater promise of egalitarian and participatory involvement to a broader sector of society (see John-Steiner, 2000).

This chapter examines one such collaborative effort between a local university, a community college, and a public elementary school. A unique web of collaboration across the three institutions was made possible by the linkage of an after-school project to a couple of undergraduate courses offered at two different institutions, the University of California, San Diego and Southwestern Community College. The research/implementation team of *La Clase Mágica*, the after-school program composed of five developmentally and culturally relevant computer-mediated activities, coordinated the relationship building, the adaptation process and the operations of the three activities chosen for the elementary school. To understand the *La Clase Mágica's* goals and objectives, I first situate it within the partnership movement that has flourished over the last 4 decades and then track its own trajectory as an innovation of the Fifth Dimension, a university-community initiative that has expanded across California, the United States, and internationally. Next, I describe the key characteristics that inform and sustain an integrative collaboration within the local ecology that pushes for stasis and conformity. The challenge, then, becomes one of maintaining the philosophical and organizational structure of the project—that is, to keep it "not school," collaborative, and spontaneous. At the end, we note small gains and high hopes, especially for the development of "people power" among the low-income, monolingual Spanish-speaking mothers who took over the responsibility of running the site when funding dried up. Drawing on data (e.g., ethnographic field notes, meeting minutes, assessments of the student-participants' reading readiness and computer literacy) collected at the site over the first 4 years, I conclude with insights into the collaboration that was achieved and some of the strategies and resources that might offer a more integrated form of collaboration with school-site personnel in the future.

AFTER-SCHOOL PROGRAMS AS VIABLE UNIVERSITY-COMMUNITY PARTNERSHIPS

Over the past decades, colleges, corporations, communities, and governmental agencies have been collaborating with American public school systems, fueling what Wilbur and Lambert (1991) have termed a "partnership movement." Although early efforts targeted high-performing students, more recently, alternative programs for low-performing minority students in grades K–12 have become more readily available and have been shown to significantly affect minority youth (Gross, 1988; Miller, 2003). Overall, collaboration between universities and local schools has produced encouraging results, enhancing student performance and improving the educational opportunities of all types of students (Miller, 2003).[2] However, the goals of many well-intentioned after-school programs focused more on building self-esteem and sports, obfuscating the impact they had on academic achievement and social intergration of minority youth.

Collaborative ventures between universities and community-based institutions also report great success in addressing the educational needs of low-income minority groups (Gallego, 2001; Vásquez, 2003; Vásquez & Dúran, 2000) and enhancing children's cognitive and school-based skills (Blanton, Moorman, Hayes, & Warner, 1997; Brown & Cole, 2002; Mayer, 1997). In particular, community-university partnerships initiated by UCSD's Laboratory of Comparative Human Cognition established cross-system collaboration to funnel educational resources to communities in need. These partnerships share many of the same goals and objectives as those between universities and schools, but they differ in significant ways. Customarily, the relations within and between educational institutions are guided by a formal and inflexible social and organizational structure and are also often constrained by predetermined curricula. The service orientation of community institutions, by contrast, allows a flexibility that can

---

[2]See "After-school programs augment studies" by Shari Rudavsky, *Boston Globe* Online, Accessed 6/8/2003.

circumvent the tacit hierarchy so deeply rooted in school-university partnerships. Informal and fluid chain of command in community-based relationships, moreover, facilitate quicker and better-targeted access to and distribution of materials and services.

The most successful of these partnerships share some of the same characteristics, Vera John-Steiner (2000) noted among members of creative communities of artists and academics labeled, "integrative collaboration." This type of joint effort, which transforms both the individual and the project, relies heavily on dialogue and "a long process of committed activity." In the course of this committed activity, John-Steiner explains:

> Collaboration partners frequently suspend their differences in style. While creating a new vision, they can experience a profound sense of bonding. This pattern contrasts with the complementary mode of collaboration, in which differences in training, skill, and temperament support a joint outcome through division of labor. (p. 70)

In community-university partnerships, integrative collaboration feeds the democratic process by drawing minority groups into civil society and public institutions as valued partners in the problem-solving process. These collaborations encourage elementary school-aged children to set their sights on a university education and, at the same time, shape forms and contexts for learning to reflect the demographic realities of the broader society. Minority members from all walks of life are given the opportunity to actively take part in solving the educational problems that plague their communities. The university, by contrast, gains the opportunity to mobilize its power and resources in the service of change.

Collaboration between community and university institutions is also economically and intellectually beneficial to both partners (Nicolopoulou & Cole, 1993; Vásquez, 1996). The university is provided access to a live laboratory in which to conduct research; a place for its students to practice developmental theories of learning; an opportunity to showcase the advantages of modern telecommunication technologies for linking diverse populations of scholars, students, and young children (Nicolopoulou & Cole, 1993; Vásquez, 2003). It also provides a venue from which to establish positive working relations with host community institutions. The partnership enables the university to provide a qualitatively different kind of undergraduate education, one based on a culturally relevant curriculum that reflects the increasing diversity in the classroom. Collaboration with the university benefits the community by enabling local institutions to target constituencies that are academically "at risk" and/or those who have been systematically excluded from access to technology and other educational resources. Organizations and groups already actively engaged in serving the social and academic needs of young people (e.g., boys and girls clubs, churches, and community centers) receive assistance in achieving their goals. At a more individual level, university-community partnerships like *La Clase Mágica* provide children and their parents with opportunities to gain and enhance essential skills in social citizenship (Camras, 2002), border crossing (Gutiérrez, Baquedano-López, & Tejada, 1999; Vásquez, 2003) and information retrieval (Vásquez, 2003; Vásquez & Dúran, 2000).

Despite the significant benefits and the promise of substantive change that accompanies these partnerships, there are—at times insurmountable—challenges, as well. Community members typically distrust the research and pedagogical styles of the university team; this is especially true in partnerships involving communities that historically have been exoticized and exploited (Iscoe, 1974).[3] The fact that they are not imbedded within the values and administrative structures of the institution, as they are in the school systems (Gomez, Bissell, Danziger, & Casselman, 1990) these concerns can be mediated through relationship building. More troublesome is the acquiescence and imbalance in the politics of collaboration between community constituencies and resource-rich partners such as higher education institutions like the University of California, San Diego. Alternative relationships, such as "principled partnerships" (i.e., those based on mutual relations of exchange) require time and intensive commitment (Smock, 1999). Trust and respect are essential components for building productive long-term relationships: trust that the known and the unknown can be shared and shaped to the participants' mutual benefit; and respect for the knowledge and experience that all members bring to the negotiation table, regardless of how and where it was acquired. Principled partnerships also require flexibility, a willingness to take risks and an openness to self-reflective change (Vásquez, 2003). It is these same characteristics that help account for the phenomenal success of the university-community collaboration represented by *La Clase Mágica* across its 15 years of existence.

---

[3]According to Iscoe, the greatest resistance comes from communities that have become "psychologically disadvantaged" because of the loss of power and hope (p. 609).

FROM EDUCATIONAL ACTIVITY TO SOCIAL ACTION PROJECT: THE EVOLUTION OF *LA CLASE MÁGICA*

La Clase Mágica, grew out of the Fifth Dimension model of community-university partnership developed in the early 1980s by collaborators at the Laboratory of Comparative Human Cognition at the University of California, San Diego (Cole, 1996; Nicolopoulou & Cole, 1993; Vásquez, 2003). Like its predecessor, *La Clase Mágica* is a computer-based activity system that uses innovative practices and tools designed to promote learners optimal learning potential (see Cole, 1996; Vásquez, 2003). Building on the success of the Fifth Dimension, *La Clase Mágica* developed independently into a bilingual/bicultural, intergenerational adaptation seeking change in the historical underachievement of bilingual children in K–12 and their underrepresentation in higher education. In including the integration and empowerment of minority communities in its aims, *La Clase Mágica* has evolved into a sufficiently potent instrument for change that fits the category of social action as described by Moyer (2000). It sets up a two-way flow of relations between mainstream institutional agents and underrepresented groups that redistributes social and cultural capital, addressing the needs of one side of the partnership and adjusting the understandings and approaches of the other.

Until its recent expansion to two public elementary schools, *La Clase Mágica* had sought to complement school instruction from afar, providing academically oriented computer-based activities for learners of all ages. The original site (and several "satellite" sites added over the years) gave researchers, undergraduate students, and participating parents the opportunity to design and study innovative learning environments without being encumbered by the constraints of a formal institution. Project members (including parents from the local community) adjusted the structure and basic principles of *La Clase Mágica's* predecessor, the Fifth Dimension, to achieve a model of five culturally and developmentally relevant activities: *Mi Clase Mágica* (MCM), for children ages 3–5; *La Clase Mágica* (LCM), for children ages 6–12 (the original target age of the Fifth Dimension project); the *Wizard Assistant* (WA) *Club*, for second-level, adolescent participants; and *La Gran Dimensión* (LGD), for adults. *Los Promotores*, a parent involvement strategy developed at the school site reported in this chapter, was subsequently adopted at all six sites where the project is hosted.

Over the course of its existence, *La Clase Mágica* has worked closely with parents and other community members to develop long-term relationships that draw on the strengths and intellectual resources of participating individuals and the host communities. From the project's inception, parents and community members have helped the university research team operate the sites and incorporate into the instructional materials the rich cultural resources found in the community. This relationship also has helped establish social relations with key figures in the community and in the host institution. With the unfolding of their partnership skills, parents and other community members have helped develop assessment tools, carry out assessments, and write quarterly and year-end summaries of experiences at the site, including developmental trajectories of child participants. Contributions from parents and community members have directly influenced the success of each of the six sites in operation.

Another distinguishing feature of *La Clase Mágica* is that all participants are guided through a prearranged set of activities using a nurturing and loving interactional style rather one based on fear or coercion (see Nicolopoulou and Cole [1993] for a discussion of key principles in "the culture of collaborative learning" developed at the Fifth Dimension). It is not enough to encourage children to work on collaborative tasks; mutual respect and genuine affection should characterize all interactions among adults and children while they are participating in the project.[4] This principle was reaffirmed at the school site and made explicit in the unfortunate, but necessary, dismissal of a parent staff member who could not be convinced that the formula for encouraging a love of learning could not include fear or harsh treatment.[5]

The warm tone and flexible structure of the project has drawn and retained both adult and child participants for extended periods of time, often for the entire 15-year term of the project. Many of the children who advanced to second-level participants have subsequently enrolled in college prep courses in high school and as they reach college-going age, are enrolling in nearby colleges and universities in high numbers. Importantly, parents who volunteered in the initial stages of the

---

[4]This principle was first modeled by El Maga, the project's electronic entity, who, in the initial stages of the project, developed into a counselor of sorts, conversing online with the children using an affectionate tone and offering the loving advice of a godparent.

[5]Interestingly, her resignation and subsequent replacement by a parent whose pedagogy aligned more closely with the principles of nurture and love freed the site of the behavioral problems that had plagued it for almost a year.

project and later joined the staff have become integral to the operations of the after-school sites not only in their local communities but also at the five other sites that sprung up across San Diego County. Similarly, the university has profited from its support of *La Clase Mágica*. The project's research and the model of practice have received wide recognition and uptake across California (see the UC Links consortium at http://www.uclinks.org/). Furthermore, many members of the university undergraduate research staff have pursued advanced degrees and now hold academic or high-ranking administrative positions in social service institutions throughout the country. The university has, in addition, gained a state-of-the-art undergraduate education and technology-based curriculum and has earned the trust and praise of community members and local institutions. In sum, through its participation in this partnership, the university has learned how best to achieve and maintain "a steady flow of qualified individuals" out of the community and into its classrooms (Moll, Anderson, & Díaz, 1985).

LA CLASE MÁGICA GOES TO SCHOOL

In the summer of 1999, the *La Clase Mágica* was invited by UCSD's Center for Research in Education Equity, Assessment, and Teaching Excellence (CREATE) to open a new site in one of the target schools in the South Bay region of San Diego County. Responding to the need for the university's involvement in serious outreach efforts in K–12 education, CREATE sought out programs that could help the school administration bring about a change in the low performance of the student population. The idea of joining forces with school personnel and CREATE to mobilize *La Clase Mágica's* raison d'être was enthusiastically embraced by both the university research staff and staff of the original project. It would be the first attempt at scaling up and the first time collaboration with a school would go beyond cooperation in testing of child participants at school.[6] After several meetings between district personnel, CREATE, and project staff, it was decided that *La Clase Mágica*

---

[6]At the original site, *La Clase Mágica* staff worked closely with the bilingual teachers to administer the Language Assessment Scale that benefited both the school's bilingual program and the project's evaluation efforts. A year after *La Clase Mágica* entered Bayside Elementary, it was again invited to participate in an effort to assist another school raise the academic achievement level of its students. The lag time between the establishment of the two sites and the difference in approach made a comparison between the two impractical at the time of this writing.

would go to Bayside Elementary, a small school of 900 students nestled along the southernmost point of San Diego Bay. Bayside's 67% percent Latino/a population, the principal's emphasis on parent involvement, and the age group of the K–6 school, corresponded closely with the project's curricular design and goals of the time. The school also met CREATE's criteria for working with underperforming schools: Bayside was ranked "low-performing" by the SAT9 test, was situated in a low-income, predominantly minority community and had a relatively small number of after-school offerings. Not insignificant, the decreasing enrollment at the school also signaled the possibility of adequate space to situate the after-school program.

The initial efforts to establish a system of collaboration with the school were slow and often bureaucratically ridden. Not only did the project have to meet the academic goals and objectives of the school; it had to meet the school's time schedule, the district's technical standards, and the teachers' needs for academic and language enrichment for their students. In spite of these formidable obstacles, several factors signaled favorable conditions for partnership building. First, there was strong support by the school site administrator, a Latino/a principal who was deeply concerned about the low-performance of his recently acquired school. The principal's high profile programs, the "Parents Center," and the "Partnership Group" involving representatives from the community, reflected a strong commitment to parent and community involvement. Technology was also a high priority at the school. The principal and the "Tech Team," a prominent component of the school site management scheme, saw the technology focus of La Clase Mágica as a means to address the technical and academic needs of the school.

Planting a new site at the school, however, required a broader network of support beyond that of the principal's. It involved a multilevel system of support across institutions and participant groups. Collaboration had to be established with the nearby community college to offer a course to help the practicum course at UCSD support the site with undergraduate student mentors. After a series of contacts and subsequent presentations, a young Latina professor and former UCSD graduate student agreed to use our new program as a practicum site for her "Introduction to Sociology" students. The principal designated the four kindergarten teachers at the school as our targeted collaborators and several parents from the Parents Center were recruited. After a full semester of relationship building, the kindergarten teachers distributed invitations to select students who they felt, "lacked appropriate access to language and literature prior to Kindergarten

[VG, 1/25/00]." The community college course was adapted and the parents enthusiastically embraced the project, contributing time and materials for the startup.

On January 25, 2000, two sessions of *Mi Clase Mágica*, an activity designed for children in early childhood were opened for students in the school's four kindergarten classrooms. The first session opened before school for eight children in the afternoon kindergarten class. Two staff members—a parent from the original site and a university undergraduate student—managed the activities with the assistance of four parents, and two community college students. The second session opened after school for 15 children in the morning kindergarten class. The same staff members and community college students participated along with two new parents. Both sessions were a great success but issues relating to the school versus community culture proved to be "overwhelming" for the project's staff. Everything moved too fast for a staff that had grown accustomed to the slow and deliberate pace of the community-based project. The time schedule was no longer in their control. Both the community college course and school schedule mandated when and how long the program could be offered. The kindergarten children were divided into two groups and the undergraduates were placed in their activities only after school had been in session for several weeks. Teachers also had very limited time for consultation: 15 minutes before school and less than an hour after school. A deceivingly simple act of shuttling child participants across the campus from the project to snack time became a nightmare for the staff who repeatedly ran head-on into invisible but formidable walls of school protocol. In fact, the protocol for movement between classes, between class and other activities, and between school and home proved to be an ever-present quagmire for the staff the entire first year.

The infractions were not lost on the ever-vigilant principal, who asked the staff for an "outline of our activities" at the end of the first day. He also admonished the staff to "use very detailed, written information and procedures" when communicating with parents to avoid confusion and presumably breaking protocol [VC, 1/25/2000]. The teachers had other concerns. They were displeased with the focus of the learning activities: they had expected "language enrichment" and had contributed books and puzzles for just that purpose. Instead, they heard the parents and project staff emphasize computer activities. What was not readily understood by them at the time, nor we believe, ever understood, was that through computer-mediated activities the project hoped to promote sustained practice in language and literacy activities; enhance on-task engagement; and, most important, develop a love for learning.

The project team, by contrast, questioned the idea of "FIT." Could the project survive under such institutional constraints? Would the staff trip once too many times over rules not visible to the outsider? And, would the project's early childhood curriculum be suitable for an older age group? We concluded that although the institutional constraints were vexing, they were not insurmountable. We also found that the curriculum designed for preschoolers at the original site was not only adequate for their older peers, it required little or no tweaking to fit the cultural and academic needs of the Kindergartners, a finding that indicated that the children's social and academic development was delayed. A resolution was made to pay closer attention to the children's readiness skills in the adaptation process.

We also concluded at the end of the year that the project could not operate independently without the integral involvement of its institutional host as it had it done at its original site for the past 10 years. Gaining entrée into the school complex had not given *La Clase Mágica* entrée into the school culture. Achieving this kind of access required us to reevaluate our theories of action. It was also not sufficient or wise, we concluded, for the project to operate primarily on the support of the principal who had welcomed the project but whose ambitions were set on higher administration. Too heavy reliance on him jeopardized the long-term uptake of the project by the teachers and community, particularly because he continued to serve as the primary motivation for teacher involvement. The lack of teacher involvement stood as the major weakness in providing an integrated system of support for the local children and their families.[7] We reasoned that a closer relationship with the teachers would facilitate a greater understanding of the needs of the targeted learners and also provide the mechanism from which to address broader issues of academic and social development in the classroom. The latter, if achieved, could provide the possibility for changing the culture of learning of the classroom to be more reflective of the needs of bilingual children from low socioeconomic backgrounds—a

---

[7]There are many reasons why teachers did not buy into an integrative form of collaboration besides the differences they noted in ideologies, curricular strategies, and approaches to learning of the project. They were short of time and at the end of the day, they were tired and their personal priorities often compelled them to leave school as soon as the bell rang. And, very importantly, we were unable to give them the time and attention that our analysis indicates they could have used.

goal that was not visibly accomplished. More realistically, a relationship with the teachers could serve to align the curriculum of both the
classroom and the after-school project for optimal support of the children's growth—a goal that was pursued and achieved for the first two
years of the project.

In the second year, three new areas of attention were added to the
project's activities at the school. The first involved finding funds to
pay teachers to work more closely with the project staff to align the
two curricula. More of the teachers' time was required beyond that
which was allowed by union-guidelines for unpaid time. A grant was
secured from the UC Office of the President (UCOP) for the second
and the third year to further develop the existing project and enhance
collaborative activities. Teachers were paid a stipend for meeting with
the staff and submitting mutually designed monthly field notes on the
progress of their students. The added strain on the teachers' time, their
tepid acceptance of the project's methodology and philosophy, as well
as their need for more consistent face-to-face contact led us, by the
second year, to focus increasingly on the ever present collaboration
with parents.

Parent involvement became one of the shining accomplishments of
the site activities at the school. UCOP monies were used to form, *Los
Promotores*, [the promoters] a parent group modeled after Paulo Freire's
literacy cadres to keep parents abreast of the goals and objectives of the
project and to inform them of school policy, structure, and their rights
as parents (see Vásquez 2004). Because many working parents were unable to attend the regular meetings, a select group of parents was trained
to train other parents at more convenient times. This small group of five
mothers became centrally involved with the everyday operations of the
site and fund raising activities. Thus, when the budget cuts threatened
to close the project at the end of the third year, these parents had no
problem understanding the educational and social consequences of the
impending closure and mobilized to keep the program open. They pe-
titioned to allow the program to stay open till the end of their track,
$2^{1}/_{2}$ months after the university-community team had closed all other
sites for the summer. When they realized they required more technical and educational expertise, they requested more training from the
project team. They received a rigorous 8-week summer training co-
sponsored by *La Clase Mágica* and one of its most supportive and ideologically aligned community partners in the South Bay, *Casa Familiar*, a
nonprofit community organization serving the Latino/a community in

the city of San Ysidro. In the fourth year of the project—the 2002–2003 academic year—eight parents managed one session of MCM and the afternoon session of LCM, often by themselves because the course at the adjacent community college also fell victim to budget cuts. They were assisted by several undergraduate students from the practicum course at UCSD, but it was the eight mothers, led by an incredible high-powered young mother, Gabriela Arce, who ran the site activities. Interestingly, without the direct involvement of the teachers and the university staff, parent volunteers were freed of the specter of institutional constraints. It was not long after they took over that behavior problems ceased and the tone and tenor of the environment shifted to love and nurture and child-directed activity.

CHALLENGES OF AN IMPROBABLE VENTURE

Ours were lofty goals. However, the linking of two sets of ideologies, two curricular strategies, and two approaches to learning threatened to subvert the possibility of building a long-term relationship with the teachers, the key players in changing the culture of learning. Trust, and for all practical purposes, respect, seemed to teeter in the balance throughout the first year as both sides slowly learned about the pedagogical and philosophical basis of the instructional approach each used in their respective learning contexts. The point of articulation was the material and philosophical motivations that both curricular offerings shared in enhancing children's achievement and social development. Outside of this commonality, each held divergent theoretical understandings regarding the abilities of the learner and the proper course of action. A case in point is the views that each group held of the learner: The school personnel labeled selected learners as "at-risk" and in need of remedial treatment. The project's undergirding theoretical foundations, by contrast, posited every learner as capable of achieving his or her optimal potential given proper assistance (see Vygotsky, 1978). From this view, the learner is in a state of readiness, willing and able to move to the next level of development with expert support. In the classroom, children actions were guided towards a specific skill by the didactic guidance of the teacher. At *La Clase Mágica*, children were guided by movement inscribed in the representation of a 20-room maze printed on an 8-by-11 sheet of paper (see Nicolopoulou & Cole, 1993; Vásquez, 2003). In the classroom, children were motivated by the individual evaluation of their performance, at the after-school program, by the movement to another collaborative activity with peers or adults. In the classroom, fear of failure and teacher disapproval motivated children to stay on task. At *La Clase Mágica* activities, love and gentle prodding, and *mucha atención y mucha paciencia* (lots of attention and lots of patience) kept children engaged in the activities of the maze.

The differences in the ideologies of social action and social enhancing reproduction that the respective partners brought to the negotiation table made for an improbable partnership in serving "at risk" children and their families.[8] The discourse of social change versus individual change repeatedly clashed in the politics of collaboration. One side sought change and transformation of the system and its content, the other sought its stability and integrity. Stasis and standardization bounded the actions of one side of the collaboration. Flexibility and creative solutions prompted the actions of the other. The institutional entrenchment of one partner and the fluid almost amorphous structure of the other stymied the process of building meaningful trusting relations across the two groups. As the project grew roots in the everyday life of the school, the relationship with the teachers became strained with the weight of the collaboration.

The effects of academic standards on the child-directed enrichment character of the after-school project also were unequivocal: learning became fettered to what Dewey (1938) would call an education of outsiders—that is, children's learning trajectory was predetermined by the teachers, not by district or state mandates, and not by the spontaneous decision-making of the children. Standards raised concerns in both material and objective terms for *La Clase Mágica*. District standards of grade level achievement, for example, not only specified what the children needed to know by the end of the year, they also influenced what *La Clase Mágica* had to emphasize in order to complement classroom instruction. Although grade level competency was not incompatible with the project's goals, it was not a curricular goal in the philosophical makeup of the project. Rather, children's academic and social development was an expected by-product of the project's focus on learning to learn. Standards imposed an extension of the school on the playful character of *La Clase Mágica*. In essence, the children's self-determined pace and curiosity were coopted by an insensitive and detached force.

---

[8]Taken from *An Improbable Venture: A History of the University of California, San Diego*. Although the effort here may be miniscule compared to the creation of a high-class university, the goals and objectives were as great—to make a significant contribution to society.

Another factor that threatened the viability of *La Clase Mágica* was the district's views and standards on technology. The district's policy specified high-end technology (IBM Pentium III) as well as socially approved software, making the technology and supportive materials of *La Clase Mágica*—Macintosh computers, some as old as Apple IIe's and the occasional shoot'-em-up-type variety computer games—unacceptable at the site. In the past and across the five other sites, these tools had served exceptionally well as mechanisms for organizing a playful environment in which undergraduates and children could form social relations that enhanced learning of both academic and social skills (Vásquez & Durán, 2000). District standards on technology not only sought to standardize the physical context, it also restricted the content of the software and Internet access. *La Clase Mágica* did not have the technical capacity nor held the views of technology that the District mandated or that the principal and technical team envisioned for the school. The district's functional views of technology, also threatened the flexibility and child-directed activities at site. For example, the project did not attribute to technology the power to accomplish social change independent of its social conditions. Rather, *La Clase Mágica* saw technology as a part, albeit a formidable one, of a larger system of mediating artifacts that function concurrently to bring about social change. Had the standards not been waved, the project would have had to fold before it started. The problem of underperformance, was of greater concern to both the school and the district and the promise of educational resources were too great to pass up. The implementation of district policy was postponed until further funding was secured; giving the research-implementation team ample time to adapt to the technical demands of the new context.

The ideologies from the sociopolitical arena also seeped into the process of relationship building. *La Clase Mágica's* focus on a Mexican origin population and its intellectual resources ran counter to the restrictive legislation of the times that prohibited minority preferences. References to Proposition 209 and Proposition 227, propositions that focused on eliminating affirmative action and bilingual education respectively, entered into the discussions periodically. For example, teachers repeatedly voiced their concern that unstructured native language use—for example, codeswitching, the form of language used in the curricular materials—could disrupt second language acquisition. They asked how the home language, in this case Spanish, could "be used in the classroom when the law prohibits it." Fortunately, for the fledgling collaboration, the principal in his wisdom reminded the group several times, that

"La Clase Mágica is after-school"; in essence he was saying that *La Clase Mágica* was outside the jurisdiction of the law. Although this clarification allowed for the use of the native language during the site sessions and served to temper the concerns of the teachers, it did not guarantee the full acceptance of the project's primary pedagogical principle of incorporating native language and culture as fundamental building blocks for curriculum development and community involvement. For all practical purposes, the teachers tolerated the policy only within the confines of the project's activities.

SMALL GAINS, HIGH HOPES

Under the conditions described above, the politics of collaboration demanded a compromise by the two participating systems—a compromise that would move each toward a more flexible and multilevel approach to solving the problem of underperformance at the school. The analysis of the data, however, pointed out that it was *La Clase Mágica* that had sustained the most change (see Figure 13.1). Influence on the content and goals of learning flowed from the classroom to *La Clase Mágica*; in direct contrast to the dialectical changes that had influenced the adaptation of the structure and content of the activities at the original site in the community setting and the course and research at the university. At the new site, what the children learned was influenced by outsiders who emphasize as Freire (2000) points out, "the mechanical memorization of contents" (p. 30) rather than by the spontaneous curiosity of the moment. This influence was noted by the staff from the early stages of the site as the staff repeatedly attempted to win the

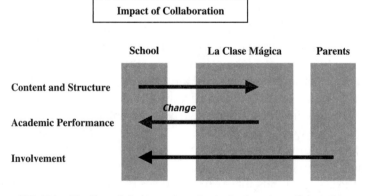

FIG. 13.1.   The flow of change as a result of school-project collaboration.

teachers' approval of the project. A case in point is the first field note written by the university staff member, where she comments that the team must plan "a tangible goal (e.g., mastering the ABC's)" to impress upon the teachers that "the program is working and at some point may support us more" [VC., 2/29/2000]. Later, it would be the district and state standards that would influence the content and language of adult-child interactions at the site, impinging further on the "curiosity that is indispensable in the cognitive process" (Freire, 2000, p. 31).

On the surface, it appeared that in this new context, *La Clase Mágica* was not an agent of change, at least not in the classroom. Rather, the intractable nature of the school culture had seeped into the everyday life of the project. Forms of address among the participants became formalized[9] and interactions with specific children became routinized—that is, the team was encouraged to apply a didactic pedagogical approach with some children using only one language at a time. According to the teachers, specific children required the sole use of one language and step-by-step instruction. The emphasis on district standards and grade level achievement also threatened the project's focus on self-direction and spontaneity. In other words, the standards specified which concepts would be introduced and in which order. Additionally, discipline issues common throughout the school and unheard of at the other community-based sites followed the children into *La Clase Mágica*. Whether or not misbehavior was a result of the children's social development or a result of the school culture will require further research. What was obvious at the time, however, was that misbehavior was affecting the social climate of the site and the social relations with other partners. The impact of the misbehavior was so strong that it generated endless discussions in staff meetings and class sessions among the undergraduates at both the community college and UCSD. It also almost cost the collaboration with the community college colleagues. In a video-conference discussion, the community college dean and the two professors of the practicum course voiced concerns that their undergraduate students were not prepared to work with "children with special needs" [video.SWC-UCSD/1/25/01]. To assuage the fears of our community college colleagues, we instituted a school-based policy for dealing with inappropriate behavior: expulsion. It would be the first and only time such policy was instituted in the project's 15-year history

---

[9]The nonhierarchical nature of *La Clase Mágica* outside of school encourages children and adults to interact on first name basis. The school, on the other, forced the team to accept being addressed by titles, Mrs. Durán, Dr. Vásquez, and so on.

and, fortunately, was applied only once. For a period of time, the conventional strategy of finding innovative ways to engage the children in activity was restricted to two or three attempts in which the children also were warned about the consequences. The project's focus on "love" as a primary motivation for building responsibility, self-direction, and learning was again overriden by school-based policy.

Despite these challenges, a closer look at the data demonstrated that *La Clase Mágica* had, however, accomplished its goals of affecting the academic achievement and social development of child participants. Individual growth seems to have flowed from the site activities to the classroom (see Fig. 13.1). Both teachers and parents repeatedly stated the positive affects on children's classroom participation and academic growth. Parents, too, noted the affects the project had on their children's intellectual and language development and became involved as a result. At the CREATE annual conference, a young mother who was to become the lead parent, told an audience of educators that she had become involved because she credited *La Clase Mágica* with teaching her child to read in English. The reading readiness and computer literacy instruments developed at the site also confirmed that all of the participants in the MCM activities had met district standards for promotion and had progressed significantly in computer knowledge and skills by the end of the academic year. A preliminary analysis of these data indicated that Spanish-dominant kindergartners were able to catch up to their English-speaking peers in reading readiness skills. In the fall of 2001, the principal recognized *La Clase Mágica* as being one of the chief resources that had helped the school relinquish its low-performing status.

Parent involvement, if not "community uptake" of the project, also was an important accomplishment of our collaboration at the school. The team had not been able to secure an integrative form of collaboration with the teachers, however it did with the parents. It was true that parents had operated the site basically by themselves during the entire fourth year, but something more profound was taking place. The small group of *Promotores* had made the project theirs and in the process transformed it and themselves. The commitment and bonding that John-Steiner recognized among communities of artists was readily evident among parents and the community at the graduation ceremony held for MCMers and their older peers in LCM at the end of the 2003–2004 academic year. As I was finishing the last pages of this chapter, I was invited to an event that reconfirmed not only my commitment to culturally and linguistically relevant curriculum but also my assertion that *La Clase Mágica* has transformative power. Over 50 parents and as many children attended the MCM graduation sponsored by *Los Promotores* and Gabriala Arce, the lead parent. The attendance was five to six times greater than the previous year and involved teachers from various grades and the principal who had already transferred out of the school several weeks prior. "It was a real graduation," as a staff member pointed out, complete with caps and gowns for the MCMers and parents pushing each other to take pictures of their loved ones. The LCMers, having no other activity to graduate to, paraded across the auditorium's floor in authentic costumes from ten or so different countries. For all practical purposes, the event was a community event independent of my research staff and the school!

Our collaboration with the school has taught us much about the politics of collaboration in achieving educational-based social action goals. First, of course, is the impact that a grassroots, cultural, linguistic, and relevant effort has on the participation and intellectual development of bilingual children and their families. And second, that a complementary type of relationship in which each party provides support according to perceived need and available resources is not an insignificant accomplishment. The project had been unable to establish a fully integrated collaboration with the teachers, but they did remain supportive of the project. And, the support did not center on the kindergarten teachers and members of the school's "Tech Team" on whom we had invested time and money. A broader network of teachers began to support *La Clase Mágica*. Periodically, other teachers participated at the end of the quarter fiestas and the end of the year MCM graduation ceremonies. The sixth-grade teachers continued to support the site activities way past the short-lived cross-aged tutoring program in which they had helped partner their brightest students with child participants. The kindergarten teachers, too, continued to keep the project staff abreast of their students' needs and repeatedly shared their books and materials with the staff. And most importantly, the principal remained an ardent supporter of the project and increasingly incorporated the project team into the school's inner circle of activities—that is, staff development, faculty meetings, and on-site committees. In January 2002, he nominated CREATE and *La Clase Mágica* for public recognition at the district's school board meeting.

The impact on research, teaching, and service by this type of project signals the beginning of a shift in paradigm and sets a new vision for minority integration into the fold of American society. It demonstrates what education practitioners, researchers, and community activists have known for some time: Minority communities have the wherewithal to rise to the occasion to not only share their intellectual and material resources as Moll and Greenberg (1990) and others (González, 1995) have shown but also to become competent partners with the school and university representatives. They can help prepare their children and themselves for active and productive involvement in the society given the opportunity (Vásquez, 2003). In other words, they can help redefine American citizenship to reflex the multiplicities out in the society at large. Additionally, this kind of educational social action helps us to search for ways to best integrate minority communities into the fold of American society at the same time that we funnel resources to help them develop their own intellectual power.

REFERENCES

Blanton, W. E., Moorman, G. B., Hayes, B. A., & Warner, M. L. (1997). Effects of participation in the Fifth Dimension on far transfer. *Journal of Educational Computing Research, 16*(4), 1–8.

Brown, C., & Cole, M. (2002). Cultural historical activity theory and the expansion of opportunities for learning after school. In G. A. Wells & G. Claxton (Eds.), *Learning for life in the 21st century: Sociocultural perspectives on the future of education* (pp. 225–238). Oxford, UK: Blackwell.

Camras, M. (2002). *Developing teen educators and advocates for community health: Fostering civic involvement in immigrant youth.* Unpublished doctoral dissertation, University of California San Diego, La Jolla.

Castells, M. (1996). *The rise of the network society.* Cambridge, MA: Blackwell.

Cole, M. (1996). *Cultural psychology: Once and future discipline.* Cambridge, MA: Harvard University Press.

Cummins, J., & Sayers, D. (1995). *Brave new schools: Challenging cultural illiteracy through global learning networks.* New York: St. Martin's Press.

Dewey, J. (1938). *Experience & education.* New York: Collier Books.

Dyke, N. B. (Ed.). (2000, August 18–20). Alleviating global poverty: Technology for economic and social uplift (a report of The Aspen Institute Conference). Aspen, CO: The Aspen Institute International Peace, Security & Prosperity Program.

Foot, K. (1999). *Writing conflicts: An activity theory analysis of the development of the network of ethnological monitoring and early warning.* Published doctoral dissertation, University of California, San Diego, La Jolla.

Freire, P. (2000). *Pedagogy of the heart.* New York: The Continuum Publishing Company.

Gallego, M. A. (2001). Is experience the best teacher? The potential of coupling community-based and conventional field experiences. *Journal of Teacher Education, 52*(4), 312–325.

Gomez, M. N., Bissell, J., Danziger, L., & Casselman, R. (1990). *To advance learning: A handbook on developing K-12-postsecondary partnerships.* Lanham, MD: University Press of America.

González, N. E. (1995). The funds of knowledge for teaching project. *Practicing Anthropology, 17*(3), 3–6.

Greenfield, P. M., & Cocking, R. R. (1994). *Cross-cultural roots of minority child development.* Hillsdale, NJ: Lawrence Erlbaum Associates.

Gross, T. L. (1988). *Partners in education: How colleges can work with schools to improve teaching and learning.* San Francisco: Jossey-Bass Publishers.

Gutiérrez, K. D., Baquedano-López, P., & Tejada, C., (1999). Rethinking diversity: Hybridity and hybrid language practices in the third space. *Mind, Culture, and Activity, 6*(4), 286–303.

Iscoe, I. (1974). Community psychology and the competent community. *American Psychologist, 29,* 607–613.

John-Steiner, V. (2000). *Creative collaboration.* New York: Oxford University Press.

Mayer, R. E. (1997). Out-of-school learning: The case of an after-school computer club. *Journal of Educational Computing Research, 16*(4): 333–336.

Miller, B. (2003, May). *Critical hours: After school programs and educational success.* Brookline, MA: Miller Midzik Research Associates.

Moll, L. C., Anderson, A., & Díaz, E. (May 1985). *Third college & CERRC: A university-community system for promoting academic excellence.* Paper presented at the University of California Linguistic Minority Conference, Lake Tahoe, CA.

Moll, L. C., & Greenberg, J. (1990). Creating zones of possibilities: Combining social contexts for instruction. In L. C. Moll (Ed.), *Vygotsky and education* (pp. 319–348). Cambridge, MA: Cambridge University Press.

Moyer, B. (2000). *Doing democracy: The map model for organizing social movements.* Gabriola Island, Canada: New Society Publishers.

Nicolopoulou, A., & Cole, M. (1993). Generation and transmission of shared knowledge in the culture of collobarative learning: The Fifth Dimension, its play-world, and its institutional contexts. In E. A. Forman, N. Minick, & C. A. Stone (Eds.), *Contexts for learning: Sociocultural dynamics in children's development* (pp. 283–314). New York: Oxford University Press.

Smock, K. (1999, June, May). *Building effective partnerships: The process and structure of collaboration.* NHI, Shelterforce online. 105.

Turkle, S. (1995). *Life on the screen: Identity in the age of the Internet.* New York: Simon & Schuster.

Vásquez, O. A. (1996). A model system of institutional linkages: Transforming the educational pipeline. In *The University of California Latino eligibility study.* Santa Cruz: University of California, Santa Cruz.

Vásquez, O. A. (2003). *La Clase Mágica: Imagining optimal possibilities in a bilingual community of learners.* Mahwah, NJ: Lawrence Erlbaum Associates.

Vásquez, O. A. (2004). A participatory perspective on parent involvement. In J. Mora & D. Díaz (Eds.), *Research in action: A participatory model for advancing Latino social policy.* Binghamton, NY: Haworth Press.

Vásquez, O. A., & Durán, R. (2000). La Clase Mágica and El Club Proteo: Multiple literacies in new community institutions. In M. A. Gallego & S. Hollingsworth (Eds.), *What counts as lit.er.a.cy: Challenging the school standard.* New York: Teachers College Press.

Vygotsky, L. S. (1978). *Mind in society: The development of higher psychological processes.* Cambridge, MA: Harvard University Press.

Wilbur, F. P., & Lambert, L. M. (1991). *Linking America's schools and colleges: Guide to partnerships and national directory.* Washington, DC: American Association for Higher Education.

14

Theoretical Perspectives on the Underachievement of Latino/a Students in U.S. Schools: Toward a Framework for Culturally Additive Schooling

Anthony De Jesús

Hunter College, City University of New York

INTRODUCTION

As the history of U.S. education unfolds, low-income, Latino/a students continue to experience enormous obstacles to their academic success in U.S. public schools. Educational policy makers express great dismay over rising indicators of failure and demand accountability for these disparities but even as the reform mantra of the current administration has become *No Child Left Behind*, through a regime that in fact leaves no child untested Latino/a students continue to experience highly disproportionate rates of school failure whether measured by standardized test scores, dropout and graduation rates, or other prevailing measures of achievement (Valenzuela, 2004).

Absent however, from the predominant discourse on school reform is the long tradition of explaining the low achievement of subordinated racial minority students by attributing academic failure to genetic inferiority or cultural deprivation.[1] These racist and refuted themes and the policies they inform underscore the urgent need for a discourse on Latino/a education that explores and acknowledges the complex structural and cultural forces that play a major role in the problem frequently referred to as "the achievement gap" between White students and students of color. By exploring economic, schooling, and social structures, and the social and cultural processes inherent within them, reproduction and resistance theories do not locate the problems of academic failure in the students themselves; rather, they provide a powerful analysis of economic, schooling, and social structures and processes that maintain socioeconomic inequality and the construction of subordinate, racialized identities, and student responses to them.

This chapter reviews and analyzes theories of reproduction and resistance and provides a synthesis of the literature most relevant to the experiences of Latino/a students. Additionally, this chapter provides a case study of a Latino/a community based school and its culturally relevant practices. The first section of this chapter examines the literature on reproduction/resistance theories (Gintis & Bowles, 1976; Willis, 1977; Giroux, 1983; Bourdieu, 1984, 1985, 1987, 1990; Giroux & Aronowitz, 1993, 1992; MacLeod, 1995) and delineates a continuum of theoretical explanations ranging from critical theory to constructivist sociological and anthropological derivatives. Although each set of theories has limitations, taken together these bodies of literature supply a rich and nuanced understanding of the social and cultural dynamics that impact U.S.-born and immigrant Latino/a students and provide the basis on which I develop a framework for transformative schooling in the final section of this chapter by analyzing the literature written about El Puente Academy for Peace and Justice, a community-based Latino/a high school in Brooklyn, New York (Dewar & Ramirez, 1996; Rivera & Pedraza, 2000). This community education initiative that seeks to privilege the social, cultural, and linguistic resources of Latino/a students informs the framework of culturally additive schooling advanced at the end of this chapter. This framework contributes to a long overdue alternative

---

[1]The genetic explanation is characterized by Hernstein and Murray (1994) in *The Bell Curve*, in which they espouse that intelligence is biologically determined and suggest that the poor academic performance of "minority" is genetically based. Although the findings and tenets of *The Bell Curve*, have been refuted (Gould, 1996), "bell curve" thinking in public schools and U.S. society endures.

discourse on Latino/a education in the United States and informs policymakers, researchers, and practitioners who are seeking more than
simple solutions to complex educational problems.

SOCIAL REPRODUCTION AND RESISTANCE
THEORIES

Theories of reproduction have been advanced by Gintis and Bowles
(1976), Althusser (1969, 1971), and Bourdieu (1973, 1977, 1987, 1990),
and begin with the premise that schools are key sites for the reproduction of social and economic inequality. According to this premise, the
role of schools is to sort individuals and groups according to the hierarchical division of labor in society. Following in this vein, schools must
shape the attitudinal and ideological dispositions and values necessary
for the maintenance of asymmetrical power relations between dominant and subordinate groups. Resistance theories seek to integrate the
idea of individual agency with understanding the complexity of social
reproduction processes.

Conceptualizations of reproduction and resistance in education are
located along a *structure/culture* continuum ranging from the highly deterministic economic reproduction model of Gintis and Bowles (*structure*) to the cultural reproductive model of Bourdieu (*culture*) to the
focus on individual agency provided by Willis (1977) and MacLeod
(1995). Each set of concepts advances important contributions to understanding the role of schooling in society, yet each also carries significant limitations. Taken together these theories represent a continuum
that provides a foundation for interpreting the behavior and academic
outcomes of marginalized youth.

Aronowitz and Giroux (1993) categorize reproduction theorists into
three models: the economic reproductive model, the cultural reproductive model, and the hegemonic-state reproductive model. The economic
reproductive model is largely characterized by the work of Gintis and
Bowles (1976) and their discussion of the correspondence principle and
the notion of the hidden curriculum. The *correspondence principle* suggests that schooling practices correspond to equivalent roles and practices in the economy, reflecting the division of labor in capitalist society.
Gintis and Bowles (1976) write:

> The educational system helps integrate youth into the economic system,
> we believe, through a structural correspondence between its social relations
> and those of production. The structure of social relations in education not

only inures the student to the discipline of the workplace, but develops the
modes of self-preservation, self-image, and social identifications which are
crucial ingredients of job adequacy. Specifically, the social relationships of
education—the relationships between administrators and teachers, teachers
and students, students and their work—replicate the hierarchical division of
labor. (p. 131)

Complementing the correspondence principle, the hidden curriculum
refers to school- and classroom-based social relations that transmit messages legitimizing class-based positionalities in regard to work, rules,
authority, and values that maintain capitalist sensibilities. Aronowitz
and Giroux (1993) observe:

The power of these messages lies in their seemingly universal qualities—
qualities that emerge as part of the structured silences that permeate all
levels of school and classroom relations. The social relations that constitute
the hidden curriculum provide ideological and material weight to questions
regarding what counts as high- versus low-status knowledge (intellectual
or manual), high- versus low-status forms of organization (hierarchical or
democratic), and, of course what counts as high- versus low-status forms of
personal interaction. (pp. 70, 71)

The hidden curriculum, then, becomes the mechanism by which students learn their place in the economy, accept their position, and develop the necessary skills for their role in the labor force. Althusser
builds on this notion by suggesting that the "school carries out two
fundamental forms of reproduction: the reproduction of the skills and
rules of labor power and the reproduction of the relations of production" (cited in Aronowitz & Giroux, 1993, p. 71). Additionally, Althusser
extends the concept of the hidden curriculum by proposing that ideology has a material existence in "the rituals, routines and social practices
that both structure and mediate the day-to-day working of schools"
(p. 72). This material existence also manifests in the architecture of
school buildings and the physical organization of classrooms that reflect the hierarchical division of labor.

The contributions of economic reproductive theorists are important
because they provide explanations for school "failure" that do not
"blame the victim" but, rather, expose structural processes of schooling that maintain social and economic inequality. These theories do,
however, have shortcomings, in that they ignore individual student
and teacher agency and the role of student resistance in disrupting

reproductive outcomes. Moreover, the theoretical outlooks forwarded by Bowles and Gintis and Althusser are rigidly deterministic, granting omnipotence to capitalist forces and leaving little room for what Aronowitz and Giroux (1993) call a "language of possibility":

> Even where the contradictions and mediations are mentioned, they generally disappear under the crushing weight of capitalist domination. As such, these accounts are marred not only by a reductionist instrumentalism regarding the meaning and role of schools but also by a form of radical pessimism that offers little hope for social change and even less reason for developing alternative educational practices. (p. 74)

Further along the *structure/culture* continuum, cultural theorists such as Bourdieu address the cultural processes at work in schools and contribute to a broader understanding of reproduction.

The cultural reproductive model, as articulated primarily by French sociologist Pierre Bourdieu, is developed around his concept of cultural capital, which is defined as cultural and linguistic knowledge, skills, and dispositions passed down from one generation to another (McLeod, 1995). Bourdieu's premise is that schools, although presenting a veneer of fairness and equality, implicitly value the cultural capital of the dominant classes and students who possess these most valued forms of cultural capital are able to translate these resources into academic success and credentials (institutionalized cultural capital). These credentials are subsequently convertible into economic capital in the labor market tacitly maintaining the social status of middle-class and affluent students and impeding students who are lacking in the cultural capital of the dominant classes. MacLeod (1995) summarizes the main characteristics of Bourdieu's model:

> First, distinctive cultural capital is transmitted by each social class. Second, the school systematically valorizes upper class cultural capital and depreciates the cultural capital of the lower classes. Third, differential academic achievement is translated back into economic wealth—the job market remunerates the superior academic credentials earned mainly by the upper classes. Finally, the school legitimates this process "by making social hierarchies and the reproduction of those hierarchies appear to be based on the hierarchy of "gifts," merits or skills established or ratified by its sanctions, or, in a word, by converting social hierarchies into academic hierarchies. (p. 14)

Although it is possible for individuals to acquire the most valued forms of cultural capital, according to Bourdieu's analysis, they are still disadvantaged because this requires large investments of time, and the natural familiarity that comes from receiving these skills and dispositions in one's family always remains elusive.[2] The cultural reproductive model, then, suggests that success or failure in school is largely determined by one's social class, yet this fact is concealed because of meritocratic ideologies that locate success or failure within individuals (or their ethnic and racial communities), rather than as a function of their inherited cultural capital.

The hegemonic-state reproductive model focuses on the role of the state in serving the interests of elites and "how the process of social and cultural reproduction operate in the political sphere" (Aronowitz & Giroux, 1993, p. 90). The hegemonic-state reproductive model is best characterized by the work of the Italian theorist Antonio Gramsci, whose analysis of state hegemony includes an understanding of the "dual use of force and ideology to reproduce societal relations between dominant classes and subordinate groups" (Aronowitz & Giroux, 1993, p. 83). In Gramsci's view, hegemony is a continuous and constant process that is actually a struggle for control of consciousness. Aronowitz and Giroux (1993) observe that in Gramsci's view: "The production of knowledge is linked to the political sphere and becomes a central element in the state's construction of power" (p. 83). As the apparatus of the state, schools embody the contradictions, ideologies, and repression practices of the state and seek to gain the consent of those subordinated through the process of socialization. Darder (1991) observes:

> With the rise of modern science and technology, social control has been exercised less through the use of physical deterrents and increasingly through the distribution of an elaborate system of norms and imperatives. Gramsci notes that—unlike fascist regimes, which control primarily through physically coercive forces and arbitrary rules and regulations—capitalist societies utilize forms of hegemonic control that function systematically by winning the consent of the subordinated to the authority of the dominant structure. (p. 34)

---

[2] A key feature of Bourdieu's analysis is his concept of the *habitus*, the embodiment or internalization of dispositions, expectations, and achievement orientations. It is "a lasting system of transposable dispositions which functions at every moment as a matrix of perceptions, appreciations and actions and makes possible the achievement of infinitely diversified tasks" (Bourdieu, 1977, p. 72). As McLeod (1995), explains: "The habitus is composed of the attitudes, beliefs, and experiences of those inhabiting one's social world. This conglomeration of deeply internalized values defines an individual's attitudes toward, for example, schooling" (p. 15). The habitus is the personification of cultural capital, which grants access to valued resources based on the subjective selection processes maintained by schools and their agents.

Giroux and Aronowitz provide an example of how the state coercively legitimizes forms of knowledge considered legitimate by the dominant class through certification:

> Through state-established certification requirements, educational systems are heavily weighted toward a highly technocratic rationality that relies on a logic drawn primarily from the natural sciences. The effect can be seen in the distinction schools make at all levels between high-status knowledge—usually the "hard sciences"—and low-status knowledge—subjects in the humanities. This bias also puts pressures on schools to utilize methods of inquiry and evaluation that stress efficiency, prediction and the logic of the mathematical formula. (p. 87)

Giroux and Aronowitz's analysis here is powerfully illustrative of the current national debate over standardization and the use of standardized tests for tracking, promotion, and graduation (McNeil, 2000; Valenzuela, 2005). By revealing how the state legitimizes the interests of elites, the hegemonic-state reproductive model explains more of the complexities involved in defining the state and explains how the interests of capital manifest in school policies and practices constructed by and through the state. However, like the economic reproductive model, the hegemonic-state reproductive model provides a rigidly deterministic view of individuals as mere cogs in the wheel of reproduction who consent to predetermined labor market roles. This failure to account for individual student and teacher agency in the form of critiquing or resisting structural (economic and political) forms of reproduction represents a major flaw in these models of reproduction and illustrates the tension that Giroux calls the *structure-agency dualism*. This dualism is well articulated by MacLeod (1995) in his discussion of structuralist and culturalist theoretical perspectives:

> Structuralist theories, which stress that history is made "behind the backs" of the members of society, overlook the significance and relative autonomy of the cultural level and the human experience of domination and resistance. "In the Structuralist perspective human agents are registered simply as the effects of structural determinants that appear to work with the certainty of biological processes. In this grimly mechanistic approach, human subjects simply act as role-bearers." Culturalist theories, on the other hand, pay too little attention to how structurally embedded material and economic forces weigh down and shape human experience. "Culturalism begins at the right place but does not go far enough theoretically—it does not dig into subjectivity in order to find is objective elements." (p. 21)

Emerging from such a critique of structuralist and culturalist limitations, resistance theorists (Giroux, 1983; Aronowitz, & Giroux, 1993; MacLeod, 1995; Willis, 1977) illuminate the importance of individual agency in response to the reproductive role of schools and balance the tension inherent within the structure/agency dualism by their interpretations of the oppositional responses of low-status students to hegemonic schooling processes. As Giroux (1983) observes, "The notion of resistance points to the need to understand more thoroughly the complex ways in which people mediate and respond to the interface between their own lived experiences and structures of domination and constraint" (p. 108). Resistance need not manifest in oppositional forms of behavior. For example, Nieto (1999) notes that "negative expectations can prove to be a motivating source to succeed" or "prove them wrong" (p. 43). Alternatively, not every oppositional behavior should be considered an act of resistance; rather, the motivating interests underlying the behavior must be assessed. Giroux (1983) observes:

> Central to analyzing any act of resistance would be a concern with uncovering the degree to which it speaks to a form of refusal that highlights, either implicitly or explicitly, the need to struggle against the social nexus of domination and submission. In other words, resistance must have a revealing function, one that contains a critique of domination and provides theoretical opportunities for self-reflection and for struggle in the interest of self-emancipation and social emancipation. (p. 109)

Examples of resistance are revealed in a brief review of *Learning to Labour*, Paul Willis's (1977) classic ethnography of working-class boys in the United Kingdom. Willis analyzes the schooling orientations of the *ear'oles* (students who conform to the school's norms) and the *lads* (students who challenge authority and defy the school culture). Willis supplies an interpretation of the logic (or what he calls *penetrations*) that motivates the *lads'* rejection of the pursuit of "qualifications" and appropriation of an immediate gratification-based lifestyle.

> The counter-school culture is involved in its own way with a relatively subtle, dynamic, and, so to speak "opportunity-costed" assessment of the rewards of the conformism and obedience to which the school seeks to exact from working class kids. In particular, this involves a deep seated skepticism about the value of qualifications in relation to what might be sacrificed to get them: a sacrifice ultimately, not of simple dead time, but of a quality of action, involvement and independence. Immediate gratification is not only immediate, it is a style of life and offers the same thing too in ten years time. To be

an 'ear'ole' now and to gain qualifications of dubious value might be to close off forever the abilities which allow and generate immediate gratifications of any kind at any stage. (p. 126)

In the case of the *lads*, as they reject the conformist orientation of the *ear'oles* they exercise agency by their acts of resistance (disrupting class by having a "laff") interpreted by Willis to represent "the struggle to win symbolic and physical space from the institution and its rules and to defeat its main purpose: to make you 'work'" (p. 26). In essence, the *lads'* behavior reflects a critique of their schooling and the labor market structures that shape it. Rather than participate in school as obedient and docile subjects, they prefer to subvert a schooling ideology, which they realize, based on their lived experience, will never work for them. According to Willis, the *lads'* behavior

is an accurate assessment of the role and importance of qualifications, it supports the view that it is unwise for working class kids to place their trust in diplomas and certificates. These things do not act to push people up—as in the official account—but to maintain there those who are already at the top. (p. 128)

Unfortunately, as rational as the *lads'* critique may be, by foregoing the opportunity to develop critical thinking skills through the pursuit of qualifications, the *lads* pretty much assure their own reproduction as working-class, low-status subjects, and their oppositional activities serve to further marginalize them. Aronowitz and Giroux (1993) acknowledge this ironic characteristic of resistance theory, which examines "how students who actively reject school culture often display a deeper logic and view of the world that confirms rather than challenges existing capitalist social relations" (p. 92). The *lads'* rationale is informed by their lived experience, but their rejection of things academic (though justifiable) is short-sighted in that it virtually guarantees that they will not apprehend a transformative analysis of their condition:

Not only do the lads reject the alleged superiority of mental labor, but they also reject its underlying ideology that respect and obedience will be exchanged for knowledge and success. The lads oppose this ideology because the counter logic embodied in the families, workplaces, and street life that make up *their* culture points to a different and more convincing reality ... but in doing so they closed off any possibility of pursuing an emancipatory relationship between knowledge and dissent. By rejecting intellectual labor, the lads discounted the power of critical thinking as a tool of social transformation. (p. 92)

Learning to Labour provides rich, nuanced accounts and interpretations of the behavior of working-class students engaged in the production of a counter-school culture. Willis presents a strong critique of the structural reproductionists as he reveals how the lads exercise agency and actively resist structures of domination, rather than acquiesce to them and makes a major contribution to the evolution of resistance theory.

Although resistance theories help balance the structure/agency dualism, they do not supply a definitive analysis of all oppositional behavior; rather, as Giroux (1983) suggests, they provide a different theoretical starting point

> that links the display of behavior to the interest it embodies. As such the emphasis is going beyond the immediacy of the behavior to the notion of interest that underlies its often hidden logic, a logic that also has to be interpreted through the historical and cultural mediations that shape it. (p. 110)

Social reproduction and resistance theories contribute to explanations of the academic success and failure of low-income students of color in that they allow for a complex understanding of structural and cultural processes that both shape and elicit a range of responses from marginalized students. The structure/culture continuum reflected in this discussion is most valuable to the extent that it reveals various forms of and responses to inequality that can illuminate a transformative framework of schooling.

CONCEPTUALIZING SOCIAL/CULTURAL CAPITAL IN EDUCATION

Over the last two decades, social scientists across a number of fields (Bourdieu, 1984, 1985, 1987, 1990, 1992; Coleman, 1988, 1990; Loury, 1977; Putnam, 1993, 2000) have increasingly utilized the theoretical construct of social capital to describe intangible resources existing between individuals and groups. Putnam (2000) simply observes that the core idea behind social capital theory is that "social networks have value":

> Whereas physical capital refers to physical objects and human capital refers to properties of individuals—social capital refers to connections among individuals—social networks and the norms of reciprocity and trustworthiness that arise from them. (p. 19)

In the realm of education, these networks of mutual obligation and trust nurture the intellectual and interpersonal development of students and gain them access to material and intangible resources. It follows then, that an invisible economy of social exchanges exists, and as it relates to schooling it supplies (and alternatively denies) important resources related to the academic achievement of students, depending on the resources available to them.

As discussed earlier, the concept of cultural capital articulated by Bourdieu (1984, 1987, 1992) consists of forms of knowledge, dialects, and dispositions that are valued by a society's dominant culture. Within academic and economic markets, cultural capital is then differentially converted into academic and occupational rewards for those who are in possession of its most valued forms (Bourdieu, 1986). A deeper understanding of social/cultural capital[3] and the ways it is created, nurtured, activated, exchanged, and diminished in schools emerges from the work of Coleman.

COLEMAN: SOCIAL CAPITAL AND CLOSURE

The sociologist James Coleman (1988), in his article "Social Capital in the Creation of Human Capital," popularized the notion of social capital related specifically to education. Building on Loury's (1977) definition of social capital, Coleman (1990) describes it as

> the set of resources that inhere in family relations and in community social organization and that are useful for the cognitive or social development of a child or young person. These resources differ for different persons and can constitute an important advantage for children and adolescents in the development of their human capital. (p. 300)

Coleman was interested in how social capital was a resource that could stimulate the academic achievement of individuals. Although he fails to provide an explicit definition of social capital, he claims it is defined by its function:

> It is not a single entity but a variety of different entities, with two elements in common: they all consist of some element of social structures, and they facilitate certain actions of actors—whether persons or corporate actors—within the structure. Like other forms of capital, social capital is productive, making possible the achievement of certain ends that in its absence would not be possible. (p. 97)

---

[3]Because of the close interaction between social and cultural capital, they will be described in this section and merged into an integrative concept, *social/cultural capital* (Lopez & Stack, 1999; Schneider, 1998).

According to Coleman (1988), community and organizational structures that foster social capital are characterized by *social closure,* a cohesive set of shared norms and sanctions characterized by "the trustwor-
thiness of social structures that allows the proliferation of obligations
and expectations" (p. 107). Within these social structures, closure allows
for the fostering of relations of trust based on norms (shared expectations) and effective sanctions that facilitate certain actions and constrain
others. Norms and sanctions are important elements of social closure.
According to Coleman (1990), an effective norm

> constitutes a powerful but sometimes fragile form of social capital. Effec-
> tive norms that inhibit crime in a city make it possible for women to walk
> freely outside at night and for old people to leave their homes without fear.
> Norms in a community that support and provide effective rewards for high
> achievement in school greatly facilitate the schools' task. (p. 311)

The concept of closure has important implications for an analysis of the
interconnectedness of relations between communities, schools, parents,
and students in supporting academic achievement.

Although a number of Coleman's insights are quite useful in understanding the role of social structures, community and family relations,
and exchanges in facilitating academic success, his treatment of social
capital is problematic because he fails to provide a critical analysis of social and economic inequality and its role in delimiting the social capital
available to disenfranchised communities and individuals. In this regard, reproduction theories, particularly Bourdieu's analysis of cultural
reproduction, are most useful in developing an understanding of how
social/cultural capital not only facilitates but also constrains academic
achievement, depending on differential economic and social advantage.

CULTURAL CAPITAL AND THE CODES
OF POWER

As discussed earlier, Bourdieu makes important contributions to our
understandings of schooling as a cultural process. In his essay "The
Forms of Capital," Bourdieu (1987) delineates his concepts of cultural
capital and social capital. Cultural capital, which manifests in three
states (embodied, objectified, and institutionalized), consists of cultural knowledge, language, dialects, and tastes (embodied within an
individual), and the ability to appropriate and utilize cultural goods
(objectified cultural capital) within an economy of cultural practices

learned in families and valued within cultural and academic markets. Through the schooling process, manifestations of embodied cultural capital are rewarded and converted into educational credentials or institutionalized cultural capital. These credentials are subsequently convertible into economic capital in the labor market, implicitly maintaining the social status of students who possess the most valued forms of cultural capital and impeding students who are lacking in the cultural capital of the dominant classes. Cultural capital consists of a set of competencies in the forms of knowledge and ideas legitimated by the dominant society (other forms of knowledge and cultural expression are subordinated to what is considered "legitimate" culture). Central to Bourdieu's understanding of reproduction is the notion of meritocracy, or what is frequently referred to in the United States as the "level playing field" on which all students allegedly compete. While presenting a veneer of fairness (as is the case with the current standardization movement), schools are key sites that reward proficiency in dominant cultural capital. Aronowitz and Giroux (1993) observe: "By appearing to be an impartial and neutral transmitter of the benefits of valued culture, schools are able to promote inequality in the name of fairness and objectivity" (p. 75). Bourdieu (1973) describes how schools maintain uneven educational achievement of students from different cultural and social class backgrounds by

> requiring initial familiarity with the dominant culture, and which proceeds by imperceptible familiarization and offers information and training which can be received and acquired only by subjects endowed with the system of predispositions that is the condition for the success of transmission and inculcation of the culture. (p. 494)

In other words, students who come from privileged classes bring to school the means to appropriate the cultural knowledge valued by schools and the educational system. Educational researcher Lisa Delpit (1995) refers to this process as the natural knowledge that comes from participating in "the culture of power," or the ability of students who come to school with valued forms of cultural capital to "cash in" the cultural currency that they bring to school. The veneer of fairness tacitly disadvantages those students who bring devalued cultural currency to school.

> This means success in institutions—schools, workplaces and so on—is predicated upon acquisition of the culture of those who are in power. Children from middle class tend to do better than children from non-middle class

homes because the culture of the school is based upon the culture of the middle and upper classes—of those in power. The middle and upper classes send their children to school with all the accoutrements of the culture of power; children from other kinds of families operate within perfectly wonderful and viable cultures but not cultures that carry the codes or rules of power. (p. 25)

Delpit points out that schools fail to provide non-middle-class students with the opportunity to learn the codes of power because middle-class educators work under the assumption that the codes are internalized. She further argues that schools must provide students of color with "discourse patterns, interactional styles, and spoken and written language codes that will allow them success in the larger society" (p. 29).

A growing number of researchers (Darder, 1991; Moll & Greenberg, 1990; Stanton-Salazar, 1997) assert the need for schools to acknowledge the social/cultural capital of students of color as a foundation for developing a bicultural network orientation, allowing Latino/a students to appropriate both the dominant discourses (codes of power) and their own familial cultural capital or funds of knowledge (Moll & Greenberg, 1990). Theories of social/cultural capital reviewed herein provide an important foundation for understanding the invisible resources that grant and deny access to educational and institutional rewards. The ways in which social/cultural capital is denigrated are revealed in the sociocultural micro-processes at Seguín High School, the basis of Valenzuela's case study of subtractive schooling, which is highly relevant to the education of Latino/a students.

SYNTHESIZING REPRODUCTION AND RESISTANCE FOR LATINOS: SUBTRACTIVE SCHOOLING

In her book *Subtractive Schooling U.S.–Mexican Students and the Politics of Caring*, the sociologist Angela Valenzuela (1999) provides a cogent theoretical analysis integrating the literature on immigrant student achievement, social capital, and adds an important dimension, the literature on caring. In her 3-year study of academic achievement and schooling orientations among immigrant Mexican and Mexican American students at Seguín High School (a pseudonym), a large, "comprehensive" high school in Houston, Texas, she found:

> Rather than functioning as a conduit for the attainment of the American dream, this large, overcrowded, and under funded urban school reproduces Mexican youth as a monolingual, English-speaking, ethnic minority, neither identified with Mexico nor equipped to function competently in America's mainstream. For the majority of Seguín High School's regular (non college-bound) track, schooling is a subtractive process. It divests these youth of important social and cultural resources, leaving them progressively vulnerable to academic failure. (p. 3)

Building on Cummins (1984, 1986) and Gibson's (1993) concept of *subtractive assimilation,* which views "assimilation as a non-neutral process and that its widespread application negatively impacts the economic and political integration of minorities" (p. 25), Valenzuela developed the term *subtractive schooling* to bring the school more clearly into focus in the broader Americanization project, suggesting that "schools may be subtractive in ways that extend beyond the concept of subtractive cultural assimilation to include the content and organization of the curriculum" (p. 27). Guadalupe San Miguel (1999), in his review of the history of schooling in the Southwest, discusses *subtractive Americanization,* which occurred when schools devalued particular minority groups and their specific cultural heritages, and when they sought to replace the identities of these groups with an idealized American one, or when they sought to remove minority communities, languages, and cultures from the curriculum and educational structures altogether (p. 38). Valenzuela argues that this is accomplished because large, urban public schools like Seguín

> are organized formally and informally in ways that fracture student's cultural and ethnic identities, creating linguistic and cultural divisions among the students and the staff. As a direct consequence of these divisions, social relationships at Seguín typically are often fragile, incomplete, or nonexistent. Teachers fail to forge meaningful connections with their students; students are alienated from their teachers and are often (especially between groups of first generation immigrants and U.S.-born) hostile toward one another as well; and administrators routinely disregard even the most basic needs of both students and staff. The feeling that "no one cares" is pervasive—and corrosive. (p. 5)

Using a framework developed by Nel Noddings (1984), Valenzuela (1999) analyzes competing notions of caring among teachers and students that are rooted in fundamentally different cultural and class-based expectations about the nature of schooling. These expectations inevitably clash at Seguín, and when they do, they fuel conflict and power struggles between teachers and students who see each other as *not caring:*

> The predominately non-Latino teaching staff sees students as not sufficiently *caring about* school, while students see teachers as not sufficiently *caring for* them. Teachers expect students to demonstrate caring about schooling with an abstract, or *aesthetic* commitment to ideas or practices that purportedly lead to achievement. Immigrant and U.S.-born youth, on the other hand, are committed to an *authentic* form of caring that emphasizes relations of reciprocity between teachers and students. (p. 61)

In order to succeed academically at Seguín, students must conform to the faculty's value of aesthetic caring "whose essence lies in an attention to things and ideas" (Valenzuela, 1999, p. 22). In general Latino/a students resist this notion and experience the cultural and social distance between them and their teachers as depersonalizing and inauthentic. Alternatively, authentic caring constitutes an essential element of what these young people consider *educación,* a term that within Mexican/Latino culture and schooling practices is strongly related to social ties and reciprocal relationships (p. 61). In other words, educación represents a form of schooling infused with reciprocal and relational social capital. As Valenzuela points out, "students' precondition to caring about school is that they be engaged in a caring relationship with an adult at school" (p. 79).

Frank, a ninth grader whom Valenzuela interviewed, illustrates the competing aesthetic and authentic caring ideologies that define what it means to be educated. A C-student who performs well below his potential, Frank presents a critique of the dominant mobility narrative in the United States, or the "out of the barrio" (p. 95) ideology, when he explains why he does not exert more energy on his studies:

> I don't get with the program because then it's doing what *they* [teachers] want for my life. I see *Mexicanos* who follow the program so they can go to college, get rich, move out of the *barrio,* and never return back to give to their *gente* [people]. Is that what this is all about? If I get with the program, I'm saying that's what it's all about and that the teachers are right when they're not. (p. 94)

Although in his critique he expresses his desire to "give back" to his community, Frank's refusal to conform to the dominant success narrative contributes to his indifference about school, read as not caring by the majority of his teachers. Reminiscent of the lads in Willis's study, this irony reinforces barriers that will make it difficult for Frank to achieve at Seguín, thus diminishing his chances of making sustained contributions to his community. However, as Valenzuela observes, "Frank is not unwilling to become a productive member of society; he is simply at odds with a definition of productivity that is divorced from the social and economic interests of the broader Mexican community" (p. 95). In this example, the definition of school success as moving out of the barrio is related to middle-class Anglo values and is interpreted by Frank as a threat to the development of his community and maintenance of his cultural integrity. This is not a rejection of education or achievement but, rather, a form of resistance. Frank (like many students at Seguín) is not opposed to education, but to the subtractive ways in which Seguín is organized. Valenzuela observes: "U.S.-born (Latino) youth I observed do not oppose education, nor are they uniformly hostile to the equation of education with upward mobility. What they reject is schooling—the content of their education and the way it is offered to them" (p. 19).

Emerging from their sense of isolation within the school and their race, class, and age biases, many teachers at Seguín have developed negative attitudes and perceptions about Latino/a students that prevent them from ever viewing them as serious learners. Additionally, students' self-representations reinforce teacher perceptions that students do not care about learning.

> Complicating most teachers' demands that students care about school is their displeasure with students' self representations, on the one hand and the debilitating institutional barriers they face on a daily basis that impede their abilities to connect effectively with youth's social world, on the other. From these adults perspective, the way youth dress, talk and generally deport themselves "proves" that they do not care about school" (p. 61).

Just as teachers are isolated victims of bureaucratic structures characterized by cynicism and lack of professional and personal support, students respond to their sense of isolation and alienation in ways that reinforce for teachers, the idea that they are not invested in learning. As Valenzuela observes: "What looks to teachers and administrators like opposition and lack of caring, feels to students like powerlessness and alienation" (p. 94). She goes on to document policies, practices, and conventions at Seguín (and the state and district level) that serve to systematically divest students of their Mexican identities and

"impede their prospects for fully vested bilingualism and biculturalism" (p. 172). In addition to the obvious tensions they create between
students and teachers, these practices facilitate even deeper divisions
between Mexican immigrant and U.S.-born youth, inserting a wedge
between students who potentially have so much to offer each other in
the development of complementary bilingual/bicultural identities. Instead, this potential is stifled by the established "pecking order, based
on the privileging of English as both the medium of instruction and the
ticket to participation in faculty sponsored school activities" (p. 186).
Consistent with a deficit orientation, ESL students are, for example,
categorized as "limited English proficient" rather than "Spanish dominant" or "English language learners." The belief that English is superior (and Spanish and things Spanish are inferior) pervades the school
culture and manifests in myriad ways, such as the subtle revisions of
students' Spanish names:

> At every turn, even well-meaning teachers "adapt" their students' names:
> "Loreto" becomes "Laredo"; "Azucena" is transformed into "Suzy." Because
> teachers and other school personnel typically lack familiarity with stress rules
> in Spanish, last names are particularly vulnerable to linguistic butchering.
> Even names that are common throughout the southwest, like Martinez and
> Perez, are pronounced as MART-I-nez and Pe-REZ (instead of Mart-I-nez
> and PE-rez). (p. 173)

Further evidence of the subordination of things "Spanish" is found in
the fact that the student handbook is only available in English, despite
the school's large Spanish dominant population. This makes it virtually
impossible for immigrant students to negotiate the school's credit
and graduation requirements. Additionally, because of the horrendous
counselor/student ratio and bureaucratic nature of the counseling department, while students are "instructed to discuss their school plans
with their pre-assigned counselor, most students know that no counselor, pre-assigned or otherwise, will actually be available for such a
discussion" (p. 174).

   The one policy at the state level that according to Valenzuela's analysis profoundly reinforces the subtractive nature of schooling at Seguín
is the Texas Assessment of Academic Skills (TAAS) examination, which
is only given in English. Seguín students are not informed of this, nor
are they informed that they must pass this state-mandated exam in order to graduate, regardless of credits earned and academic standing.
Rather than alert and prepare Latino/a students for the TAAS, the lack

of clarity in explaining the TAAS (and the tests own shortcomings) prevents many Spanish-dominant students from graduating, despite their demonstrated academic competence.

Whereas subtractive schooling policies and practices are clearly the focus of her analysis, Valenzuela also provides several examples of "additive" (authentic) educational relationships at work at Seguín. These examples begin to inform the development of a broader framework of additive schooling. One compelling example is the commitment of Mr. Sosa, the band teacher who reveals a form of authentic caring toward his students by preparing *taquitos* for them every day. Realizing early on in his work at Seguín that students were often hungry in school, he began to feed them. Spending up to two hours each night preparing the food for his students, Sosa sees it as a labor of love. As a result, he developed reciprocal, trusting relationships with his students, leading them to the city championship for three consecutive years (p. 113). In Sosa's example, it becomes clear that student success at Seguín is linked to caring relationships that they develop with adults. Valenzuela reflects:

> At Seguín, where the importance of personal worth is often overlooked, where the links between academic achievement, cultural integrity and mutual respect are so fragile, and where helpfulness and hopefulness are often in short supply, Mr. Sosa reminds us that a different, more affirming and positive world may be only one taquito away—that is if it is one made with sincerity and love. (p. 113)

Valenzuela's articulation of subtractive schooling thoughtfully defines a problem critical to the future of all Americans. The pervasiveness of noncaring, the lack of reciprocal relationships, and the systematic devaluation of students' social/cultural capital at Seguín High School serves to reproduce a subordinated cultural and linguistic identity for Mexican youth. Yet with examples of agency such as Mr. Sosa, who affirms students' cultural capital at the same time he nurtures reciprocal trust, Valenzuela contributes to a language of possibility. She provides powerful insights into the elements of additive schooling, which have the potential to transform students through the development of a bicultural network orientation. "Subtractive schooling" teems with insights into the ways we might continue to critically examine mainstream schooling practices and pleads for the development of a theoretical framework for additive schooling, which becomes clearer in the following case study.

EL PUENTE ACADEMY FOR PEACE AND JUSTICE: A PRACTICE OF ADDITIVE SCHOOLING

El Puente Academy for Peace and Justice, an innovative community school in the Williamsburg neighborhood of Brooklyn, New York is part of a community-based youth development organization, *El Puente*, which means "bridge" in Spanish.[4] El Puente is located adjacent to the Williamsburg Bridge, which links this diverse neighborhood to Manhattan. Qualitative accounts of El Puente Academy for Peace and Justice (Maeroff, 1998; Ramirez & Dewar, 1995; Rivera & Pedraza, 2000) provide valuable insights into the role that institutional agents play in creating social/cultural capital among marginalized youth. Although not an alternative school in the traditional sense (a school where students who have "failed" or "dropped out" are sent), El Puente represents a powerful alternative to traditional (subtractive) schooling.

In their report entitled *El Puente Academy of Peace and Justice: A Case Study for Building Social Capital*, Dewar and Ramirez (1995) describe how a vision of education for community development manifests in every aspect of life at El Puente:

> The Academy's emphasis on peace, justice, human rights and community development is visible throughout the school. It is reflected in the location of the school (which is located inside the same building that houses all other El Puente projects and activities); the physical setup and décor of the building (e.g. the building has an open feel; and staff are easily accessible to students; posters of Malcolm X, Martin Luther King, Rigoberta Menchu and others involved in struggles for justice are hung throughout the building); and the Academy's curriculum (e.g. students are given the opportunity to study their own as well as other cultures—including cultures related to race and national origin, as well as current youth culture). Art, writing, and health courses are also related to student's community environmental activism. (p. 17)

These physical and pedagogical structures were created by the deliberate efforts of community activists, many of whom were frustrated with the dearth of opportunities for youth in their community. They believed that building an institution like El Puente was necessary for all

---

[4]El Puente Academy is a New York City public school, which operates under the New Visions for Education, an initiative founded "to create a critical mass of small, effective schools that equitably serve the full range of children in New York City" (Rivera & Pedraza, 2000, p. 227).

aspects of their cultural and educational survival. Ramirez and Dewar observe that:

> The institution was built by long term residents who had roots that were deeply embedded in the local culture, language and civic infrastructure of Williamsburg. Most of the people who have come to work at El Puente or have become members of El Puente also have deep roots in the community, and were already known to be active in many other community efforts. Although this community of people was concerned with the education and future of its young, they were also active in addressing many issues that affected the community as a whole (i.e., cultural development, arts, crime, environment, family, race relations, human rights, poverty, housing). The case of El Puente shows that strong community work is *not* just centrally based in school settings, but proceeds from the multiple concerns and activities of a community. (p. 45)

According to Rivera and Pedraza (2000), the teaching staff at El Puente, *facilitators* as they are called because they facilitate learning, "incorporate both the cognitive and the affective into activities, use problem-posing and dialogic methods, value anti-racist multiculturalism, and emphasize critical inquiry across disciplines by implementing action research projects" (p. 223). The student-centered curriculum incorporates activist projects, the arts, holism, and rituals and celebrations into its day-to-day pedagogy. El Puente's facilitators integrate these curricular goals across subject areas and base their work on the Academy's four cornerstone principles: "love and caring, collective self-help, peace and justice, and mastery." According to Rivera and Pedraza:

> El Puente's principles are integrated into the Academy's daily life through a creative, critical pedagogy (Park, 1995). By incorporating students' realities and communities into the curriculum (i.e. housing, health, employment, and violence) and by utilizing emancipatory educational practices "by which the oppressed are equipped with the necessary tools to re-appropriate their history, culture and language practices" (Freire & Macedo, 1987, p. 157), schools can emerge as "cultural spaces" that support both personal and intellectual growth as well as community development (Freire, 1970; Giroux, 1988; Hooks, 1994; Walsh, 1996). (p. 233)

The *sankofa* curriculum, based on the Swahili word meaning "going back to the source," provides students with the opportunity to go back to their sources and explore their "historical, sociocultural and familial traditions and legacies in their global studies, English, science and art classes" (Rivera & Pedraza, 2000, p. 234). For El Puente students, the majority of whom are Latino/a (Puerto Rican, Dominican, Mexican, Central American, and Afro-Caribbean), this offers an opportunity to explore deeply their origins and establish a cultural foundation based on their community funds of knowledge. The Academy's director, Frances Lucerna, explains:

> In our ancestry/history, education happened through the telling of stories which connected us to the fabric of life in the community.... Education happens in the community, is facilitated by people in the community and should benefit the individual student, his/her family and the rest of the community. (Ramirez & Dewar, 1995; p. 16)

El Puente's community development and educational philosophy is informed by a critical appraisal of the mainstream society and its approaches to schooling and treatment of communities of color. El Puente's philosophy is politically clear and consistent with Valenzuela (and Bartolome, 1994), when she asserts that:

> Students' cultural world and their structural position must be fully apprehended, with school based adults deliberately bringing issues of race, difference and power into central focus. This approach necessitates the abandonment of a color-blind curriculum and a neutral assimilation process. The practice of individualizing collective problems must also be relinquished. A more profound and involved understanding of the socioeconomic, linguistic, sociocultural, and structural barriers that obstruct the mobility of Mexican youth needs to inform all caring relationships (Delgado-Gaitan & Trueba 1991; Phelan et al. 1993; Stanton-Salazar 1996). Authentic caring cannot exist unless it is imbued with and motivated by such political clarity. (p. 109)

A compelling example of how El Puente's curriculum integrates the cognitive and affective, students' funds of knowledge, a critical assessment of mainstream society, and the development of knowledge of core subjects (codes of power) is found in a description of the Sugar Project, a year-long integrated curriculum unit for sophomores and juniors during the 1996–1997 academic year. A Williamsburg landmark, the Domino Sugar factory, inspired the unit. Throughout the year, students studied the history of sugar and its economic relationship to slavery and colonialism in the Caribbean and Latin America. Additionally, they studied patterns of sugar consumption in the United States and how Brazilian, Caribbean, and communities have interacted with sugar. "The culmination of the Sugar Project was the Sweet Freedom

Sugar Feast, a performance and parade with student stilt walkers, Afro-Caribbean dance, spiritual songs, a skit, and a presentation of short videos about race and identity produced by young people" (Rivera & Pedraza, 2000, p. 237).

Integrated projects like the Sugar Project illuminate the ways in which El Puente creates an additive curriculum. This allows students to develop critical academic skills in core academic subjects (codes of power), yet is based on students' funds of knowledge, critical pedagogy, and a historical grounding (*sankofa*) that links their own histories and allows them to "apprehend their cultural world and structural position in an unequal society" (Valenzuela, 1999, p. 109). Moreover, a strong commitment to activism runs through the curriculum at El Puente, which is connected to a larger analysis of community concerns. Maeroff (1998) describes examples of activism that he suggests "positions a school to identify more closely with the lives of its students and their families" (p. 59).

> When sandblasting on the [Williamsburg] bridge to remove the old paint was being considered, students and faculty alerted the community to the dangers of filling the air with fragments of lead paint. The students and their allies won the battle when a judge halted the sandblasting, a ruling that was eventually expanded by the State Supreme Court to include all of New York City's bridges. Another time El Puente underscored its community connections by actively opposing the construction of a 50-story incinerator planned for the nearby Brooklyn Navy Yards. (p. 57)

El Puente staff, professional educators, most of whom are community residents, are personally identified with students and their broader struggles for community development. This exemplifies the form of social/cultural capital that Portes (1998) identifies as *bounded solidarity*

> that leads wealthy members of church groups to anonymously endow church schools and hospitals, members of a suppressed nationality to voluntarily join life threatening military activities in its defense, and industrial proletarians to take part in protest marches or sympathy strikes in support of their fellows. Identification with one's own group, sect or community can be a powerful motivational force. (p. 5)

At El Puente the creation of social/cultural capital, and generalized reciprocity is nurtured through the close associations and common struggles between staff and students. As Coleman suggests, the proliferation of obligations and expectations arise from an organization that promotes closure, in part through its commitment to community development. Moreover, these ties facilitate authentic forms of caring and an activist orientation; all bases for achievement motivation and additive schooling. As community activists, the founders of El Puente already had a critical assessment of mainstream approaches to schooling and explicitly sought to counteract their detrimental effects and develop a learning community that more authentically reflected the community's funds of knowledge. Stanton-Salazar (1997) observes that ideological forces play an important role in projects of additive schooling:

> Ideological forces of a counter-hegemonic nature and personal dispositions motivate many institutional agents to struggle against the alienating properties of their institutional roles, and to develop actively explicit agendas geared toward the transmission of institutional support of minority children and youth. (p. 25)

In this sense, the staff at El Puente takes Stanton-Salazar's analysis of institutional agents a step further. Because they reflect who the students are culturally, they are also protective agents who provide the supportive context for students to develop resiliency (and the capacity to resist) through community embedded relations, and assist them in learning to decode the dominant system of power.

Community education initiatives such as El Puente Academy for Peace and Justice reflect what Moll and Ruiz (2002) refer to as projects of *educational sovereignty*:

> Educational sovereignty requires that communities create their own infrastructures for development, including mechanisms for the education of their children that capitalize on rather than devalue their cultural resources. . . . These forms of education must address Latino's self-interest or determination, while limiting the influence of the anglocentric whims of the white majority that have historically shaped their schooling. (p. 2)

As is evident from this definition, educational sovereignty is a necessary condition for a fully additive schooling project. At El Puente Academy, this takes place through a philosophy of community development and self-determination that sees the individual students' educational success (bicultural capital development) as directly tied to community development. This collective purpose for education strongly contrasts with the *out of the barrio* individualist ideology that Valenzuela

(1999) documents in *Subtractive Schooling*. According to Rivera and Pedraza (2000):

> The goal of community development as an educational objective is implicit in pedagogical approaches that consider the sociohistorical context of students, particularly their daily life experiences, to be of paramount importance. Centering pedagogical practices on issues of language, culture and identity is an attempt to integrate these two levels, individual and communal, through a program of activities and action that fosters individual Latino/a student development. (p. 224)

Ramirez and Dewar (1995) reveal that a convention of generalized reciprocity at El Puente is manifested by a strong value attached to "giving back" to this community.

> Notions of "remembering where people came from" and "giving back to the community" are central to the philosophy, structure and activities at El Puente Academy. El Puente's philosophy is broader than "schooling." It is rooted in an understanding of young people as community members. The purposes of education are not only to enhance the success of the individual young people, but also to help advance the young person so she or he can use his or her gifts or talents to benefit the community. (p. 17)

El Puente Academy for Peace and Justice provides protective institutional agents who generate *confianza*-based social/cultural capital. As a bicultural institution, it is well equipped to educate its students in the skills that are considered important for occupational success in the mainstream society, precisely because they are grounded in their own funds of knowledge, an essential feature of additive schooling. Additionally, the purpose of education at El Puente is critically and explicitly attached to larger projects of community development and liberation, linking learning to concepts and skills that students see as essential to their survival and success in the dominant society.

TOWARD A FRAMEWORK OF ADDITIVE SCHOOLING

This chapter has sought to integrate the literature on reproduction and resistance, provide an analysis of reproduction and resistance as it relates particularly to Latinos, and explore the culturally additive and academically transformative practices documented at El Puente Academy for Peace and Justice. Valenzuela's concept of *Subtractive*

Schooling provides a compelling definition of the educational problems experienced by Latino/a students in U.S. public schools. Alternatively, according to the literature El Puente Academy for Peace and Justice reflects important elements of additive schooling that inform the framework of additive schooling. In these ways El Puente seeks to disrupt the social and cultural reproductive processes associated with subtractive schooling through *confianza*-based (Moll & Greenberg, 1990), social/cultural capital rich (Bourdieu, 1984, 1985, 1987, 1990, 1992; Coleman, 1988, 1990; Putnam, 1993, 2000), authentic caring relationships (Noddings, 1984; Valenzuela, 1999). By centering its focus on issues of importance to the broader community and human rights, El Puente defines its curriculum in ways that are politically clear (Bartolome, 1994), critical, and that privilege student cultural identities (*sankofa*, "going back to the source"). This curriculum serves as a foundation for students learning to appropriate the codes of power of the dominant society while maintaining high self-regard based upon their funds of knowledge (Stanton-Salazar; 1997).

Emerging from this analysis of the reproduction/resistance literature and El Puente Academy is a confianza-based social/cultural capital framework for additive schooling. This framework informs both policy makers and practitioners interested in social transformation of the conceptual underpinnings of school and social structures that can effectively educate Latino/a students within a broader understanding of the reproductive processes inherent in traditional schooling. This framework of additive schooling reveals tremendous potential for changing the purposes, processes, and outcomes of traditional schooling in the United States. The work of El Puente Academy represents significant advancement in supporting the academic achievement of Latino/a students in a learning context that affirms their cultural, linguistic, and social resources and provides a hope-inspiring example of a project of additive schooling. Through its effort to redefine pedagogy, social organization, and educational purpose for students of color in ways that disrupt the reproductive tendencies of schooling, it strives to create a language and practice of possibility and advances the critical discourse on Latino/a education in the United States.

REFERENCES

Aronowitz, S., & Giroux, H. A. (1993). *Education still under siege* (2nd ed.). Westport, CT: Bergin & Garvey.

Bartolome, L. I. (1996). Beyond the methods fetish: Towards a humanizing pedagogy. In P. Leistyna, A. Woodrum, & S. A. Sherblom (Eds.), *Breaking free: The transformative power of critical pedagogy* (pp. 229–252). Cambridge, MA: Harvard Educational Review.

Bourdieu, P. (1973). Cultural reproduction and social reproduction. In R. Brown (Ed.), *Knowledge, education and social change* (pp. 71–112): London: Tavistock.

Bourdieu, P. (1984). *Distinction: A social critique of the judgment of taste.* Cambridge, MA: Harvard University Press.

Bourdieu, P. (1987). The forms of capital. In J. G. Richardson (Ed.), *Handbook of theory and research for sociology of education* (pp. 241–258). New York: Greenwood Press.

Bourdieu, P., & Passeron, J. C. (1977). *Reproduction in education, society and culture* (Richard Nice, Trans., vol. 5). London: Sage.

Bourdieu, P., & Wacquant, L. J. D. (1992). *An invitation to reflexive sociology.* Chicago: University of Chicago Press.

Coleman, J. (1988). Social capital in the creation of human capital. *American Journal of Sociology, 94* [Supplement], 95–120.

Coleman, J. S. (1990). *Foundations of social theory.* Cambridge, MA: Belknap Press.

Darder, A. (1991). *Culture and power in the classroom: A critical foundation for bicultural education.* New York: Bergin & Garvey.

Delgado-Gaitan, C., & Trueba, H. (1991). *Crossing cultural borders: Education for immigrant families in America.* New York: Falmer Press.

Delpit, L. (1995). *Other people's children: Cultural conflict in the classroom.* New York: New Press.

Gintis, H. & Bowles, H. (1976). *Schooling in capitalist America.* New York: Basic Books.

Giroux, H. (1983). *Theory and resistance in education: A pedagogy for the opposition.* New York: Bergin & Garvey.

Gould, S. J. (1996). *The mismeasure of man.* New York: W. W. Norton.

Graham, P. (1993). What America has expected from its schools over the past century. *American Journal of Education, 101*(February), 83–88.

Haney, W. (2000, August 19). *The Myth of the Texas miracle in education,* Education Policy Analysis Archives. Retrieved September 1, 2000, from http://olam.ed.asu.edu/epaa/v8n41/

Hernstein, R. J., & Murray, C. A. (1994). *The bell curve: Intelligence and class structure in American life.* New York: Free Press.

Jencks, C., & Phillips, M. (1998). *The black-white test score gap.* Washington, DC: Brookings Institution Press.

King, M. H. (1980). *Chain of change.* Boston: South End Press.

Kluger, R. (1975). *Simple justice.* New York: Vintage Books.

Kohl, H. (1994). *I won't learn from you.* New York: New Press.

Loury, G. (Ed.). (1977). *A dynamic theory of racial income difference: Women, minorities, and employment discrimination.* Lexington, MA: Lexington.

Lukas, A. (1986). *Common ground: A turbulent decade in the lives of three American families.* New York: Vintage Books.

MacLeod, J. (1995). *Ain't no makin' it: Aspirations and attainment in a low-income neighborhood.* Boulder, CO: Westview Press.

Maeroff, G. I. (1998). *Altered destinies: Making life better for schoolchildren in need.* New York: St. Martin's Press.

Marshall, G. (1998). *A dictionary of sociology.* Oxford, UK: Oxford University Press.

McNeil, L. M. (2000). *Contradictions of school reform: Educational costs of standardized testing.* New York: Routledge.

McNeil, L., & Valenzuela, A. (2000). *The harmful impact of the TAAS system of testing in Texas: Beneath the accountability thetoric.* Harvard Civil Rights Project.

Retrieved August 12, 2000, from http://www.law.harvard.edu/groups/civilrights/conferences/testing98/drafts/mcneil_valenzuela.html.

Mehan, H. (1996). *Constructing school success: The consequences of untracking low-achieving students.* Cambridge: Cambridge University Press.

Moen, P., Dempster-McClain, D., & Walker, H. A. (1999). *A nation divided: Diversity, inequality, and community in American society.* Ithaca, NY: Cornell University Press.

Moll, L. C. (1990). *Vygotsky and education: Instructional implications and applications of sociohistorical psychology.* New York: Cambridge University Press.

Moll, L. C., & Greenberg, J. B. (1990). Creating zones of possibilities: Combining social contexts for instruction. In L. C. Moll (Ed.), *Vygotsky and education: Instructional implications and applications of sociohistorical psychology* (pp. 319–348). New York: Cambridge University Press.

Moll, L. C., & Ruiz, R. (2002). The schooling of Latino students. In M. Suárez-Orozco & M. Páez (Eds.), *Latinos: Remaking America* (pp. 362–374). Berkeley, CA: University of California Press.

Montero-Sieburth, M., & Batt, M. C. (2001). An overview of the educational models used to explain the academic achievement of Latino students: Implications for research and policies into the new millennium. In M. Calderon & R. Slavin (Eds.), *Effective programs for Latino students* (pp. 331–368). Mahwah, NJ: Lawrence Erlbaum Associates.

Moreno, J. (Ed.). (1999). *The elusive quest for equality: 150 years of Chicano/Chicana education.* Cambridge, MA: Harvard Educational Review.

Natriello, G., & Pallas, A. M. (1998). *The development and impact of high-stakes testing.* Harvard Civil Rights Project. Retrieved September 1, 2000, from http://www.law.harvard.edu/civilrights/conferences/testing98/drafts/natriello99.html.

Nieto, S. (1999). *The light in their eyes.* New York: Teachers College Press.

Noddings, N. (1984). *Caring: A feminine approach to ethics and moral education.* Berkeley: University of California Press.

Noddings, N. (1992). *The challenge to care in schools: An alternative approach to education.* New York: Teachers College Press.

Noguera, P., & Akom, A. (2000, June 5) Disparities demystified: Behind the racial achievement gap. *The Nation* 29–31.

Ortner, S. (1998). Identities: The hidden life of class. *Journal of Anthropological Research,* 54(1), 1–17.

Phelan, P., Davidson, A. L., & Yu, H. C. (1993). Students' multiple worlds: Navigating the borders of family, peer and school cultures. In P. Phelan & A. L. Davidson (Eds.), *Renegotiating cultural diversity in American schools* (pp. 52–88). New York: Teachers College.

Portes, A. (1998). Social capital: Its origins and applications in modern sociology. *Annual Reviews in Sociology, 22,* 1–24.

Putnam, R. D. (1993). The prosperous community: Social capital and public life. *American Prospect, 13,* 35–42.

Putnam, R. D. (1995). Bowling alone: America's declining social capital. *J. Democracy 6,* 65–78.

Putnam, R. D. (2000). *Bowling alone: The collapse and revival of American community.* New York: Simon & Schuster.

Ramirez, S., & Dewar, T. (1995). *El Puente Academy for Peace and Justice: A case study for building social capital.* Minneapolis: Rainbow Research.

Ramos-Zayas, A. Y. (1998). Nationalist ideologies, neighborhood-based activism, and educational spaces in Puerto Rican Chicago. *Harvard Educational Review, 68,* 164–192.

Ramos-Zayas, A. Y. (2000, October). *Los de aqui y los de alla: Cultural "authenticity," class identities and constructions of Puerto Rican nationalism in the U.S.* Paper presented at a meeting of the Puerto Rican Studies Association, Amherst, MA.

Rivera, M., & Pedraza, P. (2000). The spirit of transformation: An education reform movement in a New York City Latino/a community. In S. Nieto (Ed.), *Puerto Rican students in U.S. Schools* (pp. 223–243). Mahwah, NJ: Lawrence Erlbaum Associates.

Robinson, S. P. (1996). *The conditions necessary for urban students to achieve at high levels.* Washington, DC: U.S. Department of Education, Office of Educational Research and Improvement.

Rose, M. (1996). *Possible lives: The promise of public education in America.* New York: Penguin Books.

San Miguel, J. G. (1999). The schooling of Mexicanos in the Southwest, 1848–1891. In J. F. Moreno (Ed.), *The elusive quest for equality: 150 years of Chicano/a education* (pp. 31–51). Cambridge, MA: Harvard Educational Review.

Schneider, J. A. (1998, December). *Social capital and welfare reform: Examples from Pennsylvania and Wisconsin.* Paper presented at the annual meeting of the American Anthropological Association, Philadelphia.

Stack, C. B., & Lopez, L. (1999, October). *Social capital at the crossroads.* Paper presented at the Ford Foundation Conference on Social Capital and Poor Communities: Building and Using Social Capital to Combat Poverty, New York.

Stanton-Salazar, R. D. (1997). A social capital framework for understanding the socialization of racial minority children and youths. *Harvard Educational Review, 67,* 1–40.

Tyack, D. B., & Cuban, L. (1995). *Tinkering toward utopia: A century of public school reform.* Cambridge, MA: Harvard University Press.

Valenzuela, A. (1999). *Subtractive schooling: U.S.–Mexican youth and the politics of caring.* Albany: State University of New York Press.

Valenzuela, A. (2005). *Leaving children behind: Why Texas-style accountability fails Latino youth.* Albany: State University of New York Press.

Willis, P. (1977). *Learning to labour: How working class kids get working class jobs.* New York: Columbia University Press.

PART V

Actualizing the Future

15

Latino/a Families' Epistemology

Nitza M. Hidalgo
Westfield State College

Oye, Researcher
Before you go poking around the
barrio with your yellow pad
of preconceived notions
develop
an understanding
of my Mexicano
childhood fears:
El Cuco or La Llorona don't just disappear
like tooth fairies.

Before you quantitate and qualitate
my mestizo, Chicano, Mexicano, Hispanic, Latino,
lifestyle
through your narrow lens of Taco Bell lunch breaks or chic collection of
Frida Kahlo art
remember that you will
never see the:
sores on my feet after the long Bataan death march
blisters on my hands from picking chile verde in the hot New Mexican sun,
self-esteem wounds from swatting me for speaking Spanish in school,
or CONFIDENCE I have developed from coping with 200 years of your
ignorance.[1]

---

[1] Excerpt from Nicholás Retana (1996).

INTRODUCTION

The poem "Oye, Researcher" describes how Latino/as' lives, in this case Mexican Americans, have been misinterpreted by researchers using Eurocentric theoretical frameworks. Theoreticians have defined Latino/as' reality using an epistemology created out of the experience of Whites, which is believed to apply universally to all groups, as if such an epistemology wasn't based on lived experiences. Employing the Eurocentric lens, which usually comprises mainstream academic social science training, tends to distort or misinterpret Latino/a realities and perpetuate stereotypical misunderstandings of Latino/a lived experiences. These stereotypes are often misunderstood as "truths" and haunt Latino/a families, whereas Latino/a (also Black, Asian, and American Indian) forms of knowledge receive little legitimacy (Scheurich & Young, 1997). In combined quantitative/qualitative parenting style research, Arzubiaga, Ceja, and Artiles, (2000, p. 102) state: "imposing constructs generated through research conducted with White samples on minority groups limits the validity of the findings and questions the study's goals." In qualitative research with Latino/a families, researchers have to refocus the theoretical lens used to understand Latino/a families' lives, hopes, and dreams. The work of researchers, as Delgado-Gaitan states: "Begins in learning how Latino/as perceive their cultural, historical, political, and social experiences which receives little attention in the sphere of social science, social policy, and education" (1996, p. 31).

In recent years, Latino/a researchers have questioned the philosophy, methods, and purposes of qualitative research in relation to Latino/a communities. Rejecting a mainstream academic knowledge formation, Delgado Bernal (1998) promotes a Chicana epistemology that locates Chicanas at the center of a theoretical framework that includes four types of "cultural intuition," aspects of Chicana researchers' personal, professional, collective, and historical experiences, that informs the research process. In Arzubiaga, Ceja, and Artiles's (2000, p. 100) work, an ecocultural framework grounded in families' "routines, beliefs, resources, and constraints" contextualizes Latino/a parenting style away from deficit conclusions about authoritarian approaches. Villenas's (1996) work focuses on the multiple identities of the researcher vis-à-vis her informants and the academic research community; she questions her role in the marginalization of Latino/a communities as well as her own position as "other" within the academic arena. Also concerned with the role of the researcher, Delgado-Gaitan (1995) questions the researchers' assumptions about major concepts being studied, in her case, the concepts of parental involvement and leadership. Whereas Delgado-Gaitan and Trueba (1991), and Pizarro (1999) promote the ideas that the purposes of research should be community improvement and social justice, respectively.

In a previous work (Hidalgo, 1999), I explored the elements of a qualitative research paradigm geared to the study of Latino/a families (see Figure 15.1). The framework developed a preliminary formulation of its philosophical underpinning, an exploration of the purposes of the research, an inquiry of numerous elements of contextualization, and an examination of the role of the researcher. I created this

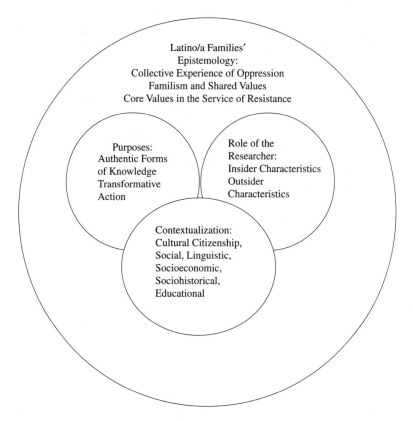

FIG. 15.1.   Toward a definition of a Latino/a family research paradigm.

framework as a result of conducting qualitative research with Puerto Rican families in Boston, and from my study of the literature in the fields of qualitative research and Latino/a studies. The framework requires the interrogation of the researcher's conceptual lens throughout the research. When the elements of the framework guide the research process, then the racial, ethnic, gendered, and class perspectives or biases (the very factors depicted in the poem, "Oye, Researcher" inherent in the research shift toward how the participants of the research understand their lived experiences. I take the position that the more one knows about the context of Latino/as lived experiences, the better one may understand their processes of adaptation and change. Latino/a knowledge creation is, in part, a process of accommodation, resistance, and change in response to the cultural and structural forces that shape the lived experiences of individuals and the collective groups. According to Hill Collins (1991), an epistemology of subordinate groups should answer three questions: "How such an epistemology enriches our understanding of how [Latino/as] create knowledge that fosters resistance? What is the process of validation of epistemology within the community? and, Does the epistemology capture or account for the contradictions within a [Latino/a] standpoint?" (p. 207). In this chapter, I examine some of the underlying standards to be utilized in the development of a Latino/a epistemology in the study of Latino/a families in the United States. Then I present a case study of a Puerto Rican family that utilizes the standards inherent in the epistemology.

The underlying standards within a Latino/a epistemology[2] are the collective experience of oppression within the U.S. racial classification system, the primacy of the family, shared cultural values, and resistance to subjugation in which Latino/a families reaffirm their culture and lay

---

[2]This paper relies on the work of feminists of color, specifically, African American, Chicana, and Puerto Rican authors who have delineated the theoretical and cultural issues that concern Black and Latino/a communities from the concerns of White feminists. Theorists such as Hill Collins (1991) and Mullings (1997) provide Afrocentric perspectives of family and community. While writers like Zambrana (1982, 1995), Baca Zinn (1995), Anzaldúa (1987), Rodríguez, Sánchez-Korrol, & Alders, (1980), and Sánchez-Korrol (1980) document the important role of women and families in the creation of resistance strategies, and they analyze the role of ethnicity, race, gender, class, and sexuality in Latino/a's lives. Furthermore, this paper is based on the literature, experiences, and research on Mexican American and Puerto Rican groups. Although there may be some similarities with some groups, such as Dominicans and Panamanians, whose countries have undergone U.S. domination and oppression, the conditions described herein may not apply to other Latino/a groups in the United States.

claim to their unique knowledge base. In this chapter, the standards are evidenced by the case study of a Puerto Rican family, and by the work of qualitative researchers who employ the standards in their work with Latino/a families.

COLLECTIVE EXPERIENCE: OPPRESSION

"I speak two languages broken into each other but my heart speaks the language of people born in oppression."[3]

Latino/as have been historically identified as a racialized ethnic group—Hispanic, nonwhite (Marable, 2000). The Hispanic classification was originally designated in 1971, under the federal Office of Management and Budget's Statistical Directive 15, as an ethnic label, but its use in popular culture has been racialized to depict a nonwhite category (Oquendo, 1998). Latino/as tend to identify using ethnic labels, not the racial categories of Black or White (Torres, 1995). In a national study of Latino/a political opinion, de la Garza, DiSipio, Chris García, García, & Falcón (1992) found that the most common identification was group specific (i.e., Mexican American) and the second most preferred term was a broad categorization (such as Hispanic or Latino). U.S.-born Latino/as were most likely to use the broad labels, such as Latino, to identify (de la Garza et al., 1992).

Latino/as have a unique interpretation of race that stems from the historic racial intermixture that comprises the Latino/a population. Massey, Zambrana, and Bell (1995) state that Latino/as view race as a "continuum" (p. 195). For Latino/as, who may have various shades of skin color within their own families, the perception of race is fluid and may be influenced by socioeconomic standing, a common phenomena in Latin America. Latino/as' foundational knowledge of race contrasts with the historical biracial perspective in the United States, where people are classified as either Black or White.

The racialized meaning of Latino/a ethnic groups has developed historically in part from their colonial relationships to the United States' power structure. Both Mexicans and Puerto Ricans have experienced colonized relationships with the United States. Shorris (1992) quotes a popular saying among Mexican Texans: "We didn't cross the border, the border crossed us" (p. 37). As Mexican lands were taken away as a

---

[3]Excerpt from Sandra María Esteves (1997).

result of American encroachment into the Southwest due to imperialist expansion though political (Manifest Destiny) or economic (gold rush and the institution of slavery) reasons, Mexican Americans were "gradually subjugated to minority status" (Acuña, 1988; Oquendo, 1998, p. 69; Shorris, 1992). Puerto Rico, by contrast, was appropriated as a result of the Spanish American War, culminating in an over 100-year heritage of U.S. domination and control of the island and its people. As immigrants/migrants, both Mexicans and Puerto Ricans have been subsequently "pulled in" or "pushed out" depending on the economic needs of this country, and of course, the conditions in the mother countries. The common colonial histories have contributed to Latino/as present racialized ethnicity and their low positioning within a social hierarchy (Córdova, 1998). Although Latino/as tend to identify as an ethnic group, they share the collective experience of racism (Torres, 1995).

Advocates of critical race theory believe the categories of race have been historically and socially constructed in the United States. Haney López (1998) defines a racial groups as "a group of people loosely bound by historically contingent, socially significant elements of their morphology and/or ancestry" (p. 9). The concept of race is created and maintained by societal institutions like families, schools, media, and government agencies. Different worth is assigned to each racial category, to particular racial features, such as skin color, and to certain ancestry to define the races (Haney López, 1998). Each group "has been racialized in its own individual way and according to the needs of the majority group at particular points in history" (Delgado & Stefancic, 2001).

Racial oppression is a relational process. The social meaning of each racial category is always in relation to another group, "each is understood by its opposition to another category" (Espinosa, 1998, p. 17). Within the U.S. context, whiteness is always at the center, whereas nonwhite people are marginalized as "other." Thus, the social construction of racial categories contains entrenched prejudicial practices, inequitable access to resources and rewards within society, and the situating of groups within a social hierarchy.

The social hierarchy positions groups of people in relation to "measures of standards of living" such as income levels, years of education, and household composition (Hurtado, 1989, p. 835). The group's position on the social hierarchy is related to the significance attached to the group's race. Social forces, such as poverty, impinge upon families to produce differences in definitions of family developed from lived experiences and from strategies created for survival. Two such forms of Latino/a family formation according to Baca Zinn (1995) are "extended kinship structures and informal support networks spread across multiple households" (p. 185). Thus, the construct of race (also ethnicity, gender and class) influence the cultural knowledge formation of Latino/as, especially as these constructs differ from the U.S. model. Qualitative research epistemology needs to consider how these categories interact and are relational to each other (Mullings, 1997).

The externally imposed classification of Latino/as as racialized ethnic group is a common element in a collective experience of oppression that shapes a Latino/a epistemology. The collective experience of oppression in the U.S. results from the historic subjugation and placement within the marginalized "other," whereby Latino/a values, histories, and knowledge have been excluded, whereas the Eurocentric experiences have been depicted as the primary form of knowledge. Qualitative researchers must deconstruct the role of race in the subjugation of Latino/as that is often hidden under the guise of objectivity and neutrality within conceptual frameworks. A Latino/a epistemology accounts for the collective experience of oppression as that experience negates Latino/a identity, history, and culture and results in an externally imposed definition of who we are, and at times, an internalization of a colonized mentality (Córdova, 1998). Latino/a families are not mere victims of racism but resist and adapt to their collective experience of oppression. Group survival requires resistance to oppressive forces via a return to core values and the formation of collective struggle to uplift community.

FAMILISM, SHARED VALUES, AND RESISTANCE

"Hoy por tí, mañana por mi."[4]

Ethnic values stem from common history, language, rituals, beliefs, and experiences that group members share; common values provide a framework in which shared meanings are tacitly understood (McGoldrick, Pearce, & Giordano, 1996). When worldviews are similar, value frameworks need not be explained. Ethnic values provide a safety net against conflicting values of the dominant society. When describing the values and behaviors of particular ethnic groups, it is important

---

[4]"Today for you, tomorrow for me." This is a common Puerto Rican saying (*refrán*).

to remember that there are as many variations and differences existing within a group as there are similarities. Intragroup differences result from various factors: the level of education, socioeconomic status, length of time in the United States, area of residence (or residence within an ethnic enclave), the generational position of individuals, and the amount of intermarriage to other ethnic groups. For Latino/as in the United States, additional factors may influence intragroup differences, such as: Spanish or English dominance, where educated (either the homeland or United States), where the formative years were spent, immigration/migration patterns, and intensity of their connection to the homeland. Thus, the core values of a group will undergo some modification within the U.S. context.

The literature on Mexican American and Puerto Rican cultures reveals a number of values that are practiced in various forms. These core values have been preserved and maintained in some form despite the transition to the United States. In a study of the effects of acculturation on Latino/as' concept of familism (see explanation below), Sabogal, Marín, Otero-Sabogal, VanOss, & Pérez-Stable (1987) found that some dimensions of the Latino/a core values were being maintained even by highly acculturated Mexican, Cuban, and Central American Latino/as. The close communication, the connections to the homeland, the existence of multigenerational, extended family, and the back and forth movement of people are all mechanisms that facilitate the maintenance of cultural values. These mechanisms interact with educational levels, language dominance, and time spent in the United States to produce significant intragroup diversity in the extent to which the values are adhered to in their pure forms.

Latino/as organize themselves around the primacy of the family in its various forms. Family unity depends on the concept of familism that is defined as "strong emotional and value commitments to family life" (Vega, 1995, p. 7). Familism is further defined by Sabogal et al. (1987) as "a strong identification and attachment of individuals with their families (nuclear and extended), and strong feelings of loyalty, reciprocity and solidarity among members of the same family" (p. 398). Family members tend to be close and to rely on relationships beyond the nuclear family context. The nuclear family may be embedded within an extended family, with flexible boundaries existing whereby numerous family members, especially females, perform many parental functions (Falicov, 1996).

Within low-income Latino/a families, the preference for familism may contain functional elements derived from their socioeconomic conditions (Vega, 1995). Andrade (1982) comments on how oppressive structural conditions can have an adverse effect on Latino/a families. She states that the "subordinate socioeconomic position, the migration experience, pervasive racism, adjustments to a highly industrialized and urban milieu," all impact heavily on the structure of Latino/a families, endangering their function as a social support system (p. 102). Families organize in response to economic opportunities that are available to them. Baca Zinn (1995) states that the diverse family forms are not inherent characteristics based on cultural differences between groups but an outcome of social forces, such as racial and socioeconomic class hierarchies.

Reciprocity and Dignity

The accompanying values of reciprocity and *dignidad* (dignity) function within the Latino/a family to maintain interpersonal relationships. Reciprocity, which refers to the genuine expression of generosity toward others, stems from a concern about closeness and caring for others, and is expected among family members and neighbors (García-Preto, 1996; Lauria, 1972). The highly valued norm of reciprocity is part of interpersonal relationships in which one is expected to reciprocate kindness. Reciprocity is taught by the example of parents and by oral expressions and sayings that are repeated during the childhood years. A good deed toward another, whatever form it takes, satisfies the norm of reciprocity, and need not be in material form, nor directed toward the same person who was kind to you.

The inner quality that defines a good person and provides a sense of personal integrity is individual dignity. Inner self-worth comes from doing what is expected, especially with regard to family obligations. For Latino/as, being poor does not diminish one's dignity (*dignidad*) (Falicov, 1996). "In Puerto Rican society, poverty is imbued with the cultural values of '*dignidad*'" (Benmayor, Torruellas, & Juarbe, 1997, p. 60). In an otherwise sensitive portrayal of the struggles of a Mexican American immigrant family to help their children academically, Carger (1996) missed subtle cultural values operating when describing the father's efforts to provide for his family. The obligation and capacity to provide for his family is a Latino's source of dignity.

An understanding of the concept of familism and its corresponding values moves qualitative researchers away from the individualistic orientation prevalent within American culture. Research philosophically grounded in the concept of familism deepens understanding of how

Latino/a norms function within families. The value of familism was present in Harry's (1992) work as Puerto Rican "parents spoke of their children's strengths and weaknesses in terms of family characteristics" (p. 32). Harry found that Puerto Ricans shared a collective identity in which the achievements or conditions ascribed to one member, such as a child, reflected back to the family as a whole. The parents traced the child's characteristics to particular family members, as traits being taken from adult members. Their sense of family identification was holistic in nature and not individualized.

Employing a cultural discontinuities framework, Ortíz Colón (1985), studied the expectations of White teachers and Puerto Rican mothers of preschool-aged children. He found subtle cultural differences in the importance placed on particular behaviors of children. Ortíz Colón found White teachers ranked behaviors based on independence and verbal assertiveness as more important, whereas mothers placed more importance on obedience and mindfulness of rules. Ortíz Colón concluded, "Cultural and socio-economic differences in ideologies about how best to socialize the child, then, are factors that influence the discontinuities between mothers and teachers" (1985, p. 111). The Puerto Rican mothers, operating from their cultural norms, believed in socializing their children within an interdependent, rather than independent framework.

Using Ogbu's theory of immigrant and caste minority, Suárez-Orozco (1997) found that Central American students' motivation for school success was driven by a sense of obligation to help family members or to repay parents for their sacrifices. The meaning of success shifted from an individual one to a family-oriented one. A Latino/a sense of identity comes from within a system of family relationships, and family obligations promote inner self-worth. Then, within that understanding, fulfilling one's responsibilities in school means fulfilling one's role in the family.

One measure of a Latino/a epistemology is the incorporation of core values into the research framework; the shared values developed from Latino/a histories, customs, languages, practices, and experiences are foundational in the creation of knowledge. The Latino/a preference for close family ties and interdependence among relations grounds a worldview that is adaptive to structural forces. Their shared values influence how they interpret experience and generate social behavior, in other words, how they express their cultural knowledge (Spradley, 1979). A Latino/a epistemology must account for how the group members' behavior reflects implicit cultural understandings. For Latino/as, the individual experience can only be understood when it is contextualized within the collective one.

Shared Values and Resistance

In the play entitled *Botánica* written by Dolores Prida (1991), the central character Milagros, anglicized to Millie, is told by Rubén, a childhood friend: "*... no hay que dejar que nos maten los búfalos ...,*"[5] to teach Millie a lesson about the connection between cultural values and identity. The lesson focused on how Native Americans experienced some loss of identity when the White man killed off all the buffalos, an essential part of their cultures. Rubén's point was Latino/as have to resist the cultural assaults[6] that strip identity and deny Latino/a cultural knowledge.

The lens of a Latino/a epistemology leads researchers to a new consciousness about how Latino/a knowledge is affirmed within the cultural and structural influences on Latino/as in the United States. Flores (1993) describes a series of interactive phases in the development of Puerto Rican identity within literature, where one faces a culture devoid of richness as it is depicted through the lens of dominant society (similar to the themes expressed in the poem, "Oye, Researcher"). To make meaning, one reaches back through time to one's ancestors, a movement that is spiritual and psychological, to the precolonized Taíno and African Caribbean peoples, in order to develop a better understanding of oneself. A new sense of "social consciousness" develops as one understands the influences of race, class, gender, and sexuality in a historical context. One develops a sense of political and national awareness along with the historical awareness of one's ancestors, that consciousness augments the foundation of Latino/a knowledge formation described in the previous section. Anzaldúa (1987) writes about the process of developing a mestiza consciousness where one has to take stock of the past and throw out damaging mythology about one's people, in order to remake oneself. Abalos (1998) details the formation of a "transformative cultural perspective" that requires critical reflection about

---

[5] "We can not allow them to kill our buffalos ... "

[6] "Cultural assaults are systematic attacks on the institutions and forms of social organizations that are fundamental to the maintenance and flourishing of the group's culture" (Baca Zinn & Thornton Dill, 1994, p. 7).

the oppressive elements within dominant *and* Latino/a cultures to rid ourselves of victim-oriented identities. Trueba (1999) also describes a similar process that Mexican Americans leaders have to undergo in forging a new Latino/a identity. The process entails understanding the overlapping oppressions faced by one's group, developing conscientization (in the Freirean sense) through education, claiming and reaffirming cultural values, and finally, forming political alliances across Latino/a groups for action and empowerment of one's communities.

Thus, Latino/a writers and social science theorists seem to revert to core values and collective forms of resistance to overcome the pressures of racial, political, and class oppressions. Latino/a writers underscore the significance of including the whole family in the struggle for social justice (Baca Zinn, 1995; Rodríguez et al., 1980; Sánchez-Korrol, 1980; Zambrana, 1982, 1995). The knowledge produced from such efforts pushes toward group empowerment. Resistance strategies include establishing networks of support among friends, neighbors and family relations "to derive a sense of security for individuals" (Hurtado, 1995, p. 409). (See Figure 15.1.)

Latino/a's strategies of resistance occur on collective levels, where local, regional, and national political organizations have surfaced; on community levels, where programs for community improvement abound; and on familial/individual levels, where families and their relations join together to overcome hardships.

On the national level, Latino/as have created organizations such as National Council of La Raza and ASPIRA to provide research, advocacy, political lobbying, and dissemination of information on and about the Latino/a condition in the United States. Latino/as have a long history of organizational development, especially labor unions, to support their communities (Acuña, 1988). Historically, many Latino/a political movements have "used the family to symbolize the need for unity, strength and struggle with adversity" (Bonilla-Santiago, 1992, p. 25). For example, the Chicano Movement of the 1970s held the concept of family unity as a core principle to promote individual and community improvement (López, 1977 as cited in Alarcón et al., 1993).

On the community level, we find movements and community activism to uplift Latino/a neighborhoods. These forms of resistance rely on core Latino/a values and forms of knowledge to fight for social justice. Often, community programs become an extension of family

(Rivera, 1999). Pizarro (1999) states that "Chicana/o epistemology [is] based on love, family, and the need for justice [and] suggests a new way of understanding of how our society is organized" (p. 72). El Barrio Popular Education Program in New York (Rivera, 1999) utilized Spanish language literacy (also critical pedagogy and popular research) to help low-income Puerto Rican and Dominican women gain critical awareness of oppressive social structures affecting their families and communities. In East Los Angeles, Castaneda (1997) documented the creation of a community-based high school that incorporated the cultural concept of *dignidad* (dignity) in carrying out its central mission with students and the surrounding community. The school provided a wide range of services for Latino/a youth and families, and had active community participation in governance, curriculum, and personnel. In Puerto Rico, Capella Noya (1997) described the "community-based, culturally responsive strategies" used in a educational program geared to assist low-income teenage mothers (p. 75). The program helped young women empower themselves with the support of a caring community of women, who collectively were learning to envision a more just social reality. Pardo (1990) documented the community activism of Mexican American mothers in East Los Angeles. She found that the women used their traditional responsibilities as nurturers of children and families to network with other women who were concerned with quality of life issues in their community. The mothers developed linkages between existing networks, like church groups, school parent councils, and neighborhood watch groups, to fight against the proposed waste incinerators and prisons being brought into their neighborhoods. According to Pardo, the mothering role was transformed into community caring where concern for family and community meshed into one motivating entity.

Research accounts show how Latino/a family forms may contain variable structures and diverse household compositions (Vega, 1995). Nevarez LaTorre (1997) found household-based networks that were maintained on the value of *confianza* (trust) between neighborhood residents. Hurtado (1989) found Mexican American mothers developed survival skills situated around family concerns "such as, sustaining informal networks of support" across multiple households, and "organizing for political and social change" (p. 852). Thus, Latino/a families build extended kinship structures and adapt their organization to fight racial and economic oppression (Baca Zinn, 1995).

According to Flores (1993), Latino/a resistance to oppressive conditions in the United States stems from awareness that one's culture was being threatened by economic and political forces. Latino/a resistance takes the form of self-affirmation, cultural maintenance, and actions toward group empowerment. The validation of resistance strategies is demonstrated by refusing to be silenced, by affirming native language, by breaking away from externally imposed definitions of Latino/a culture and identity, and by moving toward connection and collectivity (Córdova, 1998).

Realizing that no one-to-one correspondence exists between structural forces and individual response, the following case study illustrates how a young Puerto Rican family from the projects perceives and resists racism within an educational context. Paraphrasing Tate (1997), the use of individual narratives can bring light to discussions of oppressive structures and political forces in relation to the group. I am employing the experience and knowledge of a working class Puerto Rican extended family in Boston, specifically their resistence to racism, to illustrate elements of a Latino/a epistemology.

THE COLLAZO FAMILY: RESISTANCE, FAMILY, AND COMMUNITY[7]

Doña Concha Colon is Carmencita Collazo's maternal grandmother, and the matriarch of her family. She is a strong woman in her mid-40s, who migrated with her husband, from Rincón, Puerto Rico to New York when she was about 20 years old, and later moved to Boston. She and her husband, Don Pedro Juán, had four daughters. Doña Concha's involvement in public schools began when she enrolled her oldest daughter into Head Start. She became an assistant teacher at a Head Start program in the Mission Hill section of Boston, where they lived at the time. Her involvement in her daughters' early years of schooling led Doña Concha to become active in her community, her life's work.

---

[7]This case study is based on an ethnographic study that investigated how Puerto Rican families supported their children's school success during the primary grades. Qualitative, longitudinal data were collected on nine Puerto Rican families in Boston, Massachusetts between September 1991 and September 1994. The database consists of kindergarten, first, and second grade teacher interviews; yearly classroom observations; review of school records; parent (both mother and father in year one), grandparent, uncle/aunt, and child interviews in grades K, 1 and 2; field trip data; and field notes.

"Para mí, fíjate, mi vida ha sido en la comunidad, toda mi vida aquí en Boston, todo lo que yo hecho en la comunidad, este, ayudando a la gente, tú sabes."[8] When her family moved to the South End, she started working at a local community-based organization. She describes herself as a social activist, and her daily life attests to that reality. Her family struggle thus transcended personal boundaries and became the struggle for better conditions for her people.

Doña Concha believes in fostering in her children and grandchildren a sense of family unity and obligation to the Puerto Rican community. She describes how she develops Camernsita's (who is 5 years old) sense of community. *"Yo me la llevo a cuanta cosa hay de la comunidad, yo me la llevo a todos los eventos, me la he llevao pa' reuniones y todas políticas. Ella me ha ayudado hasta a repartir papeles . . . , cuando yo tengo que repartir papeles en la comunidad, lo primero que hago es, este, llevármela a ella y ella lo primero que me hace es, 'Mami, coge tu aquí que yo cojo acá,' y ayudándome a repartir papeles en la comunidad, y eso es lo que quiere hacer."*[9] Doña Concha inculcates the value of reciprocity to Carmensita as the child accompanies her to community events.

Describing a recent community organizing event, Doña Concha stated: *"Fue un éxito tremendo, el outreach que hicimos anoche aquí en Villa Victoria."* (I: *De qué era el outreach, doña Concha?*) *"El outreach era para dar información a la gente, anunciando todos los programas que hay aquí en la agencia. Tuvimos un cook-out, música, entretenimiento. Comió todo el mundo, estuvieron todos bien contentos. Estuvo bien tremendo, bien bueno, el outreach que hicimos anoche. Se necesita todo eso para que ellos vean que nosotros estamos haciendo algo por ellos y ellos mismos aprendan y se unan unos a los otros. Eso es lo que estamos haciendo ahora."*[10] Doña Concha's

---

[8] "For me, you see, my life has been in the community, all my life in Boston, what I've done in the community, um, helping people, you know."

[9] "I take her with me to everything happening in the community, I take her to all the events, I take her to meetings and political activities. She has even helped me distribute information . . . , when I distribute materials in the community, the first thing I do is, is take her and the first thing she does is, 'Mami, you take over here and I'll do there" and she helps me distribute the materials to the people, that's what she wants to do.

[10] "It was a great success, the outreach we had here last night in Villa Victoria." (I: What was the outreach for, Doña Concha?) "It was to provide information, to announce all the programs we provide in this agency. We had a cook-out, music, entertainment. Everyone ate, they were all very happy. It was tremendous, very good, the outreach we had last night. We needed that so they can see we are doing something for them, so they can learn, and become unified with each other."

community outreach includes a social component (food, music, and good times), important aspects in the development of *confianza*, a sense of confidence and trust between agency workers and the people of the community. The goal of the event expresses the value of reciprocity, helping the people of the community so they may learn to help others, and the value of community unity, so that people can come together for social improvement.

Milagros Collazo, Doña Concha's second oldest daughter, is Carmencita's mother. She is a high school graduate and works as a homemaker. Milagros has recurring back problems, which have limited her ability to work outside the home. She had previously worked as a data clerk at a Boston hospital, but was forced to quit after she injured her back in a car accident. She is in her mid-20s. Milagros is married to José Collazo who also completed high school and works at a Boston hospital in materials management. He is in his early 30s. José was born in Arecibo, Puerto Rico and came to the United States as an adolescent. Milagros and José have two daughters, Carmencita and her younger sister, Gloria, who is asthmatic. The family lives in the South End Housing Development. I followed Carmencita from the time she attended kindergarten through the second grade at the Jackson Elementary School in the South End.

Familism in Daily Life

Milagros sees her extended family daily. "I have three other sisters. They have their children. And my mother and father. And my husband and his part of the family, which is two sisters and his mother and father." (I: They're all in this area?) "Um. His family lives right in the next building. My mother lives on Tremont. And my sisters live, one in Dorchester, and the other one in Ruggle, and the other one in South Boston." Milagros also believes in maintaining close relations with her family. (I: Do you get together often?) "All the time. Every day. Every day. Like I told you we do things together. They either meet me here or I meet them at my mother's and we just go. We do a lot of things together." The desire for close relations within the family is also expressed by Doña Concha. (I: *Cuánto tiempo usted pasa con su familia?*) "*Con la familia, olvídate, todos los días, mija.*"[11] Doña Concha would like to return to

---

[11] (I: How much time do you spend with your family?) "With my family, forget about it, every day, mija."

Puerto Rico someday, but her desire to be close to her family does not allow it. *"Que por ahora mismito es como yo te digo, por mis nietos, yo no me he vuelto a mi patria, como uno dice, porque no puedo dejarlos y irme. No puedo dejarlos y irme. Ahora mismito yo estoy sola con mi esposo, porque nos podemos ir pa' donde quiera. Pero mi esposo y yo estamos dedicados a nuestros nietos y a nuestros hijos."*[12] The primacy of the family guides Doña Concha's life.

The Collazo family lives in the South End of Boston, a diverse neighborhood that has a distinctively Latino identity derived from the centrally located Villa Victoria, a housing development created from the struggles of Puerto Rican community groups who successfully defended their right to control their neighborhood's development against its proposed displacement by the Boston Development Authority (Uriarte, 1992). At the time of this study, Latino/as were 16% of the total population in the South End (Goetze & Johnson, 1993). Latino/as in the South End earned an average of $8,364 (Uriarte, Osterman, & Meléndez, 1992).

The reliance on extended family relationships lessens the impact of economic forces on low-income families. The value of familism can be seen in the Collazo family's daily lives where the mother work (Hill Collins, 1994) is divided between Milagros and Doña Concha. Carmensita is Doña Concha's first grandchild. When Milagros, at age 17, gave birth to Carmensita, Milagros, José, and Carmensita lived with Doña Concha for a year. Doña Concha described their first year together. *"Carmensita es mi primera nieta. Y se criaron en casa todos, porque Carmensita cuando nació, nació en casa. O sea, para que mi hija descansara, tú sabes, que los bebitos cuando nacen, ay Dios mío, yo me las amanecía en casa. Yo tenía que amanecerme. Entre las dos [Milagros and doña Concha] nos turneábamos, tú sabes."*[13]

The pressures of living in an economically depressed community necessitates the Collazo family dependence on the core value of familism, in order to accomplish the common goal of child development and

---

[12] "Right now, it's like I said, because of my grandchildren, I haven't returned to my homeland, like we say, because I can't leave them and go. Right now I' m alone with my husband, because we can go anywhere. But my husband and I are dedicated to our grandchildren and to our children.

[13] "Carmensita is my first granddaughter. And they were raised in my home, all of them, because when Carmensita was born, she was born in my home. That is, so that my daughter could rest, you know, how it is with a newborn, oh my God, I had many sleepless nights. I had to stay up. Between [Milagros and me] we took turns, you know."

to ensure family survival. Milagros describes the value of familism. "I have a lot of family that do a lot for me. They're really good to me. But I think being that if someone did not have any family around and had three or four kids to take care of, that would be a rough situation." Describing the kinds of interdependence between herself and her family Milagros states: "My mother, Carmensita calls her mami also. All the time everyday . . . , my mother, and my kids. Because whenever something is missing in the house, there's mom. Like I need Pampers and I don't have any money. Or I need milk and there is no money. My mother is there for me. My mother will buy anything for Carmensita no matter what it costs or what. If she doesn't have it she' ll get it for her." Thus the family joins together to overcome economic hardships.

By contrast, Doña Concha, who also has very little financial resources, but has an extensive community network of people she relies on, describes how she and her family try to support Milagros. She situates the financial problems within the context of a unified, interdependent family. Describing Milagros's situation, Doña Concha says *"Que se le ha hecho muy difícil. Que ha tenido que buscar la ayuda, tú sabes, y la ayuda mía, que yo he tenido que darle ayuda de todo financiera, de servicios, de enfermera, servicio de baby . . . , de todo, de todo, imagínate tú. Suerte que, suerte que mi hija ha tenido mucha suerte que tiene una familia bien unida, tú sabes, que todas, le ponemos, le damos, le ponemos un granito de arena o lo que sea, tú sabes, para ayudarle a ella. Pero sí, la situación es difícil en término de la economía aquí, especialmente aquí en Massachusetts y especialmente cuando uno no tiene nada, no tiene nada, tu sabes los recursos, aquí hay que pagar todo . . . y ella especialmente. Yo también, tú sabes, que ahora mismo yo tengo mi trabajo pero a mí no me da tampoco suficiente, yo no tengo Medicare, no tengo nada, tú sabes, que son . . . difícil."*[14]

Resistance Within the School Context

In kindergarten, Carmensita had a very gentle, loving teacher, who showered the children with compliments and hugs. But in the first

---

[14] "It has been difficult for [Milagros]. She has had to seek help, you know, my help, I have helped her financially, services, health care, child care, everything, imagine. Fortunately, fortunately, my daughter is fortunate to have a close family, you know, that all of us, we put, we give, we contribute a little something, or whatever, you know, to help her. But yes, the situation is economically difficult for her, especially here in Massachusetts, and especially when you don't have anything, don't have, you know, the resources, you have to pay for everything here . . . and her especially. Me too, you know, right now I have my work but I don't have enough, I don't have Medicare, I don't have anything, you know, things are . . . difficult."

grade Carmensita's new teacher was a screamer. Milagros describes the problem. "Yeah there was a problem, I guess it's just the tone of her voice that got Carmensita scared. I think it was her tone of voice and how she was saying things to her, you know, Carmensita's very sensitive, her feelings and if you just raise your voice at her, she starts you know, crying, she'll pout, and she was telling me that was what [the teacher] was doing, you know raising her voice." Doña Concha, who often took Carmensita to school and represented the family at school functions, also noticed the teacher's manner. *"Carmensita es bien buena en la escuela, tú sabes, que no hay ningún problema con ella. Pero lo único sí que, cualquier cosita que ella dice, 'Mami, no le digas a la maestra,' entonces, unas cuantas veces, dijo que la maestra le grita a los niños."*[15] The teacher's yelling frightened Carmensita and disturbed Milagros.

But Milagros perceived that there was more involved than the teacher's yelling. "I was concerned that it might have been a racial thing because Carmensita used to always tell me that um, the teacher would only say things to her and how she said it to her. Because she never called on her, she never does this, she never lets her do this, she never lets her do that. And there are only two Hispanic kids in that class. That's the reason I guess she felt kind of scared, and she couldn't say much because the teacher would never call her for anything and wouldn't do anything with her." "I thought she was a racist. I really did. I'm being very honest and frank with you. Uh, she had the tone of voice that you just disliked from the beginning." (I: What tone of voice is that?) "She's very out front with things and very open, I just didn't like her tone of voice that she spoke to me. I didn't like it at all. And I let it be known. I did confront her at once, well actually, I didn't confront her at first, I confronted the principal, and from there I confronted the teacher. . . . And I guess because I confronted the teacher, maybe she kind of like paid a little more attention [to Carmensita]."

A further rift in the parent/teacher relationship occurred when Milagros noticed Carmensita was having difficulty with mathematics. She went to speak with the teacher concerning her daughter's progress in mathematics. "Once, I told her that I think she needed more work in her Math. And she as well agreed to it. Yeh. 'Cause I know she's having problems with her Math and I wanted to address her to that so she would know to give her a little more, try to help her out more in the

---

[15] "Carmensita is real good in school, you know, there's no problem with her. But the only thing is, that, she says 'Mami, don't tell the teacher.' Then, a few times, she said, that the teacher screams at the children."

Math than in anything else." When Milagros asked the teacher to give her ideas on how to help her daughter in math, the teacher responded with generalities. Instead of providing the requested help, the teacher placed the blame for Carmensita's poor math work on the child, on her potential and performance.

Moreover, Milagros came away from the discussion believing that there was nothing she could do for her child at home. She left with the impression that the teacher perceived her as an incompetent parent, unable to participate constructively in the academic growth of her child. Milagros stated. "That's how everything, everything would always fall into a well, the parents don't take the time out to do, the parents this, the parents that. I didn't want to hear that. Just tell me what my daughter needs. She's in there almost eight hours a day. You know, and I know from my point, I'm with her the other time but I know only from home, I don't know what goes on in school unless she tells me or unless Carmensita tells me. She's in there eight hours a day and I feel, her responsibility as a teacher should be, that she should tell me what Carmensita needs. What she needs help in, what I can do to help her. Don't tell me about what, you know, what you think parents don't know. I don't want to hear that. . . . Maybe she didn't think that I knew how to be a parent. I try to do the best I can for them. And if that's not enough, I don't know what else to do." The teacher's behavior of ignoring Carmensita, screaming at her, and not being responsive to Milagros's request for math help were interpreted by Milagros, a second generation, U. S.-born Puerto Rican, as being racially motivated. The teacher's treatment of both Carmensita and Milagros was a cultural assault, an affront on Milagros' sense of dignity, which in part is derived from her role as a good mother to her children.

Milagros's response was immediate; she enlisted her mother's and the principal's help to resolve the problem. Together, Milagros and Doña Concha complained to the principal, which resulted in an observation of the teacher in her classroom by the assistant principal.

Doña Concha described the resolution in the following way. "Le llegó la queja a Ms. Willis [the assistant principal]." (I: Ustedes fueron?) "Sí, sí, sí, nosotros rapidito fuimos. Sí, nosotros mismos, le dimos la queja, porque nosotros, como yo digo, estamos interesados porque, cuál es el uso que un niño se fustre porque la maestra, o qué es lo que está pasando mal con la maestra, porque depende también de la maestra. Ok, porque si una maestra no se lleva con el niño, ahí también, tú sabes. Ahí va la, la educación de los niños, que ahí se fustran los niños. Entonces, nosotros eso estamos pendiente de que, qué *es lo que está pasando en la escuela o lo que sea, tú sabes. Inmediatamente la observamos y todo . . . no sé, si fue que ella vio que la estaban observando que no hizo nada, tú me entiendes, que se portó bien con los nenes. La cosa fue que todo bien. . . . Milagros estaba también ahí cuando Ms. Willis [the assistant principal], ellos estaban observándola. Milagros se quedó en la escuela ese día, para también observar, ok." (I: O sea que, Migdalia estuvo dentro del salón?)* "*No del salon. Se escondío acá en el hall.*"[16]

Both Milagros and Doña Concha felt the teacher changed her behavior once they brought in the school administrator. They felt the assistant principal's classroom observation and Milagros's presence in the school signaled to the teacher the gravity of their concerns. They acted collectively for the benefit of the child. Furthermore, both mother and grandmother monitored the situation in the classroom. Milagros spent the day at the school and Doña Concha keeps an eye out for future problems when she takes her to school every day. "*Si yo veo que hay algo raro, que a mí no me gusta, que yo observo algo que no me gusta, inmediatamente doy queja, lo que sea. Inmediatamente me voy pa' l principal, 'Mira esto está pasando, esto no se puede dejar así.' Tú sabes.*"[17]

Hopes for Carmensita's Future

Doña Concha's role as a mother who raised four children in a low-income neighborhood, and her experience in a unified family is projected outward toward the Latino/a community in the South End, into community caring. Her hopes for Carmencita, who spends a lot of time with her, who often sleeps over at her grandmother's home, where they do schoolwork, hand out flyers for community activities, sing, go

---

[16]"The complaint reached Ms. Willis [assistant principal]." (I: You went?) "Yes, yes, yes, we went right away, yes, we went, we complained, because we, like I say, we' re interested because, what's the use of having a child frustrated, or that the child is having a bad time with the teacher, because a lot depends on the teacher, OK, because if a teacher doesn't get along with a child, there too, you know. There goes the children's education, the children are frustrated. Then we are monitoring what is, what is happening in the school, or whatever, you know. Immediately, we observed her [the teacher] and . . . I don't know, if when she found herself being observed that she didn't do anything, you understand, that she treated the children well. So everything was fine. Milagros was there with Ms. Willis, they were observing her. Milagros was in the school all day, to watch the teacher." (I: You mean Milagros was in the classroom?) "Not inside. She stayed in the hall."

[17]"If I see something strange going on, that I don't like, if I observe something I don't like, immediately I complain, whatever it is. I go to the principal, 'Look this is happening. That can't go on.' You know."

shopping, and dance together, are tied to her life's work. Doña Concha asserts that Carmencita would like to become a social activist like herself someday, and that she encourages her to do her best in school so that she may better serve others in the future. *"Y eso es lo que ella, tú sabes, siempre hemos hablado. Ella me dice: 'Mami, yo quiero ser como tú.' Yo le dije: 'Sí mamita, por eso es que yo te traigo a ti, pa que aprendas, to' lo que yo voy hacer. Así es que mira, esto es lo que yo hago, pero para eso también tienes que estudiar,' le dije yo. 'También que llevar una carrera. Ok? Oh sí, pero yo quiero que tú la termines la carrera, ok, para que tú veas, que tú vas a ser más que yo. Y ayude a la gente.' Me gustaría que ella hiciera lo que yo estoy haciendo. Ayudar a la gente, que es mi, mi misión."*[18]

IMPLICATIONS FOR EDUCATORS

Educators may derive from research based on Latino/a epistemology an understanding of core values, such as familism, reciprocity, and dignity. There are numerous levels in which a Latino/a epistemology can inform educational practice. At the classroom level, teachers can use an awareness the importance of familism to motivate Latino/a children for family's expectations. So children can fulfill their roles as individuals within a network of relationships in their families and communities. In the area of parent participation in children's education, an element of all parent/teacher relationships, is the establishment of personal connections based on trust (*confianza*). In addition, teachers can accommodate their parental involvement expectations to be inclusive of grandparents and other relatives, and perhaps derive an understanding of how close family relationships differ from the White model. At the broader, community level, educators may incorporate community participation in school settings. And knowledge of the structural pressures that Latino/a face in an economically poor community may explain some of the strategies parents create to raise their children, such as Latino/a parents' protection of children.

---

[18] "We always talk about that. [Carmensita] tells me, 'Mami, I want to be like you.' I tell her, 'Yes, Mami, that's why I bring you with me, so you will learn all that I do. So that is, look, that's what I do, but you also have to study.' I tell her. 'Also have a career. OK? Oh yes, I want you to finish your schooling to have a career, OK, so you will see that you can be more than I am. And help the people.' I would like for her to do what I am doing. To help the people, that is my, my mission."

IMPLICATIONS FOR RESEARCHERS

What are some ramifications of enlisting a Latino/a epistemology for Latino/a researchers, for researchers of color, for White researchers, in the study of Latino/a families? Latino/a researchers must learn to be bicultural in their social lives, and once trained in traditional social science theory and methods, they must undergo a process of biculturalization in their professional lives also (Scheurich & Young, 1997). Whereas Latino/a researchers become proficient in White epistemology, developing theoretical frameworks molded from Latino/a cultural, historical, political, and social experiences is an acquired standpoint, one that has to be consciously reconstructed (Delgado-Gaitan, 1995; Villenas, 1996). Latino/a researchers may have different starting assumptions that may find validation within an epistemology grounded in the values and historical experiences of Latino/as (Andersen, 1993).

Researchers of color employing a Latino/a family epistemology may find commonalities in the experiences of different ethnic/racial groups. A Latino/a framework can provide a vision of the broader range of human experiences, of similarities and differences, for all qualitative researchers.

The ramifications of enlisting a Latino/a epistemology for White researchers is to move researchers away from the employing Eurocentric standards toward a Latino/a-based model. While some may find decentering from a Eurocentric perspective threatening, the benefits of biculturalism may outweigh the risks. The resultant grounded theory may yield less misinterpretations and distortions, more authentic information, which are, in essence, the desired goals in qualitative research.

By applying a knowledge base derived from Latino/a symbolic culture and a critical theoretical approach that contextualizes knowledge creation within racial, ethnic, class, and gendered standpoints, qualitative researchers may have a better possibility of understanding Latino/as' constructed meanings. Overall, Latino/as' knowledge will counter and demystify long held stereotypes and may lead to deeper understandings about the experiences of Latino/a families in the United States. A Latino/a family epistemology begins with the critical question of whose knowledge is central in the conceptualization and analysis of qualitative research studies (Delgado Bernal, 1998). The broad objective of this paper has been to advocate for the movement of qualitative research away from theoretical frameworks that present one standard as if that standard were divorced from the racial, ethnic, gendered, and class conditions that gave rise to it.

CONCLUSIONS

Latino/a families in the United States share core values and common experiences of oppression and resistance. Their ways of thinking about the world, their construction of meaning, their formation of knowledge, are affected by the cultural values and structural elements of their experiences. The epistemological standards depicted here include a consciousness of shared cultural values that are sources of strength and identity against the multiple oppressions impacting families. A Latino/a epistemology enriches the qualitative study of Latino/as families by changing qualitative research's underlying orientation to one centered on Latino/a knowledge. The complex understanding of the common experiences of oppression situates ethnicity, race, class, gender, and sexuality as interactive and relational constructs to help researchers analyze the conditions under which Latino/a families make meaning of their lives (Mullings, 1997). The epistemology also promotes research awareness of the processes of adaptation and resistance in the study of Latino/a families. The standards of collective experiences of racial oppression, familism, shared cultural values, and collective forms of resistance comprise the nature of knowledge for Latino/a families.

The validation of this epistemology within the Latino/a community can be documented as families change and adapt to the multiple pressures they face. Validation may be found in the past and present development of educational and social programs that incorporate into their practice core Latino/a values and forms of resistance. Qualitative research projects that confirm the difficult conditions and choices within which many Latino/a families live, how adaptation to external forces is a strength of Latino/a families, and understand how Latino/a families perceive the adaptive strategies they employ within particular contexts, will validate further the components of a Latino/a family epistemology.

There are many areas that remain unexplored in this chapter that future qualitative research incorporating the standards of a Latino/a family epistemology must address. Some of the issues include: value transformations, gender relations, immigration processes, language maintenance, and negative forms of resistance. Within the shared value of familism, how does an epistemology account for the effects of acculturation in relation to the transformation of core values? How does an epistemology explain the contradictions found within patriarchical forms of Latino/a family organization? Can a Latino/a family epistemology explain the contradictions found in newly arrived immigrants' perceptions of oppressive structures compared to Latino/as who have experienced oppression for generations? If Spanish language is at the heart of Latino/a culture and identity, does an epistemology aid understanding of an English-dominant generation's experiences? Can a Latino/a epistemology explain the contradictions found when resistance strategies are counterproductive to family and community uplift? These questions must be investigated in future elaborations of a /a family epistemology.

REFERENCES

Abalos, D. (1998). *La comunidad Latina in the United States*. Westport, CT: Praeger Publishers.

Acuña, R. (1988). *Occupied America*. New York, NY: HarperCollins.

Alarcón, N., Castro, R., Pérez, E., Pesquera, B., Sosa Riddell, A., & Zavella, P. (1993). *Chicana critical issues*. Berkeley, CA: Third Woman Press.

Andersen, M. (1993). Studying across difference: Race, class, and gender in qualitative research methods. In J. Stanfield II & R. Dennis (Eds.), *Race and ethnicity in research methods* (pp. 39–52). Newbury Park, CA: Sage Publications.

Andrade, S. (1982). Family roles of Hispanic women: Stereotypes, empirical findings, and implications for research. In R. Zambrana (Ed.), *Latina women in transition* (pp. 90–105). New York, NY: Hispanic Research Center, Fordham University.

Anzaldúa, G. (1987). *Borderlands, la frontera*. San Francisco, CA: Aunt Lute Books.

Arzubiaga, A., Ceja, M., & Artiles, A. (2000). Transcending deficit thinking about Latinos' parenting styles: Toward an ecocultural view of family life. In *Charting new terrains of Chicana(o)/Latina(o) Education* (pp. 93–106). Cresskill, NJ: Hampton Press, Inc.

Baca Zinn, M. (1995). Social science theorizing for Latino families. In R. Zambrana (Ed.), *Understanding Latino families* (pp. 177–189). Thousand Oaks, CA: Sage Publications.

Baca Zinn, M., & Eitzen, S. (1987). *Diversity in American families*. New York, NY: Harper & Row.

Baca Zinn, M., & Thornton Dill, B. (1994). Differences and domination. In M. Baca Zinn & B. Thornton Dill (Eds.), *Women of color in U.S. society* (pp. 3–12). Philadelphia, PA: Temple University Press.

Benmayor, R., Torruellas, R., & Juarbe, A. (1997). Claiming cultural citizenship in East Harlem: "Si esto puede ayudar a la comunidad mia . . . " In W. Flores & R. Benmayor (Eds.), *Latino cultural citizenship* (pp. 152–209). Boston, MA: Beacon Press.

Bonilla-Santiago, G. (1992). *Breaking ground and barriers: Hispanic women developing effective leadership*. San Diego, CA: Marin Publications.

Capella Noya, G. (1997). Proyecto aurora: Building a community of women. *Education and Urban Society, 30*(1), 75–89.

Carger, C. (1996). *Of borders and dreams*. New York, NY: Teachers College Press.

Castaneda, L. (1997). Alternative to failure: A community-based school program for Latino teens. *Education and Urban Society, 30*(1), 90–106.

Córdova, T. (1998). Power and knowledge: Colonialism in the academy. In C. Trujillo (Ed.), *Living Chicana theory* (pp. 17–45). Berkeley, CA: Third Women Press.

de la Garza, R., DiSipio, L., Chris García, F., García, J., & Falcón, A. (1992). *Latino voices: Mexican, Puerto Rican, and Cuban perspectives on American politics*. San Francisco, CA: Boulder Press.

Delgado Bernal, D. (1998). Using a Chicana epistemology in educational research. *Harvard Educational Review, 68*(4), 555–582.

Delgado-Gaitan, C. (1995). Researching change and changing the researcher. In G. Capella Noya, K. Geismar, & G. Nicoleau (Eds.), *Shifting histories: Transforming education for social change* (pp. 119–141). Cambridge, MA: Harvard Educational Review.

Delgado-Gaitan, C. (1996). *Protean literacy*. London: The Falmer Press.

Delgado-Gaitan, C., & Trueba H. (1991). *Crossing cultural borders*. London: Falmer Press.

Delgado, R., & Stefancic, J. (Eds.). (1998). *The Latino condition: A critical reader* (pp. 17–23). New York, NY: New York University Press.

Delgado, R., & Stefancic, J. (2001). *Critical race theory: An introduction*. New York, NY: New York University Press.

Espinosa, L. (1998). Latino identity and multi-identity: Community and culture. In Delgado, R. & J. Stefancic (Eds.), *The Latino condition: A critical reader* (pp. 17–23). New York, NY: New York University Press.

Esteves, S. (1997). A la mujer Borrinqueña. In H. Augenbraum & M. Fernández Olmos, *The Latino reader* (p. 384). Boston, MA: Houghton Mifflin Company.

Falicov, C. (1996). Mexican families. In M. McGoldrick, J. Pearce, & J. Giordano (Eds.), *Ethnicity and family therapy* (pp. 134–163). New York, NY: The Guilford Press.

Flores, J. (1993). *Divided borders, essays on Puerto Rican identity*. Houston, TX: Arte Público Press.

García-Preto, N. (1996). Puerto Rican families. In M. McGoldrick, J. Pearce, & J. Giordano (Eds.), *Ethnicity and family therapy* (pp. 164–186). New York, NY: The Guilford Press.

Goetze, R., & Johnson, M. (1993, January). *South End planning district*. Boston, MA: Boston Redevelopment Authority.

Haney López, I. (1998). The social construction of race. In Delgado, R. (Ed.), *Critical race theory: The cutting edge* (pp. 191–203). Philadelphia, PA: Temple University Press.

Harry, B. (1992). Making sense of disability: Low-income, Puerto Rican parents' theories of the problem. *Exceptional Children, 59*(1), 27–40.

Hidalgo, N. (1999). Toward a definition of a Latino family research paradigm. In L. Parker, D. Deyhle, & S. Villenas (Eds.), *Race is . . . race isn't: Critical race theory and qualitative studies in education* (pp. 101–124). Boulder, CO: Westview Press.

Hill Collins, P. (1991). *Black feminist thought*. New York, NY: Routledge.

Hill Collins, P. (1994). Shifting the center: Race, class, and feminist theorizing about motherhood. In E. Nakano Glenn, G. Chang, & L. Rennie Forcey (Eds.), *Mothering: Ideology, experience, and agency* (pp. 45–66). New York, NY: Routledge.

Hurtado, A. (1989). Relating to privilege: Seduction and reflection in the subordination of white women and women of color. *Signs: Journal of Women in Culture and Society, 41*(41), 833–855.

Hurtado, A. (1995). Variations, combinations, and evolutions: Latino families in the United States. In R. Zambrana (Ed.), *Understanding Latino families* (pp. 40–61). Thousand Oaks, CA: Sage Publications.

Lauria, A. (1972). Respeto, relajo and interpersonal relations in Puerto Rico. In F. Cordasco & E. Bucchioni (Eds.), *The Puerto Rican community and its children on the mainland* (pp. 36–48). Metuchen, NJ: The Scarecrow Press.

Marable, M. (2000, February 25). We need new and critical study of race and ethnicity. *Chronicle of Higher Education, 16*(25), B4–7.

Massey, D., Zambrana, R., & Bell, S. (1995). Contemporary issues in Latino families: Future directions for research, policy and practice. In R. Zambrana (Ed.), *Understanding Latino families* (pp. 190–225). Thousand Oaks, CA: Sage Publications.

McGoldrick, M., Pearce, J., & Giordano, J. (Eds.). (1996). (2nd ed.), *Ethnicity and family therapy.* New York, NY: The Guilford Press.

Montoya, M. (1995). Máscaras, trenzas, y greñas: Un/masking the self while un/braiding Latina stories and legal discourse. In R. Delgado (Ed.), *Critical race theory: The cutting edge* (pp. 529–539). Philadelphia, PA: Temple University Press.

Mullings, L. (1997). *On our own terms, race, class, and gender in the lives of African American women.* New York, NY: Routledge.

Nakano Glenn, E. (1987). Gender and the family. In B. Hess & M. Marx Ferrer (Eds.), *Analyzing gender: A handbook of social science research* (pp. 348–380). Newbury Park, CA: Sage Publications.

Nevarez La Torre, A. (1997). Influencing Latino Education: Church-based community programs. *Education and Urban Society, 30*(1), 58–74.

Oquendo, A. (1998). Re-imaging the Latino/a race. In R. Delgado & J. Stefancic (Eds.), *The Latino/a condition* (pp. 60–71). New York: New York University Press.

Ortíz-Colón, R. (1985). *Acculturation, ethnicity and education: A comparison of Anglo teachers' and Puerto Rican mothers' values regarding behaviors and skills for urban HEADSTART children.* Unpublished doctoral dissertation, Harvard University, Cambridge, MA.

Pardo, M. (1990). Mexican American women grassroots community activists: "Mothers of East Los Angeles." *Frontiers, 11*(1), 1–7.

Pizarro, M. (1999). "Adelante!": Toward social justice and empowerment in Chicana/o communities and Chicana/o studies. In L. Parker, D. Deyhle, & S. Villenas (Eds.), *Race is . . . race isn't: Critical race theory and qualitative studies in education* (pp. 53–82). Boulder, CO: Westview Press.

Prida, D. (1991). *Beautiful señoritas and other plays.* Houston, TX: Arte Público Press.

Retana, N. (1996). Oye, researcher. *Qualitative Studies in Education, 9*(3), 3.

Rivera, K. (1999). Popular research and social transformation: A community-based approach to critical pedagogy. *TESOL Quarterly, 33*(3), 485–500.

Rodríguez, C., Sánchez-Korrol, V., & Alers, J. (Eds.). (1980). *The Puerto Rican struggle: Essays on survival in the U.S.* Maplewood, NJ: Waterfront Press.

Sabogal, F., Marín, G., Otero-Sabogal, R., VanOss, B., & Pérez,-Stable, E. (1987). Hispanic familism: What changes and what doesn't? *Hispanic Journal of Behavioral Sciences, 9*(4), 397–412.

Sánchez-Korrol, V. (1980). Survival of Puerto Rican women in New York before WWII. In C. Rodríguez, V. Sánchez-Korrol, & J. Alers (Eds.), *The Puerto Rican struggle: Essays on survival in the U.S.* (pp. 47–57). Maplewood, NJ: Waterfront Press.

Scheurich, J., & Young, M. (1997). Coloring epistemologies: Are our research epistemologies racially biased? *Educational Researcher, 26*(4), 4–17.

Shorris, E. (1992). *Latinos: A biography of the people.* New York, NY: Avon Books.

Spradley, J. (1979). *The ethnographic interview.* New York, NY: Holt, Rinehart and Winston.

Suárez-Orozco, M. (1997). "Becoming somebody": Central American immigrants in U.S. inner-city schools. In M. Seller & L. Weis (Eds.), *Beyond Black and White, New faces and voices in U.S. schools* (pp. 115–130). New York, NY: State University of New York Press.

Tate, W. (1997). Critical race theory and education: History, theory, and implications. *Review of Research in Education, 22*, 195–247.

Torres, A. (1995). *Between the melting pot and mosaic, African Americans and Puerto Ricans in the New York political economy.* Philadelphia, PA: Temple University Press.

Trueba, H. (1999). *Latinos unidos: From cultural diversity to the politics of solidarity*. Lanham, MD: Rowman & Littlefield Publishers.

Uriarte, M. (1992). Contra viento y marea (against all odds): Latinos build community in Boston. In M. Uriarte, P. Osterman, & E. Meléndez (Eds.), *Latinos in Boston: Confronting poverty, building community* (pp. 1–34). Boston, MA: The Boston Foundation.

Uriarte, M., Osterman, P., & Meléndez, E. (Eds.). (1992). *Latinos in Boston: Confronting poverty, building community*. Boston, MA: The Boston Foundation.

Vega, W. (1995). The study of Latino families: A point of departure. In R. Zambrana (Ed.), *Understanding Latino families* (pp. 3–17). Thousand Oaks, CA: Sage Publications.

Villenas, S. (1996). The colonizer/colonized Chicana ethnographer: Identity, marginalization, and co-optation in the field. *Harvard Educational Review, 66*(4), 711–731.

Zambrana, R. (Ed.). (1982). *Latina Women in Transition*. New York, NY: Hispanic Research Center, Fordham University.

Zambrana, R. (Ed.). (1995). *Understanding Latino families*. Thousand Oaks, CA: Sage Publications.

16

Latino/a Education in the 21st Century

Raymond V. Padilla
University of Texas at San Antonio

The creation of a new agenda for Latino/a education in the 21st century is fundamentally a conceptual task. It involves both the clarification and resolution of historic paradoxes involving Latino/a education as experienced in the United States, and the creation of a new vision of Latino/a pedagogy that is premised on the belief that Latino/a students can be successful learners. This new vision is framed by four fundamental principles that are meant to guide the work of educators in the 21st century:

- Diverse sociocultural perspectives are to be honored, respected, and incorporated into new pedagogical models and practices.
- Latino/a education is understood in a sociopolitical and historical context that in the past often has been characterized by the struggle for opportunity and social justice.
- The active involvement of Latino/a communities is an essential element in effective education for Latino/a students.
- The public schools should function as stewards of freedom, advocates for social justice, and as the mentors of democracy.

Using these principles as a point of reference, this chapter calls for the reformulation and the reenvisioning of Latino/a pedagogy taking into account its historical and sociopolitical context. The chapter focuses on four crucial points: (1) the need to promote both multiculturalism and social unity in U.S. society—here the concepts of transculturalism and elliptic multiculturalism are introduced; (2) the need to clarify and expand, within the context of elliptic multiculturalism, core philosophical concepts in areas such as knowing, being, and learning that profoundly influence basic ideas about schooling, teaching, and learning; (3) the need to envision a pedagogy of engagement (POE) that is premised on student advocacy and the assumption that all students can learn; and (4) the need to redeploy research strategies, methods, and paradigms so that an important goal of academic research will be to promote positive social change and to improve institutional performance, especially by educational institutions. By placing these items on the table, the intent is to invite discussion from various perspectives about the shape of a new agenda for Latino/a education in the 21st century. So as a way of starting the conversation and stimulating further dialogue, each point is discussed in more detail in the sections that follow. Others are invited to contribute additional points and to think of ways in which the new agenda can be implemented.

UNITY AND DIVERSITY: A NEW *COYUNTURA*

It is reasonable to accept the idea that social unity is an important concern for any society. The question is: Can social unity be attained only through monoculturalism and monolingualism? Those who adhere to the "melting pot" view of the United States would appear to answer this question with a resounding "yes." According to this view, everyone should reject "foreign" cultural characteristics and quickly assimilate into the majority culture (Rodriguez, 1982). For the assimilationists, one culture fits all. There have been many voices raised against this monolithic view of U.S. culture (Banks, 2002; Banks & McGee Banks, 2001; Garcia, 2001; Ovando & Collier, 1998). The multiculturalists believe that pluralism is an inherent feature of U.S. society from its very founding to the present. For the multiculturists, *E Pluribus Unum* is not merely a slogan to be placed on the currency of the nation but a logo that aptly describes a basic feature of the nation in all its historic and contemporary diversity.

The critics of multiculturalism would argue that excessive attention to diversity has resulted—or at least threatens to result—in an ever greater fragmentation of the nation. They cannot see the "glue" that would unite the nation when an ever increasing number of identity groups persistently advocate for their own special interests and seemingly without regard for the common whole. Consequently, balkanization of the United States is seen as a major threat if multiculturalist perspectives are adopted. Is there no possible balance, then, between unity and diversity?

There certainly can be no balance between unity and diversity if they are seen as binary concepts with nothing to connect them. The lack of a *coyuntura* or nexus between unity and diversity is literally the missing link that has both abetted assimilationist thinking and generated a perplexing silence by multiculturalists on the potential dangers of social fragmentation (and how to avoid it). What is called for is better understanding of the *coyuntura* between unity and diversity.

Figure 16.1 shows a concept model of multicultural diversity with transcultural unity (MDTU). The *coyuntura* between diversity and unity is a transcultural foundation of ideas that is agreed to by all members

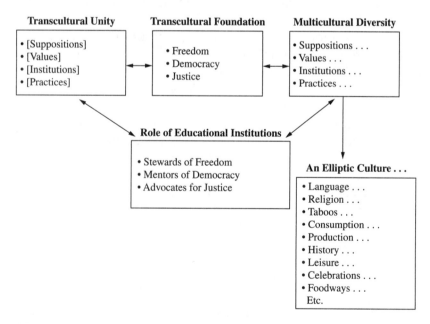

FIG. 16.1.   A concept model of multicultural diversity with transcultural unity (MDTU).

of society. The transcultural foundation includes the three pivotal ideas of freedom, democracy, and justice. These fundamental ideas are seen as transcultural because they encompass all of the various cultures existing in the society, yet they transcend the individual cultures singly and collectively. The transcultural foundation can thus be seen as a social compact agreed to by everyone as an essential part of civil society.

The existence of the transcultural foundation makes it possible to have both multicultural diversity and transcultural unity. The latter is expressed as the suppositions, values, institutions, and practices in society that directly result from the transcultural foundation and that promote its continued existence. The transcultural suppositions, values, institutions, and practices are shown in brackets to indicate that these transcultural expressions have enduring qualities that transcend any particular cultural group and that change only slowly as a result of cultural and social evolution. As such, transcultural unity represents stability and schools should be the engines that shape students into citizens who are cognizant of the transcultural common ground that binds the society. Specifically, the school curriculum and the extracurriculum are the indicated vehicles for inculcating in students awareness and appreciation of the transcultural foundation that is central to social unity.

Multicultural diversity, by contrast, expresses elliptic (. . .) culture. Elliptic suppositions, values, institutions, and practices can vary considerably from one cultural group to another so long as they are not in conflict with the transcultural foundation. Hence, under multiculturalism, suppositions, values, institutions, and practices are followed by ellipses in order to show that these cultural expressions are open ended and variable across the society. As such, multicultural diversity has the quality of experimentation, innovation, change, and exchange; it is dynamic and generative. In the school context, multicultural diversity implies a recognition, appreciation, and critical assessment of the elliptic cultural elements that make up the mosaic of society. The theories, principles, and practices developed to promote multicultural education during the twentieth century can be used as a starting point for integrating elliptic cultural elements into the school curriculum and the extracurriculum.

The MDTU model includes additional implications for educational institutions. The transcultural foundation, multicultural diversity, and transcultural unity can be maintained only if educational institutions are designed and operated as the guarantors of the social compact. In this role, educational institutions must function as the stewards of freedom, the mentors of democracy, and the advocates for justice. When functioning in this manner, educational institutions will always advocate for students and opt for their success.

The MDTU model can help to clarify difficult and troubling issues that went unresolved during the 20th century. For example, the assimilitionists properly argued for national unity but they incorrectly attributed the transcultural foundation exclusively to the Euro-Anglo cultural group. The bracketed expressions of transcultural unity were equated with Euro-Anglo elliptic cultural expressions, thus creating the hegemony of the Euro-Anglo cultural group over all the other groups. By improperly claiming to be the sole possessor of the transcultural foundation and transcultural unity, the hegemonic group could privilege its elliptic cultural expressions over the elliptic cultural expressions of all other groups. The MDTU shows that this hegemonic behavior is antithetical to both transcultural unity and multicultural diversity, as well as to civil society itself. The Civil Rights movement represents the most intense effort of the 20th century to dislodge cultural hegemony by one group and to give voice, vote, and expression to all cultural groups.

As another example, the MDTU model helps to explain why multiculturalists have done poorly in dealing with the issue of unity. Social unity can not be found in multicultural diversity itself. According to the model, social unity is a transcendent feature of multicultural diversity. In other words, multicultural diversity points to transcultural unity as something which exists beyond multicultural diversity itself. Transcultural unity is necessary if multicultural diversity is to exist in any coherent way. What makes multicultural diversity viable is its transcendent unity. By contrast, social unity that extinguishes multicultural diversity is a vacuous unity, a unity that extinguishes free cultural expression, hence the wisdom of *E Pluribus Unum*.

EXPLORING ELLIPTIC CULTURAL EXPRESSIONS

It is necessary to explore elliptic cultural expressions in order to provide viable alternatives for the cultural suppositions on which educational institutions are established and operated. In the past, the privileging of Euro-Anglo elliptic cultural suppositions often has resulted in educational institutions that operate on a deficit view of Latino/a students and in an inability of those institutions to properly deliver educational

services to diverse students (Romo & Falbo, 1996; Valencia, 1997; Valenzuela, 1999). Although there are many elliptic cultural suppositions that
could be analyzed and contrasted, the focus here will be limited to three,
namely the nature of knowing, being, and learning.

In Euro-Anglo elliptic culture, to know is to know is to know. To
know is to know positively and absolutely. By contrast, in Latino/a
elliptic culture there are two distinct ways of knowing, as expressed by
the Spanish verbs *saber* and *conocer*. A brief anecdote can illustrate the
differences between the two ways of knowing.

Suppose that a Spanish-speaking person is in a school and wants to
know about a student named Juan García. The person might go to a
Spanish-speaking Latino/a counselor and ask, "*¿Quien es Juan García?*"
(Who is Juan García?). The answer might come back: "*Se de él pero no
lo conozco.*" Now what are we to make of this response if we translate
it into English? Surely it would not be an accurate translation to say,
"I know him but I do not know him." What's the problem here? The
problem appears to be that in Spanish there are two quite different ways
of knowing which are distinguished by the words *saber* and *conocer*.
Saber is accurately translated into English by the verb "to know," but
what about conocer?

Conocer implies a more personal and interactive kind of knowing,
a situated knowing that depends on personal experience. To observe
someone or something is to know (in the sense of saber) about the person or thing, but it is not conocer. To know people or places interactively
involves conocer. Conocer implies a contextualization or mutuality of
knowing, a knowing that is achieved in a relationship that is reciprocal
between the knowing parties. Thus, conocer cannot be absolute knowing because it is premised on a relationship between the knower and
the known and the relationship cannot be one of objectivity, rather it
must be one of interconnectivity, interactivity, and perhaps even inter-
subjectivity. Conocer thus opens a new epistemological space that is
outside the elliptic Anglo epistemology of absolute, objectivist knowing. Conocer type knowing makes no claim to universality or objectivist
foundations. Consequently, universal (nomothetic) knowledge is outside the scope of conocer. Yet, it is interesting that conocer type knowing
may be used to validate saber type knowing, as in the expression "*Se
donde vive porque lo conozco.*" ("I know where he lives because I am
acquainted with [i.e., I know] him.")

The exclusive reliance by educational institutions on saber type
knowing has resulted in an elliptic culture of measurement that is

threatening to engulf all other elliptic cultures throughout the country and to overwhelm broader approaches to education. The elliptic culture of measurement is leading schools to distorted practices that predetermine the life chances of children on the basis of single-score high-stakes tests that only recognize saber type knowledge (McNeil & Valenzuela, 2000). The conocer type of knowledge, which in the context of schooling can be understood as resulting from a pedagogic relationship between the student and the teacher, the student and the parents, and the student and the community, is completely ignored by the culture of measurement. Instead, the culture of measurement can be seen as promoting a mechanistic type of teaching (usually to the test) that in the end is profoundly antidemocratic and animical to the transcultural foundation of civil society and of the Latino/a community in particular. Multiple measures in educational assessment (Valenzuela, 2002) that are based on both saber and conocer types of knowledge would be a powerful safeguard against the harmful effects of the elliptic culture of measurement and its penchant for high-stakes, single-score testing.

The bifurcated epistemological space of Latino/a elliptic culture must be taken into account in educating Latino/a students. All school knowledge can not be crammed into the limited span of saber type knowing. Conocer type knowledge should be a fundamental part of Latino/a pedagogy so that students can learn both nomothetic (saber) as well as relational (conocer) knowledge.

Latino/a and Euro-Anglo elliptic cultures also can be contrasted on their suppositions regarding the nature of being. For the Euro-Anglo culture there can be only one ontological state which is described by the verb "to be." In Latino/a elliptic culture ontology is bifurcated and the two distinct states of being are designated by the Spanish words *ser* and *estar*. Ser is correctly translated into English by the verb "to be." "To be" refers to absolute, continuous being that has no conditions placed on it. Hence, "to be or not to be" is the only possible question. What about estar? Estar denotes conditional, contingent, or temporary being. *Estoy enfermo* means "I am sick," but sickness is presumed to be temporary and something that will not exist forever, hence the use of the estar form of "to be." *Soy enfermo* is not a proper expression in Spanish because sickness can not be permanent or without contingency. By contrast, *soy mujer* means "I am a woman" and uses the ser form of "to be." The expression *estoy mujer* is not permitted because presumably the characteristic of being a woman is permanent and not contingent once established.

The hegemony of Euro-Anglo elliptic ontology has distorted the way that educational institutions function. Limited to an ontology of absolute being (ser), Euro-Anglo elliptic culture supposes that human cultures exist (in the sense of ser) in an evolutionarily determined hierarchy (see Menchaca, 1999, for a discussion of the racialization of Mexicans by the United States after 1848). Thus, various cultures can be arranged in an order of absolute superiority and inferiority. This results in a world view which announces the superiority of Euro-Anglo elliptic culture and demands the righteous imposition of this culture on all "foreign" peoples, while exterminating all "foreign" languages and cultures. Educational institutions operating under the sway of this world view implement assimilationist practices whose goal is to absorb all languages, cultures, and peoples into a "melting pot" of Eurocentric people and culture. Those people who are seen as not susceptible to assimilation are regarded as targets for destruction, enslavement, or erasure (Menchaca, 1997). Teaching in this context adopts a subtractive stance (Valenzuela, 1999). The goal is to extract and subtract from students all "foreign" language and cultural elements and replace them with "superior" elliptic Euro-Anglo language and culture. The curriculum is infused with Euro-Anglo American history and culture and there is the systematic erasure of the histories, languages, and cultures of all other groups across the land (Macedo, 1994; Menchaca, 1999; Padilla, 1993; Perez, 1999).

Latino/a education should include the ontology of both ser and estar. Under being as estar, human existence is seen as an historical, contingent, and changing set of relationships between various groups and cultures. All languages and cultures are seen as having inherent value and as needing resources in order to thrive. Under the sway of estar ontology schools recognize, embrace, and celebrate the variety of languages, cultures, and peoples across the land. They accept those who are different and promote the value of *convivencia*, that is, the notion of "live and let live." Teachers appreciate and share different languages and cultures; they practice additive pedagogy by adding language and cultural resources to what students already possess. The curriculum emphasizes multiple languages, cultures, and histories so that students from various groups can see themselves positively in the curriculum.

The last cultural supposition considered here involves learning. In Euro-Anglo elliptic culture learning is seen as something that is achieved almost exclusively within a set of positive circumstances. That is, learning occurs when learners are placed within positive environments, activities, and experiences. In behavioristic terms, learning is related to positive reinforcement and positive learning outcomes. In Latino/a elliptic culture, however, there are two distinguishable modalities of learning which are expressed by the Spanish words *aprender* and *escarmentar*. Aprender corresponds to the positive English verb "to learn." Escarmentar, by contrast, has no direct English translation and refers to the positive learning that can occur from negative environments, activities, or experiences. Escarmentar is learning in the sense of "learning one's lesson." Escarmiento perhaps reflects an Hispanic redemptive attitude which allows for positive learning to occur even in the presence of evident error or misbehavior.

In one theory of expertise (Harmon & King, 1985), expert knowledge is seen as a combination of formal, theoretical knowledge and heuristic or practical knowledge. In some ways, escarmiento may be an important source for constituting heuristic knowledge. Students succeed in schools because they become experts at being students. As experts, they must possess both the formal book knowledge required for graduation and the heuristic, experientially derived, knowledge that allows them to survive the campus. At the same time, successful students make use of heuristic knowledge that is available in their communities and that can shield them from subtractive practices often evident in the schools (Tapia, 1991). Understanding that Latino/a students learn through both aprender and escarmentar types of learning should encourage educators to revisit and reexamine the learning principles that they use in constructing the school curriculum. The Latino/a bifurcated idea of learning also has implications for student assessement. Educators need to find ways to assess heuristic knowledge so that students who lack it can be provided an opportunity to learn it. Comprehensive assessment of both aprender and escarmentar types of learning are prerequisites for the proper instruction of students so that they can gain the necessary expertise to graduate from high school and college.

The three elliptic cultural suppositions discussed here are merely examples of the many contrasts that could be drawn between various elliptic cross cultural expressions. There are many others that could be considered. For example, Latino/a elliptic culture makes sharp distinctions between education and schooling, between behavior and comportment, between obligated actions and actions voluntarily taken, between *capacitación* and *entrenamiento* (development vs training), etc. Regarding *obligación* (obligation), in Latino/a elliptic culture teachers are obligated to advocate for their students, while Euro-Anglo elliptic culture simply permits advocacy and thus not every student finds an advocate in school.

ENVISIONING A PEDAGOGY OF ENGAGEMENT (POE)

If a goal of Latino/a education in the 21st century is to ensure that every student has an advocate then it is necessary to envision a pedagogy of engagement as the vehicle that can provide such advocacy. In the latter part of the 20th century, educators and policy makers spent too much time trying to fix every fault in the schools at the expense of advocating for each and every student. The fact of the matter is that all kinds of students—rich and poor, minority and nonminority, males and females, and so on—have problems and difficulties with the schools. The students who succeed in these schools with significant organizational deficits are those students who have advocacy behind them. When parents are effective advocates for their children, it is very likely that their children will succeed in school. When such advocacy is absent or marginal, then advocacy must come from other sources or the student truly will be at risk of not succeeding in school.

Figure 16.2 shows one vision of a pedagogy of engagement which includes prominently the idea of advocacy. As shown in Figure 16.2, and as already indicated, the point of departure for a Latino/a POE is the understanding that Latino/a students must experience school success under deficit organizational resources (SUDOR). Latino/a success in school can not wait until the schools are perfectly functioning

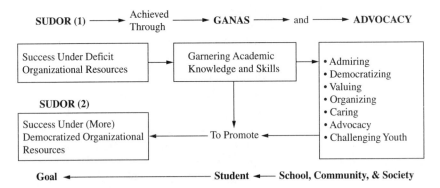

FIG. 16.2. Envisioning a pedagogy of engagement which assumes that schools are less than ideal and therefore that all students require advocacy.

organizations; instead Latino/a school success must be achieved with schools as they operate at any given time. We know that success is possible under deficit organizational conditions because there are always some students who experience success (Garcia, 2001; González, Huerta-Macías, & Villamil Tinajero, 1998; Padilla, 1999; Reyes, Scribner, & Paredes Scribner, 1999). The idea then is to shift all students in the direction of success. How can this be done?

As the model shows, success can be achieved if students as learners have the motivation to garner academic knowledge and skills (GANAS) and if they are supported in their learning through advocacy. Advocacy is the responsibility of the family, school, community, and society. Some key elements of advocacy are admiring, democratizing, valuing, organizing, caring, advocating itself, and challenging youth. Older people need to admire young people and young people need to feel that they are admired by older people (Bly, 1990; Freire, 1995). It is on the basis of this admiration that older people take younger people "under their wing" and advocate for their success. If every student is admired by someone, then student motivation to GANAS to learn will be increased.

Advocacy must be based on a profound commitment to the greater democratization of society. Immigrants often come to the United States seeking improved economic futures, but they just as often desire the benefits of a democratic society. By implementing cultural democracy in schools (Ibarra, 2001; Ramirez & Castañeda, 1974), we become advocates of both native and immigrant students who see that they are appreciated and that they have a positive role to play in the larger society. The school experience itself thus becomes the preparation for effective participation in civil society.

Students need to feel valued and validated (Rendón, 2002). They need to be valued for who they are and their life experiences need to be validated if further learning is to occur (Jalomo, 1995; Rendón, 1994). So an important part of advocacy is to show in many ways and throughout the school years that students are valuable. The obscene notion of "throw away kids" is the antithesis of valuing students. The younger generation always represents the future and valuing youth is an essential part of advocacy.

Valuing of students can come from many sources: teachers, administrators, counselors, staff, peers, family, and community. Valuing can be expressed in many ways, including affirming that students can be successful learners, acknowledging their contributions to knowledge, affirming student choices, affirming the student's culture, building the student's confidence, etc. (see Rendón, 2002). The students also should be able to see themselves in the curriculum they study and in the teachers who instruct them.

Effective advocacy always requires organization at some level. The COPS organization in San Antono, Texas is a good example of community level organization aimed at advocating for students and community. But even when advocacy is done on an individual basis, organization is required. Each student is an individual with particular needs that are expressed dynamically in the vicissitudes of life. When a student does not show up for class on a given morning, someone must advocate for that student and take the time to find out why the student is not in school. If the student's problem can be resolved in real time, then the student can be brought back to school. But this type of real-time advocacy requires organization both of schools and communities; otherwise the resources needed to overcome problems will not be available. Advocacy implies organization for advocacy. To the extent that today's schools are not organized to promote advocacy, school reform efforts should be refocused to pursue this goal.

Those who advocate do so because they care about students. The shocking lack of caring expressed by some school personnel when it comes to Latino/a students shows that such individuals have abandoned their obligations as teachers and educators (Romo & Falbo, 1996; Valenzuela, 1999). Caring means that the welfare of students is always the highest priority of educational systems. Caring means doing right by students and giving every student a genuine opportunity to learn. Caring means to read between the lines and to help students even when they have not expressed the needs that they have. Advocacy often results from caring, and without caring advocacy seems unlikely.

Advocates also challenge. Youths need to be challenged if they are to apply their copious energy to constructive purposes. Boring curricula and boring schools can not satisfy the eagerness and curiosity of young people. Spending inordinate amounts of time preparing students for single-score high-stakes tests is not a good way to challenge students (McNeil, 2000; McNeil & Valenzuela, 2000). Students are challenged when they have to reach a little bit further than what they know they can already do (Moll, 1990). They are challenged when novel possibilities are brought before them. They are challenged and inspired when they know that their performance and achievement will result in admiration from peers and adults alike. They are challenged when they see that a better future is possible for themselves and their families. The

Latino/a community is richly involved in the arts: music, art, dance, theater, sculpture, muralism, and other arts genres. Along with a challenging curriculum in science, math, and technology, Latino/a youth ought to be presented a challenging curriculum and extracurriculum in the plastic and performing arts that would include the arts traditionally encountered in the Latino/a community, but also the newer arts involving film, video, multimedia, performance art, and so on.

Advocacy, then, involves many parallel activities. If students are to garner significant amounts of academic knowledge and skills, advocacy must be deployed on many levels and in many different ways. With proper advocacy, students can succeed even in schools which are less than perfect. But advocacy also can be for school improvement, especially if such improvement is based on the lessons learned from advocating for individual student success. When advocacy shifts its focus from helping individual students to improving particular schools then there is the possibility that schools will deploy learning resources in a more democratic manner. When this happens then Latino/a students can succeed under (more) democratized and enhanced organizational resources. In this sense, school improvement can be measured by the extent to which organizational resources under a school's control are allocated democratically and sufficiently to meet the needs of students. When resources are allocated to schools democratically, justly, and sufficiently, and schools in turn do likewise with resource allocation to students and teachers, then—if students have GANAS—their achievement potential will be at maximum.

The vision of a Latino/a pedagogy of engagement undoubtedly will require a substantial retooling of the schools (Berliner & Biddle, 1995). It might be helpful to identify at least the general design parameters for an educational service delivery system that follows the ideas of the pedagogy of engagement. Table 16.1 provides one example of the general design parameters for a POE service delivery system. As can be seen from Table 16.1, action teams are seen as the vehicle for promoting student advocacy. The environment in which schools operate is assumed to be complex, dynamic, and turbulent (on complexity, see Dörner, 1996). Therefore, schools are to function as highly organized and coordinated systems but with minimal hierarchy. Schools are seen as flexible, responsive, and adaptable. And they serve to stabilize and smooth what is otherwise a turbulent environment.

Schools as stabilizing centers are seen to deliver instructional services with specific characteristics. Among these are parallel service

TABLE 16.1

General Design Parameters for a POE Service Delivery
System (SDS). Schools Operate as Service Delivery
Systems and the Challenge Is to Design Schools That
Meet the Specifications Below

Specifications. To construct a service delivery system with action teams forming
an interface between clients and the service delivery system to promote
student success under less than ideal conditions.

Environmental Assumptions. The operating environment of the service delivery
system is assumed to exhibit the following characteristics:
- Complex
- Dynamic
- Turbulent

These environmental features imply the following corresponding characteristics
of the service delivery system:
- Highly organized and coordinated but minimally hierarchical
- Flexible, responsive, and adaptable
- Stabilizing and smoothing

Characteristics of service delivery
- Parallel service delivery
- Targeted service delivery
- Resource integration and consolidation to achieve "just in time service"
- Action teams as interface between clients and service delivery system
  supported by:
  -Speciality teams
  -Training and evaluation teams
  -Volunteers
  -Parents
  -Service delivery vehicles (SDVs)
- Action triggers:
  -Client
  -Action teams (interface)
  -Service delivery vehicle
- Continuous monitoring of client status by actions teams and others

Support elements
- Online data warehouse
- Highly networked within the service delivery system and across its
  environment

delivery so that there are many paths to service, targeted service delivery so that special needs are met effectively, and "just-in-time" service so that problems are taken care of in real time. Action teams are then used as an interface between students and the service delivery system These action teams consolidate resources across schools, families, and communities. They form the core of student advocacy.

The idea of action teams as the source of advocacy for students and as an interface between schools (as service providers) and students (as clients) is shown in Figure 16.3. The proposed REACT model clearly

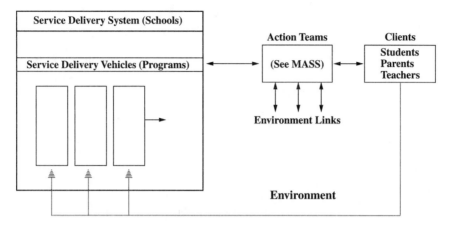

FIG. 16.3. Macroview of REACT—Resource Environment Access, Coordination, and Targeting. A service delivery system to enable a pedagogy of engagement in which action teams serve as an interface between students, communities, and the schools.

shows that schools cannot be allowed to be hermetic institutions left to their own devices to "process" students. Rather, the schools are seen as part of a community-wide effort to educate all students.

The role of action teams in the overall functioning of the schools is shown in Figure 16.4. As can be seen from the model, advocacy must help both individual students and schools to improve. In order to do so, the action teams need to include both school personnel and community volunteers. These teams will be highly networked with organizations and resources available in schools and the community at large.

The various models presented are intended merely to illustrate how a pedagogy of engagement might be designed and implemented. The task for educators during the 21st century will be to implement working models of POE. Many ideas will surely surface, and the lessons to be learned are many.

A MODEL OF RESEARCH FOR SOCIAL CHANGE

A Latino/a educational agenda for the 21st century will require attention to the role of social science research in promoting educational progress. Too often in the past, educational researchers, social scientists, and historians have used paradigms, methods, and perspectives in their research that contained inherent biases with respect to the nature of Latino/a language, culture, and history (Hernández, 1970; Limón, 1994; Macedo, 1994; Romano, 1973; Rosaldo, 1993). The deficit

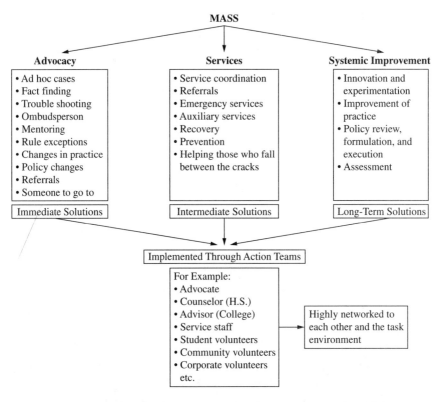

FIG. 16.4. Model of advocacy, service, and systemic improvement (MASS) for students, families, and communities in pursuit of enhanced educational achievement. Macroview of action teams and their function.

view of Latino/a students has deep roots in social science research that was not completely open to truth (Menchaca, 1997). As a result of the negative views of Latinos manufactured through biased research, too much energy has been spent by Latino/a researchers and others trying to "refute" the mistaken ideas that have driven ineffective educational policies and practices. The time has come to retool social science research methods and paradigms so that they can become useful tools for supporting an effective Latino/a pedagogy for the 21st century.

Figure 16.5 shows a concept model of social science research that uses the kaleidoscope as a metaphor for research. This model emphasizes social change as a goal and concept modeling as a technique for representing social situations in order to understand and change them. The model is premised on a distinction between the *earth* and the *world*. The earth is naturally given and human beings did nothing to create it.

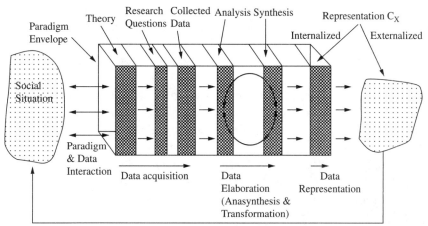

FIG. 16.5. Concept model of social science research based on the metaphor of a kaleidoscope. The model assumes the transcultural foundation (see text) as a norm and positive social change as a goal.

They simply exist in it. Researchers who study the earth are considered natural scientists. The world, by contrast, is a human construction. This means that there are many worlds, depending on the perspectives of various groups and cultures. In the extreme case, each person exists in a different world, as is recognized by the Mexican saying, *"Cada cabeza es un mundo"* (Each head is a world). These worlds are constantly changing so that an individual actually lives in many worlds across time and events. Societies also exist as many parallel worlds that are constantly shifting and changing. Researchers who study the worlds in which people live are considered social scientists, and it is these social scientists who need to upgrade their ways of doing research if it is to help improve the functioning of social institutions, including educational institutions.

Figure 16.5 shows that the focus of social science research is a specific social situation which is bracketed out of an otherwise fluid and continuous world of human affairs. The social situation by definition is local, although localness can vary widely, for example from studying a one person case to a project involving an entire community or culture. The purpose of the research is to create a concept model of the social situation so that on the basis of the understanding created by the model, effective interventions can be made in the social situation. This model of social science research is normative in the sense that it assumes that the transcultural foundation and the bracketed transcultural expressions

discussed earlier are the proper foundation and goal of society. Therefore, this model insists that social science research must promote, and
be driven by, the ideas of freedom, democracy, and justice.

What connects the social situation and its conceptual representation
is shown in the model using the metaphor of a kaleidoscopic. The outer
part of the kaleidoscopic tube represents the paradigmatic assumptions
under which a particular research project is carried out, for example,
positivism, post positivism, constructivism, critical theory, and so on.
Data are collected from the social situation and scooped into the tube.
Because paradigms can condition what one is able to see or ask about,
the double-headed arrows at the entrance of the tube show that there
is an interaction between the data collected and the paradigm that is
driving the research.

A priori theory, when used, also conditions the data that are collected. This is shown schematically in the model as the first lens in the
kaleidoscopic tube. Once data are acquired, the process of data elaboration becomes the focus of attention. Data elaboration consists of
two related processes: Data analysis, which is the breakdown of data
into its constituent parts, and data synthesis, which is the creation of a
new whole based on the data analysis. The elaboration process might
be referred to as "anasynthesis" to recognize the dialectic relationship
between analysis and synthesis. On the basis of the anasynthesis, a conceptual representation (concept model) of the social situation is made.
This concept model then can be used to institute positive changes in the
social situation under study. The research model shown in Figure 16.5
can be seen as consisting of three distinct stages in a continuous process.
First is data acquisition which includes identification of a bounded local social situation, construction of appropriate research questions, the
optional identification and use of an a priori theory, devising appropriate data collection instruments and procedures, and the actual data
collection. The second stage involves data reduction and transformation. Data reduction summarizes the essential meaning of an extensive
body of data, often by subsuming a large number of examples under a
broad category or concept, whereas data transformation looks for relationships between the concepts that can be used to form a new image
or representiaon of the social situation under study. The final stage is
the creation of a representation, or concept model, which can be used
to take action in the world. Following the action stage, the research
process may start all over again.

This model of social science research, or something along the same lines, is needed if the development of effective Latino/a pedagogy is to be driven by empirically based research. The normative stance incorporated into the model requires that elliptic cultural biases and prejudices be consciously reduced while framing all elliptic cultural selections within a consciousness of potential alternatives within the larger multiculturalism of the society. At the same time social research under this model can take advantage of diverse culturally based suppositions regarding knowing, being, learning, and so on. The model aims to support and maintain the transcultural foundation essential for a viable civil society.

SUMMARY

In this chapter, consideration is given to the creation of a new agenda for Latino/a education in the 21st century. The task is seen as involving a new conceptualization of Latino/a pedagogy, one that assumes the inherent ability of Latino/a students to learn. It eschews deficit models of Latino/a students, their families, and their various communities and cultures. A new vision of Latino/a education is presented, which calls for respect for diverse sociocultural perspectives, recognition of the sociopolitical and historical context of Latino/a education, integration of diverse communities as partners in education, and advocacy for values such as social justice and democratic ideals. With this vision as background, the chapter emphasized four critical points: the need to conceptualize a multiculturalism that entails social unity; the examination of elliptic cultural suppositions that influence the way students are taught in schools—suppositions related to knowing, being, and learning are used as examples; the envisioning and formulating of a pedagogy of engagement that is built on expanded notions of knowing, being, and learning; and the creation of a new model of social science research that takes the transcultural foundation described in the text as a norm and that has as a goal the promotion of positive social change with the expectation that social institutions, such as schools, can be improved for all students and used as the engines that promote participation in a democratic society. Suggesting an educational agenda is one thing. Putting it into action will require the hard work of many researchers, teachers, policy makers, community and business leaders, and so on. Especially needed will be the commitment and devotion of Latino/a leaders and the Latino/a community, along with progressive individuals and groups in the larger society. So, in the end, creation of an agenda is also a call to action.

REFERENCES

Banks, J. A. (2002). *An introduction to multicultural education.* Boston, MA: Allyn and Bacon.

Banks, J. A., & McGee Banks, C. A. (Eds.). (2001). *Handbook of research on multicultural education.* San Francisco: Jossey-Bass.

Berliner, D. C., & Biddle, B. J. (1995). *The manufactured crisis: Myths, fraud, and the attack on America's public schools.* New York: Addison-Wesley.

Bly, R. (1990). *A gathering of men.* (With Bill Moyers; Betsy McCarthy, Producer, & Wayne Ewing, Director). New York: Mystic Fire Video.

Dörner, D., (1996). *The logic of failure: Recognizing and avoiding error in complex situations* (Kimber, R. & R, Trans.). Cambridge, MA: Perseus Books.

Freire, P. (1995). *Pedagogy of the oppressed:* New revised 20th-anniversary edition. New York: Continuum.

García, E. (2001). *Hispanic education in the United States: Raíces y alas.* New York: Rowman & Littlefield.

González, M. L., Huerta-Macías, A., & Villamil Tinajero, J. (Eds.). (1998). *Educating Latino students: A guide to successful practice.* Lancaster, PA: Technomic Publishing Company.

Harmon, P., & King, D. (1985). *Expert systems.* New York: Wiley.

Hernández, D. (1970). *Mexican American challenge to a sacred cow: A critical review and analysis focusing on two UCLA Graduate School of Education research studies about Mexican American "values" and achievement.* Los Angeles: University of California Press.

Ibarra, R. A. (2001). *Beyond affirmative action: Reframing the context of higher education.* Madison: University of Wisconsin Press.

Jalomo, Jr., R. (1995). *Latino students in transition: An analysis of the first-year experience in community college.* Unpublished doctoral dissertation, College of Education, Arizona State University, Tempe.

Limon, J. E. (1994). *Dancing with the devil: Society and cultural poetics in Mexican-American south Texas.* Madison: University of Wisconsin Press.

Macedo, D. (1994). *Literacies of power: What Americans are not allowed to know.* Boulder, CO: Westview Press.

McNeil, L. M. (2000). *Contradictions of school reform: Educational costs of standardized testing.* New York: Routledge.

McNeil, L. M., & Valenzuela, A. (2000). *The harmful impact of the TAAS system of testing in Texas: Beneath the accountability rhetoric.* Houston, TX: Rice University. Center for Education. Occasional Papers, Vol. 1, Issue 1.

Menchaca, M. (1997). Early racist discourses: The roots of deficit thinking. In R. Valencia (Ed.), *The evolution of deficit thinking: Educational thought and practice* (pp. 13–40). Washington, DC: Falmer Press.

Menchaca, M. (1999). The Treaty of Guadalupe Hidalgo and the racialization of the Mexican population. In J. S. Moreno (Ed.), *The elusive quest for equality. 150 years of Chicano/Chicana education* (pp. 3–29). Cambridge, MA: Harvard Educational Review.

Moll, L. C. (Ed.). (1990). *Vygotsky and education: Instructional implications and applications of sociohistorical psychology.* New York: Cambridge University Press.

Ovando, C. J., & Collier, V. P. (1998). *Bilingual and ESL classrooms: Teaching in multicultural contexts* (2nd ed.). New York: McGraw-Hill.

Padilla, G. M. (1993). *My history, not yours: The formation of Mexican American autobiography.* Madison: University of Wisconsin Press.

Padilla, R. V. (1999). College student retention: Focus on success. *Journal of College Student Retention, Research, Theory & Practice, 1*(2), 131–145.

Perez, Emma. (1999). *The decolonial imaginary: Writing Chicanas into history.* Bloomington: Indiana University Press.

Ramirez, M., & Castañeda, A. (1974). *Culural democracy, bicognitive development, and education.* New York: Academic Press.

Rendón, L. I. (1994). Validating culturally diverse students: Toward a new model of learning and student development. *Innovative Higher Education, 19*(1), 23–32.

Rendón, L. I. (2002). Community college puente: A validating model of education. *Educational Policy , 16*(4), 642–667.

Reyes, P., Scribner, J. D., & Paredes Scribner, A. (1999). *Lessons from high-performing Hispanic schools.* New York: Teachers College Press.

Rodriguez, R. (1982). *Hunger of memory: The education of Richard Rodriguez. An autobiography.* Boston, MA: D. R. Godine.

Romano-V., O. I. (Ed.). (1973). *Voices: Readings from El Grito 1967–1973.* Berkeley, CA: Quinto Sol Publications.

Romo, H. D., & Falbo, T. (1996). *Latino high school graduation: Defying the odds.* Austin: University of Texas Press.

Rosaldo, R. (1993). *Culture & truth: The remaking of social analysis.* Boston, MA: Beacon Press.

Tapia, J. C. (1991). *Cultural reproduction: Funds of knowledge as survival stratgies in the Mexican American community.* Unpublished doctoral dissertation, University of Arizona, Tucson.

Valencia, R. (Ed.). (1997). *The evolution of deficit thinking: Educational thought and practice.* Washington, DC: Falmer Press.

Valenzuela, A. (1999). *Subtractive schooling: U.S.-Mexican youth and the politics of caring.* Albany: State University of New York Press.

Valenzuela, A. (2002). High-stakes testing and U.S.-Mexican youth in Texas: The case for multiple compensatory criteria for assessment. *Harvard Journal of Hispanic Policy, 14,* 97–116.

17

Democracy, Education, and Human Rights in the United States: Strategies of Latino/a Empowerment

Raymond Rocco
UCLA

INTRODUCTION

The history of Latino/a communities in the United States has been a long, complex, and diverse one in which the nature, level, and type of membership of Latinos in the larger society has been one of the contested aspects of the relationship between these communities and the dominant institutions of power and control. An extensive literature now exists that documents the various historical forms of discrimination and marginalization confronted by Latinos, as well as the continuous efforts to overcome these.[1] And one of the most important factors in understanding the particular pattern of development of Latino/a communities in the United States since the end of World War II is the role education has played in determining both the internal characteristics

---

[1] See, for example, the introduction to the edited volume by Suárez-Orozco and Páez (2002) for an excellent short summary of the challenges confronting Latinos.

of these communities as well as their relationships and access to institutions of power. It is a mixed record of expanding opportunities for a relatively small number of Latinos on the one hand and a dismal record of substandard schools and unresponsiveness to community needs on the other.[2] Whereas the gains of the Civil Rights movement stimulated the growth of a Latino/a middle and professional class by providing for the first time greater access to universities, graduate and professional schools, at the same time the majority continue to struggle with realities of faltering educational structures, restricted occupational opportunities, low incomes, substandard health care, and poor housing conditions. Despite this uneven record and the many ways that the educational system has failed Latino/a families, achieving equal access to quality educational systems continues to be one of the consistent and key elements in the strategies of empowerment embraced by Latino/a communities and has been seen as a primary means for transforming political and economic conditions and achieving both individual advancement and community development.

It should not be surprising, then, that there are an increasing number of important works such as those in this volume, that have delineated and analyzed the range of specific issues related to education in Latino/a communities in the United States, identified specific needs, and documented a host of inadequacies regarding facilities, low budgets, scarce resources, and unsound educational pedagogies. These works provide vital information and analysis for those struggling to improve the quality of education for Latino/a children and adults. But it is just as important to see that the specifics of these studies are part of a broader context of Latino/a struggles for democracy, social justice, and to achieve full membership in the society. The close relationship among education, democracy, and social justice has not only been an important principle in major educational philosophies such as those of Dewey and Freire but continues to be the focus of considerable work in political theory.[3] And one of the important strands of analysis in this latter work concerns the status of education as a human right. It is this issue that I want to take up in this chapter, developing an argument to establish education as a human right and assessing the extent to which it may apply it to the Latino/a populations of the United States. The

---

[2] A useful overview of the condition of Latino/a education can be found in Roderick (2000).
[3] See the excellent discussion of the relationship among education, democracy, and justice in Callan (1997).

latter depends to a great extent on demonstrating that the specific conditions of Latinos in the United States require this kind of intervention as well as assessing the viability and effectiveness of human rights as a political strategy. Let me then turn to the first dimension.

GLOBALIZATION AND LATINO/A COMMUNITIES

There are a wide array of forces that have affected the trajectory of Latino/a community formation in the last half century, but I want to focus on those institutional changes that have most directly impacted the economic, political, and cultural conditions in these communities and that have the greatest bearing on whether human rights, and in particular education as a human right, is a strategy that can advance the interests, access, and inclusion of Latinos in the United States. I have argued elsewhere that the complex processes of globalization and restructuring during the last 30 years have had the greatest influence on the particular pattern of development of Latino/a communities and the resulting structure of opportunities, obstacles, and resources.[4] And it is these processes and their effects on Latino/a communities, and the significance of education in particular, that I want to briefly summarize before considering the empowerment potential of human rights claims.

The globalization and restructuring processes that took root in the 1970s have transformed the economic and demographic character of the United States, and with it, have promoted a particular pattern of development in Latino/a communities. Although there is little consensus on the exact parameters and meaning of globalization, the nature of the changes normally included are fairly clear. I have found that focusing on the growth in interdependence and flows across a number of activities to be the most useful organizing concept in attempting to understand these phenomena. The flows of capital, labor, communication, networks, knowledge, culture, crime, pollutants, and communities across borders, have all accelerated significantly during the last 30 years and increased the level of interdependence between different societies and regions. At the most general level, these phenomena are what I take to be the defining characteristics of globalization.

The following lists those aspects of globalization most relevant to Latino/a communities and is adapted from Cohen's analysis of diaspora

---

[4]See Rocco (2000).

(Cohen, 1997, pp. 157–176). Most important for my purposes are the following:

1. a world economy characterized by faster and more extensive transactions made possible by advances in communication, cheaper forms of transportation, a reconfigured international division of labor, the rise of transnational corporations

2. increase in international migration from Third World countries to the major urban regions of Europe, the United States, Canada, Australia, as well as a few others

3. the development of global cities as the center of operations and coordination widely dispersed international operations

4. the formation of transnational networks of households, transactions, and political organizations

5. the emergence of social identities that challenge the hegemony of the nation-state as primary referent of political identity, and a fracturing of the Eurocentric cultural base of many of the countries.

6. the development of an array of treaties, conventions, codes, contracts, organizations and agreements between nation-states in order to deal with interdependent economic, political, and environmental destinies.

Now the impact of these on the United States and the level of interdependence that resulted is clearly discernable. For example, the proportion of the national economy, although varying by region, that is dependent on trade with other countries has increased significantly since 1970. Mexico and Canada are the largest trading partners and the viability of regional economies, for example in the Southwest, depend on maintaining a close working relationship with these states. The impetus for these processes in the United States was the reorganizational responses of the corporate sector to the sustained economic slowdown that began in the late 1960s. Initially thought of as part of a normal cycle of expansion and contraction of capitalist markets, it was soon clear that a different dynamic was at work and that corporations world wide had to adjust to the new economic order. Policies that were pursued included moving either part or all operations offshore or to regions of the country that provided more attractive competitive environments, such as lower wage rates, low tax rates, a nonunionized workforce, fewer environmental regulations, and in some cases, investment incentives provided by either or both state or city governments. And those companies that stayed put clearly moved to restructure their workforce, replacing higher paid, unionized labor with low-wage workers, made possible by technological innovations in production. Another strategy was to rely much more on subcontracting and part-time labor, as well as more flexible production and distribution strategies.

As a result of these new strategies, policies, and practices, a number of changes that have affected Latino/a communities directly have taken place. One of the most basic has been the process of "deindustrialization" and the subsequent "reindustrialization" where the manufacturing sector not only declined overall but also was reconstituted and spatially redistributed. The Fordist regime of manufacturing, characterized by its emphasis on large-scale corporate based production and facilities located largely in the northeast United States and to a lesser extent in cities like Chicago and Los Angeles, declined significantly but was replaced by the growth in so-called old industries, such as the garment sector, which were organized in nonunionized firms of much smaller size, with few or no benefits, that drew primarily on the new cheaper immigrant labor force. And this reorganization of the manufacturing sector also displaced many of the firms to areas of the South and Southwest where nonunion labor, particular women, was readily available. This was one of the elements that was part of a broader process of change in the national economy that saw a fundamental shift from manufacturing to high-technology driven and service industries that completely altered the nature of the labor market and the structure of jobs. By 1980, services had replaced manufacturing as the dominant sector in terms of employment, and by the 1990s, it also was surpassed by retail trade and government employment. These processes transformed many of the major industrial cities and gave rise to a pattern of development that promoted a bipolar economy and job market, with job growth occurring primarily in the higher wage, skilled, professional, and semiprofessional occupations in industry, the high-tech sectors, in media and communications, and finance, on the one hand, and even greater growth in the low wage, nonunionized, unskilled or semiskilled jobs in small manufacturing and services, with few or no benefits, on the other. The growth of these low-end jobs was particularly important in attracting the large-scale and rapid expansion of immigration from Latin America and the Caribbean that transformed Latino/a communities in the United States and led to the very rapid and large-scale growth, spatial dispersion, and diversification of the Latino/a population.

As a result of these patterns, the proportion of Latinos concentrated in the low-end sector of the labor market is inordinately high and has lead to greater levels of economic inequality and poverty in these communities. However, the Latino/a population is extremely heterogenous in terms of class, national origin, length of residence, and citizenship status. Despite the tendency of dominant institutions to collapse this diversity, each group of Latinos with significant numbers has a different history of articulation with U.S. society distinguished by diverse modes of incorporation, networks with country of origin, and levels of education and skills. But in spite of these differences, it is nevertheless true that for the majority of Latinos in the United States, the pattern of economic restructuring and the effects of globalization have created considerable economic hardship for many and poverty for nearly 30%. This has not been the result of joblessness but, rather, the limited access of the majority to higher income occupations and consequently, Latinos have a higher percentage of working poor than any other racial/ethnic group.[5] A sense of the disproportionate negative impact on Latinos in the workforce is provided by the following statistic. Between 1960 and 1990, the number of White males who entered the workforce at the high wage level increased by 187% whereas for Latino/a males, the figure was 100%. But the number of Latino/a males entering low-wage jobs during the same period *increased* by 376% whereas the percentage for White males in the same category actually *decreased* by 65%.[6]

Rebecca Morales, who has long studied the effects of restructuring on the socioeconomic characteristics of Latino/a populations, summarizes the impact of the changes of the national economy in the following way: "Latinos are the poorest racial/ethnic group in the country and are continuing to fall behind economically" (Morales, 2000, p. 35). And as I have discussed earlier, one of the major reasons why this is the case has to do with the changes in the nature of work and the structure of the jobs in the labor market. But this has not occurred in a political vacuum. Two other factors have contributed to the growth in the Latino/a working poor. The fundamental conservative shift in the political environment of the United States in the last 30 years has dramatically reduced the basis and availability of economic and social rights in general, and affected issues that directly impact the life conditions and opportunities of low-wage workers. For example, the neoliberal state has continued

---

[5]This is clearly described in a number of works on the Latinos and the labor market. See Morales (1998, 2000); Chapa (1998); Chapa and Wacker (2000).

[6]These percentages are based on figures provided in Table 4 in Morales (2000, p. 41).

to reject significant reform in the minimum wage and minimal benefits for low income workers, and unionization has been undercut by the forms of support provided by both the federal and state governments to the corporate sector. The welfare reforms of 1995 capped more than two decades of efforts by the political right to minimize the level of services available for the poor, working poor, and immigrants, and the Bush administration's budget proposal for the next fiscal year clearly revives the Reagan approach that transferred a greater portion of the national income to the wealthy in the name of national security. In addition to these structural and institutionally based barriers, Latinos continue to be the victims of employment and other forms of discrimination. Because of widespread use of various strategies such as tracking, job segregation, and poor recruitment, access of Latinos to a variety of positions in both the private and public sector continues to be limited.[7]

As mentioned at the outset, it is important to keep in mind that while the majority of Latinos are working class and many are working poor, there is now a middle and professional class that have made significant economic and occupational gains. And according to most of the studies on the economic profile of the Latino/a population, the factor that is most directly related to determining occupation and income is education.[8] So it is clear that the economic well-being, improved material quality of life, and full membership of Latinos in societal institutions will depend to a great extent on having access to effective education. I am not implying that the primary reason to struggle for educational rights should be simply economic mobility or that market logic should drive educational reform. Indeed, I argue here that these should be considered means to achieve conditions that promote human development rather than being the goal themselves. So my argument for education as a human right is based on the premise that in the type of globalized conditions that characterize the United States, education is a means to enable the development of the creative and critical power of every person. But to do so requires full and equal access to the major institutions and resources in a given society, including the ability to draw on political and civil rights to effectively participate in democratic governance, and all of these clearly depend on achieving some level of economic security.

---

[7]See for example, the excellent review of employment discrimination in Meléndez, Carre and Holvino (1995). Also the short but useful discussion by Morales (2000, pp. 56–58).

[8]See Roderick (2000) for a concise summary of data on this point.

But achieving this goal is jeopardized by the nature of Latino's participation in and access to educational institutions. In 2001, the Harvard Civil Rights Project published findings that indicate that the percentage of Latino/a students who attend segregated schools, particularly in poorer, inner city districts, has actually increased since the late 1960s. In 1968, 23.1% of Latino/a students attended schools with minority enrollments of over 90% and yet after 30 years of "educational reform," in 1998, that figure rose to 36.6% (Orfield, 2001, p. 31). And a more recent study by the same research project confirms that "Latino/a students are the most segregated minority group" (Frankenberg, Lee, & Orfield, pp. 2003–2004). And the highest levels of segregation are generally found in schools that are in poor and working poor communities. This is closely correlated in turn with inferior educational institutions in these areas. In her recent review of the various indices of the quality of education that Latinos received, Roderick states that they all point to the same conclusion: "Hispanic Americans—Mexicans, Puerto Ricans, and Central Americans in particular, are currently the most educationally disadvantaged group in America. Whether one looks at students' skill levels, years of school completed, or performance in school, Hispanic students fare worse than any other racial or ethnic group. The educational attainment and achievement of Hispanics has also not been improving as rapidly as other groups." (Roderick, 2000, p. 123). This is hardly the type of educational experience that is likely to facilitate the full incorporation in and access to the major institutional spheres in the United States in a period where educational attainment is highly correlated with the type of opportunity structures that promote the conditions for achieving a higher quality of life.

The generally poor quality of the education available to a majority of Latinos, however, should not only be conceived of in terms of achievement, reading scores, and other quantitative measures most often considered indicators of educational "success." This connection between Latino/a education and the broader political context has been addressed by a number of scholars in a way that I believe supports the notion that education should be established as a human right. Moll and Ruiz, for example, argue that the poor quality of educational institutions and services provided in Latino/a communities are fundamental indicators of more basic forms of control and coercion that sustain the location of Latinos in the structure of racial and class inequality (Moll & Ruiz, 2002). After summarizing some of the specific issue areas that are problematic in predominantly Latino/a schools, they state that: "It is vital to recognize the organized political forces that guide these activities as part of a broader ideological coalition and an urgent agenda to control schools" (Moll and Ruiz, 2002, p. 367). Thus, they see the poor educational experience of a majority of Latinos as symptomatic of the more fundamental reality of the disempowered condition of large sectors of Latino/a communities throughout the United States. They advance the notion of "educational sovereignty" as a way to emphasize this dimension of power relations that point to the need to develop distinct political control over those institutions and conditions that will determine the development of the Latino/a future. This emphasis on situating Latino/a education in the broader context of the realization of a more inclusive, equitable, and just democratic society, suggests that we need to conceptualize Latino/a access to effective, quality educational institutions as more than simply a desirable policy goal that will enhance labor market opportunities and occupational mobility. Instead, this perspective supports the notion that education needs to be conceived of as a process that is vital to the development of communities that can promote productive, creative, healthy lives and futures—education, in other words, as a human right for individual and community development, and full membership in a society.

HUMAN RIGHTS AND EDUCATION

In order to determine whether the notion of human rights can promote this goal of Latino/a community empowerment, we need to have a sense of the historical development of the more general role that human rights has played in promoting democratic inclusion and social justice. The generally accepted view is that although there are intimations of human rights in the cosmopolitan conceptions of international norms of justice set forth in the 18th century, the notion of human rights proper only became a significant issue in the world of politics a little over 50 years ago. One of the strongest advocates of human rights in academia, Richard Falk states in a recent work that: "It is important to remember that human rights were not even an active part of political consciousness until after World War II" (Falk, 2000, p. 4). The establishment of the United Nations and the prosecutions pursued in the Nuremberg Trials are seen as the two crucial factors that laid the foundation for the development of the contemporary "human rights regime" identified by David Beetham as including the following four dimensions: "... a philosophy, a body of international law, a set of institutions for monitoring and implementation, and as an important component, and legitimator, of an emergent global civil society" (Beetham, 1998, p. 58).

The most important documents that lay out what are normally thought of as the institutional and normative parameters of human rights in the current period are the *Universal Declaration of Human Rights* (1948), the *International Covenant on Civil and Political Rights* (1966), and the *International Covenant on Economic, Social and Cultural Rights* (1966), all passed by the General Assembly of the United Nations.[9] These instruments have established 16 groups of human rights organized within the five main categories of civil, political, economic, social, and cultural rights, and each specifies particular guarantees that all residents within individual member states should have and they thus define in normative terms the various criteria for not only monitoring but also for legislating and adjudicating according to these norms of international law.

Most of these are considered extensions of the first generation of primarily political and civil rights that emerged as part of the European revolutionary struggles of the 18th and 19th centuries as well as the social and economic second generation of rights won by the working classes in countries such as England, Germany, and France during the 19th and 20th centuries. These rights were in theory supposed to be guaranteed to each citizen of those emerging nation-states that adopted them. The initial rights-claims were primarily defined in terms in specific freedoms from state abuse, such as freedom from arbitrary arrest, freedom of religion, speech, and expression but the early documents that codified these rights, such as the English Bill of Rights of 1689, the U.S. Declaration of Independence of 1776, and the French Declaration of the Rights of Man of 1789, included few if any economic and social rights. However, during the 19th century there was an increase in the struggle for and rights-claims to entitlements and social welfare provisions based in part on the premise that effective democratic governance required a certain minimal level of material well-being. Thus, the notion of economic and social rights took root and was incorporated in

---

[9]The Universal Declaration of Human Rights, *adopted* 10 Dec. 1948, G.A. Res. 217 (III), U.N. GAOR, 3d Sess., Resolutions, pt. 1, U.N. Doc. A/810 (1948); The International Covenant on Civil and Political Rights, *adopted* 16 Dec. 1966, G.A. Res. 2200 (XXI), U.N. GAOR, 21st Sess., Supp. No. 16, U.N. Doc. A6316 (1966), 999 U.N.T.S. 171 (entered into force 23 Mar. 1976); International Covenant on Economic, Social and Cultural Rights, *adopted* 16 Dec. 1966, G.A. Res. 2200 (XXI), U.N. GAOR, 21st Sess., Supp. No. 16, U.N. Doc. A6316 (1966), 993 U.N.T.S. 3 (entered into force January 3, 1976).

the political reconfigurations in an increasing number of nation states. It was not, however, until the conclusion of World War I in the *Treaty Between the Principal Allied and Associated Powers and Poland* (1919) that there was international recognition of the right to education for the first time. Eventually, education as a human right was included in four different international instruments that provided the major foundations for the regime of international law regarding human rights: *the Universal Declaration of Human Rights* (1948); UNESCO *Convention against Discrimination in Education* (1960); *International Covenant on Economic, Social and Cultural Rights* (1966); and *the Convention on the Rights of the Child* (1989).[10] In addition to these globally defined instruments, a number of regional charters, organizations, and protocols in Latin America, Africa, and Europe also elaborated different dimensions of the notion of educational rights.

What the range of political, civil, social, economic, and cultural rights define, then, are not only the protections against the intrusions of and abuse by the state, but also what every state must provide for its members in order to maintain a minimal standard of human well-being. But it is clear that the general thrust of the human rights regime, particularly in the last 30 years is to promote international norms that go beyond a minimal standard and that the underlying premise is rather that every society has an obligation to provide conditions and resources that will provide each individual the opportunity for the full development of his or her potential. And the right to education has been a fundamental component in these efforts. This much broader aim of the right to education is clear in the range of rationales for such a right that have been included in these documents. In his detailed summary of the emergence of education as a human right, Hodgson identifies four basic rationales found in the major international human rights conventions and treaties and 13 additional ones that although not as central, are nevertheless important to note. The four major goals of the right to education are: (1) the full development of the individual's personality talents and abilities; (2) the strengthening of respect for human rights and fundamental freedoms; (3) the enabling of all persons to participate effectively and responsibly in a free society; (4) the promotion of understanding,

---

[10]This section draws on the detailed analyses provided in Chapters 4 and 5 of Hodgson (1998). As he makes clear, there were a number of additional international agencies, protocols, conventions, and documents that reinforced the rights to education elaborated by the documents referred to in this section.

tolerance, and friendship among all nations, racial, ethnic, or religious groups and the furtherance of the activities of the United Nations for the maintenance of peace. Among the other aims, the following are particularly important: the intergenerational transmission of cultural heritage; contribution to the economic and social development of the community; the development of the individual's critical ability and judgement; the development of the sense of dignity of the human personality, raising the standard of living, ability to communicate interculturally; the attainment of social justice, freedom, and peace.[11]

LIMITATIONS AND POSSIBILITIES OF RIGHTS THEORY AND PRACTICE

Although the emergence of the human rights regime now in place, including the right to an education, has been of great importance in terms of defining general norms that societies should adhere to, it is widely acknowledged that one of its major limitations revolves around the issue of implementation and enforcement. Although many if not most of the principles embodied in these norms are incorporated in the body of international law, the effective responsibility for enforcing them continues to rest with the individual nation-states that are part of an international system based on the principles of sovereignty established over 3 centuries ago in the Treaty of Westphalia, including the right of noninterference in the internal affairs of each state.[12] And although there are many examples of the United Nations acting to enforce some of these rights in smaller countries or regions, it is clear that this is simply not likely to be a feasible option to use against those states with substantial military capacity. Thus, there is considerable skepticism in many marginalized, disempowered communities regarding the potential effectiveness of human rights strategies as a resource for bringing about democratic reform, greater economic equality, and establishing secure principles of social justice.[13]

---

[11] In addition to listing all 17 of the rationales, Hodgson also indicates in which binding and nonbinding international instruments each is to be found Hodgson (1998, pp. 73–81).

[12] See the discussion by McGrew (1997).

[13] One of the few efforts in the social sciences to deal with the issue of rights as they relate to Latino/a communities is found in the various essays in Flores and Benmayor (1997). However, the notion of cultural citizenship advanced by the editors of that volume does not sufficiently examine the issue of how these cultural claims must eventually be linked to institutional structures within the political system in order to secure them.

In addition to this fundamental concern, there are a number of other important critiques of the general notion of rights as a potential empowerment strategy that apply to the more general category of human rights. As I indicated earlier, it is generally recognized that the discourse of human rights in the contemporary period developed as an extension of the first and second generation of rights that were established in the 18th and 19th centuries within the framework of the nation-state. As a recent discussion of the sociology of human rights states: "Thus, the contemporary human rights discourse did not arise in a vacuum, but emerged from the rights discourse, which, until World War II, was anchored within a nation-state (or societal) framework" (Sjoberg, Gill, & Williams, 2001, p. 20). Although there are a variety of critical arguments against the effectiveness or adequacy of rights as emancipatory resources, three of the most widely discussed have emerged from the perspective of critical legal studies, feminism, and cultural relativism.

The field of critical legal studies, which developed some 20 years ago, encompasses a broad set of critiques of rights discourse and practice, and most seem to develop from a more general critique of liberalism.[14] Some take Marx's scathing critique of rights as a point of departure, whereas others depart from the basic positions articulated by the communitarian critique of liberalism. The former hold that rights claims emerged from a very specific set of political, economic, social, and cultural circumstances and pattern of development associated with the rise of capitalism and while these claims attempted to secure civil and political freedoms, they completely ignore the fundamental reality of economic inequality. As a result, then, rights discourse simply obscure the fundamental causes of injustice, exploitation, and oppression, and thus divert the energies of social struggle away from confronting the structural root of existing social conditions. Other critical legal scholars have focused on the highly individualistic and abstract conceptions of the self that are fundamental in liberal thought and ideologies. The focus in liberalism is on the separation between the individual and community or groups, and it posits a "universalist" human nature that is incapable of providing any effective way of accounting for or incorporating any form of difference and in effect results in rationalizing the particularistic interests of those in power. The concrete lived circumstances and conditions within which the self develops, the particular

---

[14]For representative arguments in the Critical Legal Studies movement, see Boyle (1992). For recent studies and assessments, see Bauman (2002) and Brown and Halley (2002).

important defining characteristics of individuals, the mutuality and mutual dependence constitutive of social relations, all of these are simply bracketed out of the rights discourse and thus the real social nature of the self is completely occluded.

Feminist critiques of rights reflect the divergent perspectives and positions that characterize feminist theory more generally.[15] They range from those approaches that I would label liberal feminist at one end of the continuum and that share many of the principles of traditional liberalism but focus on the forms of gender-based exclusionary theories and practices of liberal societies and institutions, to more radical feminisms that reject the construction of the image of the liberal self as completely incapable of accounting for the differences based on gender and sexuality. The former concentrate on the various modes of discrimination that prevent women from gaining equal access to the traditional resources, position, and general benefits of liberal societies, and so the stress is on equality of opportunity. The critique of rights discourse developed by this approach does not reject rights per se, but instead focuses on ways to make rights more inclusive and democratic. The latter perspective, however, sees rights as part of a set of institutions that are formalistic, hierarchical, and patriarchal, and as such, constitute a system of subordination based on gender and sexuality that reflects and privileges the male viewpoint and interests. Rights are part of this complex of ideology, practices, and institutions that both rationalize and maintain the systematic subordination of women. One of the leading figures holding this view is Catherine MacKinnon, who summarizes as follows: "Abstract rights will authorize the male experience of the world" (MacKinnon, 1983, p. 635). The problem with rights according to this approach, then, is not gender differences per se but rather male dominance. Although they differ substantially in basic assumptions and emphasis, what these feminist critiques share is that "they all ask the 'woman' question. Feminist theory examines the woman's condition in a male-dominated society from a woman's perspective" (Kim, 1993, p. 55).

Another form of critique of rights also revolves around the issue of exclusion but focuses instead on cultural inequalities. As is the case with feminism, the cultural relativists' perspective on rights is part of a more

---

[15] A brief discussion of some of the different positions as they relate to the field of rights and law more generally can be found in Kim (1993, pp. 49–55).

comprehensive critique.[16] The primary axis of this view is the rejection of cultural claims advanced during the modern period by Western societies as having universal validity and being culturally superior. It considers these claims to be a defining characteristic of cultural imperialism, taking the form of a cultural essentialism that is interpreted by its critics as a strategy for rationalizing Western global hegemony and for devaluing non-Western value systems, beliefs, and social practices.[17] As one recent essay discussing Western versus Islamic conceptions of human rights puts it, "cultural relativists . . . reject universal human rights as a manifestation of Eurocentric arrogance or as an illusion doomed to collapse" (Bielefeldt, 2000, p. 91). Thus, human rights are seen by cultural relativists as being a product of the Western world and therefore reflecting the particular moral values, political principles, and historical experience foreign to much of the rest of the societies. Although there are clearly those that reject the entire concept of human rights, most of these critiques argue for a reconceptualizing of the discourse in a way that does not privilege Western cultural frameworks and call for a renegotiation of both the theoretical underpinnings and the institutional structures and conventions through which the human rights regime is implemented.

What all of these critiques share is a varying level of skepticism that rights can in practice promote social change and emancipatory goals. However, although acknowledging the validity of many of the elements of these arguments, there are those committed to bringing about social change and political empowerment in communities with histories of discrimination and political marginalization, who argue that some form of rights have been and continue to be crucial to achieving those goals. They point to the important role that rights claims have played in the struggles for inclusion and democratization waged by racial groups and women in the United States. For example, Patricia Williams writes: "For blacks in this country, politically effective action has occurred mainly in connection with asserting or extending rights" (Williams, 1991, p. 57) and continues a few pages later arguing that: "This country's worst historical moments have not been attributable to

---

[16]See Brems (1997) for a short critique and comparison between feminists and cultural relativists on human rights.

[17]For an example of the strongest forms of this type of critique, see Polis and Schwab (1979). For other critiques with variations on the main theme, see Tesón (1985), Cobbah (1987), and Donnelly (1984).

rights-*assertion*, but to a failure of rights-*commitment*" (Williams, 1991, p. 61). And in his strong critique of the critical legal studies condemnation of liberalism, rights and rights theory, law professor Robert Williams states: "For peoples of color, however, these icons mark trails along sacred ground. The attack by the Critical Legal Studies movement on rights and entitlement theory discourse can be seen as a counter crusade to the hard campaigns and long marches of minority peoples in this country. Minority people committed themselves to these struggles . . . [to attain] a seat in the front of the bus, repatriation of treaty-guaranteed sacred lands, or a union card to carry in the grape vineyards" (Williams Jr., 1987, p. 120).

What these debates illustrate is that both the theory and institutional practice of rights, including human rights, like so many other societal institutions, have played a dual and contradictory role in societies. On the one hand, they have clearly been used as mechanisms for excluding specific populations and providing judicial and even constitutional legitimation for doing so. On the other hand, as the earlier quotes emphasize, rights-claims have been crucial tools in the struggles to transform racist, sexist and other forms of institutionalized exclusionary practices. I would argue that emancipatory movements can ill afford to discard any resources, mechanisms, or strategies that may be of value in different phases of contestation. However, for rights claims to function in this way, the factors discussed by its critics that limit their effectiveness as a tool of empowerment need to be addressed. The question is whether there is an alternative way of conceptualizing and institutionalizing rights that can overcome these constraints. I believe there is, and in the next section, I want to outline some of the basic characteristics of this approach that proposes the need to engage the discourse and practice of rights in order to transform the static, male-centered, individualistic, abstract, and ethnocentric elements into an emancipatory political strategy.

RECONCEIVING RIGHTS AS
POLITICAL STRATEGIES

While there are a number of different defenses of rights, many continue to rely on some of the same assumptions that have been the basis of the critiques discussed above. One approach, however, that shifts the basic frame of reference is found in a number of essays that have attempted to develop a notion of rights that conceives of them as contested extensions of political struggles and seeks to root them within the lived experiences of disempowered sectors of the society. Let me begin by citing a recent article by Nedelsky that provides an initial step. She correctly characterizes the way that rights function politically and legally within the United States as resting on a notion of autonomy or freedom as limiting rather than enabling. This construes rights as "barriers that protect the individual from intrusion by other individuals or by the state. Rights define boundaries others cannot cross, and it is those boundaries, enforced by law, that ensure individual freedom and autonomy. This image of rights fits well with the idea that the essence of autonomy is independence, which thus requires protection and separation from others" (Nedelsky, 1996, p. 71). As long as rights are conceived of in terms of separating individuals from one another and the state, they are unlikely to be able to address the societal conditions that are the root cause of disempowerment. It is not separation but relationship, mutuality, and interdependence that characterize and define the horizon for action, and that provide the space for autonomy. This societal interdependence is the ". . . precondition in the relationships—between parent and child, student and teacher, state and citizen—which provide the security, education, nurturing, and support that make the development of autonomy possible. . . . Interdependence becomes the central fact of political life, not an issue to be shunted to the periphery in the basic question of how to ensure individual autonomy in the inevitable face of collective power" (Nedelsky, 1996, p. 71). In this view, rights are not seen as "an effort to carve out a sphere into which the collective cannot intrude, but a means of structuring the relationship between individuals and the sources of collective power so that autonomy is fostered rather than undermined" (Nedelsky, 1996, p. 72). So rights are conceived of as a particular type of mechanism whose function it is to "construct" relationships—"of power, of responsibility, of trust, of obligation" (Nedelsky, 1996, p. 75).

At first glance, this may seem to be simply a shift in perspective but in fact there are several implications of this approach for the way that rights are incorporated into the political world. First, it emphasizes the fact that the meaning of rights varies historically as societies change and is always a function of the various forms of contestation by different sectors of the population. Second, it links rights to the issue of democratic accountability by focusing on the extent to which institutions structure relations that foster inclusion and access. Third, it stresses the inherent connection between social struggles, social movements, and rights claims. And, finally, it allows us to understand rights as practices that take place in the realm of daily life within the sites of civil society.[18] From this perspective, rights are conceived of as a particular type of political strategy, not a static and reified legal claim. As one activist legal scholar states regarding her experience in both the civil rights and feminist movements, "We asserted rights not simply to advance legal argument or to win a case, but to express the politics, vision, and demands of a social movement, and to assist in the political self-definition of that movement. We understood that winning legal rights would not be meaningful without political organizing to ensure enforcement of and education concerning those rights" (Schneider, 1986, p. 605). Thus, I am proposing that rather than consider human rights as moral claims which are unlikely to be persuasive against power, the history of the role of rights in promoting forms of social justice and full inclusion in democratic nation states that are the final arbiters of such claims, suggests that human rights are better understood and more effective when they are considered and advanced as political strategies for empowerment linked to specific structural and institutional relations and contexts. These factors also imply that any assessment of the potential of the right to education as an essential component of empowerment strategies must situate rights-claims of particular groups within the specific societal position they occupy and the general societal conditions that exist at that particular time.

SOVEREIGNTY, GOVERNANCE, AND POLITICAL COMMUNITY

An earlier section of this chapter provided some indication of the particular pattern of Latino/a community development that has been greatly influenced by the internationalization of the economy. I argued earlier that the assessment of human rights regime as a potential Latino/a empowerment strategy needed to be based not only on an understanding of its nature and history, but that any such approach needed to emerge as well from an analysis of the specific societal position of Latino/a communities in the United States. As we have seen, Latinos are a vital part of an economy that is linked extensively with other countries. But

---

[18] I am here summarizing detailed discussions of these points elaborated in several different works. See, in particular, Nedelsky (1996), Villmoare (1991), and Schneider (1986).

societal transformation is not a unidimensional process and whereas the shift to global economic relationships has perhaps been the most significant cause, changes in political and cultural relationships and processes also have played a basic role. The economic dimensions of the transnationalization of capital has been fully documented but less attention has been focused on the contextual elements that influence the effectiveness and viability of highly interdependent global economic relations. Advances in transportation, communications, and technology have made the process of globalization possible. But the transnational dimension of these has not been unproblematic.

For nearly 3 centuries, the dominant Western powers have been organized politically in a system of nation-states based on the principle of absolute sovereignty within the nationally defined territory. The control of economic processes and development was conceived of as being within the province of the nation-state, and to a large extent still is. However, it is clear that in the current period, the economies of all of the major nation-states are so intertwined with other states that their political structures are incapable of controlling all elements of that process. So the globalization of capital has required a number of adjustments to this new level of interdependence with the creation of what Sassen calls the new regime of capital, consisting of new laws, agreements, treaties, and contracts that in effect constitute a transnational governing structure for the operations of capital (Sassen, 1996). Organizations like the IMF, the World Bank, and the International Economic Forum have become the primary instruments for stabilizing global capitalism. Thus, globalization has challenged the principles of territoriality and sovereignty that have been the defining characteristics of the meaning of a political community in the modern age. The question arises, then, whether this conception of political community provides the most appropriate basis for a form of democratic governance for the new pattern of relations of interdependence. It is through examining this disjunction between the levels of interdependence that characterize globalization, on the one hand, and the structure of political community, on the other, that I believe we can discover a space for promoting the use of human rights, and in particular, education as a human right, as an effective empowerment strategy for Latino/a communities.

In a recent essay on the effects of globalization on conceptions of political community, David Held argues that most contemporary notions of democracy rest on an incorrect assumption of the coincidence between political community and the territorially bounded nation-state, or as he puts it, the "uncritically appropriated concept of the territorial political community" (Held, 1999, p. 91). In fact, he claims, political communities have rarely coincided in this way with a given territorial or geographical space. Instead, political communities emerge on the basis of a complex set of interactions between social practices, economic linkages, political power, cultural and ethnic loyalties, and military conquest. The modernist notion that territorial boundaries should coincide with the right of rule and governance developed as a specific element of the processes of nation-building in Europe during the period between the 17th and 19th centuries. This is a view that has been advanced with increasing frequency in the literature on the challenges that globalization poses for democracy. One of the clearest articulations of this position is provided by R. B. J. Walker, who states that:

> It has been abundantly clear to many observers that the principle of state sovereignty is increasingly problematic. As a formalization of configurations of power and authority that emerged in a specific historical context, it has been criticized as an inappropriate guide to both theory and practice in an age of rapid transformation. It has come to seem particularly inappropriate in view of the current internationalization or globalization of economic, technological, cultural, and political processes. (Walker, 1990, pp. 161–162)

Thus, the particular way in which the relationship between power, governance, territory, identity, and membership was construed as part of what was a specific historical process of political and economic development in a limited region of the world at a particular time, has been transformed into more universalistic claims that equate the dimension of explicit power with the dimension of territorial space.

It should be recalled that this formulation and figuration of these elements was the product of a very specific set of political conflicts in 17th-century Europe that focused on rival claims precisely about the right to control and govern contested areas. The Treaty of Westphalia of 1648 was promoted and accepted as the basis for ending the Thirty Years' War and established the central principles of the nation-state that continue to be the basis of political relations 350 years later, which are: territoriality, sovereignty, autonomy, and legality (McGrew, 1997, pp. 3–60). The nation-state thus provided a particular answer to fundamental political questions such as: How should we understand the meaning of political community? Where are power and authority to be located? How is such power and authority to be legitimized? Despite the fact that this was an answer that corresponded to a specific, bounded historical set of circumstances, this model of political community and organization became the modality that was imposed on societies and nations characterized by entirely different conditions, cultures, values, and societal practices.

The effects of the processes that constitute globalization, economic restructuring, and transnationalization have given rise to a debate about the extent to which this particular construction of the principles on which the nation-state continues to function can accommodate the new patterns of relationships and linkages that have resulted from the flows of people, technologies, capital, images, and ideas that increasingly define the global map. A variety of theoretical positions have emerged that challenge the forms of political discourse that have either ignored or been insensitive to these flows and the transformations they have initiated. The critiques focus on attempting to demonstrate "how the questions to which the principle of state sovereignty has seemed to provide an uncontestable answer for so long—questions about who 'we' are, where 'we' have come from, and where 'we' might be going—might be answered differently" (Walker, 1990, p. 160).

It is precisely the constitution of the "we" that is assumed by the nation-state form that has been contested by the particular pattern of migration from non-European regions to the Euro-U.S. center. The fact that the predominant political unit is designated by the combined terms of nation and state is often overlooked. But it is clear that a foundational element of this framework was the attempt to link the dimension of identity and jurisdictional elements. The form of state nationalism in the particular context of nation-state building in Europe was essentially developed as a strategy for promoting cultural homogenization, whereas citizenship was the means for regulating the level and type of societal membership in a given nation-state, and territoriality was key in articulating these two dimensions and incorporating them into the institutional basis of governance and control. The exclusivist "we" that was privileged and granted membership in the initial formulations has been consistently contested since then by the political coalescence of a series of different types of groups, such as labor, women, racial and ethnic groups, and now by immigrants. It is clear that an essential element in the history of the development of the nation-state is the story of the various mechanisms, devices, laws, and regulations that have been created and relied on to contain the tension between independent logics of nation and state. The goal was to make the forms of social and cultural bonding and solidarity that characterize nations of peoples, coincide with the jurisdictional prerogatives that established the right to govern through the control of the political institutions, including the control of the organized means of violence. This is why the issue of membership has been such a crucial element in defining the parameters of the nation-state. The definition of the "we" is created and maintained by the nation-state's sovereignty over controlling membership, and although the means for doing so are varied, citizenship has played a particularly important role in this area.

However, there have been few instances where this control has been completely effective. In fact, the popular notion of citizenship as a rather clear-cut status is mostly fictional. Citizenship is neither singular, discrete, nor unchanging. Instead, we need to understand the theories and practices of citizenship as developed by nation-states as primarily a set of political mechanisms intended to control and regulate the level, type, and range of societal membership. And educational institutions, as Moll and Ruiz suggest, are primary mechanisms for exercising such control. Not only the dispersion of economic elements vital to the domestic system, but the wide-scale changes such as the racial and ethnic makeup of the United States that have resulted from the processes of globalization, presents nation-states with a challenge to their ability to exercise effective control over who the "we" are that constitute its normatively privileged "citizens." From this perspective, citizenship is not solely nor even primarily a legal status but, rather, a political mechanism for the control and containment of the distribution of rights, benefits, privileges, entitlements, and resources to different sectors of the population who reside within the territorial, sovereign boundaries of the nation-state.[19]

In response to these issues, an increasing body of work has been devoted to the analysis of alternative forms of determining societal membership in a global context. Drawing on these discussions, my view is that the nation-state continues to play a fundamental role in determining the configurations of power in the sphere of global politics, but the particular ways in which this occurs have changed. So the question of whether the power of the nation-state has been eroded by the processes of globalization should be reframed to ask what are the ways in which the character of the modern nation-state has changed

---

[19]One of the clearest analyses of this relationship between the nation-state, citizenship, and membership is provided by Brubaker (1989).

in response to these processes. Thus the issue is not whether the state is withering away but rather its "transformation under specific historical circumstances" (Walker, 1990, p. 167). One of the elements that has indeed changed as part of this transformation is that political authority is no longer solely exercised within clearly demarcated territorial boundaries. New regimes of the regulation, control, and organization of economic relations have been created by treaties, contracts, and agreements that nation-states have entered into during the last 30 years, and whereas most of these have been driven by economic concerns, the fact is that there is an inevitable political dimension to these. Policies and institutions such as NAFTA, the WTO, MERCURSUR, and the European Union, have all proposed that member nation-states agree to share some aspects of political authority, of their national sovereignty. The protestations or denials of some of the member states notwithstanding, the fact is that all of these efforts have created spheres of political and economic coauthority that are simply inconsistent with the claims of exclusive sovereignty that have characterized the conception of the nation-state for so long now. And the very existence of these new institutional arrangements is an indication of the growing disjunction between traditional forms of political authority tied to the nation-state and the most recent forms of global economic organization. In effect, the strategies developed to promote the viability of the global capitalist system have implicitly established the principle of shared sovereignty.

These practices and perspectives reflect the recognition that the processes of globalization and the impact they have had on the structure of societal relations require new institutional forms of governance. As I indicated earlier, nation-states have been forced to address the economic dimensions and with the participation of transnational capital, have established an extensive set of instruments that in effect create a regime of economic and political rights for transnational capital.

The logic and form of these regimes are driven by the need to respond to transnational networks, relationships, practices, that define regional communities of common *economic* interest. However, as I have stressed several times, these economic relationships do not and cannot exist or function in a vacuum. As the quote I cited from Held indicates, political communities are defined by "social practices, economic linkages, political power, cultural and ethnic loyalties" and the structures of governance, including the particular form of citizenship and the scope of rights that are its foundation, must correspond, articulate with, and reflect these patterns for society to be viable over time. Although the interests of the networks and practices of transnational capital are finding expression in sectors of the apparatus of governance, those specific forms of social relations, economic transactions, and cultural loyalties that constitute the lived reality of the majority of the population have not yet been incorporated in any systematic way into the institutions that define the official parameters of political community. As a result, there is a disjunction between the forms of governance still based on territorially defined notions of sovereignty and the actual social space created by the organic sets of relationships that define the real boundaries of a particular community. Societal relations evolve as a result of the interaction between individuals and groups with particular sets of values and beliefs, seeking to realize their goals, promote their interests, within a specific institutional context. What often occurs however, is that the latter become barriers to the kinds of strategies that individuals, families, households, and groups develop to meet changing circumstances. That is what I believe to be the case in the current period. Institutional change has occurred to facilitate the operations of transnational corporations, but not in response to the changes in the broader sectors of society. It is precisely the conception of who the "we" that should be considered as fundamental members of society that is at issue then. Although there are literally millions of households that have been and continue to be a vital part of the economic, social and cultural fabric of these regions, legal and political parameters that emerged as part of a very different societal configuration, prevent them from having equal standing and membership in the very society, the community of common linked fate that they have helped to create.[20]

Let me illustrate the argument with the example of Southern California. If the flow of goods, people, culture, capital, images, values, and so on that occur in the region and the networks that these give rise to were to be traced on a map, the territorial boundaries within which the majority of these flows occur would be clearly demarcated. In other words, these networks of interdependence are what in fact determine a community of common fate in spite of political or legal barriers that might exist. In the case of Southern California, this region of interdependence stretches from the northernmost area of Los Angeles county at the border with Ventura, all the way to the Mexican seaport of Ensenada, some 75 miles south of the international border. This argument,

---

[20] I am adapting the concept of "linked fate" developed by Michael Dawson in his analysis of racial politics in the United States. See Dawson (1994).

and the supporting evidence, has already been advanced by Wilkie in a recent volume on regional integration in North America (Wilkie, 1998). Far from being unique, Southern California is but one of several emerging sub- and transnational regions that are the basic units of political and economic reality on the continent. In the Pacific Northwest region of the United States known as Cascadia, consisting of the Canadian province of British Columbia, Washington, and the northern part of Oregon, is another region where there has been significant integration of the industrial base, including forms of unionization, as well as a high level of cross-settlement and the emergence of a common regional culture which have developed from what initially was an effort by urban areas on both sides of the international border to confront common challenges of environmental degradation. The common linkages and challenges of the tristate region consisting of New York, New Jersey, and Connecticut, although not crossing international borders, nevertheless illustrate that traditional structures of governance, in this case state governments, are no longer capable of responding effectively to what are in effect regionwide issues and challenges. And efforts to address this level of regional integration have even been undertaken within large-scale urban areas within one country, such as the case of Toronto, which created a regionwide governing structure, the Regional Municipality of Metropolitan Toronto, that shares responsibility for policy making with the various municipalities in the area.

Each of these regions constitute a community of common linked fate based on economic, cultural, and social linkages that function within a common environment. These are what I would argue define the boundaries of an organic political community that should be the basis of democratic governance. This is not to say that there are not common ties with other parts of the country, nor does it address the difficult question of the relationship between these regional political communities and the nation-state as a whole. What these do demonstrate, however, is that legally established borders and boundaries that define the jurisdictional powers of governance in these regions no longer correspond with or facilitate the development of democratic principles. This in effect has resulted in the de-democratization of regions such as Southern California where millions of the regional society's members have no opportunity to influence the decisions that affect them directly through the political process. Recent work in regional political economy now routinely operates on the assumption that regions are the basic units of the international system and the development of the European Union is but another example of attempts to create new structures of governance that can more effectively address the forms of interdependence across national boundaries that already exist in the region.

CONCLUSIONS IN STRATEGIC CONTEXT

The final issue I want to address is whether the position I am advancing is a politically feasible and viable one—the question of the potential effectiveness of adopting the specific type of human rights strategy I have proposed. The assessment of the *importance* of education for Latino/a communities ultimately depends on the normative political vision that underlies one's conception of empowerment. Although the right to a quality education can and has been defended on the basis of market logic, that is, as a form of "social capital" that is required to achieve individual economic advancement, the argument I am making here is instead based on the rationales articulated by the various human rights instruments I reviewed at the beginning of this essay, which are based on the principle of capacity development, that is, providing the conditions and resources so that each individual can realize their full capacity.[21] This is clearly a particular moral vision. However, although I do not disagree with those who attempt to convince governments to adopt these types of human rights on the basis of moral grounds, the record on implementation of these efforts has been extremely weak, as I discussed in the first part of this chapter. Instead, I have argued here that human rights should be seen as a political strategy whose potential *effectiveness* must be assessed in terms of the context within which it would be used and the social and political positioning of the groups advancing it. From my perspective, the goal of strategic political analysis is to identify those aspects within the overall institutional framework of the society that provide structurally based openings or opportunities for reform, that is, conditions or characteristics that are vital to the effective functioning of major institutional spheres, such as the economy, state, and cultural apparatus.

What I am suggesting here is that the very logic and practice of the adjustments in the notion of sovereignty adopted by nation-states, and the United States in particular, in response to the processes of globalization have themselves provided the rationale for the argument

---

[21]See the work of Amartya Sen for a defense of the notion that human rights should be based on what he terms "capabilities theory" and capacity building (Sen, 1999).

for transnational, regionally grounded rights for Latino/a communities, which would in effect establish the basis for a form of transnational or regional citizenship. Although these communities have been an integral part in the development of those regions in the United States most affected by globalization and that are most internationally interdependent, only a small percentage of Latinos have benefited from their role in that process. From a strategic perspective, the argument for the extension of rights and the development of expanded conceptions and practices of citizenship is rooted in this approach in the fact that the structure of governance has already incorporated the principle of shared sovereignty by establishing a regime of rights for transnational capital. To avoid moving in the direction of parallel rights for Latino/a communities given the vital role they play in that very transnational economy, would be to risk undermining and eroding the legitimacy of democratic governance. Although it is clear that the principles of democratic governance are not supported by transnational corporations on the basis of principle, they do, however, see these as one of the ways of securing the stability required for their effective functioning. I want to make clear that I am not endorsing the interests pursued by transnational firms but, rather, arguing that empowerment strategies should be developed that can take advantage of the structures and practices set up to advance those interests and use these to promote the well-being of Latino/a communities. Far from being a utopian vision, this approach can be promoted by educating and urging Latino/a communities, advocates, and organizations to focus on pressuring governments and firms to make the extension of the kinds of rights argued for here a part of the various treaties, conventions, laws, and so on, that are developed to promote the transnational sector of the economy and oppose any measures that do not provide for this form of inclusion. Given the demographic shift in the workforce and the interest of corporate actors in having a well-educated labor market, they can ill afford to ignore the fact that Latinos will be a major component of that workforce.

If the notion of political community I am arguing for is accepted, this then creates a space where the regime of human rights can play a role in helping to ground and legitimate strategies of empowerment on the part of Latino/a communities who are an integral part of a regional society without, however, being included as part of the governing process. For human rights basically challenge that notion that rights are the sole province of the nation-state. The essence of democracy is self-governance and requires effective participation by all members of the community that share a common, linked fate, which is what defines the effective boundaries of political community. When these boundaries of community are altered as they have been by the processes of globalization, realignments in the political structures of governance, including the nature and scope of rights, are required to maintain the legitimacy and long-term viability of a democratic polity. And it is only within this context that principles of social justice can be achieved. Although there is no one form that would be appropriate to all areas, in the context of the types of regional integration discussed here, what must begin to emerge are what I would call "regional" forms of citizenship based on a regime of transnational rights that reflect the basic principles of the human rights reviewed earlier. And in the current configuration of economic and social relations, the right to education is clearly one of the vital resources that members of these political communities must have available to them in order to not only to achieve security and advancements in the economic marketplace but also to be able to create the types of inclusive structures of governance on which a effective democracy must be based.

REFERENCES

Bauman, R. W. (2002). *Ideology and community in the first wave of critical legal studies.* Toronto: University of Toronto Press.

Bielefeldt, H. (2000). "Western" versus "Islamic" human rights conceptions? A critique of cultural essentialism in the discussion of human rights. *Political Theory, 28*, 90–121.

Binion, G. (1995). Human rights: A feminist perspective. *Human Rights Quarterly, 17*, 509–526.

Boyle, J. (Ed.). (1992). *Critical legal studies.* New York: New York University Press.

Brems, E. (1997). Enemies or allies? Feminism and cultural relativism as dissident voices in human rights discourse. *Human Rights Quarterly, 19*, 136–164.

Brown, W., & Halley, J. (Eds.). (2002). *Left legalism/left critique.* Durham, NC: Duke University Press.

Brubaker, R. (1989). Introduction. In R. Brubaker (Ed.), *Immigration and the politics of citizenship in Europe and North America.* Lanham, MD: University Press of America.

Callan, E. (1997). *Creating citizens: Political education and liberal democracy.* Oxford: Clarendon Press.

Chapa, J. (1998). The burden of interdependence: Demographic, economic, and social prospects for Latinos in the reconfigured U.S. economy. In F. Bonilla, E. Meléndez, R. Morales, & M. de los Angeles Torres (Eds.), *Borderless borders: U.S. Latinos, Latin Americans, and the paradox of interdependence* (pp. 71–82). Philadelphia: Temple University Press.

Chapa, J., & Wacker, C. (Eds.). (2000). Latino unemployment: Current issues and future concerns. In S. M. Pérez (Ed.), *Moving up the economic ladder: Latino workers and the nation's future prosperity* (pp. 61–87). Washington, DC: National Council of La Raza.

Cobbah, J.A.M. (1987). African values and the human rights debate: An African perspective. *Human Rights Quarterly, 9*, 309–331.

Cohen, R. (1997). *Global diasporas: An introduction.* Seattle: University of Washington Press.

Dawson, M. (1994). *Behind the mule: Race and class in African-American politics.* Princeton, NJ: Princeton University Press.

Donnelly, J. (1984). Cultural relativism and universal human rights. *Human Rights Quarterly, 6*, 400–419.

Falk, R. (2000). *Human rights horizons: The pursuit of justice in a globalizing world.* New York: Routledge.

Flores, W. V., & Benmayor, R. (Eds.). (1997). *Latino cultural citizenship: Claiming identity, space, and rights.* Boston: Beacon Press.

Frankenberg, E., Lee, C., & Orfield, G. (Eds.). (2003). *A multiracial society with segregated schools: Are we losing the dream?* Cambridge, MA: Civil Rights Project, Harvard University.

Held, D. (1999). The transformation of political community: Rethinking democracy in the context of globalization." In I. Shapiro and C. Hacker-Gordón, *Democracy's edges* (pp. 84–111). Cambridge, UK: Cambridge University Press.

Hodgson, D. (1998). *The human right to education.* Brookfield, VT: Ashgate Publishing.

Kim, N. (1993). Toward a feminist theory of human rights: Straddling the fence between Western imperialism and uncritical absolutism. *Columbia Human Rights Law Review, 25*, 49–105.

Künnemann, R. (1995). A coherent approach to human rights. *Human Rights Quarterly, 17*, 323–342.

MacKinnon, C. (1983). Feminism, Marxism, method and the state: Toward feminist jurisprudence. *Signs: Journal of Women, Culture, and Society, 8*, 635–658.

McCorquodale, R., & Fairbrother, R. (1999). Globalization and human rights. *Human Rights Quarterly, 21*, 735–766.

McGrew, A. (1997). Globalization and territorial democracy: An introduction. In A. McGrew (Ed.), *The transformation of democracy? Globalization and territorial democracy* (pp. 1–24). Cambridge, UK: Polity Press.

Meléndez, E., Carre, F., & Hovino, E. (1995). Latinos need not apply: The effects of industrial change and workplace discrimination on Latino employment. *New England Journal of Public Policy*, Special Issue, Latinos in a Changing Society, Part 1 (Spring/Summer).

Mills, K. (1998). *Human rights in the emerging global order: A new sovereignty?* New York: St. Martin's Press.

Minow, M. (1987). Interpreting rights: An essay for Robert Cover. *The Yale Law Journal, 96*, 1860–1915.

Moll, L. C., & Ruiz, R. (2002). The schooling of Latino children. In M. M. Suárez-Orozco & M. M. Páez (Eds.), *Latinos: Remaking America* (pp. 362–374). Berkeley: University of California Press.

Morales, R. (1998). Dependence or interdependence: Issues and policy choices facing Latin Americans and Latinos. In F. Bonilla, E. Meléndez, R. Morales, & M. de los Angeles Torres (Eds.), *Borderless borders: U.S. Latinos, Latin Americans, and the paradox of interdependence* (pp.1–14). Philadelphia: Temple University Press.

Morales, R. (2000). What a Latino worker finds in the U.S. labor market. In S. M. Pérez (Ed.), *Moving up the economic ladder: Latino workers and the nation's future prosperity* (pp. 35–60). Washington, DC: National Council of La Raza.

Nedelsky, J. (1996). Reconceiving rights as relationship. In J. Hart & R. W. Bauman (Eds.), *Explorations in difference: Law, culture, and politics* (pp. 67–88). Toronto: University of Toronto Press.

Orfield, G. (2001). *Schools more separate: Consequences of a decade of resegregation.* Cambridge, MA: Civil Rights Project, Harvard University.

Pollis, A., & Schwab, P. (1979). Human rights: A Western construct with limited applicability. In A. Pollis & P. Schwab (Eds.), *Human rights: Cultural and ideological perseptives* (pp. 1–18). New York: Praeger.

Rocco, R. (2000). Associational rights claims, civil society and place. In E. F. Isin (Ed.), *Democracy, citizenship and the global city* (pp. 218–239). London: Routledge.

Roderick, M. (2000). Hispanics and education. In P. San Juan Cafferty & D. W. Engstrom (Eds.), *Hispanics in the United States: An agenda for the twenty-first century* (pp. 123–174). New Brunswick, NJ: Transaction Publishers.

Sassen, S. (1996). *Losing control? Sovereignty in an age of globalization.* New York: Columbia University Press.

Schneider, E. (1986). The dialectic of rights and politics: Perspectives from the Women's Movement. *New York University Law Review, 61,* 589–652.

Sen, A. (1999). Development as freedom. New York: Oxford University Press.

Sjoberg, G., Gill, E. A., & Williams, N. (2001). A sociology of human rights. *Social Problems, 48,* 11–47.

Suárez-Orozco, M., & Paez, M. (Eds.). (2002). *Latinos: Remaking America.* Berkeley: University of California Press.

Tesón, F. R. (1985). International human rights and cultural relativism. *Virginia Journal of International Law, 25,* 896.

Villmoare, A. H. (1991). Women, differences, and rights as practices: An interpretative essay and proposal. *Law and Society Review, 25,* 385–410.

Walker, R. B. J. (1990). Sovereignty, identity, community: Reflections on the horizons of contemporary political practice. In R. B. J. Walker and Saul H. Mendlovitz (Eds.), *Contending sovereignties: Redefining political community* (pp. 159–185). Boulder, CO: Lynne Rienner.

Wilkie, J. W. (1998). Afterword: On studying cities and regions: Real and virtual. In J. W. Wilkie & C. E. Smith (Eds.), *Integrating cities and regions: North America faces globalization* (pp. 525–544). Los Angeles: Joint publication of Universidad de Guadalajara, UCLA Program on Mexico, and El Centro Internacional Lucas Alamán Para El Crecimiento Económico, A.C.

Williams, P. J. (1991). *The alchemy of race and rights.* Cambridge, MA: Harvard University Press.

Williams, R. A., Jr. (1987). Taking rights aggressively: The perils and promise of critical legal theory for peoples of color. *Law and Inequality, 5,* 103–134.

PART VI

Realizing the Power of Community Action

18

Reflections on Collaborative Research and the NLERAP Process

Pedro Pedraza
Center for Puerto Rican Studies, Hunter College,
City University of New York

In this final chapter, I would like to share my thoughts and insights about the NLERAP process as well as articulate, from my vantage point, important next steps in our journey. Specifically, I want to highlight three issues: (1) the consensus that emerged from our agenda document process, namely the need for a participatory approach to research; (2) the challenges that are inherent in this communal approach; and (3) what is needed to implement NLERAP's agenda.

CONSENSUS ABOUT A COLLABORATIVE APPROACH TO RESEARCH

One of the surprises of the 2-year focus group process that we undertook to produce a Latino/a education research agenda for K–12 public education (please see Appendix A) was that there lay untapped in our community a powerful collective resource. This was the consensus that we uncovered and fostered via our process of open dialogue about what should be done in education research. We discovered that for various reasons pertaining to the limitations of their institutional positions, one that no one could alone overcome, this vision was not being realized. These limitations were sometimes simply scarce physical resources, including time and place, sometimes ideological constraints on acceptable discourse, sometimes institutional role requirements and expectations, and sometimes insufficient group history, or sometimes lack of praxis, the attempt to achieve positive social change. This collective frustration with the inability to act on what one thought was needed to address the educational issues of Latino/a communities was expressed by many participants in our meetings as a lifelong challenge.

Initially, when NLERAP board members and regional meeting participants considered a Latino/a education research agenda, we produced a laundry list of issues, problems, and themes that could occupy us until the next centennial, and we ended that preliminary discussion with no decision about our agenda (not even a top-10 list). We decided to meet again and started our second set of deliberations by asking ourselves what could we recommend that probably no one else would if they were to initiate an effort on behalf of Latino/a communities. Our consensus began forming.

Part of the answer was that we did not want to do anything on behalf of, but rather with our communities, since the real untapped source of power to transform schools lay not in the reports, commissions, articles, and books emanating from research but in the effective use of those results in the mobilization of our communities as an agent of change. Research as a reflective tool to guide practice in the field, involving practitioners and community stakeholders, a grassroots bottom-up strategy for change, was for us an activity rarely undertaken in the field of education research in the United States. This was not to deny the importance of other approaches, for example, legal and legislative, but instead affirm that an effort aimed directly at the improvement of practice and policy from the perspective of those most affected by the schools via their participation in systematic investigative/scientific activity was missing and needed. As Smith (1999) states:

> In all community approaches, process—that is, methodology and method—is highly important. In many projects the process is far more important than the outcome. Processes are expected to be respectful, to enable people, to heal and to educate. They are expected to lead one small step further towards self-determination. (p. 127)

This idea of having the opportunity to work with problems in the practice of schooling and education (the two not synonymous in the eyes of our community, especially given the reductionist, skills-oriented discourse that now permeates school reform) with those actually affected by, or concretely engaged in, teaching and learning, was motivating for participants. The possibility of taking the lessons from this collaborative experience a step further to impact institutional policy at the local, state, or national level was even more attractive and inspiring.

COLLABORATIVE RESEARCH IN PRACTICE WITHIN LATINO/A COMMUNITIES

The difficulties that remain for us are actually in the details, the practice of developmental, participatory action research. Our understanding of the organization and process of studies or investigations is that questions should dictate the methods and not vice versa (please see appendix B). How would we operationalize this approach in the four areas discussed in our research agenda (please see appendix A)?

For example, how would a research project on the development of school leadership and supervision, be implemented utilizing participatory action research for the purpose of progressive community educational development? A project like this may be challenging given our current structures and institutions, requiring an altered social/institutional context to the one in which we as practitioners and academics engage daily. What new institutional relationships would be required that function on a respectful, egalitarian terrain and not on a power/authoritarian interaction model in which community insights, ideas, desires, and expectations are ignored or devalued?

One of the greatest challenges affecting our ability to implement this agenda is the construction of an infrastructure to support, nurture, and enable our learning communities of scholars, activists, practitioners, funders, and decision makers to carry out transformative research for social change. Articulating the vision and securing the funding is only the beginning of a complicated multilayered process.

Because we do not have all the experiences, conditions, knowledge, or practices readily at hand to completely inform this work, we face formidable challenges to our partnerships and collaborations. What would an alternative relationship look like, and how would it function in actual interactions in a project at a school or community site in rural Texas or Washington versus an urban setting such as Los Angeles, New York City, or Chicago?

We have a challenge on our hands to heed Padilla's call (see chapter 16) for democratic principles to guide our activities and to not lose sight "of the prize." However, we also are not beginning in a total vacuum, and we have bits and pieces of experiences, knowledge, theory, and reclaimed or rediscovered community values and practices at our disposal. These resources, though, need to be articulated, recognized, and organized in ways that make them generally useful and taken from the private to the public realm.

There is an epistemological claim here that we are making (see chapters 15 and 16, by Hidalgo and Padilla, respectively) about the lack of attention to the characteristics of the social basis of relationships that undergird and influence knowledge production in general, and education research in particular. However, our claim or desire is not to push for a new orthodoxy but, rather, to create an additional strategy for change, pulling together new combinations of our human resources, social and cultural capital, not utilized before in knowledge production for education reform in Latino/a communities.

Bensimon et al. (2004) talk about various approaches to participatory research in order to distinguish clearly their approach from others:

> To more clearly define what we mean by the practitioner-as-researcher model, we will distinguish it from other forms of action-oriented research which prioritize participants as a key feature. Reason (1944) describes three approaches to participative inquiry: cooperative inquiry, participatory action research, and action science or action inquiry. (p. 108)

She and her colleagues go on to relate the following about their project in terms of the categories mentioned earlier:

> Participatory action research operates in the political realm and is concerned with producing knowledge and empowering people and communities through genuine collaboration. This model may have been more applicable to our project had we worked directly with students of color on participating campuses who were experiencing inequities in educational outcomes. Instead we worked with faculty, administrators, and staff to conduct research on this problem. When comparing the political power of these two groups, the students appear to be those in need of empowerment in terms of making institutional change. We chose to work with the faculty ... because we felt they were closer to and could have more direct effects on the decision-making systems of the institutions. (p. 109)

This example demonstrates one of the complexities of this approach that needs explication in formulating projects: Who is the community? Who is to decide how to deal with the variation within communities and its significance for the issues being investigated? Who owns or has custodial rights over the data? Who gets to publish, and what is to be done in situations where individuals who form part of collaborations also have institutional demands that only validate and recognize individual work? How and who determines what form of collaboration is the most appropriate or feasible?

NLERAP'S NEXT STEPS

In order for NLERAP to engage in collaborative research, we first and foremost need to form networks among Latino/a youth development practitioners, community organizers, out-of-school educational program and service providers, and academic and school-based professionals at all levels. We need legislators to make claims on state resources to support these networks via events, activities, and collaborative projects that create the work environments to make these actions not just exercises in venting frustrations, but rather interventions that concretely address real needs. We should use these opportunities to organize ourselves and develop the capacity to build on each others' efforts in order to share insights, resources, and possibilities as well as goals, values, and visions.

The focus of our efforts should be ultimately to optimize individual human development, particularly youth, as a means of reaching a broader goal of community development. The idea is to strengthen our communities' social fabric (i.e., culture, language, and identity) via a vital civic life that also contributes to the political and economic systems of the local, regional, national, and now global society.

Given that the U.S. government has rarely respected the language, cultural, and educational rights of certain members of its society, particularly those included via conquest or enslavement, new contingencies created by the globalization processes of this new millennia could force a reconsideration of the policies and practices that negatively impact on the democratic ideals and rhetoric of this country. This may be wishful thinking, but together with an internal political mobilization, perhaps a human rights agenda can be seriously addressed, if even only as a tactic for the acceptance of U.S. world leadership and, therefore, beneficial for the long-term self-interest of this nation.

REFERENCES

Bensimon, E. M., Polkinghorne, D., Bauman, G., & Vallejo, E. (2004, January/February). Doing Research that Makes a Difference, *The Journal of Higher Education*, 75(1).

Smith, L. T. (1999). *Decolonizing Methodologies: Research and Indigenous Peoples*. New York and London: Zed Books Ltd. and Dunedin: Otago Press.

Afterword

A Project of Hope: Defining a New Agenda for Latino/a Education in the 21st Century

Sonia Nieto
University of Massachusetts at Amherst

When I began my teaching career in Brooklyn, New York, in 1966, all my students were Puerto Rican and African American. Yet, in my teacher preparation courses, I had read very little about African American students, and I would have been astonished to find any research at all related to Latino/a students. Once I became a teacher, no in-service workshop dealt with these topics either. It was not until a couple of years after I started teaching that I finally came across a book, *Puerto Rican Children in Mainland Schools,* edited by Francesco Cordasco and Eugene Bucchioni (1968), which was the very first book I had ever seen that concerned Latino/a students in any way. To a young Puerto Rican teacher, it was a blessing, a book for which I will always be grateful. A number of years later, in 1972, the assistant principal of my school, P.S. 25, the Bilingual School in the Bronx, placed in each teacher's mailbox a copy of a special issue of *Interracial Books for Children,* of the Council on Interracial Books for Children (CIBC) that focused on Puerto Ricans in children's books. In 1975, the CIBC published an issue devoted to Chicanos in children's books (CIBC, 1975). Except for my own experience attending public schools in New York City, these formed the extent of my knowledge about Latinos in education.

Latino/a Education: An Agenda for Community Action Research is a welcome sign that things have changed quite a bit since I started teaching, but it is also a reminder that they have not changed nearly enough. Latino/a students are still miseducated and undereducated; they still have the dubious distinction of having some of the highest dropout rates in the country; they are still underrepresented among the college-going population of young people; they still have higher retention and disciplinary rates than students from other groups; they still, in a word, have not achieved the equal education that all children in our nation are promised. Through its statistical portraits, historical analyses, and its vision for the future, this volume reviews the past while it also helps to pave the way to a more hopeful future.

The chapters in this book also make it obvious that defining a new agenda for Latino/a education in the 21st century is more than an academic exercise. It is, as I have stated in the title, a project of hope. This is because defining a new agenda for Latino/a education in no small measure also means defining a new future for Latino/a and Latina students. It is no accident that most of the authors of this volume are Latinos and Latinas. Many of us know personally what it means to be on the receiving end of the kind of destructive and soul-wrenching policies and practices that have characterized the education of Latinos. But regardless of their identities, all the authors of this book have been intimately involved in the struggle to improve the educational landscape for Latino/a students. As a result, our work is not confined to the hours of nine to five, nor is it done only for purposes of tenure, promotion, or academic honors. Our work, instead, is based on the possibility of positively influencing the future of Latino/a communities in the United States and, in the process, of the entire nation.

The work of the National Latino/a Research Agenda Project (NLERAP) thus represents a bold departure from an agenda that has heretofore been controlled by researchers and policy makers who have been detached from the Latino/a community in both affiliation and concern. This is not to imply that the authors of this volume speak with one voice. On the contrary, they are remarkably different in many ways. From passionate to measured in tone, from veteran researchers to new scholars, from teacher educators to sociologists, and representing many diverse Latino/a groups, the authors nevertheless share an unequivocal commitment to improving education for Latino/a students.

In what follows, I comment on three themes that are evident throughout this volume. Specifically, I discuss the ways in which the volume authors revisit and reframe the discourse of Latino/a education; view and discuss shifting notions of identity and culture; and challenge traditional notions of research.

REFRAMING THE DISCOURSE

Although it is rare nowadays to find the kind of blatant deficit language that was prevalent decades ago (Latino/a students as "culturally deprived," or as "problems" for schools to solve), it is still all too common to see language such as "students at risk," or even the ubiquitous "achievement gap." These terms imply, as did previous deficit terms, that the problems reside largely in the students themselves. That is, there is an implication that students are "at risk" for something they *are*, *have*, or *do*, or as if the problem of the "achievement gap" is that students are too lazy or too dumb to learn. As many of the authors in this volume make clear, risk is *created* for certain students, including Latinos. Regrettably, however, this reality has been either unacknowledged or avoided in the research literature. If it were otherwise, the "achievement gap" might instead be defined as the "resource gap" or the "fairness gap."

The NLERAP agenda changes radically the nature of the discourse concerning the education of Latinos. Rather than reinforce deficit thinking, the authors in this volume provide rich demographic data and a fertile historical context for understanding the current state of affairs of Latino/a education (see, for instance, the chapters by Cordero-Guzmán, MacDonald and Monkman, Flores, and Montero-Sieburth). At the same time, they take on both the historical baggage of the discourse (the old labels, the inherent racism, the legacy of inequality) and all the latest code words (standards, assessment, accountability) and view them in the context of a different agenda, one based on an awareness of the sociopolitical context in which Latino/a students experience education, as well as on respect and advocacy for Latinos. This approach is especially evident in the chapters by González, Rueda, and Márquez-López. In addition, a number of authors use colonization as a framework for understanding and responding to the dismal failure of education for most Latinos. In this context, education is viewed in terms of political, economic, and psychological domination, and a Latino/a research agenda is proposed as a way to decolonize education (a perspective most clearly seen in the chapters by Tejeda and Gutiérrez and Moll and Ruiz).

Changing the discourse around Latino/a education is not new, of course: Ever since fair-minded researchers began studying Latinos (whether they were Latinos themselves, such as George Sánchez, working in the Mexican American community, or non-Latinos, such as Francesco Cordasco, whose research focused on Puerto Ricans), they have insisted on viewing Latinos as more than just deficits waiting to be fixed. Moreover, they have been adamant about understanding not only students and their families, but also the *context* in which students live and learn. But the change in discourse has been particularly evident in the past 2 decades since more Latino/a and Latina researchers began joining the conversation. What makes this volume unique, however, regardless of the identity of the authors, is the resoluteness with which they make it clear that the deficit discourse is unacceptable. Given the extraordinary heterogeneity of the authors in the volume, their message is loud and clear.

SHIFTING NOTIONS OF IDENTITY

Assimilation to the cultural mainstream was a largely uncontested reality and requirement for most European immigrants to this country. Learning English while shunning one's native language; setting aside cultural traditions; even changing one's name: these were all considered necessary for acceptance and success, particularly for academic achievement. The pattern, however, has been quite distinct for people of color, and Latinos have been in the forefront of challenging the historic trend. That is, Latinos and other people of color have maintained that relinquishing one's identity is too high a price to pay for acceptance and success. Hence, another difference heralded by this volume is the historic importance of self-definition and self-determination in the Latino/a community, including the ability to define oneself in community with others rather than only in individual terms, and the significance of culture in the schooling process. The chapters by Vásquez and De Jesús are particularly insightful in this regard. Significant conceptual work in epistemological innovations by Hidalgo; the theories of *decolonizing pedagogy* and *educational sovereignty* (see the chapters by Tejeda and Gutiérrez and Moll and Ruiz), and the assertion that *coraje y pasión* are also part of the equation in promoting educational excellence among Latinos (as articulated by Grinberg, Goldfarb, and Saavedra) all add a level of richness to our understanding of Latino/a education.

At the same time, the authors in this volume make it eminently clear that Latino/a identity is neither fixed nor frozen in time. Latinos are an astonishingly diverse group, representing all social classes and races, numerous national origins, various languages and language varieties, and multiple political orientations, among other differences. The authors also acknowledge the inherent hybridity in Latino/a identity in the United States and demonstrate how Latino/a culture is multiple and changing. Rather than viewing these multiple identities as problems, Henry Trueba (2003), in an earlier article, described this reality as a "new cultural capital," maintaining that it "will be crucial for success in a modern diversified society" (p. 24). No one reading this volume can come away thinking that one strategy, one curriculum, or one policy will work for all, or that one identity describes all Latinos.

CHALLENGING TRADITIONAL NOTIONS OF RESEARCH

The NLERAP distinguishes itself from conventional research in some crucial ways. The subtitle of the volume says it all: this is "an agenda for community action research." It is an agenda that reflects an unabashed and unapologetic advocacy for Latinos, as well as a deep connection with community. This is not surprising, as many of the scholars whose work is represented here situate their intellectual and social development firmly in the Civil Rights and ethnic studies movements. Hence, the agenda is also collaborative, participatory, and action-oriented. The agenda makes it clear that the very idea of research needs to be challenged, rescued from an antiseptic notion of science as distant and disinterested. By clearly laying out and exploring the history of the education of Latinos in this country, and by providing "counterstories" to the conventional wisdom about it (a central tenet of Critical Race Theory and one that serves Latinos well also; see Delgado, and Stefancic, 2001, this volume), provides a compelling rationale for continuing to expand research and action in Latino/a education. This is an agenda for study, reflection, and action. It is, in a word, an agenda for social justice, a point of view very different from a traditional research orientation.

The roots of the NLERAP help explain this orientation, and they help readers understand how the chapters in the book respond to the development of the agenda. The NLERAP was designed from the beginning as a participatory and action-oriented process, something that in academia is nothing short of a revolutionary process. It was grounded in a Latino/a vision of community activism and inclusion. Many of the chapters reflect this vision, both inside the traditional educational system and outside of it. In this agenda, education and empowerment go hand in hand (the chapters by Padilla and Rocco describe this reality well).

Likewise, the NLEPAP maintains that no research can be disconnected from the classroom, school, and district context, or from the policy framework. This claim is demonstrated in several chapters in the volume, for instance, those by De Jesús and Vásquez. As well, the agenda proposes an intellectual/emotional/soulful connection, a connection that is clear in the articulation of guiding principles (Pedraza and Rivera) as well the chapter by Grinberg, Goldfarb, and Saavedra. Rather than separating these, scholars concerned about the progress of Latinos celebrate this connection.

Latinos are not alone in insisting that research and advocacy be linked. As Mercado and Johnson Santamaría demonstrate in their chapter, African American and Native American scholars, also tired of the educational abuse suffered by the young people in their communities, have made similar demands. Making this kind of assertion is not only unusual; it also flies in the face of a conventional research stance. Unlike traditional research that may claim to be objective or unbiased, the NLERAP maintains that no research can be disconnected from the goals, wishes, dreams, and even the biases of those who do the research. The NLERAP does not propose "neutral" research but, rather, research that is in the interests of those being researched. This is a dramatic departure from conventional research that proclaims a detachment and impartiality from its "subjects." Rather than subjects of research, the NLERAP proposes that the objects of our research also become collaborators and decision makers. This is a remarkable deviation from the norm, and it may help challenge the vision of other researchers who work in our communities.

CONCLUDING THOUGHTS

Latino/a Education: An Agenda for Community Action Research is a valuable and timely book. Through its description of the National Latino/a Education Research Agenda Project, the volume celebrates the work of a number of veteran scholars who have been working for many years to improve the education of Latino/a youngsters at the same time that it heralds a new generation of researchers whose work and commitment are squarely in the arena of Latino/a education. Having Latinos at the center will certainly help change the nature of the conversation. Nevertheless, having Latinos at the center is no guarantee, by itself, that the situation will improve. Working alone, we still lack the political power to make change. Forming alliances with others, particularly with African American and other communities of color (a point made by Ruiz and Moll in this volume), as well as with other researchers and policymakers who support our work, is absolutely essential. This volume is a first vital step in defining ourselves and our agenda; the next step is to bring others in to work with us to achieve it. At the same time, we need to understand that research alone is not enough. To take just one example: There has been abundant evidence that bilingual education works (Beykont, 2000; Cummins, 2000), but the research by itself has not led to a change in policy. On the contrary, because native language instruction has been such a contentious issue in our society since its beginnings, the research has fueled cries of bias and self-interest, largely from non-Latinos but also from a small number of Latinos. As a result, today there are fewer bilingual programs, and less support for them, than at the beginning of the most recent bilingual education movement 3 decades ago. This is a good lesson that it is only when the political will is in tandem with the research that change happens, a message we cannot afford to ignore.

Nearly 40 years ago, Richard Margolis, asked to prepare a report about the status of Puerto Ricans in U.S. schools, wrote a powerful but gloomy assessment of their progress. Called *The Losers* (Margolis, 1968), the report chronicled the many ways in which Puerto Rican students and their families were shortchanged by the public schools. In explaining his choice of a title, Margolis wrote, "'The Losers' refers to us all. The children are losing all hopes of learning or succeeding; the schools are losing all hopes of teaching; and the nation is losing another opportunity, perhaps its last, to put flesh on the American dream" (Margolis, 1968, p. i).

The National Latino/a Research Agenda Project is a new attempt to "put flesh on the American dream." It is concerned with precisely this: the opportunity to make democracy and equal opportunity a reality for Latinos in the United States. Rather than a selfish self-interest, this is a vision for the greater public good. Given the statistical portrait provided in this volume, given our history and our future, it is obvious that educating Latinos well means that we all—Latinos and non-Latinos, young and old, and those at every level of society—benefit. A society in which nearly half of all Latinos fail to graduate from high school or in which only a tiny percentage have had postsecondary education will mean that we are all indeed "losers," because no society can function while a substantial portion of its members are undereducated or unprepared for the challenges of democracy and citizenship.

This volume makes it clear that we need a new vision of the education of Latino/a students, one that will make them winners. Rather than blame the victims of inferior education and limited educational opportunities, the researchers in this book have focused their lens on the strengths of Latino/a students and their communities. The authors, and the NLERAP agenda in general, provide directions for the future that may well shape the way that research on, about, for, and with Latinos is carried out in the 21st century. They paint a picture of a new research paradigm, one that is respectful and collaborative, purposeful and humble, hopeful and visionary. Our young people, our communities, and our nation will all surely be the winners.

REFERENCES

Beykont, Z. (Ed.). (2000). *Lifting every voice: Pedagogy and politics of bilingual education.* Cambridge, MA: Harvard Education Publishing Group.

Cordasco, F., & Bucchioni, E. (Eds.). (1968). *Puerto Rican children in mainland schools.* Metuchen, NJ: Scarecrow Press.

Council on Interracial Books for Children. (1972). Special issue on Puerto Rican materials. *Interracial Books for Children* (4), 1 & 2.

Council on Interracial Books for Children. (1975). Special issue on Chicano materials. *Bulletin,* (5), 7 & 8.

Cummins, J. (2000). *Language, power, and pedagogy: Bilingual children in the crossfire.* Clevedon, UK: Multilingual Matters.

Delgado, R. D., & Stefancic, J. (2001). *Critical race theory: An introduction.* New York: New York University Press.

Margolis, R. J. (1968). *The losers: A report on Puerto Ricans and the public schools.* New York: ASPIRA.

Trueba, H. T. (2003). Multiple ethnic, racial, and cultural identities in action: From marginality to a new cultural capital in modern society. *Journal of Latinos and Education, 1*(1), 7–28.

Appendix A

NLERAP

NATIONAL LATINO/A EDUCATION RESEARCH AGENDA PROJECT

EDUCATIONAL RESEARCH FRAMEWORK AND AGENDA

NLERAP Staff

Pedro Pedraza, Project Director
Melissa Rivera, Assistant Director
Victoria Núñez, Project Associate

For more information on NLERAP contact:
Victoria Núñez   vnunez@hunter.cuny.edu
Pedro Pedraza   ppedraza@hunter.cuny.edu

ISBN: 1-878483-71-4
©2003 Centro de Estudios Puertorriqueños &
Research Foundation, City University of New York
695 Park Avenue
New York, New York 10021
212-772-5688

web: http://NLERAP.hunter.cuny.edu

Spanish Translation of Agenda Document

Patricia Fernández
patriciafernandez@earthlink.net

Layout and Design:

somos arte
www.somosarte.com
design@somosarte.com
917-208-3058

INTRODUCTION

The National Latino/a Education Research Agenda Project (NLERAP) was founded in 2000 to voice a Latino/a perspective on school reform and the knowledge base needed to sustain that vision. NLERAP's efforts focus on research and school reform to improve academic outcomes and the long-term life chances of Latino/a students, their families and communities. The project has brought together various constituencies within the broader Latino/a community, all concerned with primary and secondary public education, into a process of dialogue and consensus building. Initiated by staff at the Centro de Estudios Puertorriqueños at Hunter College, NLERAP has been guided from the start by a national advisory board that includes academic scholars, practitioners and community advocates. It is this group that developed a first draft of a Latino research agenda. That document was discussed and modified by participants in nine regional gatherings around the United States, gatherings that brought together a diversity of stakeholders in the education of Latino students. The process yielded an amazing consensus within the national Latino/a community about the type of educational research needed and the issues to be addressed.

The Latino/a community has not been and continues not to be well served by U.S. public school systems. This miseducation of Latino/a communities is reflective of larger sociohistorical and economic inequalities that have resisted various remedies over the decades. As a result, by most measures of academic success, large numbers of Latino/a students in the U.S. are failing miserably, or rather, as NLERAP believes, U.S. public schools are miserably failing Latino/a students. As we begin a new century, more attention to these educational issues is required due to the tremendous population increase and projected growth of Latino/a communities in the U.S. This reality reinforces a sense of urgency within our community and informs the desperate need to create schools that are responsive to an increasingly multicultural, multilingual and transnational population.

For decades, research that sought to improve education for Latino/a students was conducted by non-Latino/a academics on issues ranging from bilingual education to immigration to standardized testing and has been based on unquestioned assumptions about the educational needs of Latino/a communities. This research has shaped both public opinion and social policy regarding the educational issues of Latino/a students and has left our community with the challenges imposed by the legacy of deficit models, among others. Further, in our experiences as Latino/a researchers, educators and activists, governmental and philanthropic infrastructures are not designed in ways that allow Latino/a communities (nor other non-dominant communities) to evaluate or define our own educational problems and solutions. Such approaches have served to marginalize the perspectives of Latino/a community members. We believe that the maintenance of poor educational outcomes for Latino/a students attending U.S. public schools is partly related to the existing culturally myopic research practices and policymaking structures in the U.S. Because the Latino/a community now possesses the human and intellectual capital in the form of academic researchers, educators and community advocates, we believe it is imperative that we work within a framework that we create and own. To this end, the NLERAP began a process of dialogue with the aim of constructing a framework and plan for the design, implementation, and assessment of pedagogical innovation, practice and educational policy, by and for Latinos/as.

NLERAP is the work of many different people representing diverse constituencies and stakeholders in the education of Latino/a communities across the U.S. However, this research agenda is meant to be neither an all-inclusive agenda, nor a prioritized listing of projects, as important an endeavor as those might be. Rather, the agenda is our effort to define an approach to inquiry to serve the more immediate concern of affecting current educational outcomes. The purpose is to document much that we know already works and to learn as much as we can about other possibilities for positive human development for the members of our communities.

AGENDA DEVELOPMENT PROCESS

The National Latino/a Education Research Agenda Project officially started in February 2000, though it had existed as an idea for years. NLERAP's goal was to articulate a Latino/a perspective on research-based school reform and to use research as a guide to improve the public school systems that serve Latino/a students and communities. The project began with a planning meeting with support from the Centro de Estudios Puertorriqueños at Hunter College and the Annie E. Casey Foundation. At this seminal gathering, educators, policy advocates, foundation representatives, and community activists decided that in order for this effort to be most meaningful and productive for our communities as well as educational contexts in general, we would have to adopt a new approach, in essence, that the agenda development process would be supremely important to the outcome of the document. That is, what the agenda said (its vision and priorities) would be determined by how it was created and who participated in its creation. Thus began the two-year process of gathering hundreds of folks involved in and impacted by

the education of Latino/a communities to discuss, imagine and innovate.

In March 2000 an advisory board was developed for NLERAP with a commitment to equitable representation with regard to gender, ethnicity, culture, region, and diversity of roles within the educational process. Our board members include university researchers, policy advocates, school faculty and personnel, education administrators, community organization representatives, local activists and artists from various Latino/a cultural groups (including Chicanos/as and Mexican Americans, Puerto Ricans, South and Central Americans, Cubans and Dominicans and others) as well as nine U.S. regions, including Puerto Rico (see Appendix B for list of board members).

Between April 2000 and January 2002, NLERAP gathered folks from these nine regions:
Northwest
Southern California
Midwest
Southwest
Northeast

New York metropolitan area
Washington D.C. area
Southeast
Puerto Rico

These focus groups created spaces to initiate dialogues among regional meeting participants about what is most needed in Latino/a educational communities. Though there were regional variations, overall, a consensus emerged about K-12 educational research for Latinos/as and is outlined in this document. We hope that this research framework and agenda will advise and guide researchers, policy makers, educators and institutions on important educational issues relating to and impacting on Latino/a communities. Mostly, we hope it will inspire readers like you to actively engage in efforts to improve the education and lives of Latinos/as and others.

OVERVIEW
OF DOCUMENT

The agenda is organized into four parts. In Part I, the Purpose and Goal of the initiative are presented. Parts II and III illuminate NLERAP's approach to research, highlighting the research process as a central tenet of our work. How and with whom the research is designed and conducted are equally important to the actual research questions. This orientation towards community participation and collective movement is the soul of NLERAP's vision and action plan.

In Part II four Guiding Principles are shared. These principles emerged from lively thinking and discussions about how NLERAP's vision of research would differ from others, in essence, what this collective effort could contribute to both Latino/a communities as well as educational practices and policies. In Part III, NLERAP's Methodological Principles are described, illuminating our commitment to developmental, community-engaged, action-oriented research that aspires to impact on issues of educational equity and social justice.

Part IV presents the first four Areas of Research NLERAP proposes to address in research projects. Instead of creating an infinite list of research

topics, NLERAP board members and regional meeting participants worked to first develop a framework for all research (as evidenced by the guiding principles and methodology). Eventually, some areas of research were identified and prioritized in order to begin projects with schools, communities and universities.

Some questions that guided the development of our areas of research include: What are the current, pressing policies to which we must respond as a community? What local issues do we have information about that can and should be shared with broader audiences? What questions do we have that few others are asking and that would benefit our communities?

Some areas of research (for instance, assessment and accountability) emerged in response to salient practices and policies severely impacting on Latino/a students and communities. Others (such as arts in education) emerged organically from the indigenous wisdom within Latino/a communities' history and culture. That is, there was a simultaneous top down (response to imposed structures and processes) and grassroots (affirmation of our communities' knowledge and assets) perspective on the selection of these areas of research. This list was conceived as a starting point for our collective work, not as a comprehensive list of issues NLERAP community researchers will address.

Part IV also presents NLERAP's current Action Plan for implementing the collective vision of the agenda, including the development of action research projects with local communities in Latino/a schools and neighborhoods. The aim of NLERAP's research efforts is to contribute to and impact on classroom and school practices, local community issues, state educational policies, and the field of educational research.

Finally, in the Appendices section, in addition to our board members, volume authors, acknowledgements and contact information, there is a more comprehensive view of the multitude of ideas, thoughts, musings, and discussion points that were shared during our regional gatherings.

PART I:
PURPOSE, GOAL AND OBJECTIVES OF THE AGENDA

PURPOSE

To generate an organic research framework, agenda and action plan for Latino/a, publicly-funded K-12 educational research that honors the participation of Latino/a community members and practitioners as well as university-based researchers. This framework and agenda can advise and guide researchers, policy makers, educators, families, community organizations and other institutions on important educational issues relating to and impacting on Latino/a communities.

GOAL

To design and conduct research that ensures Latino/a students are educated in a way that provides for their holistic development as well as their full and equal participation in broader social, economic and national and international political contexts.

By holistic development we mean that Latino/a students will be able to:

- affirm and build upon their linguistic and cultural heritage in school;
- develop critical literacies in the areas of reading, writing, numeracy, science, and sociocultural and political awareness;
- apply critical thinking skills in their intellectual and social endeavors;
- nurture a commitment to participate in community action and civic engagement; and
- develop physical, spiritual and emotional well-being.

OBJECTIVES

Some research processes that support NLERAP's goal include:

- identifying and helping improve educational conditions that support Latino/a students and communities;

- working with educators, community advocates and families to investigate and improve educational practices and policies; and
- documenting and disseminating processes and practices of action-oriented research with Latino/a communities.

Four principles guide the National Latino/a Education Research Agenda Project (NLERAP). These principles all focus on creating, forging and strengthening Latino/a communities.

1. HONOR SOCIOCULTURAL PERSPECTIVES

NLERAP projects examine and integrate the sociocultural perspectives of the students, educators and community members.

Our projects...

- affirm and engage cultural assets within Latino/a communities;
- respect linguistic variations, such as Spanish, English, bilingualism, bidialecticism, and, youth language; and
- recognize and respect commonalties and differences in origins and experiences, especially the variation, diversity and heterogeneity within and across Latino/a communities.

2. RECOGNIZE THE SOCIOPOLITICAL AND HISTORICAL CONTEXT OF LATINO/A EDUCATION

NLERAP projects integrate the social, economic, structural and political contexts that impact on the education of Latinos/as.

Our projects...

- appreciate, acknowledge and respect the similarities, differences and historical and current relationships to other communities, in particular with communities of African and indigenous ancestries.

3. CO-EDUCAR CON LAS COMUNIDADES

NLERAP projects incorporate community perspectives and voices in collaborative research and mentor all participants throughout the process.

482

Our projects...

- engage with communities and their constituents in collaborative and transformative research;
- affirm Latino/a researchers as a significant force for transforming education and assure that our research agenda actively involves Latino/a researchers; and
- mentor new generations of Latino/a researchers and leaders from diverse institutions and communities by involving them in research design, implementation and dissemination.

4. PROMOTE SOCIAL JUSTICE AND DEMOCRATIC IDEALS

NLERAP projects are based on a philosophy of equity, self-determination, human rights, and collective transformation.

Our projects...

- challenge existing research and policy agendas that do not serve the needs of Latino/a communities;
- build upon the assets, resources and knowledge bases in Latino/a learning communities as well as develop alternatives to the current educational systems;
- affirm human dignity and advocate for Latinos/as' rights to determine their own destinies; and
- promote the development of an informed and active Latino/a citizenry.

PART III:
APPROACHES TO RESEARCH

This National Latino/a Education Research Agenda is grounded in the principles of developmental, participatory action research where community researchers engage collaboratively with public school educators, parents, students and community activists in the design, implementation and analysis of education projects. This research approach is an especially important one for Latino/a communities in the United States whose voices are rarely acknowledged or valued.

We support educational research projects that:

- are collaborative and participatory;
- are interdisciplinary;
- are longitudinal (lasting between five and ten years);
- recognize Latino/a group variation;
- use appropriate and/or innovative methodologies;
- address ethical issues such as insider/outsider researcher roles/identities;
- encourage the reflective process and transform research and teaching;
- generate new understandings and theories that support the improvement of Latino/a education;
- influence educational public policy; and
- are responsive, maintain integrity and protect human rights.

PART IV:

AREAS OF RESEARCH

These four areas of research were selected after a long process of discussing and prioritizing the external policies and practices impacting on Latino/a educational communities (such as the standardization movement) as well as the organic and indigenous themes inherent in our communities (such as the creative arts).

1. ASSESSMENT AND ACCOUNTABILITY

Research will include investigation of the current movement to rely on standardized exams as the dominant mode of student assessment, the creation of standardized curriculums, and the use of high stakes testing to determine grade promotion and graduation eligibility, especially the impact standardization has on Latino/a students. In addition, extensive research on innovative and holistic assessments as alternatives or additions to standardized assessments, including the use of multiple measures to assess more holistically students' learning development over time, will be studied.

2. TEACHER AND ADMINISTRATOR EDUCATION AND PROFESSIONAL DEVELOPMENT

Research will address issues regarding the recruitment, preparation and retention of Latino/a educators, administrators and school personnel as well as the best ways to prepare and support all educators to work with Latino/a students.

3. ARTS IN EDUCATION

Research will focus on best practices and challenges to infusing and integrating the visual and performing arts as well as creative processes throughout the curriculum and holistic forms of assessment.

4. SOCIOCULTURAL, POLITICAL, ECONOMIC AND HISTORICAL CONTEXT OF LATINO/A EDUCATION

Research will address the historical placement of Latino/a groups as well as their present social and political position and how these conditions impact on their education. The nature of social relations among all stakeholders in the education of Latino/a students will be integrated into these studies, including governing structures of school systems.

LEVELS OF RESEARCH

Each area of research will address the following three levels: institutional, in-structional, and interpersonal. (For examples of possible research themes, please see the appendices section.)

- Institutional: to reconfigure schools and other social institutions to better and more effectively serve Latino/a students and communities;
- Instructional: to search for innovative pedagogies and practices that engage students and improve educational outcomes and community development for Latino/a populations; and
- Interpersonal: to consider assets and needs of Latino/a communities as well as important relationships within them.

RESEARCH ACTION PLAN

The current action plan for implementing NLERAP's vision includes the following six steps.

I. NATIONAL ADVISORY BOARD AND NATIONAL NETWORK

NLERAP's national advisory board was formed in February 2000. In addition to continuing our annual work with board members regarding fiscal, organi-zational and research issues, NLERAP intends to develop a national network of schools, communities and organizations working together on collaborative research projects to help improve Latino/a education in the U.S. (i.e. LEARN: Latino/a Education and Action Research Network).

2. COMMUNITY RESEARCH PROJECTS

Action research projects will be developed in collaboration with local communities in Latino/a schools and neighborhoods. Each research project will be a collaborative effort, including university researchers, school administrators and faculty, parents, community advocates, and in some cases, students. The research teams will develop a question to explore and investigate what is important and meaningful to the local school and community and that has implications for regional and state policy.

3. RESEARCH AND PUBLIC POLICY COMMITTEE

A national policy advisory committee met in December 2000 with representatives from various Latino/a advocacy organizations. NLERAP will continue developing direct links between research and public policy in both local and national arenas.

4. RESEARCH DESIGN GUIDELINES

NLERAP will convene a group of scholars and veteran community researchers to design and develop a set of methodological guidelines to ensure the rigor of all of NLERAP's research projects. In addition, research design teams, composed of researchers, policymakers and practitioners with extensive knowledge and experience in the specific areas of research will develop a design framework for NLERAP projects. The designs will be open and flexible to allow for regional variation and local issues, yet remain structured in order for NLERAP to build a collective story about Latinos/as across the United States and in Puerto Rico.

5. REGIONAL BOARDS

NLERAP will develop regional boards to design, implement and oversee all of the community research projects in their areas (i.e. Northeast, New York area, Southeast, Puerto Rico, Midwest, Southwest, Northwest and Southern California). For instance, the Southwest regional board will be responsible for the projects in Arizona, New Mexico, Colorado and Texas. National board members will also participate in their regional boards.

6. RESEARCH DISSEMINATION

NLERAP will continue to share its work with others through publications and presentations (such as with our edited scholarly volume published by Lawrence Erlbaum Associates). In addition, NLERAP participants will continue to present at local community venues and national forums.

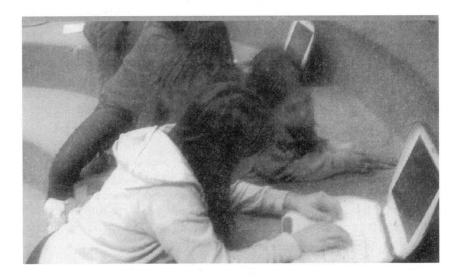

This section presents initial ideas, issues and concerns that were brainstormed during our regional focus group meetings as important topics that could and should be researched. The research themes are presented within each area of research as well as according to each level of research.

AREA OF RESEARCH # 1:
ASSESSMENT AND ACCOUNTABILITY

LEVEL # 1: INSTITUTIONAL

Theme: High stakes testing and accountability practices

Example Research Questions:
- What are the implications of the current standardization movement for Latino/a students and their teachers? For instance, what is the impact of high stakes testing on administrators, teachers, students and schools in a community with a large Latino/a population?

  [For instance, this can refer to standardized and high stakes testing that carry accountability policies, including implications for requirements for graduation and diplomas, grade level promotion and retention rates, funding sources for tutoring and enrichment programs as well as teacher support, etc.]

- What has occurred with Latino/a students and Latino/a serving schools in instances where insufficient progress (according to state standards) is being demonstrated?
- How do different partners perceive the impact on Latino/a educational communities?

Theme: Institutional ideologies, polices and practices (including educational reform efforts, movements and initiatives) that promote or prevent Latinos/as' education

Example Research Questions:
- What is the impact of multiple reform efforts that are implemented simultaneously in Latino/a serving schools?
- How has the overrepresentation of Latino/a students in special education changed in the current environment of standardization and high stakes testing?
- How successful have "scaling up" efforts been in Latino/a serving schools and districts?
  [Note: Scaling up refers to moving successful innovative practices at local levels to systemic-wide school reform.]

LEVEL #2: INSTRUCTIONAL

Theme: Successful, innovative and culturally responsive pedagogy, learning environments and assessment processes

Example Research Questions:
- Do project-based and service-learning curricula improve Latino/a student achievement?
- What instructional and assessment practices work best for the following Latino/a student populations: students with low levels of formal schooling, students with low literacy levels (especially those who are over-age for their grade), and bilingual students (or English Language Learners)?
- What are the most critical educational issues facing Latino/a students and their teachers in small schools and schools in rural towns?
- What are the most effective literacy practices for bilingual and dual language education?

Theme: Holistic student assessment

Example Research Question:
- How can graduation portfolios and performance assessment processes help us better understand student development?

LEVEL #3: INTERPERSONAL

Theme: Educator, parent, and community values, attitudes, and beliefs and their impact on educational attainment and student learning

Example Research Question:
- What do Latino/a parents view as the purpose of education (for instance, what should and should not be taught in school)?

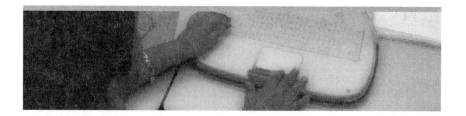

AREA OF RESEARCH #2:
TEACHER EDUCATION AND PROFESSIONAL DEVELOPMENT

LEVEL # 1: INSTITUTIONAL

Theme: Teacher and administrator education and professional development for community empowerment

Example Research Question:
- How can we better recruit and retain Latino/a educators and bilingual/bicultural educators?
- What are the benefits and drawbacks of emergency credentialing as a response to teacher shortages in Latino/a communities?
- What are new, twenty-first century issues for education administrators in Latino/a schools and districts?

LEVEL #2: INSTRUCTIONAL

Theme: Teacher and administrator education and professional development for community empowerment within Latino/a serving schools

Example Research Question:
- What are some best practices in the preparation of new Latino/a educators (bilingual/bicultural educators) and non-Latino educators who will work in Latino serving schools?
- What are effective supports for principals working in Latino serving schools?
- How do we best prepare educators for special areas (such as math, science and technology, special education, dual language education, and the visual and performing arts) and for combining these disciplines with holistic student development in Latino/a serving schools?

LEVEL #3: INTERPERSONAL

Theme: Relationships (the nature/quality of personal and institutional relationships over time)

Example Research Question:
- How can we improve teacher/student, student/student, and teacher/family/community relationships in Latino/a schools and neighborhoods?

- What are the multiracial and multiethnic relationships within Latino/a communities (i.e. nationality, immigrant status) and with other groups (i.e. African Americans, non-Spanish speaking Caribbean Americans, Asian Americans, Native Americans, and whites) and how do they impact on schooling?
- How will biracial Latino/a communities redefine racial issues in schools?
- How are educators nurturing gay, lesbian, bisexual and transgender Latino students?
- What structures are supporting Latino/a youth empowerment and student leadership within schools and the communities they serve?

AREA OF RESEARCH #3:
ARTS IN EDUCATION

LEVEL #1: INSTITUTIONAL

Theme: Collaboration on integrated arts curricula among various constituencies (schools, communities, school districts, and non-governmental organizations)

Example Research Question:
- How have/can schools and community organizations create educational projects that centralize the arts in the curriculum and learning process with Latino/a students?
- What type of administrative support is needed for integrated arts projects and programs?
- What processes and systems support the successful recruitment of Latino/a educators and artists (especially bicultural and bilingual teaching artists)?

LEVEL #2: INSTRUCTIONAL

Theme: Integration of arts disciplines and creative processes throughout academic curricula

Example Research Question:
- What role do/can arts concepts have in the learning process? For instance, what are the implications for cognitive, social, emotional development?
- How can the incorporation of the visual and performing arts improve learning for Latino/a students?
- How can teachers and schools best assess arts-based projects? What assessment processes are best suited for arts curricula?
- What type of professional development is needed to help schools develop collaborations between educators and artists in Latino/a serving schools?
- What is the role of popular youth culture (music, literature, dance) in classrooms with Latino/a students?

LEVEL #3: INTERPERSONAL

Theme: Diversity within the schooling environment

Example Research Question:
- How can arts-based curricula validate Latino/a culture and encourage respect among diverse communities?
- How can integrated arts projects support Latino/a student leadership within schools and communities?
- How can the integration of the arts help facilitate Latino/a families' involvement in their children's learning experiences?

AREA OF RESEARCH #4:
SOCIOPOLITICAL AND HISTORICAL CONTEXT
OF LATINO/A EDUCATION

LEVEL #1: INSTITUTIONAL

Theme: Governance and the politics of education and case law

Example Research Question:
- What impact has Proposition 227 (the eradication of bilingual education) had on California's Latino/a students and Latino/a serving schools and school districts?

  [Note: The same question could be asked of Proposition 209 (the elimination of affirmative action policies) and 187 (anti-immigration legislation) in California.]
- To what degree is there equitable access to high-level curriculum (such as advanced placement courses) in Latino/a serving schools? What policies can help insure equitable access to these courses?
- What is the role of community-elected school boards?

Theme: Mobility and Equity

Example Research Question:
- What are best practices for working with circular migrant, immigrant, and undocumented students?
- What is the relationship between housing policies and educational access for Latino/a students?

LEVEL #2: INSTRUCTIONAL

Theme: Examination of multiple paths and options to learning and success for diverse students, families and community members.

Example Research Question:
- What innovative educational options are available for high-level, untracked curriculum in vocational education?
- What are some successful academic practices for students in rural districts and students in geographic areas with small Latino/a populations?

LEVEL #3: INTERPERSONAL

Theme: The nature and quality of personal and institutional relationships over time

Example Research Question:

- How can schools better honor, affirm and integrate the complexities of Latino/a identities (including multiple nationalities, economic/social class, race and gender, religion, sexual orientation, region and type of school) into school culture?
- How can we use the notion of funds of knowledge in new and emerging Latino/a communities? How does the use of this notion improve Latino/a student success?
- How can parents and community members work in partnership with schools to develop successful schools that are connected to improving the quality of life of the neighborhoods in which they are located?
- What are similarities and differences in educator, parent, and community values, attitudes, and beliefs and their impact on educational attainment, learning experiences, school conditions, and student relationships among Latino/a students?

NAME	AFFILIATION
Ursula Berliner	Arizona State University
Miguel Carranza	University of Nebraska, Lincoln
María Casillas	Families in Schools
José Cintrón	California State University, Sacramento
Esperanza De La Vega	Lewis and Clark College
Barbara Flores	California State University, San Bernardino
Nilda Flores González	University of Illinois, Chicago
Ofelia García	Columbia University, Teachers College
Kris Gutierrez	University of California, Los Angeles
Frances Lucerna	El Puente Academy for Peace and Justice, New York
Victoria-María MacDonald	Florida State University
Luis Moll	University of Arizona, Tucson
Marta Montero Sieburth	University of Massachusetts, Boston
Sonia Nieto	University of Massachusetts, Amherst
Raymund Paredes	Hispanic Scholarship Fund
Sonia Pérez	National Council of La Raza
Harriet Romo	University of Texas, San Antonio
Richard Ruiz	University of Arizona, Tucson
Nora Sabelli	SRI International, Center for Technology in Learning
Virginia Valdez	Aspira of Illinois
Angela Valenzuela	University of Texas, Austin
Henry Trueba	Emeritus

NLERAP STAFF

Pedro Pedraza
Melissa Rivera
Victoria Núñez

NLERAP ACKNOWLEDGMENTS

We would like to thank all those who participated in our focus groups around the country: teachers, principals, counselors, school board members, state educational agency employees, advocates, funding agency officers, parents, legislators, and academics.

This agenda document was made possible with the financial and in-kind support of the following organizations, institutions, and individuals.

Centro de Estudios Puertorriqueños, Hunter College, City University
   of New York
Escuela Juan Ponce de León, Puerto Rico and Ana Maria Garcia Blanco
National Council of La Raza and Raúl González
The University of New Mexico, Albuquerque
The University of California, Los Angeles
The University of Massachusetts, Boston
The Inter-University Program for Latino Research at the University of Notre
   Dame (and Philip García)
The University of Texas, San Antonio
Hunter College, City University of New York and Carmen Mercado
The University of South Florida, David Anshen Center
The University of Puerto Rico
The University of Washington and Lila Jacobs

The Annie E. Casey Foundation
The Ford Foundation
The Edward W. Hazen Foundation
The Rockefeller Foundation

NLERAP Advisory Board Members (see appendix B)

NLERAP

PROYECTO DE AGENDA NACIONAL LATINA PARA LA INVESTIGACIÓN EDUCATIVA

AGENDA Y MARCO DE TRABAJO PARA LA INVESTIGACIÓN EDUCATIVA

Personal de NLERAP

Pedro Pedraza, Director Ejecutivo
Melissa Rivera, Directora Asociada
Victoria Núñez, Coordinadora

Para más información, puede comunicarse con:
Victoria Núñez   vnunez@hunter.cuny.edu
Pedro Pedraza   ppedraza@hunter.cuny.edu

ISBN: 1-878483-71-4
© 2003 Centro de Estudios Puertorriqueños &
Research Foundation, City University of New York
695 Park Avenue
New York, New York 10021
212-772-5688

web: http://NLERAP.hunter.cuny.edu

Traducción de este documento
Patricia Fernández
patriciafernandez@earthlink.net

Diseño del documento

somos Arte
Somos Arte
www.somosarte.com
design@somosarte.com
917-208-3058

INTRODUCCIÓN

El Proyecto de Agenda Nacional Latina para la Investigación Educativa (NLERAP, por sus siglas en inglés) se fundó en el año 2000 con el propósito de aportar una perspectiva latina sobre reforma educativa y los conocimientos fundamentales para respaldar tal visión. NLERAP ha centrado sus esfuerzos en la investigación y la reforma educativa con el fin de mejorar los resultados académicos y las oportunidades a largo plazo de los estudiantes latinos, sus familias y sus comunidades. Este proyecto ha reunido a una gran variedad de sectores de la comunidad latina, todos ellos relacionados con la educación pública primaria y secundaria, dando lugar a un proceso de diálogo y consenso democrático. Puesto en marcha por el personal del Centro de Estudios Puertorriqueños del Hunter College, NLERAP ha sido guiado por una junta asesora nacional que incluye a académicos, educadores y activistas que abogan por la comunidad latina. Este grupo de expertos redactó el primer borrador de la agenda, el cual se discutió y modificó durante nueve encuentros regionales a través de los Estados Unidos; encuentros que reunieron a una gran variedad de representantes dedicados a la educación de estudiantes latinos, dando como resultado un consenso extraordinario dentro de la comunidad latina nacional sobre el tipo de investigación educativa necesaria, así como los temas a tratar.

FUNDAMENTO de NLERAP

La comunidad latina nunca ha recibido y continúa sin recibir un buen servicio por parte de los sistemas de educación pública estadounidenses. Estas deficiencias educativas en la comunidad latina reflejan las grandes desigualdades económicas y sociohistóricas que no se han podido subsanar con diferentes medidas emprendidas en décadas pasadas. Como resultado, de acuerdo a casi todos los indicadores de logros académicos, una grandísima parte del cuerpo estudiantil latino en los EE.UU. fracasa rotundamente. O, según el punto de vista de NLERAP, las escuelas públicas de EE.UU. fallan rotundamente en su servicio a los estudiantes latinos. Con el comienzo de este nuevo siglo, es necesario prestar más atención a esta problemática educativa, sobre todo teniendo en cuenta el impresionante aumento en la población y la proyección de crecimiento dentro de las comunidades latinas en los EE.UU. Esta realidad refuerza la necesidad urgente de resolver esta problemática dentro de nuestras comunidades y pone en evidencia la necesidad apremiante de crear escuelas que respondan de forma efectiva a una población cada vez más multicultural, bilíngüe y transnacional.

Durante décadas, la investigación dirigida a mejorar la educación recibida por estudiantes latinos fue desarrollada por académicos cuyo origen no era latino. Los temas en los que se concentraban estos estudios incluían la educación bilíngüe, la inmigración y los exámenes estandarizados, pero siempre basándose en supuestos indiscutidos sobre las necesidades educativas de las comunidades latinas. Estos estudios han determinado tanto la opinión pública como la política social en lo referente a la educación de los estudiantes latinos, haciendo que nuestra comunidad se tenga que enfrentar sola a los desafíos impuestos por el legado de modelos deficientes, entre otros. Además, como nos demuestran nuestras experiencias como investigadores, educadores y activistas latinos, las infraestructuras gubernamentales y filantrópicas no están diseñadas para facilitar que las comunidades latinas (u otras comunidades que no son predominantes) evalúen o definan sus propios problemas y soluciones en lo que se refiere a lo educativo. Tales planteamientos sólo han servido para marginar las perspectivas de los integrantes de las comunidades latinas. Estamos convencidos de que los bajos resultados académicos de los estudiantes latinos en escuelas públicas estadounidenses están relacionados, al menos en parte, con las prácticas de investigación y estructuras de elaboración de política social, de carácter culturalmente míope. Dado que, en la actualidad, la comunidad latina en EE.UU. posee un rico capital humano e intelectual compuesto, entre otros, de investigadores académicos, educadores y activistas, creemos que es fundamental desarrollar esta labor dentro de un marco de trabajo generado por nosotros mismos. Con este propósito en mente, NLERAP comenzó un proceso de diálogo con la meta de construir un marco de trabajo y un plan de acción para el diseño, la implementación y la evaluación de políticas, prácticas e innovaciones pedagógicas, desarrolladas por y para los latinos.

NLERAP es la labor de una gran variedad de personas que representan a diversos sectores e intereses en relación a la educación dentro de las comunidades latinas de todo EE.UU. No obstante, esta agenda de investigación no pretende ser completa ni detallada ni pretende ser un listado de proyectos en orden de prioridad, aunque dichos cometidos sean de gran importancia. Más bien, esta agenda constituye un esfuerzo por nuestra parte de definir un planteamiento investigativo que aborde la preocupación más inmediata de mejorar los resultados académicos actuales. Nuestro propósito es documentar todo aquello que ya sabemos que funciona e indagar en todo lo posible otras posibilidades que fomenten un desarrollo humano positivo en las personas que componen nuestras comunidades.

PROCESO DE DESARROLLO DE LA AGENDA

El Proyecto de Agenda Nacional Latina para la Investigación Educativa comenzó de forma oficial en febrero del año 2000, aunque ya había existido como idea durante años. La meta de NLERAP era expresar una perspectiva latina en lo referente a la reforma educativa como resultado de la investigación correspondiente y utilizar dicha investigación como guía para mejorar los sistemas de

educación pública que prestan sus servicios a estudiantes latinos y sus comunidades. El proyecto se inició con una reunión de planificación con el apoyo del Centro de Estudios Puertorriqueños del Hunter College y la Annie E. Casey Foundation. En esta reunión seminal, educadores, expertos en política social, representantes de fundaciones y activistas de la comunidad latina decidieron que, para que este esfuerzo fuera realmente importante y productivo para nuestras comunidades, así como para los contextos educativos en general, habría que adoptar un nuevo planteamiento. Para nosotros, el proceso de desarrollo de la agenda sería tan importante como el resultado del documento. En otras palabras, lo que la agenda expresase (su visión y sus prioridades) vendría determinado por cómo se creó y quién participó en su creación. Así comenzó un proceso de dos años que reuniría a cientos de personas relacionadas y afectadas por la educación de las comunidades latinas para discutir, imaginar e innovar.

En marzo del año 2000, se creó una junta asesora para NLERAP con un compromiso hacia la representación equitativa en términos de género, grupo étnico, cultura, región y diversidad de roles dentro del proceso educativo. Los miembros de nuestra junta incluyen a investigadores académicos, expertos en política social, personal administrativo y docente universitario, administradores educativos, representantes de organizaciones comunitarias, activistas locales y artistas de diversos grupos culturales latinos (incluyendo chicanos/as y mexico-americanos/as, puertorriqueños/as, sur y centroamericanos/as, cubanos/as y dominicanos/as, entre otros), así como de nueve regiones de los EE.UU., incluyendo Puerto Rico (ver el Apéndice B para un listado de los miembros de la junta).

Entre abril del año 2000 y enero del año 2002, NLERAP reunió a personas de estas nueve regiones:
Noroeste
Sur de California
Medio Oeste
Suroeste
Noreste
Área metropolitana de New York
Washington D.C.
Sureste
Puerto Rico

Estos grupos dieron lugar a diálogos entre los participantes regionales sobre cuáles eran las necesidades más apremiantes en las comunidades educativas latinas. Aunque se registraron diferencias a nivel regional, se llegó a un consenso general, expuesto en este documento, sobre la investigación educativa para los grados K-12 en lo que concierne a la comunidad latina. Esperamos que esta agenda y marco de trabajo para la investigación sirva para asesorar y guiar a investigadores, legisladores, educadores e instituciones en lo referente a importantes temas educativos relacionados o incidentes en las comunidades latinas. Por encima de todo, esperamos que inspire a lectores como Ud. a involucrarse de forma más activa en la mejora de la educación y las vidas de los latinos y de otros grupos.

PERSPECTIVA GENERAL DEL DOCUMENTO

La agenda se divide en cuatro secciones. En la Parte I, se presenta el Propósito y meta de esta iniciativa, mientras que las Partes II y III explican el enfoque investigativo que siguió NLERAP, con particular énfasis en el proceso investigativo como principio fundamental de nuestro trabajo. De igual importancia para las cuestiones abordadas en la investigación son los aspectos de cómo y con quién se diseña y se realiza la investigación. Esta orientación hacia la participación comunitaria y la mobilización colectiva constituye el alma de la visión y el plan de acción de NLERAP.

En la Parte II se exponen los cuatro Principios rectores, los cuales surgieron de estimulantes reflexiones y conversaciones sobre cómo se diferenciaría la visión investigativa de NLERAP frente a otras; es decir, cuál sería la contribución de este esfuerzo colectivo tanto a las comunidades latinas como a las prácticas y políticas educativas en general. En la Parte III, se describen los Principios metodológicos de NLERAP, ilustrando nuestro compromiso con un tipo de investigación que se centra en el desarrollo, involucra a la comunidad, se orienta hacia la acción y aspira a crear un impacto en cuestiones de igualdad educativa y justicia social.

La Parte IV presenta las primeras cuatro Áreas de investigación propuestas por NLERAP como proyectos investigativos. En lugar de crear una lista infinita de temas de investigación, los participantes en las reuniones regionales y los miembros de la junta asesora de NLERAP se concentraron en el desarrollo previo de un marco de trabajo para todas las investigaciones (como prueban los principios rectores y metodológicos). Finalmente, se identificaron por orden de prioridad ciertas áreas de investigación con el propósito de iniciar proyectos con escuelas, comunidades y universidades.

Algunas de las cuestiones que han guiado el desarrollo de nuestras áreas de investigación son: ¿Cuáles son las políticas actuales más apremiantes a las que debemos responder como comunidad? ¿Qué cuestiones locales pueden y deben ser compartidas con una audiencia más general? ¿Qué preguntas nos hacemos que otros no se están cuestionando y que podrían beneficiar a nuestras comunidades?

Algunas áreas de investigación (por ejemplo, evaluación y responsabilidad) surgieron en respuesta a prácticas y políticas destacadas que perjudican seriamente a los estudiantes latinos y sus comunidades. Otras (como la presencia de las artes en la educación) surgieron de forma orgánica de la propia sabiduría de la cultura e historia de la comunidad latina. Es decir, hubo una perspectiva simultánea dirigista (respuesta a los procesos y estructuras impuestas) y de base (afirmación de los conocimientos y bienes de nuestras comunidades) en el proceso de selección de estas áreas de investigación. Esta lista se concibió como punto de partida para una labor colectiva, no como una lista completa y detallada de todos los temas que abordarán los investigadores comunitarios de NLERAP.

La Parte IV también presenta el actual Plan de acción de NLERAP para la implementación de la visión colectiva de la agenda, incluyendo el desarrollo de proyectos de investigación con miras a la acción en conjunto con comunidades locales en escuelas y barrios latinos. La meta de los esfuerzos investigativos de NLERAP es contribuir e incidir en las prácticas educativas en las clases y en las escuelas, en asuntos de las comunidades locales, en políticas educativas estatales y en el campo de la investigación educativa.

Por último, los Apéndices, además de proporcionar los nombres de los miembros de nuestra junta asesora y de los autores del documento, los reconocimientos y la información de contacto, también ofrecen un recuento más completo de la multitud de ideas, reflexiones, meditaciones y puntos de debate compartidos durante nuestras reuniones regionales.

PARTE I:
PROPÓSITO, META Y OBJETIVOS DE LA AGENDA

PROPÓSITO

Generar, con carácter orgánico, un marco de trabajo, agenda y plan de acción para una investigación educativa para latinos, financiada con fondos públicos, que abarque los grados K-12 y que respete la participación de los miembros de la comunidad latina, así como de investigadores adscritos al ámbito universitario. Esta agenda y marco de trabajo pueden servir para asesorar y guiar a investigadores, legisladores, educadores, familias, organizaciones comunitarias y otras instituciones en lo referente a importantes temas educativos relacionados o incidentes en las comunidades latinas.

META

Diseñar y llevar a cabo investigaciones que aseguren que los estudiantes latinos reciben una educación que propicie su desarrollo holístico, así como su participación completa e igualitaria en contextos más amplios: social, económico y político, tanto a nivel nacional como internacional.

Al decir desarrollo holístico, nos referimos a que estudiantes los latinos puedan:

- afirmar y fundamentarse en su patrimonio lingüístico y cultural en el contexto escolar
- desarrollar conocimientos competentes en los campos de la lectura, escritura, matemáticas y ciencias, así como concientización política y sociocultural
- ejercer capacidad crítica en sus actividades sociales e intelectuales
- fomentar un sentido positivo de obligación con respecto a la participación en acciones comunitarias y en el compromiso cívico
- desarrollar su bienestar físico, espiritual y emocional.

OBJECTIVOS

A continuación se enumeran algunos de los procesos investigativos fundamentales para cumplir la meta de NLERAP:

- identificar y ayudar a mejorar las condiciones educativas que beneficiarían a los estudiantes latinos y sus comunidades
- colaborar con profesores, miembros de la comunidad y familias con el fin de investigar y mejorar la política y práctica educativa
- documentar y divulgar en las comunidades latinas los procesos y aplicaciones de esta investigación, cuyo resultado debe ser la toma de medidas prácticas

PARTE II:
PRINCIPIOS RECTORES DE LA AGENDA

Los cuatro principios que guían el Proyecto de Agenda Nacional Latina para la Investigación Educativa se concentran en crear, construir y fortalecer las comunidades.

1. RESPETAR LAS PERSPECTIVAS SOCIOCULTURALES

Los proyectos desarrollados por NLERAP examinan e integran las perspectivas socioculturales de estudiantes, profesores y miembros de la comunidad.

Nuestros proyectos...

- afirman y aprovechan los bienes culturales que poseen las comunidades latinas
- respetan las diferentes expresiones lingüísticas, como el español, inglés, bilingüismo, bidialectismo y jergas juveniles
- reconocen y respetan las similitudes y diferencias de nuestros orígenes y experiencias, sobre todo el carácter variado, diverso y hetereogéneo de las comunidades latinas

2. RECONOCER EL CONTEXTO HISTORICO Y SOCIOPOLITICO DE LA EDUCACION LATINA

Los proyectos desarrollados por NLERAP integran todos aquellos contextos (social, económico, estructural, político) que inciden en la educación de los latinos.

Nuestros proyectos...

- aprecian, reconocen y respetan las similitudes, diferencias y relaciones actuales e históricas con otras comunidades, en concreto con las comunidades de ascendencia indígena y africana (no latinas).

3. CO-EDUCAR CON LAS COMUNIDADES

Los proyectos desarrollados por NLERAP incorporan las voces y perspectivas de la comunidad mediante el carácter colaborativo de sus investigaciones, y guían a todos los participantes durante la totalidad del proceso.

510

Nuestros proyectos...

- establecen colaboraciones con las comunidades con el fin de desarrollar investigaciones verdaderamente colaborativas y transformadoras
- afirman que los investigadores latinos constituyen una importante fuerza transformadora de la educación y aseguran su participación activa en la agenda de investigación
- guían a las nuevas generaciones de investigadores y líderes latinos provenientes de diversas instituciones y comunidades al facilitarles su participación en el diseño, implementación y divulgación de las investigaciones

4. FOMENTAR LA JUSTICIA SOCIAL Y LOS IDEALES DEMOCRÁTICOS

Los proyectos desarrollados por NLERAP se basan en una filosofía de equidad, autodeterminación, derechos humanos y transformación colectiva.

Nuestros proyectos...

- cuestionan las agendas políticas e investigativas existentes, las cuales no satisfacen las necesidades de las comunidades latinas
- se fundamentan en los bienes, recursos y conocimientos acumulados en las comunidades latinas, así como también desarrollan alternativas a los sistemas educativos actuales
- afirman la dignidad humana y defienden los derechos de los latinos a determinar sus propios destinos
- fomentan el desarrollo de los latinos como ciudadanosactivos e informados

PARTE III:
PRINCIPIOS METODOLÓGICOS

La Agenda Nacional Latina para la Investigación Educativa se basa en principios de investigación participativa. Esta metodología se fundamenta en la participación de miembros de la comunidad y se orienta hacia la acción. Los investigadores establecen colaboraciones con educadores, padres, estudiantes y activistas, todos ellos relacionados con la comunidad y afectados por el sistema de educación pública, con el propósito de diseñar, implementar y analizar proyectos educativos. Estos principios metodológicos son de suma importancia para las comunidades latinas de los EE.UU., cuyas voces rara vez se escuchan o se valoran.

Apoyamos proyectos de investigación educativa que:

- tienen un carácter colaborativo y participativo
- tienen un carácter interdisciplinario
- tienen un desarrollo a largo plazo, con una duración de entre cinco y diez años
- reconocen la diversidad entre los diferentes grupos que componen la comunidad latina
- utilizan metodologías innovadoras
- tienen en cuenta cuestiones éticas, tales como los roles y identidades de los investigadores ("insider/outsider")
- fomentan procesos de reflexión y transforman la enseñanza y la investigación

- generan nuevas teorías e interpretaciones que promueven mejoras educativas en las comunidades latinas
- ejercen influencia sobre la elaboración de política pública educativa
- demuestran sensibilidad, mantienen integridad y protegen los derechos humanos

PARTE IV:
ÁREAS DE INVESTIGACIÓN Y PLAN DE ACCIÓN

ÁREAS DE INVESTIGACIÓN

Se seleccionaron estas cuatro áreas de investigación tras un largo proceso de debate sobre las políticas y prácticas externas con incidencia en las comunidades educativas latinas (como la estandarización), así como de los temas internos y orgánicos inherentes a nuestras comunidades (como las artes creativas).

1. EVALUACIÓN Y RESPONSABILIDAD

Las investigaciones incluirán el estudio de la tendencia actual hacia la utilización de exámenes estandarizados como la forma dominante de evaluación del estudiante, la creación de planes de estudios estandarizados y el uso de exámenes de alto impacto ("high stakes testing") para determinar el paso a grados más avanzados y la elegibilidad para la graduación, prestando particular atención al impacto que causa la estandarización en los estudiantes latinos. También se llevarán a cabo extensos estudios sobre evaluaciones innovadoras y holísticas como alternativas o extensiones a las evaluaciones estandarizadas, incluyendo el uso de medidas múltiples para evaluar el desarrollo de los estudiantes durante un largo período de tiempo y según métodos más holísticos.

2. DESARROLLO PROFESIONAL Y EDUCATIVO DEL PERSONAL DOCENTE Y ADMINISTRATIVO

Las investigaciones abarcarán temas relacionados con la contratación, preparación y retención de educadores, administradores y demás personal latino en el ámbito escolar, así como las mejores vías de preparación y apoyo a todos los educadores en su trabajo con estudiantes latinos.

3. LAS ARTES EN LA EDUCACIÓN

Las investigaciones se concentrarán en aquellas prácticas y desafíos que infunden e integran las artes plásticas e interpretativas y los procesos creativos en todo el plan de estudios y en las formas holísticas de evaluación.

4. CONTEXTO HISTÓRICO, ECONÓMICO, POLÍTICO Y SOCIOCULTURAL DE LA EDUCACIÓN DE LOS LATINOS

Las investigaciones tratarán la ubicación histórica de los diferentes grupos latinos, así como su posición social y política actual y el impacto que estas condiciones tienen sobre su educación. Estos estudios integrarán los tipos de relaciones sociales existentes entre todas las personas relacionadas con la educación de los estudiantes latinos, incluyendo las estructuras de gobierno dentro de los sistemas de educación.

NIVELES DE INVESTIGACIÓN

Cada área de investigación tendrá en cuenta los siguientes tres niveles: institucional, docente e interpersonal. (El Apéndice A ofrece un listado de ejemplos de posibles temas de investigación)

- **Institucional:** Reconfigurar las escuelas y otras instituciones sociales con el fin de prestar servicios de mayor calidad y eficacia a los estudiantes latinos y sus comunidades
- **Docente:** Buscar prácticas pedagógicas innovadoras que despierten el interés de los estudiantes y mejoren los resultados académicos y el desarrollo educativo de la población latina
- **Interpersonal:** Tener en cuenta las ventajas, necesidades y relaciones presentes en las comunidades latinas

PLAN DE ACCIÓN

El actual plan de acción para implementar la visión de NLERAP incluye los siguientes seis pasos:

1. JUNTA ASESORA NACIONAL Y RED NACIONAL

La junta asesora nacional de NLERAP se formó en febrero del año 2000. Además de continuar nuestra labor anual con los miembros de la junta en lo referente a temas fiscales, organizativos e investigativos, NLERAP planea establecer una red nacional de escuelas, comunidades y organizaciones, las cuales participarán en proyectos de investigación colaborativos con el fin de mejorar la educación de los latinos en los EE.UU. (por ejemplo, Red Latina de Investigación para la Acción y Educación o LEARN, por sus siglas en inglés).

2. PROYECTOS INVESTIGATIVOS COMUNITARIOS

Se desarrollarán proyectos investigativos orientados a la acción con la colaboración de comunidades locales en escuelas y barrios latinos. Cada proyecto investigativo será un esfuerzo colaborativo, incluyendo a investigadores universitarios, personal administrativo y docente de centros educativos, padres, activistas comunitarios y, en algunos casos, estudiantes. Cada equipo de investigación se concentrará en una cuestión en concreto, explorando e investigando los aspectos más importantes y relevantes para la comunidad y escuela local correspondiente y su posible impacto en la política regional y estatal.

3. COMITÉ DE INVESTIGACIÓN Y POLÍTICA PÚBLICA

Un comité asesor de política pública se reunió en diciembre del año 2000 con representantes de varias organizaciones activistas latinas. NLERAP continuará estableciendo contactos directos entre la investigación y la política pública tanto a nivel local como nacional.

4. PAUTAS DE DISEÑO DE LA INVESTIGACIÓN

NLERAP convocará a un grupo de expertos académicos e investigadores comunitarios veteranos con el propósito de diseñar y desarrollar un conjunto de pautas metodológicas que garanticen el rigor profesional de los proyectos investigativos de NLERAP. Además, se crearán grupos de diseño investigativo, compuestos por investigadores, legisladores y educadores, todos ellos expertos con amplios conocimientos y experiencia en las áreas de investigación, que desarrollarán un marco de trabajo en lo que se refiere al diseño de los proyectos investigativos de NLERAP. Estos diseños tendrán un carácter abierto y flexible, dando espacio a las variaciones regionales y la diversidad de temáticas locales, sin que eso implique una pérdida de la estructura, de manera que NLERAP logre construir un cuadro colectivo de los latinos en los EE.UU. y Puerto Rico.

5. JUNTAS REGIONALES

NLERAP desarrollará juntas regionales para el diseño, implementación y supervisión de todos los proyectos investigativos comunitarios en sus zonas correspondientes (por ejemplo, Noreste, área metropolitana de Nueva York, Sureste, Puerto Rico, Medio Oeste, Suroeste, Noroeste y Sur de California). Por ejemplo, la junta regional del Suroeste se responsabilizará de aquellos proyectos desarrollados en Arizona, Nuevo Mexico, Colorado y Texas. Los miembros de la junta nacional también participarán en sus juntas regionales correspondientes.

6. DIVULGACIÓN DE LA INVESTIGACIÓN

NLERAP continuará compartiendo su proceso de trabajo mediante publicaciones y presentaciones (como nuestro volumen de edición académica y de próxima publicación por Lawrence Erlbaum Associates). Además, los participantes de NLERAP continuarán realizando presentaciones en locales comunitarios y foros nacionales.

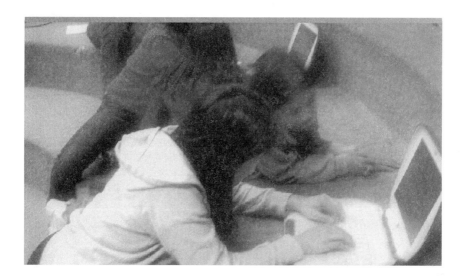

Esta sección presenta una serie de ideas, temas e inquietudes que surgieron de nuestras reuniones regionales como temas de importancia que podrían y deberían ser estudiados. Estos temas de investigación están organizados por áreas y, a su vez, por niveles de investigación.

ÁREA DE INVESTIGACIÓN N° I:
EVALUACIÓN Y RESPONSABILIDAD

NIVEL I: INSTITUCIONAL

Tema: Exámenes de alto riesgo ("high stakes testing") y prácticas de responsabilidad

Ejemplos de preguntas para la investigación:
- ¿Cuáles son las repercusiones de la tendencia actual hacia la estandarización para los estudiantes latinos y sus maestros? Por ejemplo, ¿cuál es el impacto de los exámenes de alto riesgo en los administradores, maestros, estudiantes y escuelas en comunidades con una población mayoritariamente latina?

  [Por ejemplo, puede referirse a exámenes estandarizados y de alto riesgo que conllevan políticas de responsabilidad, incluyendo repercusiones en los requisitos de graduación y obtención de diplomas, porcentajes de retención y paso a grados más avanzados, fuentes de fondos para programas extracurriculares y de tutoría o apoyo al maestro, etc.]

- ¿Qué ha pasado con los estudiantes latinos y con las escuelas que prestan servicios a la comunidad latina en aquellos casos en que no ha habido el suficiente progreso (según los estándars estatales)?
- ¿Cómo perciben las diferentes partes afectadas el impacto en las comunidades educativas latinas?

Tema: Ideologías, políticas y prácticas institucionales (incluyendo esfuerzos, movimientos e iniciativas de reforma educativa) que fomentan o que obstaculizan la educación de los latinos

Ejemplos de preguntas para la investigación:

- ¿Cuál es el impacto de los múltiples esfuerzos de reforma puestos en práctica simultáneamente en las escuelas que prestan servicios a comunidades latinas?
- En el clima escolar actual, dominado por la estandarización y los exámenes de alto riesgo, ¿cuáles han sido los cambios en la sobrerrepresentación de latinos en la educación especial?
- ¿Han tenido éxito los intentos de reforma en escala (*"scaling up"*) en las escuelas y distritos hispanos?
  [Nota: Reforma en escala ("scaling up") se refiere a prácticas innovadoras con un efecto positivo a nivel local que se incorporan a nivel sistemático en forma de reforma escolar.]

NIVEL 2: DOCENTE

Tema: Métodos pedagógicos, contextos de enseñanza y procesos de evaluación que demuestran un carácter innovador, capacidad de éxito y sensibilidad cultural

Ejemplos de preguntas para la investigación:

- El aprendizaje basado en proyectos interdisciplinarios y servicio a la comunidad, ¿mejora los logros académicos de los estudiantes latinos?
- ¿Qué prácticas docentes y de evaluación funcionan mejor con los siguientes grupos de estudiantes latinos: estudiantes con bajos niveles de educación formal, estudiantes con bajos niveles de alfabetismo (sobre todo aquellos que tienen una edad más avanzada que la que les corresponde por su grado) y estudiantes bilingües (o estudiantes que aún están aprendiendo inglés)?
- ¿Cuáles son las cuestiones educativas de importancia crítica a las que se enfrentan los estudiantes latinos y sus maestros en escuelas pequeñas y en escuelas rurales?
- ¿Cuáles son las prácticas más eficaces para la alfabetización en relación a la educación bilingüe?

Tema: Evaluación holística del estudiante

Ejemplos de preguntas para la investigación:

- ¿Cómo nos pueden ayudar a entender mejor el desarrollo del estudiante los portafolios de graduación y los procesos de evaluación de logros académicos?

NIVEL 3: INTERPERSONAL

Tema: Las creencias, actitudes y valores de los educadores, los padres y la comunidad y su impacto en los logros académicos y el aprendizaje de los estudiantes

Ejemplos de preguntas para la investigación:
*   ¿Cuál es la visión que tienen los padres latinos del propósito de la educación (por ejemplo, qué debería o no enseñarse en la escuela)?

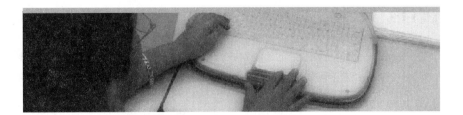

ÁREA DE INVESTIGACIÓN N° 2:
DESARROLLO PROFESIONAL Y EDUCATIVO DEL PERSONAL DOCENTE

NIVEL 1: INSTITUCIONAL

Tema: Desarrollo profesional y educativo del personal docente y administrativo para que la comunidad adquiera más poder

Ejemplos de preguntas para la investigación:
* ¿Cómo se pueden mejorar las prácticas de contratación y retención de educadores latinos y educadores bilíngües/biculturales?
* ¿Cuáles son las ventajas e inconvenientes de otorgar credenciales de emergencia como respuesta a la escasez de maestros en las comunidades latinas?
* ¿Cuáles son los nuevos temas, propios del siglo XXI, a los que se enfrentan los administradores educativos en las escuelas y distritos latinos?

NIVEL 2: DOCENTE

Tema: Desarrollo profesional y educativo del personal docente y administrativo dentro de las escuelas que prestan servicios a la comunidad latina

Ejemplos de preguntas para la investigación:
* ¿Cuáles son las mejores prácticas a la hora de preparar a nuevos educadores latinos (educadores bilingües/biculturales) y no latinos para su trabajo en escuelas que prestan servicios a la comunidad latina?
* ¿Cuáles son los apoyos más eficaces para los directores de escuelas que prestan servicios a la comunidad latina?
* ¿Cuál es la mejor preparación para los educadores especializados (por ejemplo, en matemáticas, ciencia y tecnología, educación especial, educación bilíngüe, artes creativas e interpretativas) y para la combinación de estas disciplinas con el desarrollo holístico de los estudiantes en escuelas que prestan servicios a la comunidad latina?

NIVEL 3: INTERPERSONAL

Tema: Relaciones (el tipo y calidad de relaciones personales e institucionales a lo largo del tiempo)

(CONTINUA EN LA PAGINA SIGUIENTE)

Ejemplos de preguntas para la investigación:

- ¿Cómo se pueden mejorar las relaciones maestro/estudiante, estudiante/estudiante y maestro/familia/comunidad en las escuelas y barrios latinos?
- ¿Qué relaciones multiraciales y multiétnicas existen dentro de las comunidades latinas (por ejemplo, nacionalidad, estatus inmigratorio) y con otros grupos (por ejemplo, afroamericanos, caribeño-americanos que no hablan español, asiático-americanos, nativoamericanos (indígenas norteamericanos) y angloamericanos (blancos) y qué impacto tienen en la educación?
- ¿Cómo pueden redefinir la problemática racial las comunidades latinas biraciales?
- ¿Qué tipo de contexto positivo crean los educadores para los estudiantes que se identifican como gays, lesbianas, bisexuales y transgéneros?
- ¿Qué estructuras fomentan que los jóvenes latinos tengan más voz y posibilidades de liderazgo dentro de las escuelas y sus comunidades?

ÁREA DE INVESTIGACIÓN N° 3:
LAS ARTES EN LA EDUCACION

NIVEL 1: INSTITUCIONAL

Tema: Colaboración con varios sectores (escuelas, comunidades, distritos escolares y organizaciones no gubernamentales) en la creación de planes de estudios que integren las artes

Ejemplos de preguntas para la investigación:
- ¿Cómo han desarrollado o pueden desarrollar las escuelas y organizaciones comunitarias proyectos educativos que den prioridad a las artes en sus planes de estudios y procesos de aprendizaje con estudiantes latinos?
- ¿Qué tipo de apoyo administrativo se necesita para el desarrollo de programas y proyectos artísticos integrados?
- ¿Cuáles serían los procesos y sistemas de apoyo necesarios para lograr atraer y contratar a educadores y artistas latinos (sobre todo artistas docentes bilíngües y biculturales)?

NIVEL 2: DOCENTE

Tema: Integración de disciplinas artísticas y procesos creativos en todos los planes de estudios

Ejemplos de preguntas para la investigación:
- ¿Qué papel juegan o pueden jugar los conceptos artísticos en el proceso de aprendizaje? Por ejemplo, ¿qué implicaciones pueden tener en el desarrollo emocional, social, cognitivo?
- ¿Cómo se puede mejorar el aprendizaje de los latinos mediante la incorporación de las artes plásticas e interpretativas y visuales?
- ¿Cómo se puede optimizar la evaluación de proyectos fundamentados en las artes por parte de maestros y escuelas? ¿Qué procesos de evaluación son los más adecuados para un plan de estudios fundamentado en las artes?
- ¿Qué tipo de desarrollo profesional se necesita para que las escuelas puedan establecer colaboraciones entre educadores y artistas en escuelas que prestan servicios a la comunidad latina?
- ¿Qué papel juega la cultura juvenil popular (música, literatura, danza) en clases con estudiantes latinos?

(CONTINUA EN LA PAGINA SIGUIENTE)

NIVEL 3: INTERPERSONAL

Tema: Diversidad dentro del contexto escolar

Ejemplos de preguntas para la investigación:
* ¿Cómo pueden validar la cultura latina y fomentar el respeto entre comunidades diversas los planes de estudios fundamentados en las artes?
* ¿Cómo pueden apoyar los proyectos artísticos integrados el liderazgo estudiantil latino dentro de las escuelas y comunidades?
* ¿Cómo puede la integración de las artes facilitar la participación de las familias latinas en el aprendizaje de sus hijos?

ÁREA DE INVESTIGACIÓN N° 4:
CONTEXTO HISTORICO Y SOCIOPOLITICO DE LA EDUCACION DE LOS LATINOS

NIVEL 1: INSTITUCIONAL

Tema: Gobierno y política educativa y casos legales

Ejemplos de preguntas para la investigación:
- ¿Qué impacto ha tenido la Proposición 227 (la eliminación de la educación bilíngüe) en los estudiantes latinos y en las escuelas que prestan servicios a las comunidades y distritos latinos de California?

 [Nota: Podría hacerse la misma pregunta en relación a la Proposición 209 (la eliminación de políticas de acción afirmativa) y 187 (legislación anti-inmigrante) en California.]
- ¿Hasta qué punto hay acceso equitativo a planes de estudio de alto nivel (como cursos avanzados) en las escuelas que prestan servicios a las comunidades latinas? ¿Qué políticas pueden ayudar a asegurar el acceso equitativo a este tipo de cursos?
- ¿Qué papel juegan las juntas escolares elegidas por la comunidad?

Tema: Mobilidad y equidad

Ejemplos de preguntas para la investigación:
- ¿Cuáles son los mejores recursos prácticos a la hora de trabajar con estudiantes indocumentados, inmigrantes o con un patrón de migración circular?
- ¿Qué relación hay entre la política de la vivienda y el acceso a la educación por parte de los estudiantes latinos?

NIVEL 2: DOCENTE

Tema: Exámen de los múltiples caminos y opciones al aprendizaje y al éxito para una gran diversidad de estudiantes, familias y miembros de la comunidad.

Ejemplos de preguntas para la investigación:
- ¿Con qué tipo de innovaciones educativas se podrían modificar los planes de estudios de alto nivel (pero sin seguimiento) de la educación vocacional?

- ¿Cuáles son algunas de las prácticas académicas que producen resultados positivos en estudiantes pertenecientes a distritos rurales y a zonas geográficas con bajo procentaje de latinos?

NIVEL 3: INTERPERSONAL

Tema: Tipo y calidad de relaciones personales e institucionales a lo largo del tiempo

Ejemplos de preguntas para la investigación:

- ¿Cómo podrían las escuelas respetar, afirmar e integrar mejor en la cultura escolar las complejidades inherentes a las identidades latinas (incluyendo múltiples nacionalidades, clases sociales y económicas, razas y géneros, orientaciones sexuales, regiones y tipos de escuelas)?
- ¿Cómo se puede utilizar el concepto de fondos de conocimientos en comunidades hispanos nuevas? ¿Cómo se podrían mejorar los resultados académicos de los estudiantes hispanos mediante el uso de este concepto?
- ¿Cómo podrían colaborar las escuelas con los padres y miembros de la comunidad para desarrollar escuelas competentes que mejoren la calidad de vida de los barrios en los que se encuentran ubicadas?
- ¿Qué similitudes y diferencias hay en las creencias, actitudes y valores de los educadores, padres y su comunidad y qué impacto tienen en los logros educativos, procesos de aprendizaje, condiciones escolares y en las relaciones entre los estudiantes latinos?

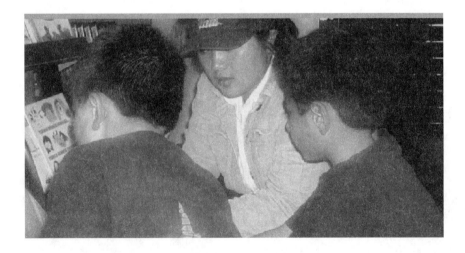

NOMBRE	AFILIACIÓN
Ursula Berliner	Arizona State University
Miguel Carranza	University of Nebraska, Lincoln
María Casillas	Families in Schools
José Cintrón	California State University, Sacramento
Esperanza De La Vega	Lewis and Clark College
Bárbara Flores	California State University, San Bernardino
Nilda Flores González	University of Illinois, Chicago
Ofelia García	Columbia University, Teachers College
Kris Gutiérrez	University of California, Los Angeles
Frances Lucerna	El Puente Academy for Peace and Justice, New York
Victoria-María MacDonald	Florida State University
Luís Moll	University of Arizona, Tucson
Marta Montero Sieburth	University of Massachusetts, Boston
Sonia Nieto	University of Massachusetts, Amherst
Raymund Paredes	Hispanic Scholarship Fund
Sonia Pérez	National Council of La Raza
Harriet Romo	University of Texas, San Antonio
Richard Ruiz	University of Arizona, Tucson
Elizabeth Saavedra	University of New Mexico, Albuquerque
Nora Sabelli	SRI International, Center for Technology in Learning
Virginia Valdez	Aspira of Illinois
Ángela Valenzuela	University of Texas, Austin
Henry Trueba	Emeritus

Personal de NLERAP

Vicky Nuñez
Pedro Pedraza
Melissa Rivera

RECONOCIMIENTOS DE NLERAP

Esta agenda pudo llevarse a cabo gracias al apoyo económico y táctico de las siguientes organizaciones, instituciones e individuos:

Centro de Estudios Puertorriqueños, Hunter College, City University of New York
Escuela Juan Ponce de León, Puerto Rico and Ana Maria Garcia Blanco
National Council of La Raza (y Raúl González)
The University of New Mexico, Albuquerque
The University of California, Los Angeles
The University of Massachusetts, Boston
The Inter-University Program for Latino Research at the University of Notre Dame (y Philip García)
The University of Texas, San Antonio
Hunter College, City University of New York y Carmen Mercado
The University of South Florida
The University of Puerto Rico
University of Washington y Lila Jacobs

The Annie E. Casey Foundation
The Ford Foundation
The Edward W. Hazen Foundation
The Rockefeller Foundation

Miembros de la Junta Asesora de NLERAP (ver Apéndice B)

Autores del libro de NLERAP (ver volumen de próxima publicación por Lawrence Erlbaum Associates)

Appendix B

Incorporating Latino/a Communities Into Educational Research: Statement on Methodology

The National Latino/a Education Research
and Policy Project (NLERAP) Subcommittee
on Research Design and Methods May, 2004

The National Latino/a Education Research and Policy Project (NLERAP) was founded in 2000 to voice a Latino/a perspective on school reform and the knowledge base needed to sustain that vision. Through research, NLERAP works to improve the academic outcomes and the well being of Latino/a students, their families, and communities. The project has brought together various constituencies within the broader Latino/a community, all concerned with public education, into a process of dialogue and consensus building. Initiated by staff at the Centro de Estudios Puertorriqueños at Hunter College, NLERAP is guided by a national advisory board that includes academic scholars, practitioners, and community advocates. It is this group that developed a first draft of a Latino/a research agenda. That document was discussed and modified by participants in nine regional gatherings around the United States. The process yielded an amazing consensus within the national Latino/a community about the type of educational research needed and the issues to be addressed. The approach is outlined in this document.

This statement was initially developed by a subcommittee of the National Latino/a Education Research and Policy Project that was convened in November, 2003.

The subcommittee was convened thanks to the gracious support of the Spencer Foundation.

NLERAP Subcommittee on Research Design and Methods

- Dr. Hector Cordero-Guzmán, associate professor and chair, Department of Black and Hispanic Studies, Baruch College/City University of New York
- Dr. Anthony de Jesús, education researcher, Center for Puerto Rican Studies, Hunter College/City University of New York
- Dr. Michelle Fine, professor, Social/Personality Psychology Program Graduate Center, City University of New York
- Dr. Carmen Mercado, associate professor, School of Education, Hunter College, City University of New York
- Dr. Pedro Noguera, Steinhardt School of Education, New York University
- Dr. Robert Rueda, professor, Rossier School of Education, University of Southern California
- Dr. Ángela Valenzuela, associate professor of education, University of Texas, Austin

This statement was written by Victoria Núñez and Pedro Pedraza.

We also thank the Rockefeller Foundation for support of this subcommittee.

The following individuals participated in the development of this document: NLERAP National Advisory board; Esperanza de la Vega, Lewis and Clark College; Odalys Diaz, CUNY-ENLACE; Fred Frelow, Rockefeller Foundation; Barbara Flores, California State University; Úrsula Casanova, Arizona State University; Martha Montero-Sieburth, University of Massachusetts; Melissa Rivera, NLERAP; Victoria-María MacDonald, Florida State University.

© May, 2004 Centro de Estudios Puertorriqueños & Research Foundation, City University of New York, New York, New York

The Collaborative Parent Empowerment Project (1999–2002) conducted research and trained Latino/a parents in Massachusetts in the use of observation, the mapping of schools, and interviewing. The intent was to build upon the knowledge that Latino/a parents have of the schools their children attend and provide them with the tools to become "researchers" as a means of increasing their involvement in the schools and in their children's education. The project trained three groups of Latino/a parents in Massachusetts including Latinos who had been in the United States for more than one generation and first generation immigrant parents. Only one group of parents went forward to conduct research. One of those parents reported, "when I interviewed the principal directly about his views on bilingual education, he said everyone has a right to their own language. But when I asked the teachers what books they used, they stated they were told to only use English textbooks and put the Spanish ones away. This seems to be a big contradiction and I would like to know why." In this example, the personal beliefs of educators demonstrate a respect for bilingualism yet the educational policies of using books only in English communicates the message that schools only value literacy in English. Parents are among the stakeholders who wrestle most directly with the contradictions of the educational system, and the power of this approach to research is that parents can explore those contradictions that researchers so routinely uncover.—Professor Martha Montero-Sieburth, University of Massachusetts, Boston.

Since its inception, the National Latino/a Education Research and Policy Project has promoted stronger links between research, the improvement of educational practice, and public school system policies. The project's national board believes that in order to realize significant improvements in Latino/a academic achievement, Latinos need to move to the forefront of the planning, decision making, and implementation of education reform plans. Our interest is in creating stronger links between educational research and education reform plans, particularly those in which Latinos are major stakeholders.

NLERAP's vision of educational research that can better support schools is one that includes parents, educators, and community educational advocates as potential participants in designing educational research projects. The present research design statement provides detail to the concept of research that includes the participation of Latino/a community members, outlining what this type of research looks like and explaining why NLERAP promotes this type of research. We believe the following principles will help distinguish educational research projects that include Latino/a communities as collaborators and active participants:

1. involve the groups most affected by the research in framing research questions;

2. develop skills of critical inquiry among the participants work-
    ing on the research project, for example, through training work-
    shops and written materials accessible to lay people;

3. share drafts of the findings with the affected communities be-
    fore the interpretation of findings is complete. Similarly, share
    a draft of written results with the affected community before
    those results are published;

4. seek out ways that the research findings can be connected to
    resolving or improving conditions locally that go beyond schol-
    arly papers;

5. negotiate some form of reciprocity with the community most
    directly affected by the research, acknowledging the benefits
    that professional researchers accrue from their research.

Our adoption of this research paradigm emerged from focus groups
with over 200 Latino/a community members who are deeply engaged
in Latino/a education. These discussions occurred in nine regions
around the United States. We repeatedly heard frustration about
top-down research projects that leave out the voices of Latino/a
community members.

DISCUSSION OF NLERAP METHODOLOGICAL
PRINCIPLES

Involve the Groups Most Affected by the Research
in Framing Research Questions

One premise of this research paradigm is that connecting a broad base
of stakeholders to educational research will link educational research to
an often overlooked and untapped source of power to change schools:
the school community broadly defined. NLERAP's approach is to link
educational researchers to multiple stakeholders including school administrators, practitioners, advocates, parents/families, and advocates,
in order to increase the possibilities that educational research can support needed changes and reforms.

This principle proposes research projects as a way of increasing community involvement in public education and more broadly, in building
civic capacity. This emphasis on a participatory research paradigm is
not intended to devalue research that is carried out using other approaches, nor research that comes from outsider perspectives. Rather,

it asserts research that involves communities as collaborative partners as an overlooked and underutilized approach in educational research in the United States.

> *University of Arizona researchers collaborated with students at Cholla High School (Tucson, Arizona) to implement a yearlong study, the Social Justice Education Project. The project investigated how students of color experience racial inequalities in education. The research adopted the unique approach of positioning students, rather than the usual adult "experts," in the forefront of designing and implementing the research. Students became education researchers by learning ethnographic research methods including participant observation, interview techniques and photo documentation. The goal of the project is for students to use their research as a vehicle for action that will address the inequalities that Latina/os experience in public schools. With students leading the way and conducting the study, SJEP provides the opportunity for student voices to enter the official dialogue on school policy and reform. The students will meet with local, state and national policymakers and officials to discuss their key findings along with specific recommendations for improving educational polices for students of color in Tucson and across the nation.—Professor Julio Cammarota, University of Arizona, Tucson.*

Develop Skills of Critical Inquiry Among the Participants Working on the Research Project Through Training Workshops and Written Materials Accessible to Lay People

A second premise is our projects' acknowledgment of the socially constructed nature of knowledge, and the incomplete nature of knowledge generated about our Latino/a communities when Latino/as are not involved in the research that produces that knowledge. Training can be offered to school community members so that they can fully participate in research projects and to improve their ability to help interpret and draw conclusions from the data.

> *Researchers at Centro de Estudios Puertorriqueños joined together with staff at El Puente Academy for Peace and Justice, an innovative high school in Brooklyn, New York, to carry out a research action project (1997–2000). El Puente Academy's principal, six facilitator/teachers and two Centro researchers joined together in a collaborative research group known as the biliteracy collective, and their objective was to use the research process as a learning opportunity for improving the educational experiences of bilingual/bicultural students. The biliteracy research collective completed activities together in four areas: (1) reviewing the scholarly literature on language acquisition and biliteracy development; (2) research at El Puente Academy on the language strengths and needs of students; (3) using the lessons learned from the research*

to train other facilitator/teachers at El Puente Academy; and (4) academic program development based on the research findings. In this way, a research project helped create a shared learning space where school staff participated alongside researchers in the entire research process (background study, research design, data collection and analysis, dissemination of outcomes, and implementation of findings).—Dr. Melissa Rivera, NLERAP associate director.

Share Drafts of the Findings With the Affected Communities Before the Interpretation of Findings Is Complete. Similarly, Share a Draft of Written Results With the Affected Community Before Those Results Are Published

School community members hold indigenous knowledge about their schools and the children and families that are served. They also hold the power to use new knowledge as a lever for change. Although they may not have training to analyze results, they will have the background knowledge to help researchers interpret their findings. At moments, critical research may identify what the school community does not want to acknowledge. Presenting findings before they are finalized is not intended as a moment of seeking approval, rather, of giving a community an opportunity to react to findings and allowing researchers to decide in what ways, if any, this feedback will be incorporated. This principle connects closely to the following principle that suggests that research written about local schools should not circulate above the school community, but should become a part of the school community's dialogue about itself.

Seek Out Ways That the Research Findings Can Be Connected to Resolving or Improving Conditions Locally That Go Beyond Scholarly Papers

In order for educational research to be most useful to Latino/a communities, the findings of the research need to move in a feedback loop back into the local school communities from which the data came. Presentations of research results that move in an upward manner (to academic conferences, journals, or to regional and national level policy makers) often leave individual school communities disconnected from the research to which they contributed. Using educational research as a tactic for school reform means that there are efforts made to share the research in ways that are accessible and interesting to local school communities that make day to day decisions about the education of children as well as to broader policy making bodies that will determine the policies in districts and states.

> More than 30 teachers, students, parents, school board members and university researchers participated in a research project on race and academic achievement entitled The Diversity Project (based at Berkeley High School, 1996–2000). Our plan was to use findings generated from our research to guide and influence changes at the school.

> Drawing from 1990 U.S. Census data, we obtained a very rough indication of the students' socioeconomic status based on where they lived. Students from homes in South and West Berkeley, the poorest sections of the city with the highest African American and Latino/a populations had the lowest grade point averages, while students in North Berkeley and the affluent Berkeley Hills had the highest GPAs. It turned out to be such a powerful illustration of the relationship between social class and academic achievement that the San Francisco Chronicle featured it in a front page article.—Professor Pedro Noguera, New York University.

Negotiate Some Form of Reciprocity With the Community Most Directly Affected by the Research, Acknowledging the Benefits That Professional Researchers Accrue From Their Research

The approach embodied by these principles seeks to counter long-standing power differentials in educational research in terms of who benefits from the process and the products of research. Our committee had a spirited discussion of what reciprocity might mean in an educational research project. For some researchers, presenting the new information that is generated through research back to the school community under study is sufficient to meet the need to "give back." For other researchers, building the skills of research project participants is an alternative way of giving back. Including school community members who participated in the research in public presentations can help raise the visibility of multiple research project participants, not just the visibility of the professional researcher. Paying research committee members a stipend, if research funding permits, is another means of addressing reciprocity.

In 2004, the current environment for educational research is strongly influenced by the position taken by the federal government, and the style of educational research it most strongly promotes is that of large-scale, randomized, field-based trials. This model of research has been broadly accepted and is familiar to the general public and to business leaders as one closely associated with the medical sciences. NLERAP acknowledges the usefulness of randomized field-based trials along with a wide variety of other research designs that can generate useful information, although we join others like the American Educational Research Association,[1] the premier network of educational researchers in the nation, in expressing dismay at the overemphasis on one type of research design. No one type of research design should be declared the most rigorous or the most scientific as it is the research question that should determine what research design is best for any particular project.

NLERAP promotes educational research as a key tool for improving the public education of Latino/a students, prioritizing an approach to research that "assumes that the purpose of research is not only to gain knowledge, but to use that knowledge to produce change that is consistent with a vision of a more equitable society . . . "[2] The inclusion of those affected by the practices and policies of our publicly financed educational institutions is fundamental to this approach, which is true for either quantitative, qualitative, or multiple method inquiries. We envision research as projects that hold the potential to build organizational alliances within school communities, helping to stretch the understanding of those who are the interested stakeholders in school communities. We plan a network of research projects in which school community members are invited to participate in forming the questions that get asked and in analyzing the significance of the results that researchers produce.

An Invitation: We invite researchers working with Latino/a communities to connect their research projects to the National Latino/a Education Research and Policy Project. The development of our capacity to initiate and complete these types of studies can be seen as an additional tactic for achieving greater social justice via improved public schooling throughout the United States. To the multiple strategies for social change that exist, legal, legislative, and top-down policy making, we can add bottom-up policy-making research. To develop the capacity to initiate and build on existing collaborations at the local level while drawing out the state and national implications requires an infrastructure of relationships, practices, and institutional arrangements that often does not exist, but needs to be organized and implemented. This is the goal of NLERAP.

---

[1] http://www.aera.net/meeting/councilresolution03.htm

[2] Center for Popular education and Participatory Research, http://www.cpepr.net, screen 1, 2/23/04

NLERAP National Advisory Board Members, 2004

Úrsula Casanova, Professor Emerita
Arizona State University, College of Education

Miguel Carranza, Professor
University of Nebraska, Lincoln

Maria A. Casillas, President
Families in Schools
Los Angeles, CA

José Cintrón, Professor
Chair of Bilingual/Multicultural Education
California State University, Sacramento

Esperanza De La Vega, Assistant Professor
Lewis and Clark College

Barbara Flores, Professor
California State University, San Bernardino

Nilda Flores González, Associate Professor
University of Illinois, Chicago

Ofelia García, Professor
Teachers College, Columbia University

Kris Gutierrez, Associate Professor
University of California, Los Angeles

Frances Lucerna, Director
El Puente Academy for Peace and Justice

Victoria-María MacDonald, Associate Professor
Florida State University, Tallahassee

Luis Moll, Professor
The University of Arizona

Martha Montero-Sieburth, Associate Professor
University of Massachusetts, Boston

Sonia Nieto, Professor
University of Massachusetts, Amherst

Raymund Paredes, Commissioner of Higher Education
Texas Higher Education Coordinating Board, Austin

Pedro Pedraza, NLERAP Director
Center for Puerto Rican Studies
Hunter College, CUNY

Sonia Pérez
National Council of La Raza
San Juan, Puerto Rico

Melissa Rivera, Associate Director
NLERAP, La Mesa, CA

Richard Ruiz, Professor
University of Arizona, Tucson

Harriet Romo
The University of Texas, Houston

Ángela Valenzuela, Associate Professor
University of Texas, Austin

For more information on the National Latino/a Education Research and
Policy Project:

Pedro Pedraza, Project   or   Victoria Núñez, Project
   Director   Associate
212-772-5711   212-772-5692
ppedraza@hunter.cuny.edu   vnunez@hunter.cuny.edu

Both can be contacted through NLERAP
Centro de Estudios Puertorriqueños
Hunter College, City University of New York
695 Park Avenue
New York, NY 10021

http://NLERAP.hunter.cuny.edu

About the Contributors

José Cintrón

Dr. Cintrón is a professor of education at California State University, Sacramento, College of Education and chair of the Bilingual/Multicultural Education Department. He teaches multicultural education, bilingual education, and social/psychoeducational foundations courses in the multiple subjects B/CLAD (Bilingual Culture Language Academic Development) and CLAD Certificate (Culture Language Academic Development) teacher credential program. In addition, he teaches advanced multicultural education and sociolinguistics courses in the Multicultural Education Master's Program.

Dr. Cintrón received his Ph.D. (1985) from the University of California, Santa Barbara, in Educational Psychology with specialization in Bilingual and Cross-Cultural Education. He has a B.A. in Spanish and M.A.T. from Purdue University. His academic interests include critical/multicultural education theory and curriculum integration, race theory, bilingual education, second language acquisition, teacher preparation, and school/classroom ethnography.

He recently completed a 5-year stint as co-director (with Dr. Nadeen Ruiz, CSUS) of the Migrant/Optimal Learning Environment (M/OLE) Project at CSU, Sacramento, funded through the California Department of Education, Migrant Education and International Office. M/OLE is a literacy staff development-training project for classroom personnel working with K–12 migrant students in California.

Dr. Cintrón's most recent work is a coedited volume (with Drs. Lila Jacobs and Cecil Canton, CSUS) about faculty of color in American universities entitled *The Politics of Survival in Academia: Narratives of Inequity, Resilience, and Success* (Rowman & Littlefield, 2002).

Héctor R. Cordero-Guzmán

Dr. Héctor R. Cordero-Guzmán is an associate professor and chair of the Black and Hispanic Studies Department at Baruch College of the City University of New York and a member of the faculty in the Ph.D. Programs in Sociology and Urban Education at the CUNY Graduate Center. He received his M.A. and Ph.D. degrees in Sociology from The University of Chicago.

Anthony De Jesús

Dr. Anthony De Jesús is a research associate at the Centro de Estudios Puertorriqueños at Hunter College (CUNY). A recent graduate of the Harvard Graduate School of Education, his dissertation presented an ethnographic case study of El Puente Academy for Peace and Justice in Williamsburg, Brooklyn, and explored the school's history and the ways in which students respond to its innovative, culturally responsive formal and informal curriculum. His current research interests include education policy, the sociology of education, Puerto Rican/Latino/a education and multicultural education. He is developing a research agenda at the Centro that explores the impact of the New York City Department of Education's "Children First" Reforms on Latino/a students and creating opportunities for Puerto Rican and Latino/a youth to engage in critical research in their schools and communities.

Barbara M. Flores

Dr. Barbara Flores, professor of education at California State University, San Bernardino, is a teacher educator in the areas of first and second language and literacy development. She has worked collaboratively with children, teachers, parents, and administrators in the development of effective pedagogy and assessment practices. She is also a scholar activist, community researcher, and writer.

Raúl González

Raúl González is legislative director with the National Council of La Raza (NCLR). In this capacity, he coordinates NCLR's federal legislative agenda. Focusing on education policy, Mr. González works with Congress, the administration, advocacy groups, and NCLR's affiliated community-based organizations to improve educational opportunities for Hispanic Americans. Before joining NCLR in 1998, Mr. González was a legislative assistant in the office of Representative Major R. Owens, for whom he worked on legislation to increase the academic achievement and attainment of poor children. As a teacher in the New York City public schools, Mr. González taught writing, algebra, and special education. This allowed him to learn firsthand about the needs of economically disadvantaged students. Mr. González was born in Puerto Rico, and was raised in Brooklyn, New York. He is a graduate of the City College of New York, with degrees in English and Psychology.

Jaime G. A. Grinberg

Dr. Jaime Grinberg is an associate professor of educational foundations at Montclair State University and the co-director of the New Jersey Network for Educational Renewal, a partnership between the university and 20 urban and suburban school districts. Dr. Grinberg has lectured in many countries, including Argentina, Mexico, and Israel. His research has been published in journals such as *Review of Educational Research, Teachers College Record, Educational Administration Quarterly, School Leadership*, and *Theory into Practice*, among others, and also has published his work in Spanish. He serves on the editorial boards of the journals *Youth and Society* and *Taboo*. He has published two books with Peter Lang Publications. A father of three school-aged children, presently his scholarship focuses on the history and genealogies of educational policies, politics and practices of teachers' and principals' preparation programs via cultural, social and political local and global contexts, and on the education of Latinos/as and immigrant students.

Kris Gutierrez

Dr. Kris Gutierrez, professor of education at the University of California, Los Angeles, focuses her research on studying the literacy practices of urban schools. In particular, her research concerns itself with the social and cognitive consequences of literacy practices in formal and nonformal learning contexts. Across her work, she examines the relationship between literacy, culture, and human development. She has conducted long-term ethnographic studies in Los Angeles area schools across various school districts. Issues of equity and excellence become important and recurrent themes throughout her work. She is a leader in the area of literacy, biliteracy, and urban education, and serves on a number of national policy-making and academic advisory boards/committees, is a keynote speaker at a number of state, national, and international conferences, and has had her research published in numerous educational journals.

Nitza M. Hidalgo

Dr. Nitza Hidalgo received her doctorate from Harvard University and is presently professor of education at Westfield State College, Westfield, Massachusetts. She teaches in the areas of multicultural education, foundations of education, and Latino/a studies. She is the director of the Westfield Professional Development School Network, a partnership between Westfield State College and five Westfield Public Elementary Schools. She is currently writing a memoir of growing up in El Barrio, New York.

Lila Jacobs

Dr. Jacobs received her Ph.D. in Education from the University of California, Santa Barbara in 1987, with an emphasis in Organizational Change and Cross-Cultural Education. She is a professor in the College of Education at California State University, Sacramento, and the former Chair of the Department of Educational Leadership and Policy Studies. She is the founder and Coordinator of the Urban Leadership Program, now in its 8th year succesfully graduating educational leaders for districts in northern California such as Sacramento, Grant, Oakland, and San Francisco. In the fall of 2004, she implemented a cohort with a focus on teachers of high-risk youth in the Los Angeles area Dr. Jacobs was the Co-Director of the K-12 Leadership Institute at the University of Washington with Dr. Rudy Crew, and has taught and conducted research for the Social Process Research Institute at the UC Santa Barbara, the Institute of Social Change at UC Berkeley, the Rockefeller Foundation, and Paul Allen's Vulcan, Inc. Dr. Jacobs is the editor of a volume entitled, *The Politics of Survival in Academia: Narratives of Inequity, Resilience, and Success* and the co-author of the book, *Cultural Conflict and Adaptation: The Case of Hmong Children in American Society.*

Lorri M. Johnson Santamaría

Dr. Lorri Johnson Santamaría is a professional educator with more than a decade of experience working with learners from K-HE. Currently she is an assistant professor of multicultural/multilingual education at California State University, San Marcos, where she teaches courses in the College of Education Teacher Preparation Program, conducts research, and writes with a focus on diversity and schooling, theory and methods of bilingual/multilingual education, the complexity of elementary multicultural/multilingual education, and assessment including over- and underrepresentational issues for children of color in special education programs.

Victoria-María MacDonald

Dr. Victoria-María MacDonald is associate professor, History and Philosophy of Education, at Florida State University. Her research examines the historical factors influencing Latino/a and African American children's educational experiences. She is the author of *Latino/a Education in the United States: A Narrative History, 1513–2000* (Palgrave-Macmillan, 2004).

Teresa Márquez-López

Dr. Teresa Márquez-López received her doctorate from Teachers College, Columbia University, in Educational Leadership and Bilingual/ Bicultural Education. Currently, Dr. Márquez López is the director of the Two-Way Immersion Biliteracy Specialist Institue (TWIBSI) at the University of California, Riverside, Graduation School of Education. She has served as principal investigator for a number of research projects and has taught graduate-level courses at Teachers College, Columbia University; University of California, Riverside; California State University, Long Beach; and Pepperdine University in Educational Administration and Teacher Education.

Carmen I. Mercado

Carmen I. Mercado received her Ph.D. from Fordham University in Language, Literacy and Learning. She has been affiliated with the programs in teacher education at Hunter College of CUNY since 1977, and as a faculty member in the Department of Curriculum and Teaching since 1988. Currently, Dr. Mercado also teaches in the Urban Education Ph.D. Program at the Graduate School of the City University of New York. Over the past two decades, Dr. Mercado has engaged in participatory community research with bilingual and mainstream teachers, students, with an eye toward understanding students' homes and communities as resources for academic learning.

Luis C. Moll

Dr. Luis Moll, professor at the University of Arizona, Tucson, was born in Puerto Rico. He has conducted educational research with language minority students for the past 22 years. Among other studies, he has analyzed the quality of classroom teaching, examined literacy instruction in English and Spanish, studied how literacy takes place in the broader social contexts of households and community life, and attempted to establish pedagogical relationships among these domains of study. He is presently conducting a longitudinal study of biliteracy development in children and the language ideologies that mediate that development. He has served on the editorial boards of several journals, and his most recent book, a coedited volume titled, *Theorizing Practices: Funds of Knowledge in Households and Classrooms*, will be published by Hampton Press. He was elected to membership in the National Academy of Education in 1998.

Karen Monkman

Dr. Karen Monkman is an associate professor of Social and Cultural Foundations of Education at DePaul University. Her research focuses on immigration and education, transnationalism and globalization, gender, international & comparative education, and critical perspectives of education. She is co-editor of *Globalization and Education: Integration and Contestation Across Cultures* (with Nelly P. Stromquist, Rowman & Littlefield, 2000).

Martha Montero-Sieburth

Dr. Martha Montero-Sieburth currently teaches in the Leadership in Urban Schools Doctoral Program and in the Education Leadership Master's Program at the University of Massachusetts, Boston. She is also an affiliate with the Mauricio Gastón Institute for Latino/a Community Development and Public Policy at the University of Massachusetts. Her research and teaching focus is on curriculum theory, bilingual and multicultural education, urban education, and community-based research, training Latino/a parents how to use qualitative research. She had coedited books with Gary Anderson, *Educational Qualitative Research in Latin America: The Struggle for a New Paradigm* (1998) and with Francisco Villaruel, *Making Invisible Latino/a Adolescents Visible: A Critical Approach Building upon Latino/a Diversity* (2000) and is working on a volume describing U.S.-born and immigrant Latinos.

Sonia Nieto

Dr. Sonia Nieto has been a teacher and teacher educator for over 35 years. She is currently professor of education at the University of Massachusetts, Amherst. Her research focuses on multicultural education and on the education of Latinos, immigrants, and other students of culturally and linguistically diverse backgrounds. Her books include *Affirming Diversity: The Sociopolitical Context of Multicultural Education* (4th ed., 2004), *The Light in Their Eyes: Creating Multicultural Learning Communities* (1999), *Puerto Rican Students in U.S. Schools,* an edited volume (2000), and *What Keeps Teachers Going?* (2003). She serves on several national advisory boards that focus on educational equity and social justice, and she has received many awards for her advocacy, activism, and research.

Raymond V. Padilla

Dr. Raymond V. Padilla is a professor in the Department of Educational Leadership and Policy Studies at the University of Texas, San Antonio. He developed the Student Success Model (SSM), which uses qualitative research methods to construct empirical models of student success. He is also the developer of HyperQual and Super HyperQual software for the management and analysis of qualitative data. He coauthored (with Miguel Montiel) *Debatable Diversity, Critical Dialogues on Change in American Universities (1998).* He also coedited (with Rudolfo Chávez Chávez) *The Leaning Ivory Tower, Latino/a Professors in American Universities (1995).* Through research and teaching over several decades, he has contributed to the fields of bilingual education, Chicana/o studies, higher education, and qualitative research methods.

Katia Paz Goldfarb

Dr. Katia Paz Goldfarb is an associate professor in family and child studies, Human Ecology Department at Montclair State University. Her teaching concentrates on issues of diversity and the importance of preparing future teachers to work with families. Her research and publications focus on school-home/families-community relationships with a specific interest in Latino/a immigrant families. She is a mother of three children, two daughters (14 and 10 years old), and one son (5 years old).

Pedro Pedraza

Dr. Pedro Pedraza, research director of education at the Centro de Estudios Puertorriqueños, Hunter College (CUNY) and director of NLERAP, has developed projects and published work on issues of language, culture identity, and education within the Puerto Rican and Latino/a communities in New York City, Puerto Rico, and Cuba for the past 30 years. He has designed and developed programs in the Puerto Rican community for children and adults, including the Young

Scientist Club and El Barrio Education Program. In addition, he has served on many boards of educational, advocacy, youth, and community organizations such as Advocates for Children, Educators for Social Responsibility, the Puerto Rican/Latino/a Education Roundtable, and New Visions for Public Schools.

Melissa Rivera

Dr. Melissa Rivera, currently the associate director for NLERAP, has worked for over 10 years as an educator and activist on many participatory research projects within youth programs, community-based organizations, prisons, public schools, and universities. Her research focuses on Latino/a youth, the performing arts, community development, and social justice and human rights efforts in educational contexts. She has a doctorate in education from the Harvard University Graduate School of Education.

Raymond Rocco

Dr. Raymond Rocco is an associate professor of political science at the University of California at Los Angeles. His work focuses on the relationships between globalization, democracy, citizenship, human rights, and marginalized communities, with an emphasis on Latin American communities in the United States. Recent publications include "Reframing Postmodernist Constructions of Difference: Subaltern Spaces, Power and Citizenship."

Robert Rueda

Dr. Robert Rueda is a professor in the areas of educational psychology and language, literacy and learning at the Rossier School of Education at the University of Southern California. He completed his doctoral work at the University of California at Los Angeles in educational psychology and special education, and completed a postdoctoral fellowship at the Laboratory of Comparative Human Cognition at the University of California at San Diego. His research has focused on the sociocultural basis of learning as mediated by instruction, with a focus on reading and literacy in English learners, students in at-risk conditions, and students with mild learning handicaps. He has most recently been affiliated with two major national research centers, CREDE (Center for Excellence, Diversity, and Education at the University of California at Santa Cruz) and CIERA (Center for the Improvement of Early Reading Achievement at the University of Michigan) and serves on the Advisory Board of CREST (Center for Research on Evaluation, Standards, and Student Testing at the University of California at Los Angeles). His most recent work has focused on how paraeducators mediate instruction and provide cultural scaffolding to English-learners and on issues of reading engagement among inner-city immigrant students in a central city community. He has consulted with a variety of professional, educational, and government organizations, has spoken at a wide range of professional meetings, and has published widely in the previously mentioned areas. He served as a panel member on the National Academy of Science Report on the Overrepresentation of Minority Students in Special Education, and is currently serving as a member of the National Literacy Panel (SRI International and Center for Applied Linguistics), looking at issues in early reading with English Language Learners.

Richard Ruiz

Richard Ruiz is professor of Language, Reading and Culture and interim head of the Department of Teaching and Teacher Education at the University of Arizona. His principal research interests are the education of language minority students and language planning and policy development. His international research includes literacy development projects in Guatemala and Mexico.

Elizabeth Saavedra

Dr. Elizabeth Saavedra is an associate professor of education at the University of New Mexico, Albuquerque. She has worked throughout her career with teachers in a process of transformative learning within contexts such as study groups and through ongoing inquiry. She has conducted research in the areas of teacher transformation and teacher study groups. She has completed and published research on the historical and genealogical constitution of Bilingual/ESL education in New Mexico. Other areas of specialization include literacy, biliteracy, teacher transformation and leadership, and social and cultural aspects of organizations and schools, discourse analysis, and issues of equity, social justice, and diversity. Her work had been published in numerous journals, including *Review of Educational Research*, *Theory into Practice*, and *Scholar-Practitioner Quarterly*. Her current research examines the historical and contemporary of an inner-city elementary school within the current economic, political, and social agenda. She has a Ph.D. in Education from the University of Arizona, Tucson.

Carlos Tejeda

Carlos Tejeda is an associate professor at the California State University, Los Angeles, where he is the Coordinator of an M.A. program in Educational Foundations and teaches courses in the social foundations of education, the history of education, educational sociology, and human development. He has been affiliated with the UCLA Statewide Migrant Student Leadership Institute since its inception in 1996, serving as a curriculum designer, social science and humanities instructor, Lead Instructor, and Associate Director. He is the originator and lead investigator of an emerging line of theorization, research, and practice defined as decolonizing pedagogy. He is an editor of *Charting new terrains of Chicana(o)/Latina(o) Education* and has published various articles and book chapters calling for and explicating the notion of a decolonizing pedagogy.

Enrique Trueba

Dr. Enrique "Henry" Trueba was a leader in the field of Latino/a education, especially language and culture issues. He has published over 20 books and numerous chapters and journal articles on bilingual and multicultural education. His most recent books include *Latinos Unidos: From Cultural Diversity to Political Solidarity*, *Immigrant Voices: In Search of Educational Equity* (with Bartolomé) and *Educational Ethnograpy* (with Zou). He has received many honors, awards, and fellowships for his research from organizations, including the American Educational Research Association, the American Anthropological Association, and the Center for Urban Ethnography, and University of Pennsylvania.

Olga A. Vásquez

Dr. Olga A. Vásquez, who received her doctorate at Stanford University, is an associate professor in the Department of Communication at the University of California, San Diego. Her research is best characterized as ethnography of education of minority group integration and learning. Her latest book, *La Clase Mágica: Imagining Optimal Possibilities in a Bilingual Community of Learn*ers, exemplifies the multiple ways in which minority communities can partner with educational institutions to provide Latinos and other minority communities with educational resources and institutional support. Vásquez's work touches on the fields of education, bilingual education, literacy, and community studies, and, more recently, on the impact that globalization is having on education in general and minority education specifically.

Author Index

Subject Index